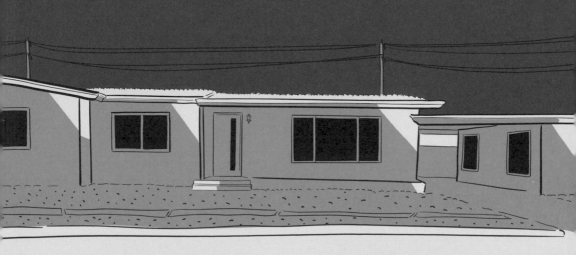

SEEK YOU

ALSO BY KRISTEN RADTKE

IMAGINE WANTING ONLY THIS

SEEK YOU

A JOURNEY THROUGH AMERICAN LONELINESS

KRISTEN RADTKE

PANTHEON BOOKS
NEW YORK

PUBLISHED IN THE UNITED STATES BY PANTHEON BOOKS, A DIVISION OF
PENGUIN RANDOM HOUSE LLC, NEW YORK, AND DISTRIBUTED IN
CANADA BY PENGUIN RANDOM HOUSE CANADA LIMITED, TORONTO.

PANTHEON BOOKS AND COLOPHON ARE REGISTERED TRADEMARKS
OF PENGUIN RANDOM HOUSE LLC.

LIBRARY OF CONGRESS CATALOGING-IN-PUBLICATION DATA
NAME: RADTKE, KRISTEN, AUTHOR, ARTIST.
TITLE: SEEK YOU : A JOURNEY THROUGH AMERICAN LONELINESS / KRISTEN RADTKE.
DESCRIPTION: FIRST EDITION. NEW YORK : PANTHEON BOOKS, 2021.
IDENTIFIERS: LCCN 2020040878 (PRINT). LCCN 2020040879 (EBOOK).
ISBN 9781524748067 (HARDCOVER). ISBN 9781524748050 (EBOOK).
SUBJECTS: LCSH: LONELINESS—COMIC BOOKS, STRIPS, ETC. GRAPHIC NOVELS.
CLASSIFICATION: LCC PN6727.R334 S44 2021 (PRINT) | LCC PN6727.R334 (EBOOK) |
DDC 741.5/973—DC23
LC RECORD AVAILABLE AT LCCN.LOC.GOV/2020040878
LC EBOOK RECORD AVAILABLE AT LCCN.LOC.GOV/2020040879

WWW.PANTHEONBOOKS.COM

PRINTED IN CHINA
FIRST EDITION
2   4   6   8   9   7   5   3   1

FOR MY DAD,
WHO KEEPS SEEKING

AUTHOR'S NOTE

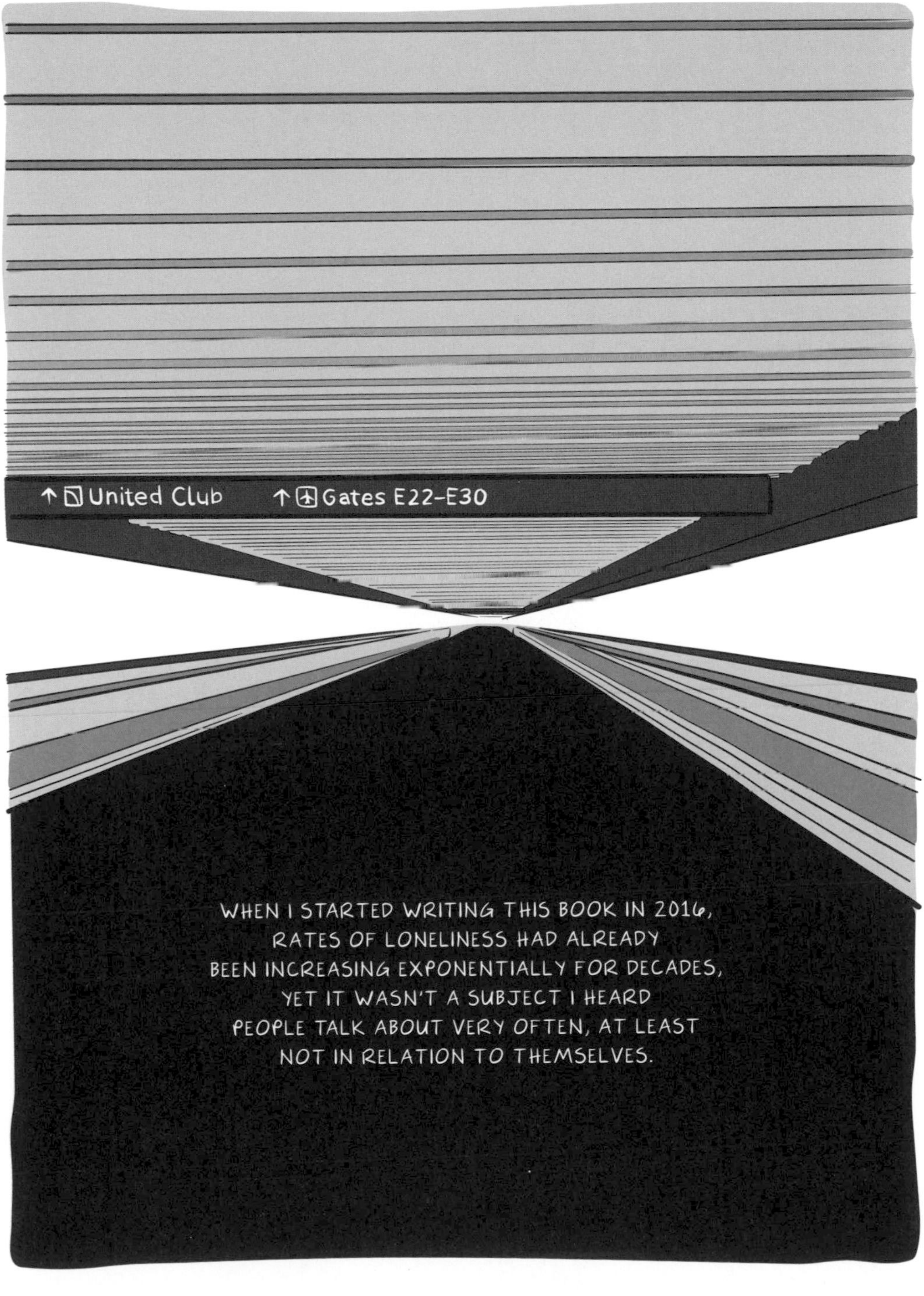
↑ United Club
↑ Gates E22–E30
WHEN I STARTED WRITING THIS BOOK IN 2016, RATES OF LONELINESS HAD ALREADY BEEN INCREASING EXPONENTIALLY FOR DECADES, YET IT WASN'T A SUBJECT I HEARD PEOPLE TALK ABOUT VERY OFTEN, AT LEAST NOT IN RELATION TO THEMSELVES.

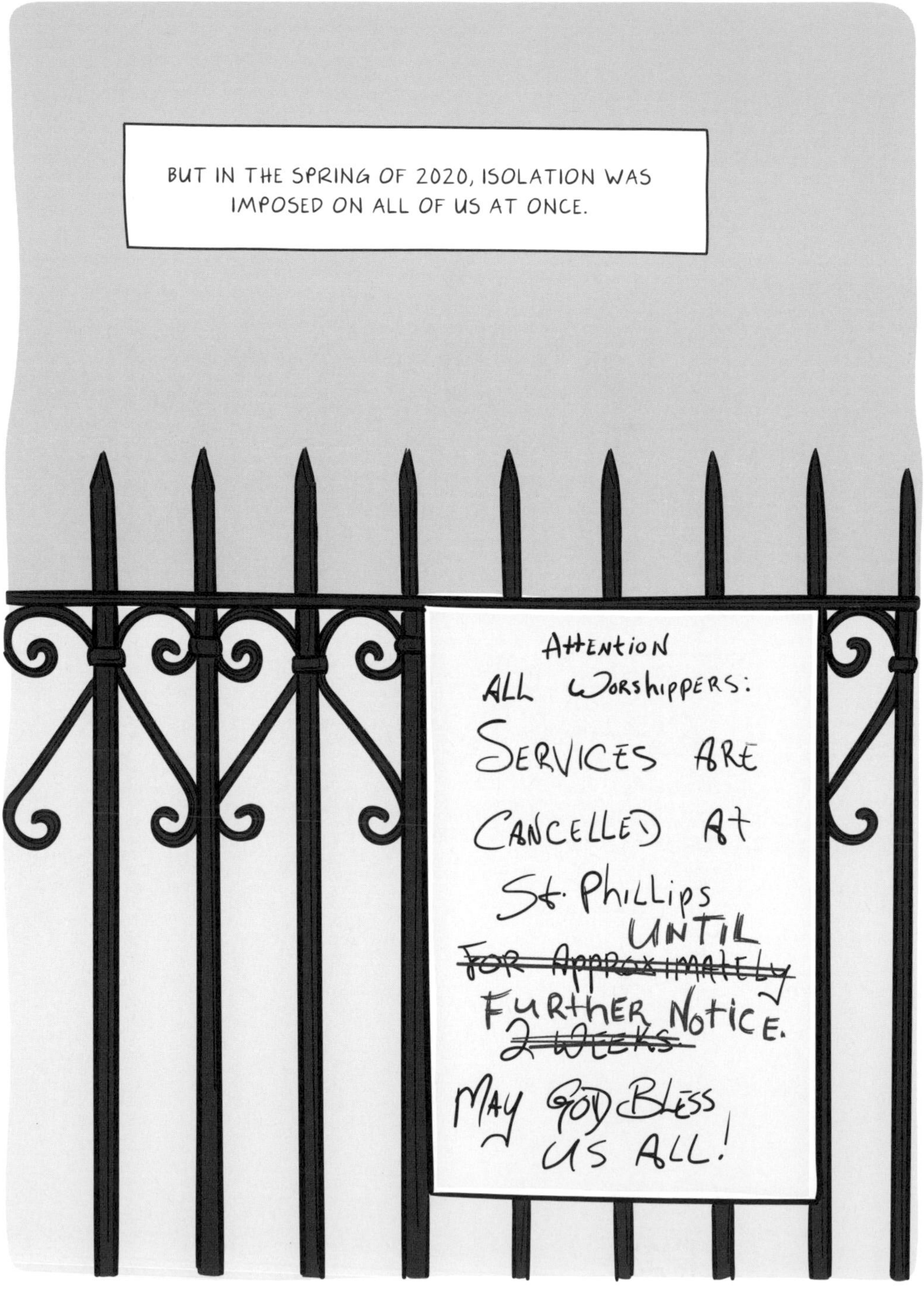
BUT IN THE SPRING OF 2020, ISOLATION WAS IMPOSED ON ALL OF US AT ONCE.
Attention ALL Worshippers:
SERVICES ARE CANCELLED At St. PhiLLips UNTIL ~~FOR Approximately~~ FURther Notice. ~~2 WEEKS~~
MAY GOD BLESS US ALL!

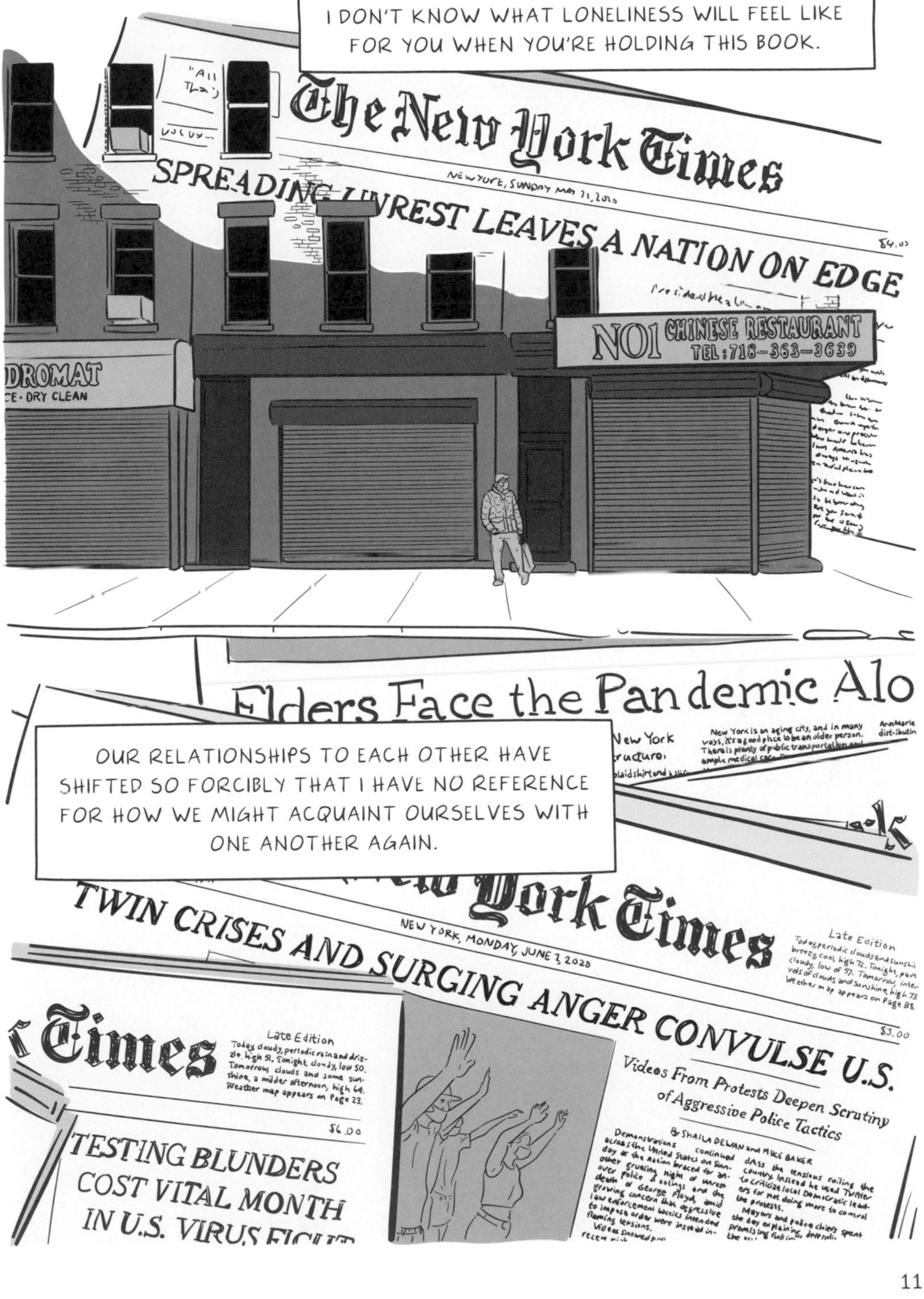
I DON'T KNOW WHAT LONELINESS WILL FEEL LIKE FOR YOU WHEN YOU'RE HOLDING THIS BOOK.
The New York Times
NEW YORK, SUNDAY MAY 31, 2020
SPREADING UNREST LEAVES A NATION ON EDGE
NO1 CHINESE RESTAURANT TEL: 718-363-3639
DROMAT
CE · DRY CLEAN
Elders Face the Pandemic Alo
OUR RELATIONSHIPS TO EACH OTHER HAVE SHIFTED SO FORCIBLY THAT I HAVE NO REFERENCE FOR HOW WE MIGHT ACQUAINT OURSELVES WITH ONE ANOTHER AGAIN.
York Times
NEW YORK, MONDAY, JUNE 1, 2020
Late Edition
TWIN CRISES AND SURGING ANGER CONVULSE U.S.
$3.00
Times
Late Edition
$6.00
TESTING BLUNDERS COST VITAL MONTH IN U.S. VIRUS FIGHT
Videos From Protests Deepen Scrutiny of Aggressive Police Tactics
By SHAILA DEWAN and MIKE BAKER

LONELINESS IS OFTEN EXACERBATED BY A PERCEPTION
THAT ONE IS LONELY WHILE EVERYONE ELSE IS CONNECTED.
IT'S EXAGGERATED BY A SENSATION OF BEING OUTSIDE
SOMETHING THAT OTHERS SEEM TO BE IN ON:
A FAMILY, A COUPLE, A FRIENDSHIP, A JOKE.

PERHAPS NOW WE CAN LEARN HOW FLAWED
THAT KIND OF THINKING IS, BECAUSE
LONELINESS IS ONE OF THE MOST UNIVERSAL
THINGS ANY PERSON CAN FEEL.

LISTEN

I

IN AMATEUR RADIO, OPERATORS CALL OUT ACROSS FREQUENCIES WITH A SERIES OF PUNCTUATED, MONOTONE BEEPS KNOWN AS A "CQ CALL." WHEN PRONOUNCED IN FRENCH, THE OFFICIAL LANGUAGE FOR INTERNATIONAL TELECOMMUNICATIONS, "CQ" SOUNDS LIKE THE FIRST TWO SYLLABLES OF "SÉCURITÉ," USED TO MEAN "PAY ATTENTION."

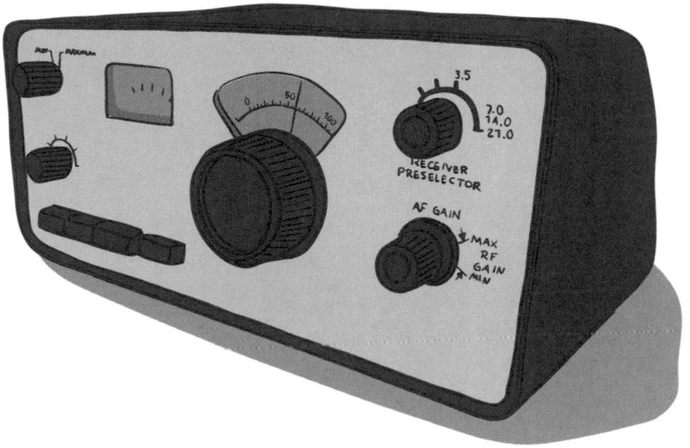
3.5
7.0
14.0
27.0
RECEIVER PRESELECTOR
AF GAIN
MAX
RF GAIN
MIN

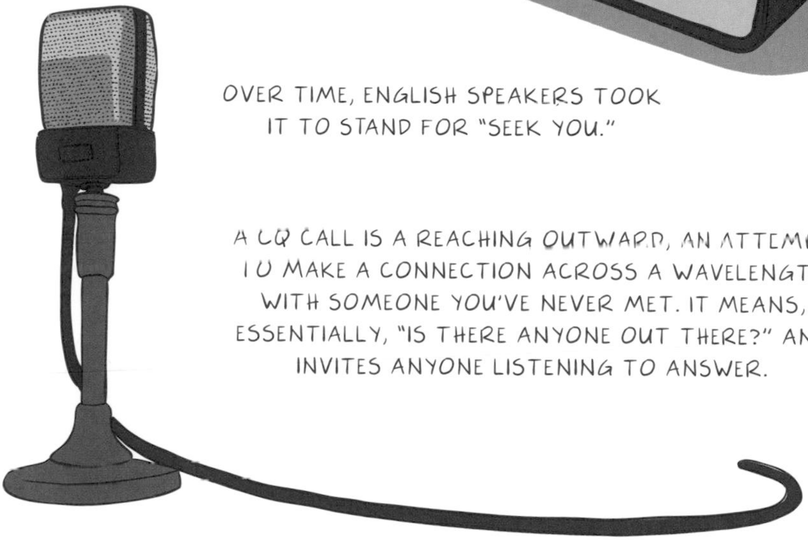

OVER TIME, ENGLISH SPEAKERS TOOK IT TO STAND FOR "SEEK YOU."

A CQ CALL IS A REACHING OUTWARD, AN ATTEMPT TO MAKE A CONNECTION ACROSS A WAVELENGTH WITH SOMEONE YOU'VE NEVER MET. IT MEANS, ESSENTIALLY, "IS THERE ANYONE OUT THERE?" AND INVITES ANYONE LISTENING TO ANSWER.

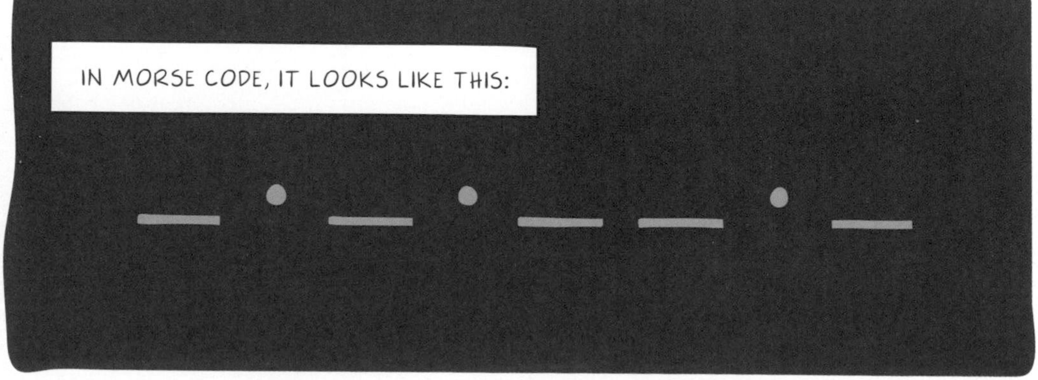
IN MORSE CODE, IT LOOKS LIKE THIS:

IF THE CALLER IS LUCKY, ANOTHER USER WILL HEAR AND
LATCH ON, REPORTING THEIR HANDLE AND LOCATION.

THESE CALLS ARE BROADCAST ACROSS LOW FREQUENCIES,
WHICH BEND WITH EASE AROUND THE CURVATURE OF THE EARTH,
ALLOWING FOR CONTACT ACROSS THOUSANDS OF MILES.

CALLERS MAY SPEAK INTO A HANDHELD RECEIVER, BUT MORSE
CODE TAKES LESS POWER AND CUTS THROUGH NOISIER STATIONS,
PUSHING AUDIBLE MESSAGES ATOP THE STATIC.

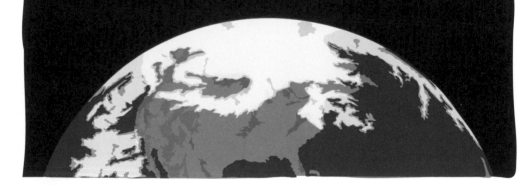

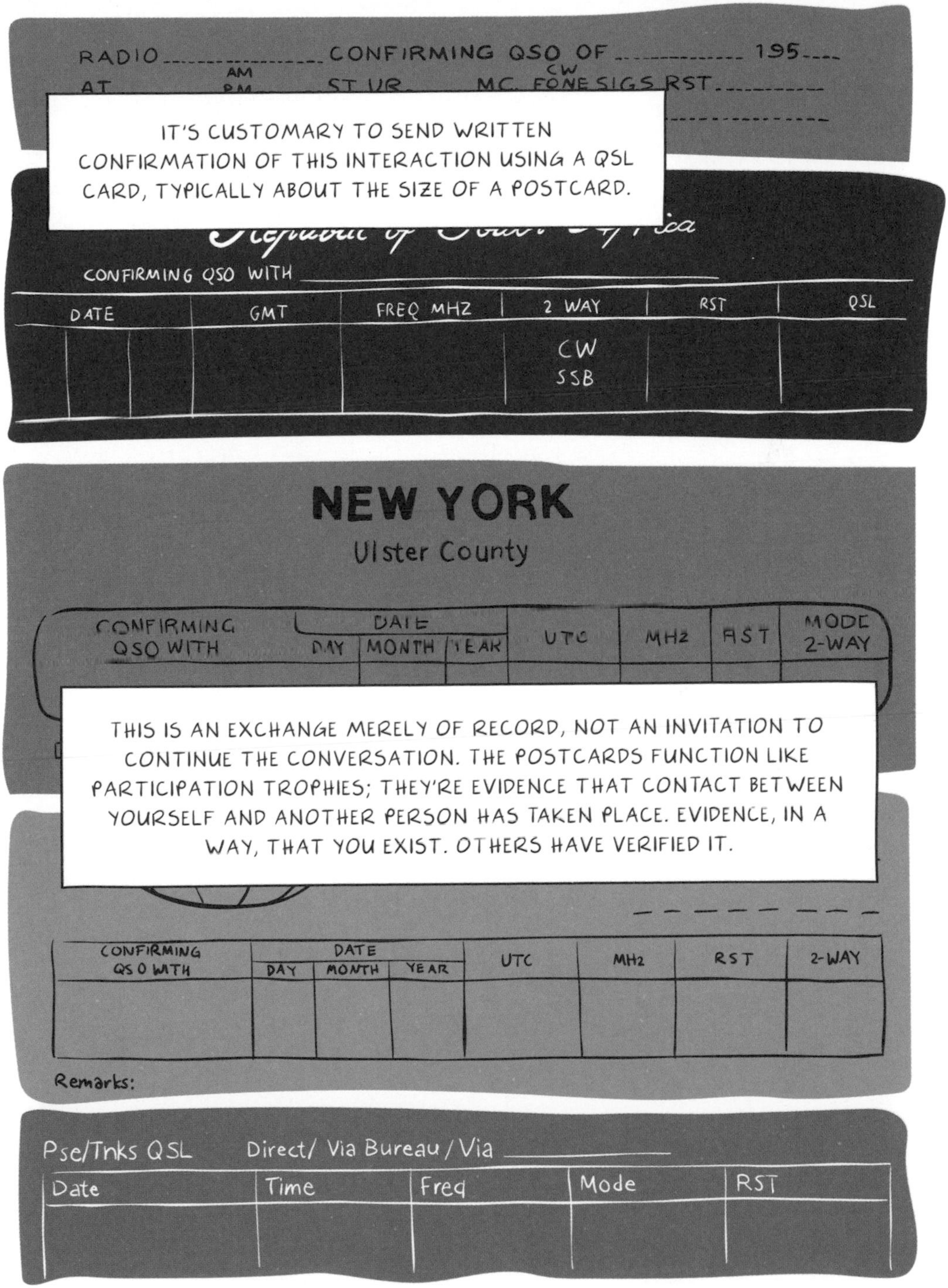

RADIO_____ CONFIRMING QSO OF _____ 195___

AT   AM   CW
      PM   ___ ST UR ___ MC. FONE SIGS RST _____

> IT'S CUSTOMARY TO SEND WRITTEN CONFIRMATION OF THIS INTERACTION USING A QSL CARD, TYPICALLY ABOUT THE SIZE OF A POSTCARD.

Republic of South Africa

CONFIRMING QSO WITH _____

DATE		GMT	FREQ MHZ	2 WAY	RST	QSL
				CW		
				SSB		

NEW YORK
Ulster County

CONFIRMING QSO WITH	DATE			UTC	MHz	RST	MODE 2-WAY
	DAY	MONTH	YEAR				

> THIS IS AN EXCHANGE MERELY OF RECORD, NOT AN INVITATION TO CONTINUE THE CONVERSATION. THE POSTCARDS FUNCTION LIKE PARTICIPATION TROPHIES; THEY'RE EVIDENCE THAT CONTACT BETWEEN YOURSELF AND ANOTHER PERSON HAS TAKEN PLACE. EVIDENCE, IN A WAY, THAT YOU EXIST. OTHERS HAVE VERIFIED IT.

CONFIRMING QSO WITH	DATE			UTC	MHz	RST	2-WAY
	DAY	MONTH	YEAR				

Remarks:

Pse/Tnks QSL   Direct/ Via Bureau /Via _____

Date	Time	Freq	Mode	RST

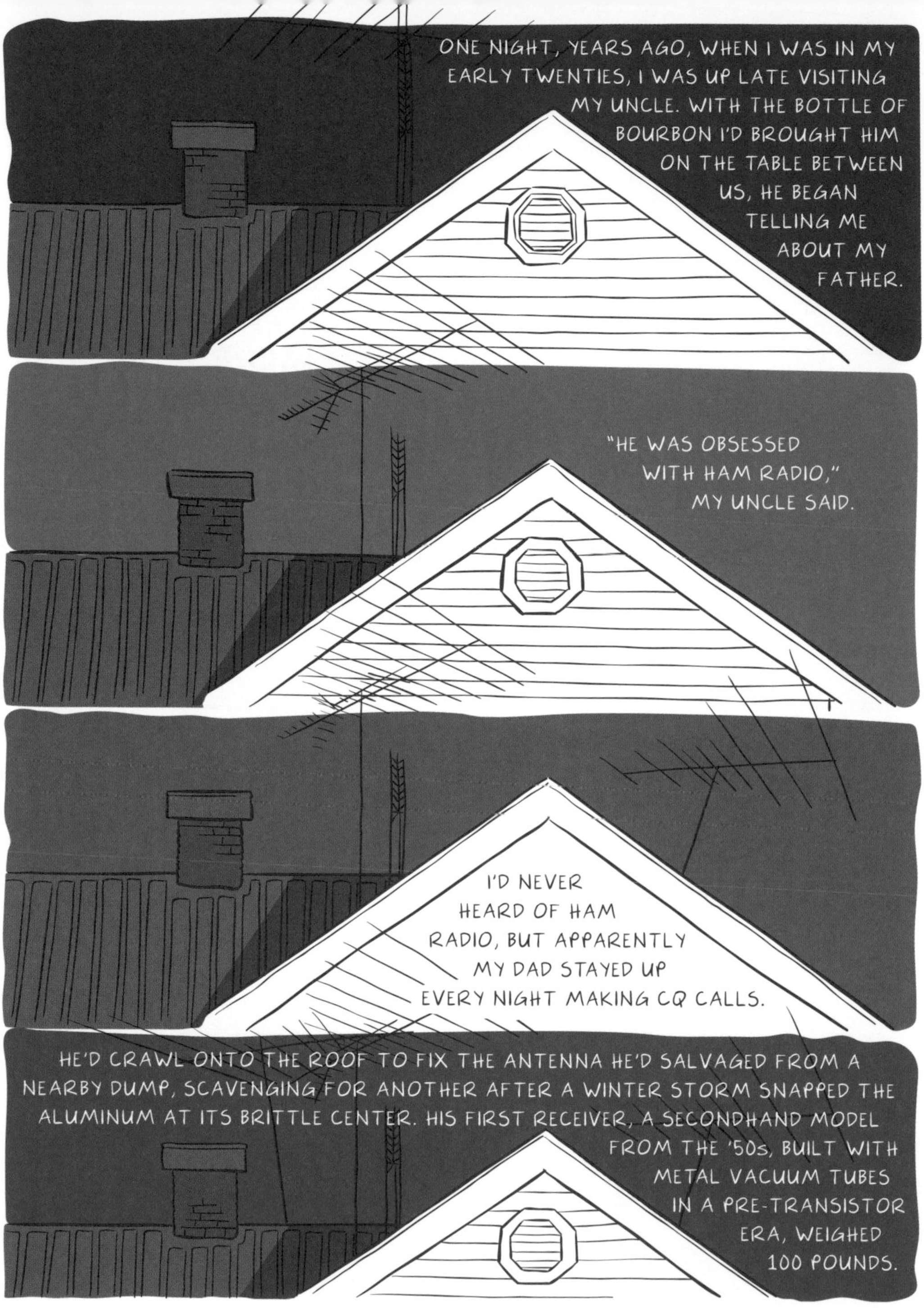
ONE NIGHT, YEARS AGO, WHEN I WAS IN MY EARLY TWENTIES, I WAS UP LATE VISITING MY UNCLE. WITH THE BOTTLE OF BOURBON I'D BROUGHT HIM ON THE TABLE BETWEEN US, HE BEGAN TELLING ME ABOUT MY FATHER.
"HE WAS OBSESSED WITH HAM RADIO," MY UNCLE SAID.
I'D NEVER HEARD OF HAM RADIO, BUT APPARENTLY MY DAD STAYED UP EVERY NIGHT MAKING CQ CALLS.
HE'D CRAWL ONTO THE ROOF TO FIX THE ANTENNA HE'D SALVAGED FROM A NEARBY DUMP, SCAVENGING FOR ANOTHER AFTER A WINTER STORM SNAPPED THE ALUMINUM AT ITS BRITTLE CENTER. HIS FIRST RECEIVER, A SECONDHAND MODEL FROM THE '50s, BUILT WITH METAL VACUUM TUBES IN A PRE-TRANSISTOR ERA, WEIGHED 100 POUNDS.

THEY GREW UP IN A FAMILY OF FIVE BOYS IN AN ECONOMICALLY DECREPIT PART OF RURAL WISCONSIN. THEIR FATHER DRANK, THEIR PARENTS DIVORCED, AND THEY SPOKE OF THEIR LATE MOTHER WITH REVERENCE TO HER SAINTHOOD THE WAY MANY MEN TALK ABOUT THEIR DEAD MOTHERS.

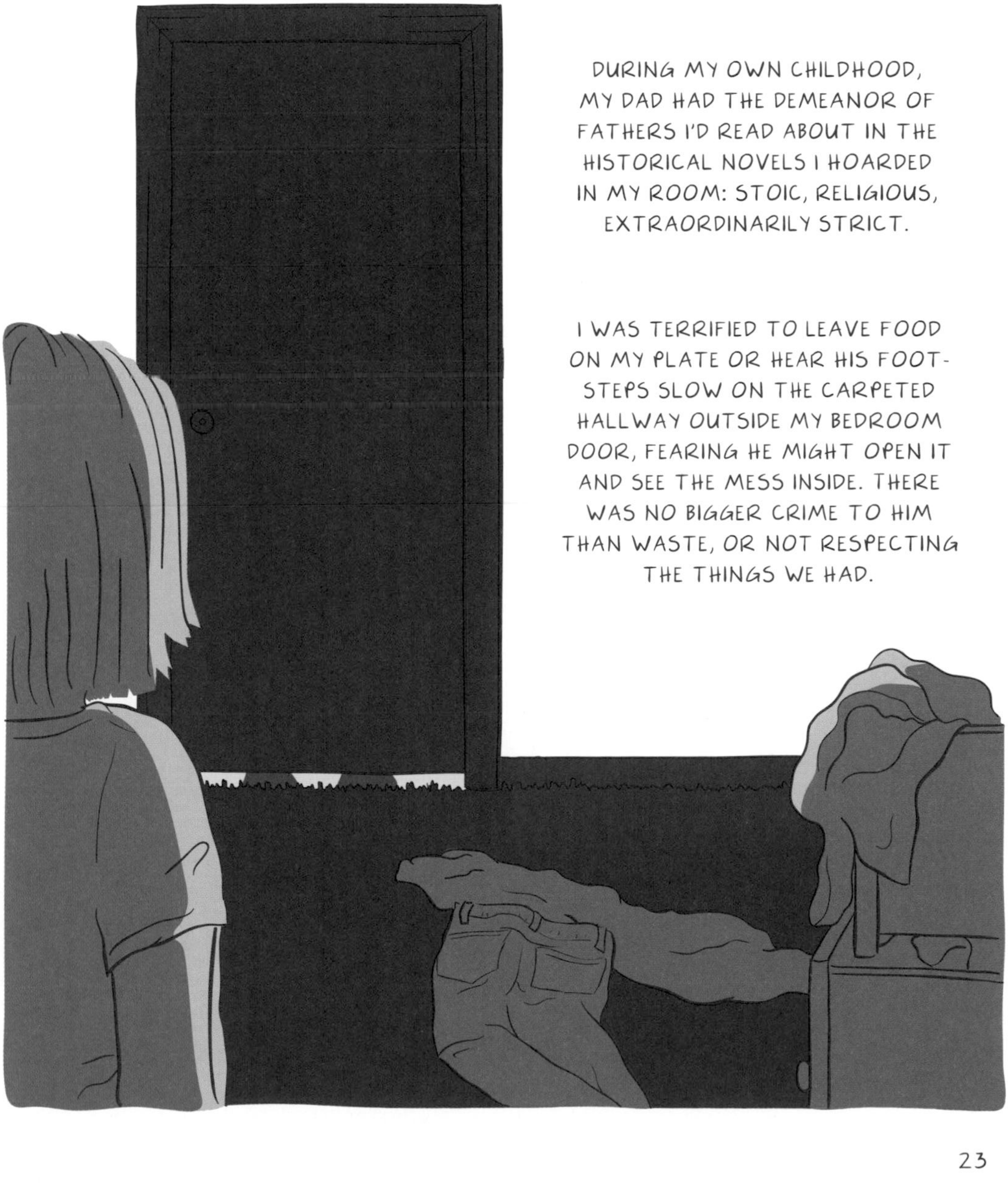

DURING MY OWN CHILDHOOD, MY DAD HAD THE DEMEANOR OF FATHERS I'D READ ABOUT IN THE HISTORICAL NOVELS I HOARDED IN MY ROOM: STOIC, RELIGIOUS, EXTRAORDINARILY STRICT.

I WAS TERRIFIED TO LEAVE FOOD ON MY PLATE OR HEAR HIS FOOT-STEPS SLOW ON THE CARPETED HALLWAY OUTSIDE MY BEDROOM DOOR, FEARING HE MIGHT OPEN IT AND SEE THE MESS INSIDE. THERE WAS NO BIGGER CRIME TO HIM THAN WASTE, OR NOT RESPECTING THE THINGS WE HAD.

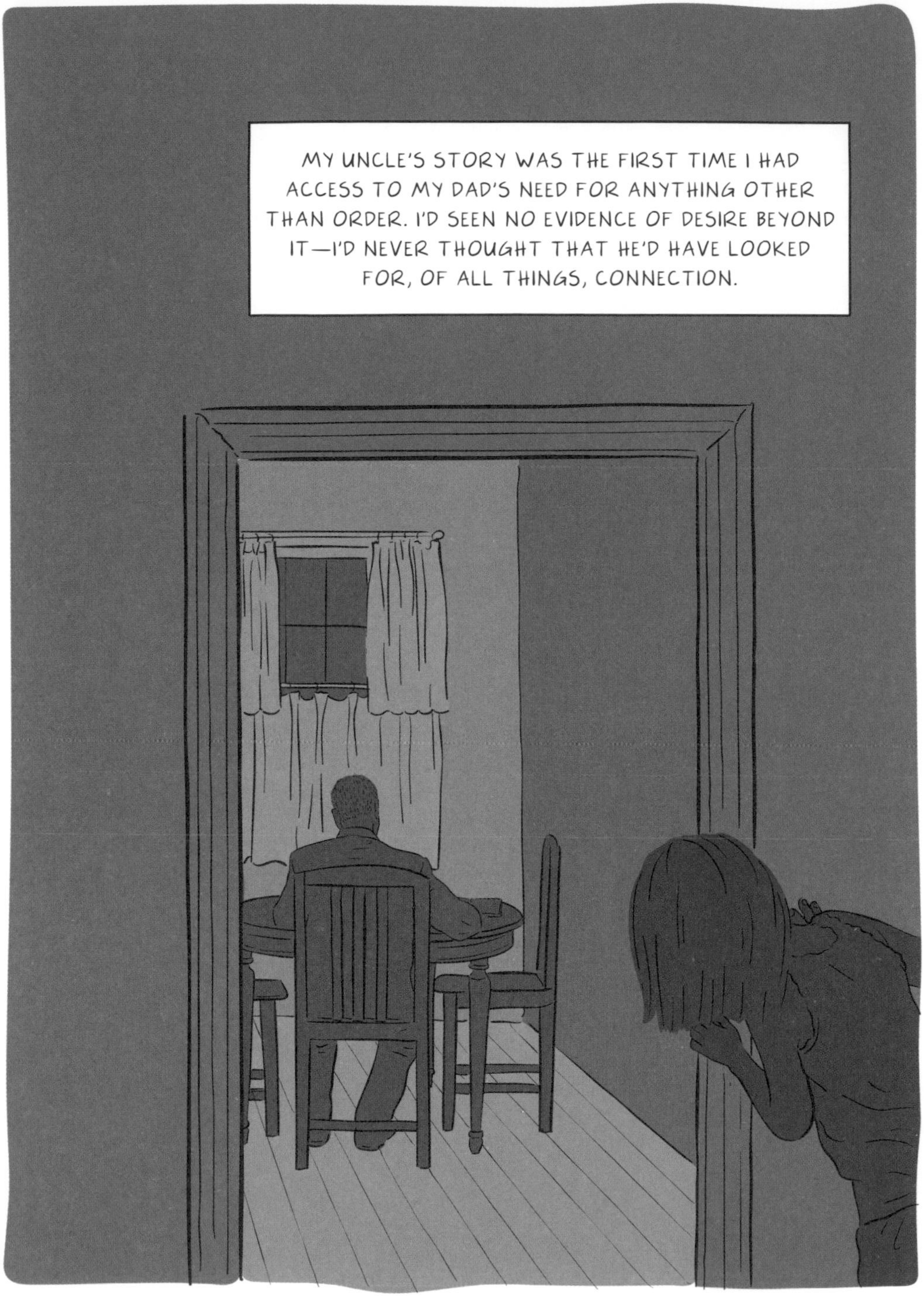
MY UNCLE'S STORY WAS THE FIRST TIME I HAD ACCESS TO MY DAD'S NEED FOR ANYTHING OTHER THAN ORDER. I'D SEEN NO EVIDENCE OF DESIRE BEYOND IT—I'D NEVER THOUGHT THAT HE'D HAVE LOOKED FOR, OF ALL THINGS, CONNECTION.

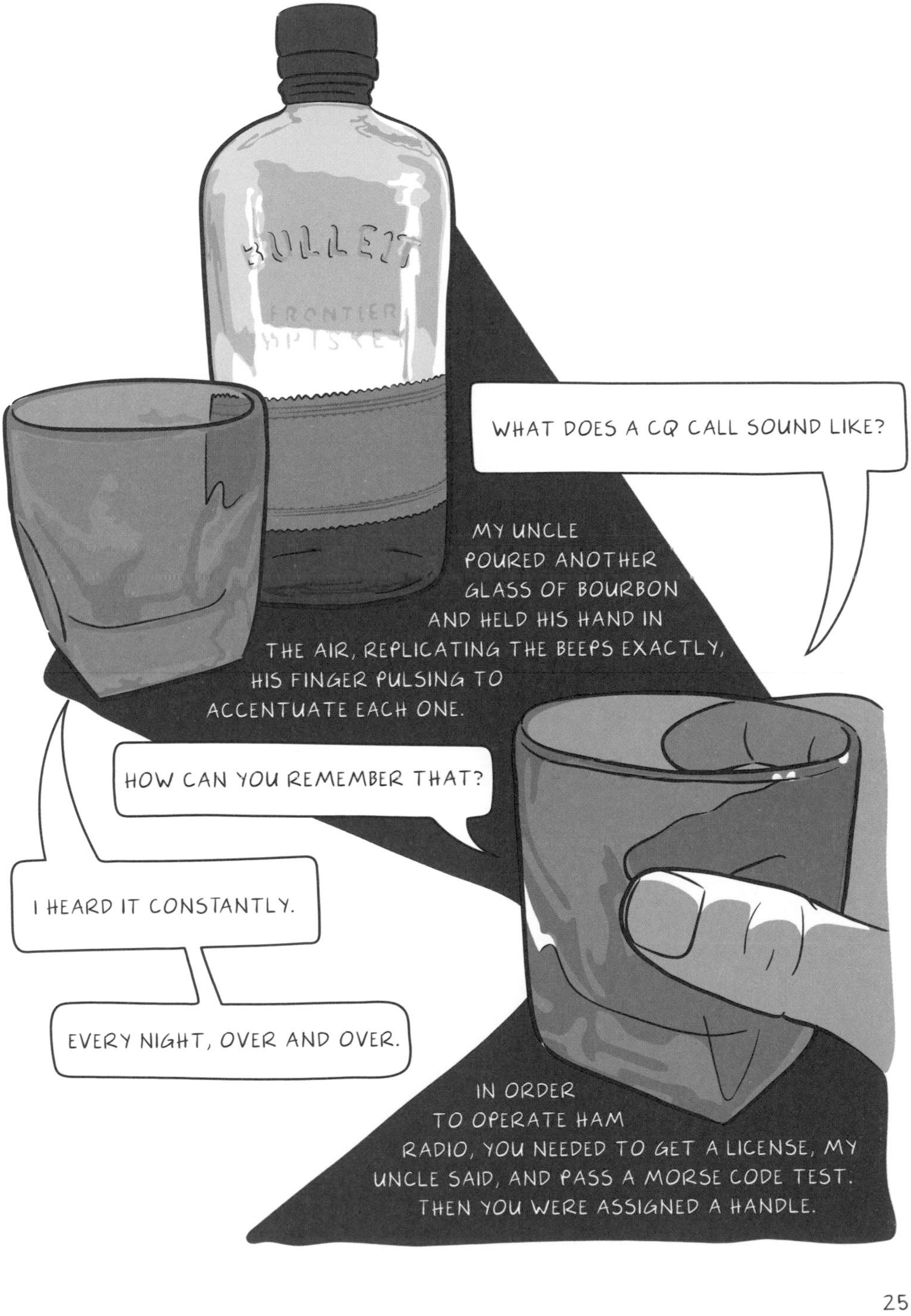
BULLEIT
FRONTIER
WHISKEY
WHAT DOES A CQ CALL SOUND LIKE?
MY UNCLE POURED ANOTHER GLASS OF BOURBON AND HELD HIS HAND IN THE AIR, REPLICATING THE BEEPS EXACTLY, HIS FINGER PULSING TO ACCENTUATE EACH ONE.
HOW CAN YOU REMEMBER THAT?
I HEARD IT CONSTANTLY.
EVERY NIGHT, OVER AND OVER.
IN ORDER TO OPERATE HAM RADIO, YOU NEEDED TO GET A LICENSE, MY UNCLE SAID, AND PASS A MORSE CODE TEST. THEN YOU WERE ASSIGNED A HANDLE.

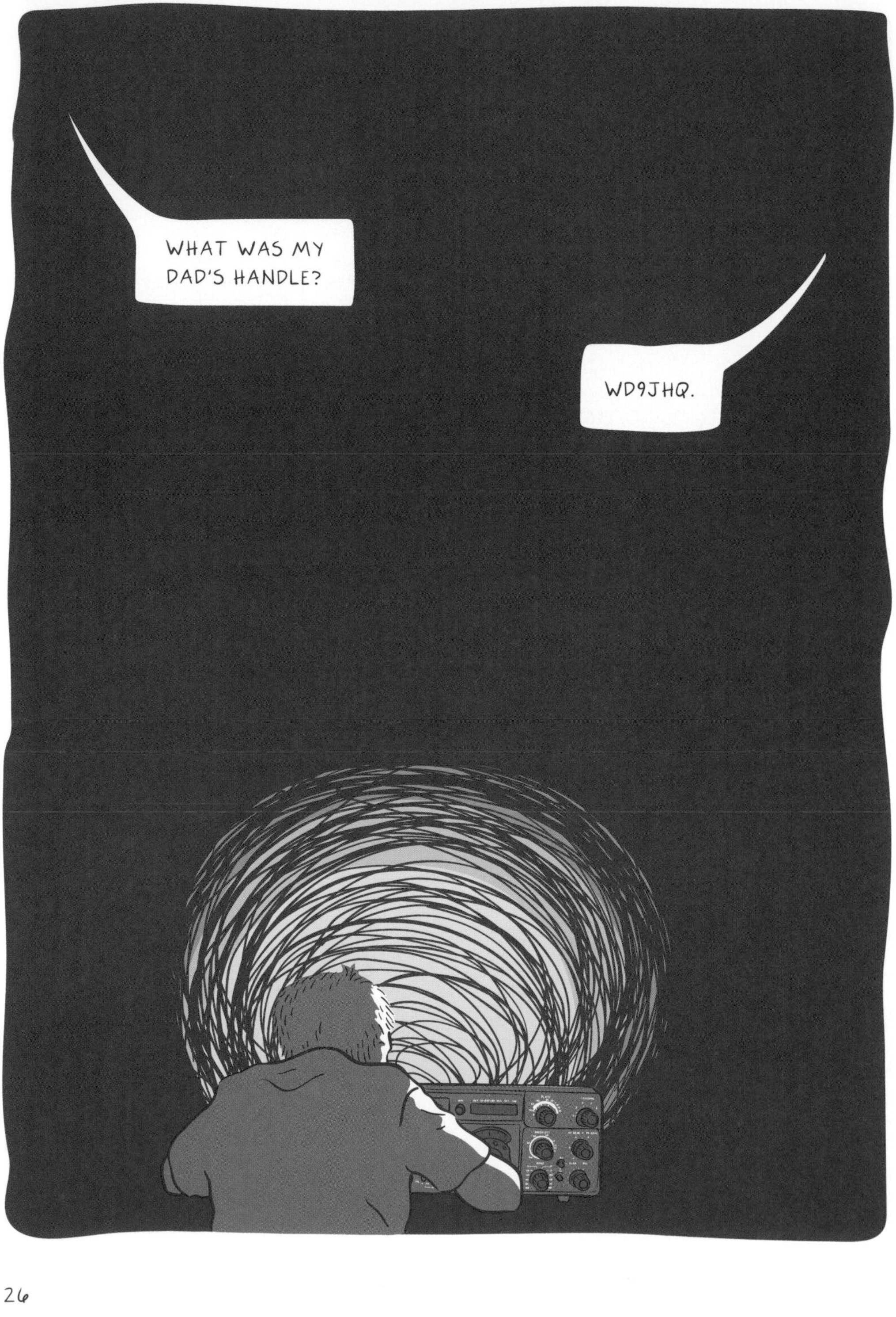
WHAT WAS MY DAD'S HANDLE?
WD9JHQ.

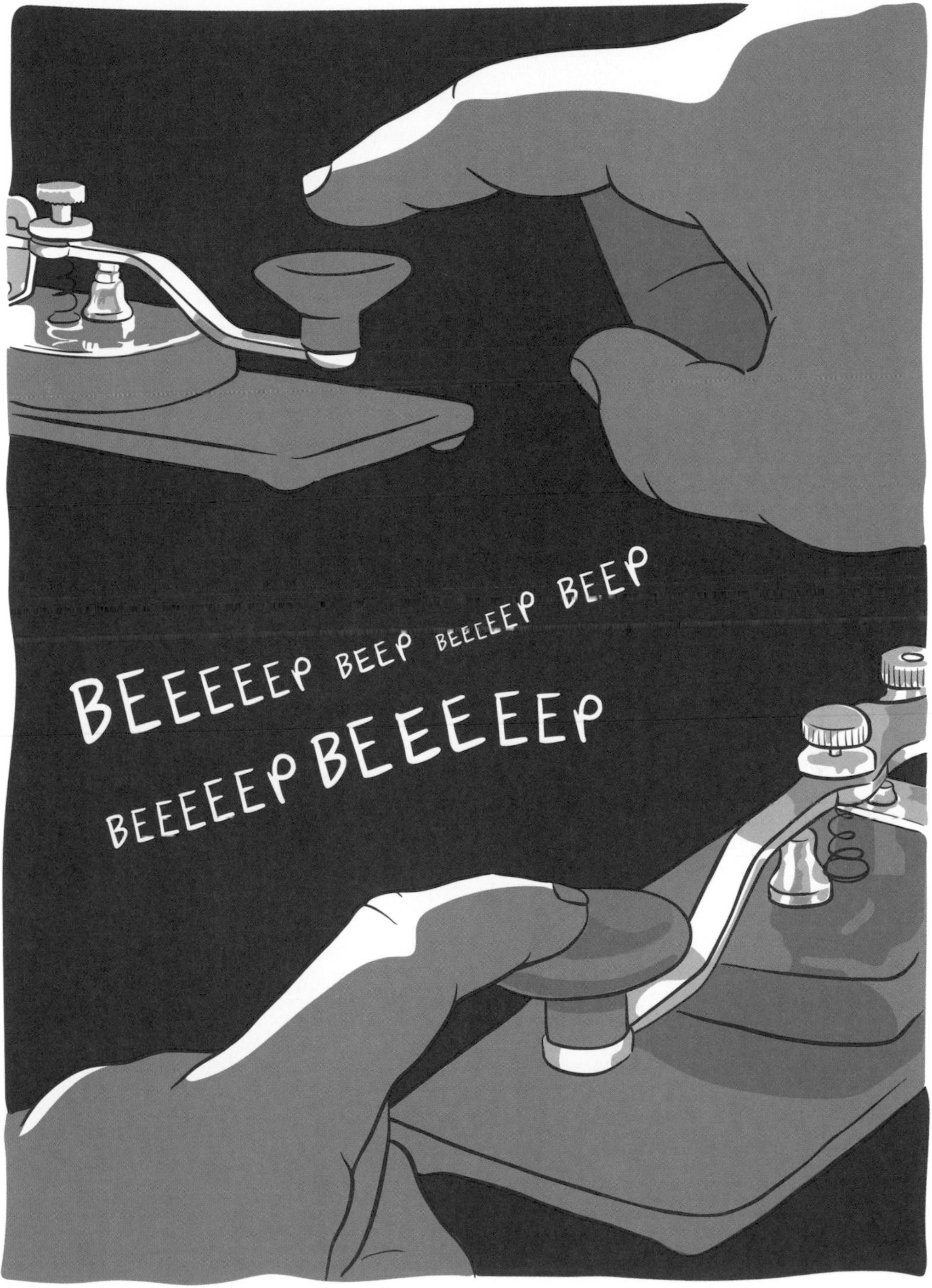
BEEEEEP BEEP BEEEEEP BEEP
BEEEEEP BEEEEEP

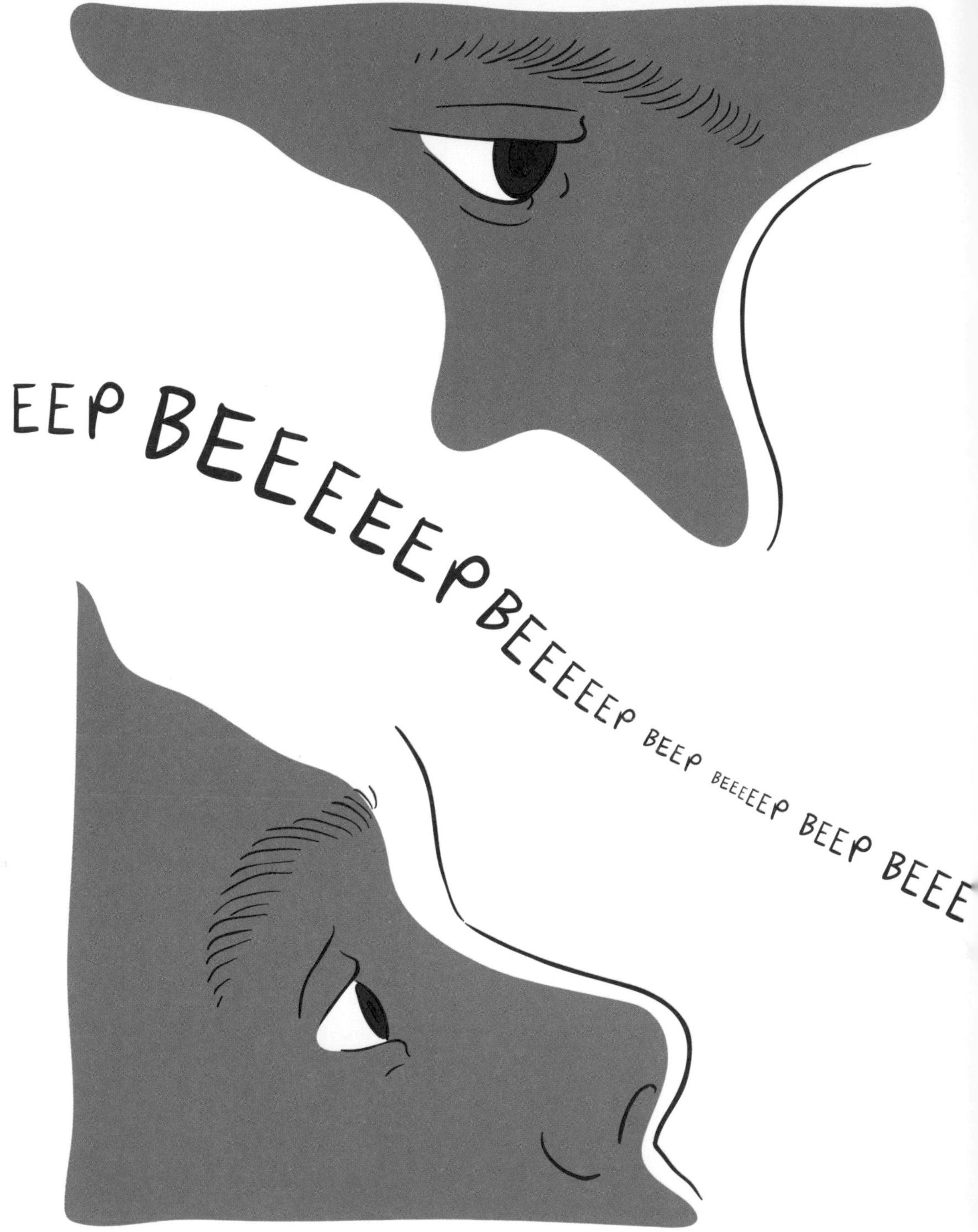
EEP BEEEEEEP BEEEEEEP BEEP BEEEEEP BEEP BEEE

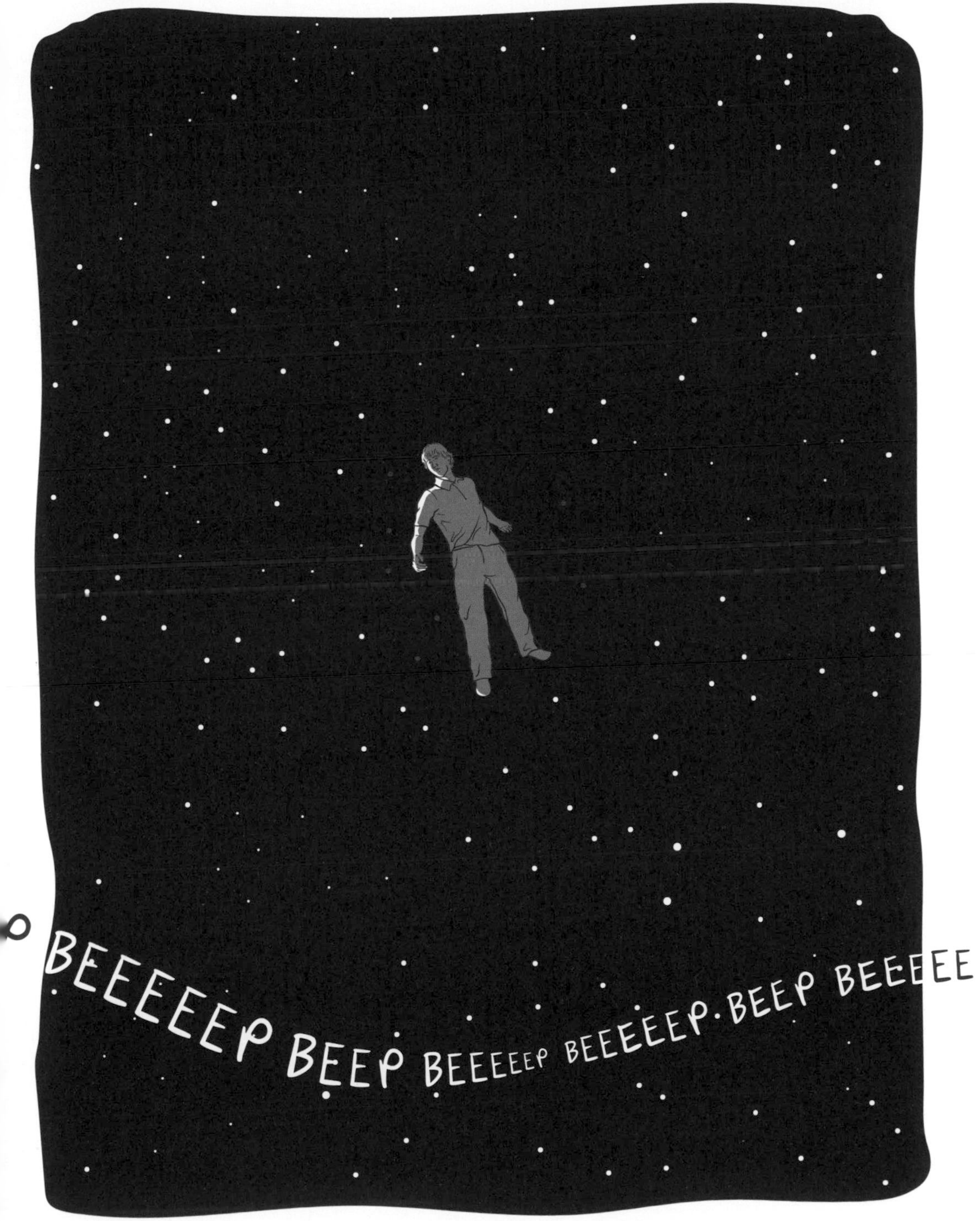
BEEEEEEP BEEP BEEEEEP BEEEEEEP BEEP BEEEEE

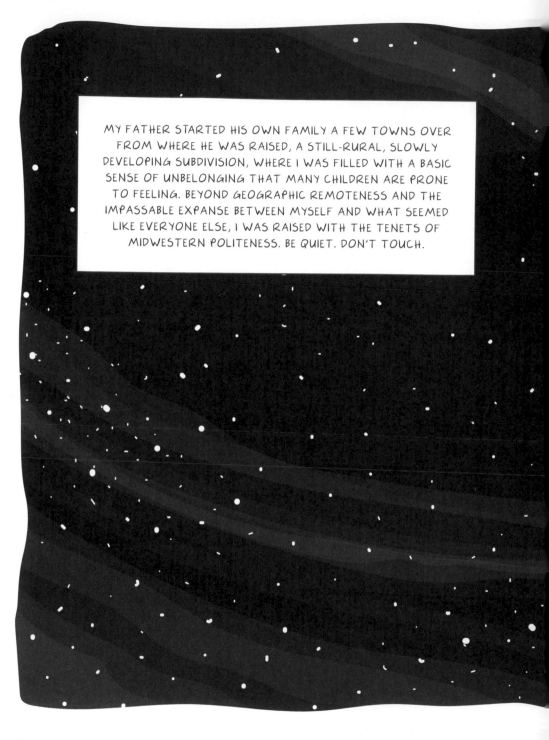

MY FATHER STARTED HIS OWN FAMILY A FEW TOWNS OVER
FROM WHERE HE WAS RAISED, A STILL-RURAL, SLOWLY
DEVELOPING SUBDIVISION, WHERE I WAS FILLED WITH A BASIC
SENSE OF UNBELONGING THAT MANY CHILDREN ARE PRONE
TO FEELING. BEYOND GEOGRAPHIC REMOTENESS AND THE
IMPASSABLE EXPANSE BETWEEN MYSELF AND WHAT SEEMED
LIKE EVERYONE ELSE, I WAS RAISED WITH THE TENETS OF
MIDWESTERN POLITENESS. BE QUIET. DON'T TOUCH.

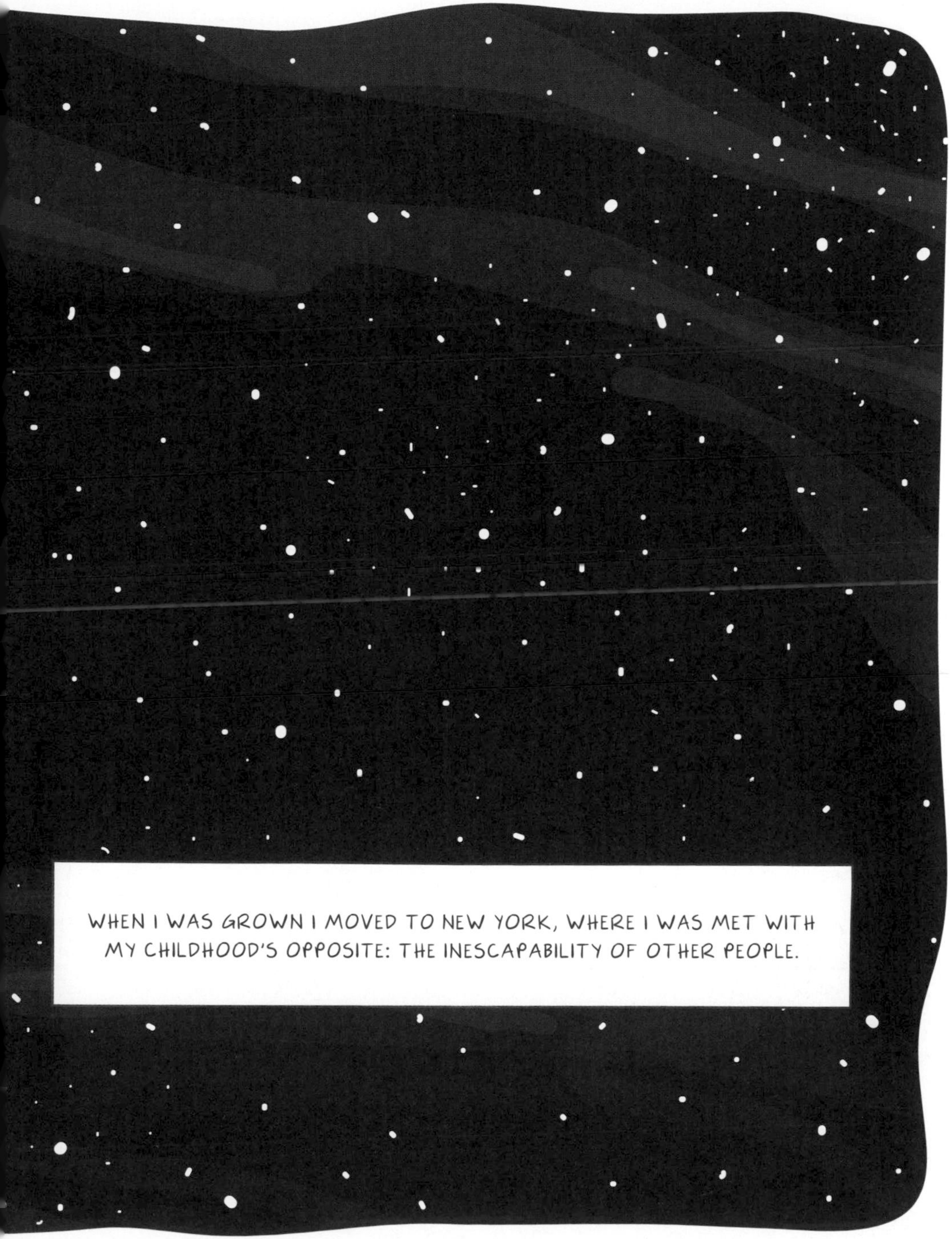
WHEN I WAS GROWN I MOVED TO NEW YORK, WHERE I WAS MET WITH MY CHILDHOOD'S OPPOSITE: THE INESCAPABILITY OF OTHER PEOPLE.

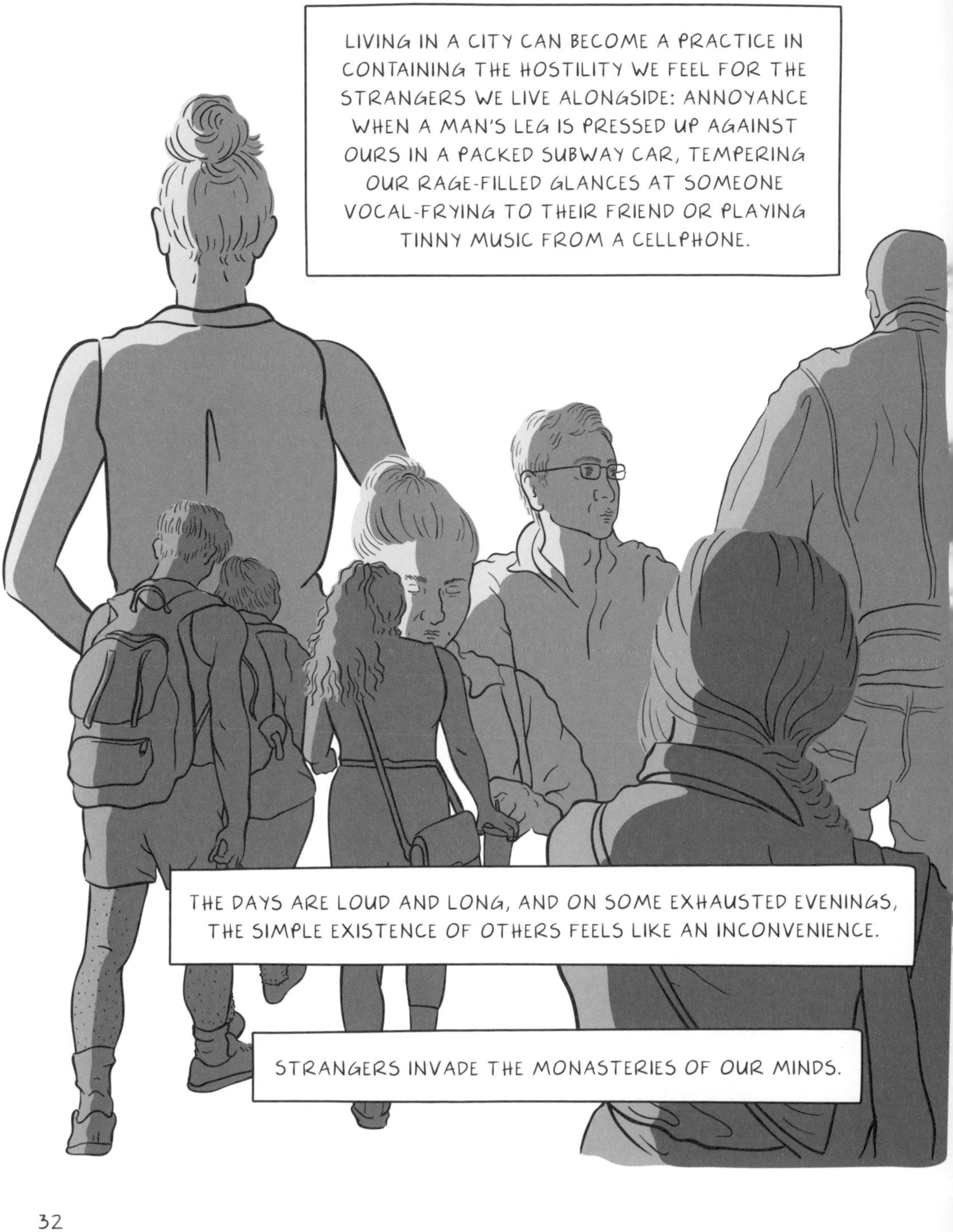
LIVING IN A CITY CAN BECOME A PRACTICE IN CONTAINING THE HOSTILITY WE FEEL FOR THE STRANGERS WE LIVE ALONGSIDE: ANNOYANCE WHEN A MAN'S LEG IS PRESSED UP AGAINST OURS IN A PACKED SUBWAY CAR, TEMPERING OUR RAGE-FILLED GLANCES AT SOMEONE VOCAL-FRYING TO THEIR FRIEND OR PLAYING TINNY MUSIC FROM A CELLPHONE.
THE DAYS ARE LOUD AND LONG, AND ON SOME EXHAUSTED EVENINGS, THE SIMPLE EXISTENCE OF OTHERS FEELS LIKE AN INCONVENIENCE.
STRANGERS INVADE THE MONASTERIES OF OUR MINDS.

CONGESTION PUTS THOSE WE DON'T KNOW AND WILL LIKELY NEVER SPEAK TO ON BRIEF AND SHIFTING STAGES, LIKE DEPARTMENT STORE WINDOWS ABOUT TO BE REDRESSED AT THE END OF A SEASON: A GIRL SLUMPED TO HER SIDE ON THE SUBWAY, ASLEEP ON HER WAY BACK FROM SCHOOL; A MAN'S FACE ILLUMINATED BY HIS LAPTOP'S GLOW THROUGH A GROUND-FLOOR WINDOW AS HE SITS ALONE IN HIS APARTMENT; A WOMAN LEANING INTO A POST AS SHE HOLDS HER CELLPHONE TIGHTLY TO HER EAR IN AN EMPTY PARKING LOT.

I DIDN'T EXPECT THE EASE WITH WHICH I'D COME TO PROJECT LONELINESS ONTO THESE MOMENTS, APPLY AN EDWARD HOPPER GLAZE OVER THE CRYSTALLINE BANALITY OF A STRANGER'S ROUTINE.

WHEN I WALK DOWN A STREET AT NIGHT AND CATCH THE CORNER OF A BEDROOM BEYOND A WINDOW'S CURTAIN, OR SEE A WOMAN FUMBLING FOR HER KEYS ON HER APARTMENT'S FRONT STOOP, I'M SURPRISED BY THE LONGING I FEEL FOR THE PEOPLE I PASS, AND THE HOMES I'LL NEVER BE INVITED INTO—OR, PERHAPS MORE ACCURATELY, FOR THE LIVES I'LL NEVER LIVE.

33

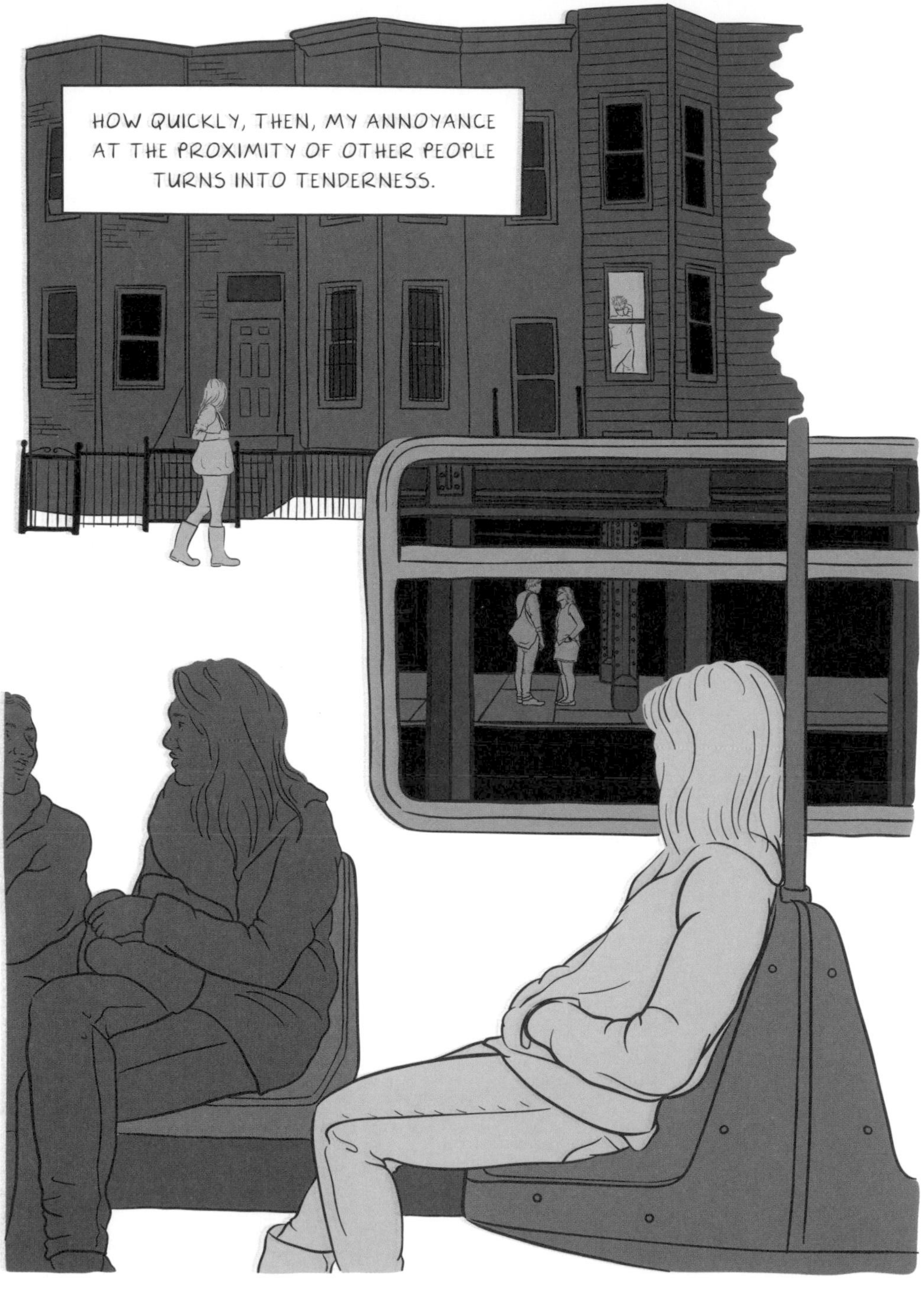
HOW QUICKLY, THEN, MY ANNOYANCE AT THE PROXIMITY OF OTHER PEOPLE TURNS INTO TENDERNESS.

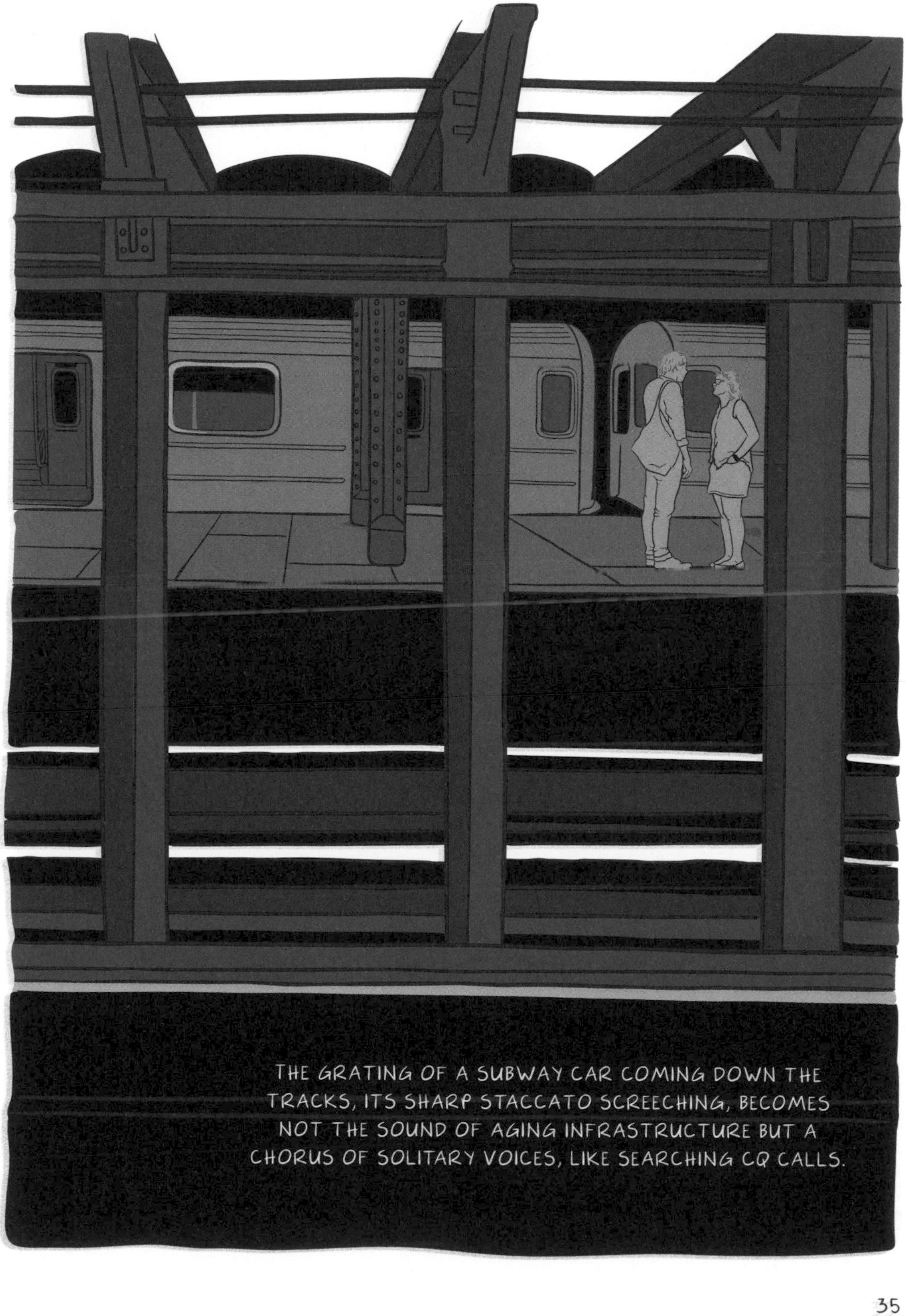
THE GRATING OF A SUBWAY CAR COMING DOWN THE TRACKS, ITS SHARP STACCATO SCREECHING, BECOMES NOT THE SOUND OF AGING INFRASTRUCTURE BUT A CHORUS OF SOLITARY VOICES, LIKE SEARCHING CQ CALLS.

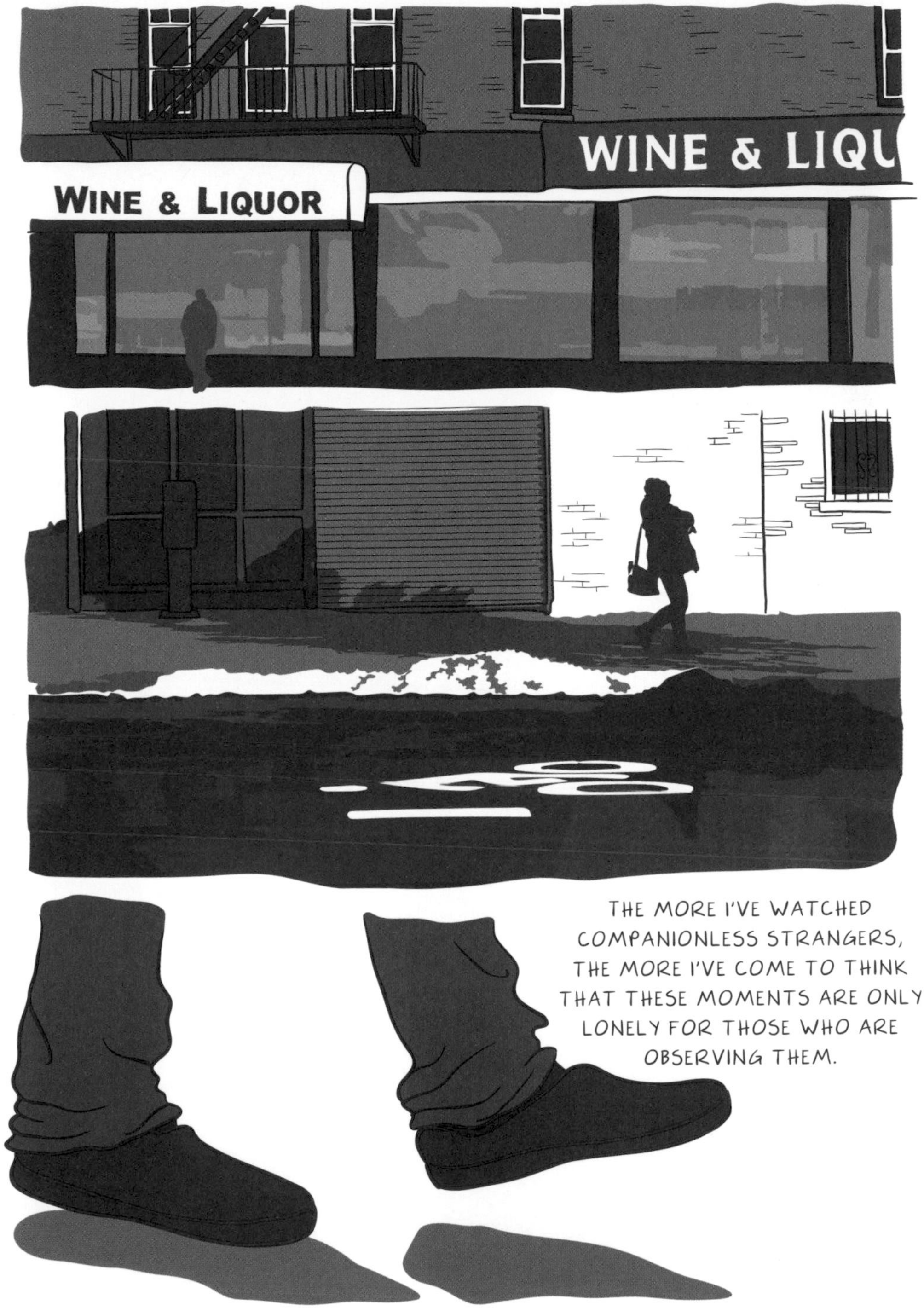
WINE & LIQU
WINE & LIQUOR
THE MORE I'VE WATCHED COMPANIONLESS STRANGERS, THE MORE I'VE COME TO THINK THAT THESE MOMENTS ARE ONLY LONELY FOR THOSE WHO ARE OBSERVING THEM.

PERHAPS WE SEE LONELINESS IN OTHERS SIMPLY
TO FEEL LESS LONELY OURSELVES.

II

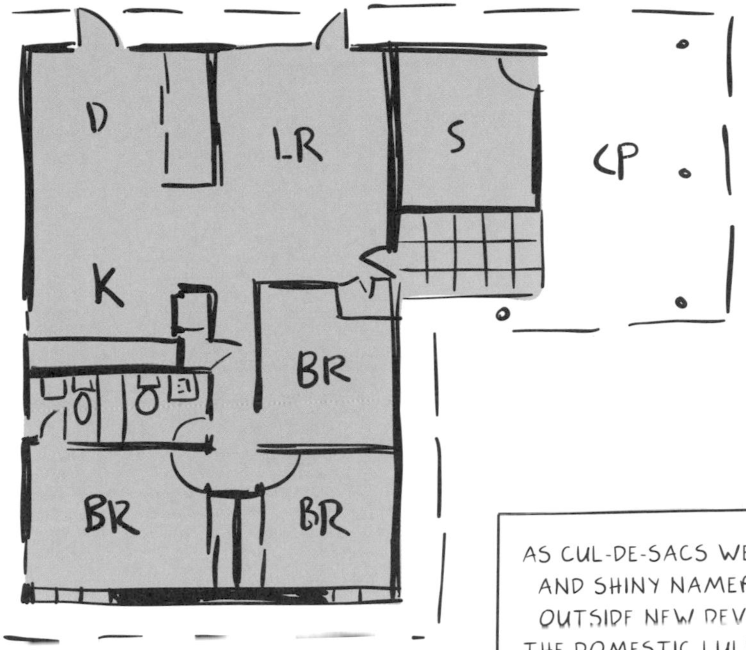
D
LR
S
CP
K
BR
BR
BR

AS CUL-DE-SACS WERE BEING PAVED AND SHINY NAMEPLATES STAKED OUTSIDE NEW DEVELOPMENTS IN THE DOMESTIC LULL AFTER WORLD WAR II, THE TELEVISION LAUGH TRACK WAS BORN.

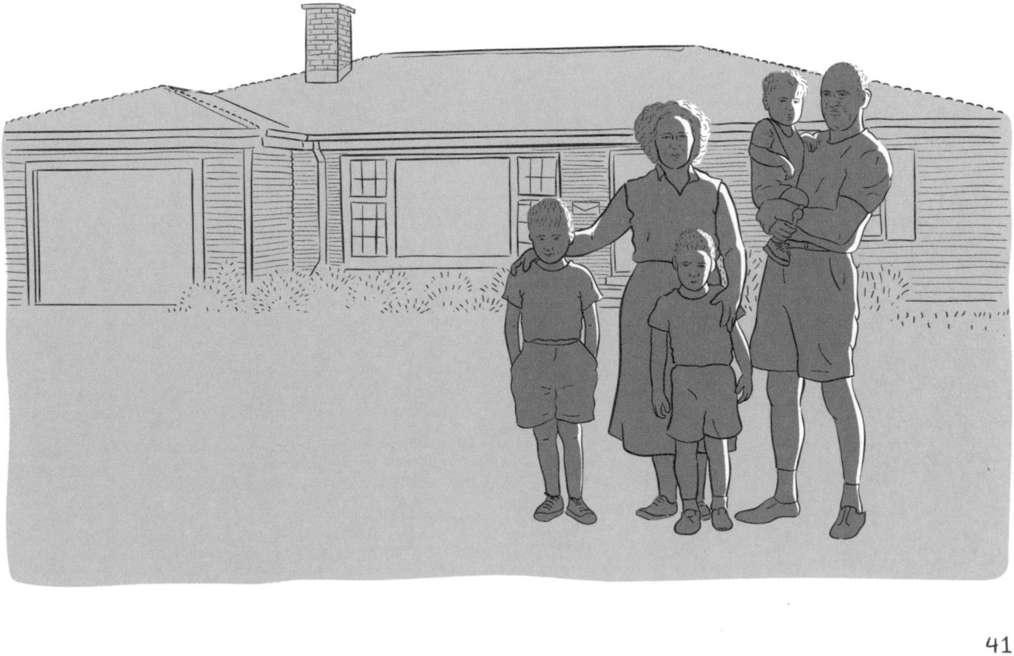

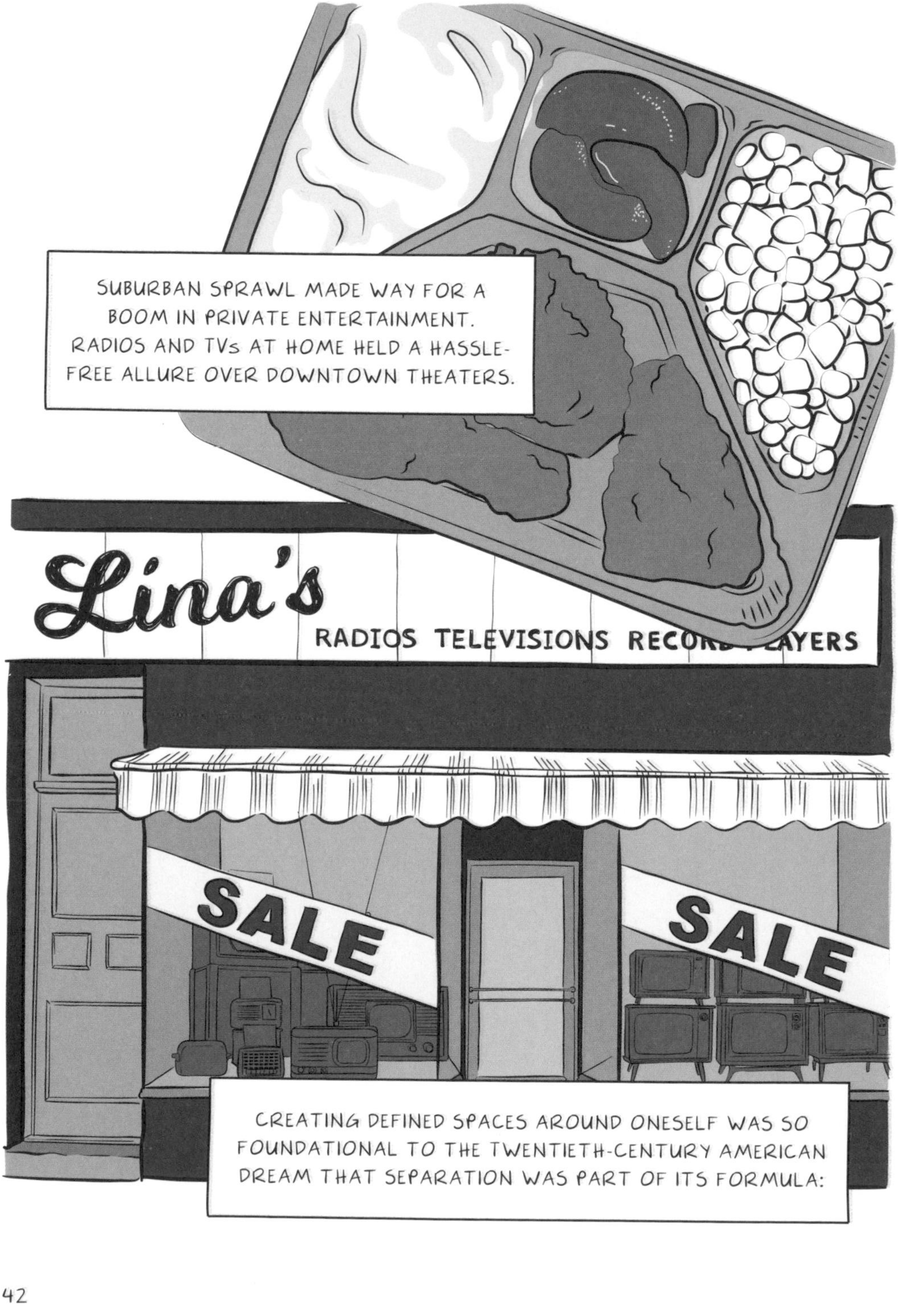
SUBURBAN SPRAWL MADE WAY FOR A BOOM IN PRIVATE ENTERTAINMENT. RADIOS AND TVs AT HOME HELD A HASSLE-FREE ALLURE OVER DOWNTOWN THEATERS.
Lina's
RADIOS TELEVISIONS
SALE
SALE
CREATING DEFINED SPACES AROUND ONESELF WAS SO FOUNDATIONAL TO THE TWENTIETH-CENTURY AMERICAN DREAM THAT SEPARATION WAS PART OF ITS FORMULA:

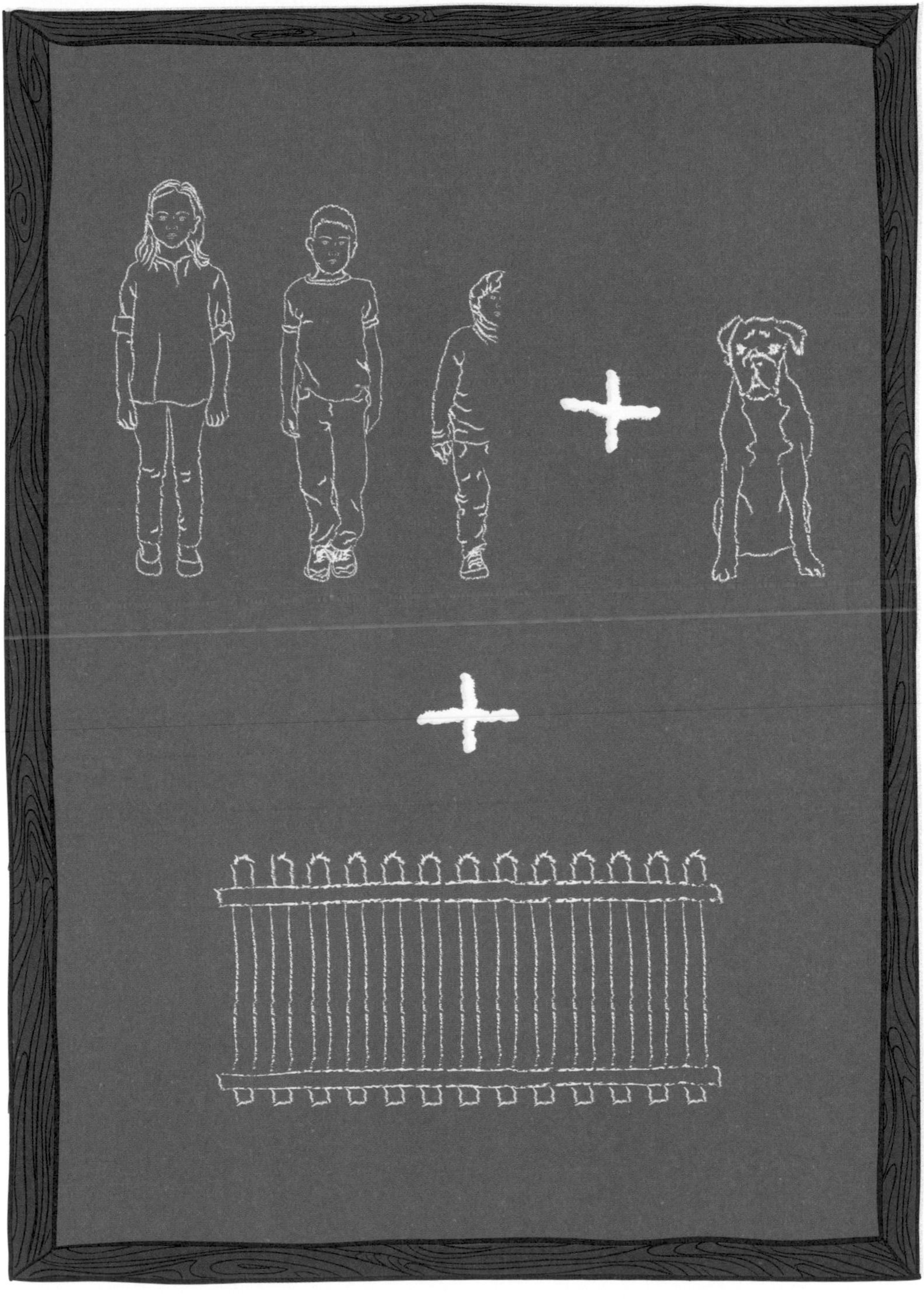

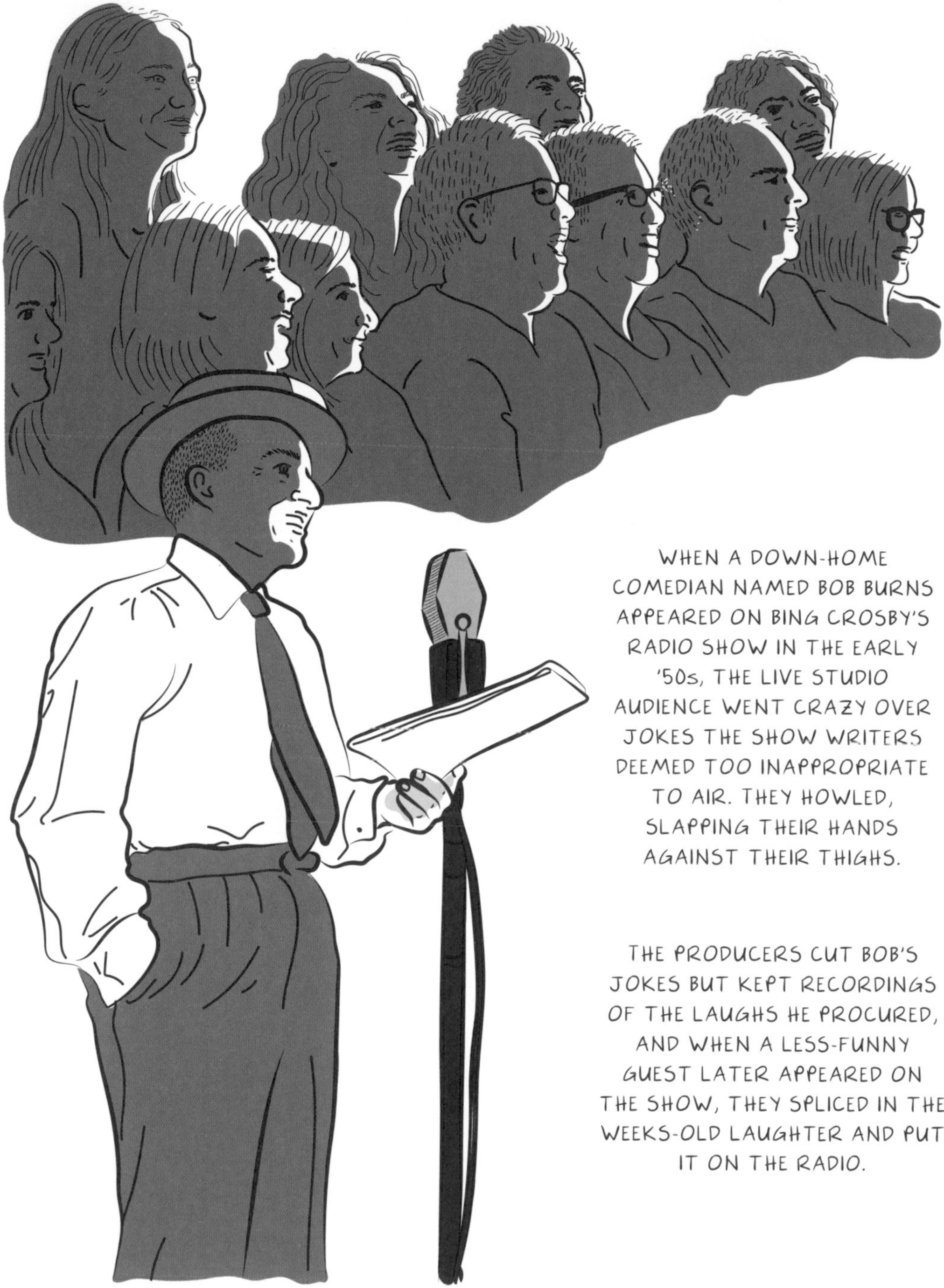

WHEN A DOWN-HOME COMEDIAN NAMED BOB BURNS APPEARED ON BING CROSBY'S RADIO SHOW IN THE EARLY '50s, THE LIVE STUDIO AUDIENCE WENT CRAZY OVER JOKES THE SHOW WRITERS DEEMED TOO INAPPROPRIATE TO AIR. THEY HOWLED, SLAPPING THEIR HANDS AGAINST THEIR THIGHS.

THE PRODUCERS CUT BOB'S JOKES BUT KEPT RECORDINGS OF THE LAUGHS HE PROCURED, AND WHEN A LESS-FUNNY GUEST LATER APPEARED ON THE SHOW, THEY SPLICED IN THE WEEKS-OLD LAUGHTER AND PUT IT ON THE RADIO.

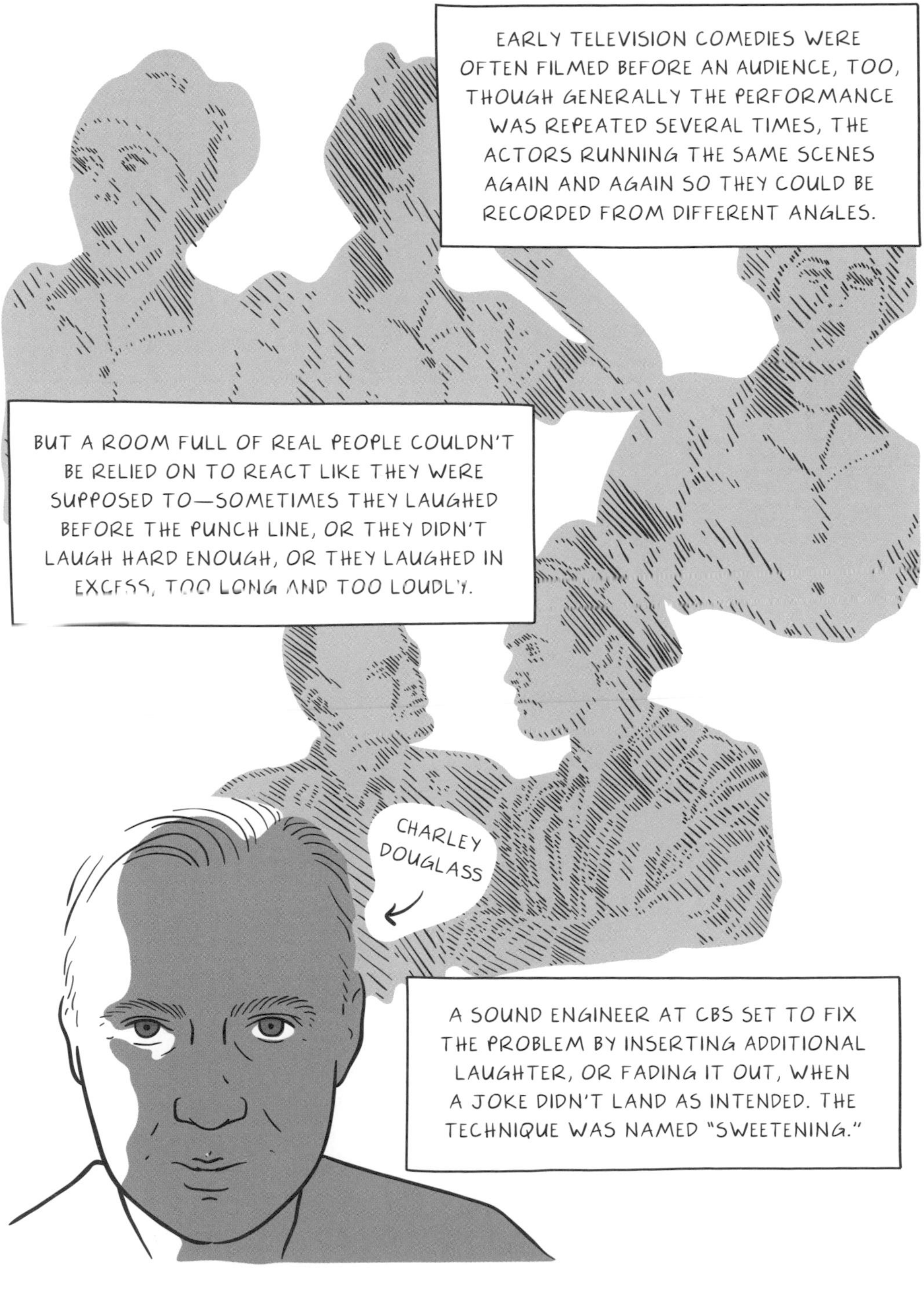
EARLY TELEVISION COMEDIES WERE OFTEN FILMED BEFORE AN AUDIENCE, TOO, THOUGH GENERALLY THE PERFORMANCE WAS REPEATED SEVERAL TIMES, THE ACTORS RUNNING THE SAME SCENES AGAIN AND AGAIN SO THEY COULD BE RECORDED FROM DIFFERENT ANGLES.
BUT A ROOM FULL OF REAL PEOPLE COULDN'T BE RELIED ON TO REACT LIKE THEY WERE SUPPOSED TO—SOMETIMES THEY LAUGHED BEFORE THE PUNCH LINE, OR THEY DIDN'T LAUGH HARD ENOUGH, OR THEY LAUGHED IN EXCESS, TOO LONG AND TOO LOUDLY.
CHARLEY DOUGLASS
A SOUND ENGINEER AT CBS SET TO FIX THE PROBLEM BY INSERTING ADDITIONAL LAUGHTER, OR FADING IT OUT, WHEN A JOKE DIDN'T LAND AS INTENDED. THE TECHNIQUE WAS NAMED "SWEETENING."

HE BUILT A MACHINE THAT PRODUCED LAUGHTER WITH THE TURN OF A WHEEL:

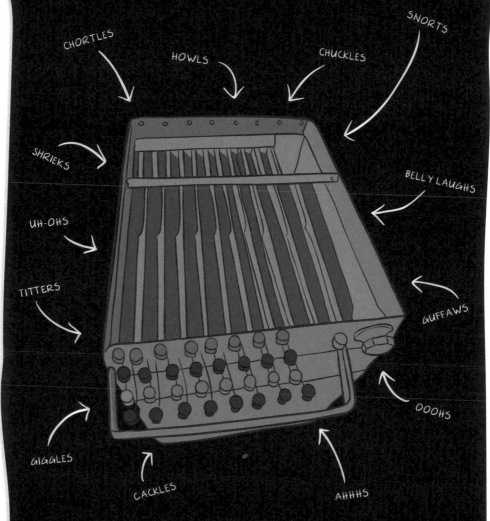

CHORTLES

HOWLS

CHUCKLES

SNORTS

SHRIEKS

BELLY LAUGHS

UH-OHS

TITTERS

GUFFAWS

GIGGLES

CACKLES

AHHHS

OOOHS

THE DEVICE CONTAINED HUNDREDS OF DISTINCT LAUGHS, ALL
DESIGNED TO SOUND LIKE REAL PEOPLE, OR PROTOTYPES OF REAL
PEOPLE—ONE WAS NAMED "HOUSEWIFE GIGGLES"; ANOTHER WAS
CONSTRUCTED TO REPLICATE THE HOLLOW RESPONSE OF SOMEONE
WHO DOESN'T GET THE JOKE BUT LAUGHS ALONG ANYWAY.

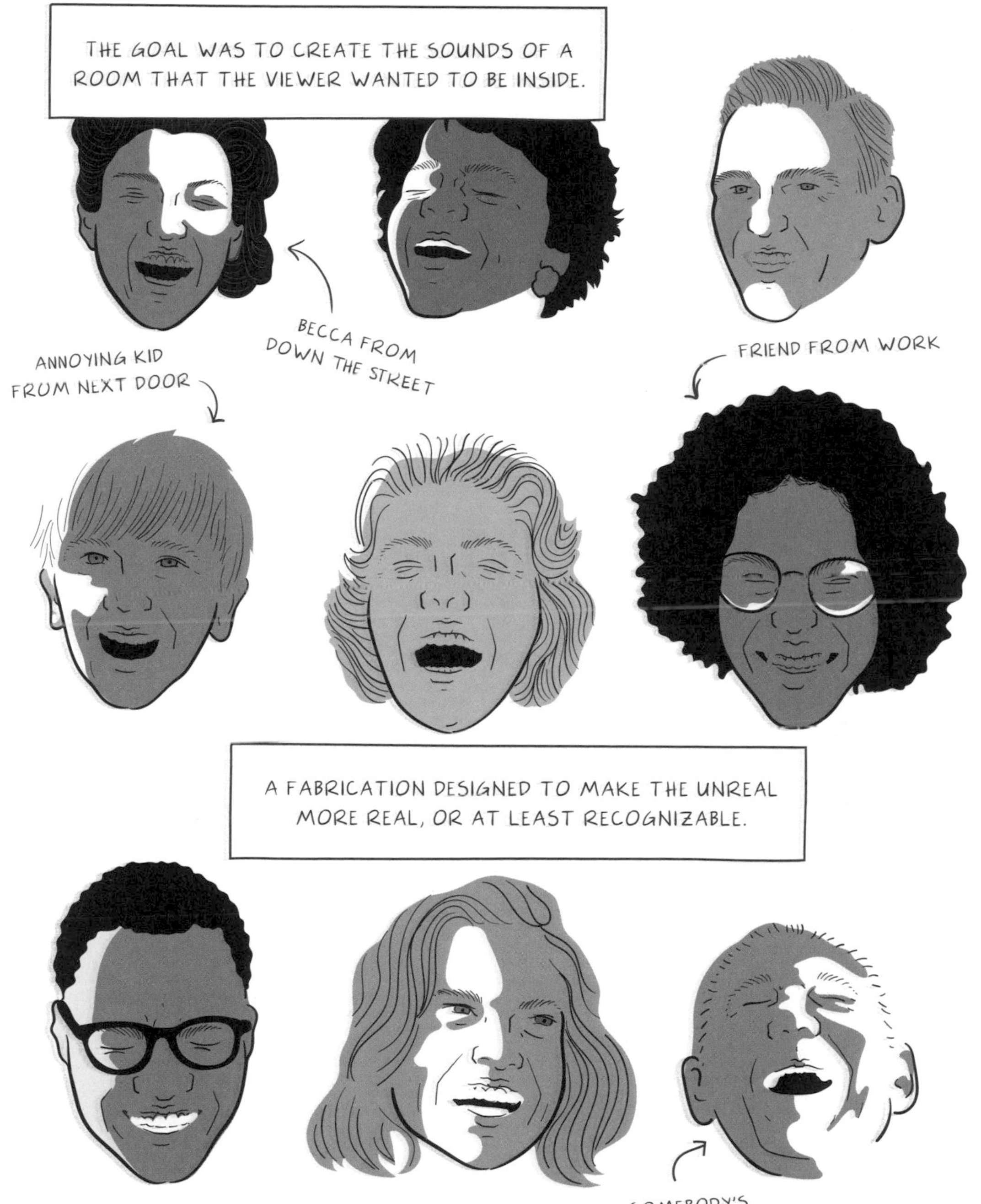
THE GOAL WAS TO CREATE THE SOUNDS OF A ROOM THAT THE VIEWER WANTED TO BE INSIDE.
BECCA FROM DOWN THE STREET
ANNOYING KID FROM NEXT DOOR
FRIEND FROM WORK
A FABRICATION DESIGNED TO MAKE THE UNREAL MORE REAL, OR AT LEAST RECOGNIZABLE.
SOMEBODY'S GRANDPA

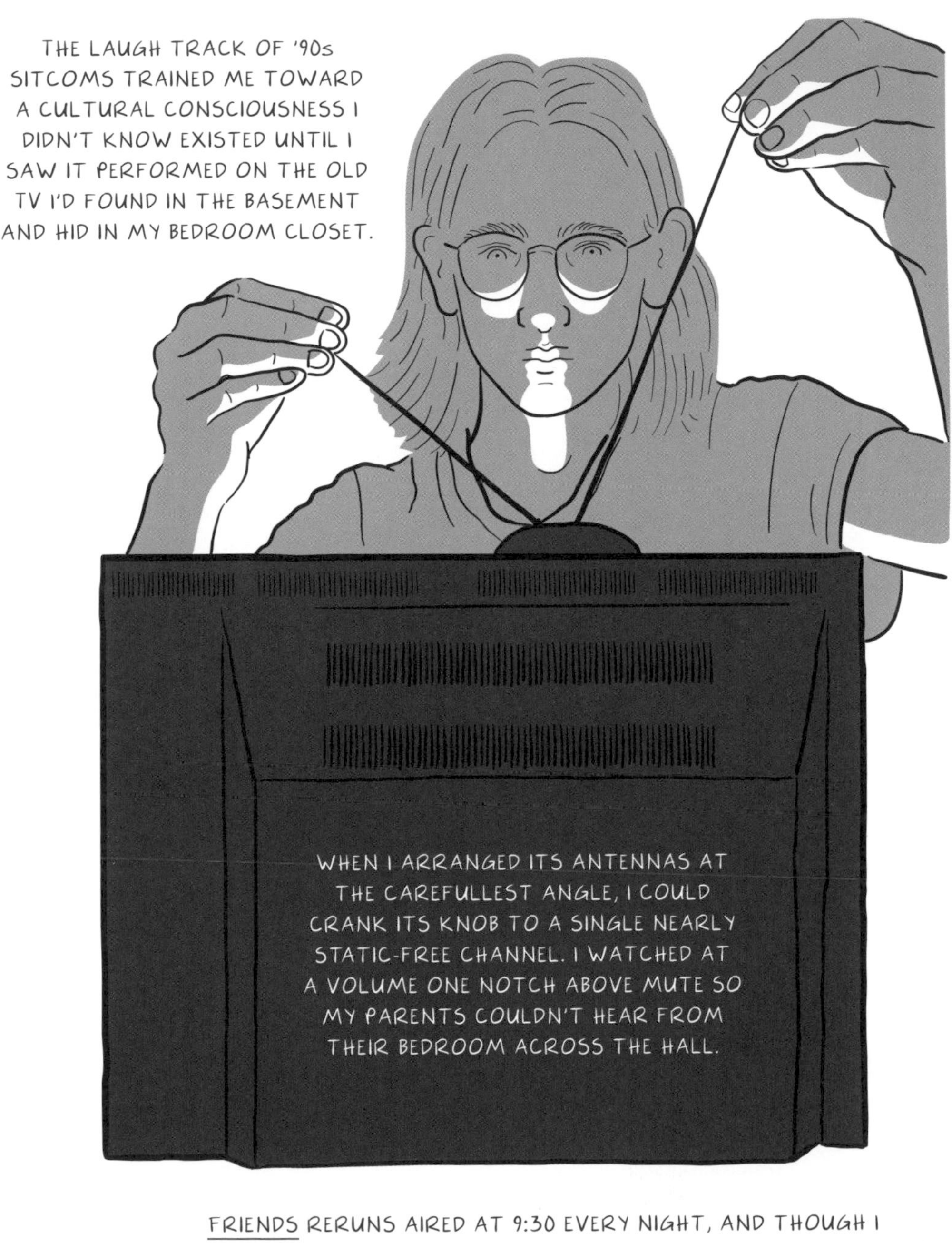
THE LAUGH TRACK OF '90s SITCOMS TRAINED ME TOWARD A CULTURAL CONSCIOUSNESS I DIDN'T KNOW EXISTED UNTIL I SAW IT PERFORMED ON THE OLD TV I'D FOUND IN THE BASEMENT AND HID IN MY BEDROOM CLOSET.
WHEN I ARRANGED ITS ANTENNAS AT THE CAREFULLEST ANGLE, I COULD CRANK ITS KNOB TO A SINGLE NEARLY STATIC-FREE CHANNEL. I WATCHED AT A VOLUME ONE NOTCH ABOVE MUTE SO MY PARENTS COULDN'T HEAR FROM THEIR BEDROOM ACROSS THE HALL.

FRIENDS RERUNS AIRED AT 9:30 EVERY NIGHT, AND THOUGH I DIDN'T UNDERSTAND MANY OF THE JOKES, THE AUDIENCE'S LAUGHTER TAUGHT ME WHAT I WAS SUPPOSED TO FIND FUNNY.

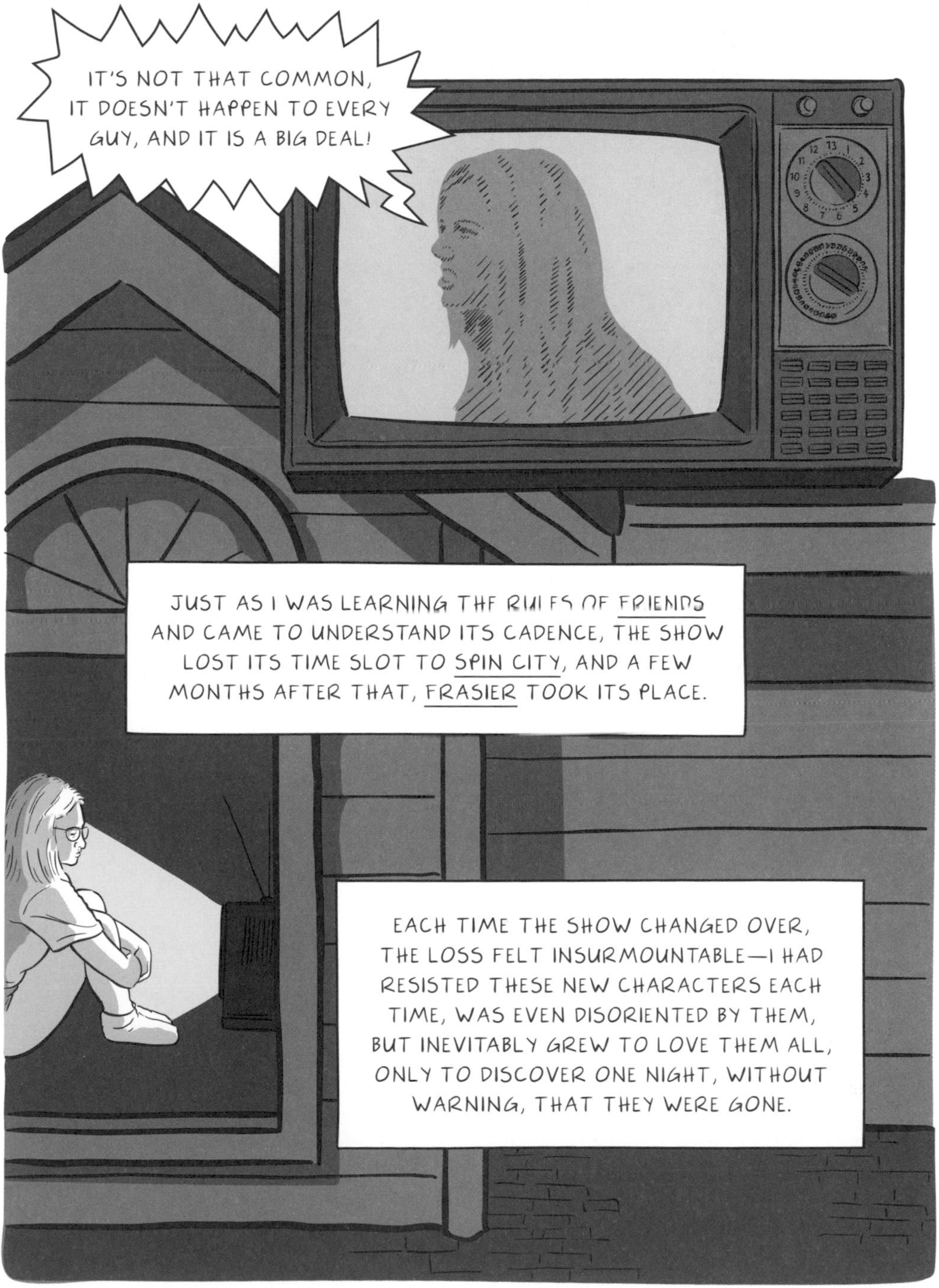
IT'S NOT THAT COMMON, IT DOESN'T HAPPEN TO EVERY GUY, AND IT IS A BIG DEAL!
JUST AS I WAS LEARNING THE RULES OF FRIENDS AND CAME TO UNDERSTAND ITS CADENCE, THE SHOW LOST ITS TIME SLOT TO SPIN CITY, AND A FEW MONTHS AFTER THAT, FRASIER TOOK ITS PLACE.
EACH TIME THE SHOW CHANGED OVER, THE LOSS FELT INSURMOUNTABLE—I HAD RESISTED THESE NEW CHARACTERS EACH TIME, WAS EVEN DISORIENTED BY THEM, BUT INEVITABLY GREW TO LOVE THEM ALL, ONLY TO DISCOVER ONE NIGHT, WITHOUT WARNING, THAT THEY WERE GONE.

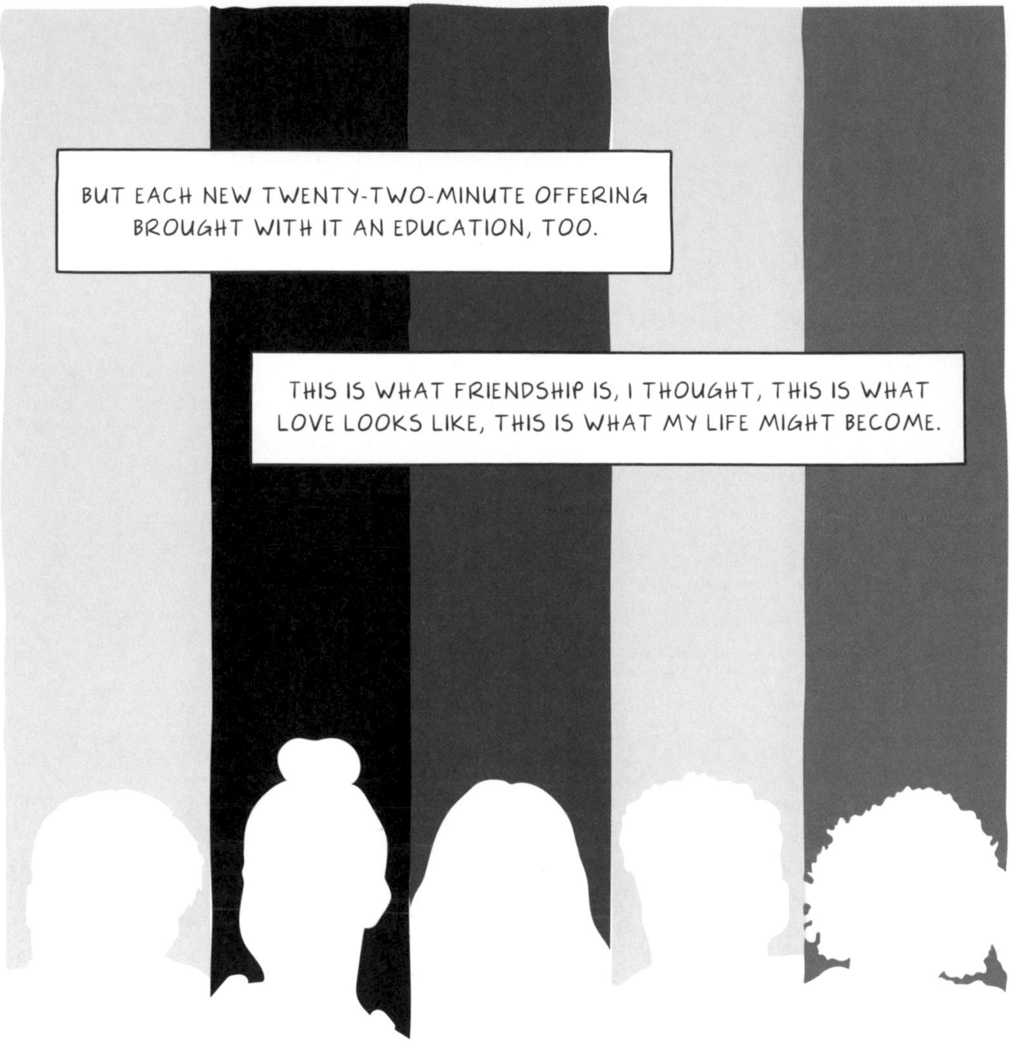
BUT EACH NEW TWENTY-TWO-MINUTE OFFERING BROUGHT WITH IT AN EDUCATION, TOO.
THIS IS WHAT FRIENDSHIP IS, I THOUGHT, THIS IS WHAT LOVE LOOKS LIKE, THIS IS WHAT MY LIFE MIGHT BECOME.

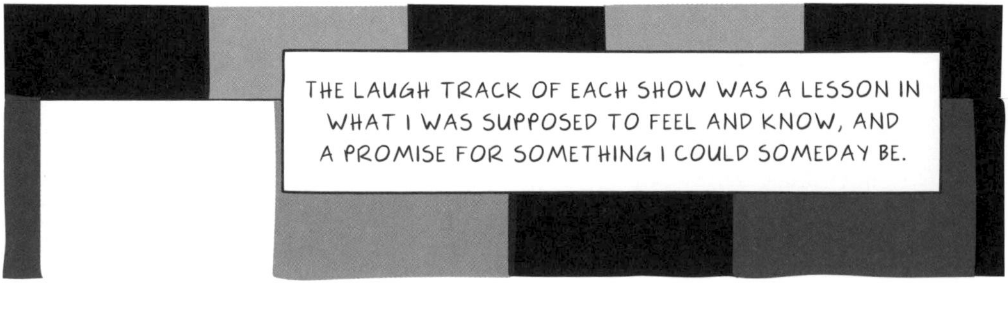
THE LAUGH TRACK OF EACH SHOW WAS A LESSON IN WHAT I WAS SUPPOSED TO FEEL AND KNOW, AND A PROMISE FOR SOMETHING I COULD SOMEDAY BE.

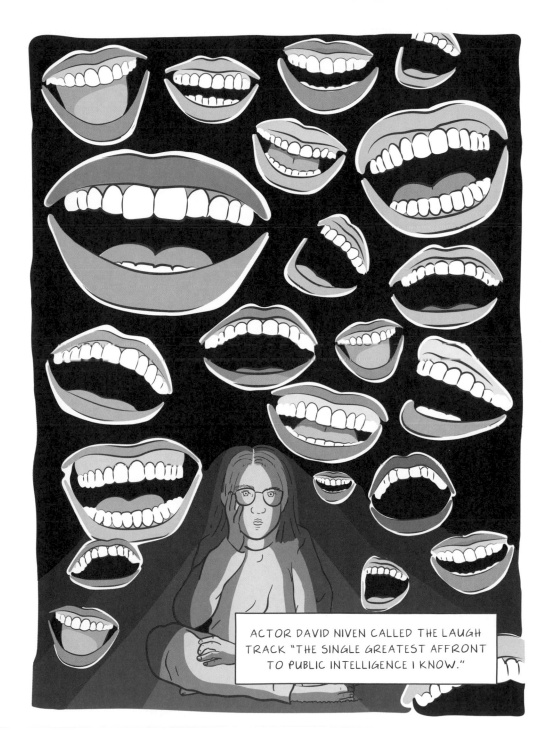

ACTOR DAVID NIVEN CALLED THE LAUGH TRACK "THE SINGLE GREATEST AFFRONT TO PUBLIC INTELLIGENCE I KNOW."

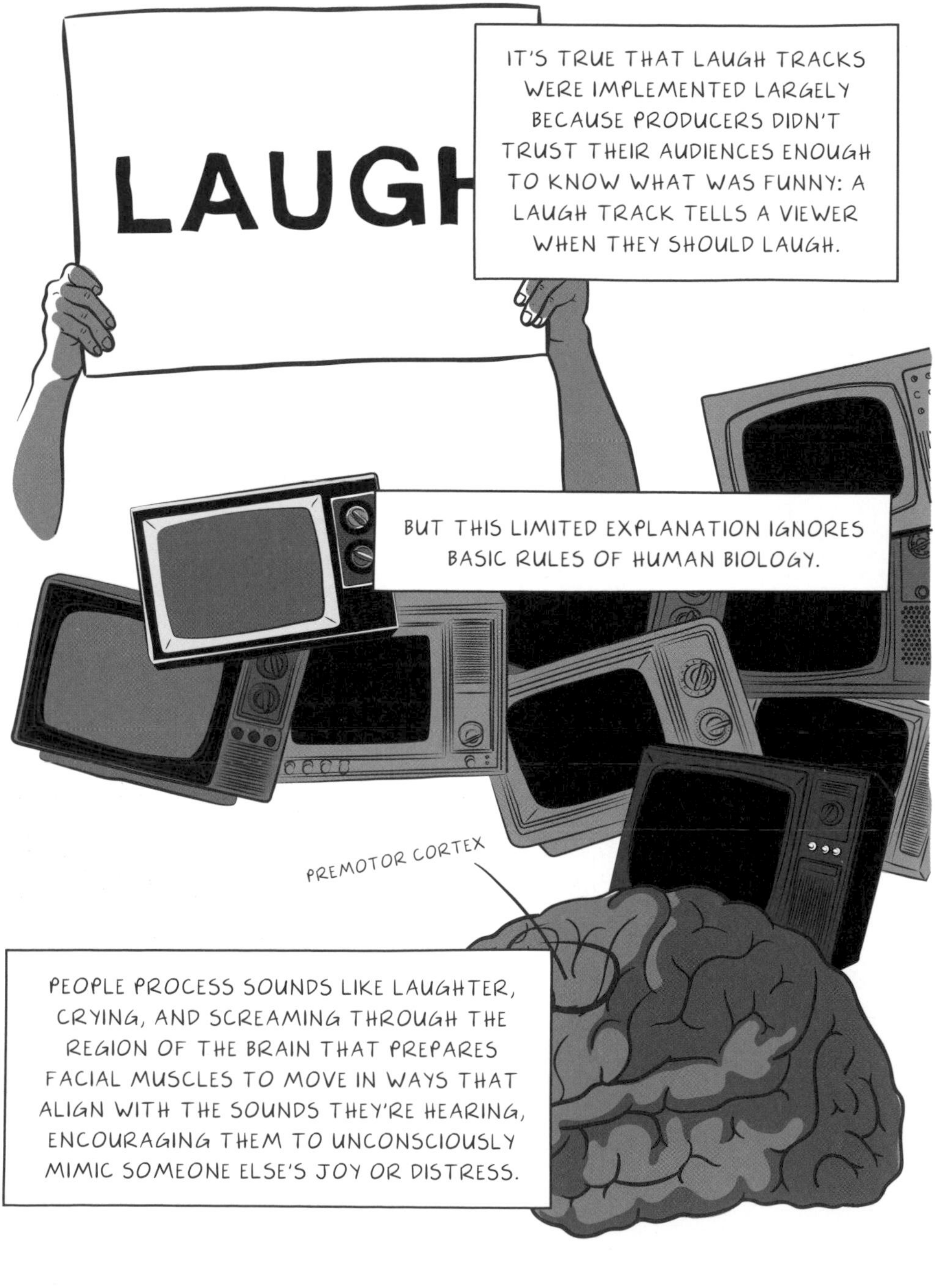
LAUGH
IT'S TRUE THAT LAUGH TRACKS WERE IMPLEMENTED LARGELY BECAUSE PRODUCERS DIDN'T TRUST THEIR AUDIENCES ENOUGH TO KNOW WHAT WAS FUNNY: A LAUGH TRACK TELLS A VIEWER WHEN THEY SHOULD LAUGH.
BUT THIS LIMITED EXPLANATION IGNORES BASIC RULES OF HUMAN BIOLOGY.
PREMOTOR CORTEX
PEOPLE PROCESS SOUNDS LIKE LAUGHTER, CRYING, AND SCREAMING THROUGH THE REGION OF THE BRAIN THAT PREPARES FACIAL MUSCLES TO MOVE IN WAYS THAT ALIGN WITH THE SOUNDS THEY'RE HEARING, ENCOURAGING THEM TO UNCONSCIOUSLY MIMIC SOMEONE ELSE'S JOY OR DISTRESS.

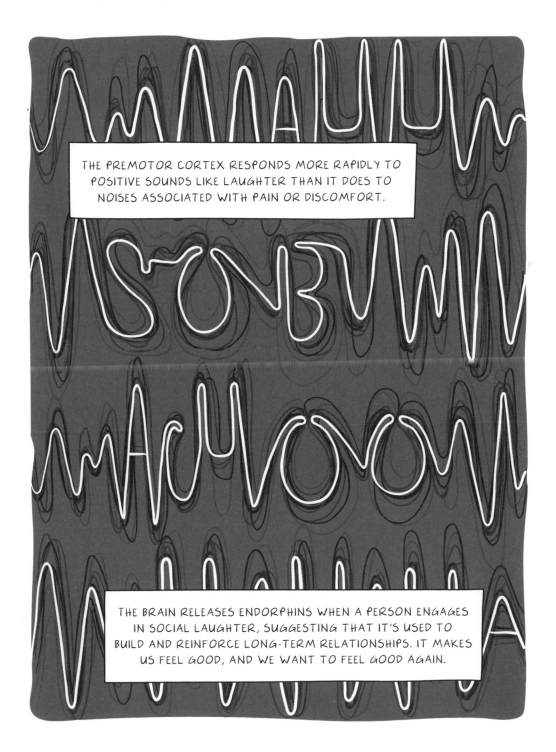

THE PREMOTOR CORTEX RESPONDS MORE RAPIDLY TO POSITIVE SOUNDS LIKE LAUGHTER THAN IT DOES TO NOISES ASSOCIATED WITH PAIN OR DISCOMFORT.

THE BRAIN RELEASES ENDORPHINS WHEN A PERSON ENGAGES IN SOCIAL LAUGHTER, SUGGESTING THAT IT'S USED TO BUILD AND REINFORCE LONG-TERM RELATIONSHIPS. IT MAKES US FEEL *GOOD*, AND WE WANT TO FEEL *GOOD* AGAIN.

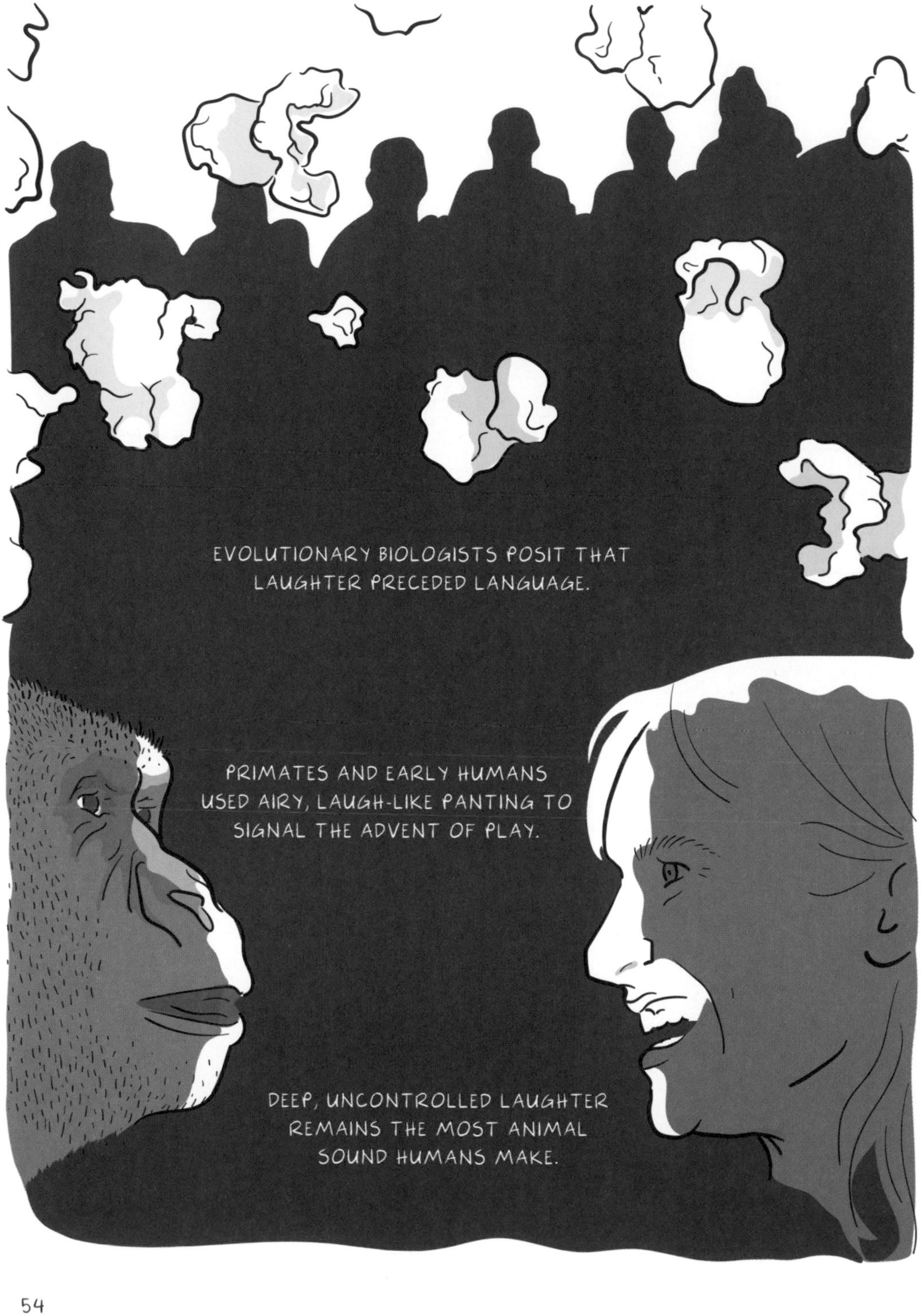
EVOLUTIONARY BIOLOGISTS POSIT THAT LAUGHTER PRECEDED LANGUAGE.
PRIMATES AND EARLY HUMANS USED AIRY, LAUGH-LIKE PANTING TO SIGNAL THE ADVENT OF PLAY.
DEEP, UNCONTROLLED LAUGHTER REMAINS THE MOST ANIMAL SOUND HUMANS MAKE.

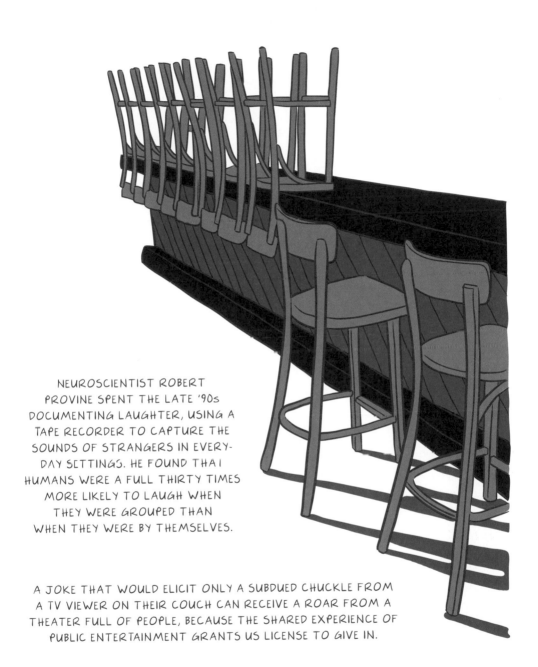

NEUROSCIENTIST ROBERT PROVINE SPENT THE LATE '90s DOCUMENTING LAUGHTER, USING A TAPE RECORDER TO CAPTURE THE SOUNDS OF STRANGERS IN EVERY-DAY SETTINGS. HE FOUND THAT HUMANS WERE A FULL THIRTY TIMES MORE LIKELY TO LAUGH WHEN THEY WERE GROUPED THAN WHEN THEY WERE BY THEMSELVES.

A JOKE THAT WOULD ELICIT ONLY A SUBDUED CHUCKLE FROM A TV VIEWER ON THEIR COUCH CAN RECEIVE A ROAR FROM A THEATER FULL OF PEOPLE, BECAUSE THE SHARED EXPERIENCE OF PUBLIC ENTERTAINMENT GRANTS US LICENSE TO GIVE IN.

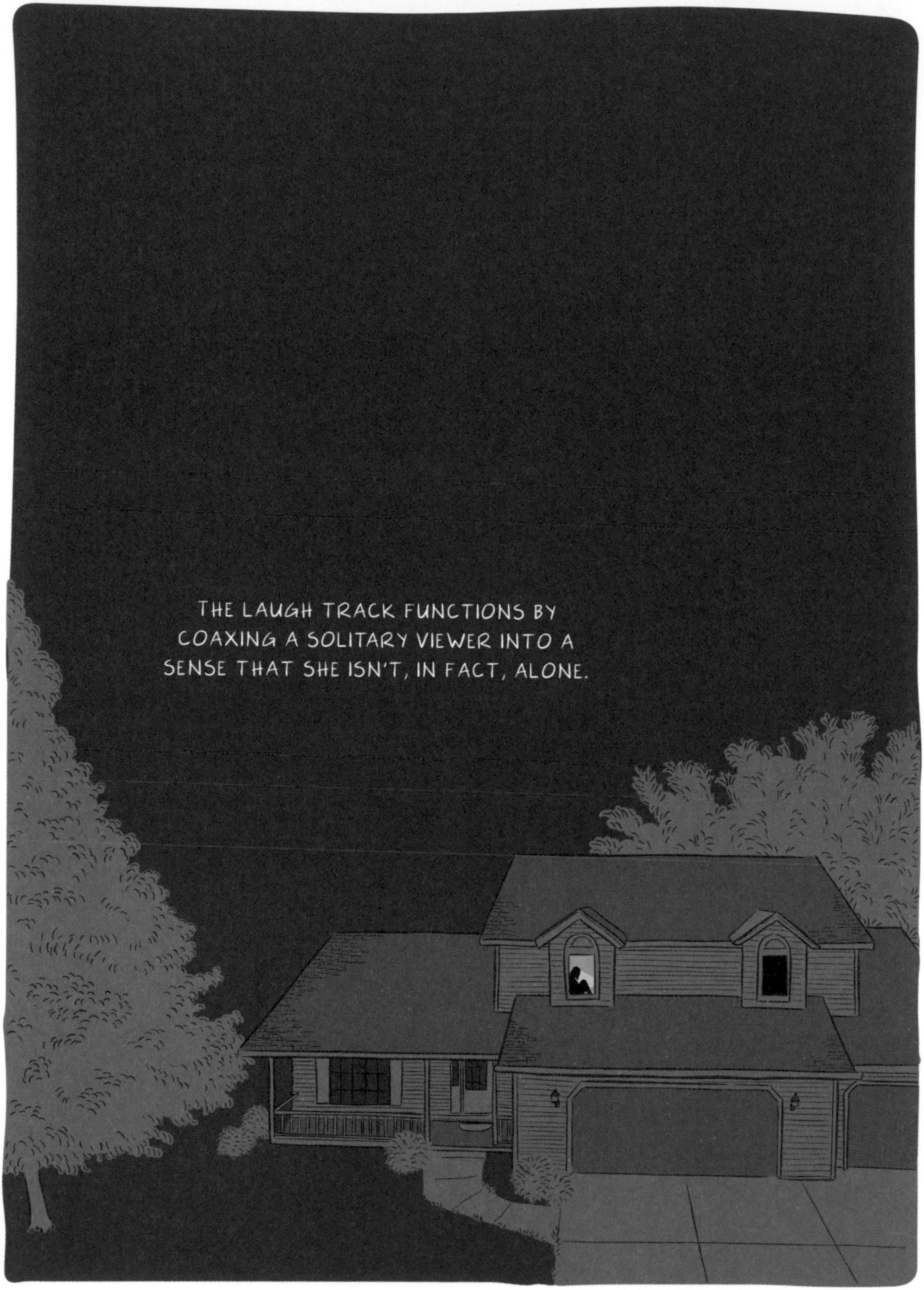
THE LAUGH TRACK FUNCTIONS BY COAXING A SOLITARY VIEWER INTO A SENSE THAT SHE ISN'T, IN FACT, ALONE.

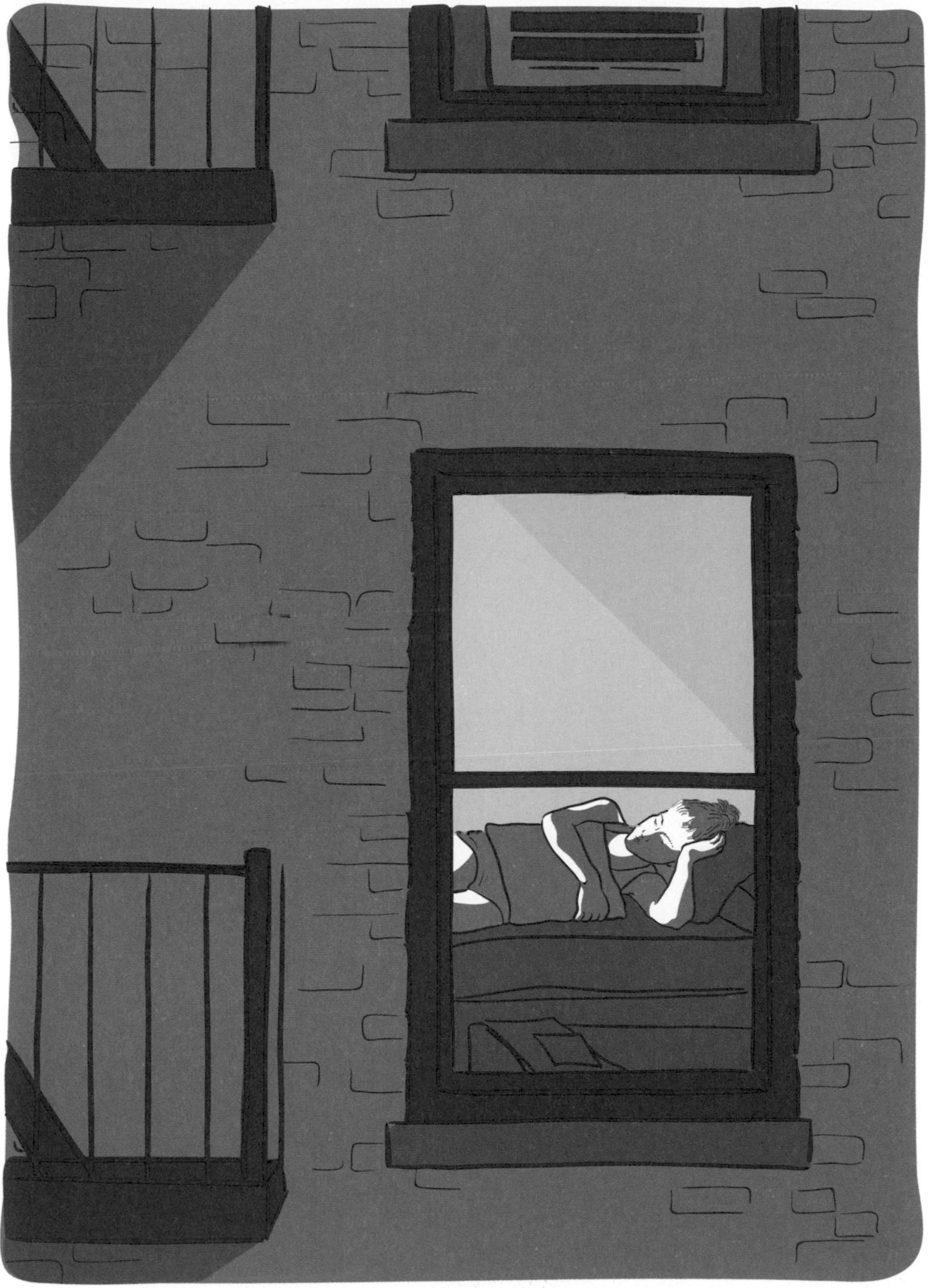

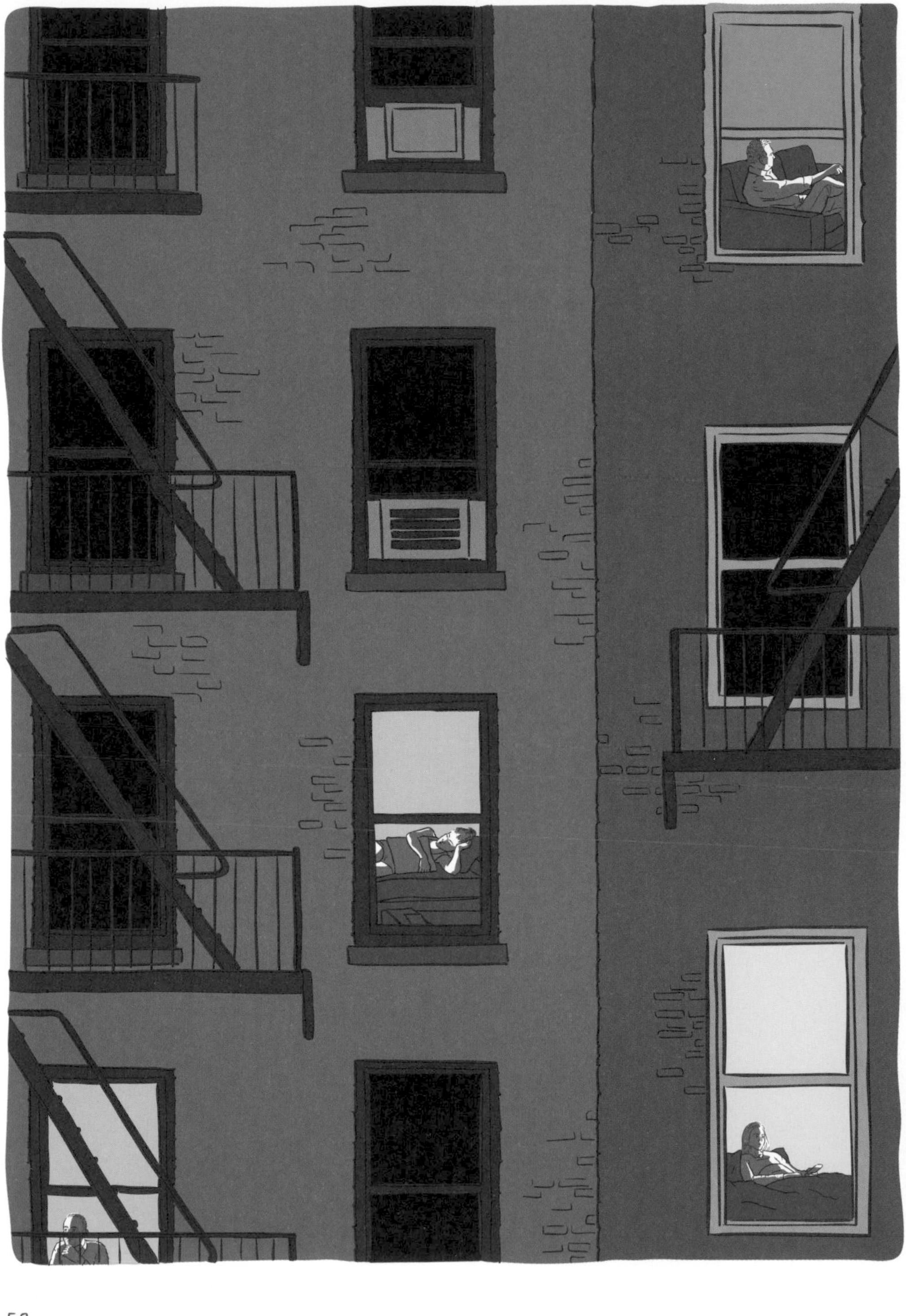

III

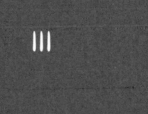

Loneliness triggers biological changes which cause illness and early death

Dang... nals activated in the brain by loneliness ulti...y affect the immu...syste...ientists have found.

VIVEK MURTHY, A FORMER SURGEON GENERAL, HAS SAID THAT THE MOST PREVALENT HEALTH ISSUE IN AMERICA IS ISOLATION.

Big

Vhy Loneliness May L Public-Health Issue

Loneliness May Warp Our Genes, and Our Immune Systems

LONELINESS WILL BE CLASSIFIED AS AN EPIDEMIC BY 2030.

U.K. Appoints a Minister for Loneliness

Loneliness makes cancer 'more likely and deadly'

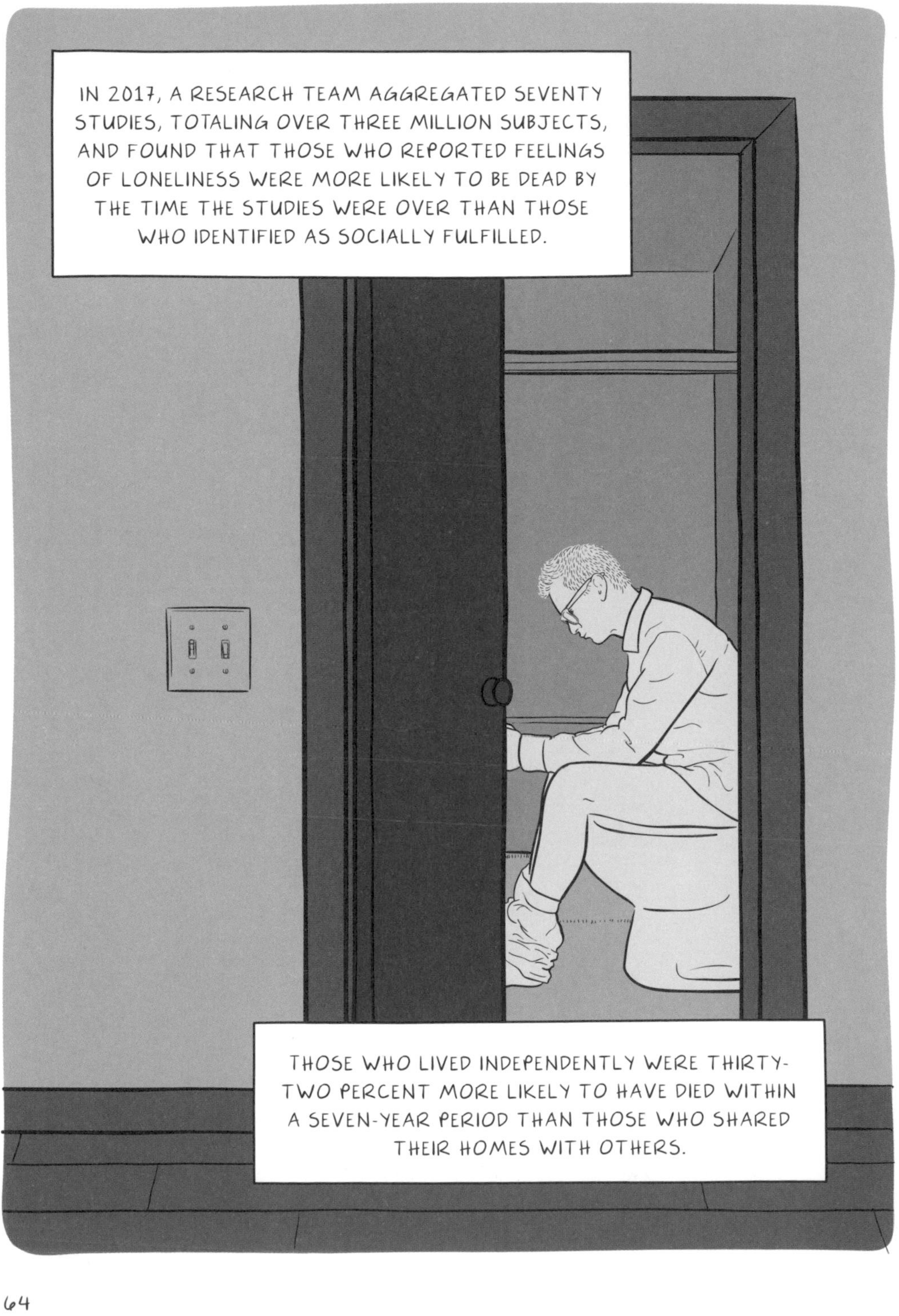
IN 2017, A RESEARCH TEAM AGGREGATED SEVENTY STUDIES, TOTALING OVER THREE MILLION SUBJECTS, AND FOUND THAT THOSE WHO REPORTED FEELINGS OF LONELINESS WERE MORE LIKELY TO BE DEAD BY THE TIME THE STUDIES WERE OVER THAN THOSE WHO IDENTIFIED AS SOCIALLY FULFILLED.
THOSE WHO LIVED INDEPENDENTLY WERE THIRTY-TWO PERCENT MORE LIKELY TO HAVE DIED WITHIN A SEVEN-YEAR PERIOD THAN THOSE WHO SHARED THEIR HOMES WITH OTHERS.

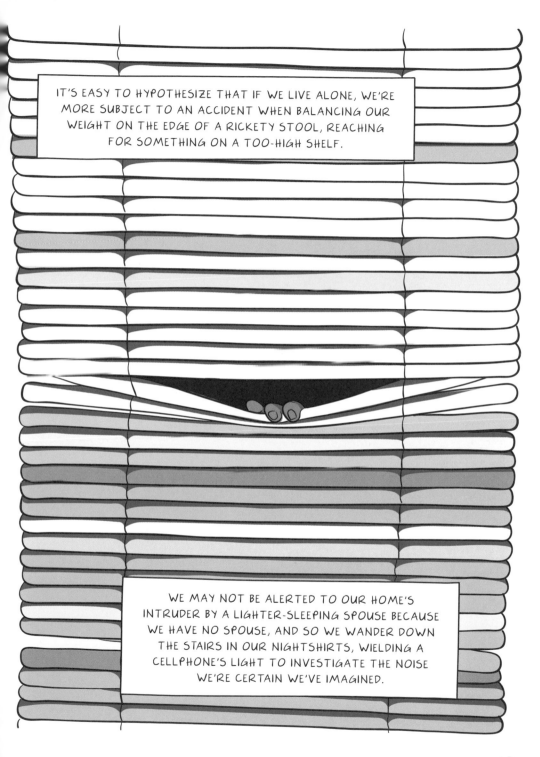

IT'S EASY TO HYPOTHESIZE THAT IF WE LIVE ALONE, WE'RE MORE SUBJECT TO AN ACCIDENT WHEN BALANCING OUR WEIGHT ON THE EDGE OF A RICKETY STOOL, REACHING FOR SOMETHING ON A TOO-HIGH SHELF.

WE MAY NOT BE ALERTED TO OUR HOME'S INTRUDER BY A LIGHTER-SLEEPING SPOUSE BECAUSE WE HAVE NO SPOUSE, AND SO WE WANDER DOWN THE STAIRS IN OUR NIGHTSHIRTS, WIELDING A CELLPHONE'S LIGHT TO INVESTIGATE THE NOISE WE'RE CERTAIN WE'VE IMAGINED.

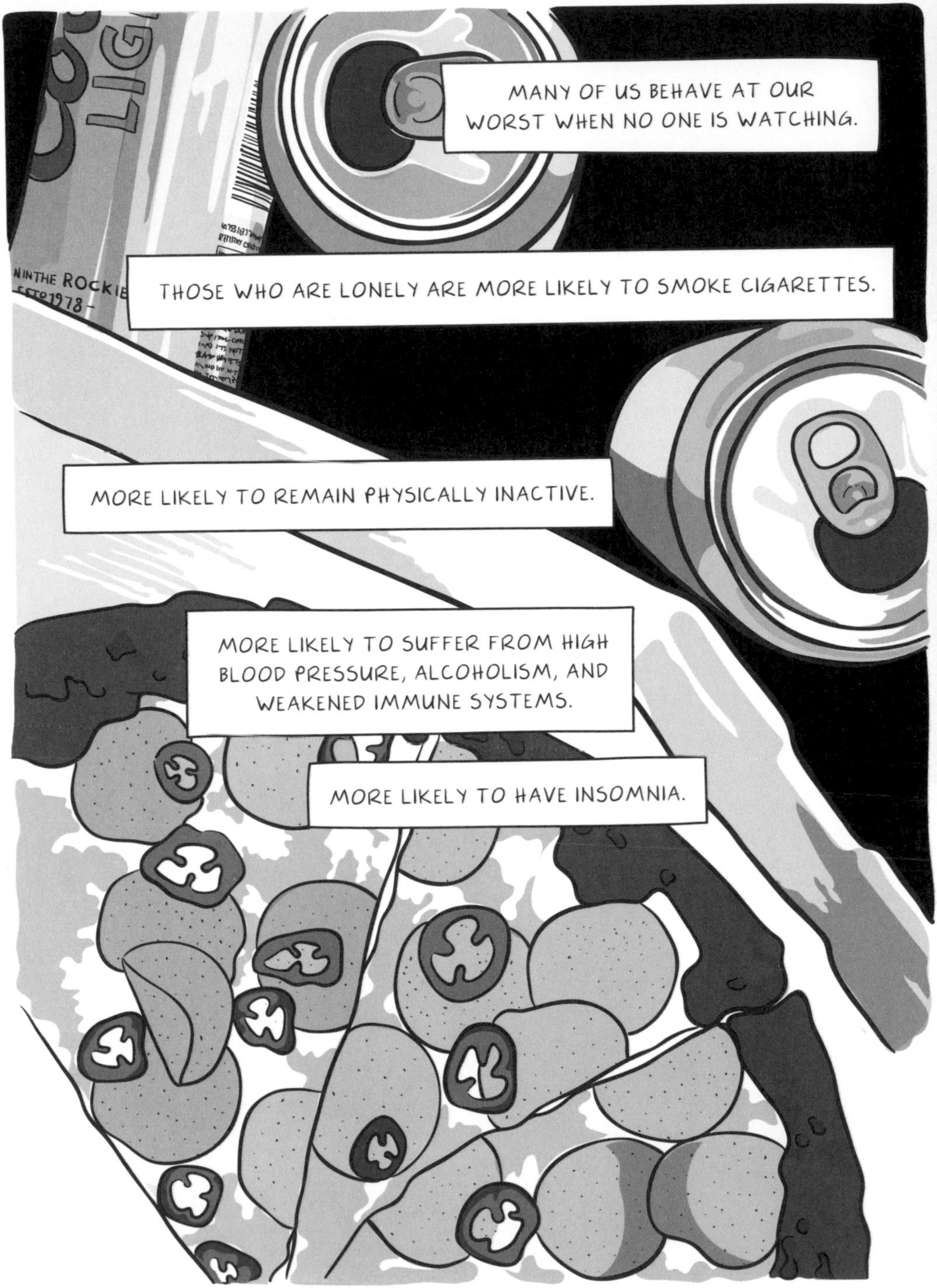
MANY OF US BEHAVE AT OUR WORST WHEN NO ONE IS WATCHING.
THOSE WHO ARE LONELY ARE MORE LIKELY TO SMOKE CIGARETTES.
MORE LIKELY TO REMAIN PHYSICALLY INACTIVE.
MORE LIKELY TO SUFFER FROM HIGH BLOOD PRESSURE, ALCOHOLISM, AND WEAKENED IMMUNE SYSTEMS.
MORE LIKELY TO HAVE INSOMNIA.

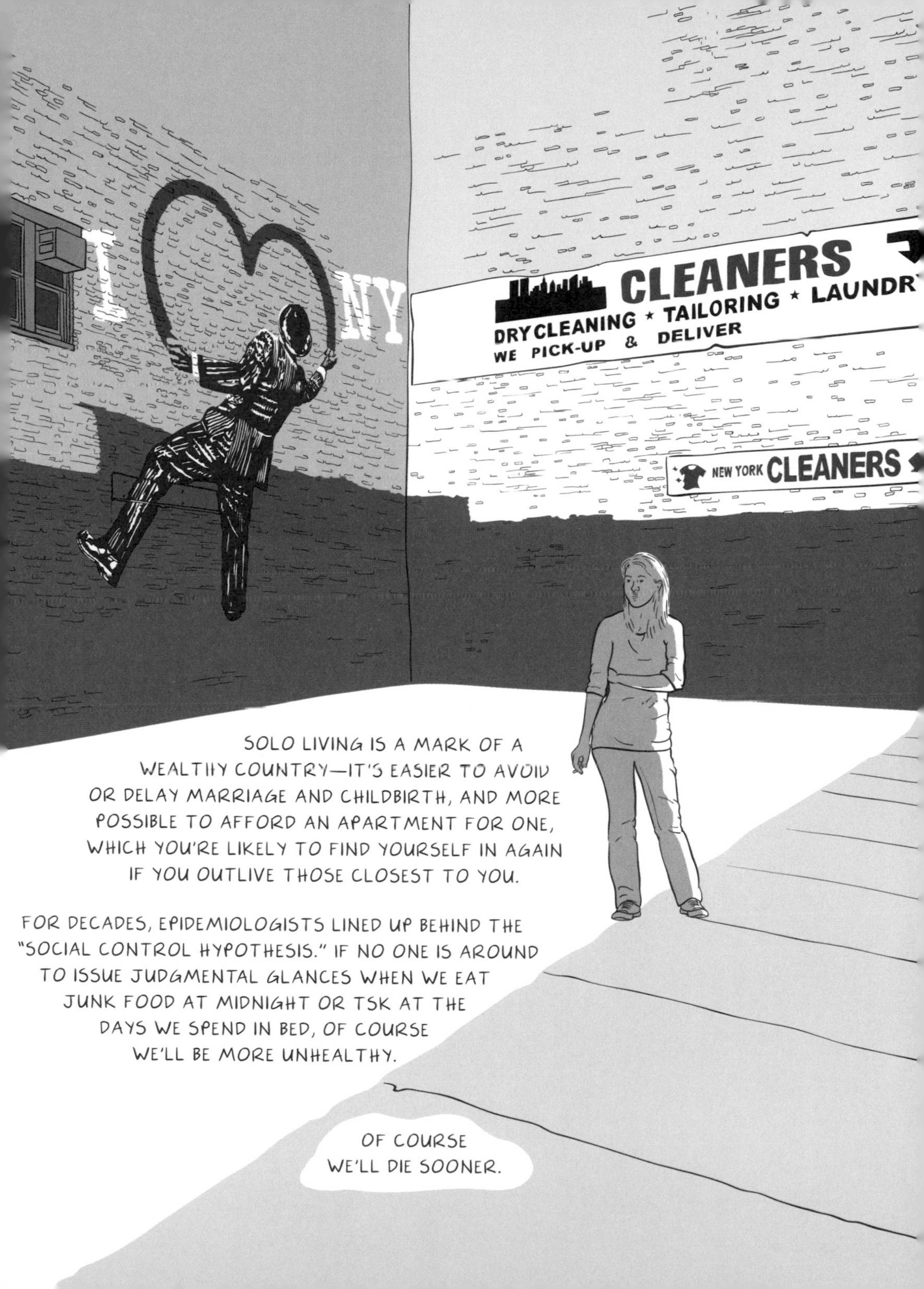
I NY
CLEANERS
DRYCLEANING ★ TAILORING ★ LAUNDR
WE PICK-UP & DELIVER
NEW YORK CLEANERS
SOLO LIVING IS A MARK OF A WEALTHY COUNTRY—IT'S EASIER TO AVOID OR DELAY MARRIAGE AND CHILDBIRTH, AND MORE POSSIBLE TO AFFORD AN APARTMENT FOR ONE, WHICH YOU'RE LIKELY TO FIND YOURSELF IN AGAIN IF YOU OUTLIVE THOSE CLOSEST TO YOU.
FOR DECADES, EPIDEMIOLOGISTS LINED UP BEHIND THE "SOCIAL CONTROL HYPOTHESIS." IF NO ONE IS AROUND TO ISSUE JUDGMENTAL GLANCES WHEN WE EAT JUNK FOOD AT MIDNIGHT OR TSK AT THE DAYS WE SPEND IN BED, OF COURSE WE'LL BE MORE UNHEALTHY.
OF COURSE WE'LL DIE SOONER.

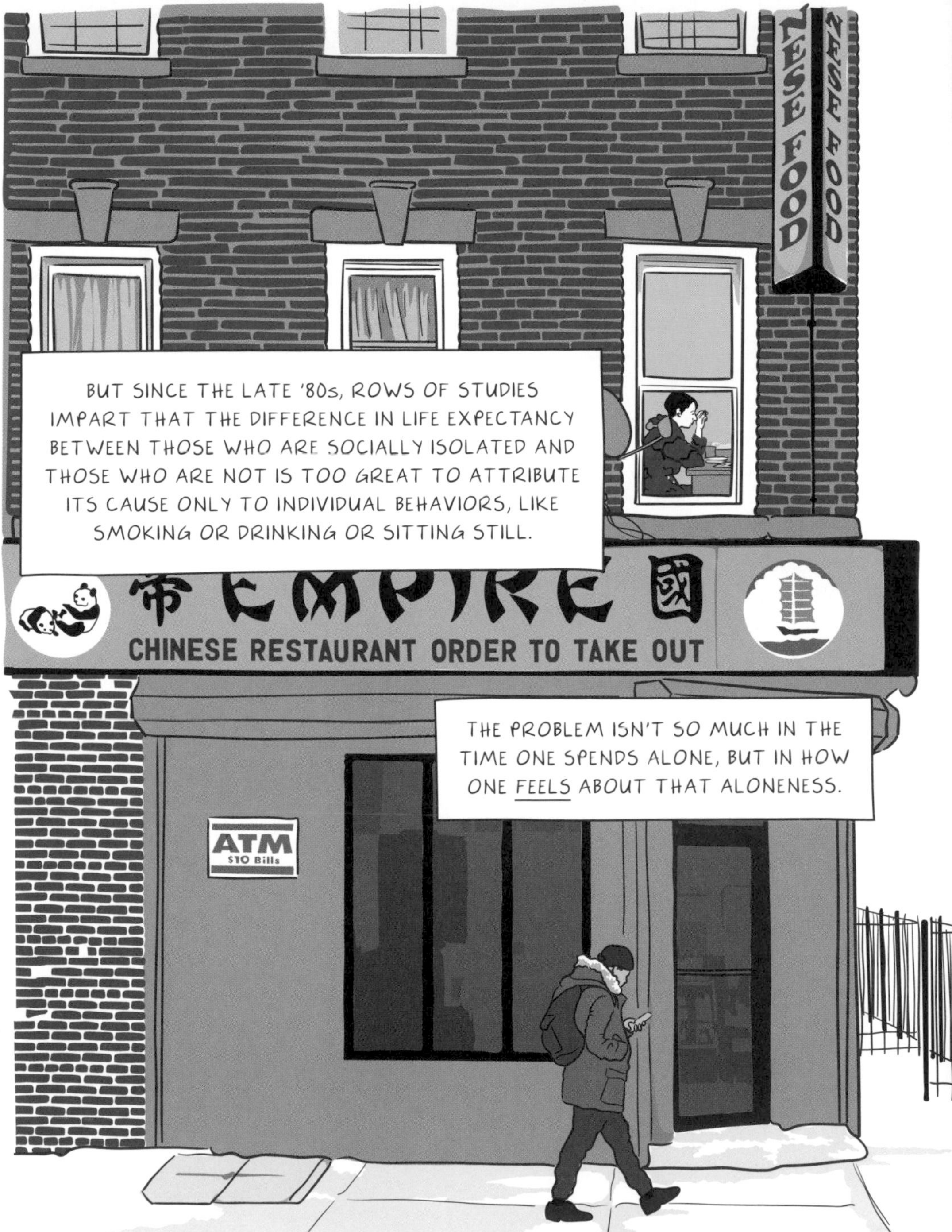
NESE FOOD
BUT SINCE THE LATE '80s, ROWS OF STUDIES IMPART THAT THE DIFFERENCE IN LIFE EXPECTANCY BETWEEN THOSE WHO ARE SOCIALLY ISOLATED AND THOSE WHO ARE NOT IS TOO GREAT TO ATTRIBUTE ITS CAUSE ONLY TO INDIVIDUAL BEHAVIORS, LIKE SMOKING OR DRINKING OR SITTING STILL.
帝 EMPIRE 國
CHINESE RESTAURANT ORDER TO TAKE OUT
THE PROBLEM ISN'T SO MUCH IN THE TIME ONE SPENDS ALONE, BUT IN HOW ONE FEELS ABOUT THAT ALONENESS.
ATM
$10 Bills

UCLA LONELINESS SCALE

Scale:

INSTRUCTIONS: Indicate how often each of the statements below is descri

O indicates "I often feel this way"
S indicates "I sometimes feel this way"
R indicates "I rarely feel this way"
N indicates "I never feel this way"

1. I am unhappy doing so many things alone
2. I have nobody to talk to
3. I cannot tolerate being so alone
4. I lack companionship
5. I feel as if nobody really understands me
6. I find myself waiting for people to call or write
7. There is no one I can turn to
8. I am no longer close to anyone
9. My interests and ideas are not shared by those around me
10. I feel left out
11. I feel completely alone
12. I am unable to reach out and communicate with those around me
13. My social relationships are superficial
14. I feel starved for company
15. No one really knows me well
16. I feel isolated from others
17. I am unhappy being so withdrawn
8. It is difficult for me to make friends
9. I feel shut out and excluded by others
. People are around me but not with me

g:

l O's =3, all S's =2, all R's =1, and all N's =0.

O S
O S
O S
O S
O S R
O S R
O S R
O S R N
O S R N
O S R N
O S R N
O S R N
O S R N
O S R N
O S R N
O S R N
O S R N
O S R N
O S R N
O S R N

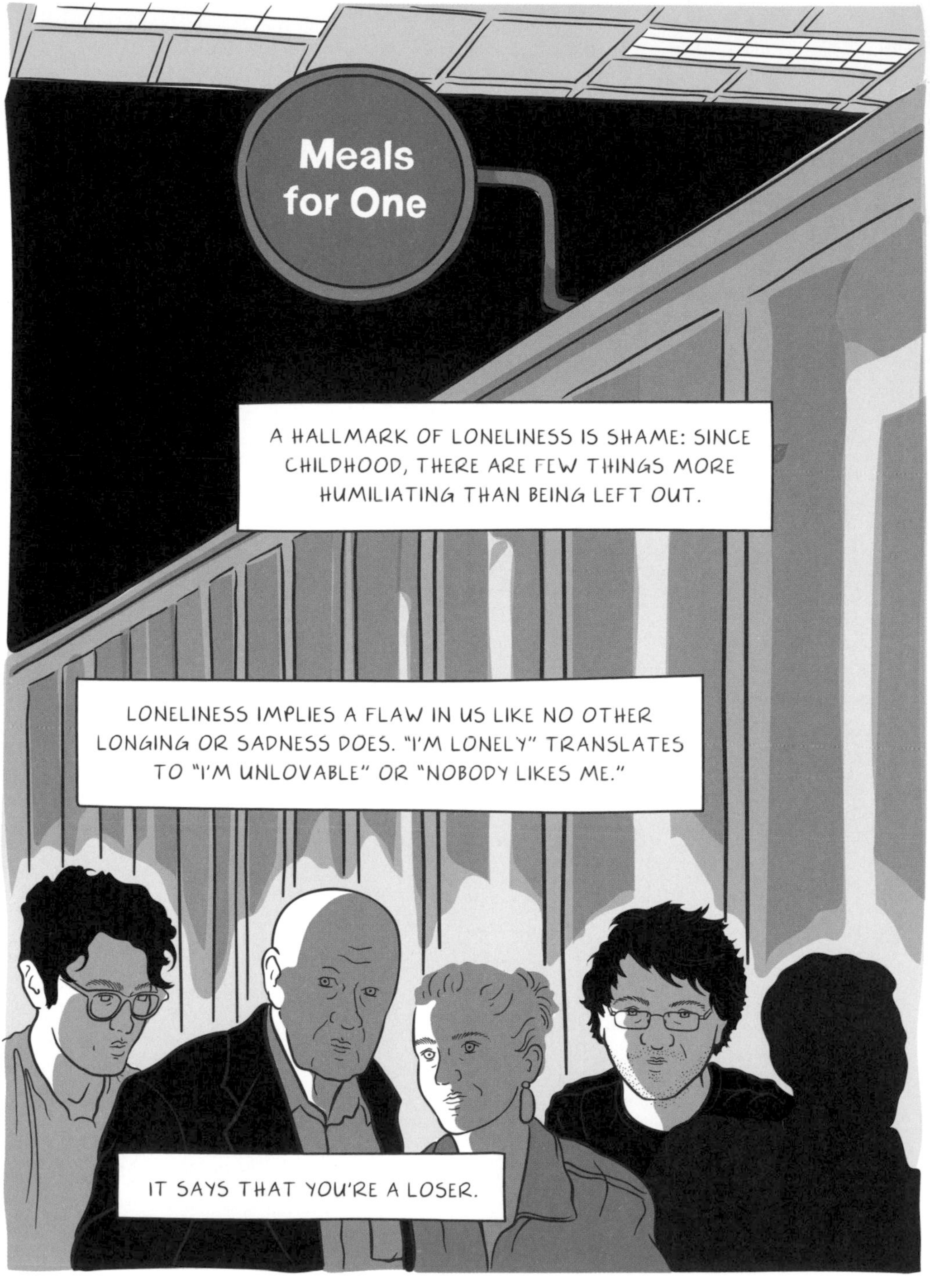
Meals for One
A HALLMARK OF LONELINESS IS SHAME: SINCE CHILDHOOD, THERE ARE FEW THINGS MORE HUMILIATING THAN BEING LEFT OUT.
LONELINESS IMPLIES A FLAW IN US LIKE NO OTHER LONGING OR SADNESS DOES. "I'M LONELY" TRANSLATES TO "I'M UNLOVABLE" OR "NOBODY LIKES ME."
IT SAYS THAT YOU'RE A LOSER.

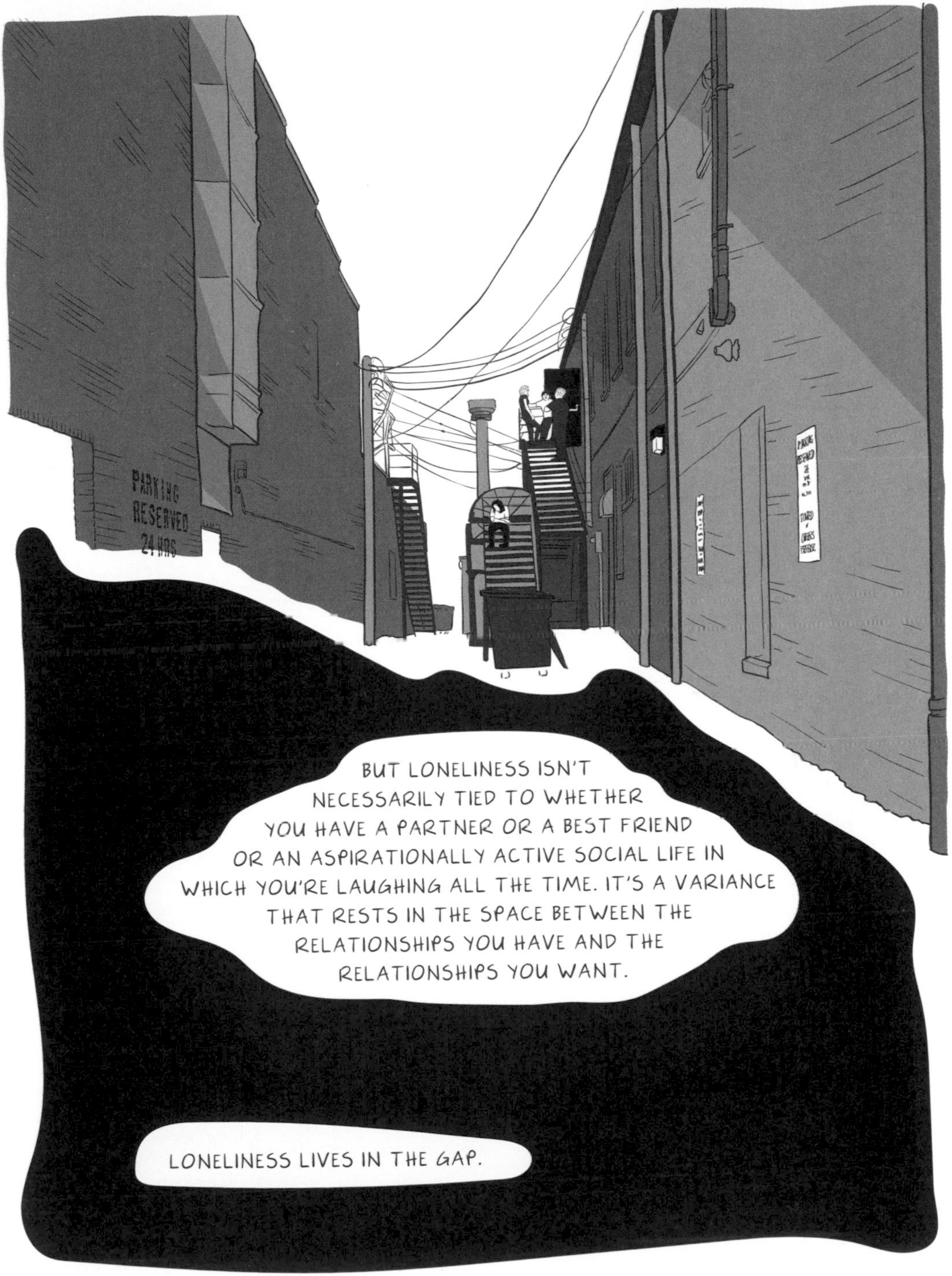
PARKING RESERVED 24 HRS
BUT LONELINESS ISN'T NECESSARILY TIED TO WHETHER YOU HAVE A PARTNER OR A BEST FRIEND OR AN ASPIRATIONALLY ACTIVE SOCIAL LIFE IN WHICH YOU'RE LAUGHING ALL THE TIME. IT'S A VARIANCE THAT RESTS IN THE SPACE BETWEEN THE RELATIONSHIPS YOU HAVE AND THE RELATIONSHIPS YOU WANT.
LONELINESS LIVES IN THE GAP.

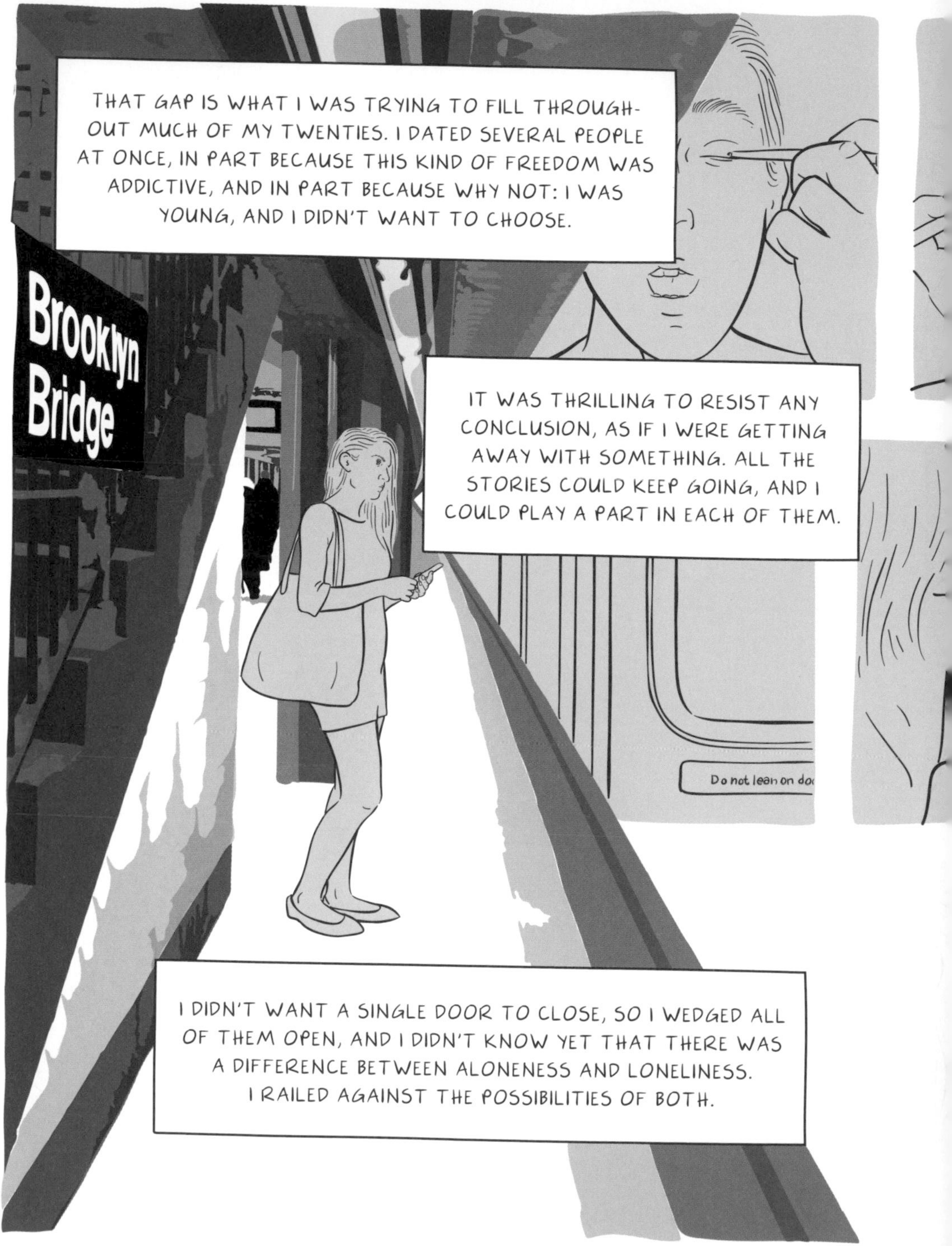
THAT GAP IS WHAT I WAS TRYING TO FILL THROUGHOUT MUCH OF MY TWENTIES. I DATED SEVERAL PEOPLE AT ONCE, IN PART BECAUSE THIS KIND OF FREEDOM WAS ADDICTIVE, AND IN PART BECAUSE WHY NOT: I WAS YOUNG, AND I DIDN'T WANT TO CHOOSE.
Brooklyn Bridge
IT WAS THRILLING TO RESIST ANY CONCLUSION, AS IF I WERE GETTING AWAY WITH SOMETHING. ALL THE STORIES COULD KEEP GOING, AND I COULD PLAY A PART IN EACH OF THEM.
Do not lean on do
I DIDN'T WANT A SINGLE DOOR TO CLOSE, SO I WEDGED ALL OF THEM OPEN, AND I DIDN'T KNOW YET THAT THERE WAS A DIFFERENCE BETWEEN ALONENESS AND LONELINESS. I RAILED AGAINST THE POSSIBILITIES OF BOTH.

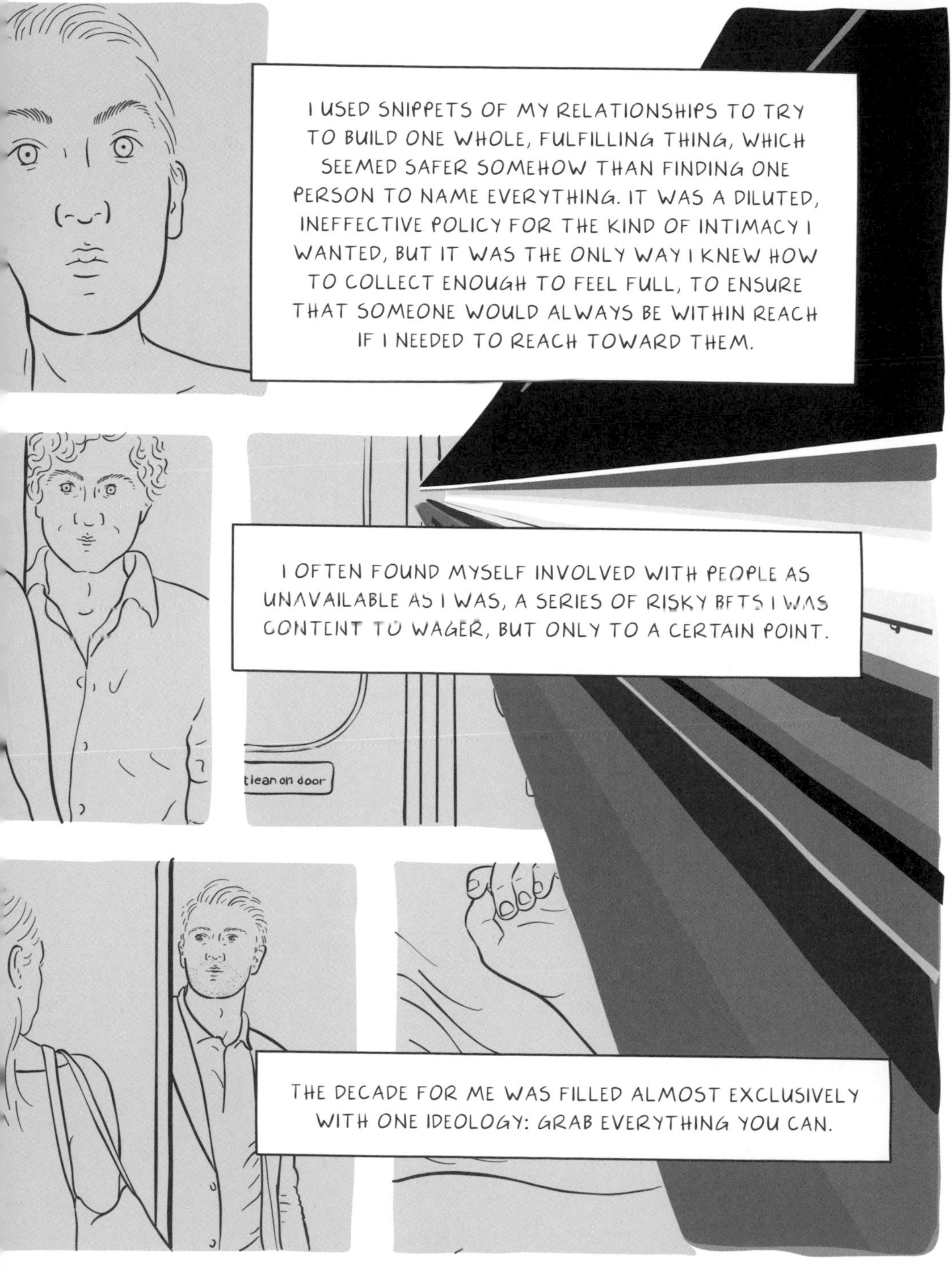
I USED SNIPPETS OF MY RELATIONSHIPS TO TRY TO BUILD ONE WHOLE, FULFILLING THING, WHICH SEEMED SAFER SOMEHOW THAN FINDING ONE PERSON TO NAME EVERYTHING. IT WAS A DILUTED, INEFFECTIVE POLICY FOR THE KIND OF INTIMACY I WANTED, BUT IT WAS THE ONLY WAY I KNEW HOW TO COLLECT ENOUGH TO FEEL FULL, TO ENSURE THAT SOMEONE WOULD ALWAYS BE WITHIN REACH IF I NEEDED TO REACH TOWARD THEM.
I OFTEN FOUND MYSELF INVOLVED WITH PEOPLE AS UNAVAILABLE AS I WAS, A SERIES OF RISKY BETS I WAS CONTENT TO WAGER, BUT ONLY TO A CERTAIN POINT.
t lean on door
THE DECADE FOR ME WAS FILLED ALMOST EXCLUSIVELY WITH ONE IDEOLOGY: GRAB EVERYTHING YOU CAN.

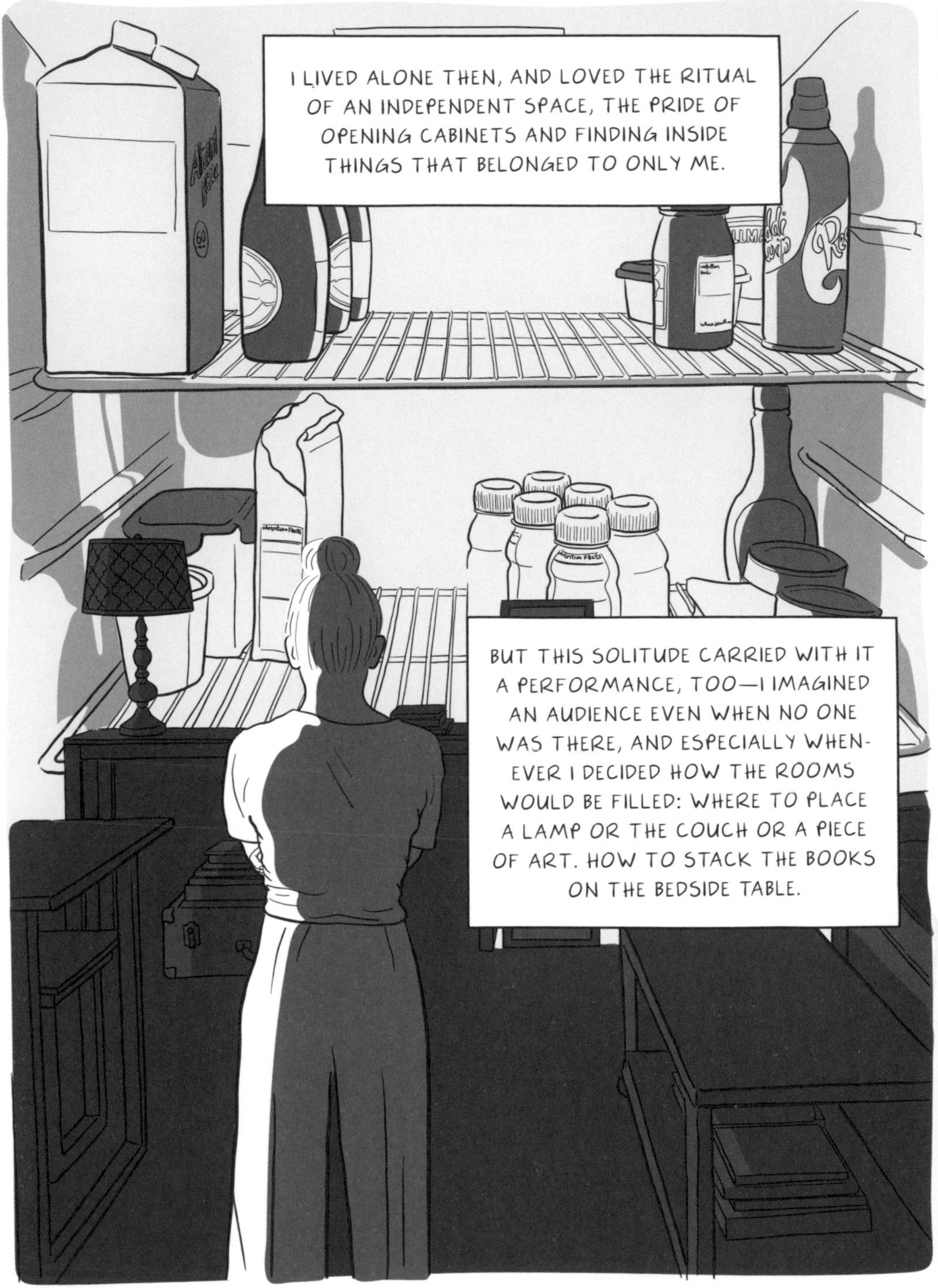
I LIVED ALONE THEN, AND LOVED THE RITUAL OF AN INDEPENDENT SPACE, THE PRIDE OF OPENING CABINETS AND FINDING INSIDE THINGS THAT BELONGED TO ONLY ME.
BUT THIS SOLITUDE CARRIED WITH IT A PERFORMANCE, TOO—I IMAGINED AN AUDIENCE EVEN WHEN NO ONE WAS THERE, AND ESPECIALLY WHENEVER I DECIDED HOW THE ROOMS WOULD BE FILLED: WHERE TO PLACE A LAMP OR THE COUCH OR A PIECE OF ART. HOW TO STACK THE BOOKS ON THE BEDSIDE TABLE.

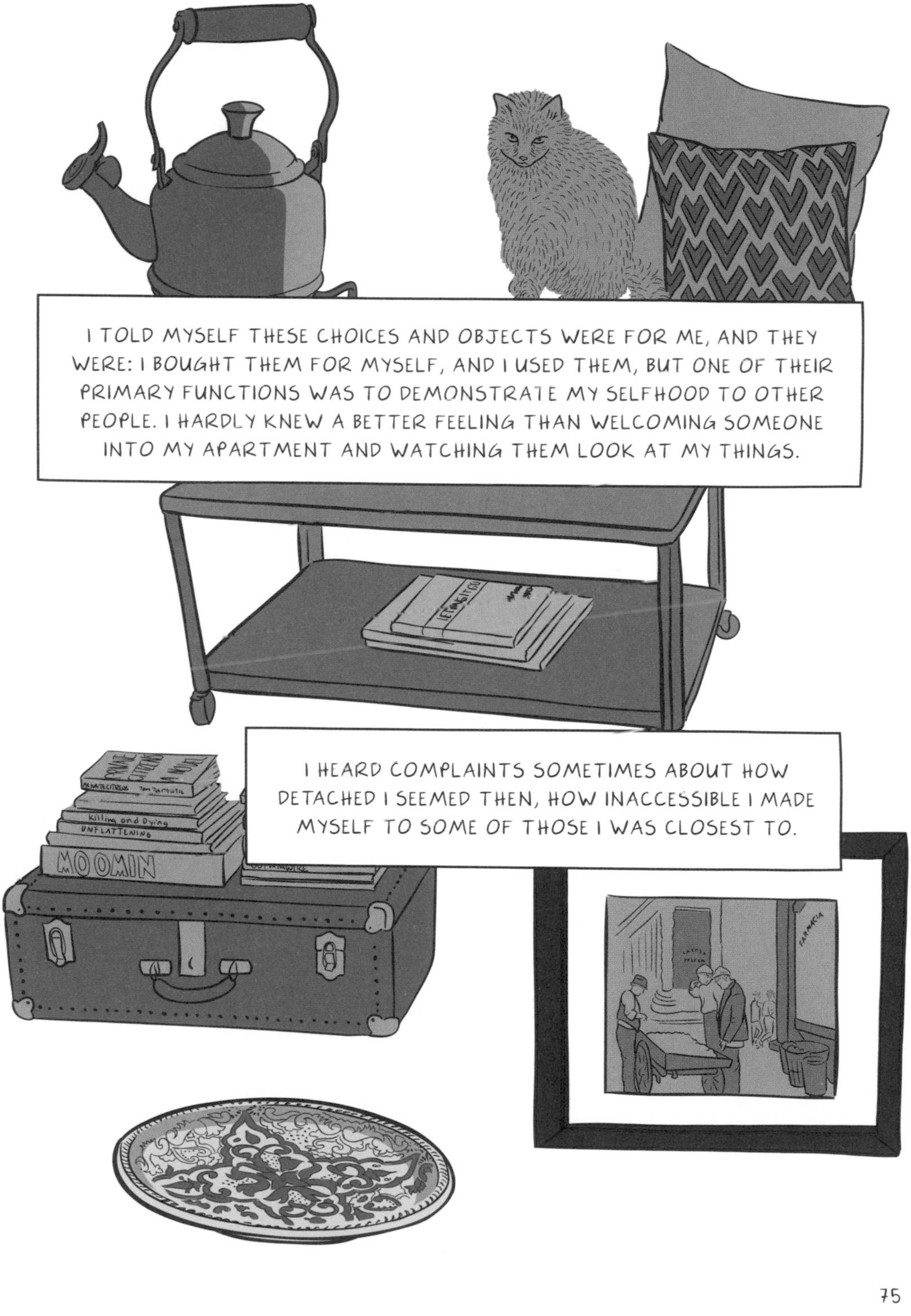
I TOLD MYSELF THESE CHOICES AND OBJECTS WERE FOR ME, AND THEY WERE: I BOUGHT THEM FOR MYSELF, AND I USED THEM, BUT ONE OF THEIR PRIMARY FUNCTIONS WAS TO DEMONSTRATE MY SELFHOOD TO OTHER PEOPLE. I HARDLY KNEW A BETTER FEELING THAN WELCOMING SOMEONE INTO MY APARTMENT AND WATCHING THEM LOOK AT MY THINGS.
I HEARD COMPLAINTS SOMETIMES ABOUT HOW DETACHED I SEEMED THEN, HOW INACCESSIBLE I MADE MYSELF TO SOME OF THOSE I WAS CLOSEST TO.
PRIVATE CITIZENS A NOVEL
Killing and Dying
UNFLATTENING
MOOMIN
FARMACIA

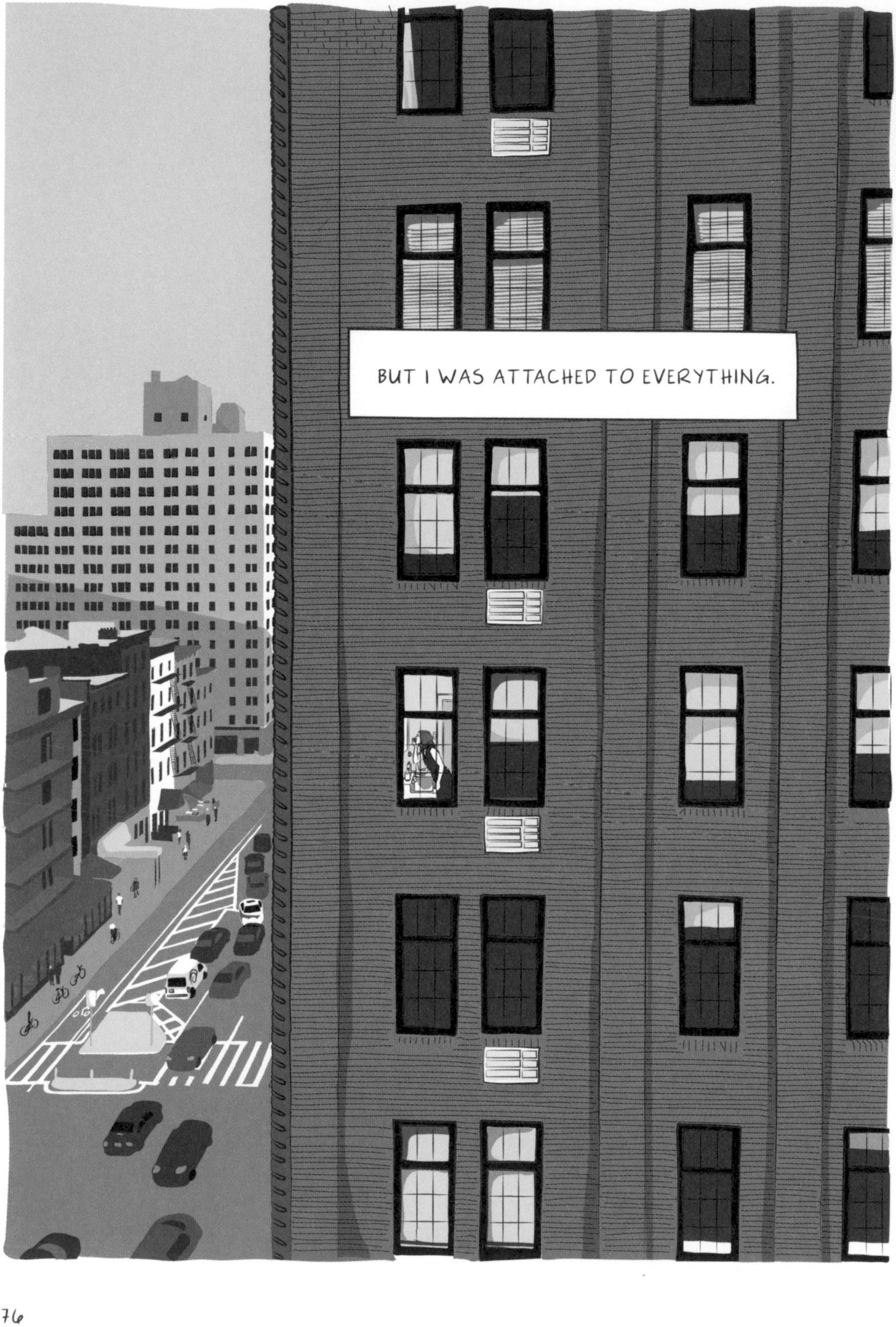
BUT I WAS ATTACHED TO EVERYTHING.

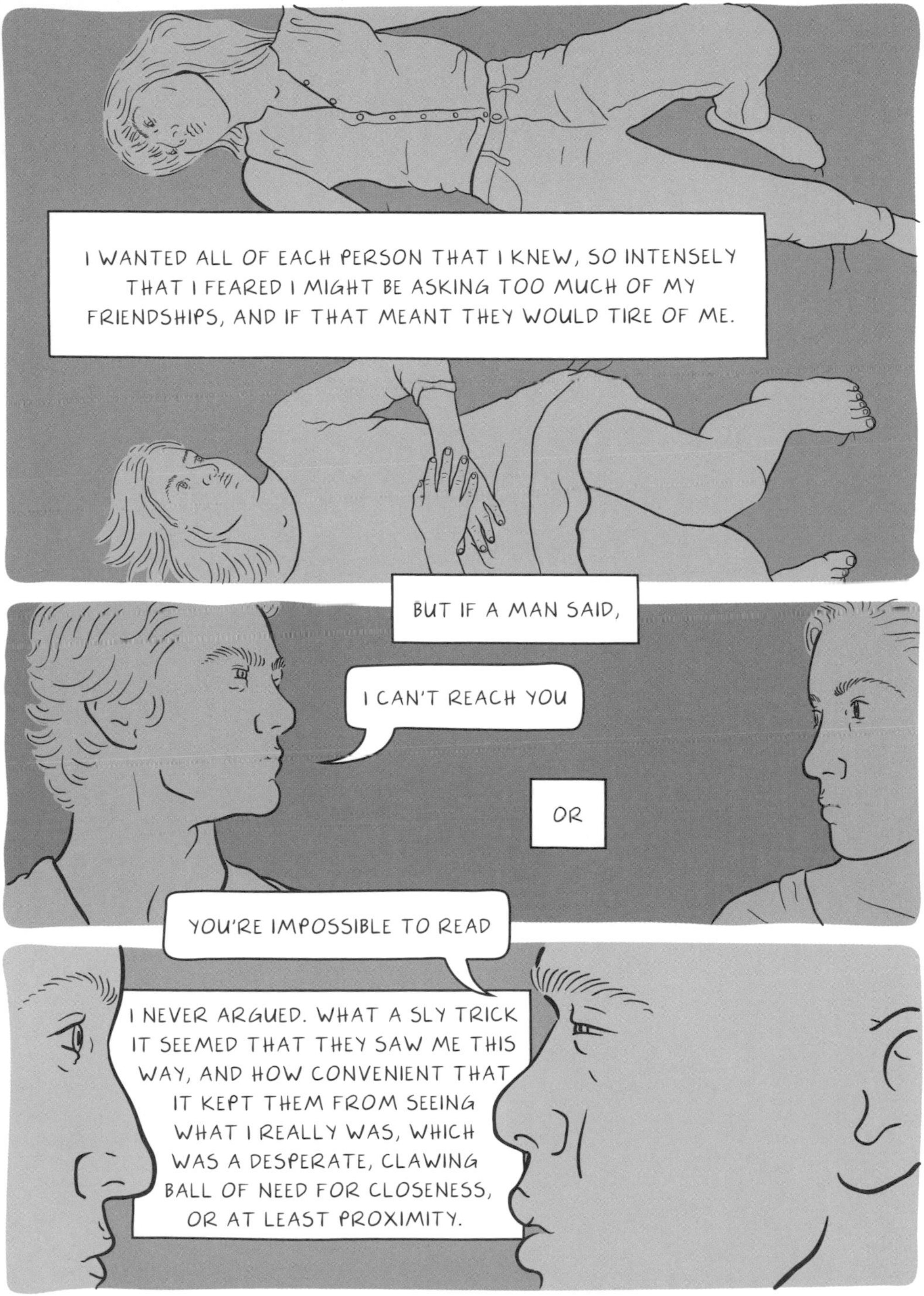
I WANTED ALL OF EACH PERSON THAT I KNEW, SO INTENSELY THAT I FEARED I MIGHT BE ASKING TOO MUCH OF MY FRIENDSHIPS, AND IF THAT MEANT THEY WOULD TIRE OF ME.
BUT IF A MAN SAID,
I CAN'T REACH YOU
OR
YOU'RE IMPOSSIBLE TO READ
I NEVER ARGUED. WHAT A SLY TRICK IT SEEMED THAT THEY SAW ME THIS WAY, AND HOW CONVENIENT THAT IT KEPT THEM FROM SEEING WHAT I REALLY WAS, WHICH WAS A DESPERATE, CLAWING BALL OF NEED FOR CLOSENESS, OR AT LEAST PROXIMITY.

THE SENSATION OF DISCONNECTION I WAS FEELING IS AN EVOLUTIONARY TRIGGER AT THE BASE OF ATTACHMENT THEORY. THROUGHOUT MOST POINTS IN THE BRIEF CURVE OF HUMAN HISTORY, IT WAS DANGEROUS TO BE ALONE.

THAT DISCOMFORTING TWINGE DESIGNED TO PULL US BACK INTO OUR COMMUNITIES AND TRIBES IS A STRESS RESPONSE THAT PUMPS HORMONES THROUGH OUR BODIES AND PUSHES BLOOD INTO OUR HEARTS AT A MORE FORCEFUL RATE.

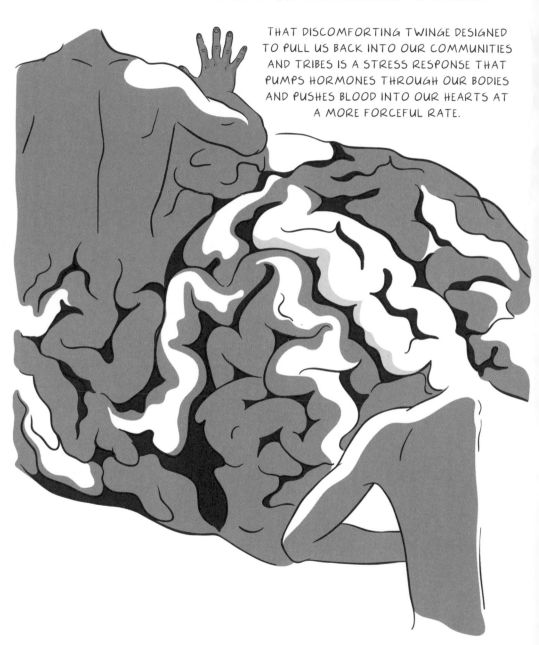

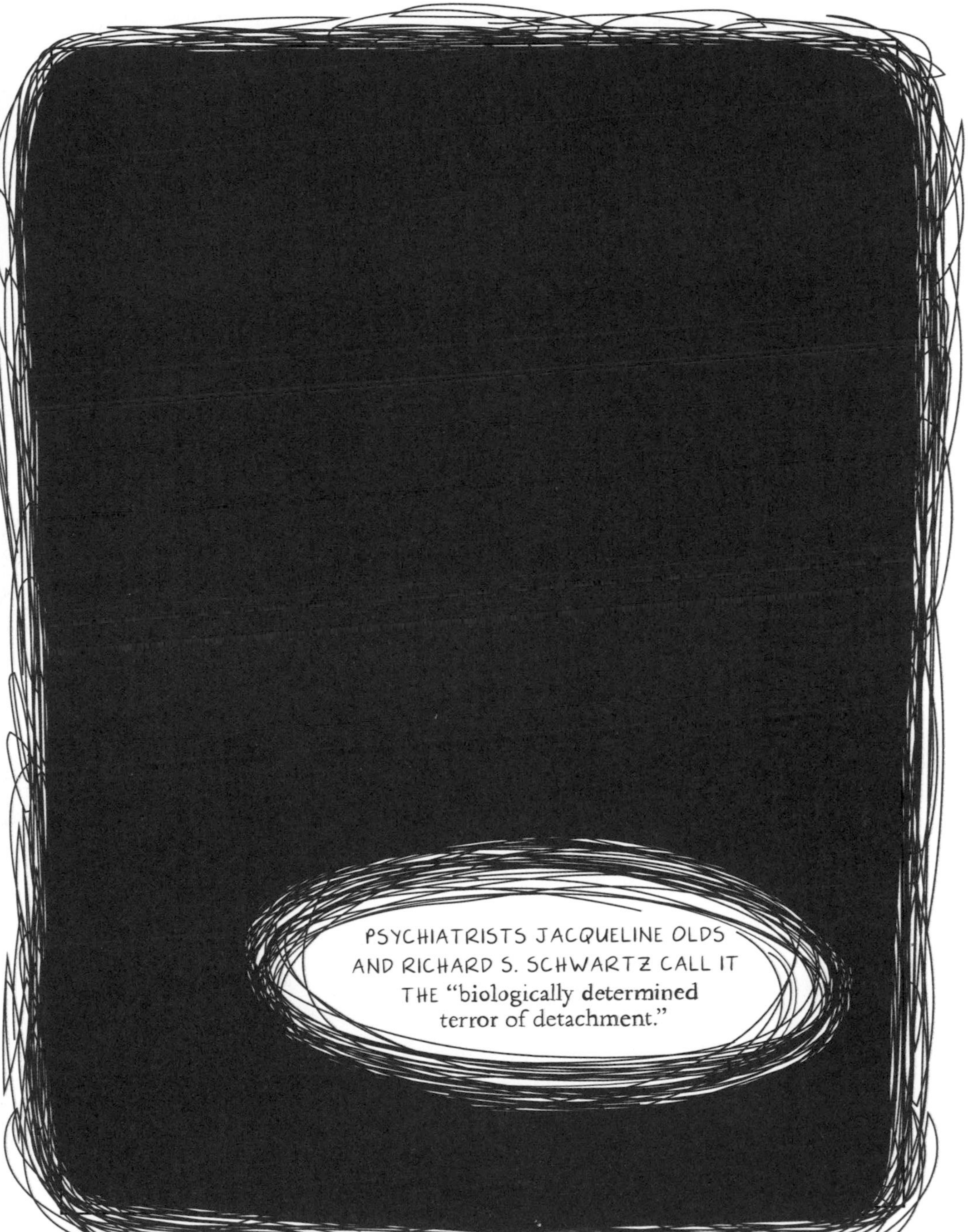
PSYCHIATRISTS JACQUELINE OLDS AND RICHARD S. SCHWARTZ CALL IT THE "biologically determined terror of detachment."

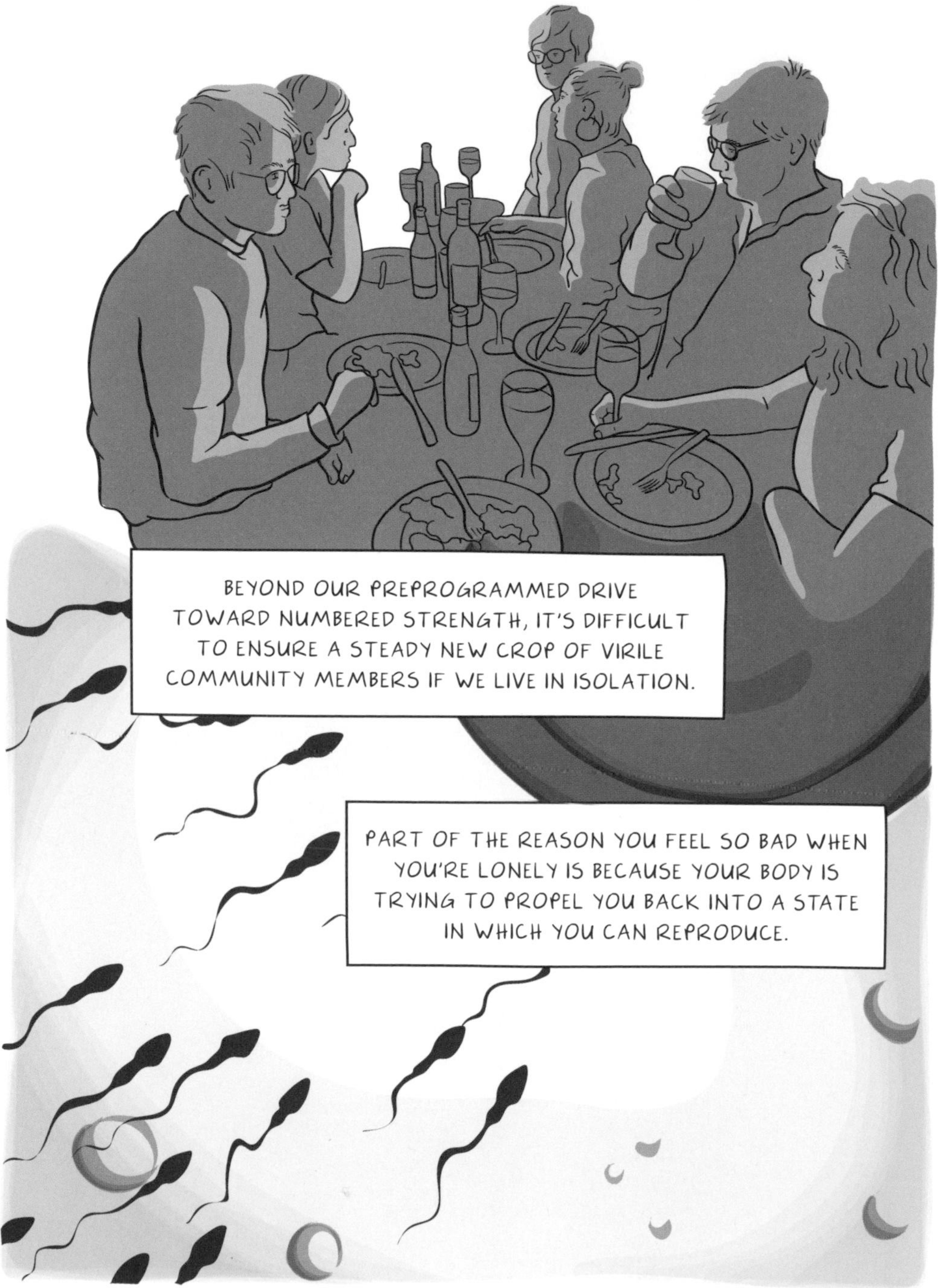
BEYOND OUR PREPROGRAMMED DRIVE TOWARD NUMBERED STRENGTH, IT'S DIFFICULT TO ENSURE A STEADY NEW CROP OF VIRILE COMMUNITY MEMBERS IF WE LIVE IN ISOLATION.
PART OF THE REASON YOU FEEL SO BAD WHEN YOU'RE LONELY IS BECAUSE YOUR BODY IS TRYING TO PROPEL YOU BACK INTO A STATE IN WHICH YOU CAN REPRODUCE.

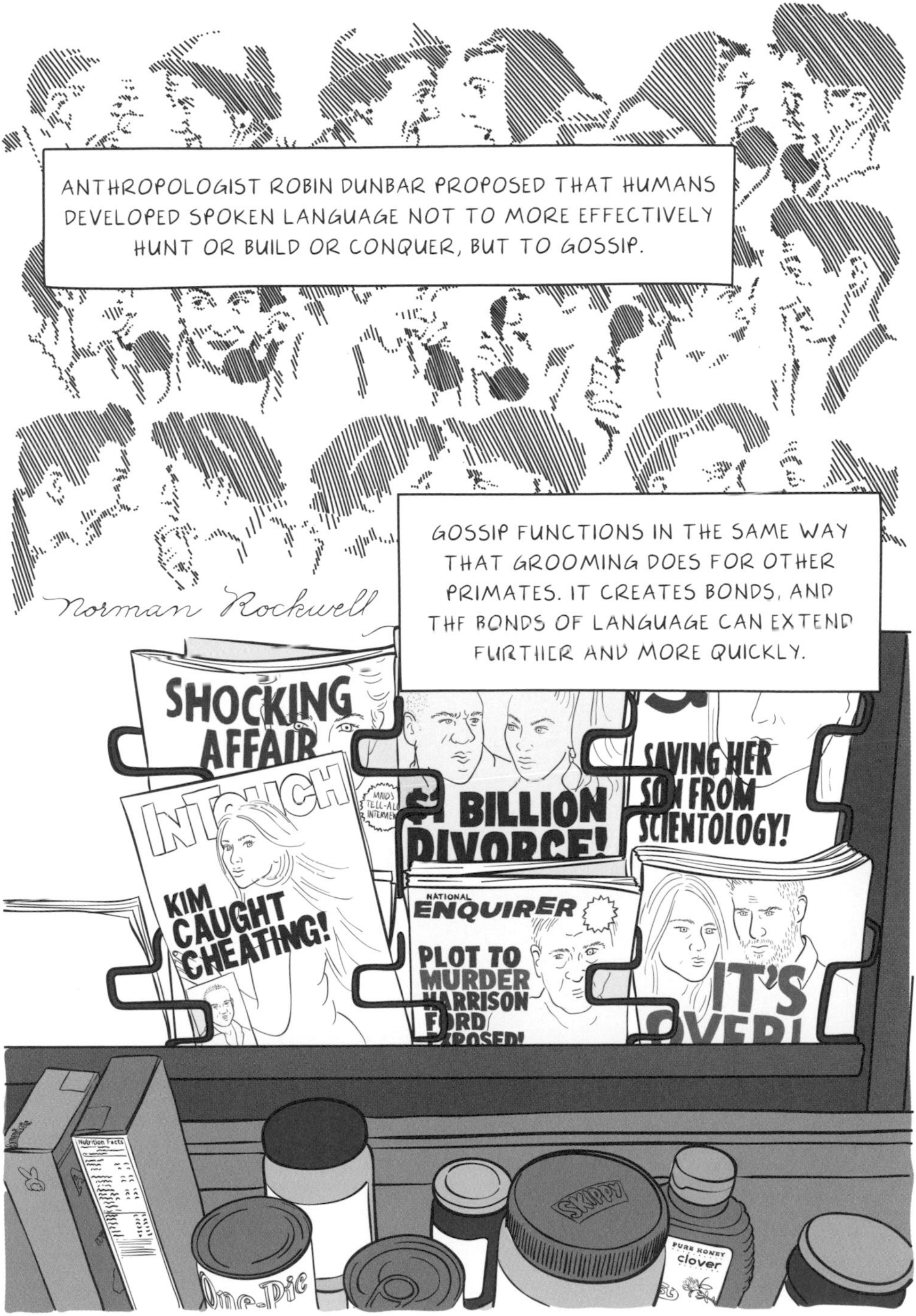

ANTHROPOLOGIST ROBIN DUNBAR PROPOSED THAT HUMANS DEVELOPED SPOKEN LANGUAGE NOT TO MORE EFFECTIVELY HUNT OR BUILD OR CONQUER, BUT TO GOSSIP.
Norman Rockwell
GOSSIP FUNCTIONS IN THE SAME WAY THAT GROOMING DOES FOR OTHER PRIMATES. IT CREATES BONDS, AND THE BONDS OF LANGUAGE CAN EXTEND FURTHER AND MORE QUICKLY.
SHOCKING AFFAIR
BILLION
SCIENTOLOGY!
KIM CAUGHT CHEATING!
NATIONAL ENQUIRER
PLOT TO MURDER HARRISON FORD
IT'S
Nutrition Facts
SKIPPY
PURE HONEY
clover

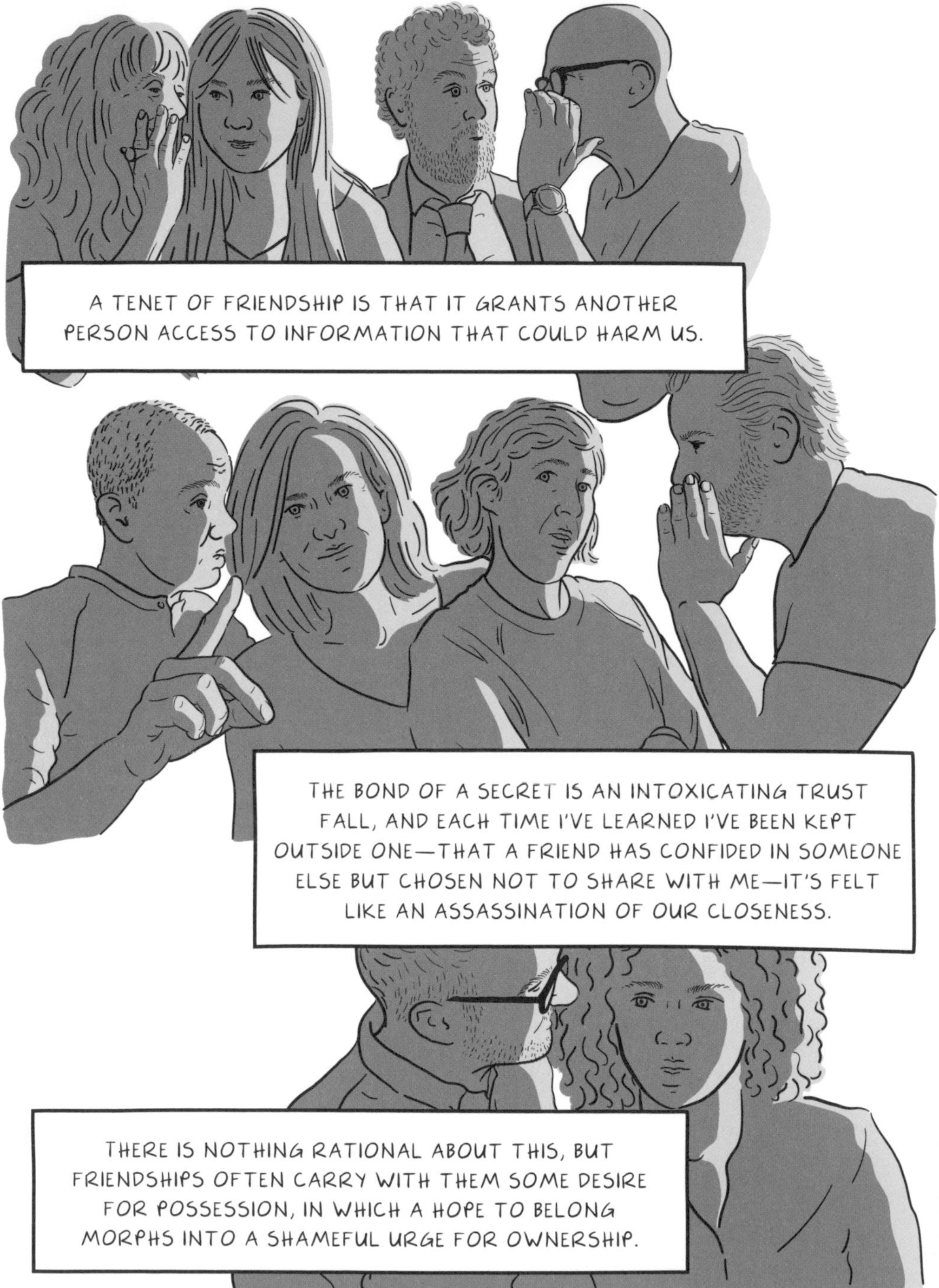
A TENET OF FRIENDSHIP IS THAT IT GRANTS ANOTHER PERSON ACCESS TO INFORMATION THAT COULD HARM US.
THE BOND OF A SECRET IS AN INTOXICATING TRUST FALL, AND EACH TIME I'VE LEARNED I'VE BEEN KEPT OUTSIDE ONE—THAT A FRIEND HAS CONFIDED IN SOMEONE ELSE BUT CHOSEN NOT TO SHARE WITH ME—IT'S FELT LIKE AN ASSASSINATION OF OUR CLOSENESS.
THERE IS NOTHING RATIONAL ABOUT THIS, BUT FRIENDSHIPS OFTEN CARRY WITH THEM SOME DESIRE FOR POSSESSION, IN WHICH A HOPE TO BELONG MORPHS INTO A SHAMEFUL URGE FOR OWNERSHIP.

THE DEVELOPMENT OF LANGUAGE BROUGHT ABOUT A FRESH
SET OF SOCIAL PROBLEMS, WHAT LINGUIST STEVEN PINKER
PUT SIMPLY AS "A CONCERN WITH ONE'S REPUTATION."

NO PARKING

YEAH? WELL, SHE CAN SAY
THAT TO MY FACE.

IF WE'RE GOING TO MAINTAIN OUR POSITION WITHIN A GROUP—WHICH IS TO SAY, FED AND WARM AND LESS LIKELY TO BE CORNERED BY BEARS WITHOUT BACKUP OR LEFT OFF THE COWORKER TEXT CHAIN ARRANGING 5 P.M. DRINKS—WE NEED TO FEEL DEEPLY TROUBLED WHEN WE OBSERVE MINOR SOCIAL SHUNS SO WE CAN CORRECT OUR BEHAVIOR.

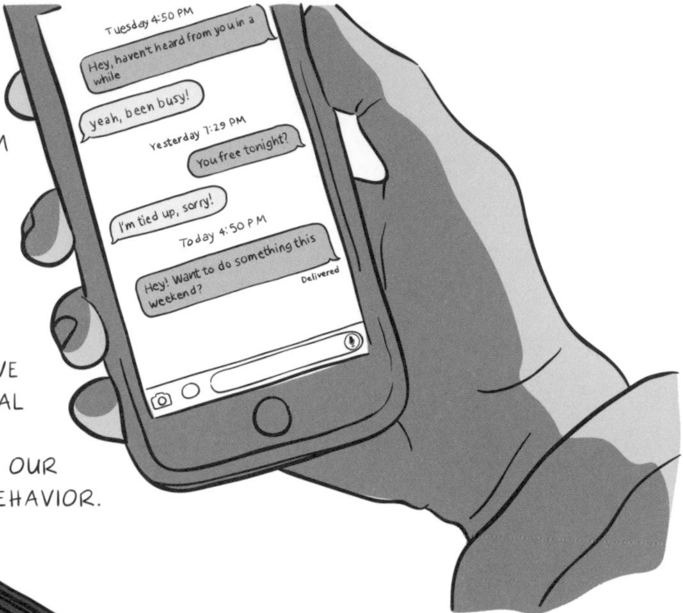
Tuesday 4:50 PM
Hey, haven't heard from you in a while
yeah, been busy!
Yesterday 7:29 PM
You free tonight?
I'm tied up, sorry!
Today 4:50 PM
Hey! Want to do something this weekend?
Delivered

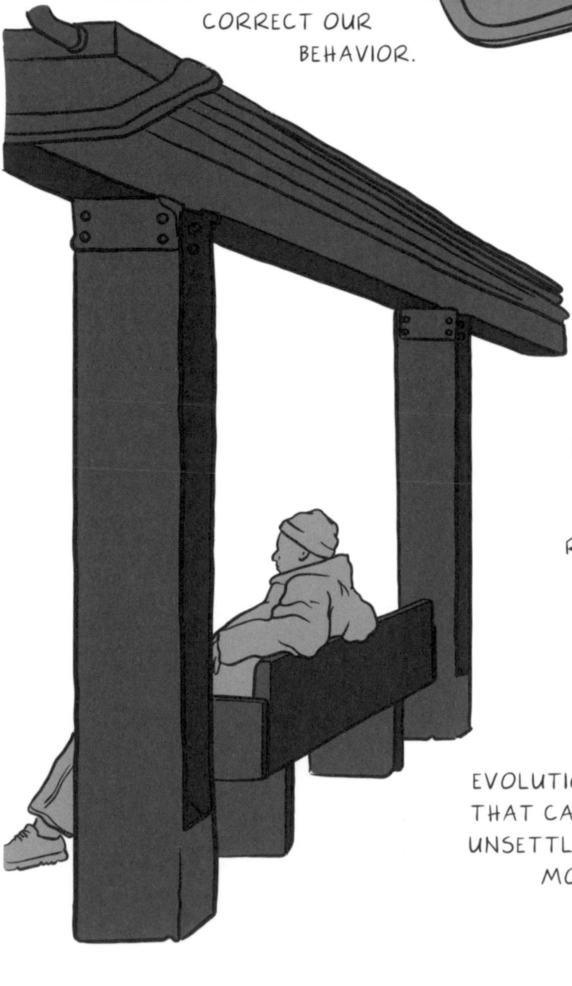

WE MUST NOTICE FACIAL CUES THAT SIGNIFY DISINTEREST, REGISTER BODY LANGUAGE THAT SUGGESTS WE SHOULD BACK UP.

EARLY HUMANS OFTEN MIGRATED FROM PLACE TO PLACE, BUT THE BANDS THEY TRAVELED WITH REMAINED THE SAME. AS OUR BODY HAIR GREW THINNER AND OUR TEETH MORE ROUNDED, SO TOO DID WE BECOME MORE UNABLE TO SURVIVE ON OUR OWN.

EVOLUTION SHOVED US INTO MOLDS THAT CAUSED US TO FEEL NOT ONLY UNSETTLED BY REJECTION, BUT ALSO MORTALLY THREATENED.

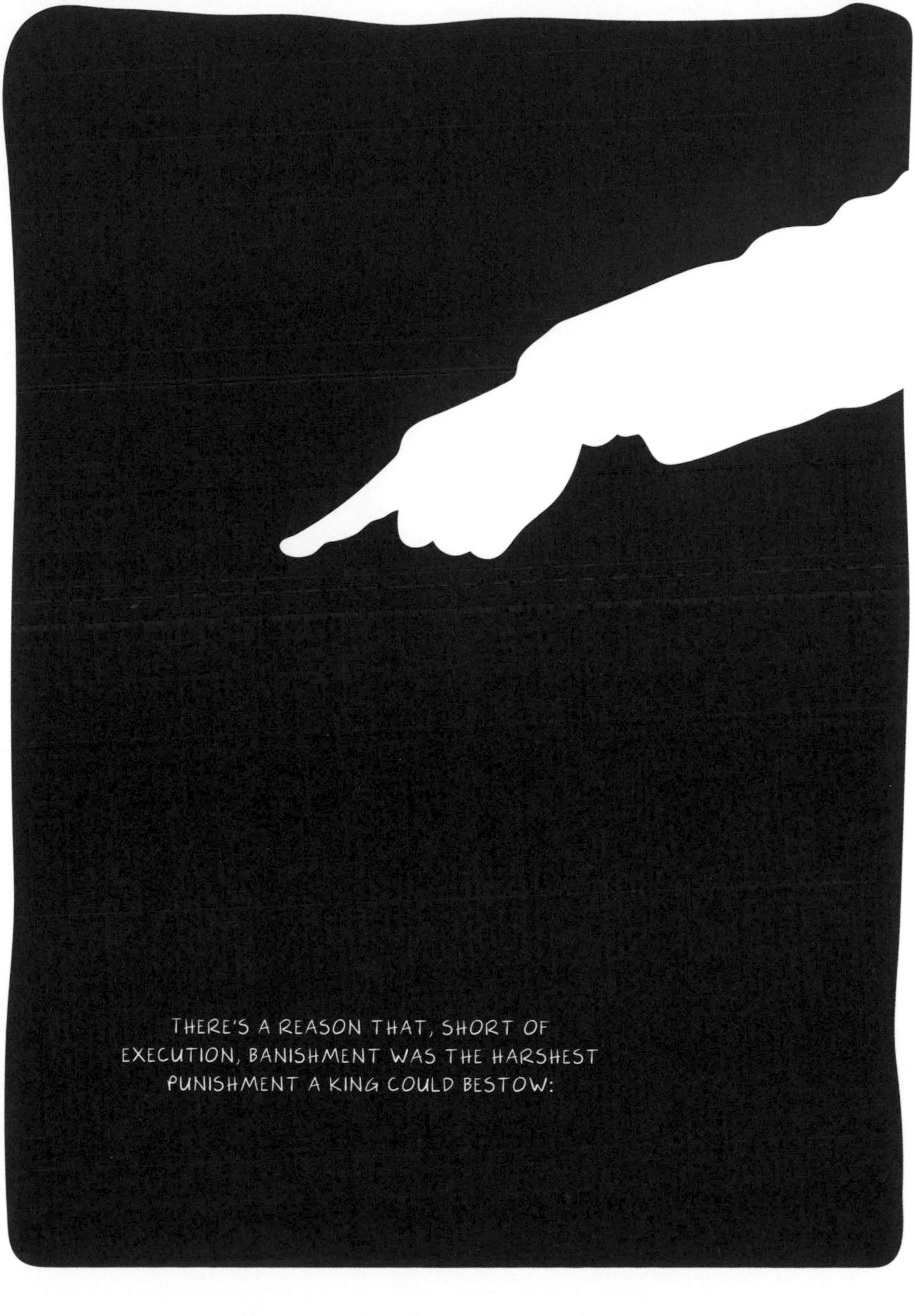
THERE'S A REASON THAT, SHORT OF EXECUTION, BANISHMENT WAS THE HARSHEST PUNISHMENT A KING COULD BESTOW:

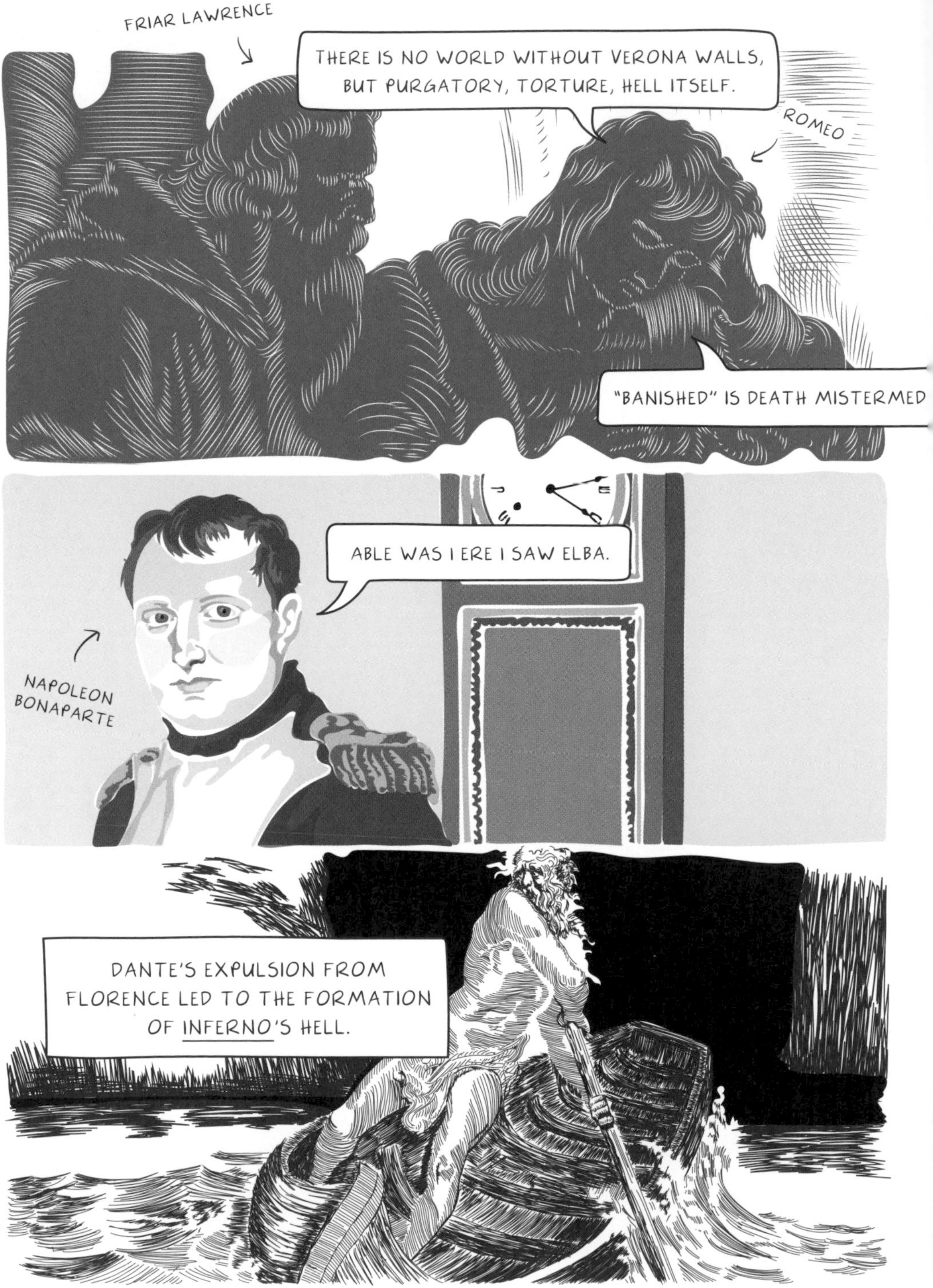
FRIAR LAWRENCE
THERE IS NO WORLD WITHOUT VERONA WALLS, BUT PURGATORY, TORTURE, HELL ITSELF.
ROMEO
"BANISHED" IS DEATH MISTERMED
ABLE WAS I ERE I SAW ELBA.
NAPOLEON BONAPARTE
DANTE'S EXPULSION FROM FLORENCE LED TO THE FORMATION OF INFERNO'S HELL.

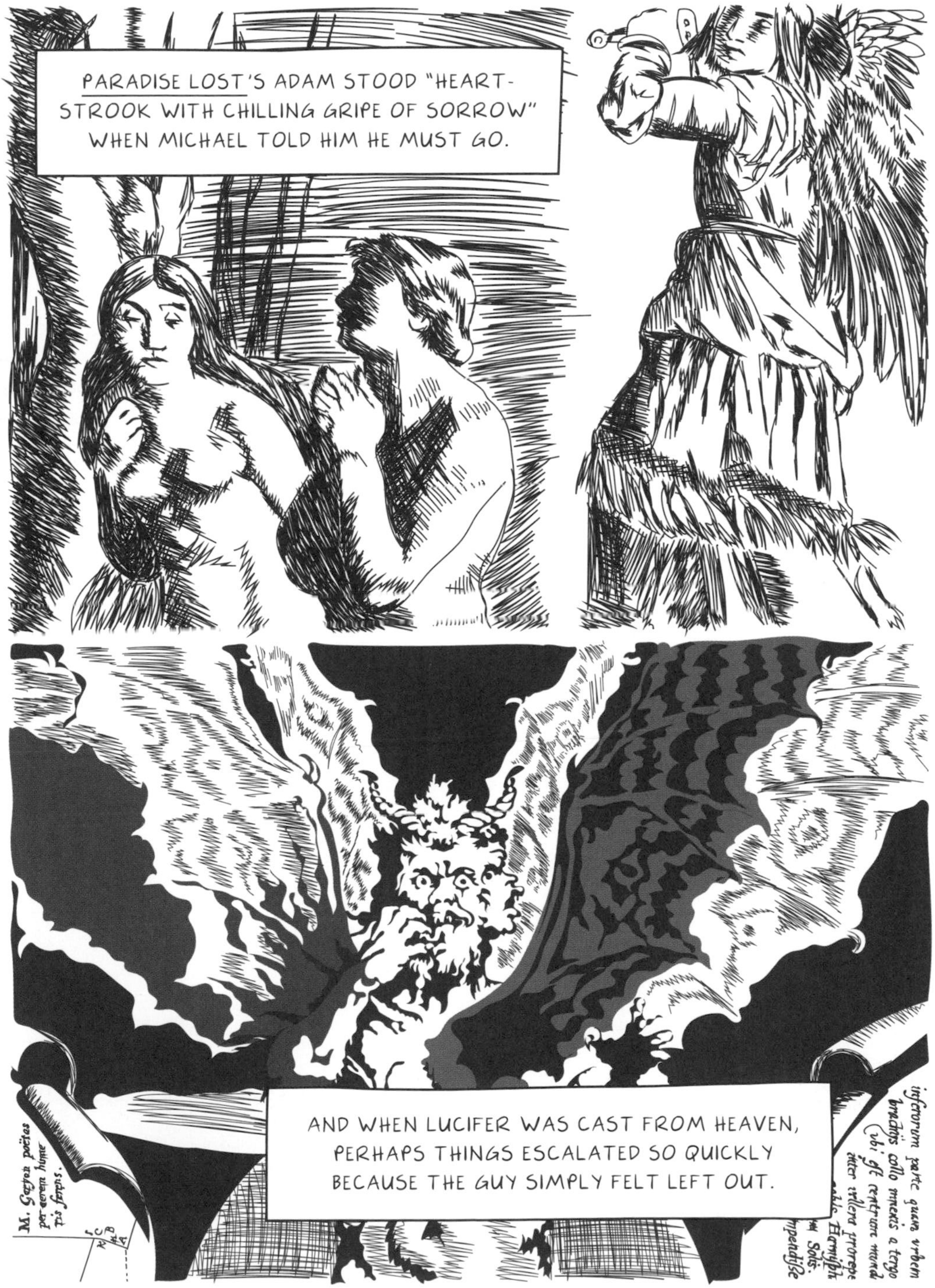
PARADISE LOST'S ADAM STOOD "HEART-STROOK WITH CHILLING GRIPE OF SORROW" WHEN MICHAEL TOLD HIM HE MUST GO.
AND WHEN LUCIFER WAS CAST FROM HEAVEN, PERHAPS THINGS ESCALATED SO QUICKLY BECAUSE THE GUY SIMPLY FELT LEFT OUT.

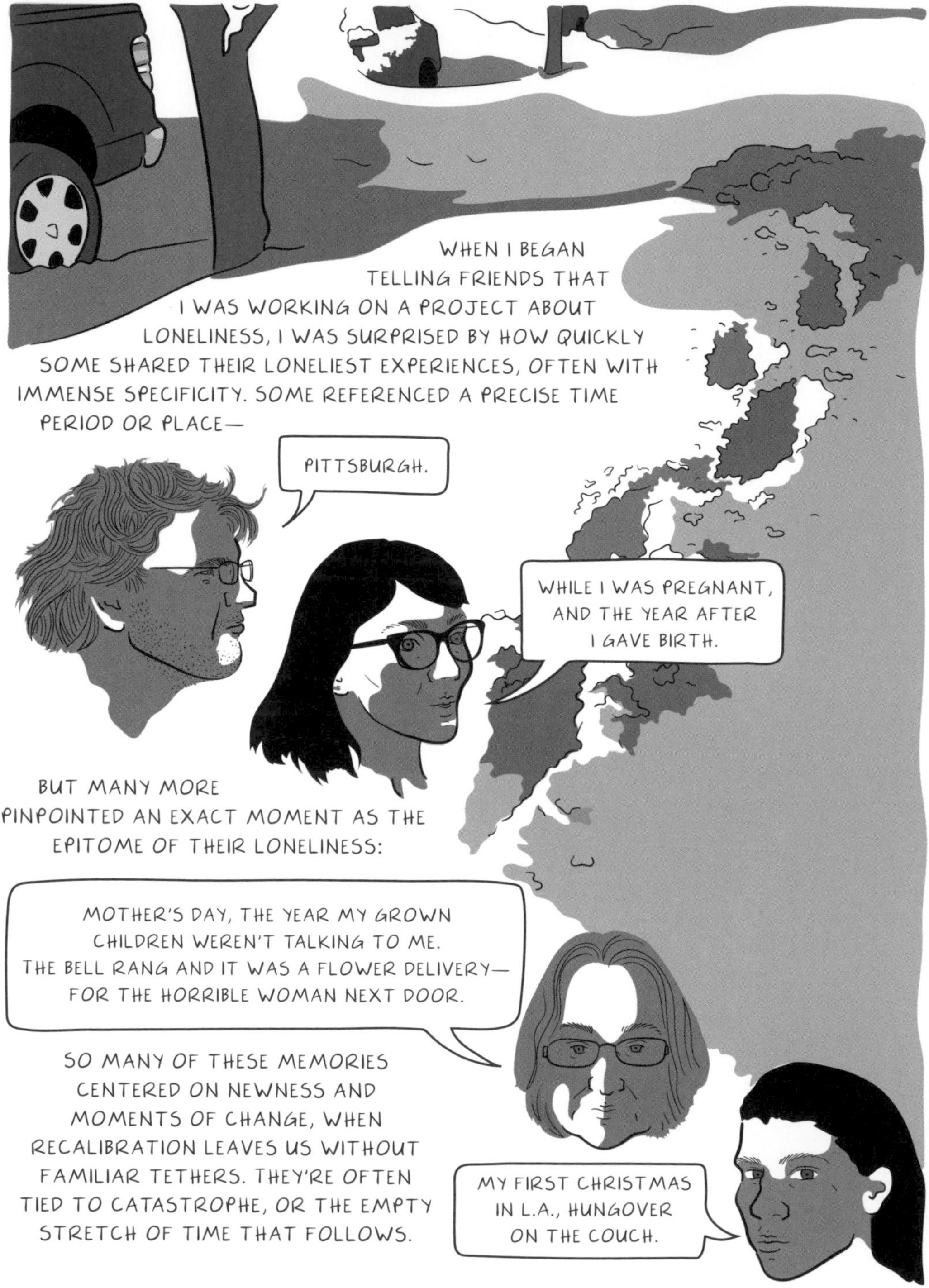
WHEN I BEGAN TELLING FRIENDS THAT I WAS WORKING ON A PROJECT ABOUT LONELINESS, I WAS SURPRISED BY HOW QUICKLY SOME SHARED THEIR LONELIEST EXPERIENCES, OFTEN WITH IMMENSE SPECIFICITY. SOME REFERENCED A PRECISE TIME PERIOD OR PLACE—
PITTSBURGH.
WHILE I WAS PREGNANT, AND THE YEAR AFTER I GAVE BIRTH.
BUT MANY MORE PINPOINTED AN EXACT MOMENT AS THE EPITOME OF THEIR LONELINESS:
MOTHER'S DAY, THE YEAR MY GROWN CHILDREN WEREN'T TALKING TO ME. THE BELL RANG AND IT WAS A FLOWER DELIVERY— FOR THE HORRIBLE WOMAN NEXT DOOR.
SO MANY OF THESE MEMORIES CENTERED ON NEWNESS AND MOMENTS OF CHANGE, WHEN RECALIBRATION LEAVES US WITHOUT FAMILIAR TETHERS. THEY'RE OFTEN TIED TO CATASTROPHE, OR THE EMPTY STRETCH OF TIME THAT FOLLOWS.
MY FIRST CHRISTMAS IN L.A., HUNGOVER ON THE COUCH.

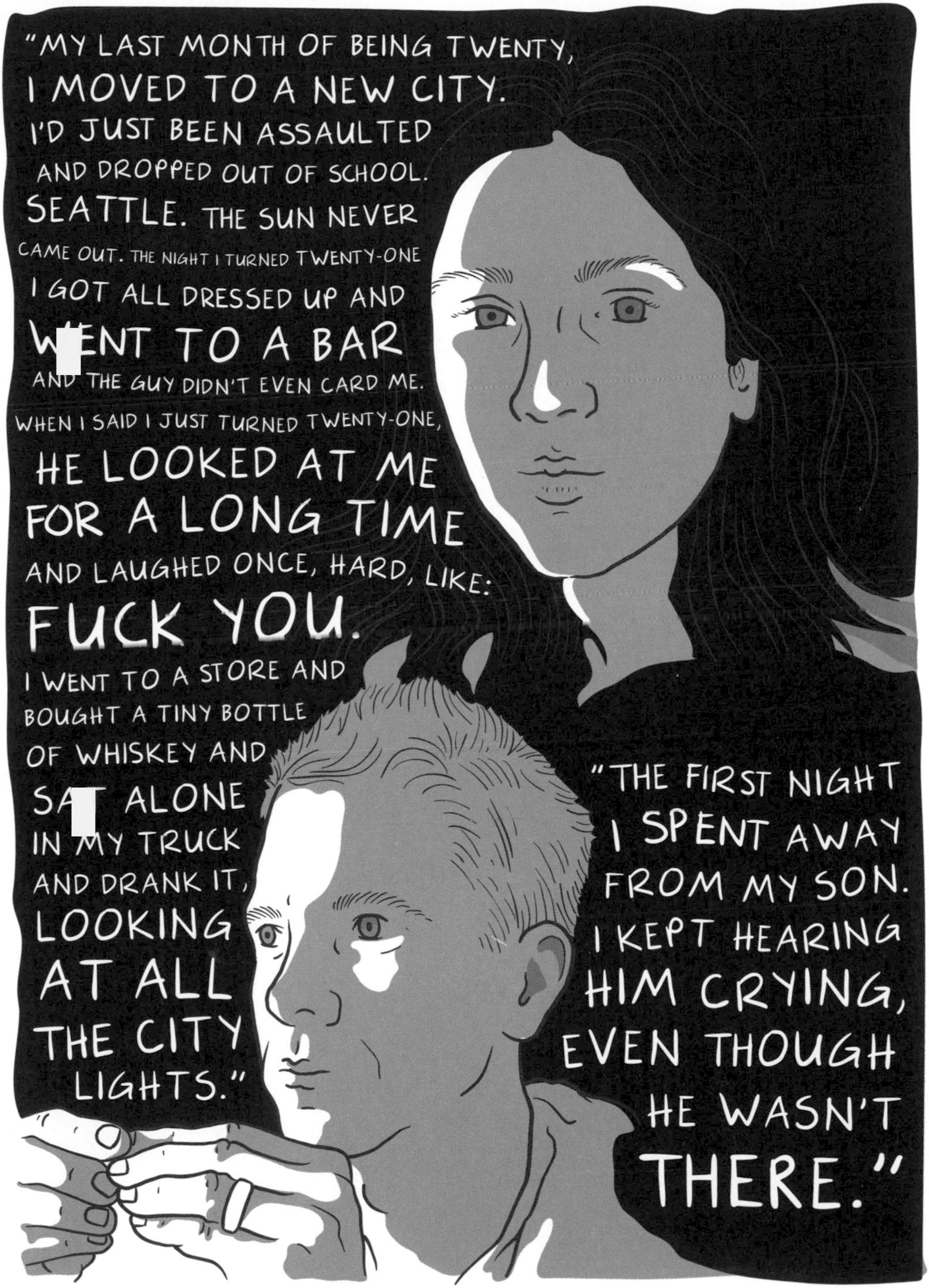
"MY LAST MONTH OF BEING TWENTY, I MOVED TO A NEW CITY. I'D JUST BEEN ASSAULTED AND DROPPED OUT OF SCHOOL. SEATTLE. THE SUN NEVER CAME OUT. THE NIGHT I TURNED TWENTY-ONE I GOT ALL DRESSED UP AND WENT TO A BAR AND THE GUY DIDN'T EVEN CARD ME. WHEN I SAID I JUST TURNED TWENTY-ONE, HE LOOKED AT ME FOR A LONG TIME AND LAUGHED ONCE, HARD, LIKE: FUCK YOU. I WENT TO A STORE AND BOUGHT A TINY BOTTLE OF WHISKEY AND SAT ALONE IN MY TRUCK AND DRANK IT, LOOKING AT ALL THE CITY LIGHTS."
"THE FIRST NIGHT I SPENT AWAY FROM MY SON. I KEPT HEARING HIM CRYING, EVEN THOUGH HE WASN'T THERE."

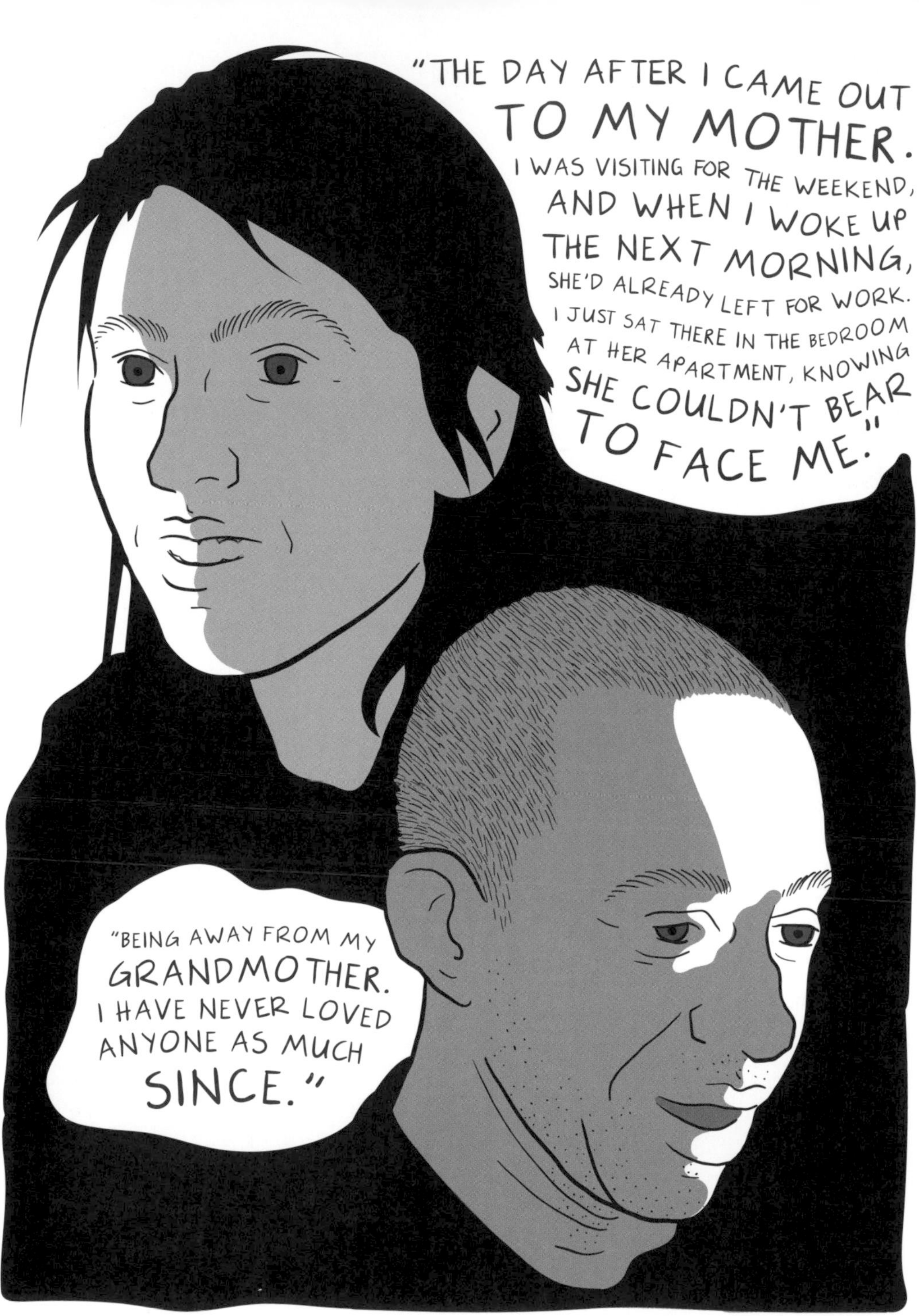
"THE DAY AFTER I CAME OUT TO MY MOTHER. I WAS VISITING FOR THE WEEKEND, AND WHEN I WOKE UP THE NEXT MORNING, SHE'D ALREADY LEFT FOR WORK. I JUST SAT THERE IN THE BEDROOM AT HER APARTMENT, KNOWING SHE COULDN'T BEAR TO FACE ME."
"BEING AWAY FROM MY GRANDMOTHER. I HAVE NEVER LOVED ANYONE AS MUCH SINCE."

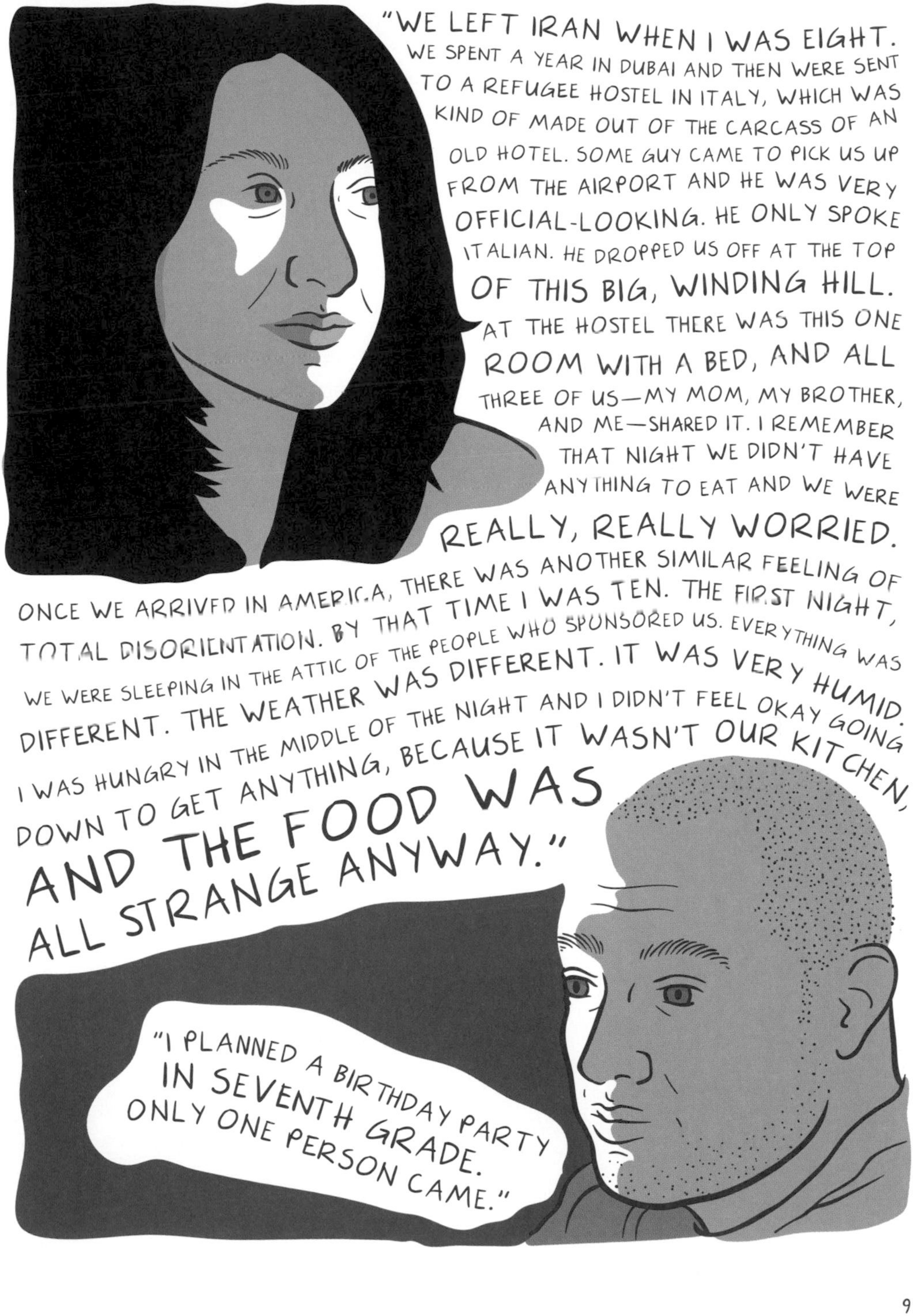
"WE LEFT IRAN WHEN I WAS EIGHT. WE SPENT A YEAR IN DUBAI AND THEN WERE SENT TO A REFUGEE HOSTEL IN ITALY, WHICH WAS KIND OF MADE OUT OF THE CARCASS OF AN OLD HOTEL. SOME GUY CAME TO PICK US UP FROM THE AIRPORT AND HE WAS VERY OFFICIAL-LOOKING. HE ONLY SPOKE ITALIAN. HE DROPPED US OFF AT THE TOP OF THIS BIG, WINDING HILL. AT THE HOSTEL THERE WAS THIS ONE ROOM WITH A BED, AND ALL THREE OF US—MY MOM, MY BROTHER, AND ME—SHARED IT. I REMEMBER THAT NIGHT WE DIDN'T HAVE ANYTHING TO EAT AND WE WERE REALLY, REALLY WORRIED.
ONCE WE ARRIVED IN AMERICA, THERE WAS ANOTHER SIMILAR FEELING OF TOTAL DISORIENTATION. BY THAT TIME I WAS TEN. THE FIRST NIGHT, WE WERE SLEEPING IN THE ATTIC OF THE PEOPLE WHO SPONSORED US. EVERYTHING WAS DIFFERENT. THE WEATHER WAS DIFFERENT. IT WAS VERY HUMID. I WAS HUNGRY IN THE MIDDLE OF THE NIGHT AND I DIDN'T FEEL OKAY GOING DOWN TO GET ANYTHING, BECAUSE IT WASN'T OUR KITCHEN, AND THE FOOD WAS ALL STRANGE ANYWAY."
"I PLANNED A BIRTHDAY PARTY IN SEVENTH GRADE. ONLY ONE PERSON CAME."

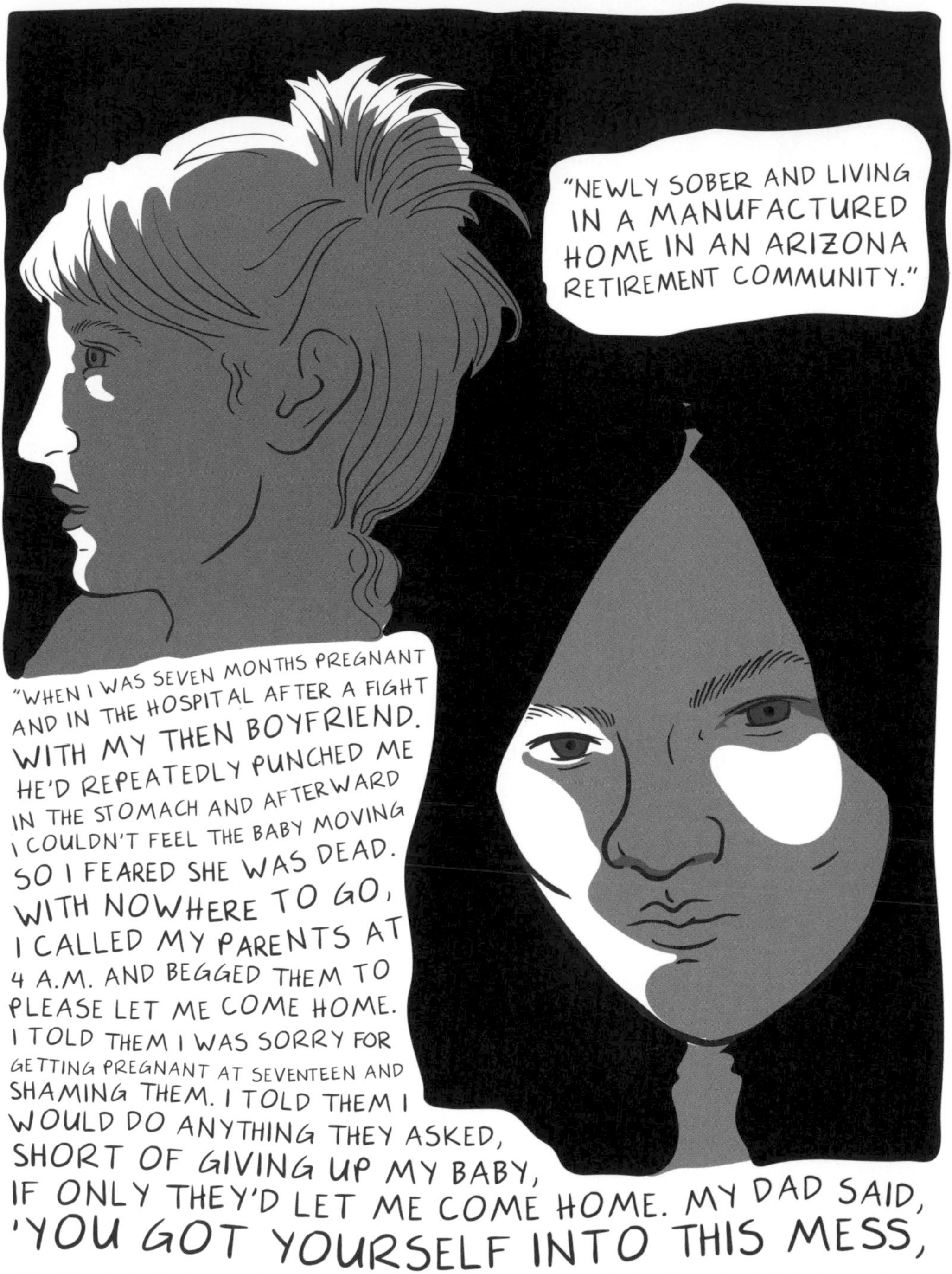
"NEWLY SOBER AND LIVING IN A MANUFACTURED HOME IN AN ARIZONA RETIREMENT COMMUNITY."
"WHEN I WAS SEVEN MONTHS PREGNANT AND IN THE HOSPITAL AFTER A FIGHT WITH MY THEN BOYFRIEND. HE'D REPEATEDLY PUNCHED ME IN THE STOMACH AND AFTERWARD I COULDN'T FEEL THE BABY MOVING SO I FEARED SHE WAS DEAD. WITH NOWHERE TO GO, I CALLED MY PARENTS AT 4 A.M. AND BEGGED THEM TO PLEASE LET ME COME HOME. I TOLD THEM I WAS SORRY FOR GETTING PREGNANT AT SEVENTEEN AND SHAMING THEM. I TOLD THEM I WOULD DO ANYTHING THEY ASKED, SHORT OF GIVING UP MY BABY, IF ONLY THEY'D LET ME COME HOME. MY DAD SAID, 'YOU GOT YOURSELF INTO THIS MESS, NOW GET YOURSELF OUT,' BEFORE HE HUNG UP."

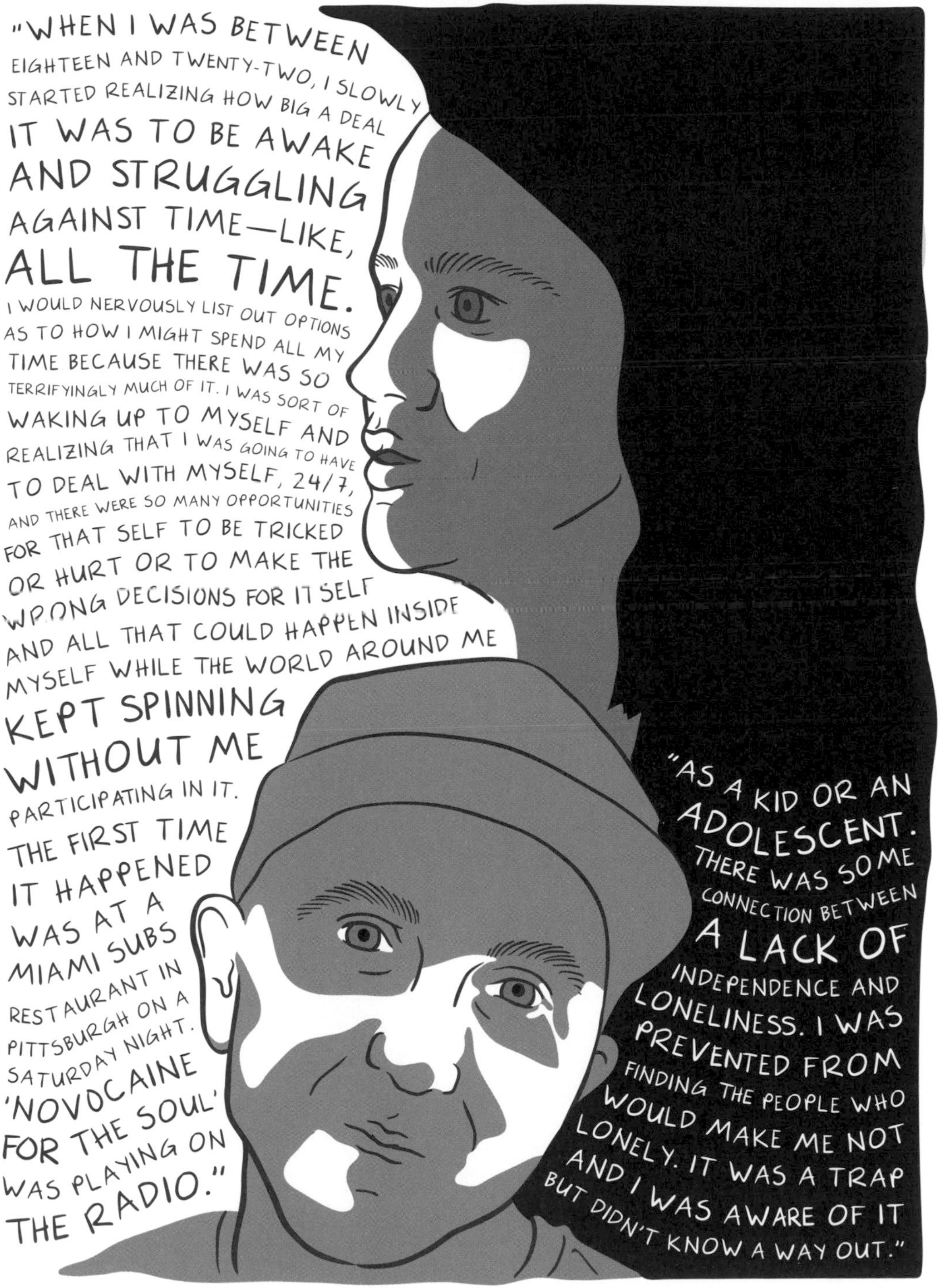
"WHEN I WAS BETWEEN EIGHTEEN AND TWENTY-TWO, I SLOWLY STARTED REALIZING HOW BIG A DEAL IT WAS TO BE AWAKE AND STRUGGLING AGAINST TIME—LIKE, ALL THE TIME. I WOULD NERVOUSLY LIST OUT OPTIONS AS TO HOW I MIGHT SPEND ALL MY TIME BECAUSE THERE WAS SO TERRIFYINGLY MUCH OF IT. I WAS SORT OF WAKING UP TO MYSELF AND REALIZING THAT I WAS GOING TO HAVE TO DEAL WITH MYSELF, 24/7, AND THERE WERE SO MANY OPPORTUNITIES FOR THAT SELF TO BE TRICKED OR HURT OR TO MAKE THE WRONG DECISIONS FOR IT SELF AND ALL THAT COULD HAPPEN INSIDE MYSELF WHILE THE WORLD AROUND ME KEPT SPINNING WITHOUT ME PARTICIPATING IN IT. THE FIRST TIME IT HAPPENED WAS AT A MIAMI SUBS RESTAURANT IN PITTSBURGH ON A SATURDAY NIGHT. 'NOVOCAINE FOR THE SOUL' WAS PLAYING ON THE RADIO."
"AS A KID OR AN ADOLESCENT. THERE WAS SOME CONNECTION BETWEEN A LACK OF INDEPENDENCE AND LONELINESS. I WAS PREVENTED FROM FINDING THE PEOPLE WHO WOULD MAKE ME NOT LONELY. IT WAS A TRAP AND I WAS AWARE OF IT BUT DIDN'T KNOW A WAY OUT."

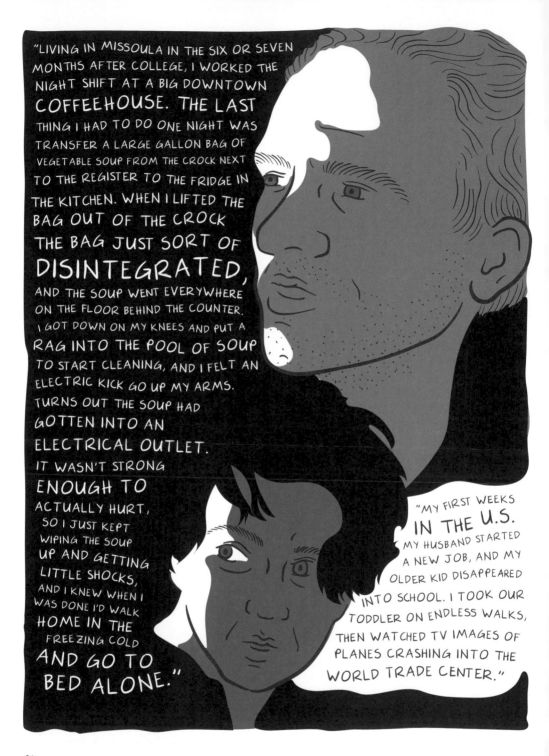

"LIVING IN MISSOULA IN THE SIX OR SEVEN MONTHS AFTER COLLEGE, I WORKED THE NIGHT SHIFT AT A BIG DOWNTOWN COFFEEHOUSE. THE LAST THING I HAD TO DO ONE NIGHT WAS TRANSFER A LARGE GALLON BAG OF VEGETABLE SOUP FROM THE CROCK NEXT TO THE REGISTER TO THE FRIDGE IN THE KITCHEN. WHEN I LIFTED THE BAG OUT OF THE CROCK THE BAG JUST SORT OF DISINTEGRATED, AND THE SOUP WENT EVERYWHERE ON THE FLOOR BEHIND THE COUNTER. I GOT DOWN ON MY KNEES AND PUT A RAG INTO THE POOL OF SOUP TO START CLEANING, AND I FELT AN ELECTRIC KICK GO UP MY ARMS. TURNS OUT THE SOUP HAD GOTTEN INTO AN ELECTRICAL OUTLET. IT WASN'T STRONG ENOUGH TO ACTUALLY HURT, SO I JUST KEPT WIPING THE SOUP UP AND GETTING LITTLE SHOCKS, AND I KNEW WHEN I WAS DONE I'D WALK HOME IN THE FREEZING COLD AND GO TO BED ALONE."

"MY FIRST WEEKS IN THE U.S. MY HUSBAND STARTED A NEW JOB, AND MY OLDER KID DISAPPEARED INTO SCHOOL. I TOOK OUR TODDLER ON ENDLESS WALKS, THEN WATCHED TV IMAGES OF PLANES CRASHING INTO THE WORLD TRADE CENTER."

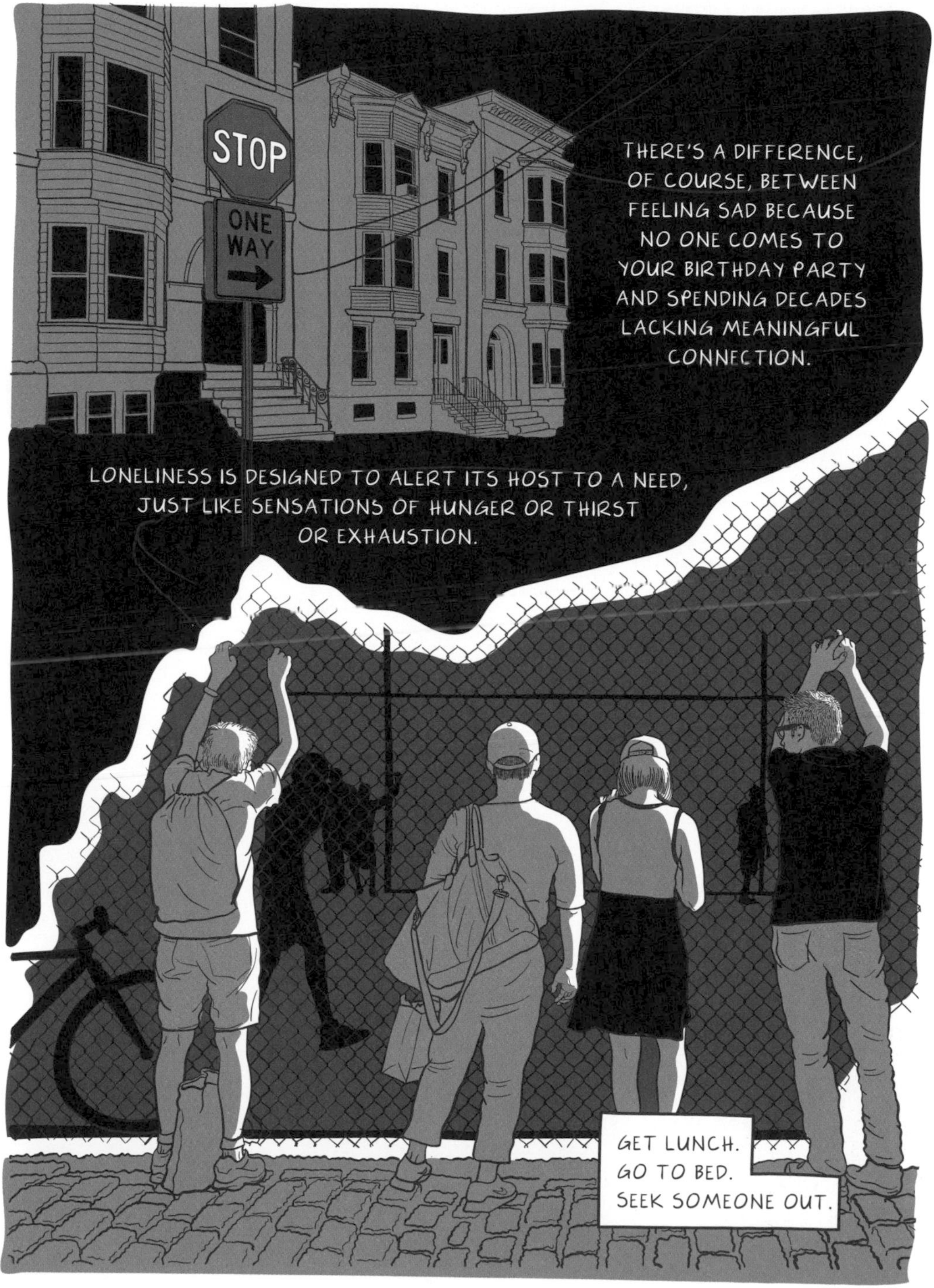
STOP
ONE WAY
THERE'S A DIFFERENCE, OF COURSE, BETWEEN FEELING SAD BECAUSE NO ONE COMES TO YOUR BIRTHDAY PARTY AND SPENDING DECADES LACKING MEANINGFUL CONNECTION.
LONELINESS IS DESIGNED TO ALERT ITS HOST TO A NEED, JUST LIKE SENSATIONS OF HUNGER OR THIRST OR EXHAUSTION.
GET LUNCH.
GO TO BED.
SEEK SOMEONE OUT.

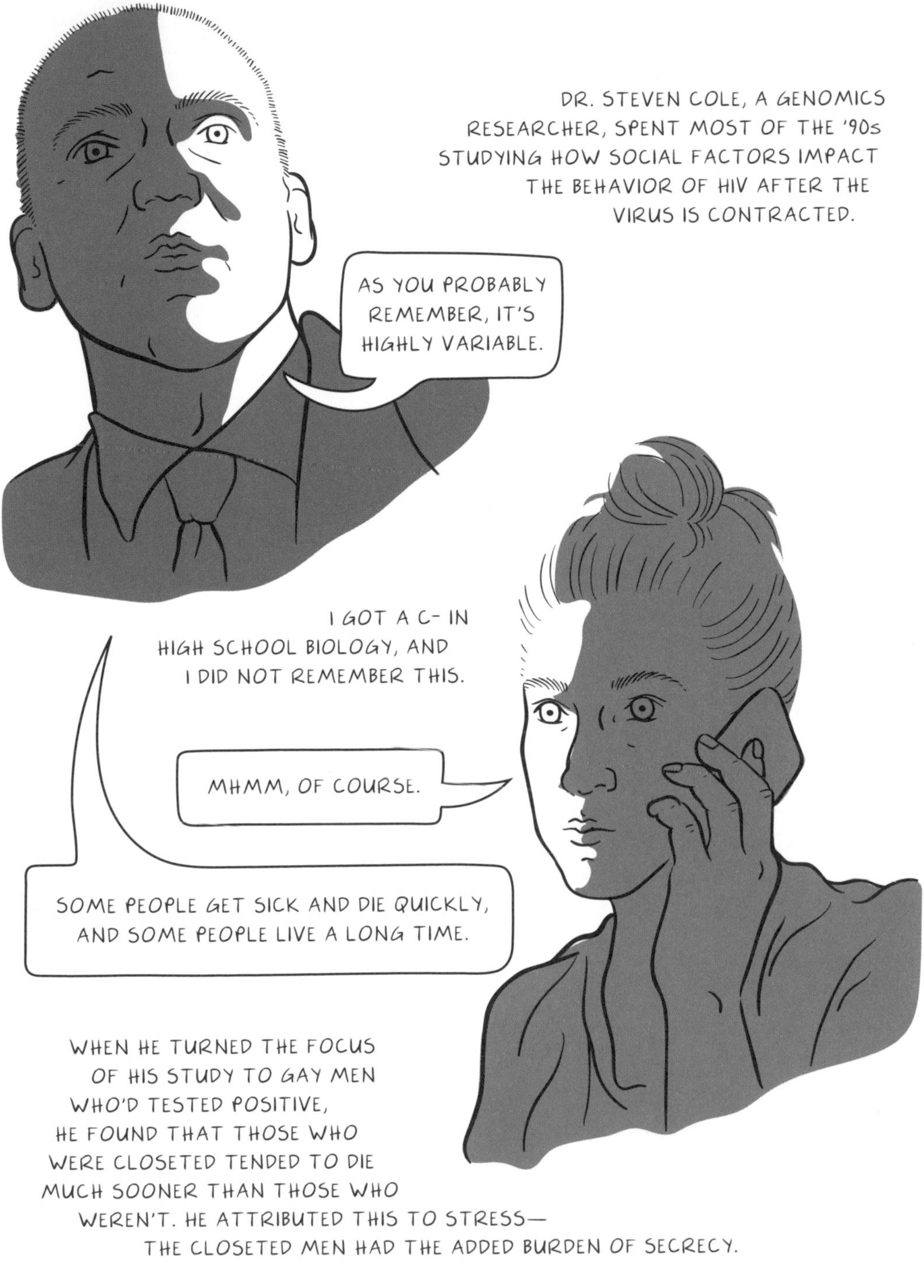

DR. STEVEN COLE, A GENOMICS RESEARCHER, SPENT MOST OF THE '90s STUDYING HOW SOCIAL FACTORS IMPACT THE BEHAVIOR OF HIV AFTER THE VIRUS IS CONTRACTED.
AS YOU PROBABLY REMEMBER, IT'S HIGHLY VARIABLE.
I GOT A C- IN HIGH SCHOOL BIOLOGY, AND I DID NOT REMEMBER THIS.
MHMM, OF COURSE.
SOME PEOPLE GET SICK AND DIE QUICKLY, AND SOME PEOPLE LIVE A LONG TIME.
WHEN HE TURNED THE FOCUS OF HIS STUDY TO GAY MEN WHO'D TESTED POSITIVE, HE FOUND THAT THOSE WHO WERE CLOSETED TENDED TO DIE MUCH SOONER THAN THOSE WHO WEREN'T. HE ATTRIBUTED THIS TO STRESS— THE CLOSETED MEN HAD THE ADDED BURDEN OF SECRECY.

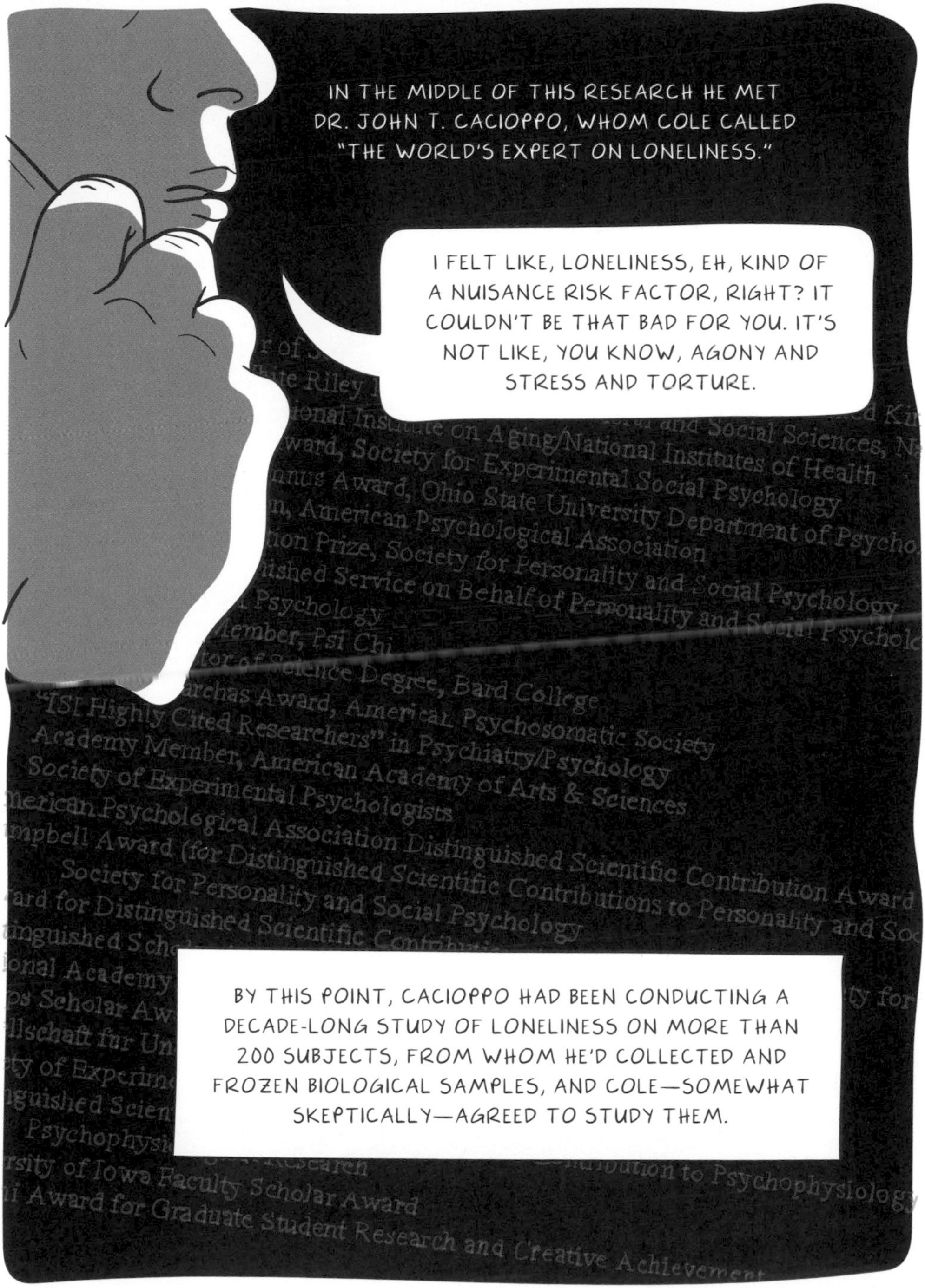
IN THE MIDDLE OF THIS RESEARCH HE MET DR. JOHN T. CACIOPPO, WHOM COLE CALLED "THE WORLD'S EXPERT ON LONELINESS."
I FELT LIKE, LONELINESS, EH, KIND OF A NUISANCE RISK FACTOR, RIGHT? IT COULDN'T BE THAT BAD FOR YOU. IT'S NOT LIKE, YOU KNOW, AGONY AND STRESS AND TORTURE.
BY THIS POINT, CACIOPPO HAD BEEN CONDUCTING A DECADE-LONG STUDY OF LONELINESS ON MORE THAN 200 SUBJECTS, FROM WHOM HE'D COLLECTED AND FROZEN BIOLOGICAL SAMPLES, AND COLE—SOMEWHAT SKEPTICALLY—AGREED TO STUDY THEM.

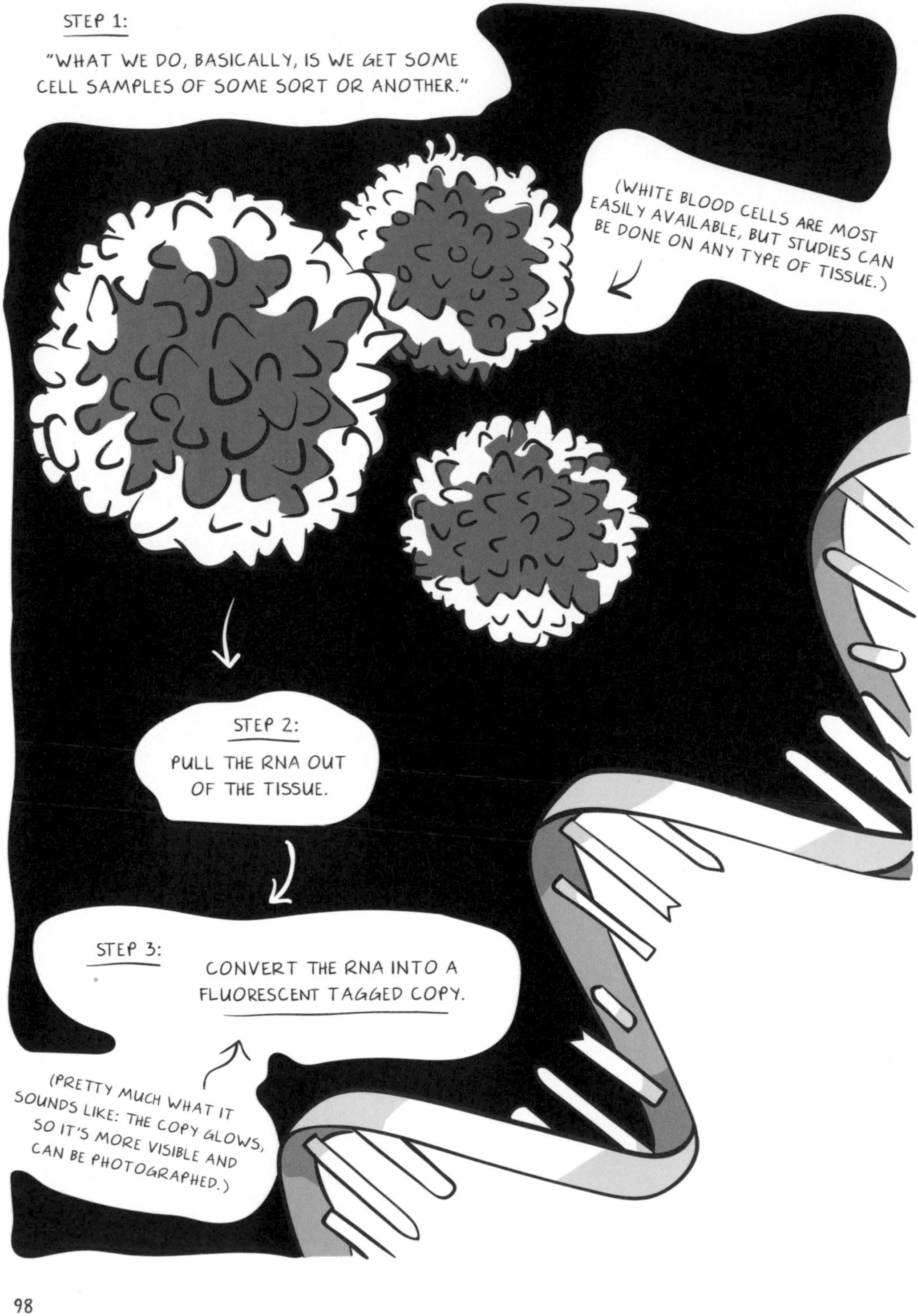
STEP 1:
"WHAT WE DO, BASICALLY, IS WE GET SOME CELL SAMPLES OF SOME SORT OR ANOTHER."
(WHITE BLOOD CELLS ARE MOST EASILY AVAILABLE, BUT STUDIES CAN BE DONE ON ANY TYPE OF TISSUE.)
STEP 2:
PULL THE RNA OUT OF THE TISSUE.
STEP 3:
CONVERT THE RNA INTO A FLUORESCENT TAGGED COPY.
(PRETTY MUCH WHAT IT SOUNDS LIKE: THE COPY GLOWS, SO IT'S MORE VISIBLE AND CAN BE PHOTOGRAPHED.)

STEP 4:

STICK THE FLUORESCENT COPY OF
THE RNA TO A <u>MICROARRAY</u>

(A TINY PLATFORM OF PROBES ENGINEERED TO
DETECT ALL 20,000 KNOWN HUMAN GENES).

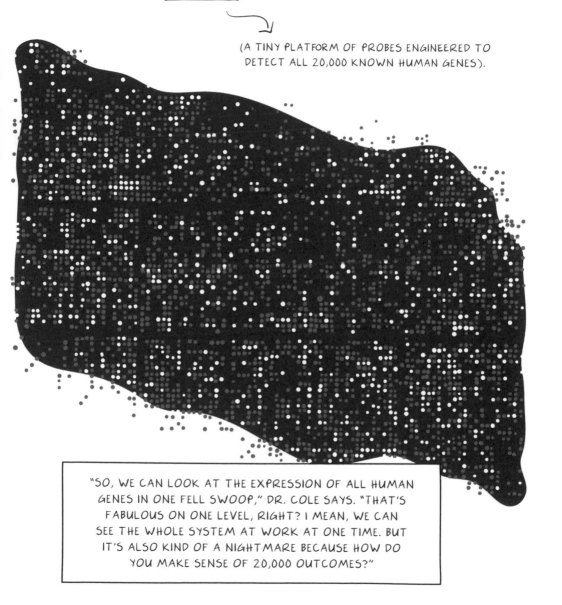

"SO, WE CAN LOOK AT THE EXPRESSION OF ALL HUMAN
GENES IN ONE FELL SWOOP," DR. COLE SAYS. "THAT'S
FABULOUS ON ONE LEVEL, RIGHT? I MEAN, WE CAN
SEE THE WHOLE SYSTEM AT WORK AT ONE TIME. BUT
IT'S ALSO KIND OF A NIGHTMARE BECAUSE HOW DO
YOU MAKE SENSE OF 20,000 OUTCOMES?"

DR. COLE CALLS THE EXPRESSION OF HUMAN
GENES "A BIG, COMPLEX CONSPIRACY OF LOTS
OF DIFFERENT INFLUENCES." HE THINKS OF THEM
LIKE OCTOPI SYSTEMS, OR SPAGHETTI DIAGRAMS
THAT CONVERGE TO BUILD A HUMAN LIFE.

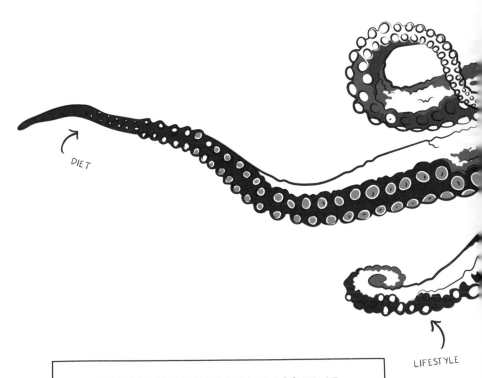

DIET

LIFESTYLE

MOST OF THE TIME, WHEN HE LOOKED AT
GENOMICS DATA, HE WAS USED TO SEEING
CHAOS—MEANING THE GENES WEREN'T
EXPRESSING ANYTHING THAT SPECIFIC. BUT
WHEN HE TESTED FOR LONELINESS, HE SAID, THAT
SIGNAL WAS MUCH CLEARER THAN HE'D EXPECTED.

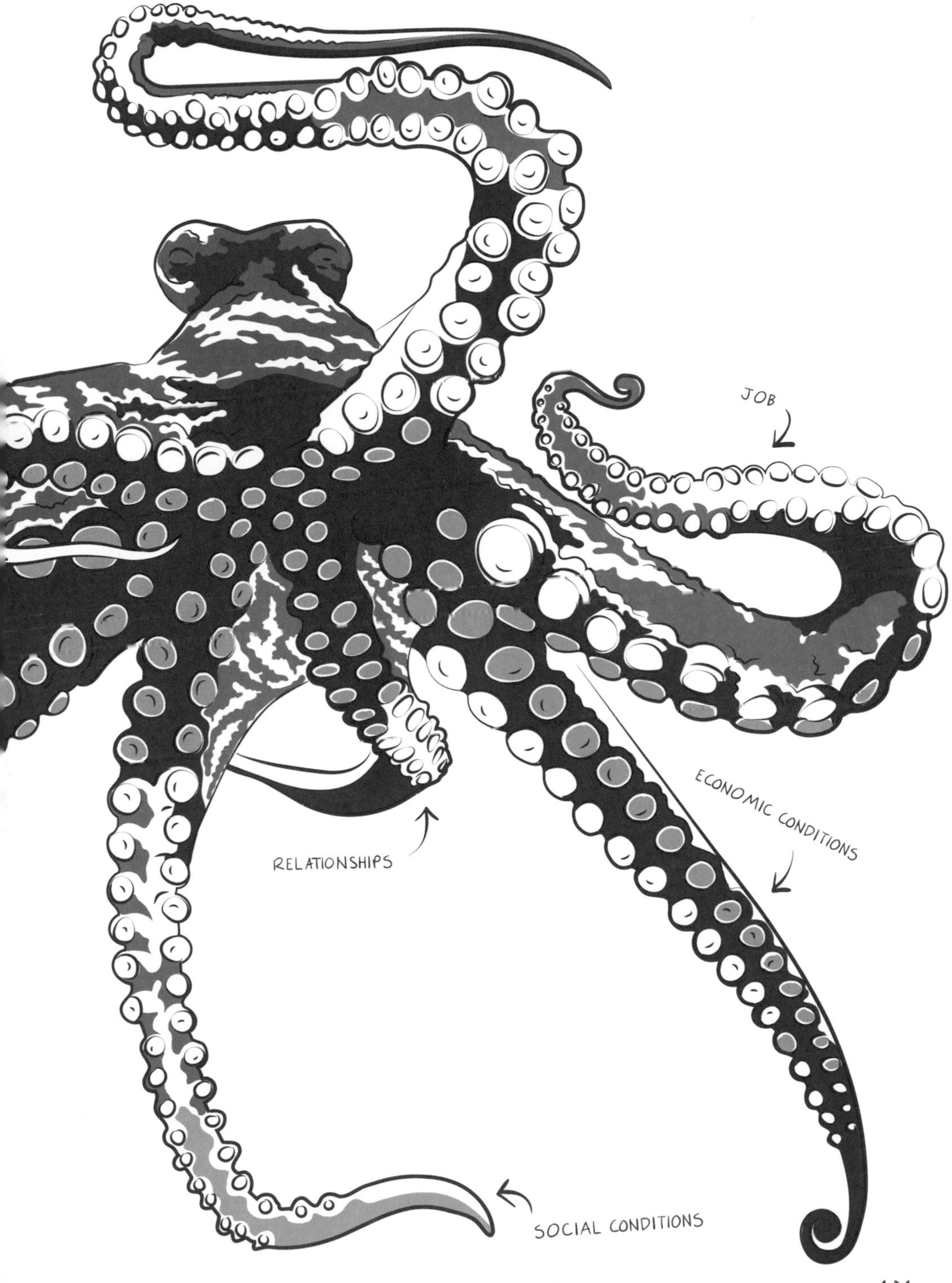
JOB
ECONOMIC CONDITIONS
RELATIONSHIPS
SOCIAL CONDITIONS

THAT CLARITY SETTLED ON ONE PRIMARY CONCERN: IN THOSE WHO ARE CHRONICALLY LONELY, DR. COLE TOLD ME, "JUST ABOUT EVERY HIGH-PREVALENCE KILLER IN CONTEMPORARY EPIDEMIOLOGY GETS YOU FASTER."

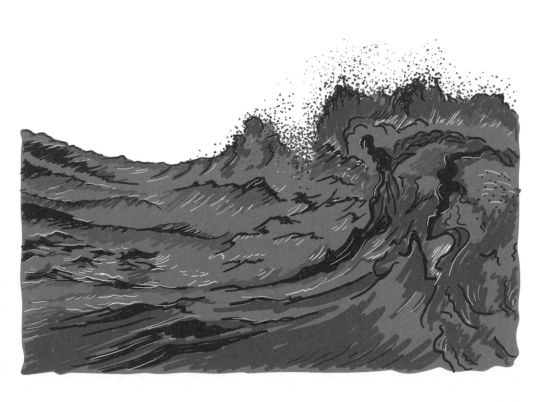

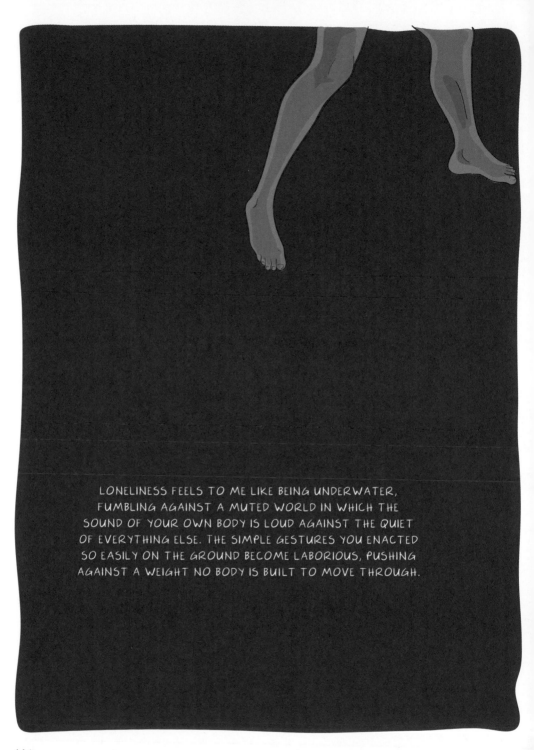

LONELINESS FEELS TO ME LIKE BEING UNDERWATER,
FUMBLING AGAINST A MUTED WORLD IN WHICH THE
SOUND OF YOUR OWN BODY IS LOUD AGAINST THE QUIET
OF EVERYTHING ELSE. THE SIMPLE GESTURES YOU ENACTED
SO EASILY ON THE GROUND BECOME LABORIOUS, PUSHING
AGAINST A WEIGHT NO BODY IS BUILT TO MOVE THROUGH.

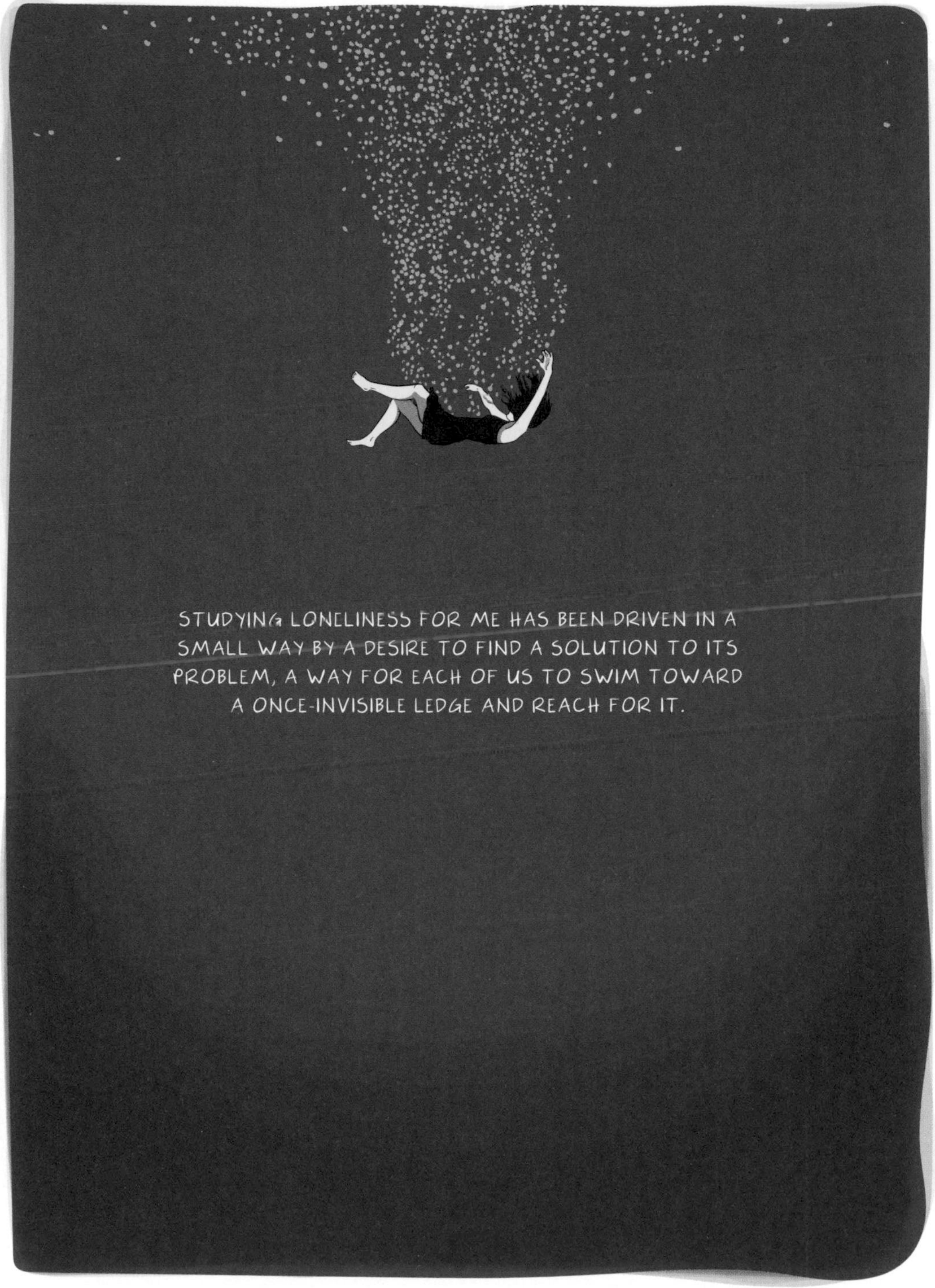
STUDYING LONELINESS FOR ME HAS BEEN DRIVEN IN A SMALL WAY BY A DESIRE TO FIND A SOLUTION TO ITS PROBLEM, A WAY FOR EACH OF US TO SWIM TOWARD A ONCE-INVISIBLE LEDGE AND REACH FOR IT.

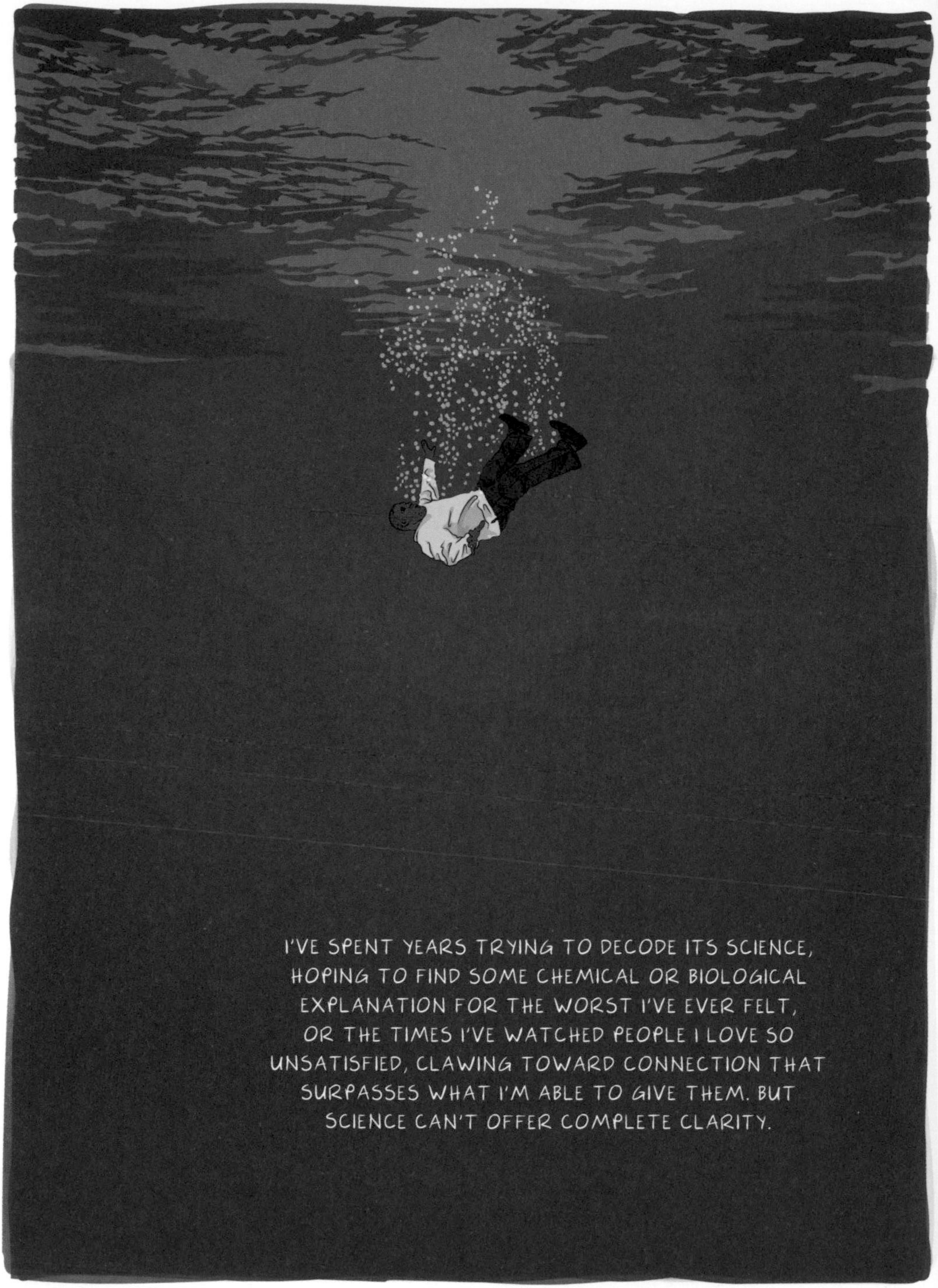
I'VE SPENT YEARS TRYING TO DECODE ITS SCIENCE, HOPING TO FIND SOME CHEMICAL OR BIOLOGICAL EXPLANATION FOR THE WORST I'VE EVER FELT, OR THE TIMES I'VE WATCHED PEOPLE I LOVE SO UNSATISFIED, CLAWING TOWARD CONNECTION THAT SURPASSES WHAT I'M ABLE TO GIVE THEM. BUT SCIENCE CAN'T OFFER COMPLETE CLARITY.

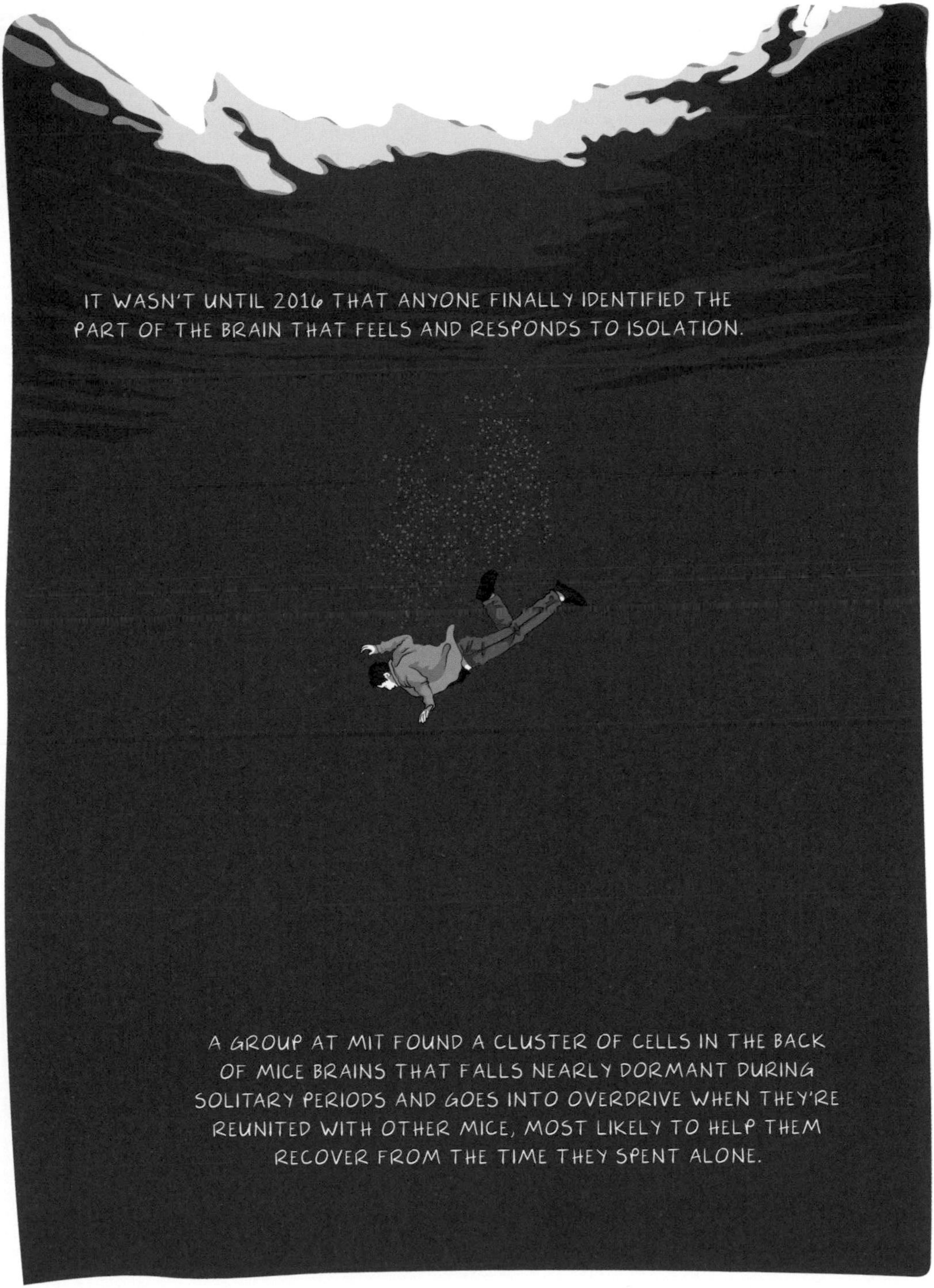
IT WASN'T UNTIL 2016 THAT ANYONE FINALLY IDENTIFIED THE PART OF THE BRAIN THAT FEELS AND RESPONDS TO ISOLATION.
A GROUP AT MIT FOUND A CLUSTER OF CELLS IN THE BACK OF MICE BRAINS THAT FALLS NEARLY DORMANT DURING SOLITARY PERIODS AND GOES INTO OVERDRIVE WHEN THEY'RE REUNITED WITH OTHER MICE, MOST LIKELY TO HELP THEM RECOVER FROM THE TIME THEY SPENT ALONE.

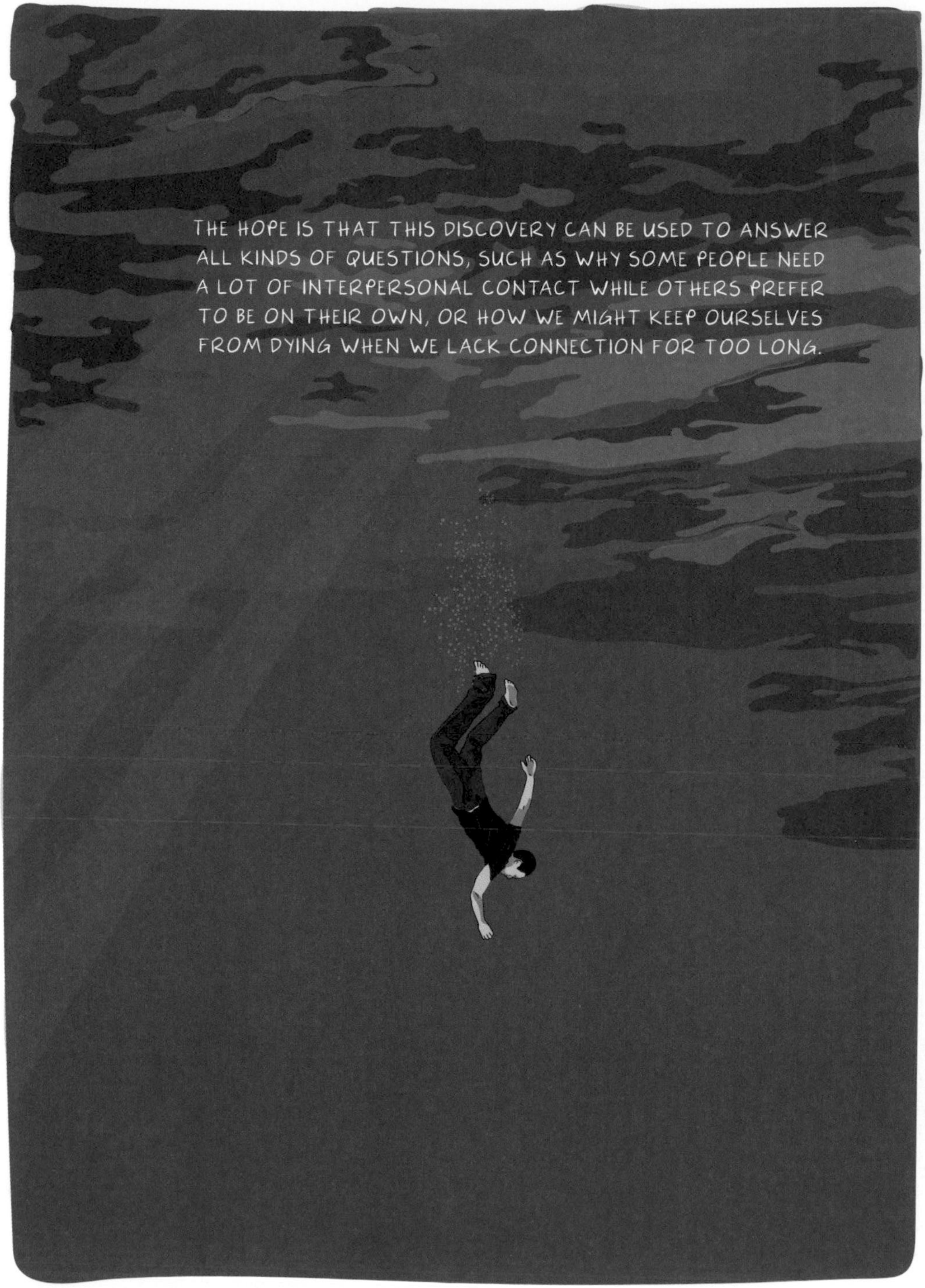
THE HOPE IS THAT THIS DISCOVERY CAN BE USED TO ANSWER ALL KINDS OF QUESTIONS, SUCH AS WHY SOME PEOPLE NEED A LOT OF INTERPERSONAL CONTACT WHILE OTHERS PREFER TO BE ON THEIR OWN, OR HOW WE MIGHT KEEP OURSELVES FROM DYING WHEN WE LACK CONNECTION FOR TOO LONG.

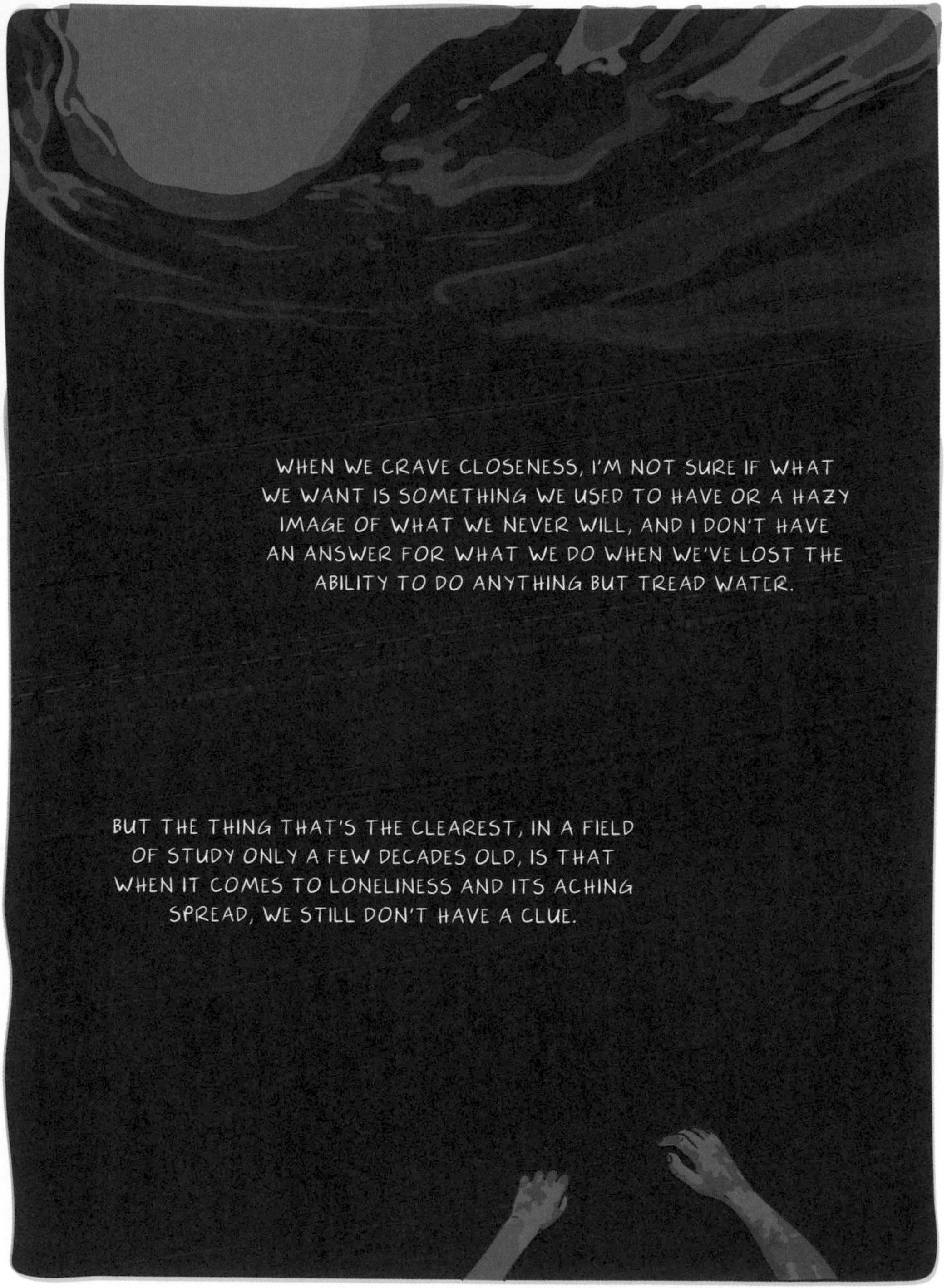
WHEN WE CRAVE CLOSENESS, I'M NOT SURE IF WHAT WE WANT IS SOMETHING WE USED TO HAVE OR A HAZY IMAGE OF WHAT WE NEVER WILL, AND I DON'T HAVE AN ANSWER FOR WHAT WE DO WHEN WE'VE LOST THE ABILITY TO DO ANYTHING BUT TREAD WATER.
BUT THE THING THAT'S THE CLEAREST, IN A FIELD OF STUDY ONLY A FEW DECADES OLD, IS THAT WHEN IT COMES TO LONELINESS AND ITS ACHING SPREAD, WE STILL DON'T HAVE A CLUE.

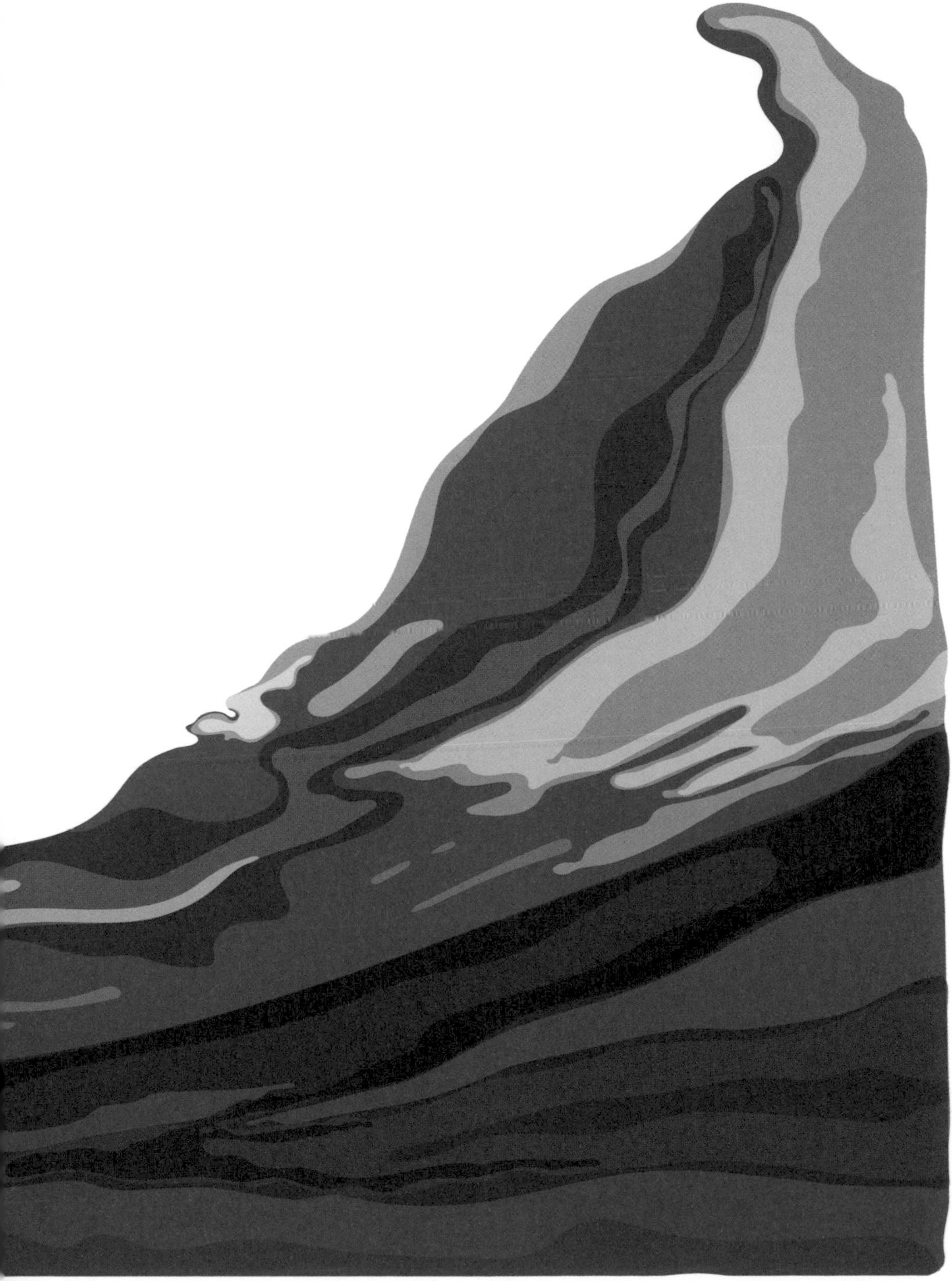

WATCH

I

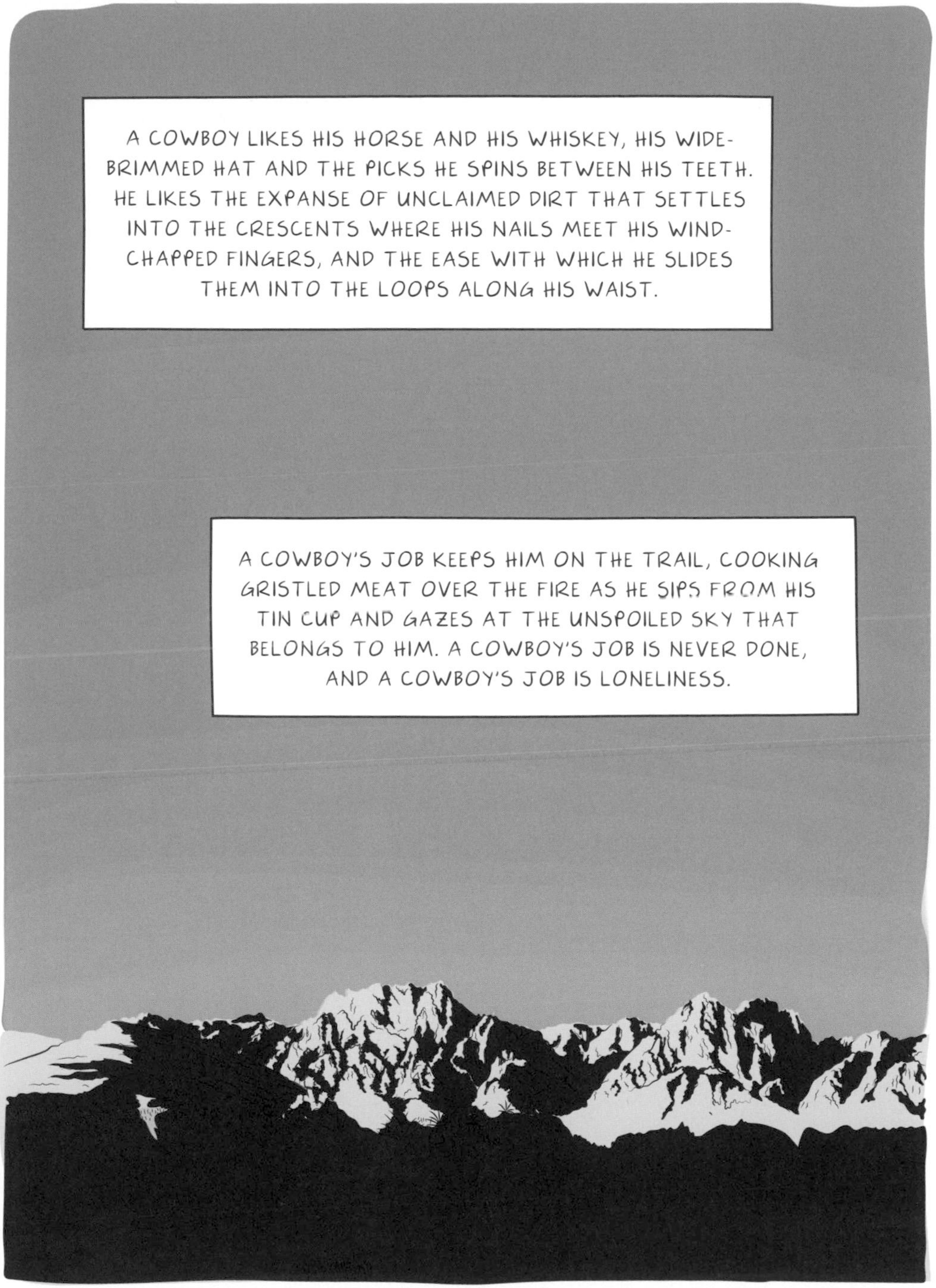
A COWBOY LIKES HIS HORSE AND HIS WHISKEY, HIS WIDE-BRIMMED HAT AND THE PICKS HE SPINS BETWEEN HIS TEETH. HE LIKES THE EXPANSE OF UNCLAIMED DIRT THAT SETTLES INTO THE CRESCENTS WHERE HIS NAILS MEET HIS WIND-CHAPPED FINGERS, AND THE EASE WITH WHICH HE SLIDES THEM INTO THE LOOPS ALONG HIS WAIST.
A COWBOY'S JOB KEEPS HIM ON THE TRAIL, COOKING GRISTLED MEAT OVER THE FIRE AS HE SIPS FROM HIS TIN CUP AND GAZES AT THE UNSPOILED SKY THAT BELONGS TO HIM. A COWBOY'S JOB IS NEVER DONE, AND A COWBOY'S JOB IS LONELINESS.

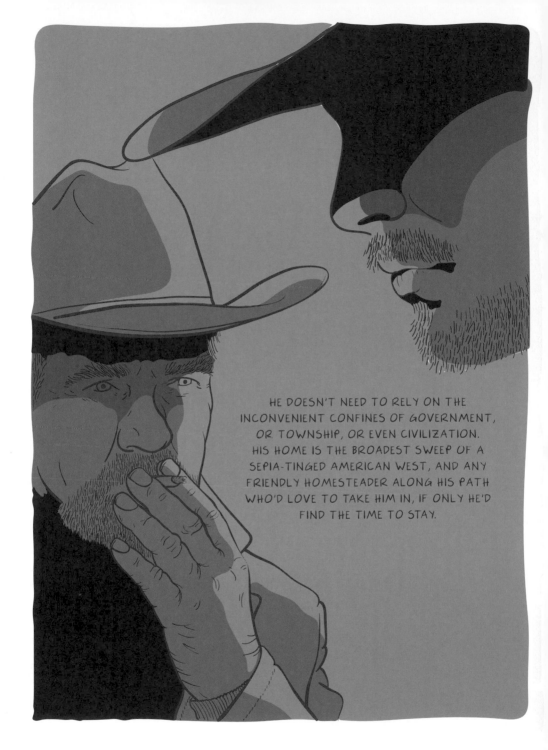

HE DOESN'T NEED TO RELY ON THE INCONVENIENT CONFINES OF GOVERNMENT, OR TOWNSHIP, OR EVEN CIVILIZATION. HIS HOME IS THE BROADEST SWEEP OF A SEPIA-TINGED AMERICAN WEST, AND ANY FRIENDLY HOMESTEADER ALONG HIS PATH WHO'D LOVE TO TAKE HIM IN, IF ONLY HE'D FIND THE TIME TO STAY.

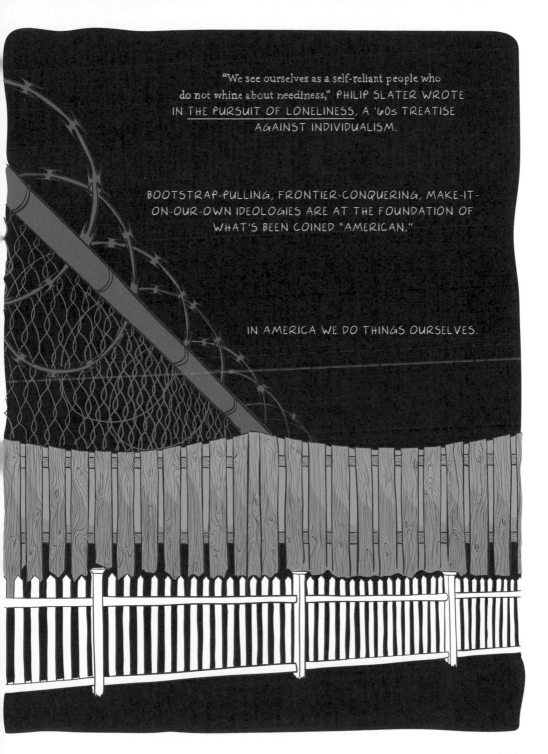

"We see ourselves as a self-reliant people who do not whine about neediness," PHILIP SLATER WROTE IN THE PURSUIT OF LONELINESS, A '60s TREATISE AGAINST INDIVIDUALISM.

BOOTSTRAP-PULLING, FRONTIER-CONQUERING, MAKE-IT-ON-OUR-OWN IDEOLOGIES ARE AT THE FOUNDATION OF WHAT'S BEEN COINED "AMERICAN."

IN AMERICA WE DO THINGS OURSELVES.

THE MYTH OF THE OLD WEST'S STRONG-AND-SILENT
COWBOY WAS SO INTOXICATING TO ANGLO-AMERICA THAT
IT SUCCESSFULLY SOLD CIGARETTES AND PRESIDENTS,
BRANDING AN ENTIRE GENRE OF MUSIC AROUND
SUN-BLEACHED DRAWLS AND WAYWARD CHIVALRY.

AMERICA

REAGAN COUNTR

IN THE COUNTRY'S REAL HISTORY,
THE REIGN OF THE COWBOY AS WE KNOW
HIM WAS HALTED BY THE INVENTION OF BARBED
WIRE, ENDING THE ERA OF FREE-RANGE CATTLE. THE MEN
WHO TENDED TO THEM WEREN'T THE TYPE TO SPIN THEIR PISTOLS
IN THE TOWN SQUARE, TIPPING THEIR HATS TO THE LADIES. RUNNING
A RANCH WAS ABOUT AS ARDUOUSLY AROUND-THE-CLOCK AS ANY
OCCUPATION INVOLVING MANUAL LABOR AND LIVESTOCK.

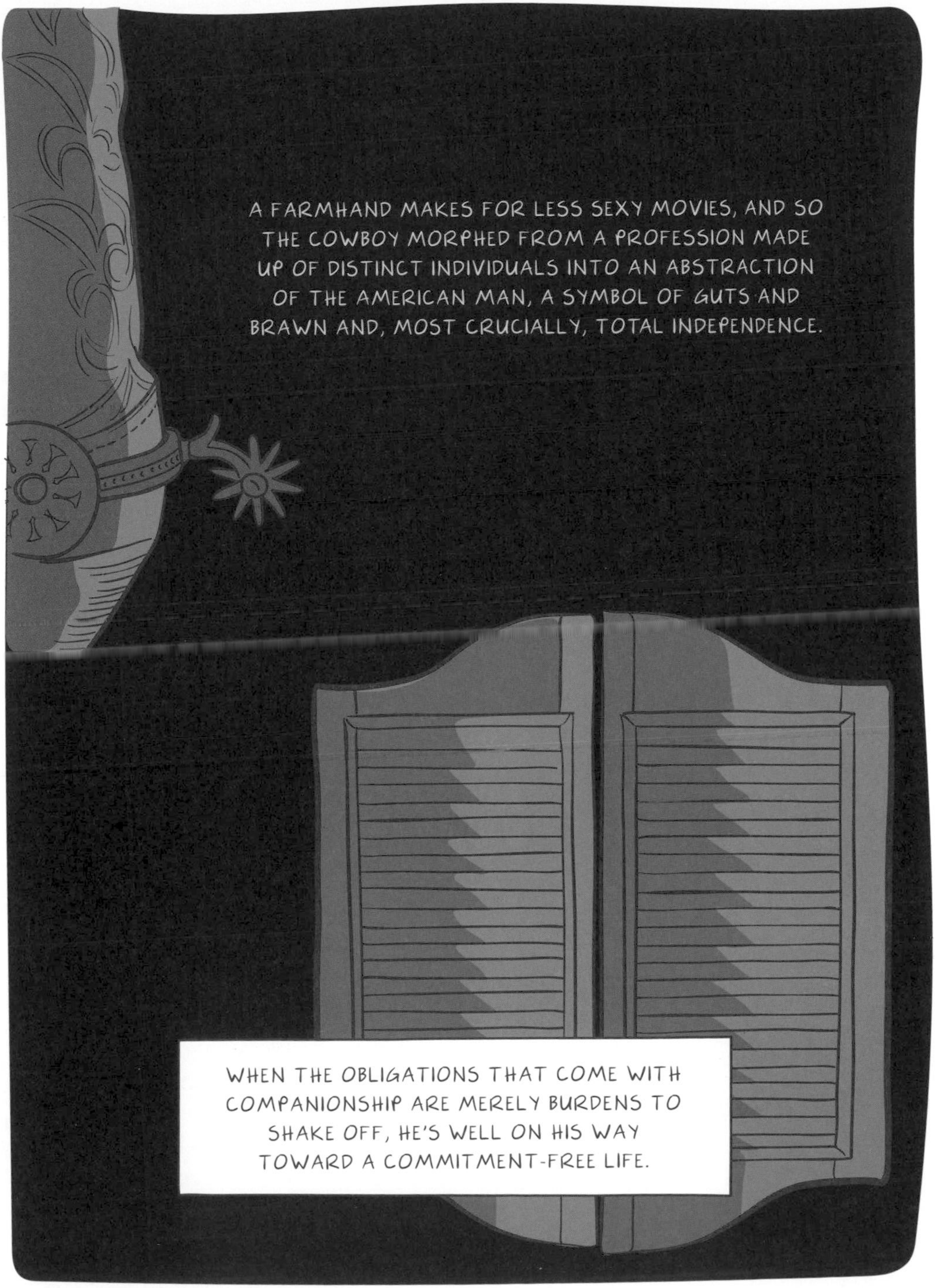
A FARMHAND MAKES FOR LESS SEXY MOVIES, AND SO THE COWBOY MORPHED FROM A PROFESSION MADE UP OF DISTINCT INDIVIDUALS INTO AN ABSTRACTION OF THE AMERICAN MAN, A SYMBOL OF GUTS AND BRAWN AND, MOST CRUCIALLY, TOTAL INDEPENDENCE.
WHEN THE OBLIGATIONS THAT COME WITH COMPANIONSHIP ARE MERELY BURDENS TO SHAKE OFF, HE'S WELL ON HIS WAY TOWARD A COMMITMENT-FREE LIFE.

I WAS RAISED ON WESTERNS THAT IDEALIZED THE HANDSOME OUTSIDER, GALLOPING INTO TOWN AND PUTTING THE BAD GUYS IN THEIR PLACE, SNAGGING THE AFFECTION OF A DAME, AND GETTING THE JOB DONE RIGHT BEFORE HE RIDES OFF ALONE.

JOHN WAYNE

in the masterpiece of four-time Academy Award winner

JOHN FORD

The Man Who Shot Liberty

GOOD GUYS WEAR WHITE HATS

TRYING ON HIS BIRTHDAY PRESENT

MY GRANDPA PASSIVELY EXPLAINED THE NARRATIVES AS WE WATCHED, WHICH I STRUGGLED TO FOLLOW. IT WAS HARD FOR ME TO TELL THE DIFFERENCE BETWEEN THE HERO AND THE VILLAIN, BECAUSE THEY ACTED MUCH THE SAME: THEY BOTH HAD GUNS, AND THEY BOTH SEEMED UNBURDENED BY THEIR FREQUENT USE OF THEM. THEY WHIPPED OUT PISTOLS FROM THEIR HOLSTERS WITH EASE IN SALOONS, AND STOOD OVER THE BODIES OF THEIR KILLS WITH DISREGARD.

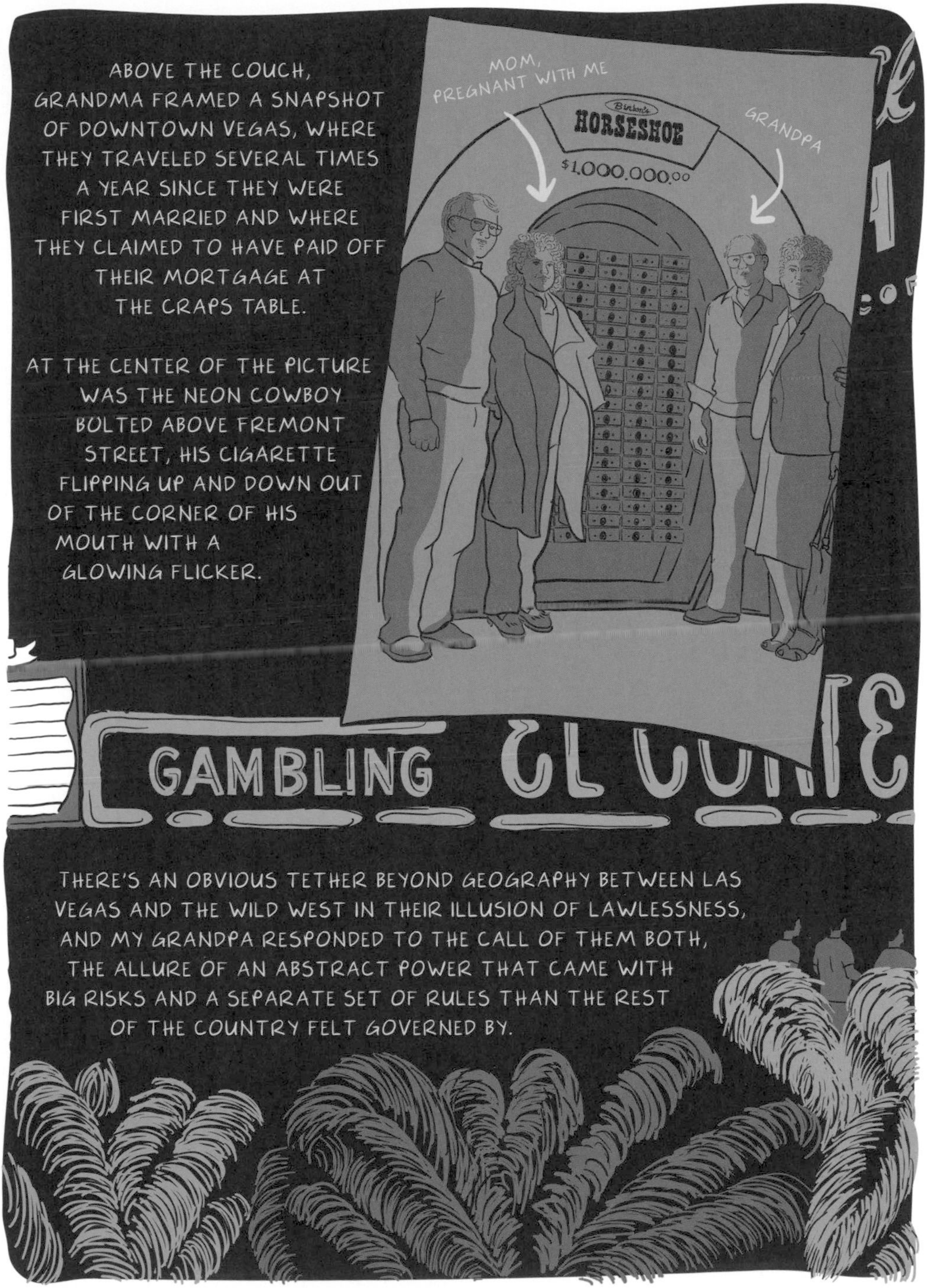
ABOVE THE COUCH, GRANDMA FRAMED A SNAPSHOT OF DOWNTOWN VEGAS, WHERE THEY TRAVELED SEVERAL TIMES A YEAR SINCE THEY WERE FIRST MARRIED AND WHERE THEY CLAIMED TO HAVE PAID OFF THEIR MORTGAGE AT THE CRAPS TABLE.
MOM, PREGNANT WITH ME
GRANDPA
Binion's
HORSESHOE
$1,000,000.00
AT THE CENTER OF THE PICTURE WAS THE NEON COWBOY BOLTED ABOVE FREMONT STREET, HIS CIGARETTE FLIPPING UP AND DOWN OUT OF THE CORNER OF HIS MOUTH WITH A GLOWING FLICKER.
GAMBLING
THERE'S AN OBVIOUS TETHER BEYOND GEOGRAPHY BETWEEN LAS VEGAS AND THE WILD WEST IN THEIR ILLUSION OF LAWLESSNESS, AND MY GRANDPA RESPONDED TO THE CALL OF THEM BOTH, THE ALLURE OF AN ABSTRACT POWER THAT CAME WITH BIG RISKS AND A SEPARATE SET OF RULES THAN THE REST OF THE COUNTRY FELT GOVERNED BY.

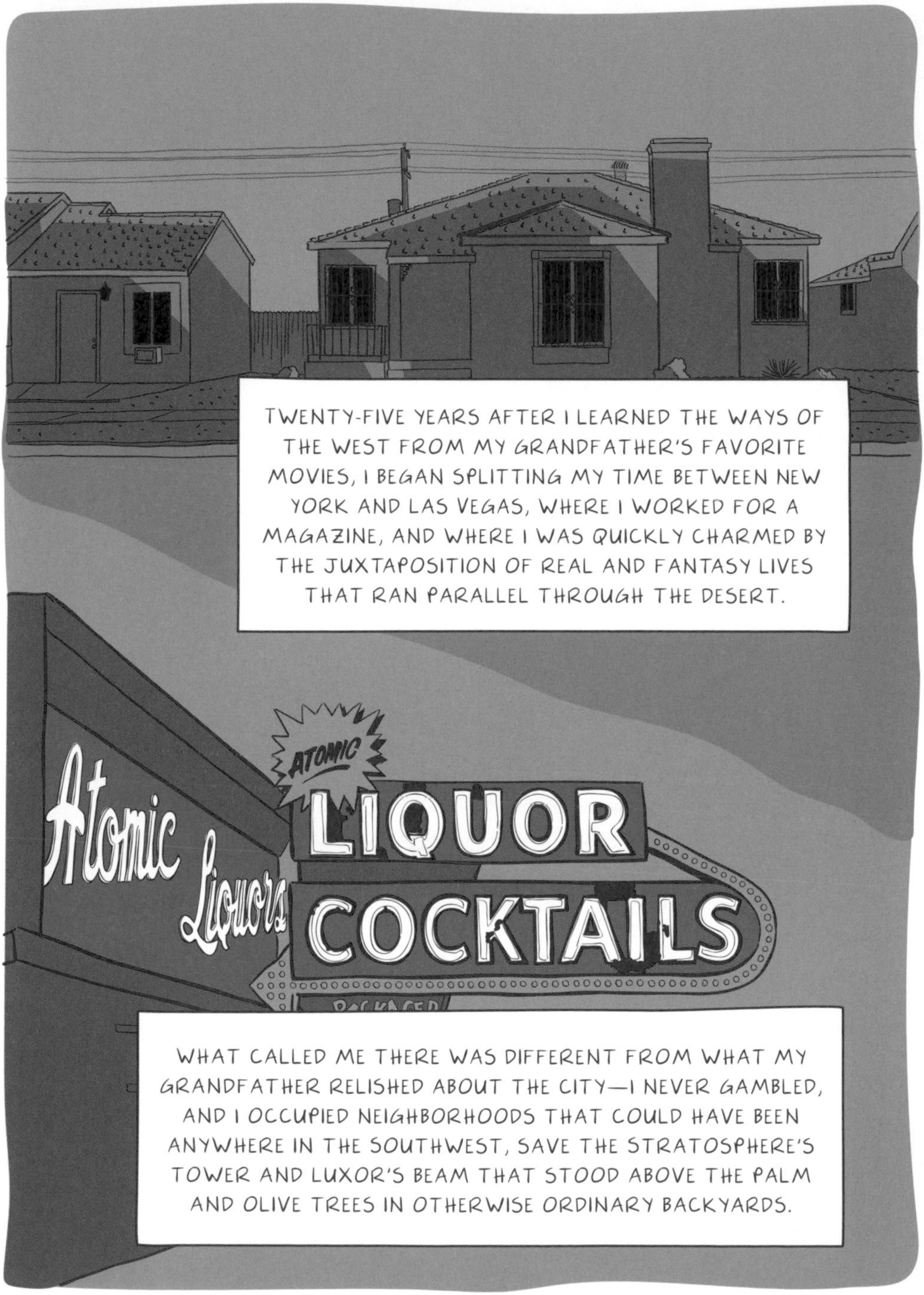
TWENTY-FIVE YEARS AFTER I LEARNED THE WAYS OF THE WEST FROM MY GRANDFATHER'S FAVORITE MOVIES, I BEGAN SPLITTING MY TIME BETWEEN NEW YORK AND LAS VEGAS, WHERE I WORKED FOR A MAGAZINE, AND WHERE I WAS QUICKLY CHARMED BY THE JUXTAPOSITION OF REAL AND FANTASY LIVES THAT RAN PARALLEL THROUGH THE DESERT.
Atomic Liquors
ATOMIC
LIQUOR
COCKTAILS
WHAT CALLED ME THERE WAS DIFFERENT FROM WHAT MY GRANDFATHER RELISHED ABOUT THE CITY—I NEVER GAMBLED, AND I OCCUPIED NEIGHBORHOODS THAT COULD HAVE BEEN ANYWHERE IN THE SOUTHWEST, SAVE THE STRATOSPHERE'S TOWER AND LUXOR'S BEAM THAT STOOD ABOVE THE PALM AND OLIVE TREES IN OTHERWISE ORDINARY BACKYARDS.

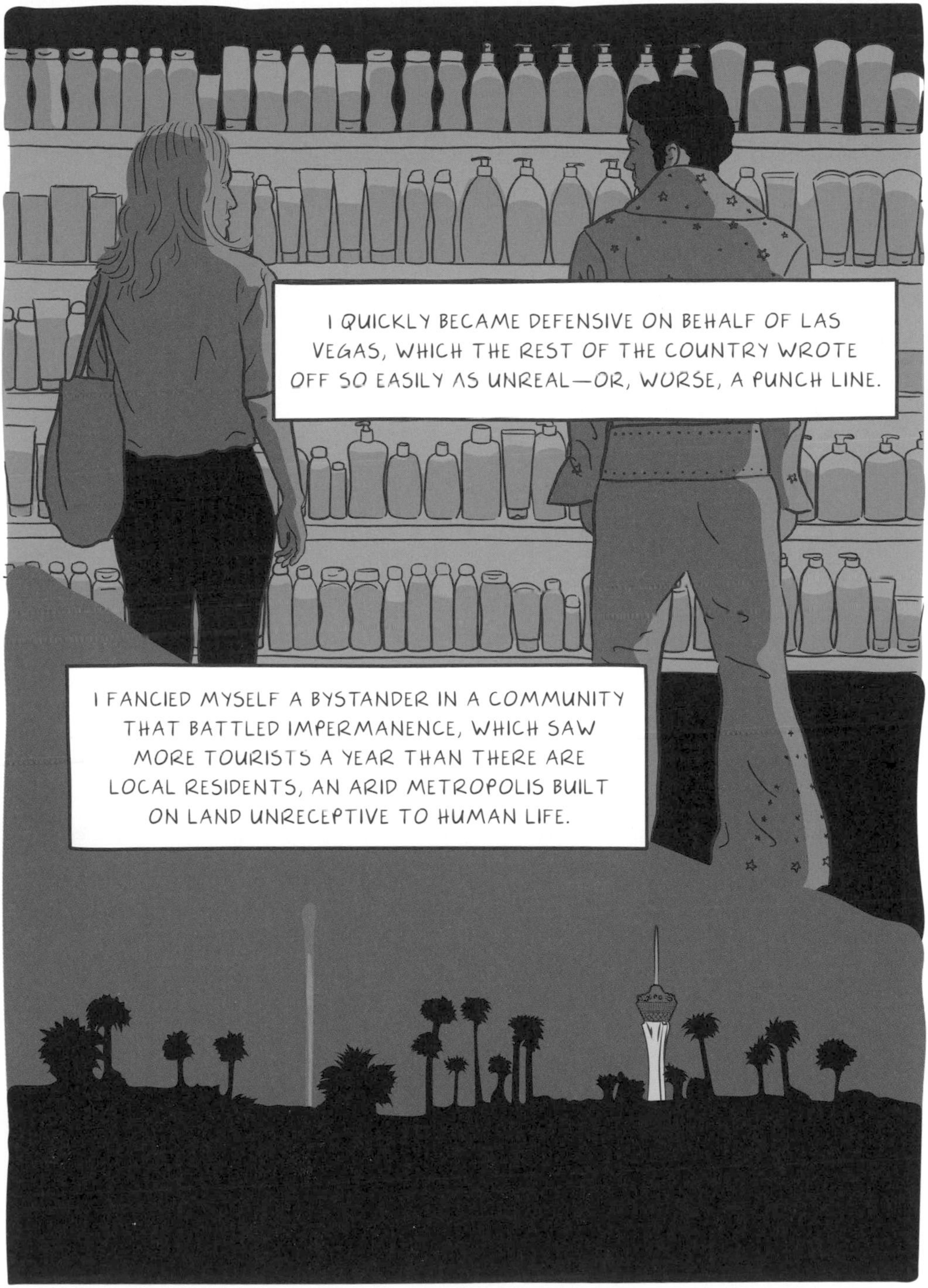
I QUICKLY BECAME DEFENSIVE ON BEHALF OF LAS VEGAS, WHICH THE REST OF THE COUNTRY WROTE OFF SO EASILY AS UNREAL—OR, WORSE, A PUNCH LINE.
I FANCIED MYSELF A BYSTANDER IN A COMMUNITY THAT BATTLED IMPERMANENCE, WHICH SAW MORE TOURISTS A YEAR THAN THERE ARE LOCAL RESIDENTS, AN ARID METROPOLIS BUILT ON LAND UNRECEPTIVE TO HUMAN LIFE.

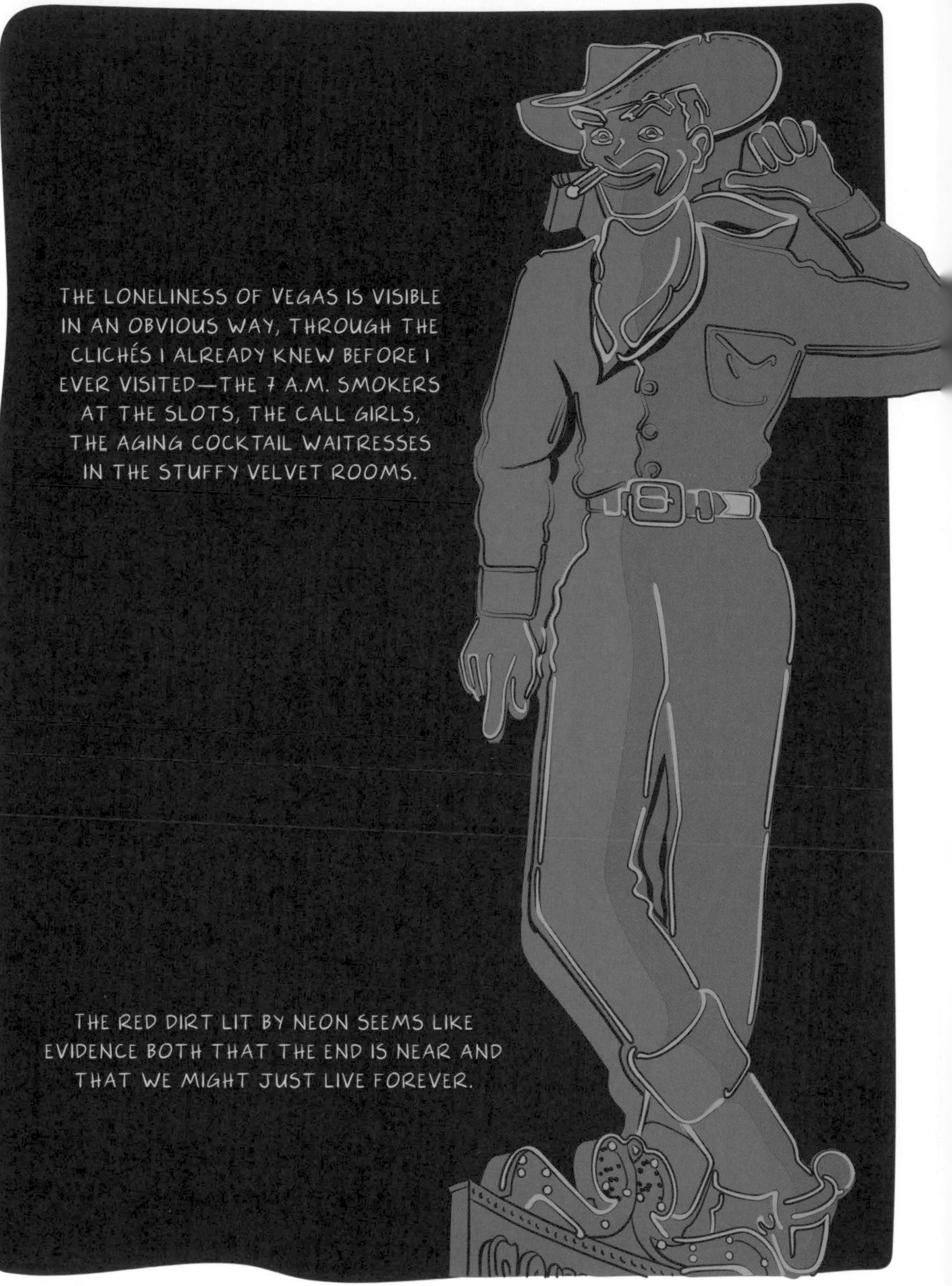
THE LONELINESS OF VEGAS IS VISIBLE IN AN OBVIOUS WAY, THROUGH THE CLICHÉS I ALREADY KNEW BEFORE I EVER VISITED—THE 7 A.M. SMOKERS AT THE SLOTS, THE CALL GIRLS, THE AGING COCKTAIL WAITRESSES IN THE STUFFY VELVET ROOMS.
THE RED DIRT LIT BY NEON SEEMS LIKE EVIDENCE BOTH THAT THE END IS NEAR AND THAT WE MIGHT JUST LIVE FOREVER.

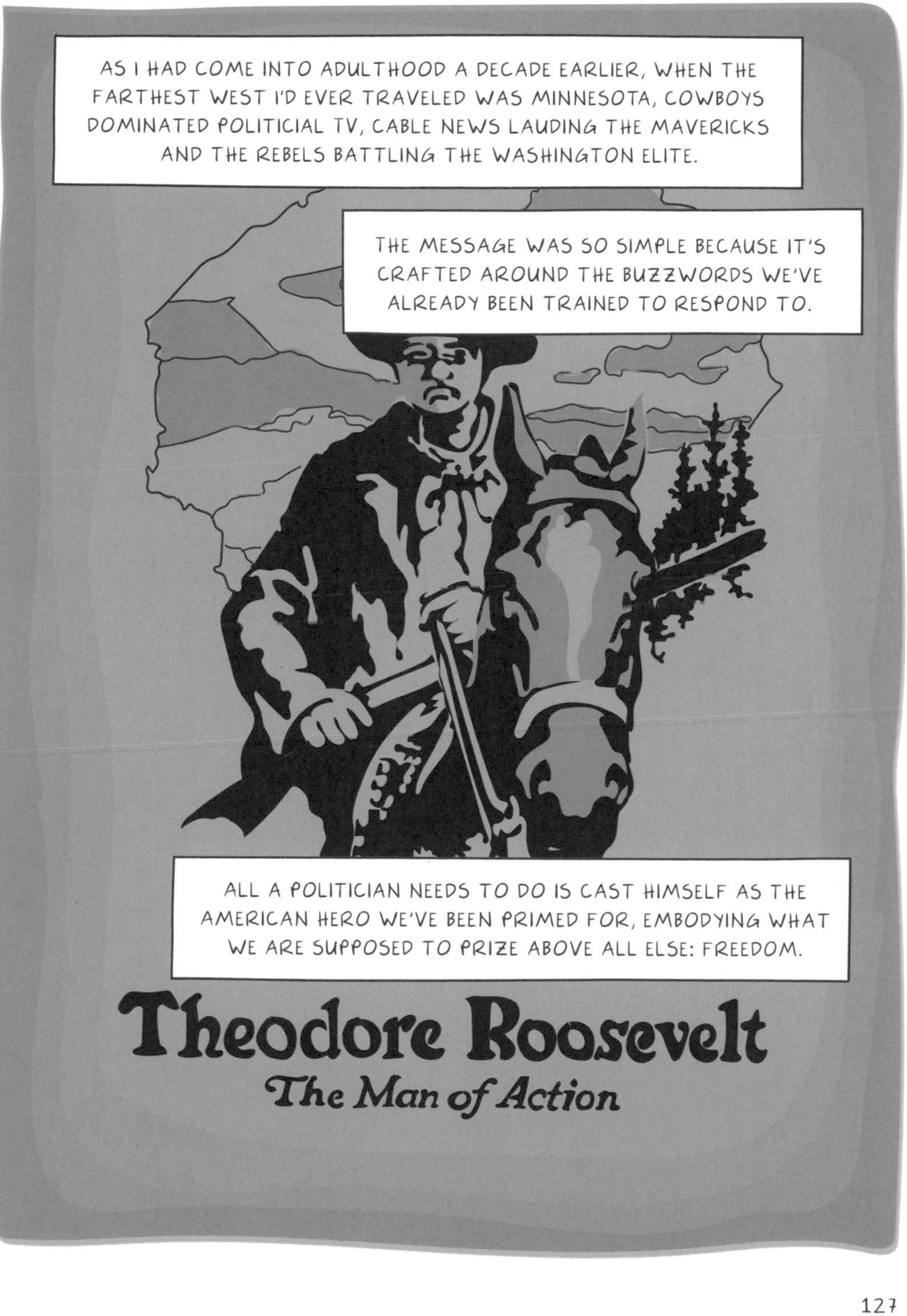
AS I HAD COME INTO ADULTHOOD A DECADE EARLIER, WHEN THE FARTHEST WEST I'D EVER TRAVELED WAS MINNESOTA, COWBOYS DOMINATED POLITICIAL TV, CABLE NEWS LAUDING THE MAVERICKS AND THE REBELS BATTLING THE WASHINGTON ELITE.
THE MESSAGE WAS SO SIMPLE BECAUSE IT'S CRAFTED AROUND THE BUZZWORDS WE'VE ALREADY BEEN TRAINED TO RESPOND TO.
ALL A POLITICIAN NEEDS TO DO IS CAST HIMSELF AS THE AMERICAN HERO WE'VE BEEN PRIMED FOR, EMBODYING WHAT WE ARE SUPPOSED TO PRIZE ABOVE ALL ELSE: FREEDOM.
Theodore Roosevelt
The Man of Action

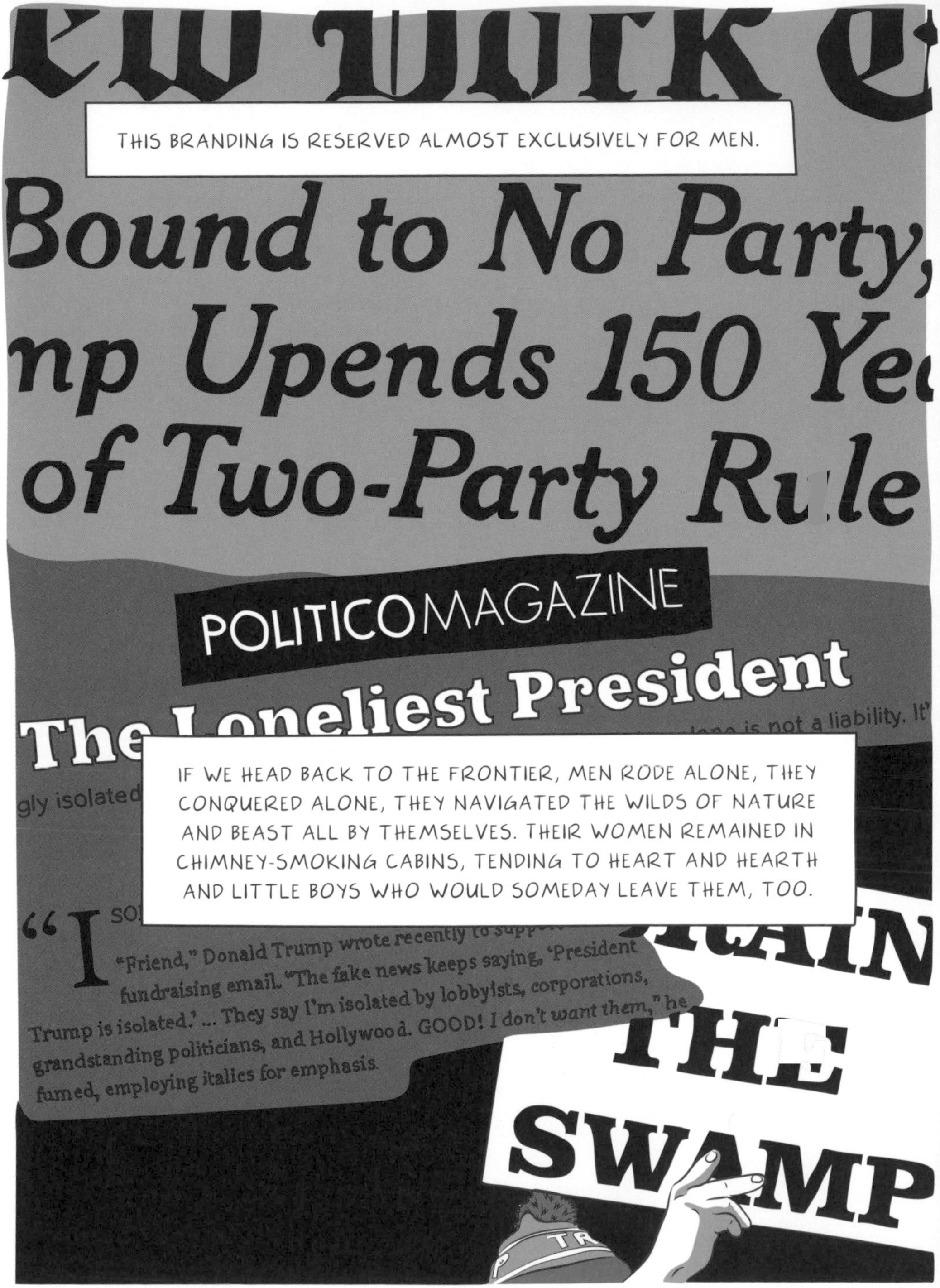

THIS BRANDING IS RESERVED ALMOST EXCLUSIVELY FOR MEN.
Bound to No Party,
np Upends 150 Ye
of Two-Party Rule
POLITICOMAGAZINE
Loneliest President
IF WE HEAD BACK TO THE FRONTIER, MEN RODE ALONE, THEY CONQUERED ALONE, THEY NAVIGATED THE WILDS OF NATURE AND BEAST ALL BY THEMSELVES. THEIR WOMEN REMAINED IN CHIMNEY-SMOKING CABINS, TENDING TO HEART AND HEARTH AND LITTLE BOYS WHO WOULD SOMEDAY LEAVE THEM, TOO.
"Friend," Donald Trump wrote recently
fundraising email. "The fake news keeps saying, 'President Trump is isolated.' ... They say I'm isolated by lobbyists, corporations, grandstanding politicians, and Hollywood. GOOD! I don't want them," he fumed, employing italics for emphasis.
THE
SWAMP

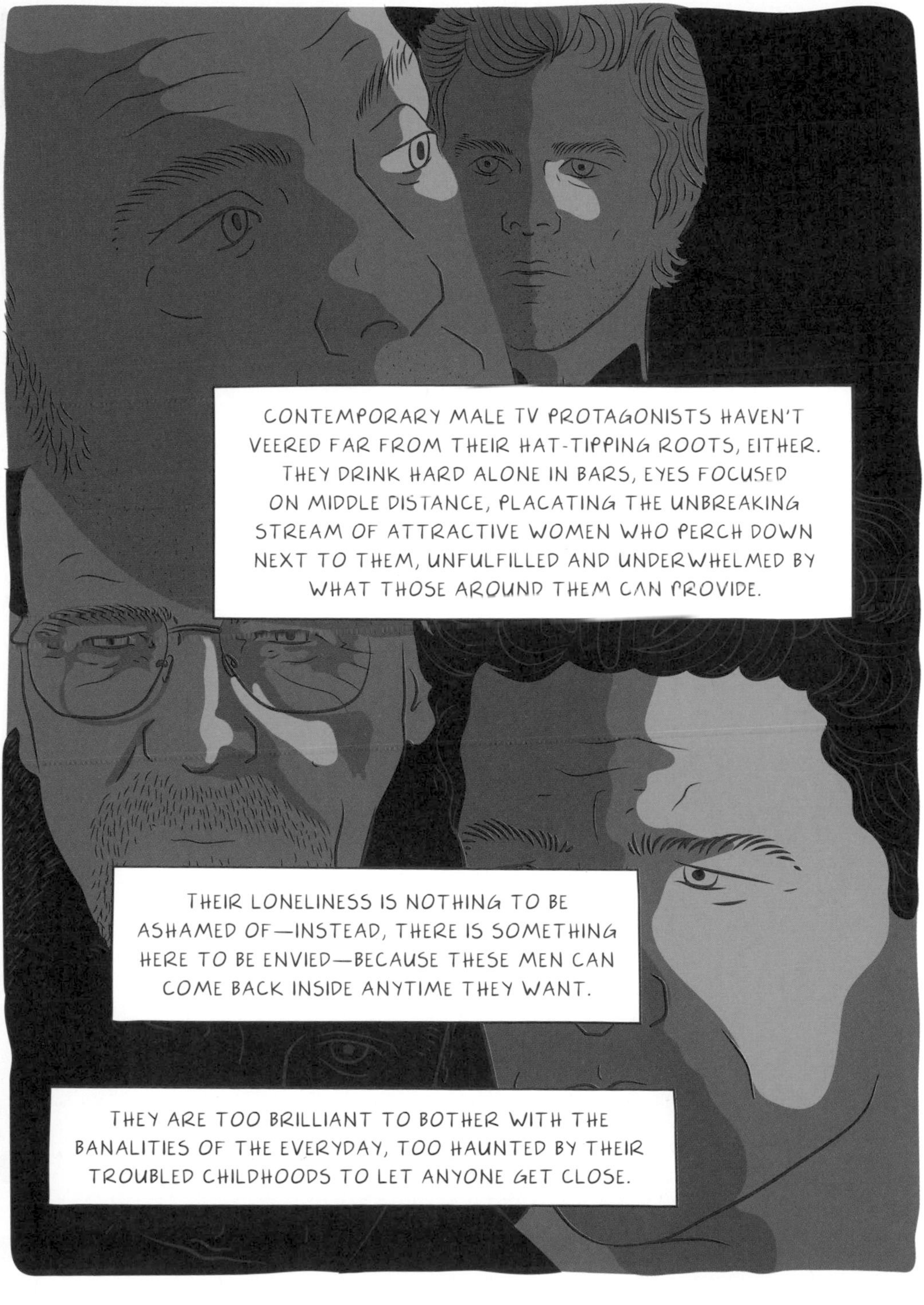
CONTEMPORARY MALE TV PROTAGONISTS HAVEN'T VEERED FAR FROM THEIR HAT-TIPPING ROOTS, EITHER. THEY DRINK HARD ALONE IN BARS, EYES FOCUSED ON MIDDLE DISTANCE, PLACATING THE UNBREAKING STREAM OF ATTRACTIVE WOMEN WHO PERCH DOWN NEXT TO THEM, UNFULFILLED AND UNDERWHELMED BY WHAT THOSE AROUND THEM CAN PROVIDE.
THEIR LONELINESS IS NOTHING TO BE ASHAMED OF—INSTEAD, THERE IS SOMETHING HERE TO BE ENVIED—BECAUSE THESE MEN CAN COME BACK INSIDE ANYTIME THEY WANT.
THEY ARE TOO BRILLIANT TO BOTHER WITH THE BANALITIES OF THE EVERYDAY, TOO HAUNTED BY THEIR TROUBLED CHILDHOODS TO LET ANYONE GET CLOSE.

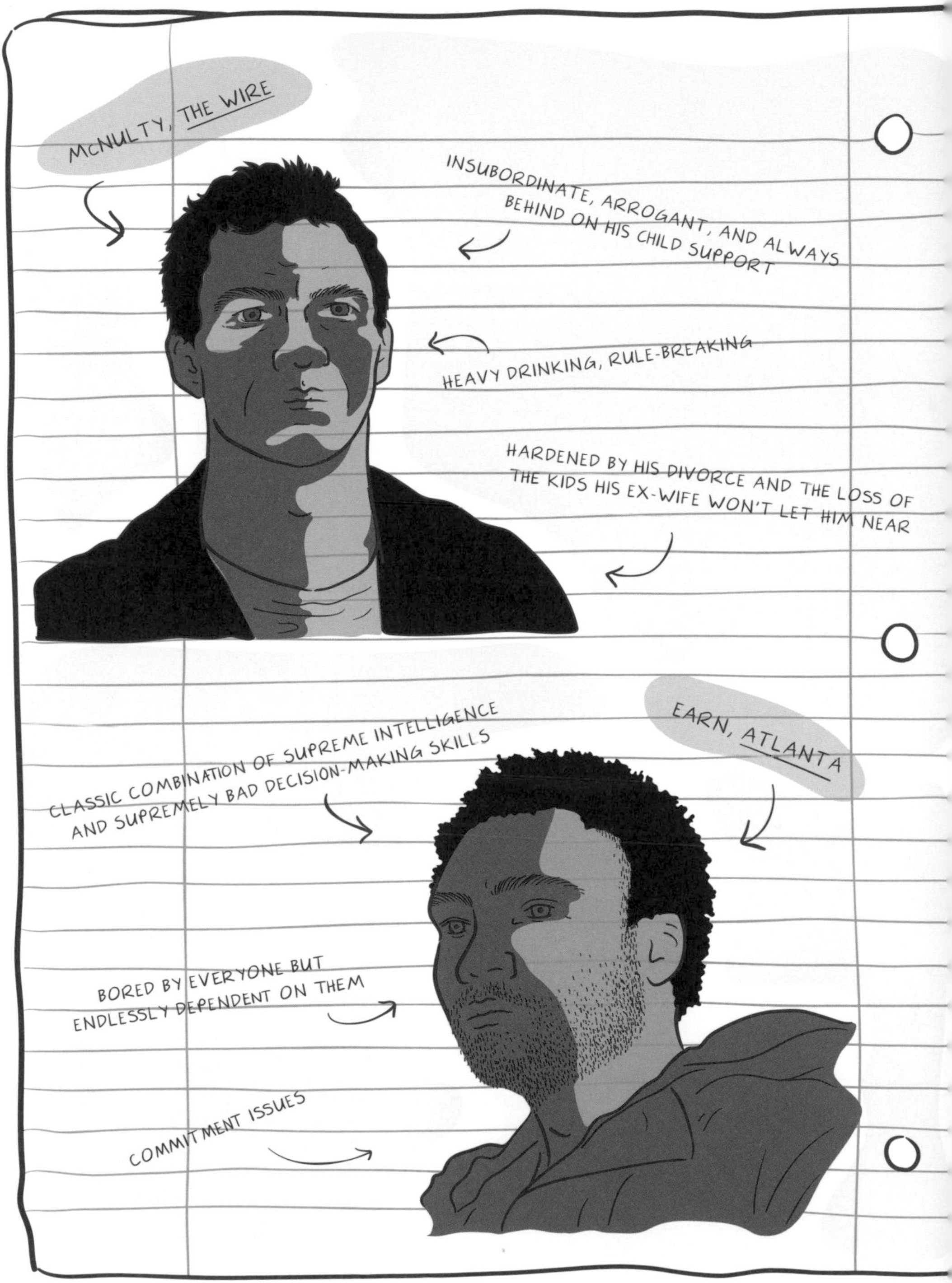

McNULTY, THE WIRE
INSUBORDINATE, ARROGANT, AND ALWAYS BEHIND ON HIS CHILD SUPPORT
HEAVY DRINKING, RULE-BREAKING
HARDENED BY HIS DIVORCE AND THE LOSS OF THE KIDS HIS EX-WIFE WON'T LET HIM NEAR
EARN, ATLANTA
CLASSIC COMBINATION OF SUPREME INTELLIGENCE AND SUPREMELY BAD DECISION-MAKING SKILLS
BORED BY EVERYONE BUT ENDLESSLY DEPENDENT ON THEM
COMMITMENT ISSUES

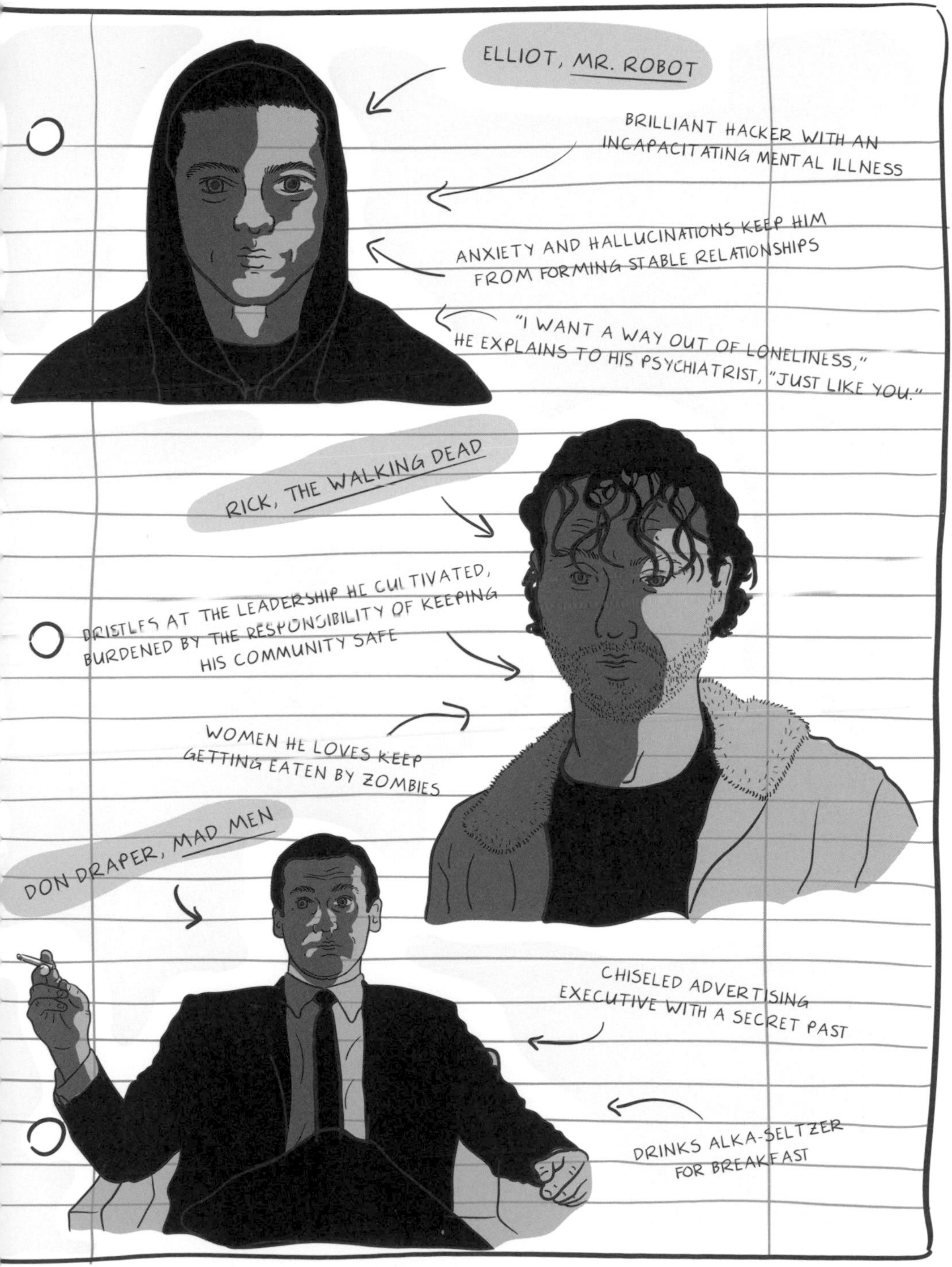
ELLIOT, MR. ROBOT
BRILLIANT HACKER WITH AN INCAPACITATING MENTAL ILLNESS
ANXIETY AND HALLUCINATIONS KEEP HIM FROM FORMING STABLE RELATIONSHIPS
"I WANT A WAY OUT OF LONELINESS," HE EXPLAINS TO HIS PSYCHIATRIST, "JUST LIKE YOU."
RICK, THE WALKING DEAD
BRISTLES AT THE LEADERSHIP HE CULTIVATED, BURDENED BY THE RESPONSIBILITY OF KEEPING HIS COMMUNITY SAFE
WOMEN HE LOVES KEEP GETTING EATEN BY ZOMBIES
DON DRAPER, MAD MEN
CHISELED ADVERTISING EXECUTIVE WITH A SECRET PAST
DRINKS ALKA-SELTZER FOR BREAKFAST

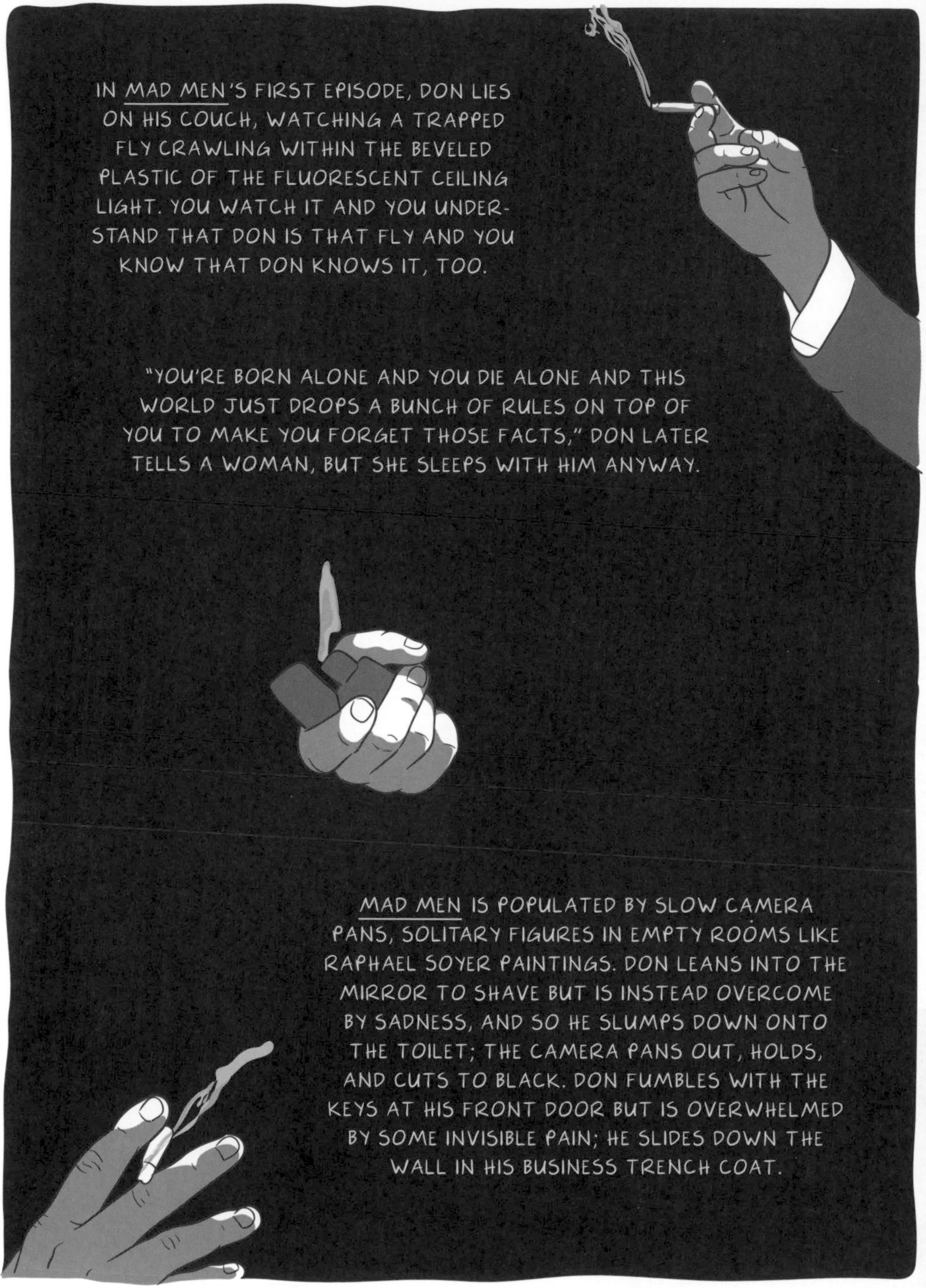
IN MAD MEN'S FIRST EPISODE, DON LIES ON HIS COUCH, WATCHING A TRAPPED FLY CRAWLING WITHIN THE BEVELED PLASTIC OF THE FLUORESCENT CEILING LIGHT. YOU WATCH IT AND YOU UNDERSTAND THAT DON IS THAT FLY AND YOU KNOW THAT DON KNOWS IT, TOO.
"YOU'RE BORN ALONE AND YOU DIE ALONE AND THIS WORLD JUST DROPS A BUNCH OF RULES ON TOP OF YOU TO MAKE YOU FORGET THOSE FACTS," DON LATER TELLS A WOMAN, BUT SHE SLEEPS WITH HIM ANYWAY.
MAD MEN IS POPULATED BY SLOW CAMERA PANS, SOLITARY FIGURES IN EMPTY ROOMS LIKE RAPHAEL SOYER PAINTINGS. DON LEANS INTO THE MIRROR TO SHAVE BUT IS INSTEAD OVERCOME BY SADNESS, AND SO HE SLUMPS DOWN ONTO THE TOILET; THE CAMERA PANS OUT, HOLDS, AND CUTS TO BLACK. DON FUMBLES WITH THE KEYS AT HIS FRONT DOOR BUT IS OVERWHELMED BY SOME INVISIBLE PAIN; HE SLIDES DOWN THE WALL IN HIS BUSINESS TRENCH COAT.

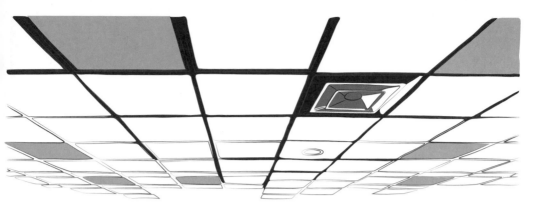

THE CAMERA PANS OUT, HOLDS, AND CUTS TO BLACK.

AS THE SERIES PROGRESSES, DON SPENDS MORE
TIME IN HOTELS, SIGHING INTO THE PHONE AS HE
RECEIVES INCONVENIENT NEWS. HE DIVORCES HIS
WIFE AND THEN ANOTHER WIFE AND HAS MORE
AFFAIRS THAN YOU CAN COUNT. TOO MUCH
DRINKING PULLS AT THE SKIN BELOW HIS EYES.

ALMOST ALL OF HIS ACTIONS ARE LACED WITH A DISINTEREST
IN OTHERS, BUT THIS IS THE IMPORTANT PART: IT IMPLIES
SUPERIORITY, AND ONLY WHEN A MAN IS SUPERIOR TO OTHERS
IS HIS LONELINESS MEANINGFUL INSTEAD OF PATHETIC.

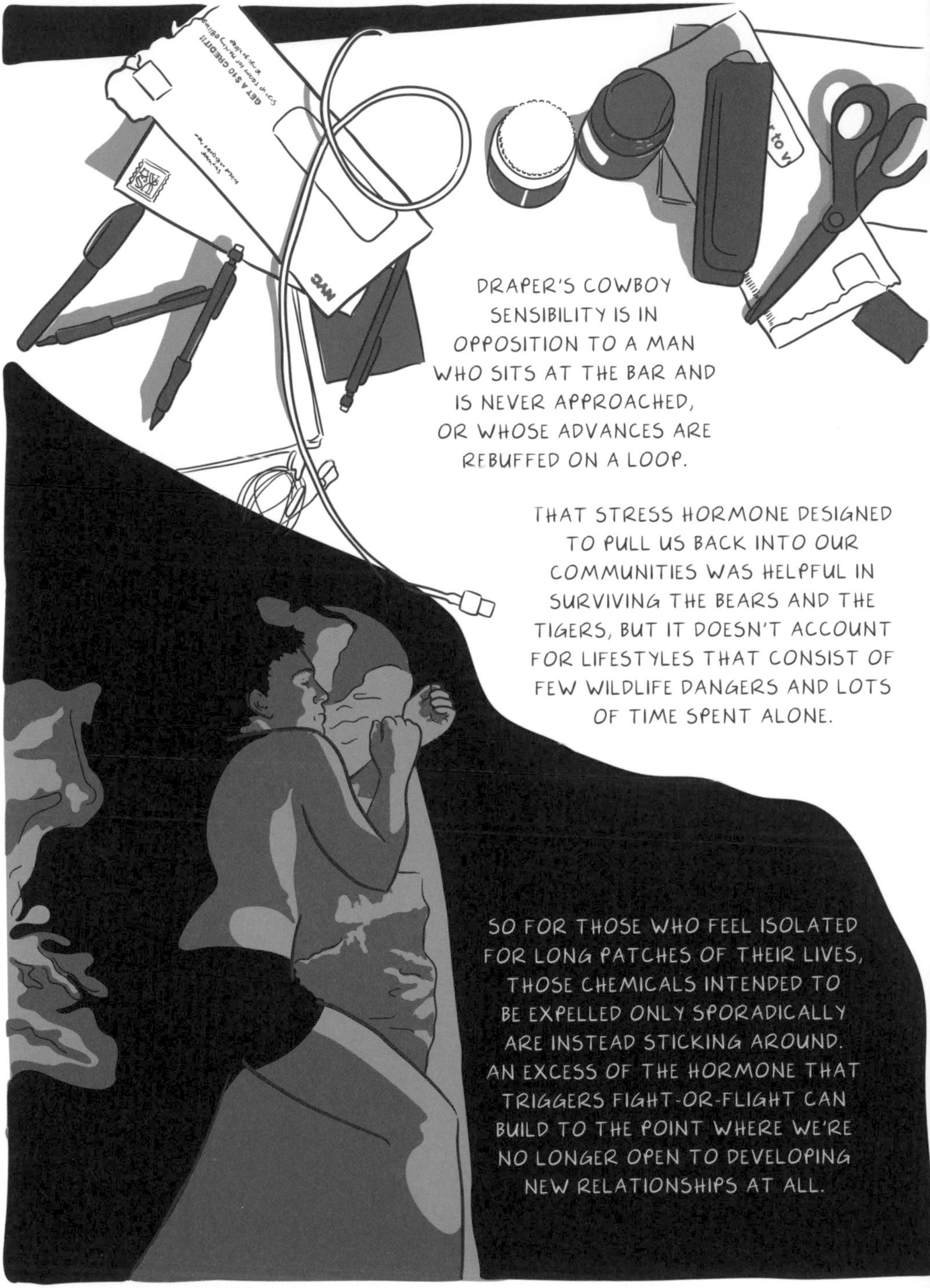
DRAPER'S COWBOY SENSIBILITY IS IN OPPOSITION TO A MAN WHO SITS AT THE BAR AND IS NEVER APPROACHED, OR WHOSE ADVANCES ARE REBUFFED ON A LOOP.
THAT STRESS HORMONE DESIGNED TO PULL US BACK INTO OUR COMMUNITIES WAS HELPFUL IN SURVIVING THE BEARS AND THE TIGERS, BUT IT DOESN'T ACCOUNT FOR LIFESTYLES THAT CONSIST OF FEW WILDLIFE DANGERS AND LOTS OF TIME SPENT ALONE.
SO FOR THOSE WHO FEEL ISOLATED FOR LONG PATCHES OF THEIR LIVES, THOSE CHEMICALS INTENDED TO BE EXPELLED ONLY SPORADICALLY ARE INSTEAD STICKING AROUND. AN EXCESS OF THE HORMONE THAT TRIGGERS FIGHT-OR-FLIGHT CAN BUILD TO THE POINT WHERE WE'RE NO LONGER OPEN TO DEVELOPING NEW RELATIONSHIPS AT ALL.

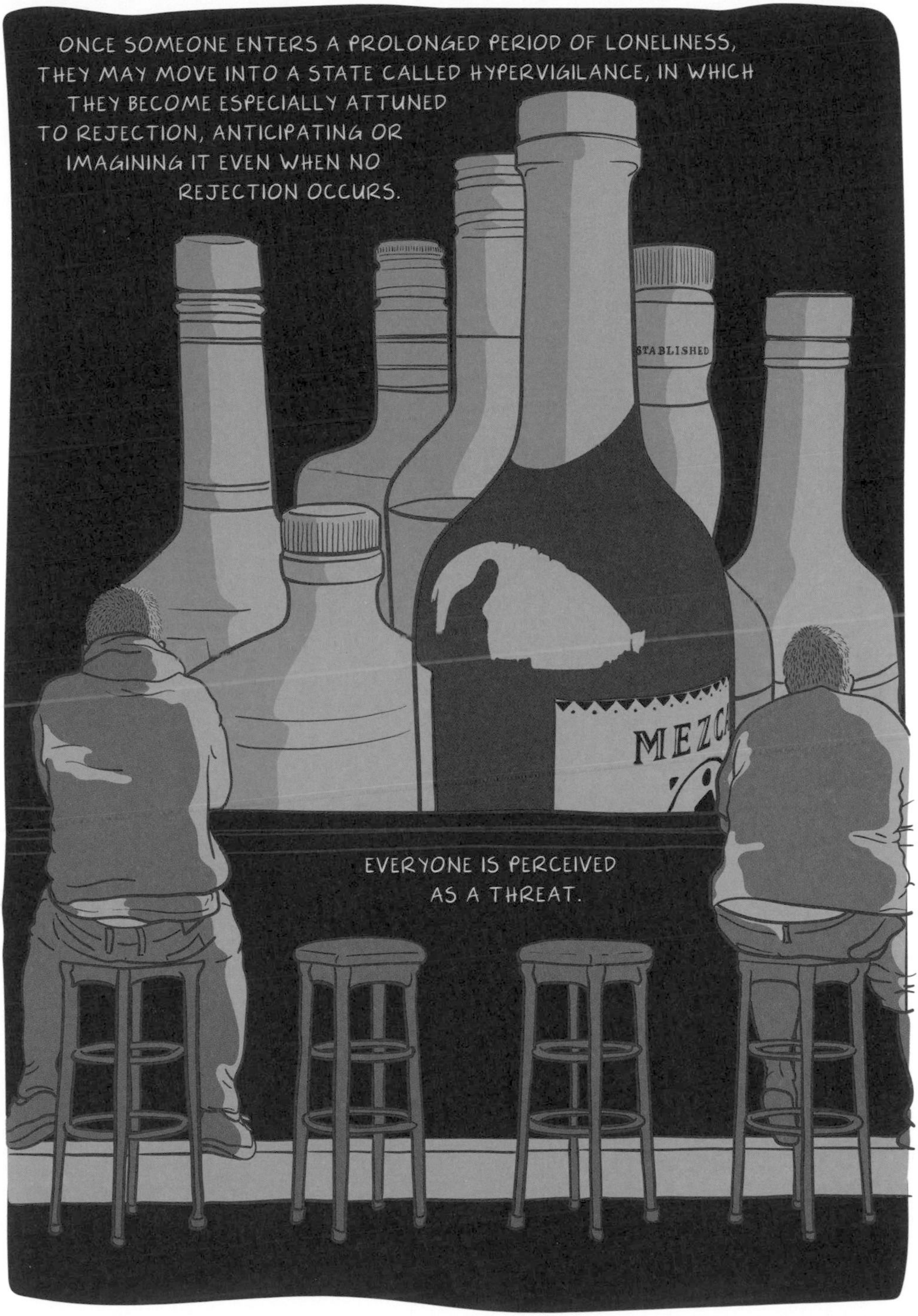
ONCE SOMEONE ENTERS A PROLONGED PERIOD OF LONELINESS, THEY MAY MOVE INTO A STATE CALLED HYPERVIGILANCE, IN WHICH THEY BECOME ESPECIALLY ATTUNED TO REJECTION, ANTICIPATING OR IMAGINING IT EVEN WHEN NO REJECTION OCCURS.
STABLISHED
MEZCA
EVERYONE IS PERCEIVED AS A THREAT.

II

THE BRAIN'S REACTION TO SOCIAL REJECTION IS ALMOST
IDENTICAL TO HOW IT EXPERIENCES PHYSICAL PAIN.

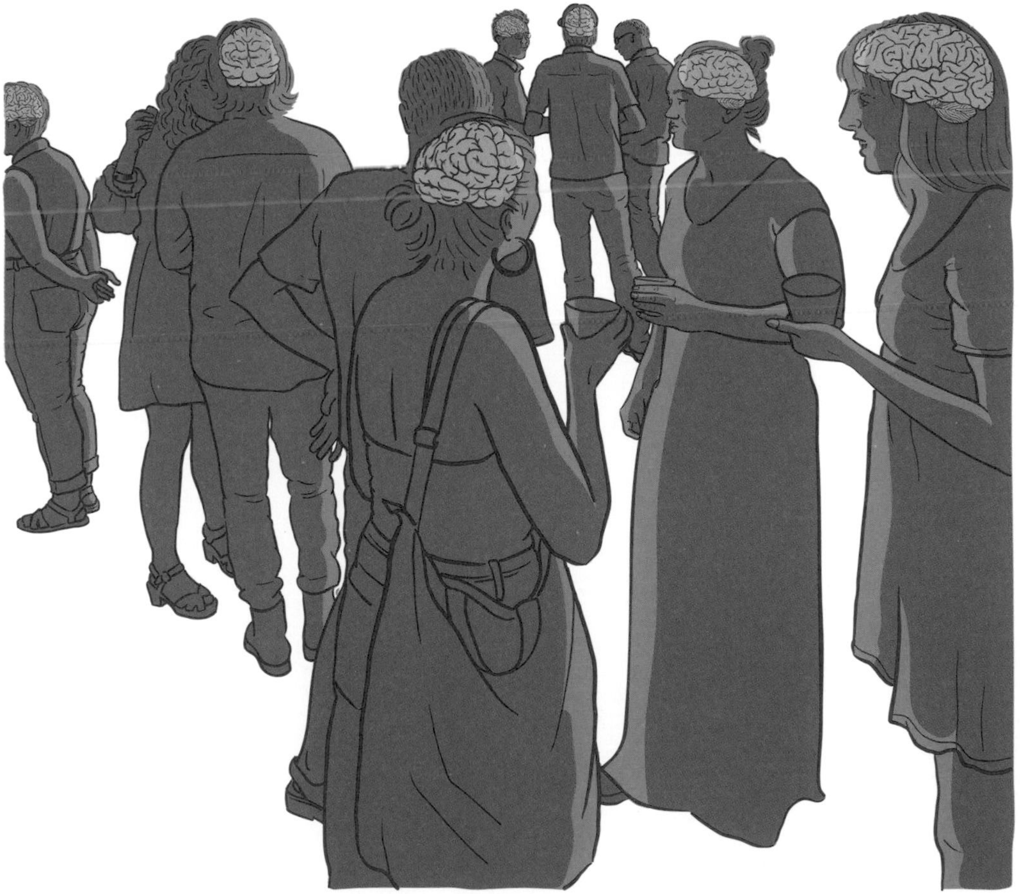

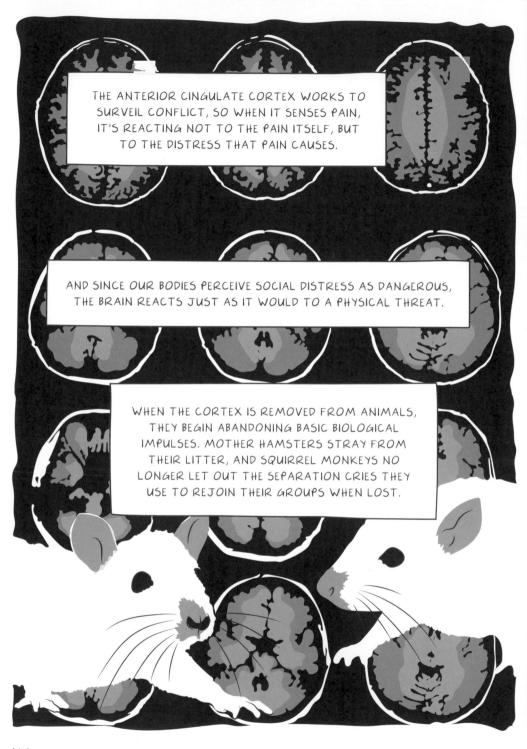

THE ANTERIOR CINGULATE CORTEX WORKS TO SURVEIL CONFLICT, SO WHEN IT SENSES PAIN, IT'S REACTING NOT TO THE PAIN ITSELF, BUT TO THE DISTRESS THAT PAIN CAUSES.

AND SINCE OUR BODIES PERCEIVE SOCIAL DISTRESS AS DANGEROUS, THE BRAIN REACTS JUST AS IT WOULD TO A PHYSICAL THREAT.

WHEN THE CORTEX IS REMOVED FROM ANIMALS, THEY BEGIN ABANDONING BASIC BIOLOGICAL IMPULSES. MOTHER HAMSTERS STRAY FROM THEIR LITTER, AND SQUIRREL MONKEYS NO LONGER LET OUT THE SEPARATION CRIES THEY USE TO REJOIN THEIR GROUPS WHEN LOST.

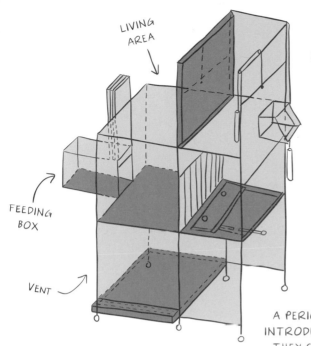

LIVING AREA

FEEDING BOX

VENT

IN A FAMOUSLY CONTROVERSIAL STUDY, RHESUS MONKEYS WERE KEPT IN TOTAL SOLITUDE BY A GROUP OF SCIENTISTS AT THE UNIVERSITY OF WISCONSIN. LED BY PSYCHOLOGIST HARRY HARLOW, THE TEAM SEPARATED THE ANIMALS SHORTLY AFTER BIRTH AND OBSERVED HOW THEIR BEHAVIOR CHANGED IN RELATIONSHIP TO THE AMOUNT OF TIME THEY'D BEEN ALONE.

MONKEYS WHO WERE IN ISOLATION FOR FEWER THAN SIX MONTHS WENT THROUGH A PERIOD OF SHOCK WHEN THEY WERE INTRODUCED TO NON-ISOLATED PEERS— THEY CLUTCHED THEMSELVES, THEY ROCKED. ONE MONKEY STARVED HIMSELF TO DEATH WHEN HE WAS PLACED WITH OTHERS BECAUSE THE ACT OF SOCIALIZING WAS SO OVERWHELMING.

RESEARCHERS BEGAN FORCE-FEEDING THE OTHER SUBJECTS TO KEEP THE EXPERIMENT MOVING, AND OVER TIME THE MONKEYS PERKED THEIR HEADS UP A LITTLE MORE, CURIOUSLY EYEING THEIR ESTRANGED SIBLINGS. WITHIN A FEW WEEKS, MOST HAPPILY JOINED THE COLONY.

BUT THOSE WHO WERE ALONE FOR A FULL YEAR WERE WORSE OFF. SCIENTISTS USED THE TERM "OBLITERATED."

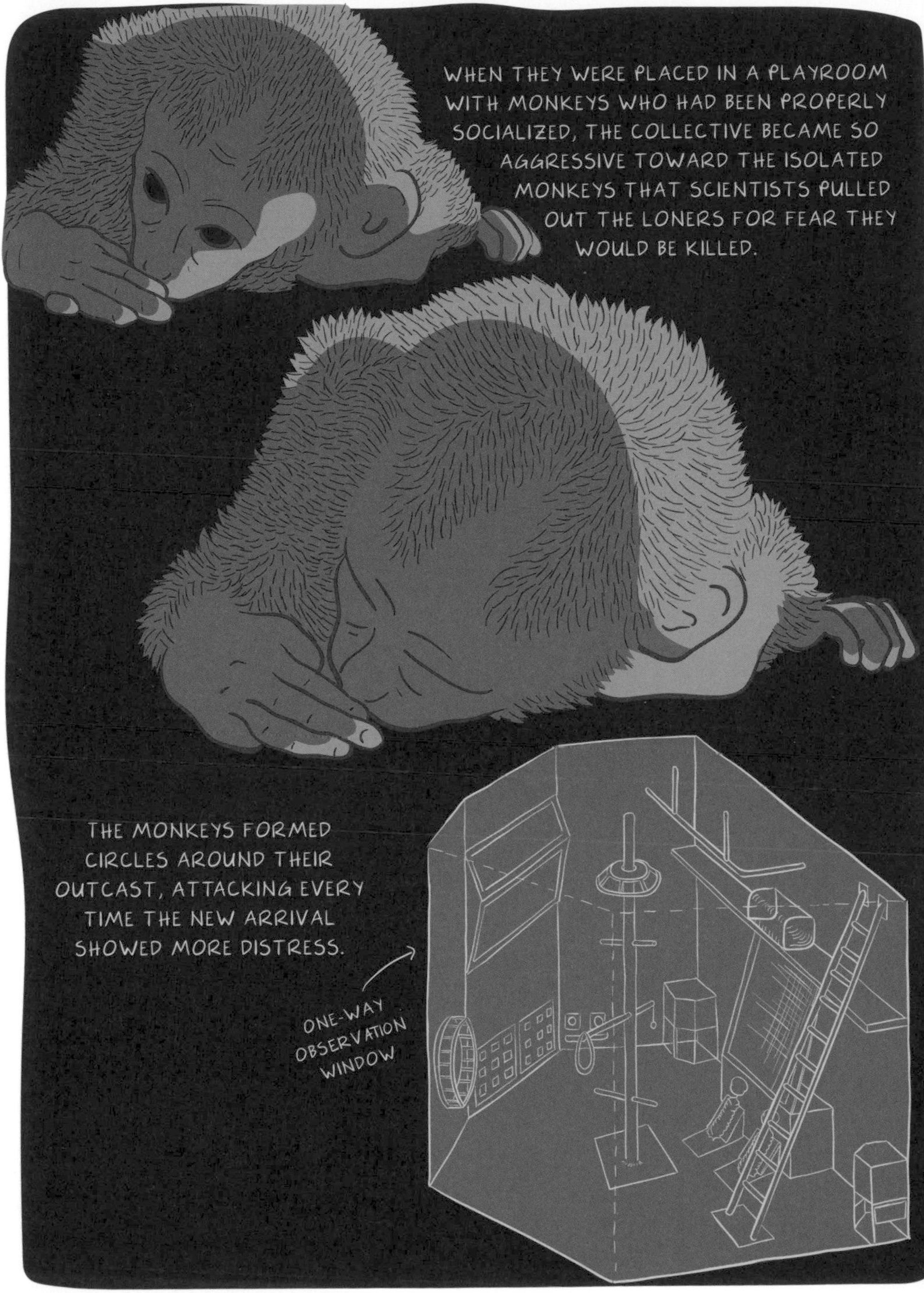
WHEN THEY WERE PLACED IN A PLAYROOM WITH MONKEYS WHO HAD BEEN PROPERLY SOCIALIZED, THE COLLECTIVE BECAME SO AGGRESSIVE TOWARD THE ISOLATED MONKEYS THAT SCIENTISTS PULLED OUT THE LONERS FOR FEAR THEY WOULD BE KILLED.
THE MONKEYS FORMED CIRCLES AROUND THEIR OUTCAST, ATTACKING EVERY TIME THE NEW ARRIVAL SHOWED MORE DISTRESS.
ONE-WAY OBSERVATION WINDOW

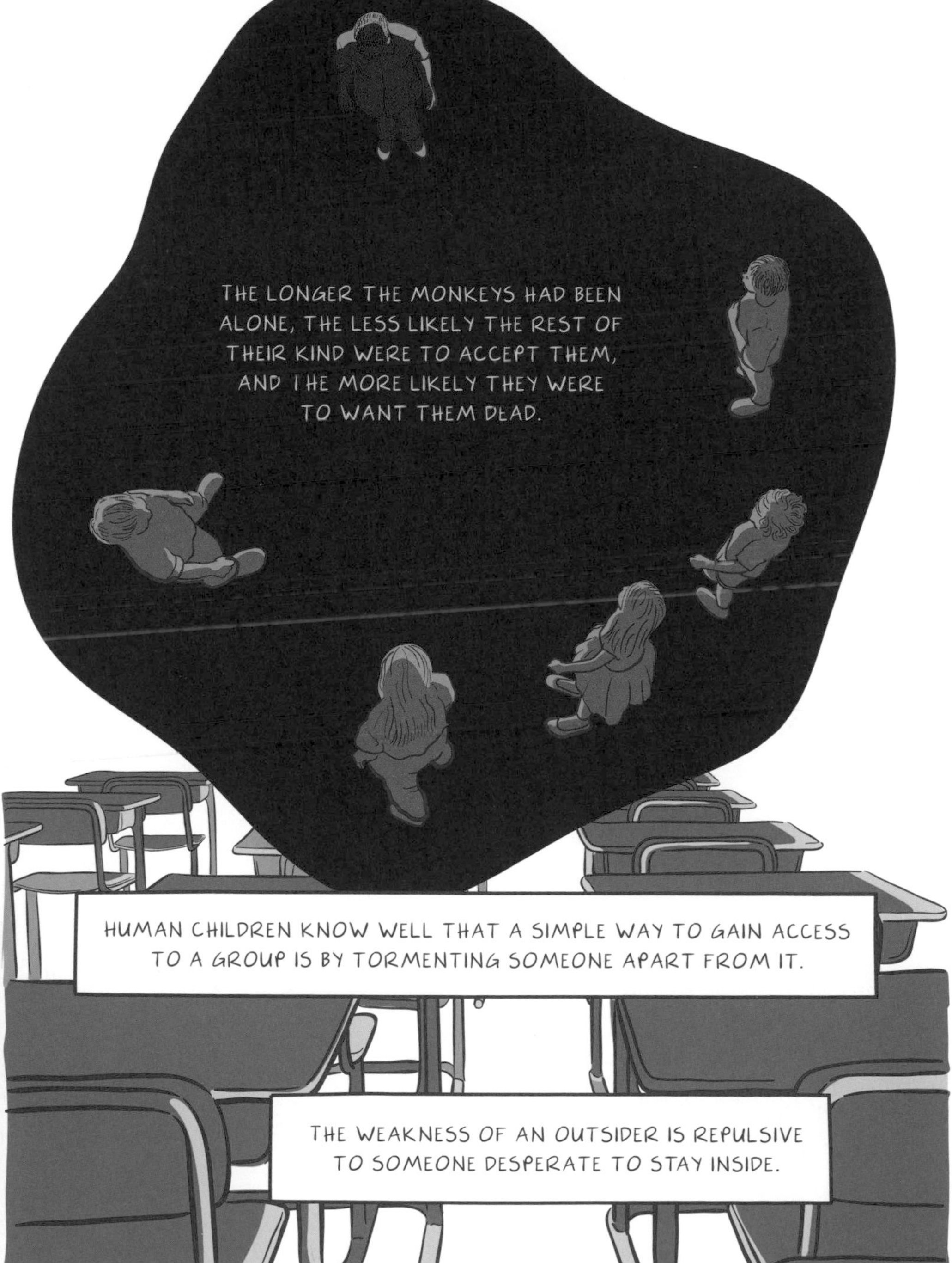

THE LONGER THE MONKEYS HAD BEEN ALONE, THE LESS LIKELY THE REST OF THEIR KIND WERE TO ACCEPT THEM, AND THE MORE LIKELY THEY WERE TO WANT THEM DEAD.
HUMAN CHILDREN KNOW WELL THAT A SIMPLE WAY TO GAIN ACCESS TO A GROUP IS BY TORMENTING SOMEONE APART FROM IT.
THE WEAKNESS OF AN OUTSIDER IS REPULSIVE TO SOMEONE DESPERATE TO STAY INSIDE.

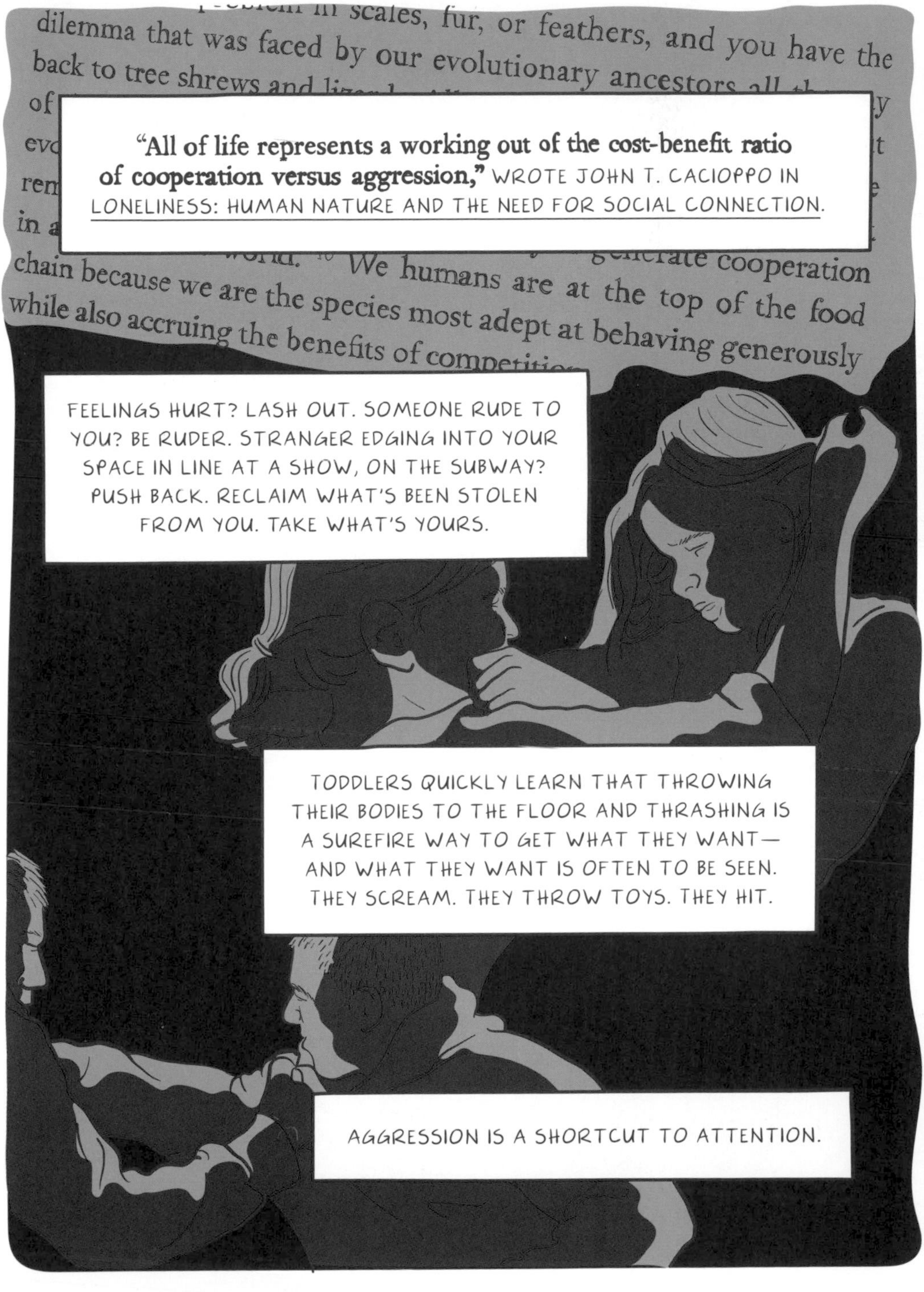
dilemma that was faced by our evolutionary ancestors
back to tree shrews and
chain because we are the species most adept at behaving generously
while also accruing the benefits of competition
We humans are at the top of the food
"All of life represents a working out of the cost-benefit ratio of cooperation versus aggression," WROTE JOHN T. CACIOPPO IN LONELINESS: HUMAN NATURE AND THE NEED FOR SOCIAL CONNECTION.
FEELINGS HURT? LASH OUT. SOMEONE RUDE TO YOU? BE RUDER. STRANGER EDGING INTO YOUR SPACE IN LINE AT A SHOW, ON THE SUBWAY? PUSH BACK. RECLAIM WHAT'S BEEN STOLEN FROM YOU. TAKE WHAT'S YOURS.
TODDLERS QUICKLY LEARN THAT THROWING THEIR BODIES TO THE FLOOR AND THRASHING IS A SUREFIRE WAY TO GET WHAT THEY WANT—AND WHAT THEY WANT IS OFTEN TO BE SEEN. THEY SCREAM. THEY THROW TOYS. THEY HIT.
AGGRESSION IS A SHORTCUT TO ATTENTION.

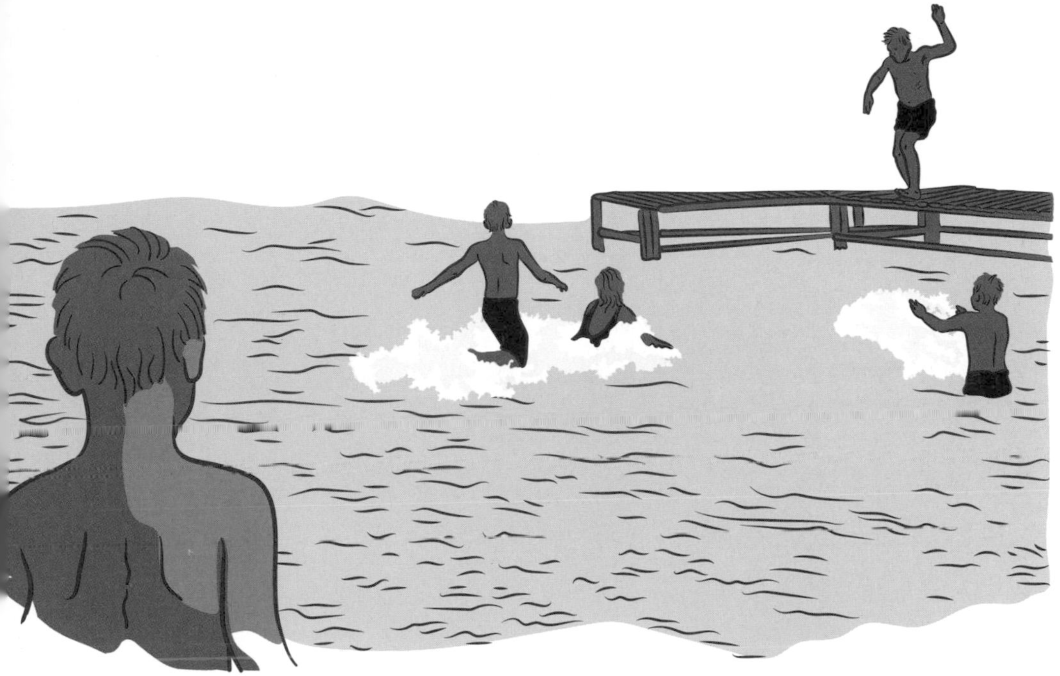

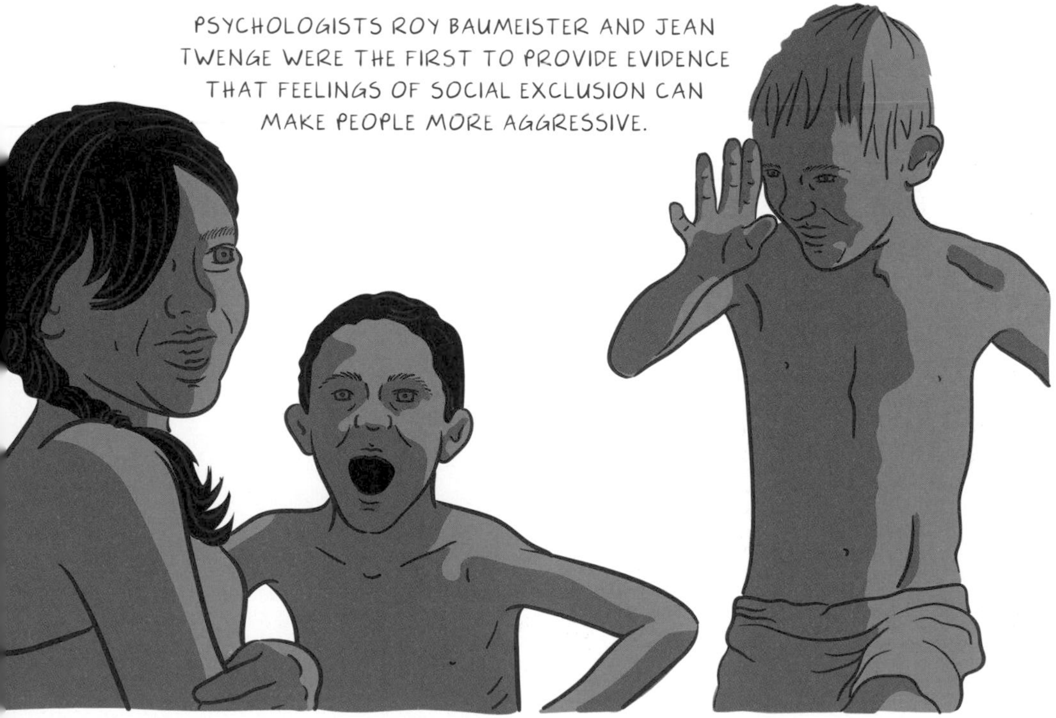
PSYCHOLOGISTS ROY BAUMEISTER AND JEAN TWENGE WERE THE FIRST TO PROVIDE EVIDENCE THAT FEELINGS OF SOCIAL EXCLUSION CAN MAKE PEOPLE MORE AGGRESSIVE.

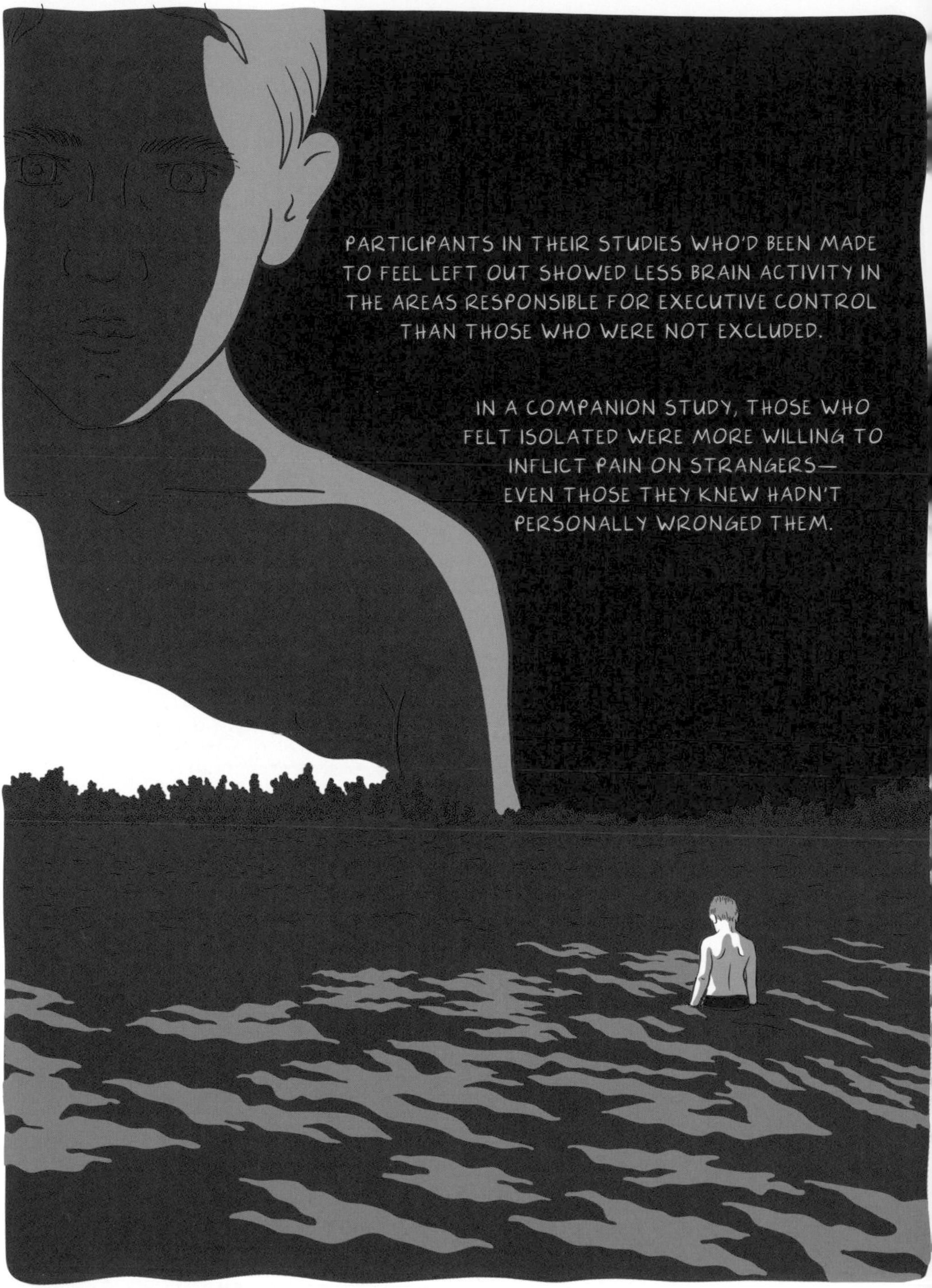
PARTICIPANTS IN THEIR STUDIES WHO'D BEEN MADE TO FEEL LEFT OUT SHOWED LESS BRAIN ACTIVITY IN THE AREAS RESPONSIBLE FOR EXECUTIVE CONTROL THAN THOSE WHO WERE NOT EXCLUDED.
IN A COMPANION STUDY, THOSE WHO FELT ISOLATED WERE MORE WILLING TO INFLICT PAIN ON STRANGERS— EVEN THOSE THEY KNEW HADN'T PERSONALLY WRONGED THEM.

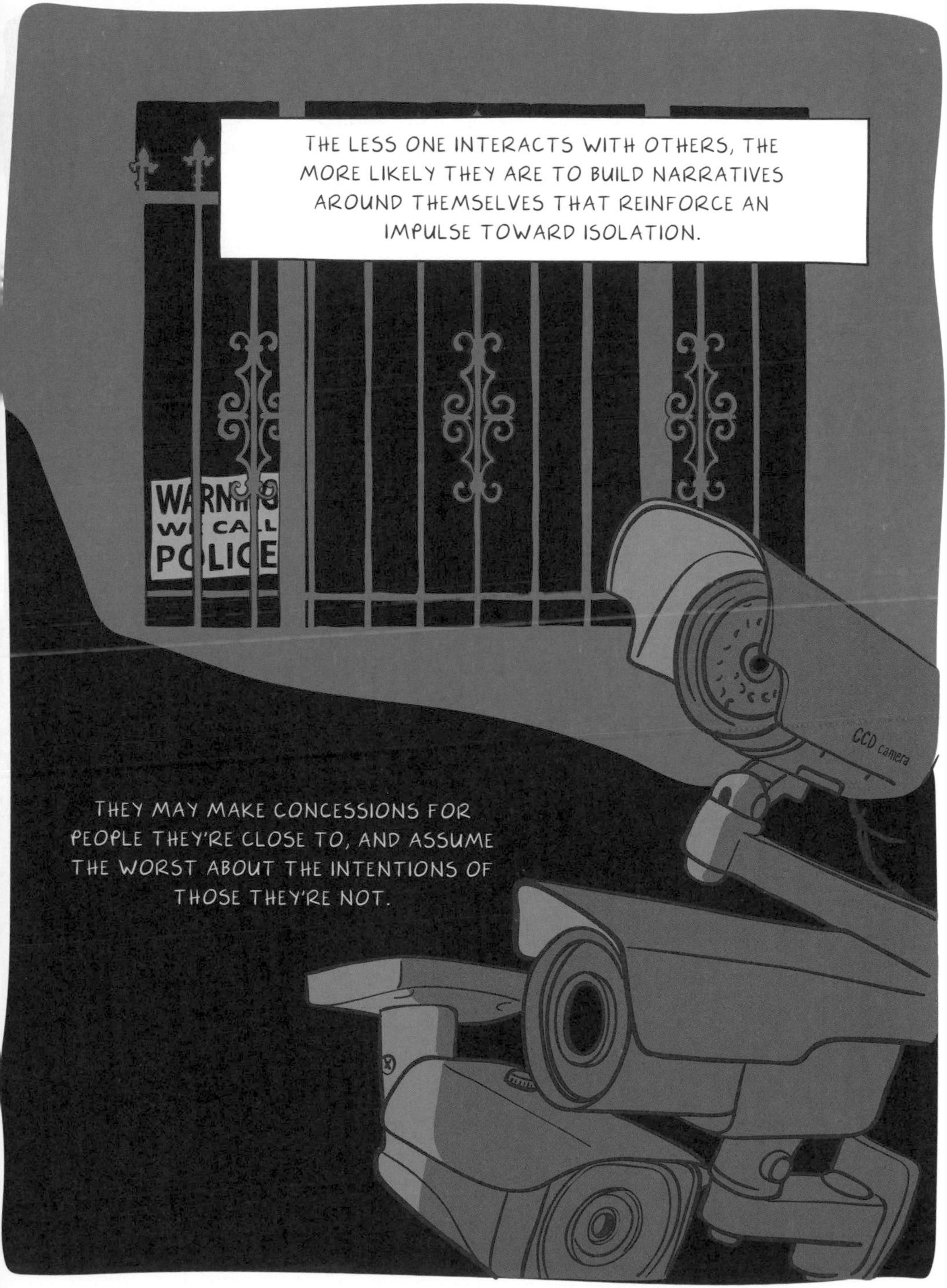
THE LESS ONE INTERACTS WITH OTHERS, THE MORE LIKELY THEY ARE TO BUILD NARRATIVES AROUND THEMSELVES THAT REINFORCE AN IMPULSE TOWARD ISOLATION.
CCD camera
THEY MAY MAKE CONCESSIONS FOR PEOPLE THEY'RE CLOSE TO, AND ASSUME THE WORST ABOUT THE INTENTIONS OF THOSE THEY'RE NOT.

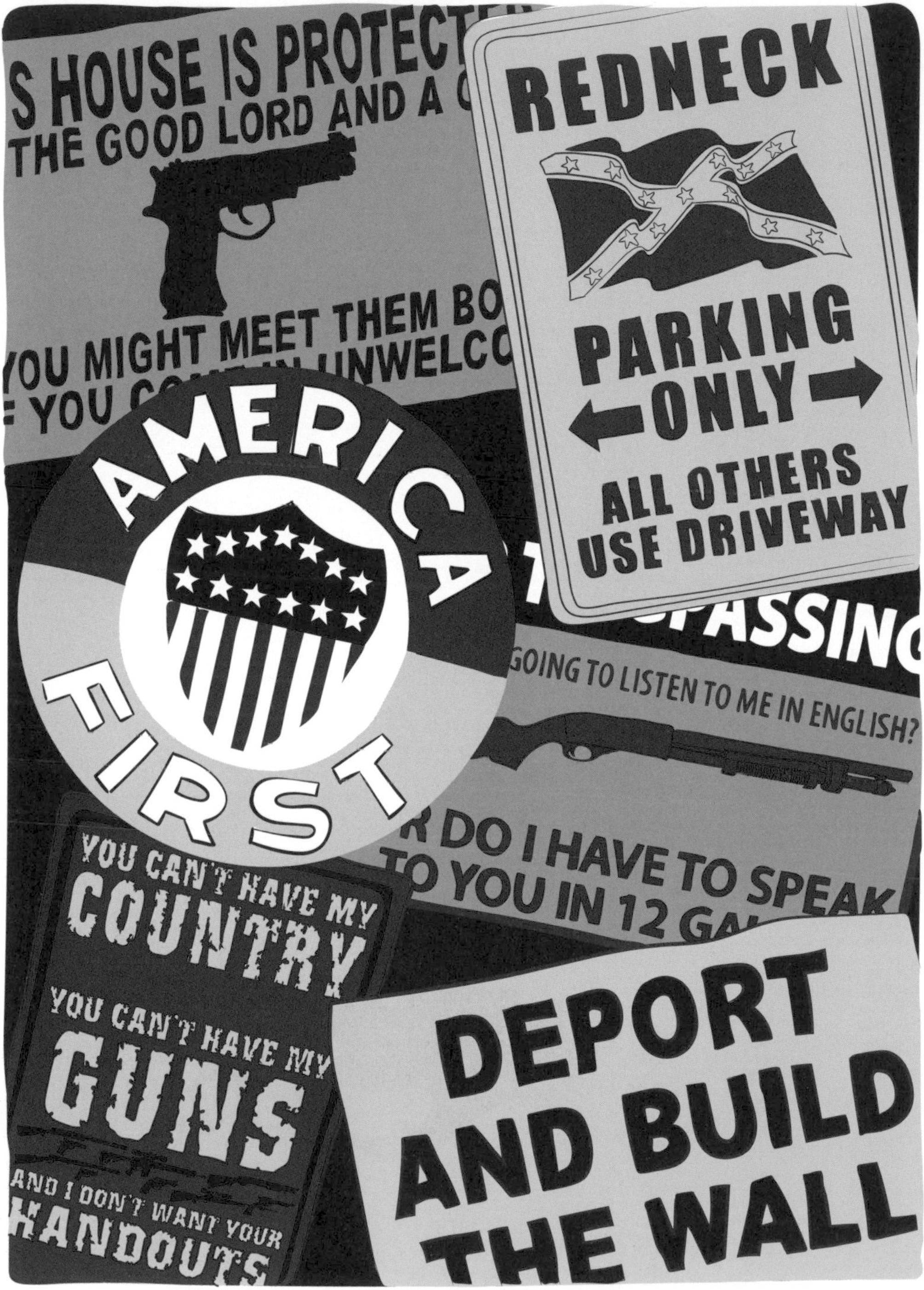
S HOUSE IS PROTECT
THE GOOD LORD AND A
YOU MIGHT MEET THEM BO
REDNECK
PARKING
ONLY
ALL OTHERS
USE DRIVEWAY
AMERICA
FIRST
PASSING
GOING TO LISTEN TO ME IN ENGLISH?
R DO I HAVE TO SPEAK
TO YOU IN 12 GA
YOU CAN'T HAVE MY
COUNTRY
YOU CAN'T HAVE MY
GUNS
AND I DON'T WANT YOUR
HANDOUTS
DEPORT
AND BUILD
THE WALL

IN HER 1951 BOOK, HANNAH ARENDT WRITES THAT LONELINESS IS **"the common ground for terror."** AS WE LOSE CONTACT WITH ONE ANOTHER, SO TOO DO WE BEGIN TO PERFORATE OURSELVES FROM REALITY.

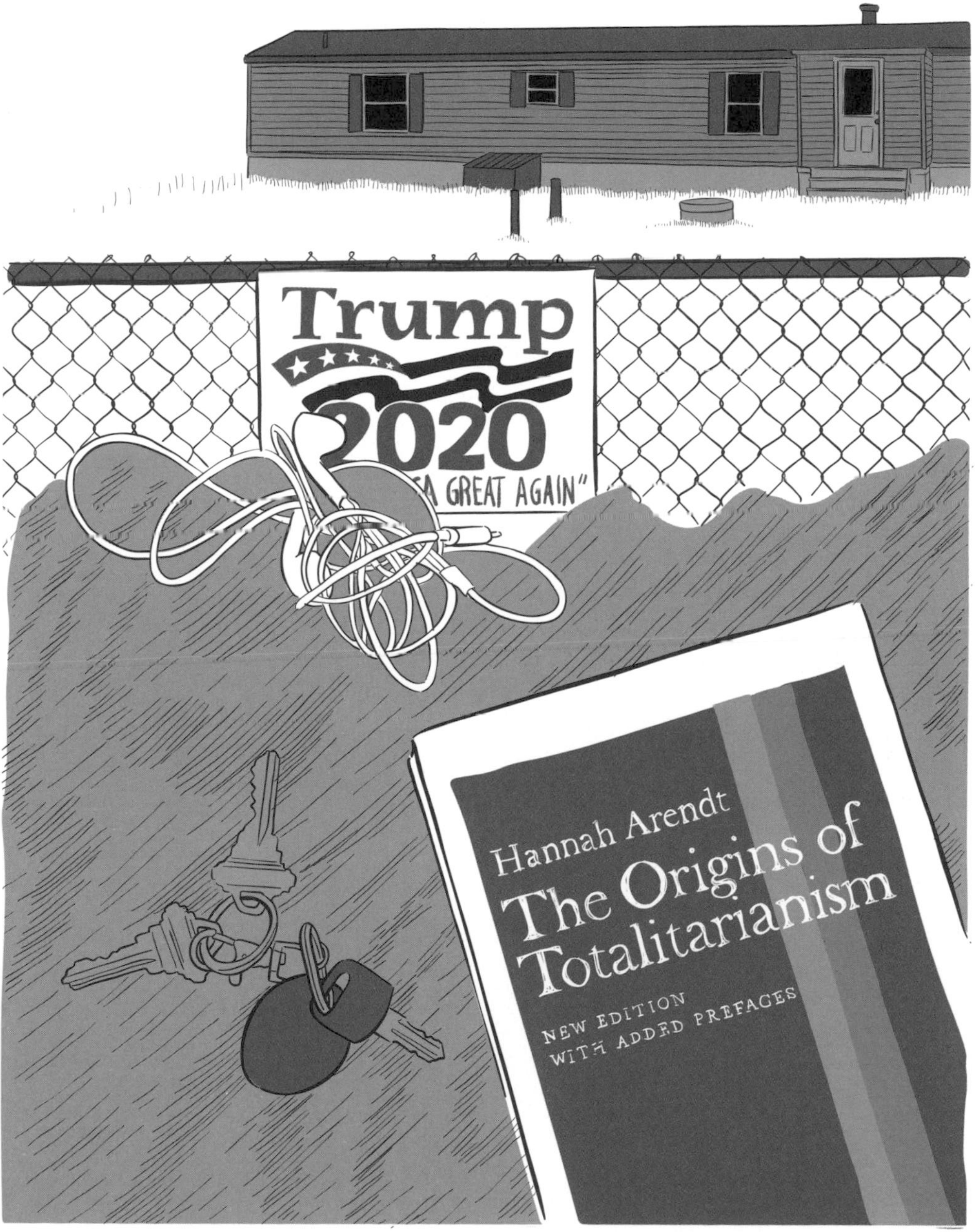
Trump
2020
GREAT AGAIN"
Hannah Arendt
The Origins of Totalitarianism
NEW EDITION
WITH ADDED PREFACES

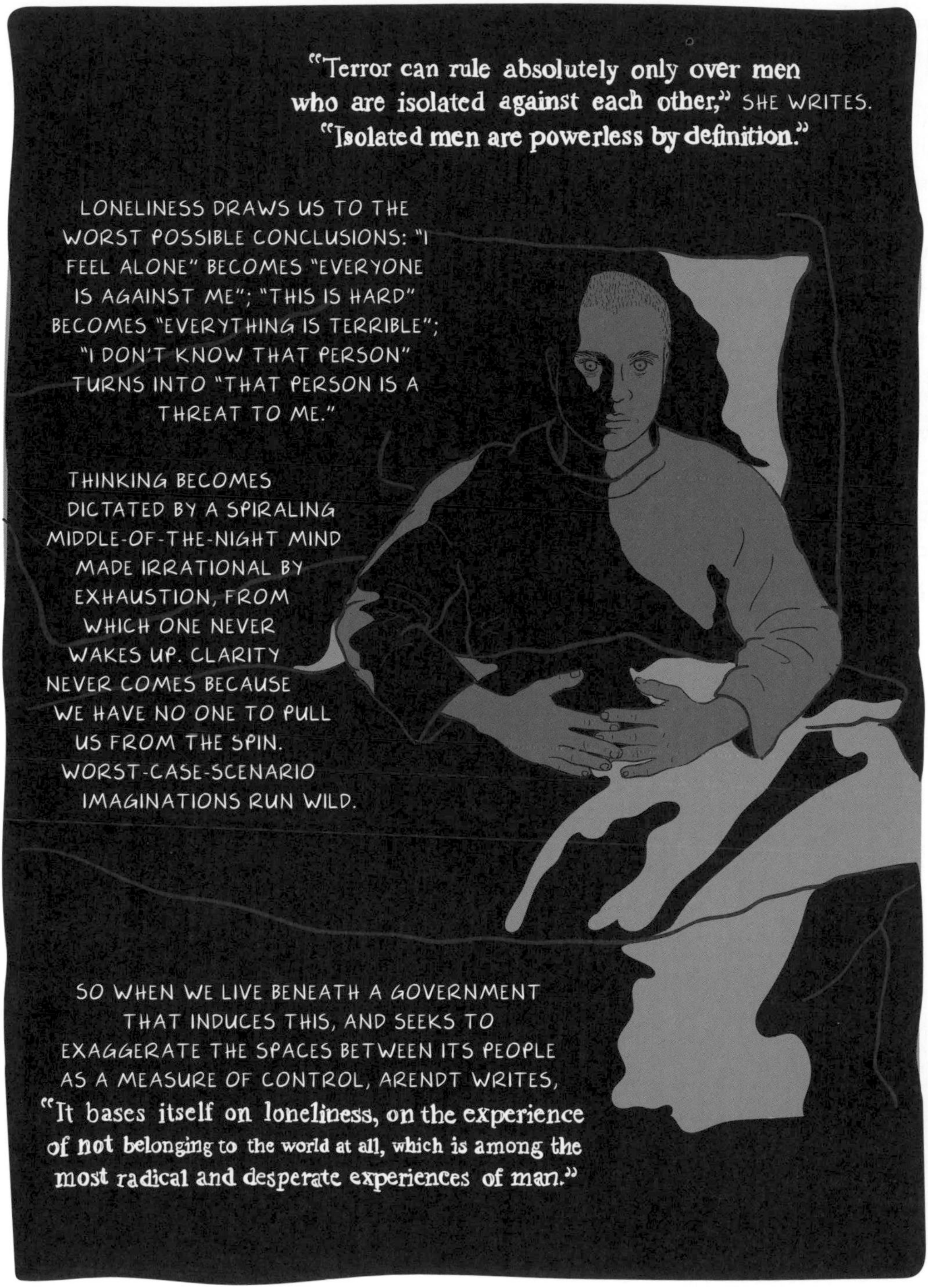
"Terror can rule absolutely only over men who are isolated against each other," SHE WRITES. "Isolated men are powerless by definition."
LONELINESS DRAWS US TO THE WORST POSSIBLE CONCLUSIONS: "I FEEL ALONE" BECOMES "EVERYONE IS AGAINST ME"; "THIS IS HARD" BECOMES "EVERYTHING IS TERRIBLE"; "I DON'T KNOW THAT PERSON" TURNS INTO "THAT PERSON IS A THREAT TO ME."
THINKING BECOMES DICTATED BY A SPIRALING MIDDLE-OF-THE-NIGHT MIND MADE IRRATIONAL BY EXHAUSTION, FROM WHICH ONE NEVER WAKES UP. CLARITY NEVER COMES BECAUSE WE HAVE NO ONE TO PULL US FROM THE SPIN. WORST-CASE-SCENARIO IMAGINATIONS RUN WILD.
SO WHEN WE LIVE BENEATH A GOVERNMENT THAT INDUCES THIS, AND SEEKS TO EXAGGERATE THE SPACES BETWEEN ITS PEOPLE AS A MEASURE OF CONTROL, ARENDT WRITES, "It bases itself on loneliness, on the experience of not belonging to the world at all, which is among the most radical and desperate experiences of man."

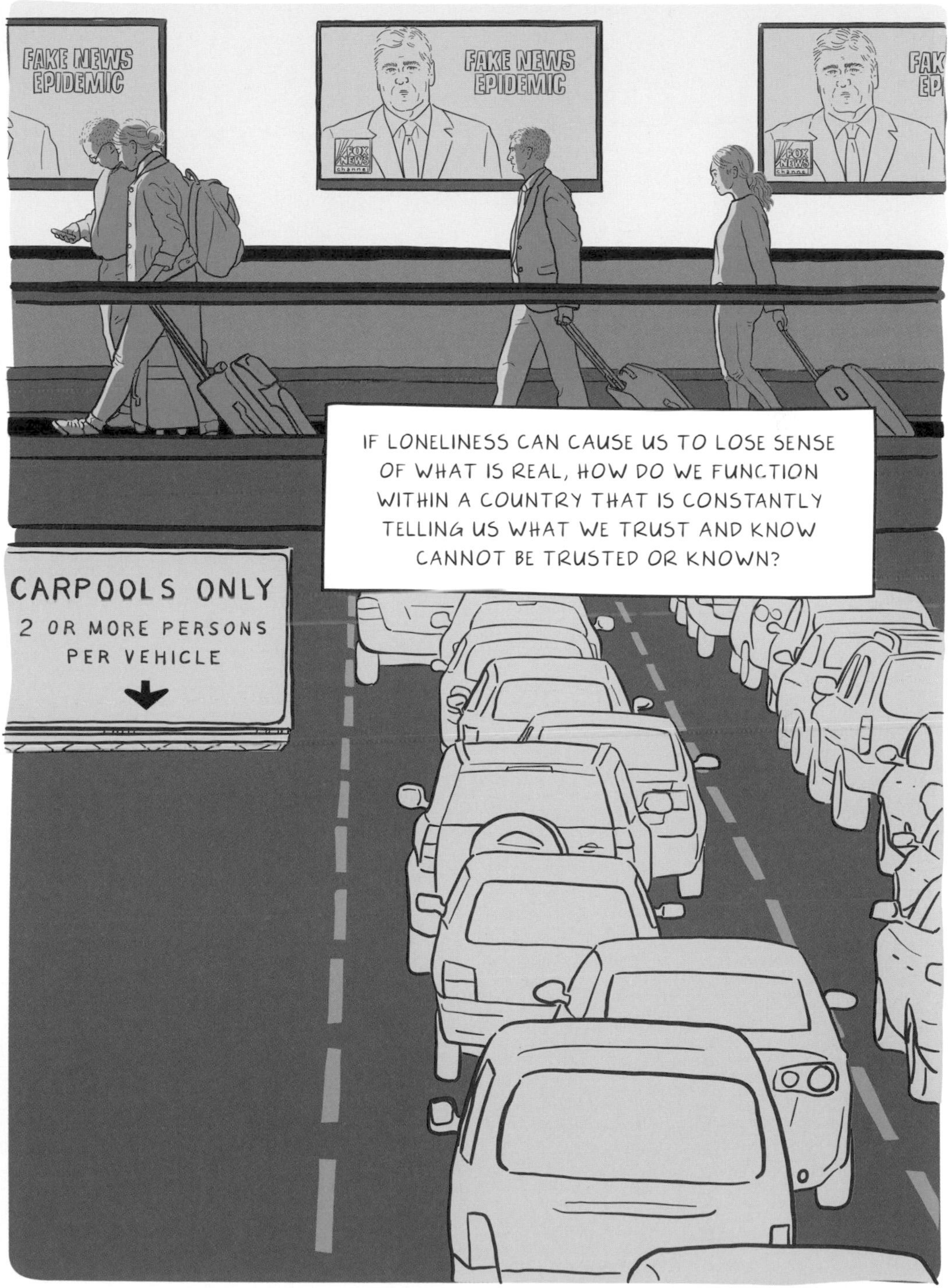
FAKE NEWS EPIDEMIC
FAKE NEWS EPIDEMIC
FOX NEWS channel
IF LONELINESS CAN CAUSE US TO LOSE SENSE OF WHAT IS REAL, HOW DO WE FUNCTION WITHIN A COUNTRY THAT IS CONSTANTLY TELLING US WHAT WE TRUST AND KNOW CANNOT BE TRUSTED OR KNOWN?
CARPOOLS ONLY
2 OR MORE PERSONS PER VEHICLE

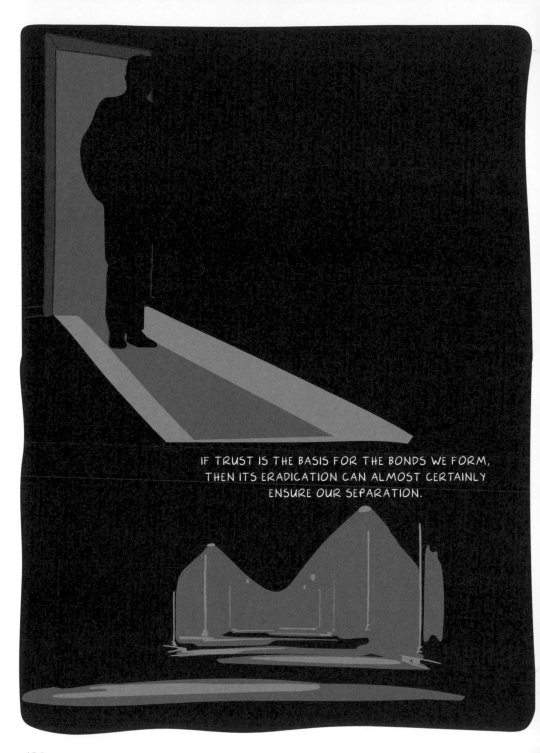

IF TRUST IS THE BASIS FOR THE BONDS WE FORM,
THEN ITS ERADICATION CAN ALMOST CERTAINLY
ENSURE OUR SEPARATION.

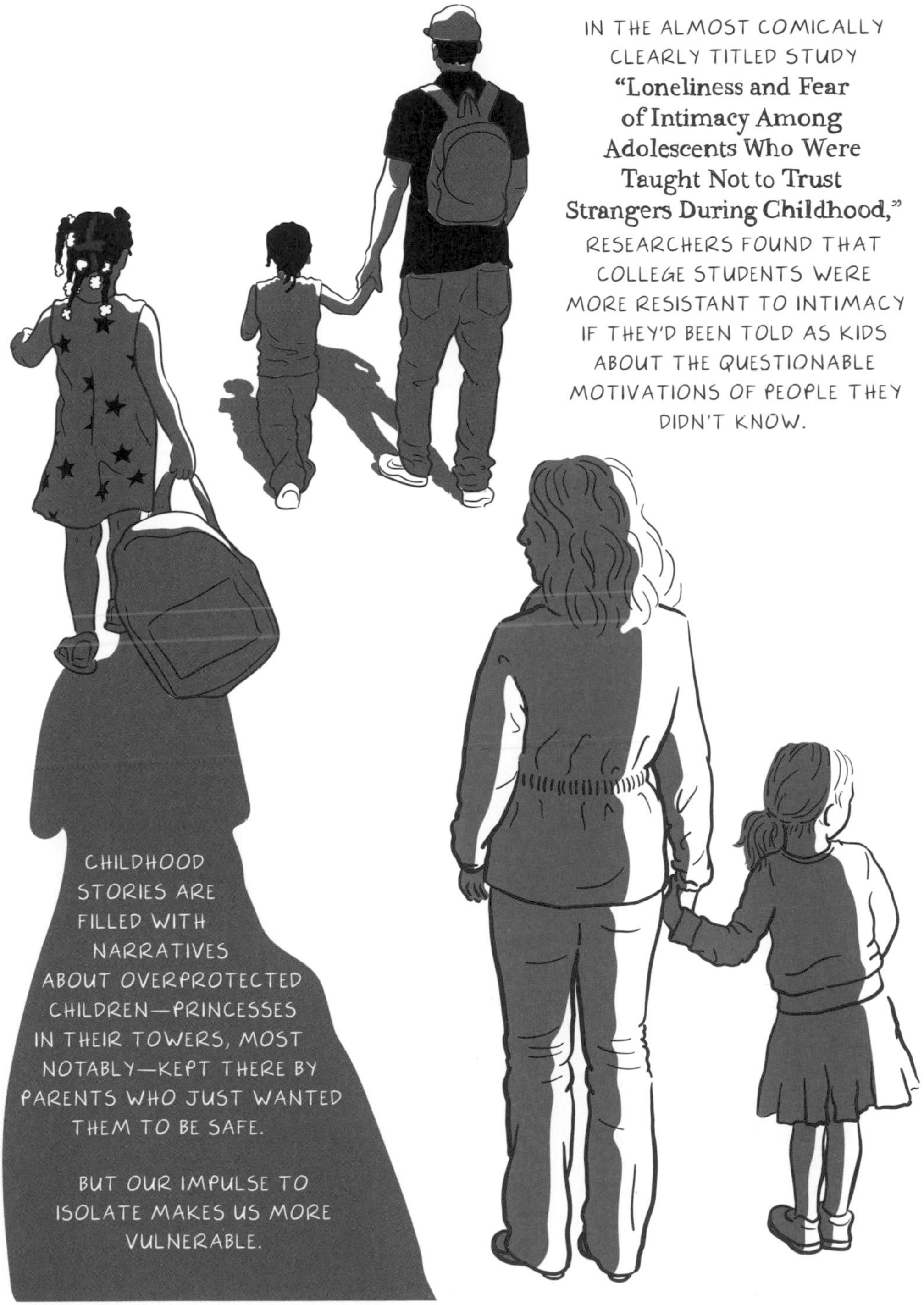
IN THE ALMOST COMICALLY CLEARLY TITLED STUDY "Loneliness and Fear of Intimacy Among Adolescents Who Were Taught Not to Trust Strangers During Childhood," RESEARCHERS FOUND THAT COLLEGE STUDENTS WERE MORE RESISTANT TO INTIMACY IF THEY'D BEEN TOLD AS KIDS ABOUT THE QUESTIONABLE MOTIVATIONS OF PEOPLE THEY DIDN'T KNOW.
CHILDHOOD STORIES ARE FILLED WITH NARRATIVES ABOUT OVERPROTECTED CHILDREN—PRINCESSES IN THEIR TOWERS, MOST NOTABLY—KEPT THERE BY PARENTS WHO JUST WANTED THEM TO BE SAFE.
BUT OUR IMPULSE TO ISOLATE MAKES US MORE VULNERABLE.

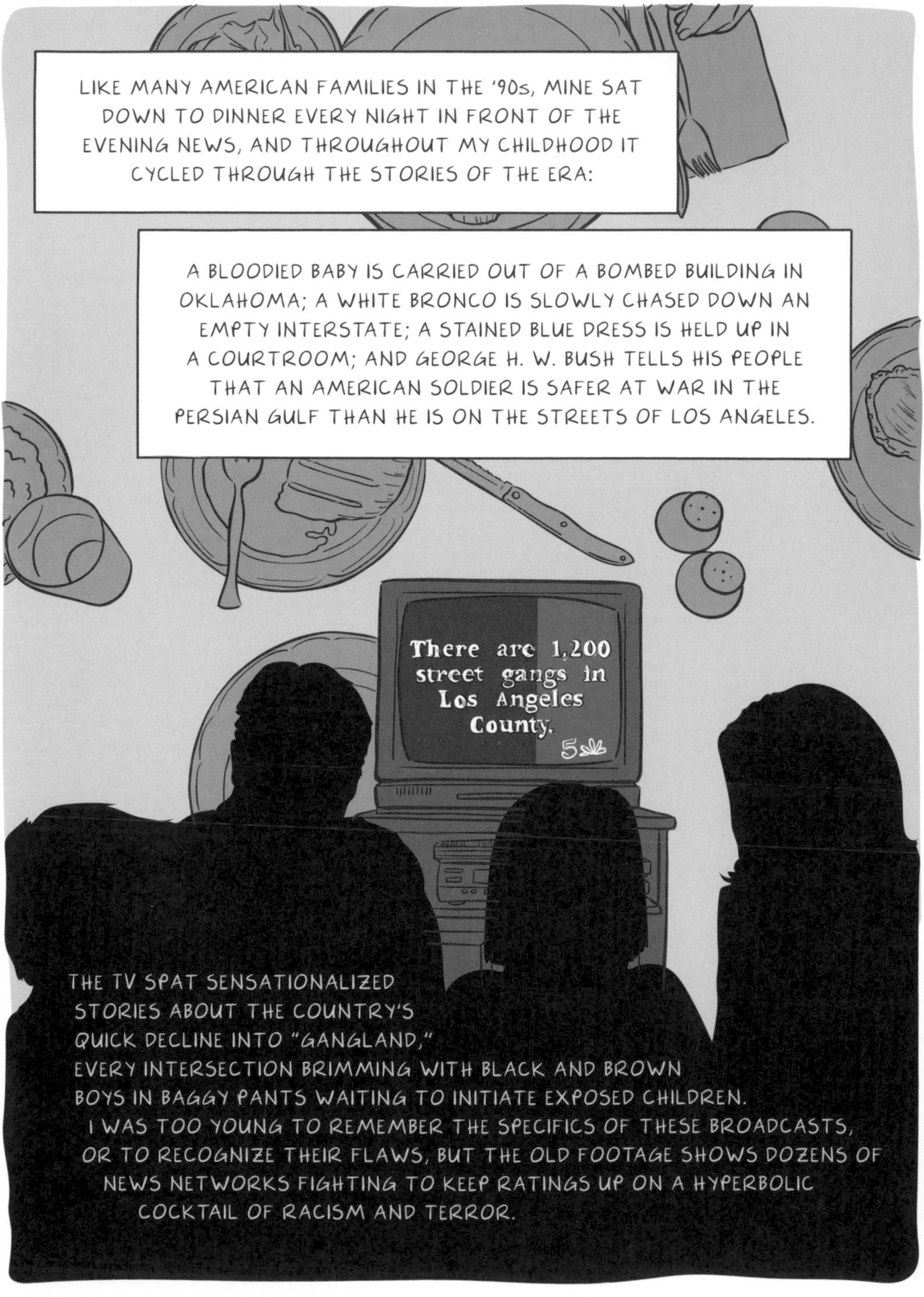
LIKE MANY AMERICAN FAMILIES IN THE '90s, MINE SAT DOWN TO DINNER EVERY NIGHT IN FRONT OF THE EVENING NEWS, AND THROUGHOUT MY CHILDHOOD IT CYCLED THROUGH THE STORIES OF THE ERA:
A BLOODIED BABY IS CARRIED OUT OF A BOMBED BUILDING IN OKLAHOMA; A WHITE BRONCO IS SLOWLY CHASED DOWN AN EMPTY INTERSTATE; A STAINED BLUE DRESS IS HELD UP IN A COURTROOM; AND GEORGE H. W. BUSH TELLS HIS PEOPLE THAT AN AMERICAN SOLDIER IS SAFER AT WAR IN THE PERSIAN GULF THAN HE IS ON THE STREETS OF LOS ANGELES.
There are 1,200 street gangs in Los Angeles County.
THE TV SPAT SENSATIONALIZED STORIES ABOUT THE COUNTRY'S QUICK DECLINE INTO "GANGLAND," EVERY INTERSECTION BRIMMING WITH BLACK AND BROWN BOYS IN BAGGY PANTS WAITING TO INITIATE EXPOSED CHILDREN. I WAS TOO YOUNG TO REMEMBER THE SPECIFICS OF THESE BROADCASTS, OR TO RECOGNIZE THEIR FLAWS, BUT THE OLD FOOTAGE SHOWS DOZENS OF NEWS NETWORKS FIGHTING TO KEEP RATINGS UP ON A HYPERBOLIC COCKTAIL OF RACISM AND TERROR.

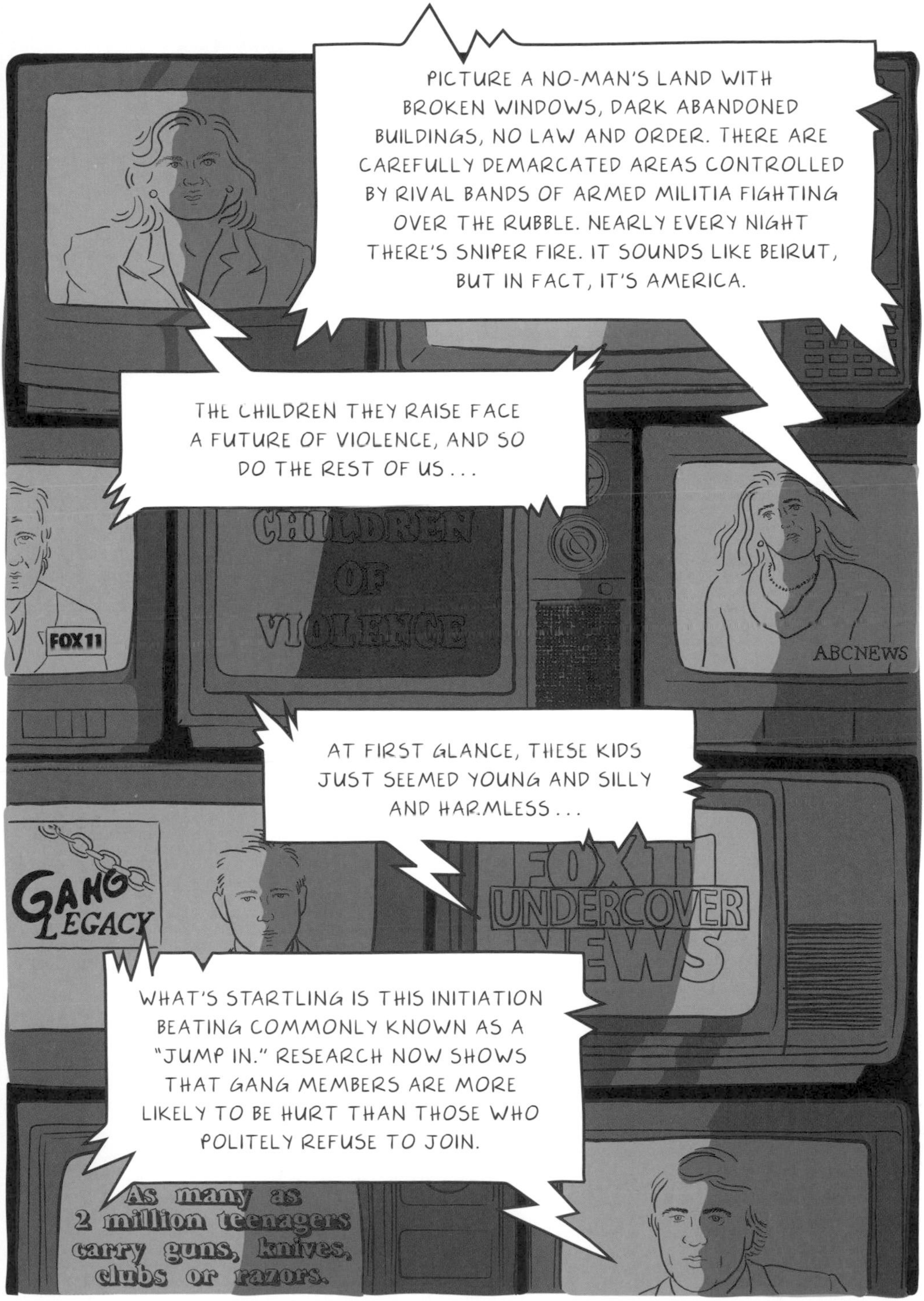
PICTURE A NO-MAN'S LAND WITH BROKEN WINDOWS, DARK ABANDONED BUILDINGS, NO LAW AND ORDER. THERE ARE CAREFULLY DEMARCATED AREAS CONTROLLED BY RIVAL BANDS OF ARMED MILITIA FIGHTING OVER THE RUBBLE. NEARLY EVERY NIGHT THERE'S SNIPER FIRE. IT SOUNDS LIKE BEIRUT, BUT IN FACT, IT'S AMERICA.
THE CHILDREN THEY RAISE FACE A FUTURE OF VIOLENCE, AND SO DO THE REST OF US . . .
FOX11
CHILDREN OF VIOLENCE
ABCNEWS
AT FIRST GLANCE, THESE KIDS JUST SEEMED YOUNG AND SILLY AND HARMLESS . . .
GANG LEGACY
FOX11 UNDERCOVER NEWS
WHAT'S STARTLING IS THIS INITIATION BEATING COMMONLY KNOWN AS A "JUMP IN." RESEARCH NOW SHOWS THAT GANG MEMBERS ARE MORE LIKELY TO BE HURT THAN THOSE WHO POLITELY REFUSE TO JOIN.
As many as 2 million teenagers carry guns, knives, clubs or razors.

HEEDING THE WARNINGS OF THE NIGHTLY NEWS, MY MOTHER
INSTRUCTED ME ON HOW TO BEHAVE SO I WOULDN'T BE INITIATED.
I NEEDED TO ACT CONFIDENTLY, SHE SAID. GANGS PREY ON THE
INSECURE, SHE'D HEARD, SEEKING OUT THOSE DESPERATE FOR
COMPANIONSHIP AND GIVING IT TO THEM AT THE COST OF HOLDING
UP LIQUOR STORES AND STANDING LOOKOUT AND HOT-WIRING
CARS AND WHICHEVER OTHER VAGUE PRIME-TIME SCENES SHE USED
TO FORMULATE A PICTURE OF WHAT A GANG MEMBER WAS.

ASSIGNMENT TO HELP ME "PRACTICE"
WHAT I MIGHT SAY IF I WERE
ASKED TO JOIN

NO tHANKS I WANt to ROLLerSKAte

MY MOTHER'S ANXIETIES WERE MISPLACED—THERE WERE NO
REPORTS OF GANG VIOLENCE IN RURAL WISCONSIN, DESPITE THE
WHISPERS ABOUT MEN WAITING BENEATH CARS IN THE EAST TOWN
MALL PARKING LOT, PRIMED TO SLICE UNSUSPECTING ANKLES
WITH RAZOR BLADES AND SPEED OFF IN YOUR MINIVAN.

WHAT MY MOTHER AND THE NEWS BOTH FAILED TO RECOGNIZE WAS THAT THE REAL GANG VIOLENCE THAT RAVAGED THE '90s PREYED ON ITS MOST VULNERABLE CHILDREN, WHO WERE RARELY THE SAME CHILDREN THE COUNTRY SEEMED INTERESTED IN PROTECTING. THE PROGRAMS IGNORED THEIR CONTRIBUTIONS TO PUBLIC PRESSURE FOR A WAVE OF MASS INCARCERATION THAT WOULD ISOLATE AMERICA'S YOUNG MEN MORE THAN THEY'D EVER BEEN BEFORE.

WHEN NEWS ANCHORS REPORTED ON FACELESS PRETEENS DESPERATE TO BELONG, THEY WERE ALSO REPORTING ON A FEAR OF THE VULNERABILITY THAT LONELINESS CAN CREATE. WITHOUT A COMMUNITY TO KEEP THEM IN LINE, THE SEGMENTS SEEMED TO SAY, GOOD KIDS COULD GO BAD.

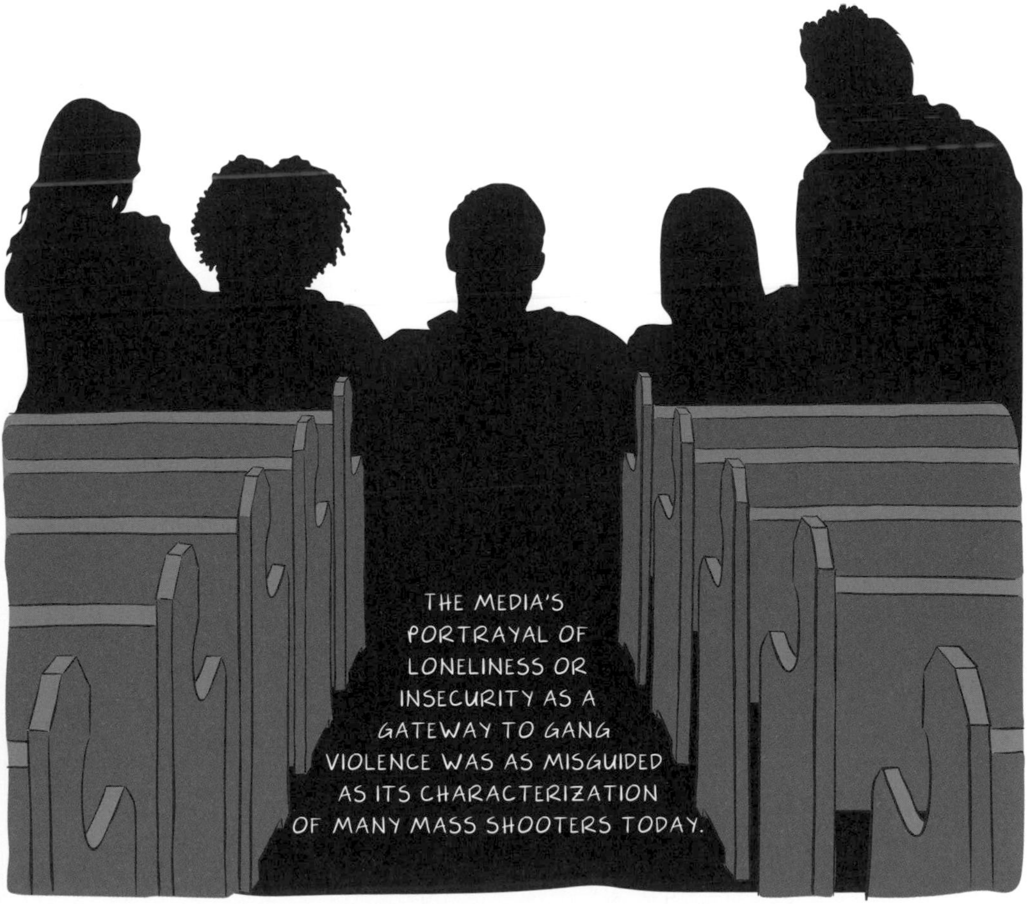
THE MEDIA'S PORTRAYAL OF LONELINESS OR INSECURITY AS A GATEWAY TO GANG VIOLENCE WAS AS MISGUIDED AS ITS CHARACTERIZATION OF MANY MASS SHOOTERS TODAY.

Neighbors Of Shooter Gary Martin Describe Him As a 'Loner'

Roommates Describe Gunman as Loner

BLACKSBURG, Va., April 17 — He was a stranger in a crowd of 26,000. Cho Seung-Hui was even unknown to the young man who for nearly a year slept just feet away from him.

James Holmes, Aurora shooting suspect, was grad school dropout and loner, say neighbors

The sole suspect of the Quebec mosque shooting described as a 'loner' and anti-feminist 'troll'

Dallas Shooter Micah Johnson Army Veteran and 'Loner'

Gilroy Festival Killer Described as 'Kind of a Loner,' Motive for Shooting Remains a Myst

El Paso shooter was anti-social loner, former classmate says

'Loner' Dallas gunman had bomb materials and kept journal of combat tactics

'Loner' student shoots and kills 10
at Texas school

Munich shooting: killer was bullied teen
loner obsessed with mass murder

Elliott Rodger, a quiet, troubled loner,
plotted rampage for months

**Planned Parenthood shooter
described as a 'loner'**

Why Many Mass Shooters Are 'Loners'

Social rejection can fuel violence, but only if the perpetrator has access to a
deadly weapon.

...oenix Serial Street Shooter sus...
...med to live in isolation

EXCLUSIVE: Congress shooter was 5'6" rude loner
who creeped out female bar staff at BBQ restaurant
where he spent Happy Hours - after moving to D.C.
to protest against the president he hated

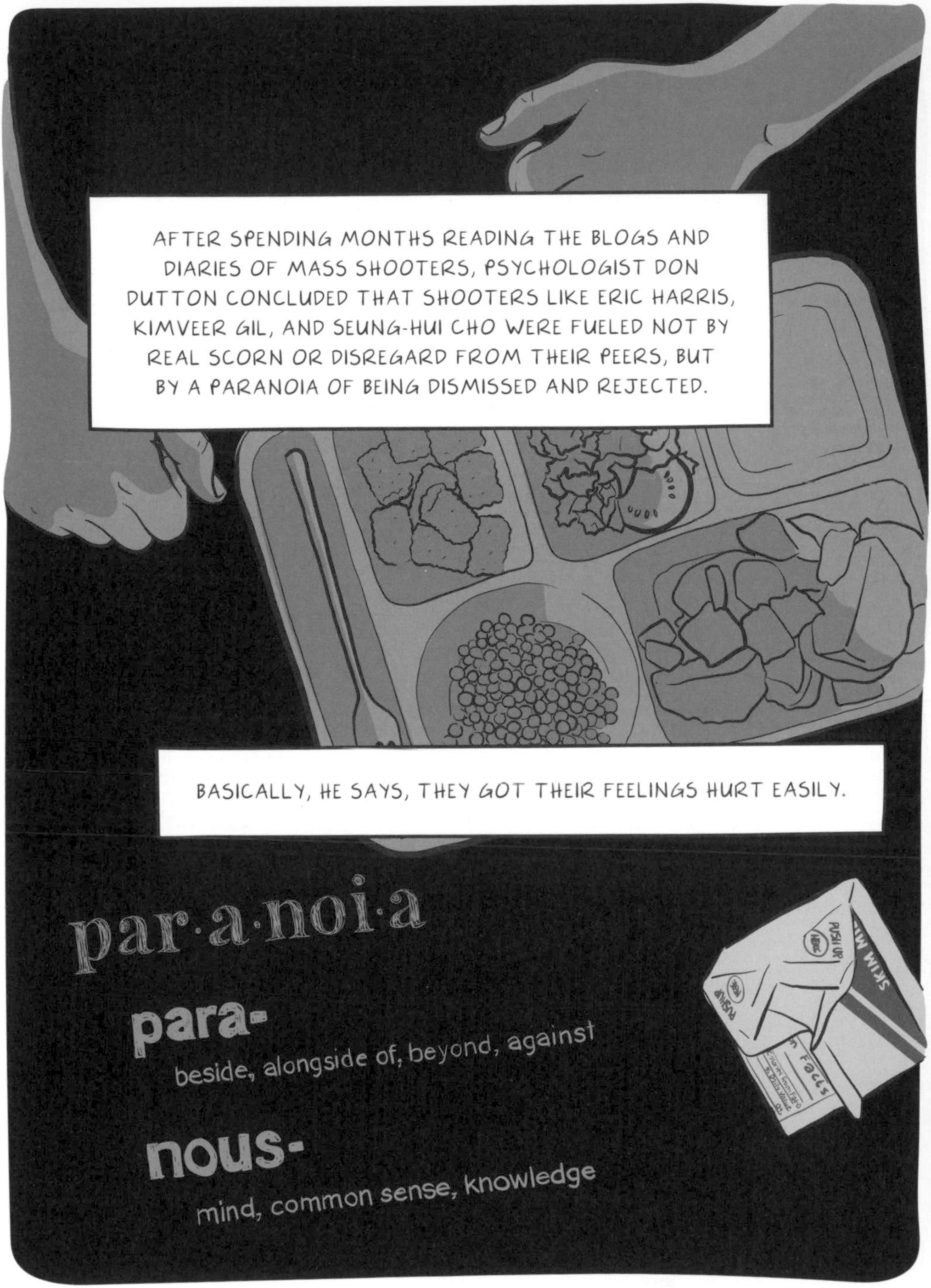
AFTER SPENDING MONTHS READING THE BLOGS AND DIARIES OF MASS SHOOTERS, PSYCHOLOGIST DON DUTTON CONCLUDED THAT SHOOTERS LIKE ERIC HARRIS, KIMVEER GIL, AND SEUNG-HUI CHO WERE FUELED NOT BY REAL SCORN OR DISREGARD FROM THEIR PEERS, BUT BY A PARANOIA OF BEING DISMISSED AND REJECTED.
BASICALLY, HE SAYS, THEY GOT THEIR FEELINGS HURT EASILY.
par·a·noi·a
para-
beside, alongside of, beyond, against
nous-
mind, common sense, knowledge
PUSH UP
SKIM MI

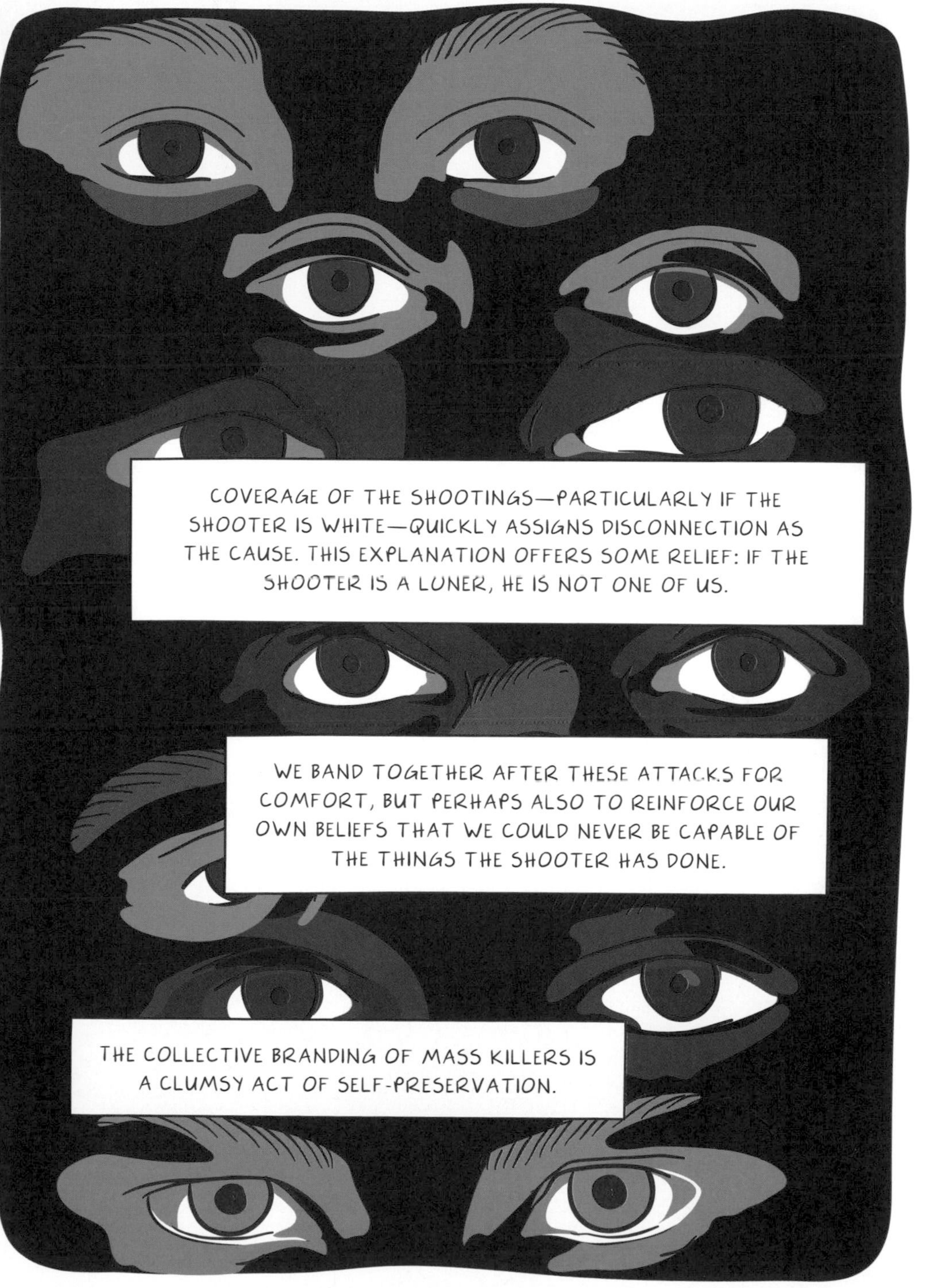
COVERAGE OF THE SHOOTINGS—PARTICULARLY IF THE SHOOTER IS WHITE—QUICKLY ASSIGNS DISCONNECTION AS THE CAUSE. THIS EXPLANATION OFFERS SOME RELIEF: IF THE SHOOTER IS A LONER, HE IS NOT ONE OF US.
WE BAND TOGETHER AFTER THESE ATTACKS FOR COMFORT, BUT PERHAPS ALSO TO REINFORCE OUR OWN BELIEFS THAT WE COULD NEVER BE CAPABLE OF THE THINGS THE SHOOTER HAS DONE.
THE COLLECTIVE BRANDING OF MASS KILLERS IS A CLUMSY ACT OF SELF-PRESERVATION.

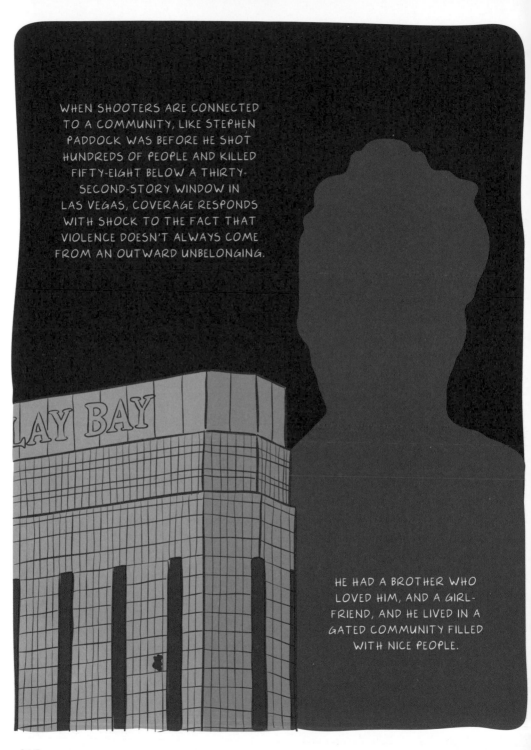

WHEN SHOOTERS ARE CONNECTED
TO A COMMUNITY, LIKE STEPHEN
PADDOCK WAS BEFORE HE SHOT
HUNDREDS OF PEOPLE AND KILLED
FIFTY-EIGHT BELOW A THIRTY-
SECOND-STORY WINDOW IN
LAS VEGAS, COVERAGE RESPONDS
WITH SHOCK TO THE FACT THAT
VIOLENCE DOESN'T ALWAYS COME
FROM AN OUTWARD UNBELONGING.

HE HAD A BROTHER WHO
LOVED HIM, AND A GIRL-
FRIEND, AND HE LIVED IN A
GATED COMMUNITY FILLED
WITH NICE PEOPLE.

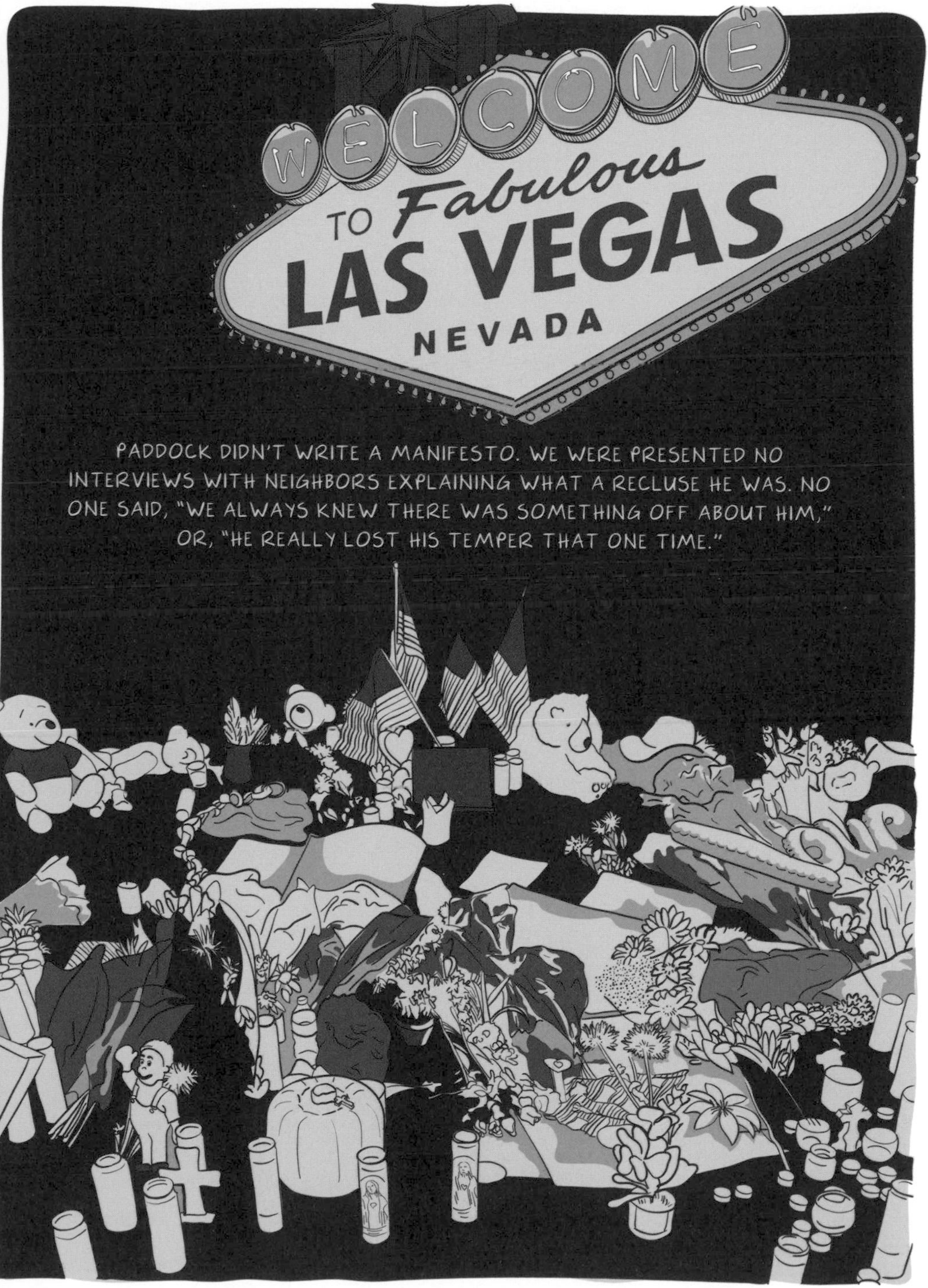
WELCOME
TO Fabulous
LAS VEGAS
NEVADA
PADDOCK DIDN'T WRITE A MANIFESTO. WE WERE PRESENTED NO INTERVIEWS WITH NEIGHBORS EXPLAINING WHAT A RECLUSE HE WAS. NO ONE SAID, "WE ALWAYS KNEW THERE WAS SOMETHING OFF ABOUT HIM," OR, "HE REALLY LOST HIS TEMPER THAT ONE TIME."

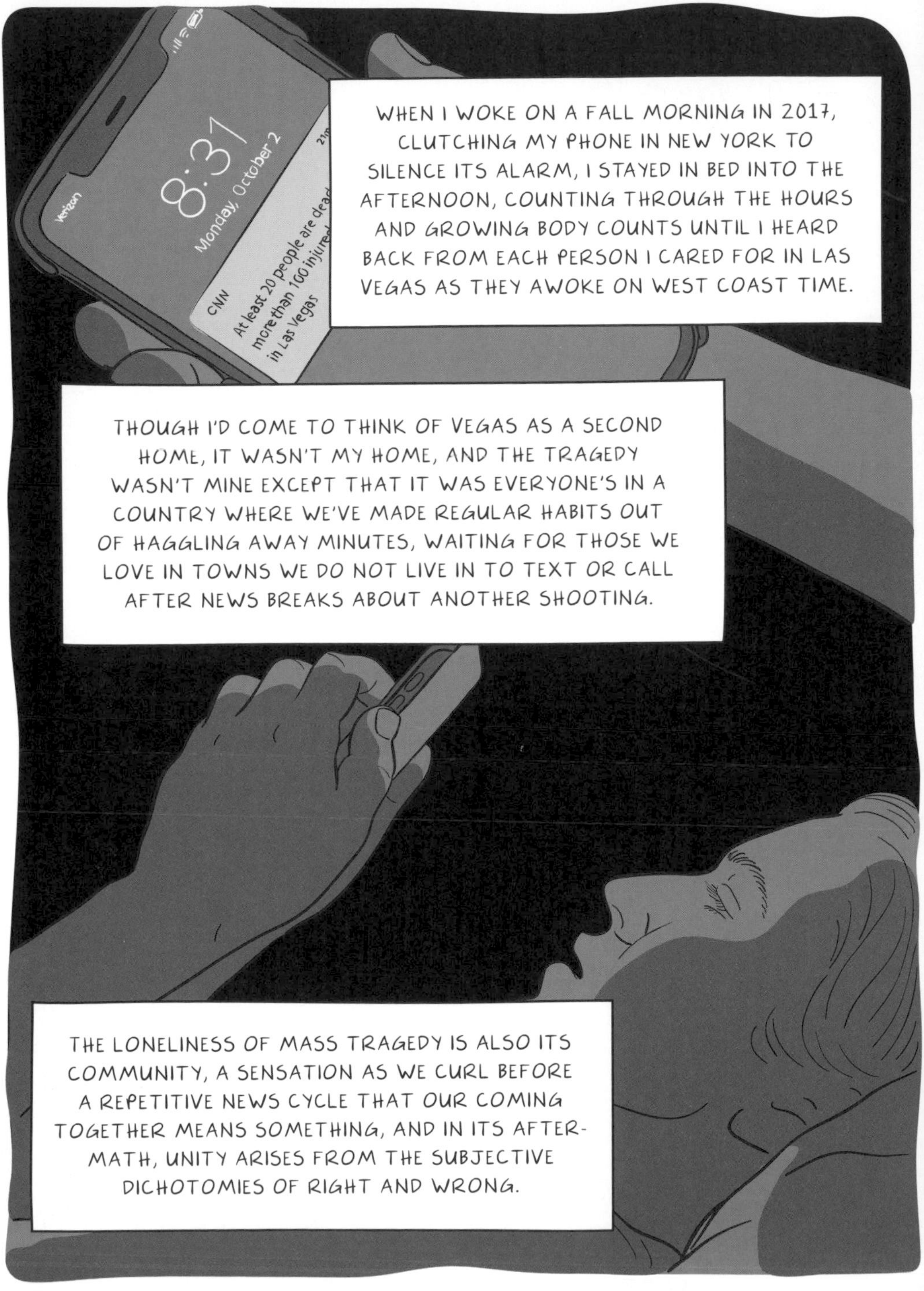
8:31
Monday, October 2
CNN
At least 20 people are dead
more than 100 injured
in Las Vegas
WHEN I WOKE ON A FALL MORNING IN 2017, CLUTCHING MY PHONE IN NEW YORK TO SILENCE ITS ALARM, I STAYED IN BED INTO THE AFTERNOON, COUNTING THROUGH THE HOURS AND GROWING BODY COUNTS UNTIL I HEARD BACK FROM EACH PERSON I CARED FOR IN LAS VEGAS AS THEY AWOKE ON WEST COAST TIME.
THOUGH I'D COME TO THINK OF VEGAS AS A SECOND HOME, IT WASN'T MY HOME, AND THE TRAGEDY WASN'T MINE EXCEPT THAT IT WAS EVERYONE'S IN A COUNTRY WHERE WE'VE MADE REGULAR HABITS OUT OF HAGGLING AWAY MINUTES, WAITING FOR THOSE WE LOVE IN TOWNS WE DO NOT LIVE IN TO TEXT OR CALL AFTER NEWS BREAKS ABOUT ANOTHER SHOOTING.
THE LONELINESS OF MASS TRAGEDY IS ALSO ITS COMMUNITY, A SENSATION AS WE CURL BEFORE A REPETITIVE NEWS CYCLE THAT OUR COMING TOGETHER MEANS SOMETHING, AND IN ITS AFTERMATH, UNITY ARISES FROM THE SUBJECTIVE DICHOTOMIES OF RIGHT AND WRONG.

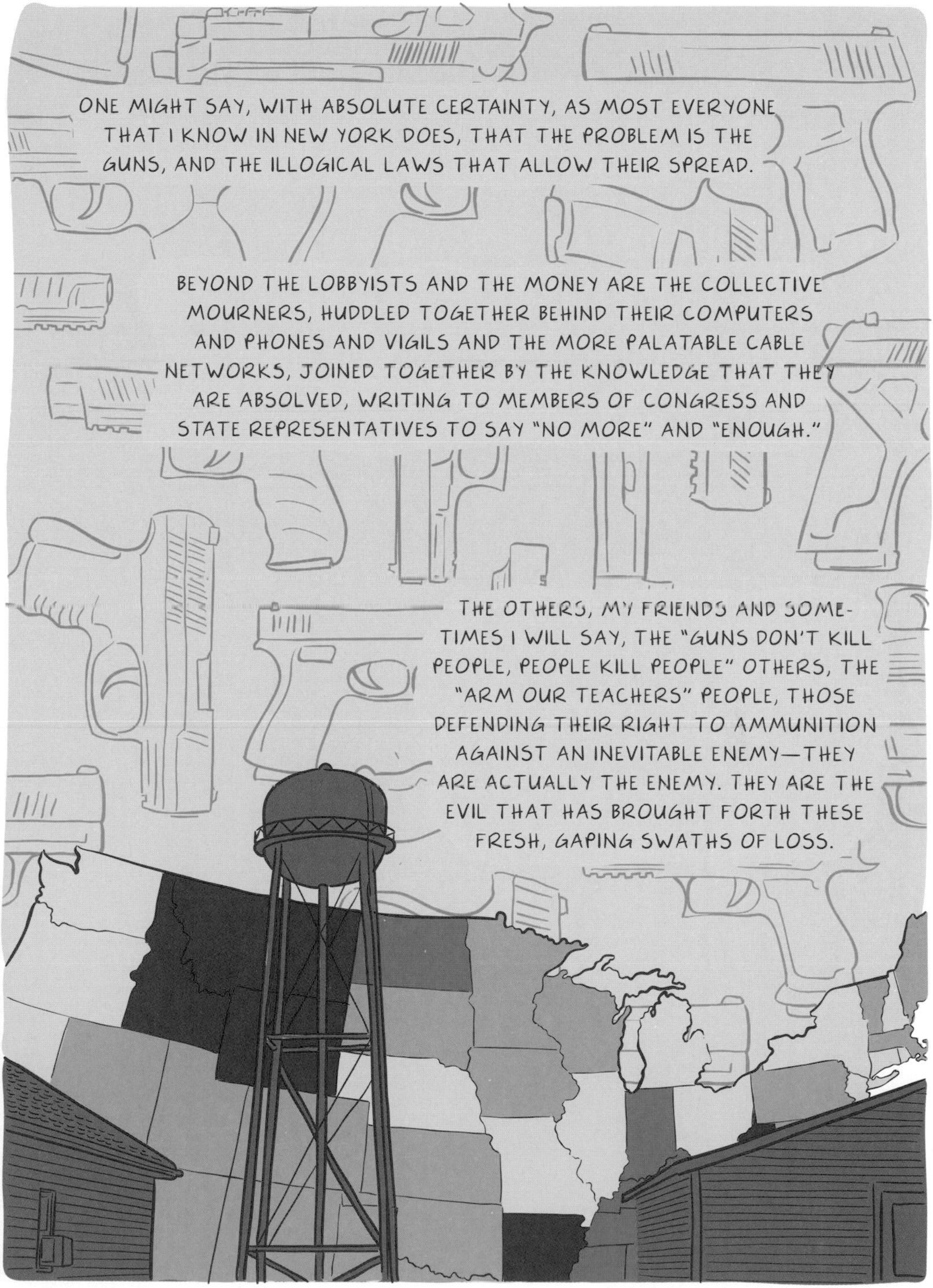
ONE MIGHT SAY, WITH ABSOLUTE CERTAINTY, AS MOST EVERYONE THAT I KNOW IN NEW YORK DOES, THAT THE PROBLEM IS THE GUNS, AND THE ILLOGICAL LAWS THAT ALLOW THEIR SPREAD.
BEYOND THE LOBBYISTS AND THE MONEY ARE THE COLLECTIVE MOURNERS, HUDDLED TOGETHER BEHIND THEIR COMPUTERS AND PHONES AND VIGILS AND THE MORE PALATABLE CABLE NETWORKS, JOINED TOGETHER BY THE KNOWLEDGE THAT THEY ARE ABSOLVED, WRITING TO MEMBERS OF CONGRESS AND STATE REPRESENTATIVES TO SAY "NO MORE" AND "ENOUGH."
THE OTHERS, MY FRIENDS AND SOMETIMES I WILL SAY, THE "GUNS DON'T KILL PEOPLE, PEOPLE KILL PEOPLE" OTHERS, THE "ARM OUR TEACHERS" PEOPLE, THOSE DEFENDING THEIR RIGHT TO AMMUNITION AGAINST AN INEVITABLE ENEMY—THEY ARE ACTUALLY THE ENEMY. THEY ARE THE EVIL THAT HAS BROUGHT FORTH THESE FRESH, GAPING SWATHS OF LOSS.

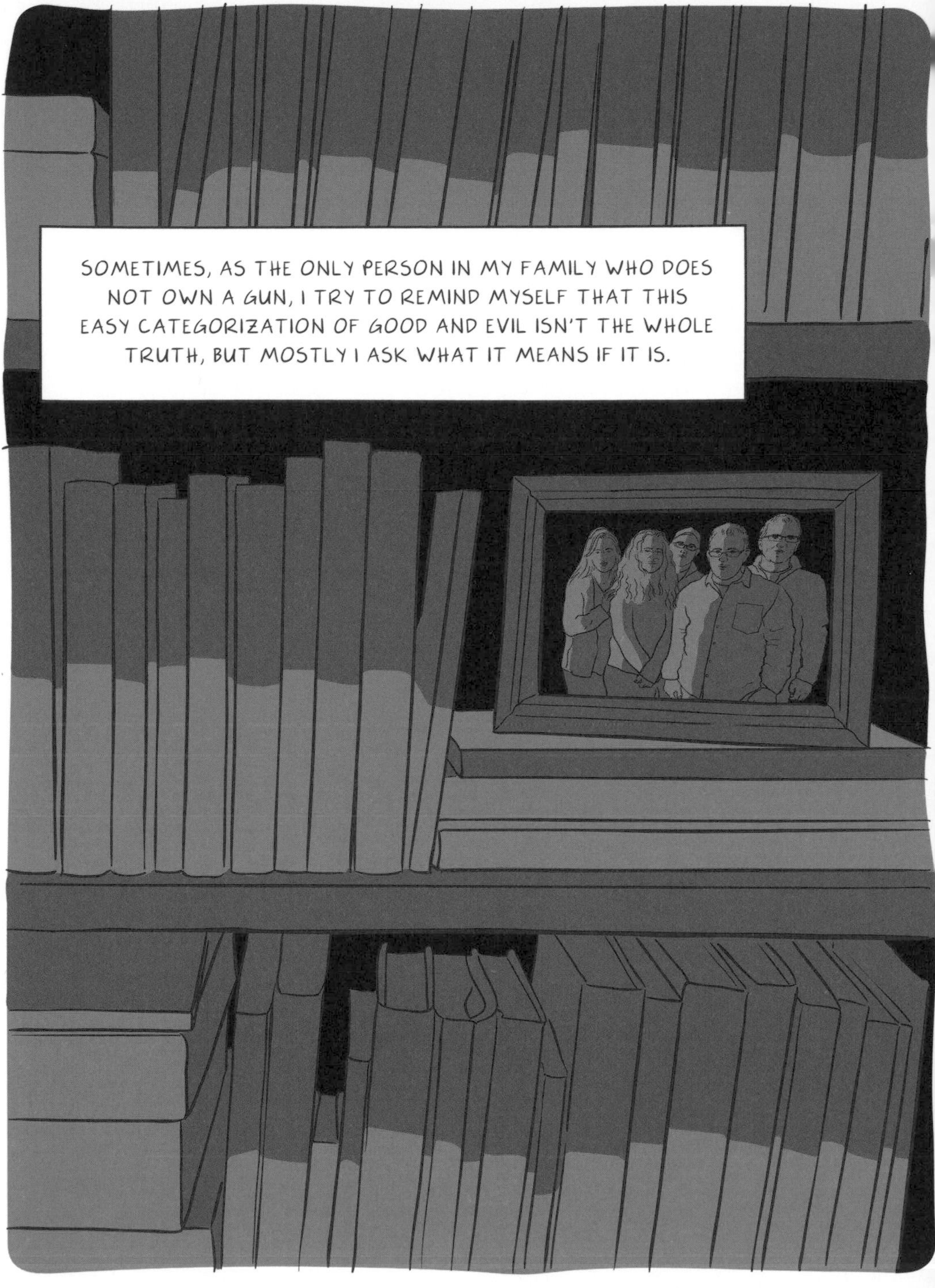
SOMETIMES, AS THE ONLY PERSON IN MY FAMILY WHO DOES NOT OWN A GUN, I TRY TO REMIND MYSELF THAT THIS EASY CATEGORIZATION OF GOOD AND EVIL ISN'T THE WHOLE TRUTH, BUT MOSTLY I ASK WHAT IT MEANS IF IT IS.

IN SOUTHERN NEVADA, MOTIVATIONAL MOURNING BILLBOARDS APPEARED OVERNIGHT ACROSS THE DESERT LIKE A FLUSH OF GREEN PUSHED THROUGH THE DIRT AFTER RAIN.

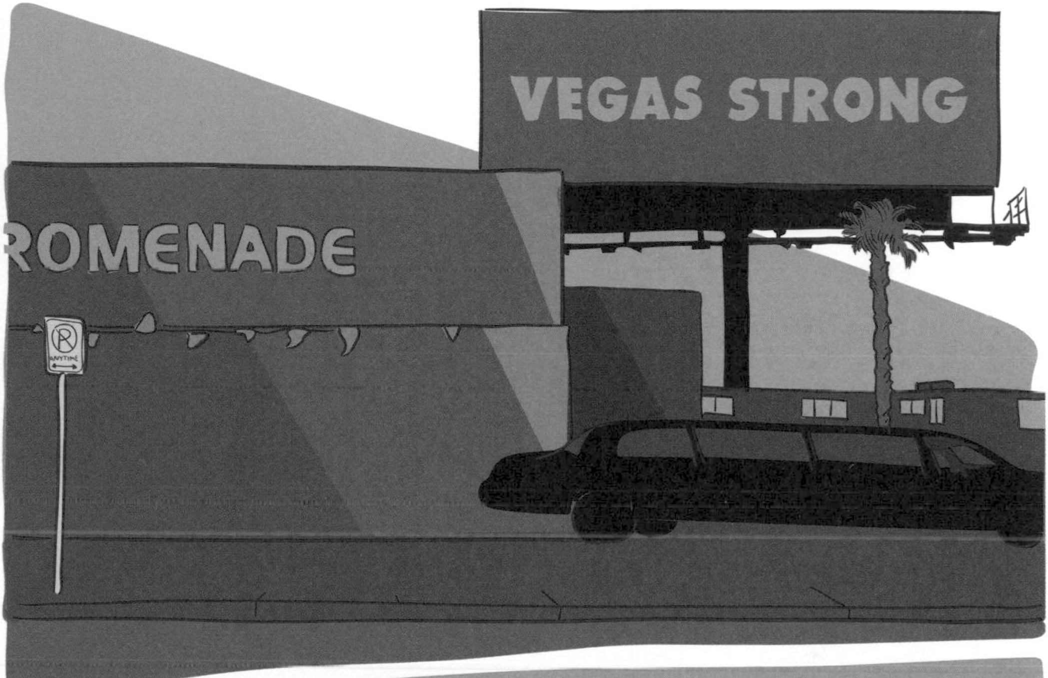
VEGAS STRONG
ROMENADE
ANYTIME

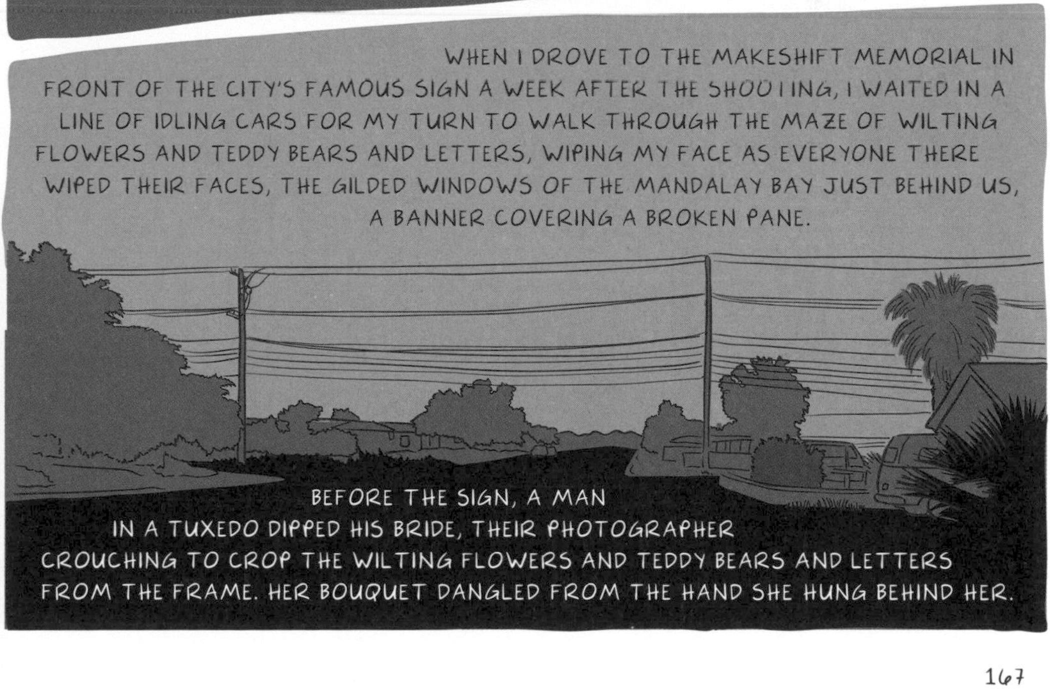
WHEN I DROVE TO THE MAKESHIFT MEMORIAL IN FRONT OF THE CITY'S FAMOUS SIGN A WEEK AFTER THE SHOOTING, I WAITED IN A LINE OF IDLING CARS FOR MY TURN TO WALK THROUGH THE MAZE OF WILTING FLOWERS AND TEDDY BEARS AND LETTERS, WIPING MY FACE AS EVERYONE THERE WIPED THEIR FACES, THE GILDED WINDOWS OF THE MANDALAY BAY JUST BEHIND US, A BANNER COVERING A BROKEN PANE.
BEFORE THE SIGN, A MAN IN A TUXEDO DIPPED HIS BRIDE, THEIR PHOTOGRAPHER CROUCHING TO CROP THE WILTING FLOWERS AND TEDDY BEARS AND LETTERS FROM THE FRAME. HER BOUQUET DANGLED FROM THE HAND SHE HUNG BEHIND HER.

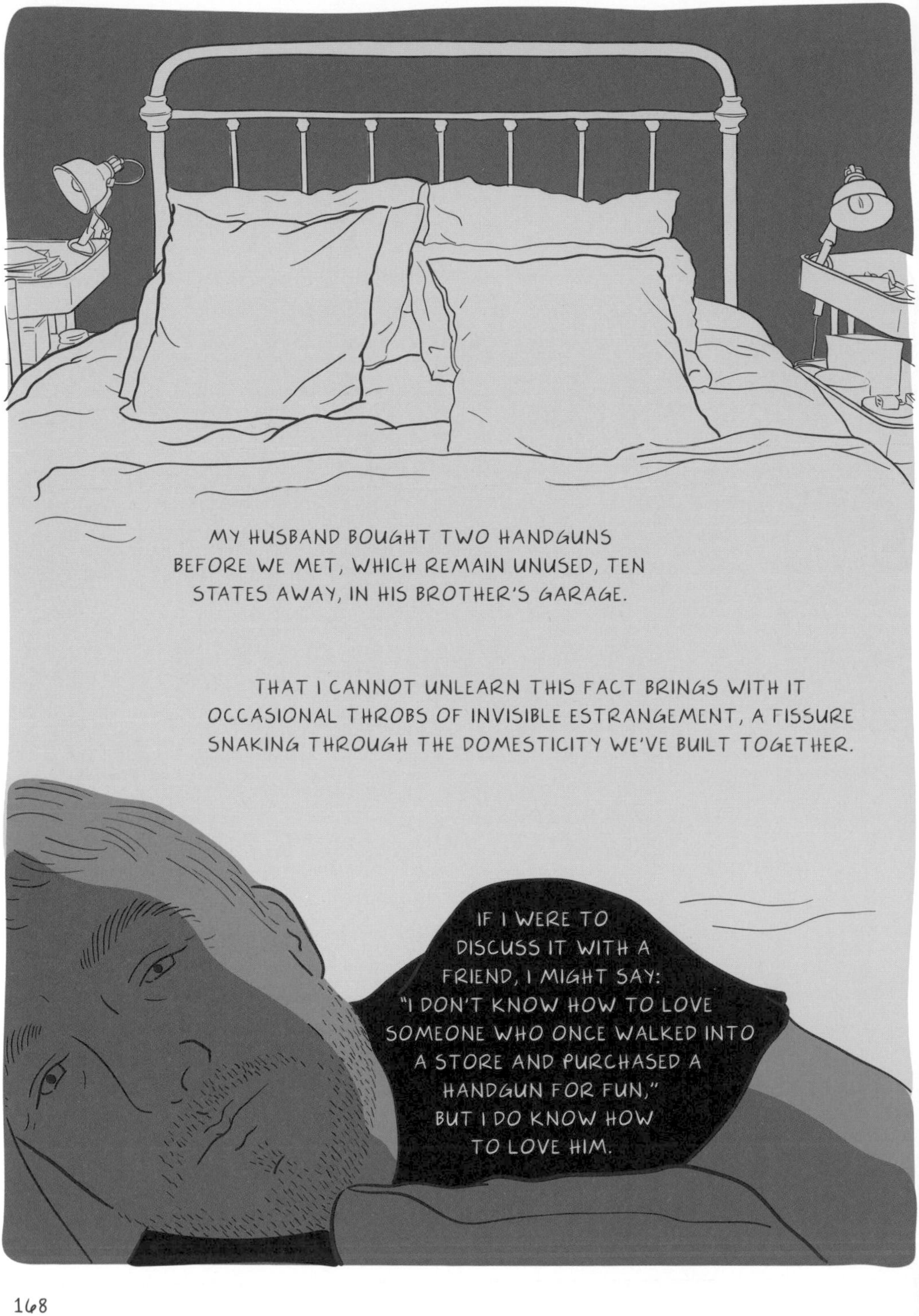
MY HUSBAND BOUGHT TWO HANDGUNS BEFORE WE MET, WHICH REMAIN UNUSED, TEN STATES AWAY, IN HIS BROTHER'S GARAGE.
THAT I CANNOT UNLEARN THIS FACT BRINGS WITH IT OCCASIONAL THROBS OF INVISIBLE ESTRANGEMENT, A FISSURE SNAKING THROUGH THE DOMESTICITY WE'VE BUILT TOGETHER.
IF I WERE TO DISCUSS IT WITH A FRIEND, I MIGHT SAY: "I DON'T KNOW HOW TO LOVE SOMEONE WHO ONCE WALKED INTO A STORE AND PURCHASED A HANDGUN FOR FUN," BUT I DO KNOW HOW TO LOVE HIM.

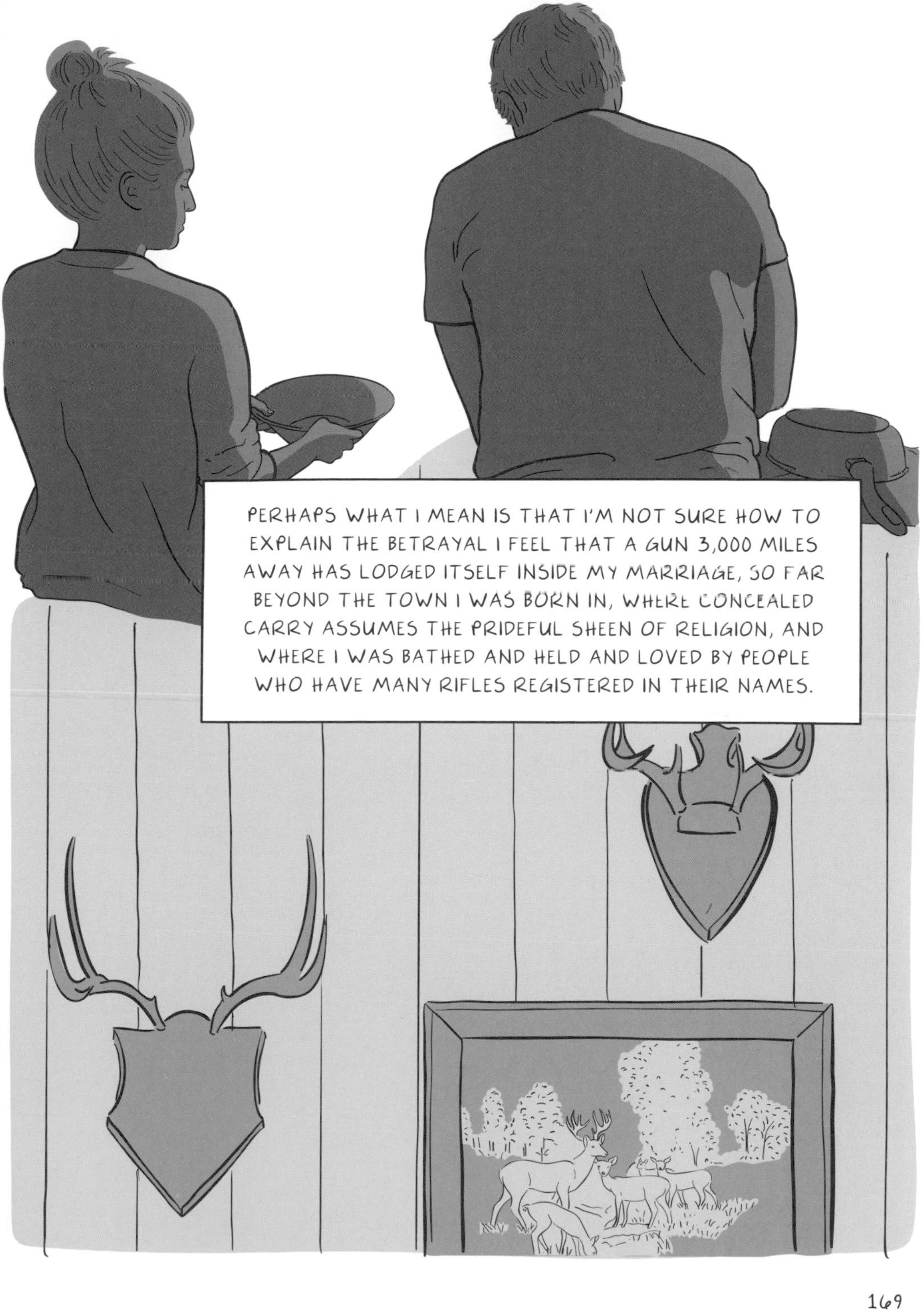
PERHAPS WHAT I MEAN IS THAT I'M NOT SURE HOW TO EXPLAIN THE BETRAYAL I FEEL THAT A GUN 3,000 MILES AWAY HAS LODGED ITSELF INSIDE MY MARRIAGE, SO FAR BEYOND THE TOWN I WAS BORN IN, WHERE CONCEALED CARRY ASSUMES THE PRIDEFUL SHEEN OF RELIGION, AND WHERE I WAS BATHED AND HELD AND LOVED BY PEOPLE WHO HAVE MANY RIFLES REGISTERED IN THEIR NAMES.

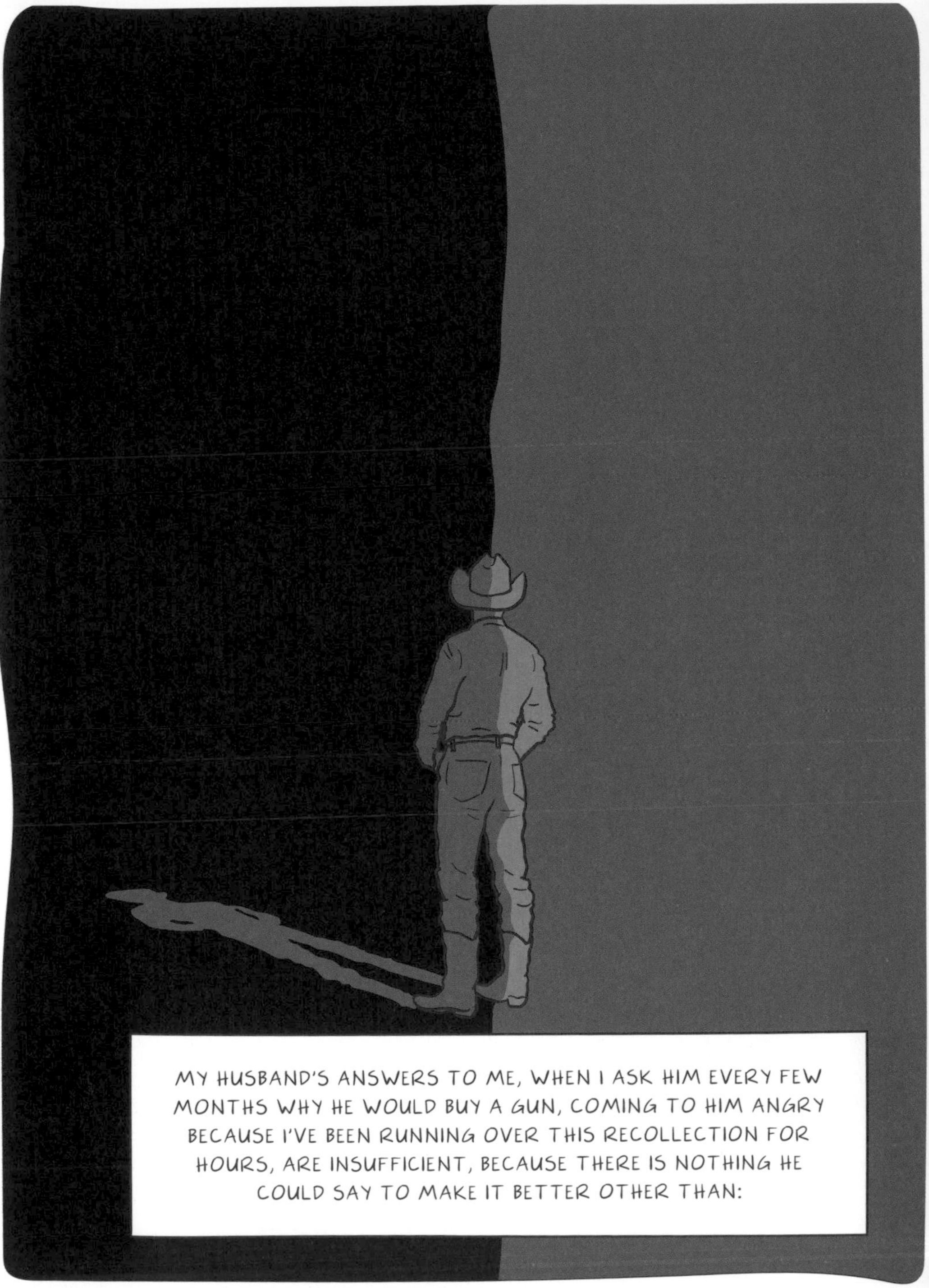
MY HUSBAND'S ANSWERS TO ME, WHEN I ASK HIM EVERY FEW MONTHS WHY HE WOULD BUY A GUN, COMING TO HIM ANGRY BECAUSE I'VE BEEN RUNNING OVER THIS RECOLLECTION FOR HOURS, ARE INSUFFICIENT, BECAUSE THERE IS NOTHING HE COULD SAY TO MAKE IT BETTER OTHER THAN:

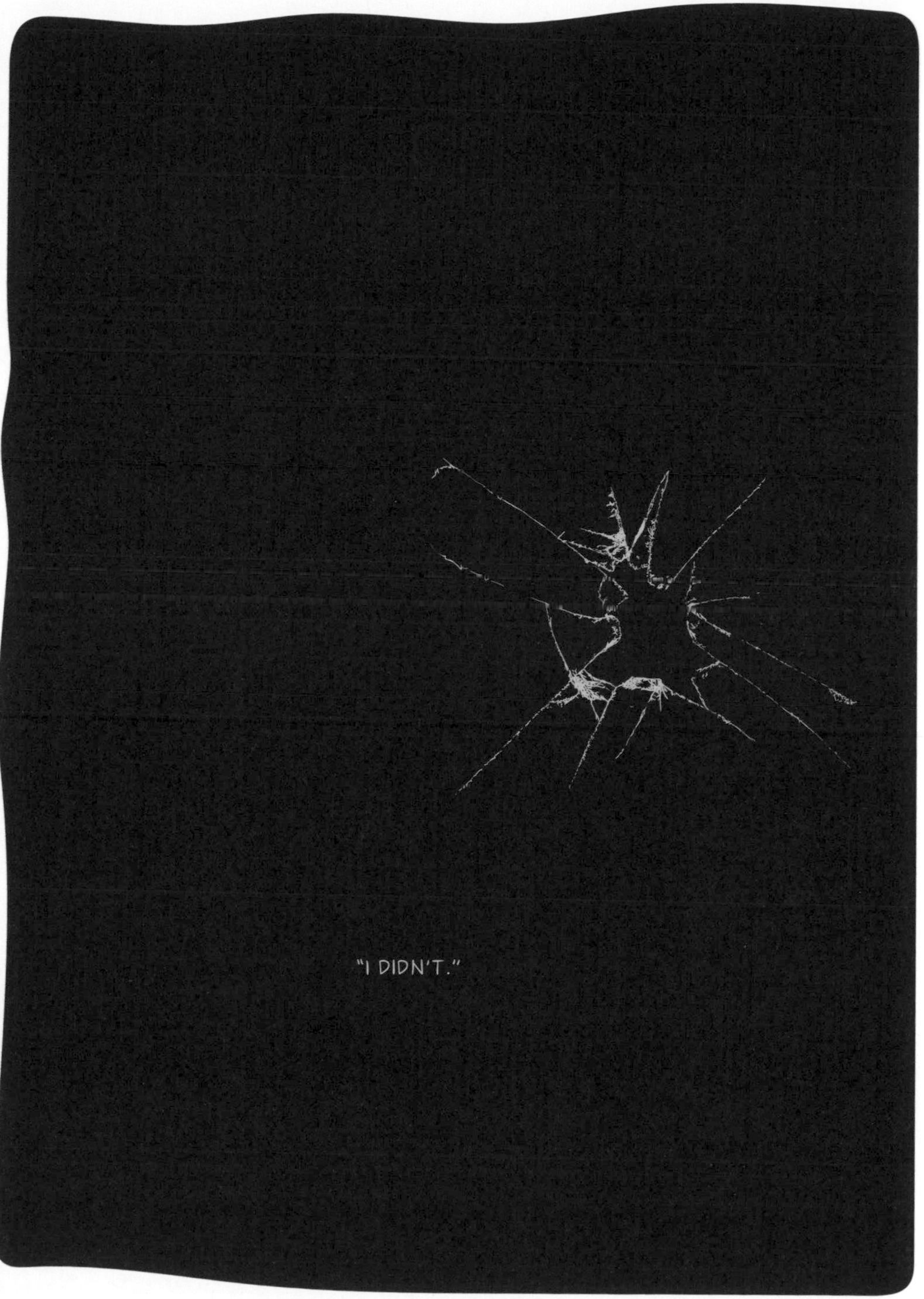
"I DIDN'T."

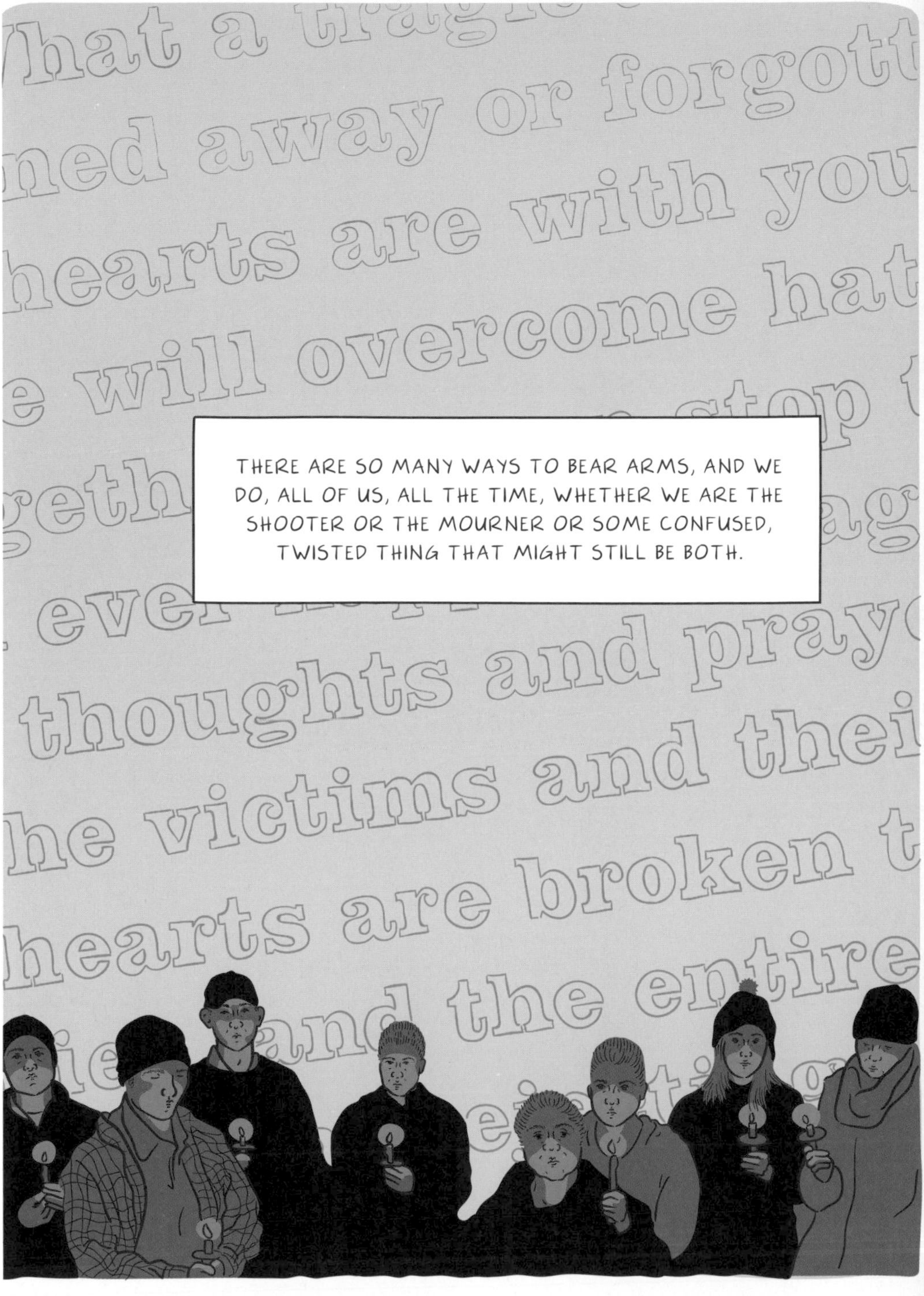
away or
hearts are with
will overcome
thoughts and
victims and
hearts are broken
the
THERE ARE SO MANY WAYS TO BEAR ARMS, AND WE DO, ALL OF US, ALL THE TIME, WHETHER WE ARE THE SHOOTER OR THE MOURNER OR SOME CONFUSED, TWISTED THING THAT MIGHT STILL BE BOTH.

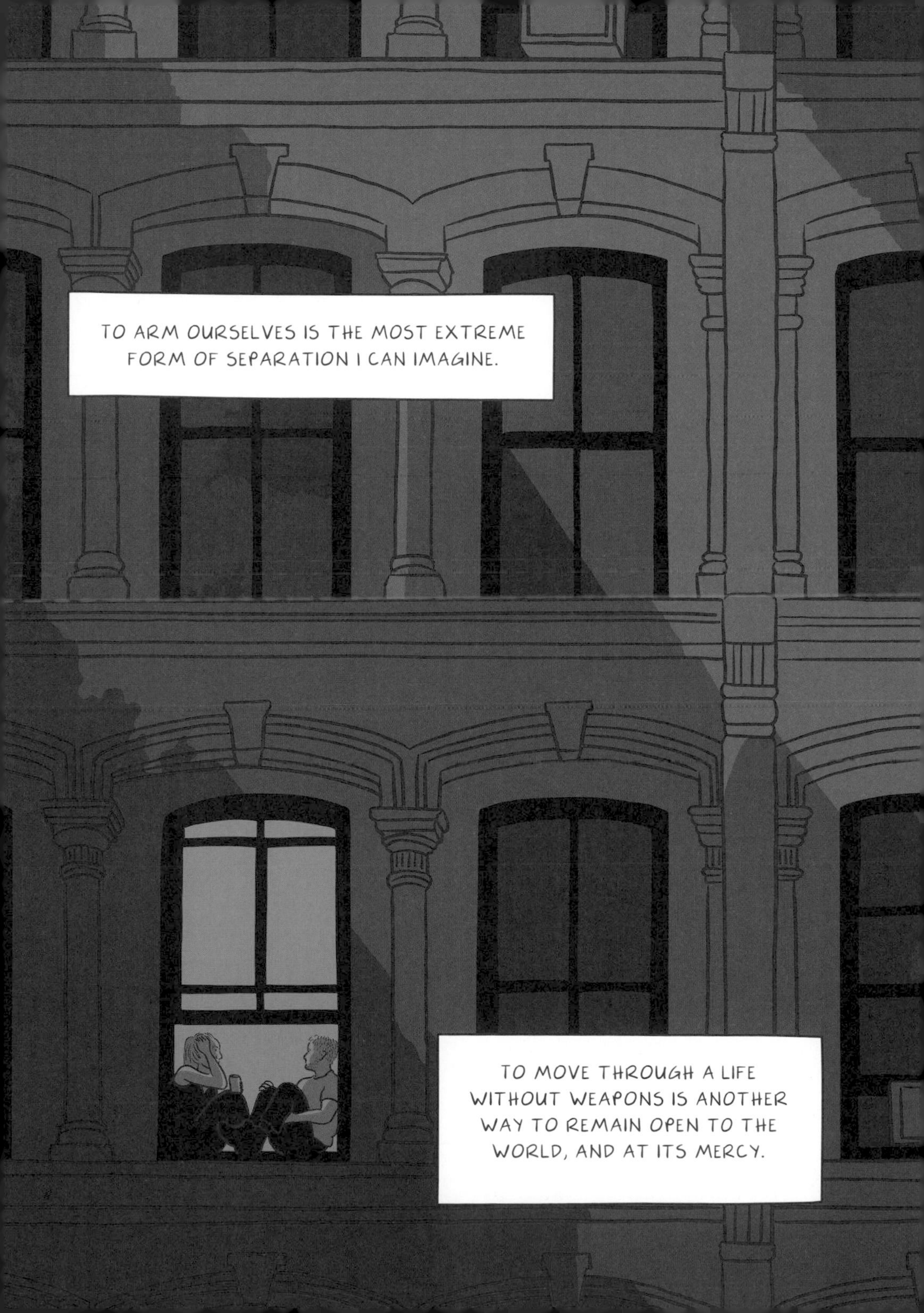
TO ARM OURSELVES IS THE MOST EXTREME FORM OF SEPARATION I CAN IMAGINE.
TO MOVE THROUGH A LIFE WITHOUT WEAPONS IS ANOTHER WAY TO REMAIN OPEN TO THE WORLD, AND AT ITS MERCY.

CLICK

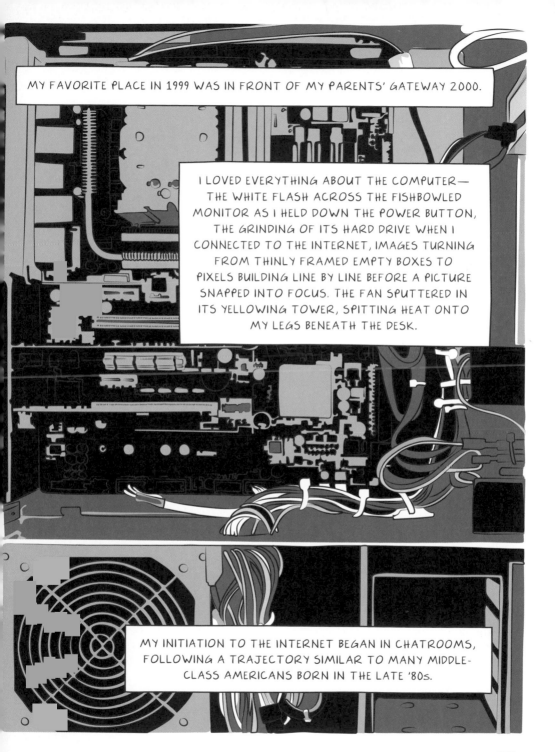

MY FAVORITE PLACE IN 1999 WAS IN FRONT OF MY PARENTS' GATEWAY 2000.

I LOVED EVERYTHING ABOUT THE COMPUTER— THE WHITE FLASH ACROSS THE FISHBOWLED MONITOR AS I HELD DOWN THE POWER BUTTON, THE GRINDING OF ITS HARD DRIVE WHEN I CONNECTED TO THE INTERNET, IMAGES TURNING FROM THINLY FRAMED EMPTY BOXES TO PIXELS BUILDING LINE BY LINE BEFORE A PICTURE SNAPPED INTO FOCUS. THE FAN SPUTTERED IN ITS YELLOWING TOWER, SPITTING HEAT ONTO MY LEGS BENEATH THE DESK.

MY INITIATION TO THE INTERNET BEGAN IN CHATROOMS, FOLLOWING A TRAJECTORY SIMILAR TO MANY MIDDLE-CLASS AMERICANS BORN IN THE LATE '80s.

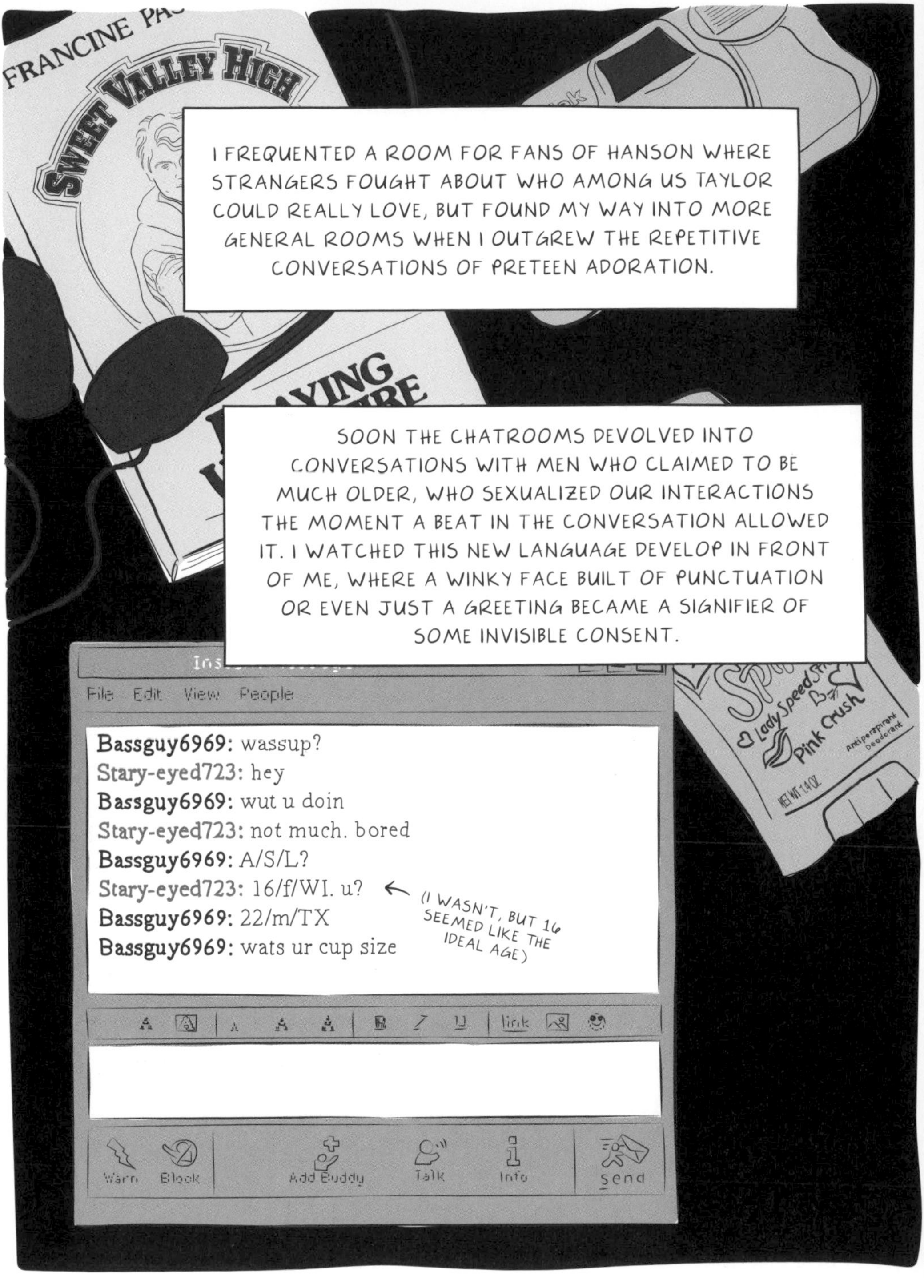
FRANCINE PAS
SWEET VALLEY HIGH
I FREQUENTED A ROOM FOR FANS OF HANSON WHERE STRANGERS FOUGHT ABOUT WHO AMONG US TAYLOR COULD REALLY LOVE, BUT FOUND MY WAY INTO MORE GENERAL ROOMS WHEN I OUTGREW THE REPETITIVE CONVERSATIONS OF PRETEEN ADORATION.
SOON THE CHATROOMS DEVOLVED INTO CONVERSATIONS WITH MEN WHO CLAIMED TO BE MUCH OLDER, WHO SEXUALIZED OUR INTERACTIONS THE MOMENT A BEAT IN THE CONVERSATION ALLOWED IT. I WATCHED THIS NEW LANGUAGE DEVELOP IN FRONT OF ME, WHERE A WINKY FACE BUILT OF PUNCTUATION OR EVEN JUST A GREETING BECAME A SIGNIFIER OF SOME INVISIBLE CONSENT.
File Edit View People
Bassguy6969: wassup?
Stary-eyed723: hey
Bassguy6969: wut u doin
Stary-eyed723: not much. bored
Bassguy6969: A/S/L?
Stary-eyed723: 16/f/WI. u?
Bassguy6969: 22/m/TX
Bassguy6969: wats ur cup size
(I WASN'T, BUT 16 SEEMED LIKE THE IDEAL AGE)
link
Warn Block Add Buddy Talk Info Send
Lady Speed Stick Pink Crush
Antiperspirant Deodorant
NET WT 1.4 OZ

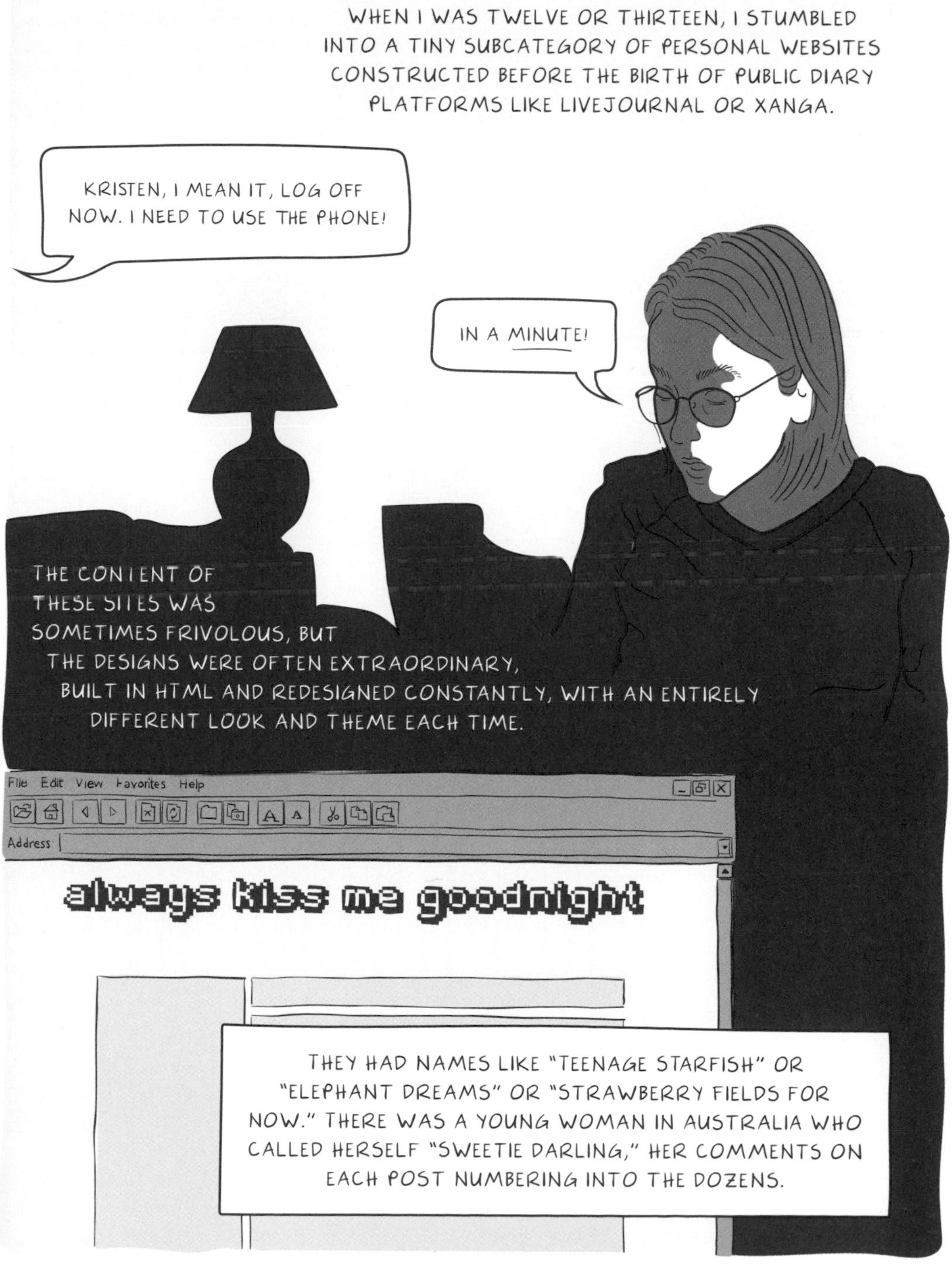

WHEN I WAS TWELVE OR THIRTEEN, I STUMBLED INTO A TINY SUBCATEGORY OF PERSONAL WEBSITES CONSTRUCTED BEFORE THE BIRTH OF PUBLIC DIARY PLATFORMS LIKE LIVEJOURNAL OR XANGA.
KRISTEN, I MEAN IT, LOG OFF NOW. I NEED TO USE THE PHONE!
IN A MINUTE!
THE CONTENT OF THESE SITES WAS SOMETIMES FRIVOLOUS, BUT THE DESIGNS WERE OFTEN EXTRAORDINARY, BUILT IN HTML AND REDESIGNED CONSTANTLY, WITH AN ENTIRELY DIFFERENT LOOK AND THEME EACH TIME.
File Edit View Favorites Help
Address
always kiss me goodnight
THEY HAD NAMES LIKE "TEENAGE STARFISH" OR "ELEPHANT DREAMS" OR "STRAWBERRY FIELDS FOR NOW." THERE WAS A YOUNG WOMAN IN AUSTRALIA WHO CALLED HERSELF "SWEETIE DARLING," HER COMMENTS ON EACH POST NUMBERING INTO THE DOZENS.

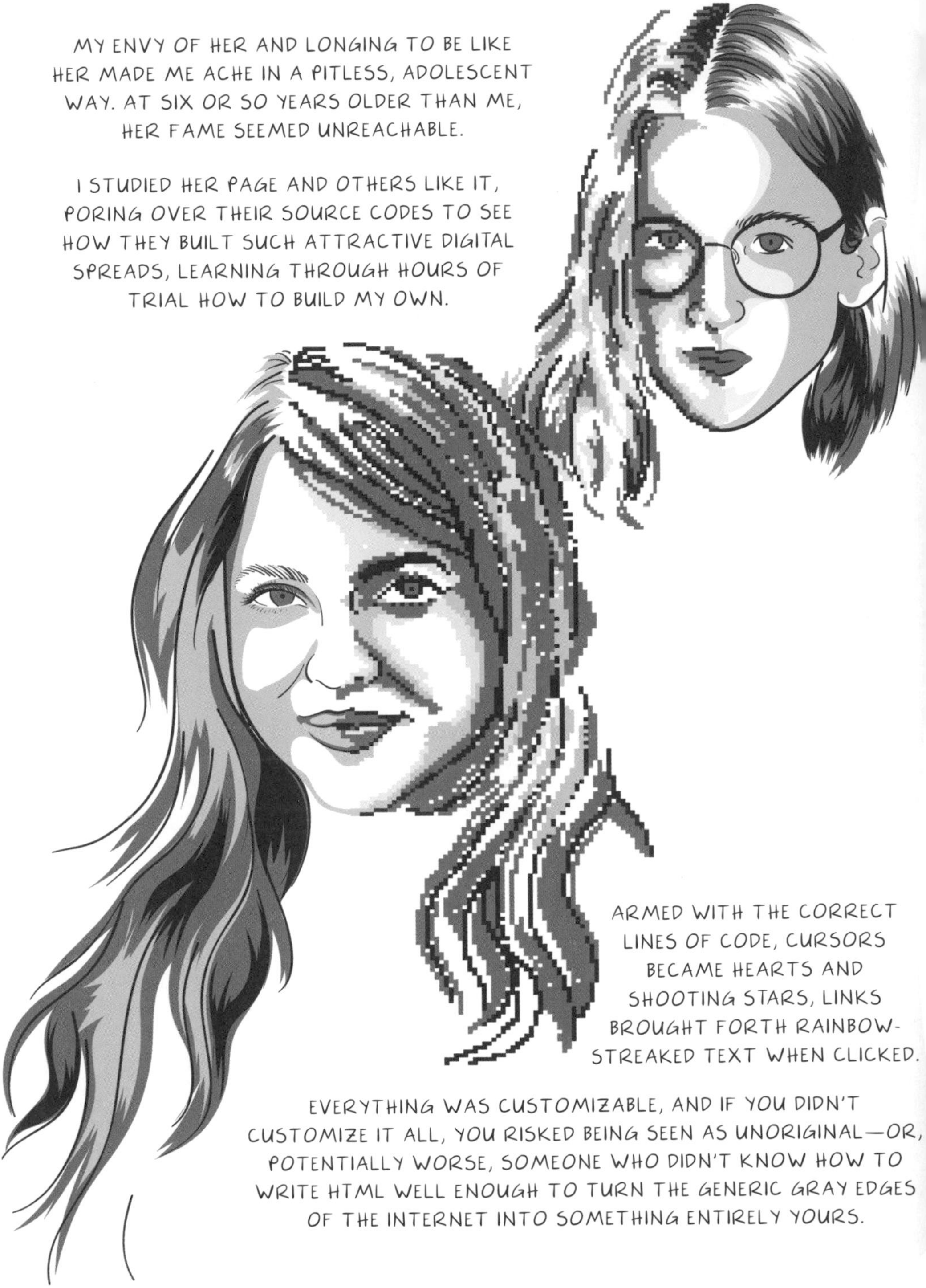
MY ENVY OF HER AND LONGING TO BE LIKE HER MADE ME ACHE IN A PITLESS, ADOLESCENT WAY. AT SIX OR SO YEARS OLDER THAN ME, HER FAME SEEMED UNREACHABLE.
I STUDIED HER PAGE AND OTHERS LIKE IT, PORING OVER THEIR SOURCE CODES TO SEE HOW THEY BUILT SUCH ATTRACTIVE DIGITAL SPREADS, LEARNING THROUGH HOURS OF TRIAL HOW TO BUILD MY OWN.
ARMED WITH THE CORRECT LINES OF CODE, CURSORS BECAME HEARTS AND SHOOTING STARS, LINKS BROUGHT FORTH RAINBOW-STREAKED TEXT WHEN CLICKED.
EVERYTHING WAS CUSTOMIZABLE, AND IF YOU DIDN'T CUSTOMIZE IT ALL, YOU RISKED BEING SEEN AS UNORIGINAL—OR, POTENTIALLY WORSE, SOMEONE WHO DIDN'T KNOW HOW TO WRITE HTML WELL ENOUGH TO TURN THE GENERIC GRAY EDGES OF THE INTERNET INTO SOMETHING ENTIRELY YOURS.

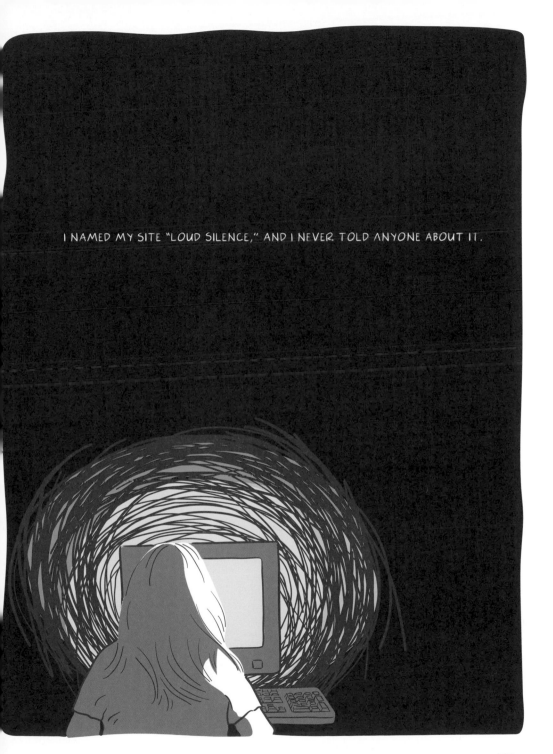

I NAMED MY SITE "LOUD SILENCE," AND I NEVER TOLD ANYONE ABOUT IT.

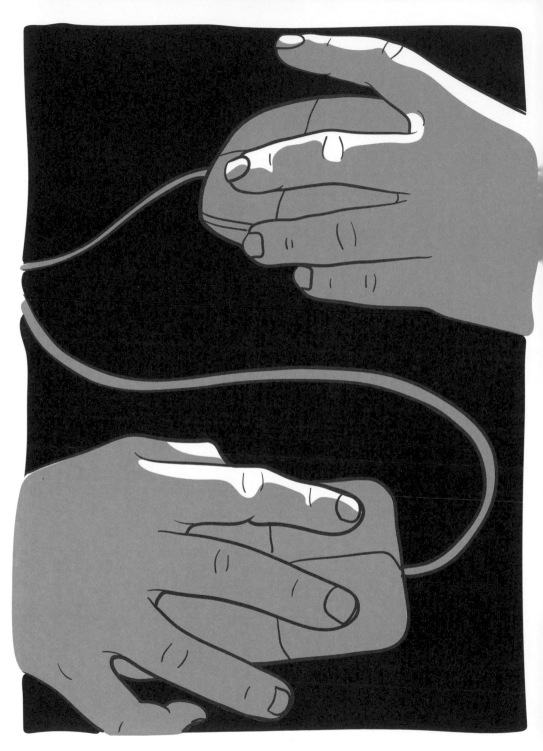

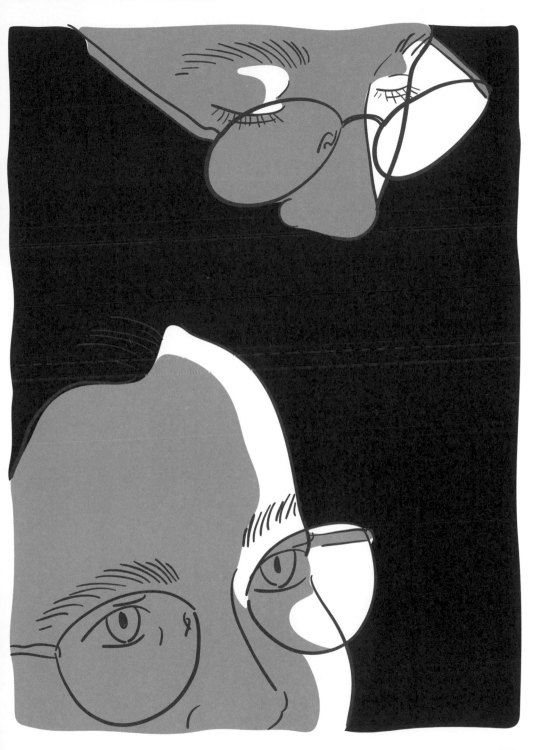

185

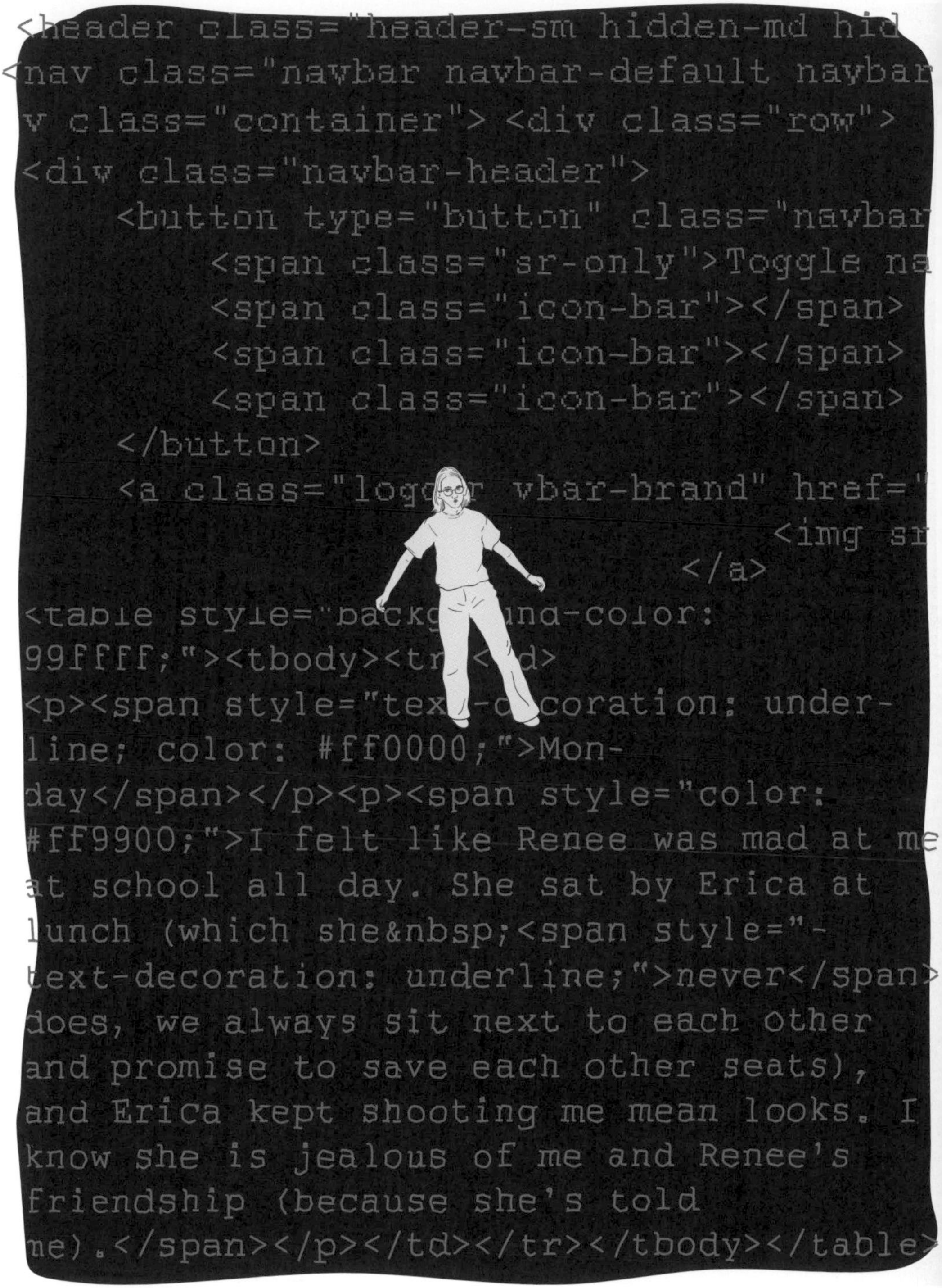

```html
<header class="header-sm hidden-md hid
<nav class="navbar navbar-default navbar
v class="container"> <div class="row">
<div class="navbar-header">
    <button type="button" class="navbar
        <span class="sr-only">Toggle na
        <span class="icon-bar"></span>
        <span class="icon-bar"></span>
        <span class="icon-bar"></span>
    </button>
    <a class="logo     vbar-brand" href="
                        <img sr
                   </a>
<table style="background-color:
99ffff;"><tbody><tr><td>
<p><span style="text-decoration: under-
line; color: #ff0000;">Mon-
day</span></p><p><span style="color:
#ff9900;">I felt like Renee was mad at me
at school all day. She sat by Erica at
lunch (which she <span style="-
text-decoration: underline;">never</span>
does, we always sit next to each other
and promise to save each other seats),
and Erica kept shooting me mean looks. I
know she is jealous of me and Renee's
friendship (because she's told
me).</span></p></td></tr></tbody></table>
```

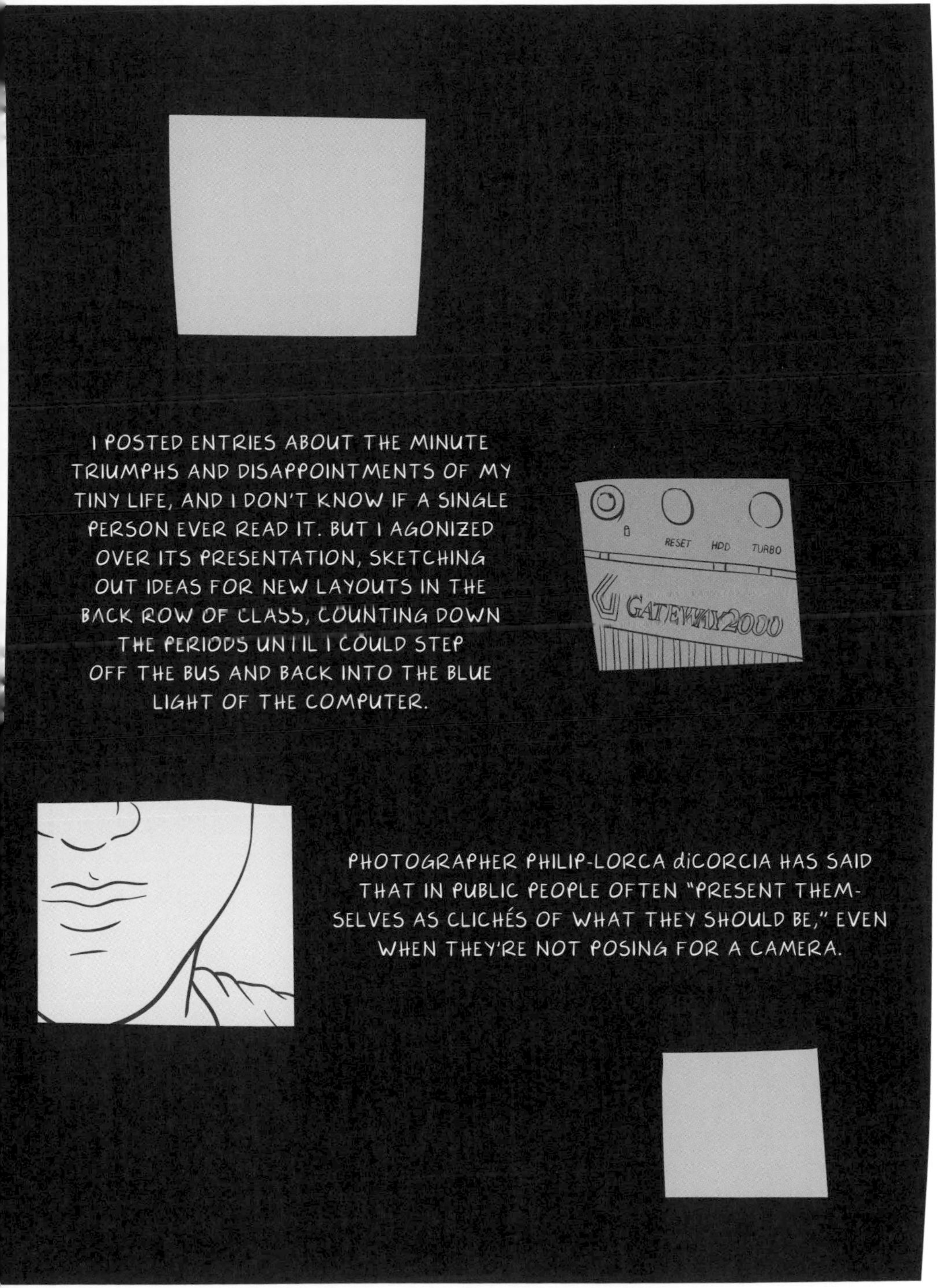
I POSTED ENTRIES ABOUT THE MINUTE TRIUMPHS AND DISAPPOINTMENTS OF MY TINY LIFE, AND I DON'T KNOW IF A SINGLE PERSON EVER READ IT. BUT I AGONIZED OVER ITS PRESENTATION, SKETCHING OUT IDEAS FOR NEW LAYOUTS IN THE BACK ROW OF CLASS, COUNTING DOWN THE PERIODS UNTIL I COULD STEP OFF THE BUS AND BACK INTO THE BLUE LIGHT OF THE COMPUTER.
RESET
HDD
TURBO
GATEWAY2000
PHOTOGRAPHER PHILIP-LORCA diCORCIA HAS SAID THAT IN PUBLIC PEOPLE OFTEN "PRESENT THEMSELVES AS CLICHÉS OF WHAT THEY SHOULD BE," EVEN WHEN THEY'RE NOT POSING FOR A CAMERA.

WE PERFORM FOR ONE ANOTHER ALL THE TIME, EVEN WHEN WE'RE ALONE, OR WHEN MASKED BY A CROWD'S ANONYMITY, IMPOSING THE VANTAGE POINT OF A NONEXISTENT VIEWER, PRETENDING AT LIFE THE WAY WE'VE SEEN IT ONSCREEN OUR WHOLE LIVES.

"LOUD SILENCE" WAS LIKE THIS FOR ME DURING MY PRETEEN YEARS. I'VE NEVER SPENT SO MUCH TIME MANUFACTURING VISIBILITY WITH LOWER STAKES.

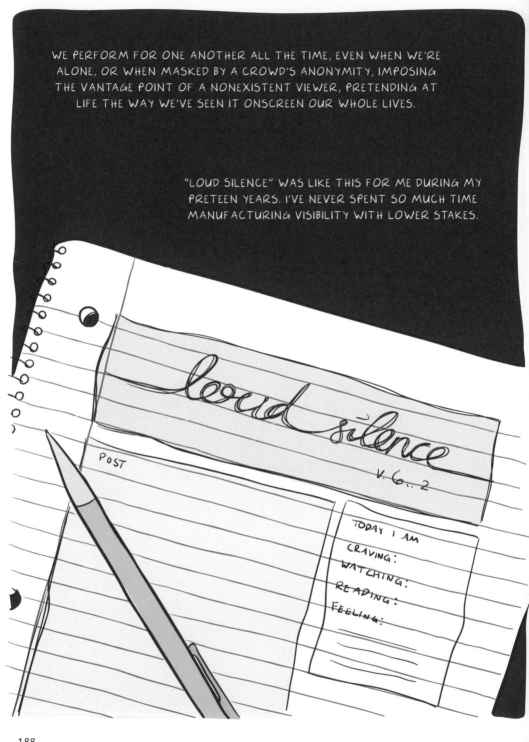

loud silence

v. 6.. 2

POST

TODAY I AM
CRAVING:
WATCHING:
READING:
FEELING:

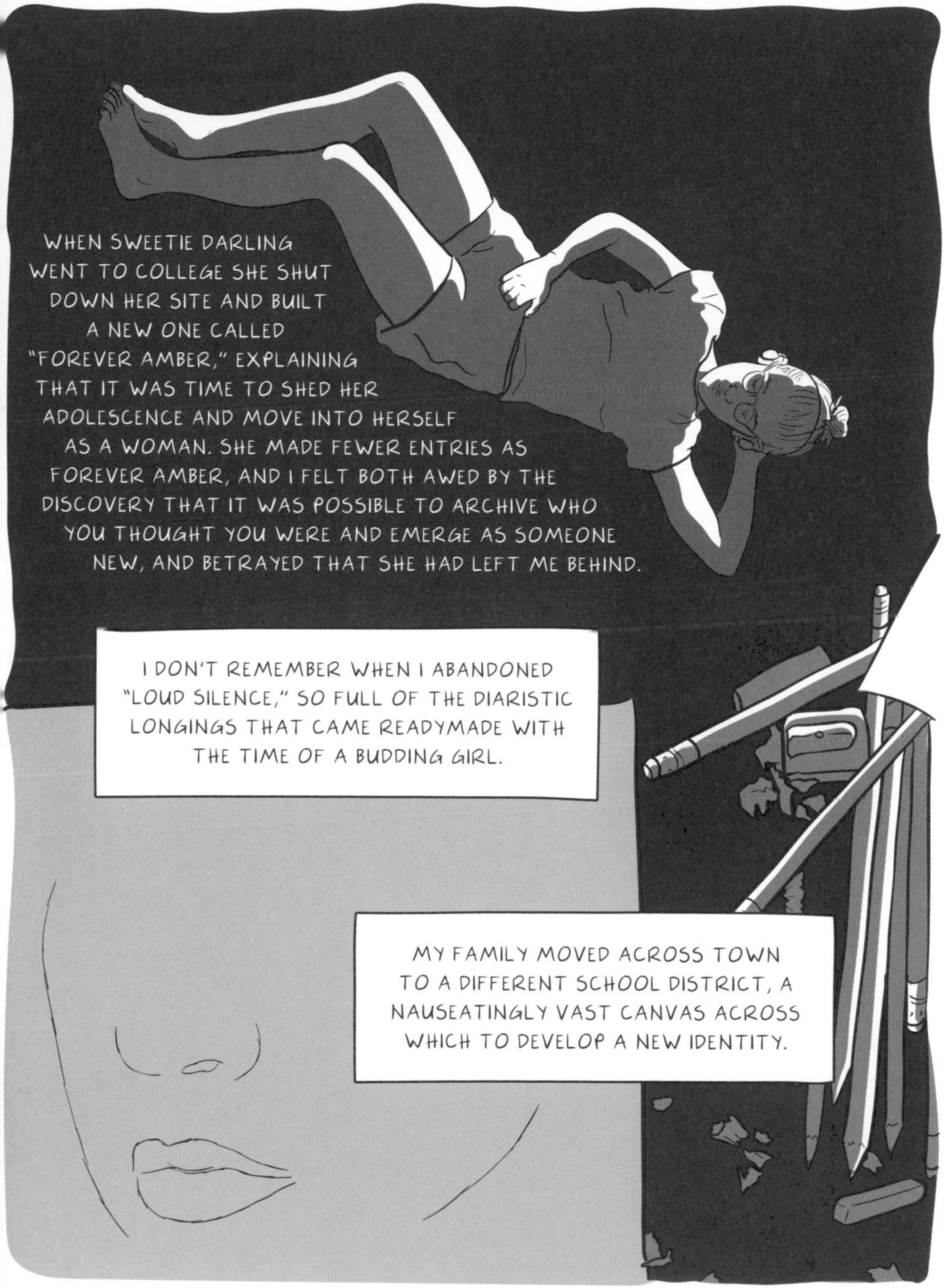
WHEN SWEETIE DARLING WENT TO COLLEGE SHE SHUT DOWN HER SITE AND BUILT A NEW ONE CALLED "FOREVER AMBER," EXPLAINING THAT IT WAS TIME TO SHED HER ADOLESCENCE AND MOVE INTO HERSELF AS A WOMAN. SHE MADE FEWER ENTRIES AS FOREVER AMBER, AND I FELT BOTH AWED BY THE DISCOVERY THAT IT WAS POSSIBLE TO ARCHIVE WHO YOU THOUGHT YOU WERE AND EMERGE AS SOMEONE NEW, AND BETRAYED THAT SHE HAD LEFT ME BEHIND.
I DON'T REMEMBER WHEN I ABANDONED "LOUD SILENCE," SO FULL OF THE DIARISTIC LONGINGS THAT CAME READYMADE WITH THE TIME OF A BUDDING GIRL.
MY FAMILY MOVED ACROSS TOWN TO A DIFFERENT SCHOOL DISTRICT, A NAUSEATINGLY VAST CANVAS ACROSS WHICH TO DEVELOP A NEW IDENTITY.

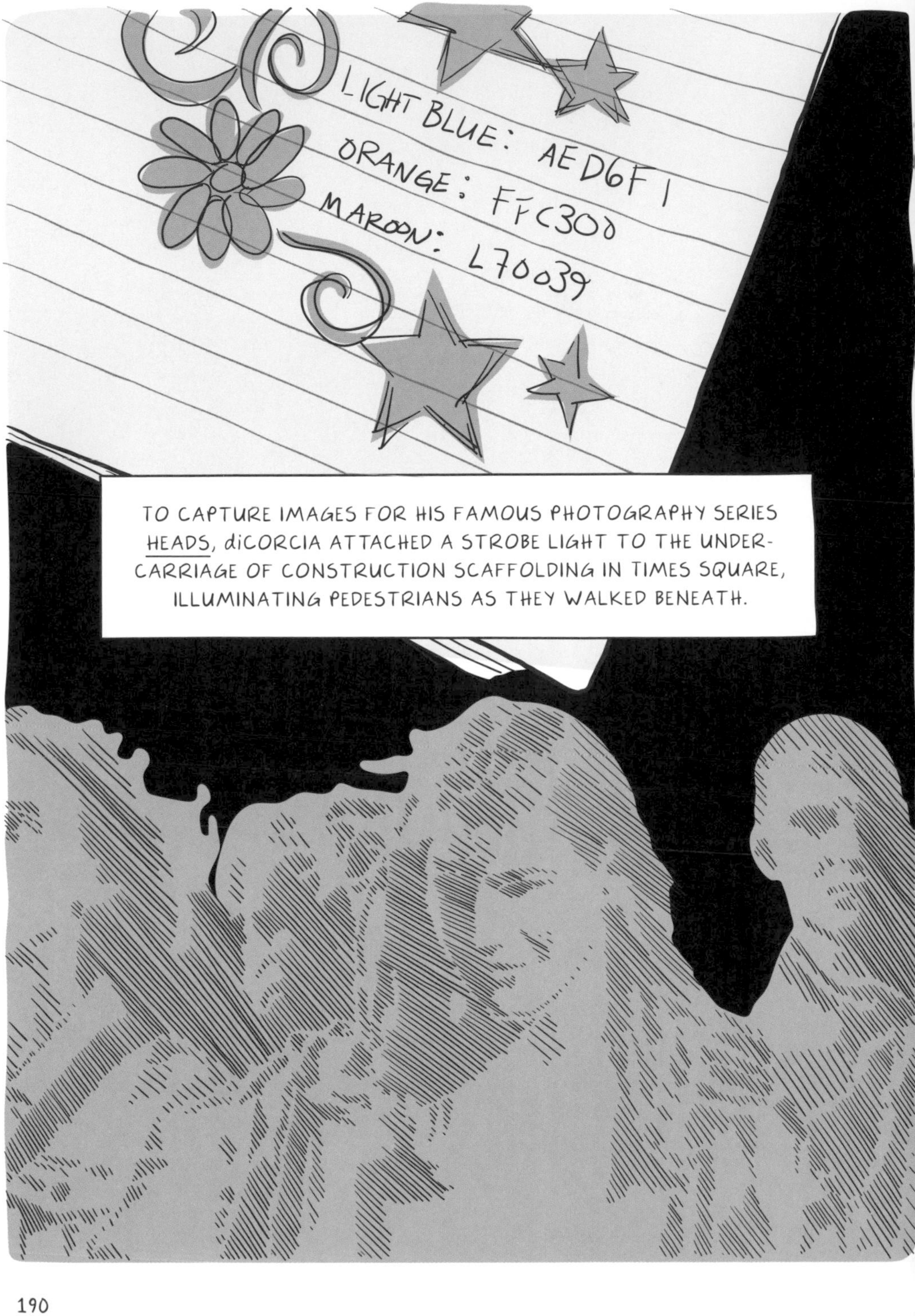
LIGHT BLUE: AED6F1
ORANGE: FFC300
MAROON: C70039
TO CAPTURE IMAGES FOR HIS FAMOUS PHOTOGRAPHY SERIES HEADS, diCORCIA ATTACHED A STROBE LIGHT TO THE UNDER-CARRIAGE OF CONSTRUCTION SCAFFOLDING IN TIMES SQUARE, ILLUMINATING PEDESTRIANS AS THEY WALKED BENEATH.

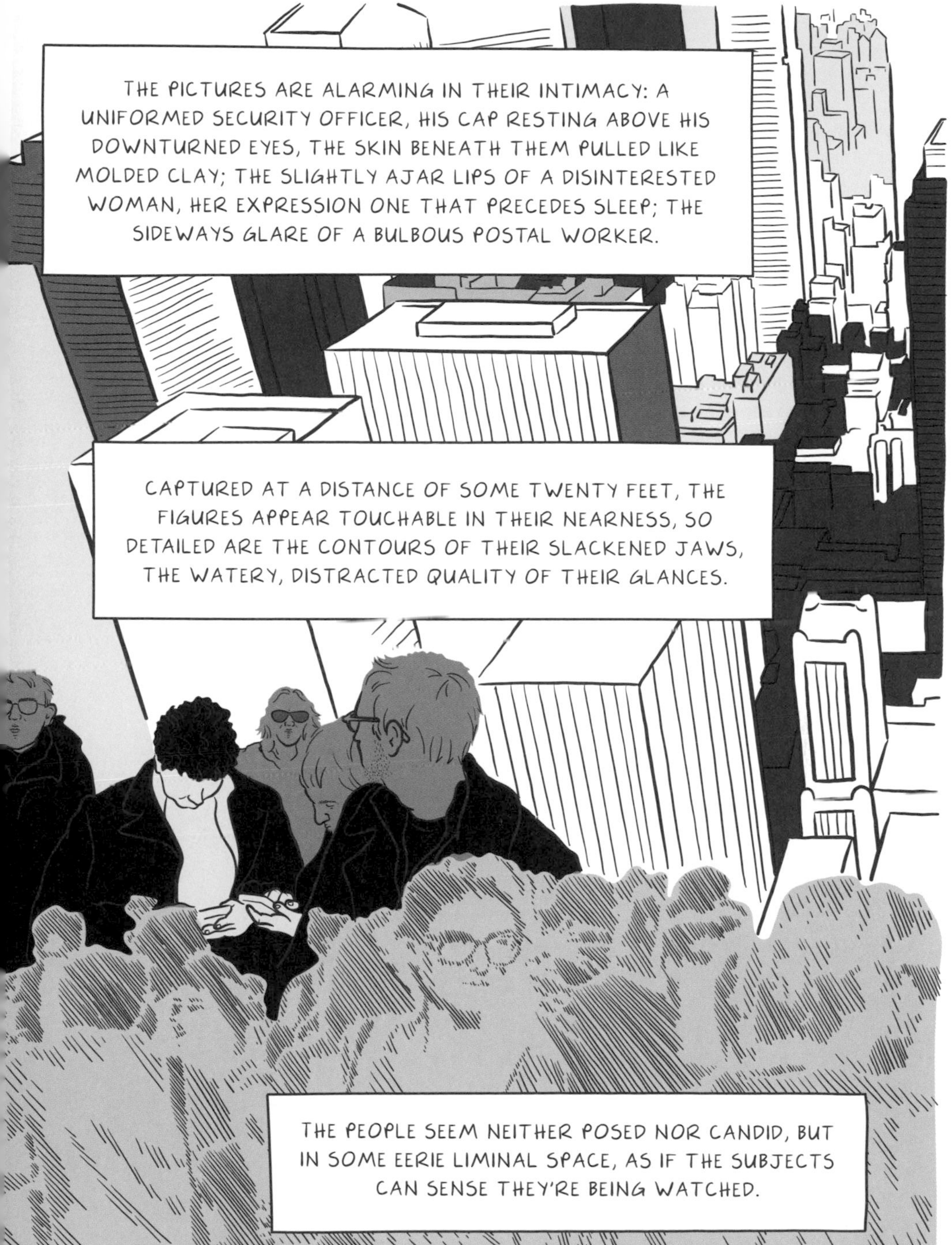
THE PICTURES ARE ALARMING IN THEIR INTIMACY: A UNIFORMED SECURITY OFFICER, HIS CAP RESTING ABOVE HIS DOWNTURNED EYES, THE SKIN BENEATH THEM PULLED LIKE MOLDED CLAY; THE SLIGHTLY AJAR LIPS OF A DISINTERESTED WOMAN, HER EXPRESSION ONE THAT PRECEDES SLEEP; THE SIDEWAYS GLARE OF A BULBOUS POSTAL WORKER.
CAPTURED AT A DISTANCE OF SOME TWENTY FEET, THE FIGURES APPEAR TOUCHABLE IN THEIR NEARNESS, SO DETAILED ARE THE CONTOURS OF THEIR SLACKENED JAWS, THE WATERY, DISTRACTED QUALITY OF THEIR GLANCES.
THE PEOPLE SEEM NEITHER POSED NOR CANDID, BUT IN SOME EERIE LIMINAL SPACE, AS IF THE SUBJECTS CAN SENSE THEY'RE BEING WATCHED.

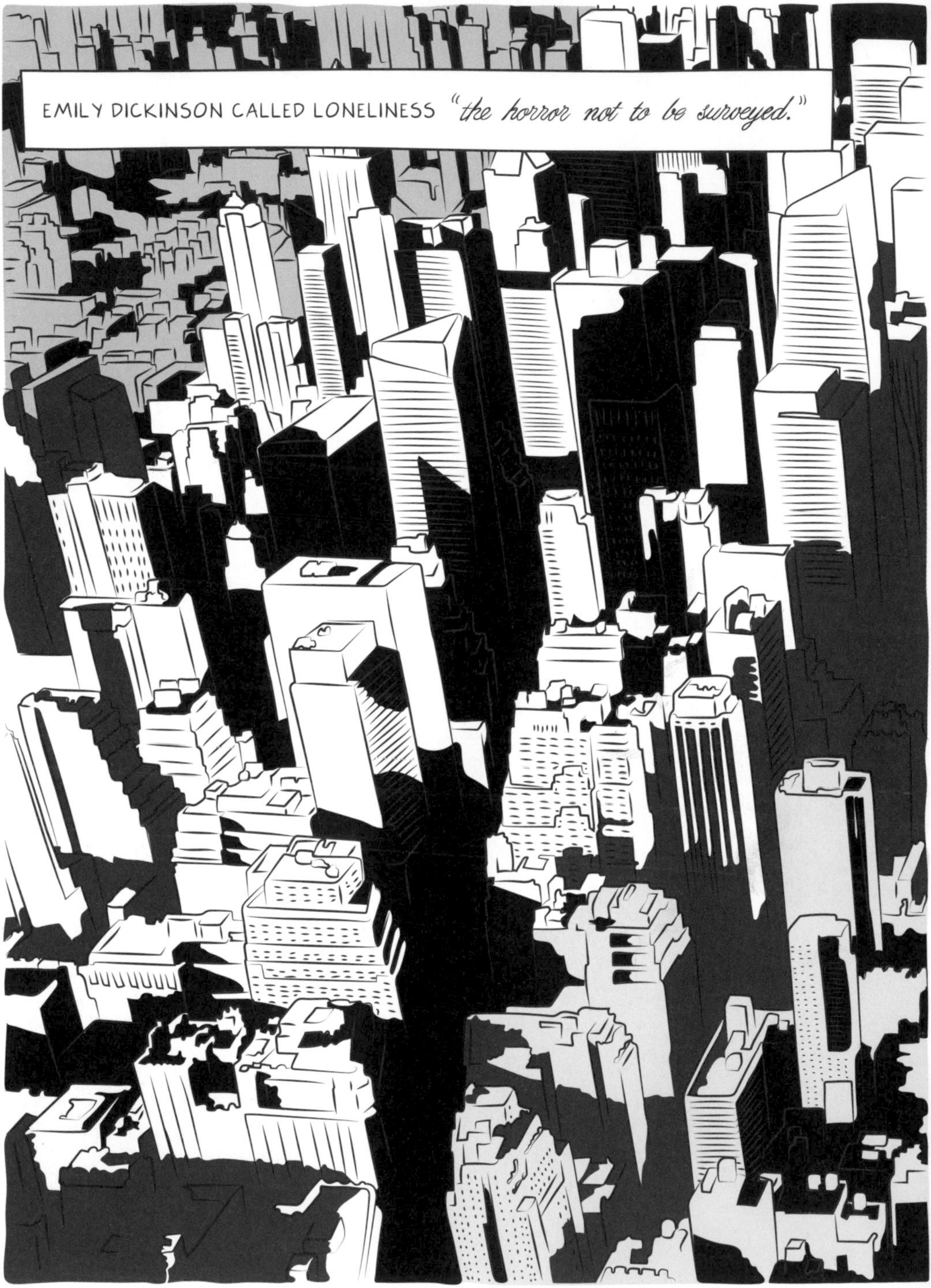
EMILY DICKINSON CALLED LONELINESS "the horror not to be surveyed."

I LOVE THIS DEFINITION, THE IDEA THAT TO BE UNSEEN IS THE PUNCTURE FROM WHICH LONELINESS UNSPOOLS.

IN CHILDHOOD WE ARE OFTEN MORE SURVEILLED THAN SURVEYED. I IMAGINED MY PERFECTLY COMFORTABLE LIFE TO BE FILLED WITH A SUFFERING NO ONE UNDERSTOOD SIMPLY BECAUSE MY LIFE DIDN'T MEAN ANYTHING YET, POPULATED BY CHOICES OTHERS HAD MADE FOR ME.

ADOLESCENCE WAS CHARTED BY THE QUIET HYSTERIA OF UNPUNCTUATED TIME MIXED WITH THRILLS OF FRUSTRATION WHEN I WAS FORCED OUTSIDE MY BROODING TOWARD FAMILY DINNER OR CHORES OR, WORSE, A LONG CAR RIDE TOWARD A LOCATION WITH EVEN LESS TO OFFER, LIKE MY GRAND- MOTHER'S HOUSE, OR A ROADSIDE MOTEL WITHOUT CABLE OR A POOL.

EVEN MOMENTS OF TRIUMPH BRIMMED WITH UNCERTAINTY, LIKE WHEN I'D CONVINCE MY PARENTS TO GRANT ME ATTENDANCE TO A SLEEPOVER, ONLY TO FACE THE ANXIETY OF WAKING UP IN AN UNFAMILIAR HOUSE BEFORE MY FRIENDS, NOT KNOWING WHAT TO DO WITH MYSELF IN A STRANGE ROOM WITH SOMEONE ELSE'S GRANDFATHER CLOCK CHIMING DOWN THE HALL.

The Barn
RESTAURANT
GREAT FOOD
OPEN

WHEN I OBSERVE TEENAGERS IN PUBLIC NOW, I SOMETIMES WONDER IF THEIR EXPERIENCE OF ADOLESCENCE HAS ANY OVER-LAP WITH MINE, BECAUSE THE ACCESS I HAD TO THE WORLD— OR EVEN INFORMATION—SEEMS DOWNRIGHT QUAINT WHEN JUXTAPOSED WITH WHAT'S AVAILABLE TO A BORED THIRTEEN-YEAR-OLD TODAY.

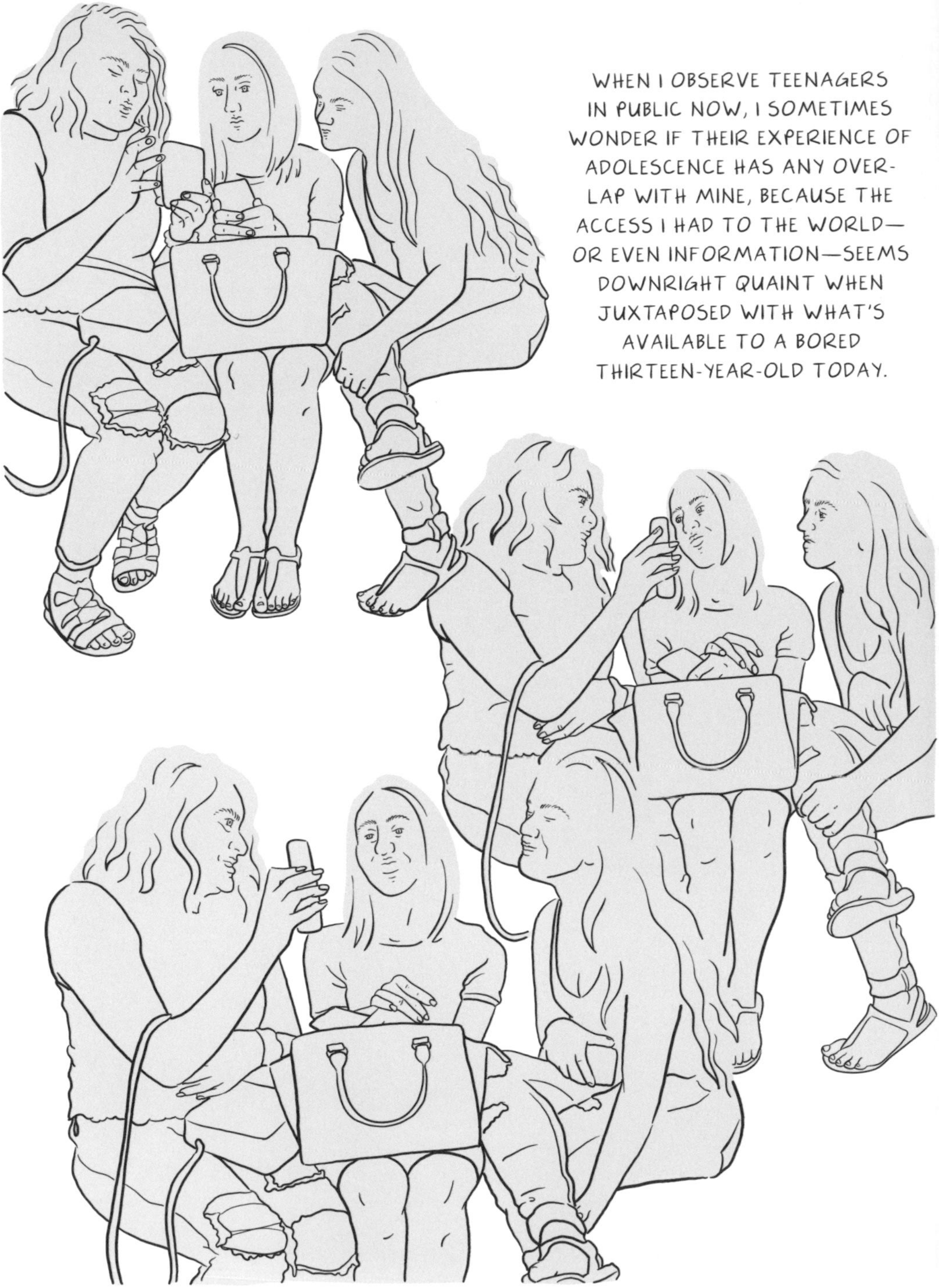

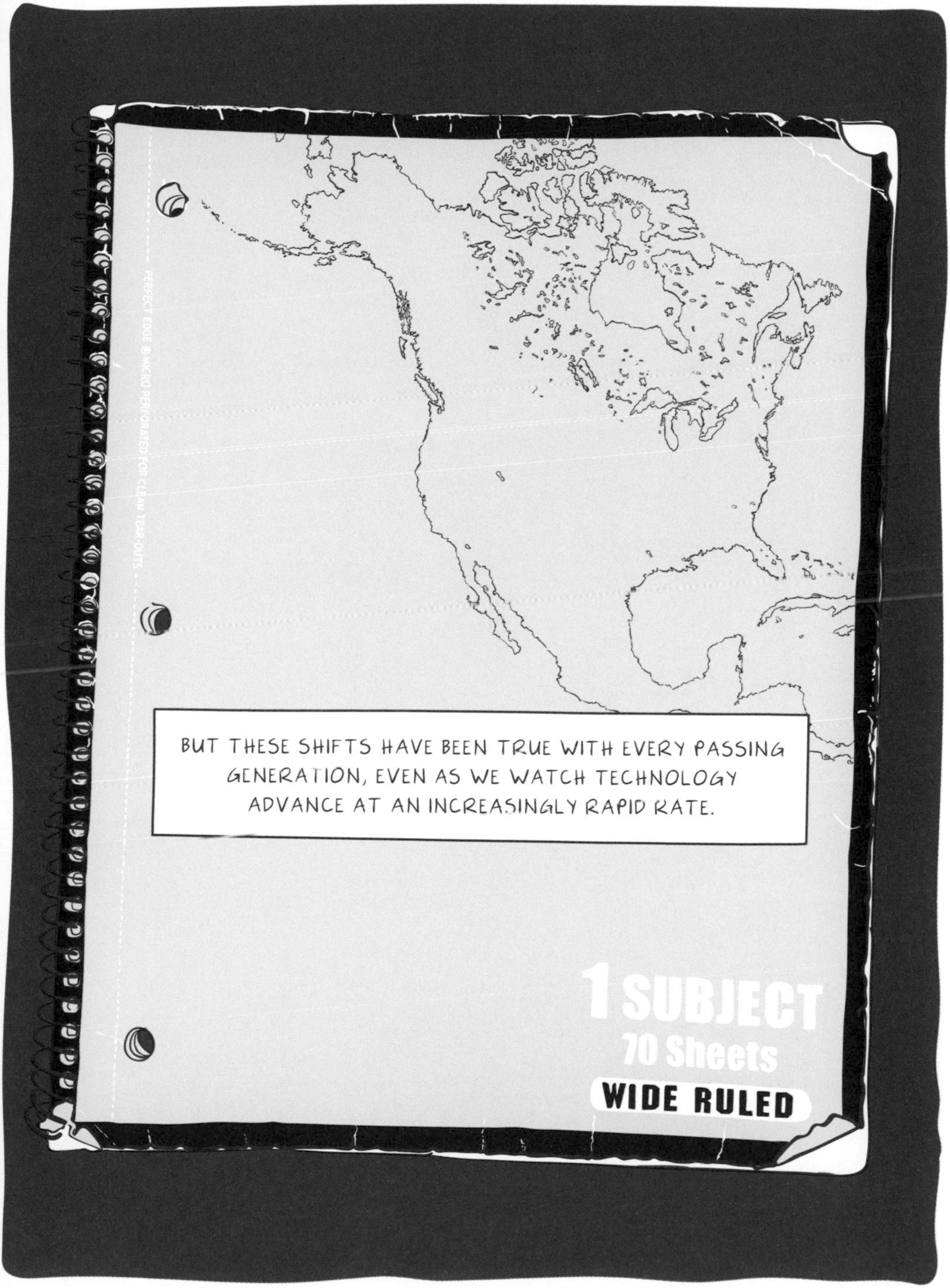

PERFECT EDGE ® MICRO PERFORATED FOR CLEAN TEAR-OUTS
BUT THESE SHIFTS HAVE BEEN TRUE WITH EVERY PASSING GENERATION, EVEN AS WE WATCH TECHNOLOGY ADVANCE AT AN INCREASINGLY RAPID RATE.
1 SUBJECT
70 Sheets
WIDE RULED

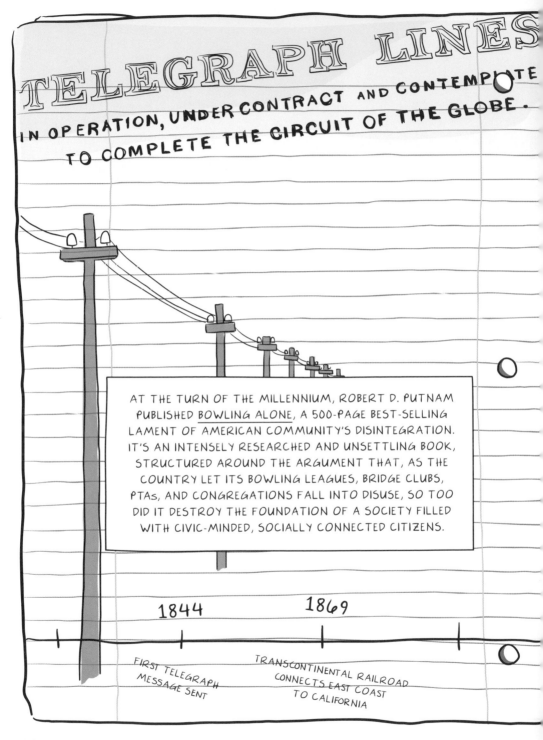

TELEGRAPH LINES

IN OPERATION, UNDER CONTRACT AND CONTEMPLATE TO COMPLETE THE CIRCUIT OF THE GLOBE.

AT THE TURN OF THE MILLENNIUM, ROBERT D. PUTNAM PUBLISHED BOWLING ALONE, A 500-PAGE BEST-SELLING LAMENT OF AMERICAN COMMUNITY'S DISINTEGRATION. IT'S AN INTENSELY RESEARCHED AND UNSETTLING BOOK, STRUCTURED AROUND THE ARGUMENT THAT, AS THE COUNTRY LET ITS BOWLING LEAGUES, BRIDGE CLUBS, PTAs, AND CONGREGATIONS FALL INTO DISUSE, SO TOO DID IT DESTROY THE FOUNDATION OF A SOCIETY FILLED WITH CIVIC-MINDED, SOCIALLY CONNECTED CITIZENS.

1844

1869

FIRST TELEGRAPH MESSAGE SENT

TRANSCONTINENTAL RAILROAD CONNECTS EAST COAST TO CALIFORNIA

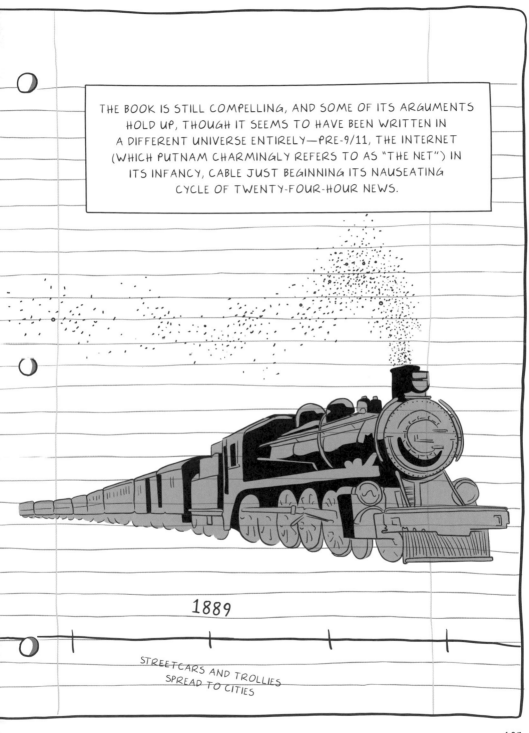

THE BOOK IS STILL COMPELLING, AND SOME OF ITS ARGUMENTS HOLD UP, THOUGH IT SEEMS TO HAVE BEEN WRITTEN IN A DIFFERENT UNIVERSE ENTIRELY—PRE-9/11, THE INTERNET (WHICH PUTNAM CHARMINGLY REFERS TO AS "THE NET") IN ITS INFANCY, CABLE JUST BEGINNING ITS NAUSEATING CYCLE OF TWENTY-FOUR-HOUR NEWS.

1889

STREETCARS AND TROLLIES
SPREAD TO CITIES

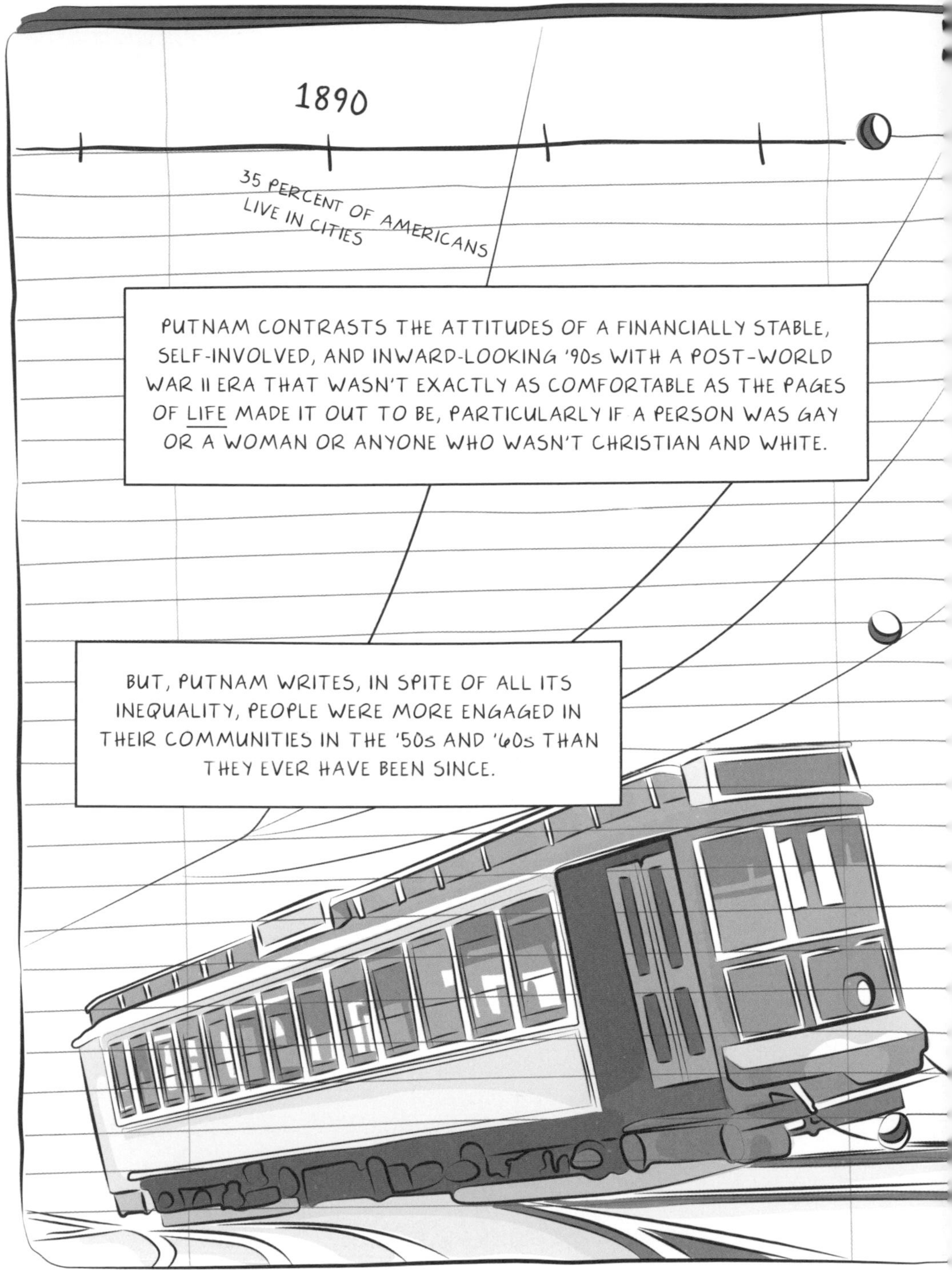
1890
35 PERCENT OF AMERICANS LIVE IN CITIES
PUTNAM CONTRASTS THE ATTITUDES OF A FINANCIALLY STABLE, SELF-INVOLVED, AND INWARD-LOOKING '90s WITH A POST-WORLD WAR II ERA THAT WASN'T EXACTLY AS COMFORTABLE AS THE PAGES OF LIFE MADE IT OUT TO BE, PARTICULARLY IF A PERSON WAS GAY OR A WOMAN OR ANYONE WHO WASN'T CHRISTIAN AND WHITE.
BUT, PUTNAM WRITES, IN SPITE OF ALL ITS INEQUALITY, PEOPLE WERE MORE ENGAGED IN THEIR COMMUNITIES IN THE '50s AND '60s THAN THEY EVER HAVE BEEN SINCE.

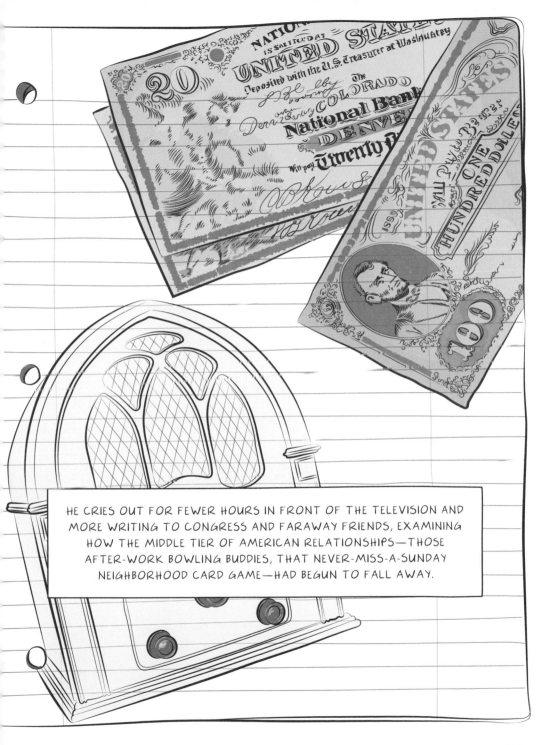

HE CRIES OUT FOR FEWER HOURS IN FRONT OF THE TELEVISION AND MORE WRITING TO CONGRESS AND FARAWAY FRIENDS, EXAMINING HOW THE MIDDLE TIER OF AMERICAN RELATIONSHIPS—THOSE AFTER-WORK BOWLING BUDDIES, THAT NEVER-MISS-A-SUNDAY NEIGHBORHOOD CARD GAME—HAD BEGUN TO FALL AWAY.

SCHOLARS OF EVERY ERA BEMOAN THE PERCEIVED DOWNFALL OF THEIR COLLECTIVE CULTURES, YEARNING FOR A TIME WHEN PEOPLE WERE LESS DETACHED AND LESS DEPRAVED.

"WE SHALL SOON BE NOTHING BUT TRANSPARENT HEAPS OF JELLY TO EACH OTHER," THE NEW YORK TIMES REPORTED IN A SPECTACULARLY VIVID RESPONSE TO THE TELEPHONE'S INVENTION, FEARING IT'D DEMOLISH OUR ABILITY FOR COMMUNICATION BUILT ON GESTURE AND FACE-TO-FACE CONTACT.

THE RADIO WAS MET WITH SIMILAR CONCERNS THAT WE'D NEVER AGAIN APPROACH OUR LIVES UNDISTRACTED.

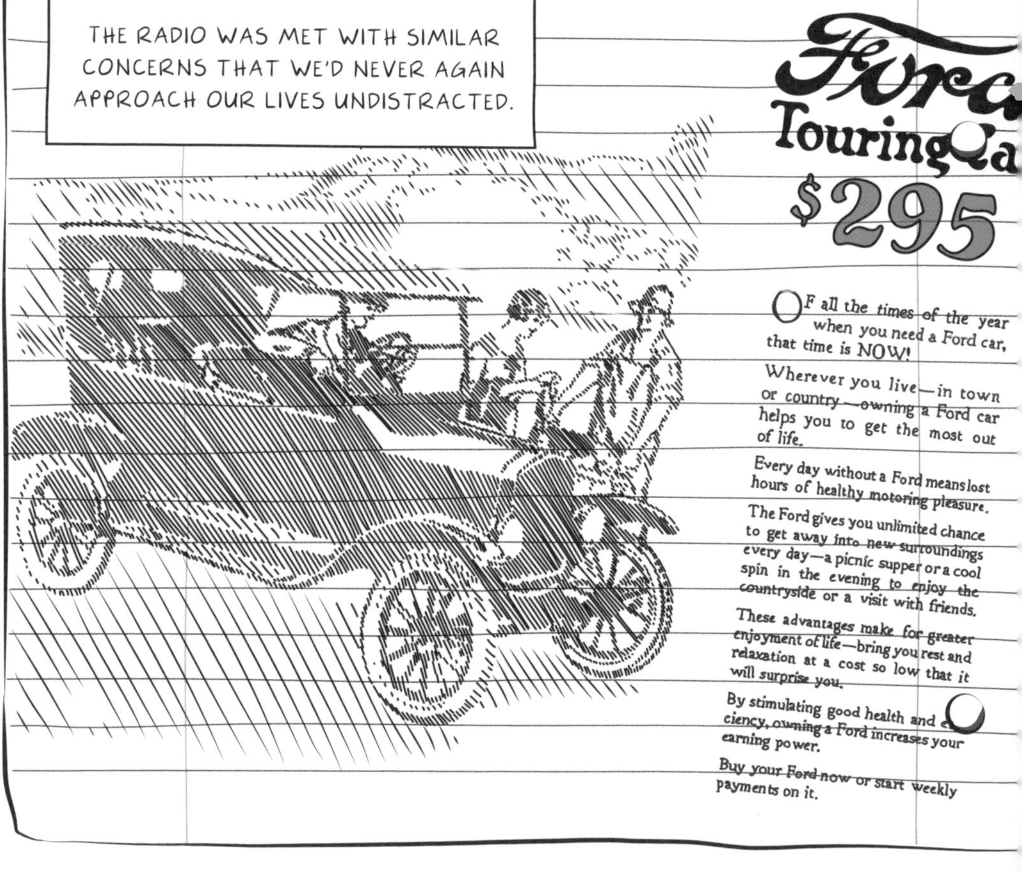

Touring
$295
OF all the times of the year when you need a Ford car, that time is NOW!
Wherever you live—in town or country—owning a Ford car helps you to get the most out of life.
Every day without a Ford means lost hours of healthy motoring pleasure.
The Ford gives you unlimited chance to get away into new surroundings every day—a picnic supper or a cool spin in the evening to enjoy the countryside or a visit with friends.
These advantages make for greater enjoyment of life—bring you rest and relaxation at a cost so low that it will surprise you.
By stimulating good health and e ciency, owning a Ford increases your earning power.
Buy your Ford now or start weekly payments on it.

"OF COURSE I CAN!

ANY NEW TOOL—A TRAIN, A TELEGRAPH, A TELEVISION—
CAN BE USED, ULTIMATELY, TO ESCAPE, OR TO BYPASS THOSE
AROUND US MOST IMMEDIATELY IN FAVOR OF SOMEONE OR
SOMETHING WHOSE COMPANY WE'D PREFER ELSEWHERE.

I'm patriotic as can be —
And ration points won't worry me!"

1950s   1960s

ORGANIZED LABOR
MAKES UP A THIRD
OF THE WORKFORCE

COMMERCIAL
AIRLINE TRAVEL
POPULARIZED

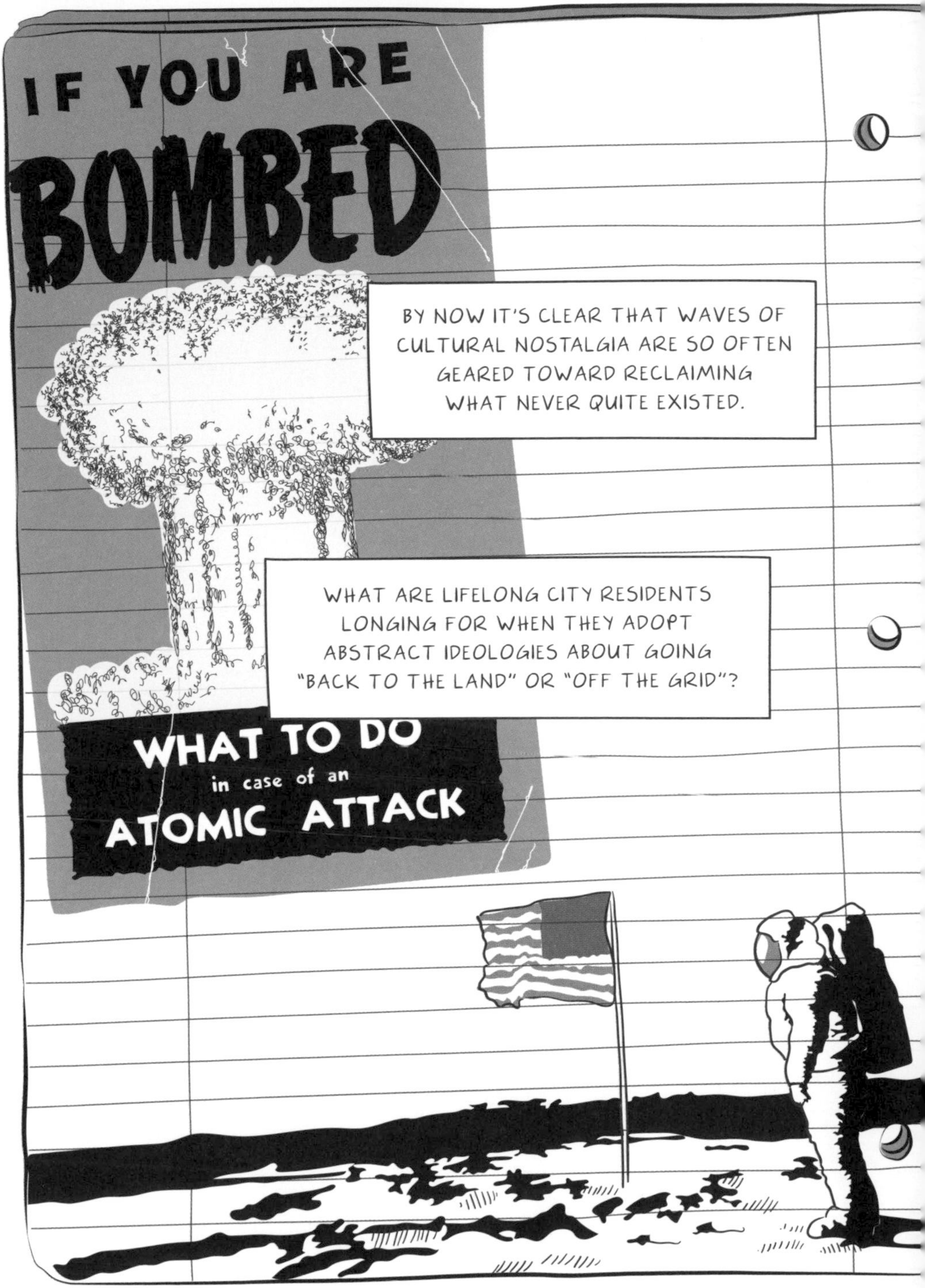
IF YOU ARE
BOMBED
BY NOW IT'S CLEAR THAT WAVES OF CULTURAL NOSTALGIA ARE SO OFTEN GEARED TOWARD RECLAIMING WHAT NEVER QUITE EXISTED.
WHAT ARE LIFELONG CITY RESIDENTS LONGING FOR WHEN THEY ADOPT ABSTRACT IDEOLOGIES ABOUT GOING "BACK TO THE LAND" OR "OFF THE GRID"?
WHAT TO DO
in case of an
ATOMIC ATTACK

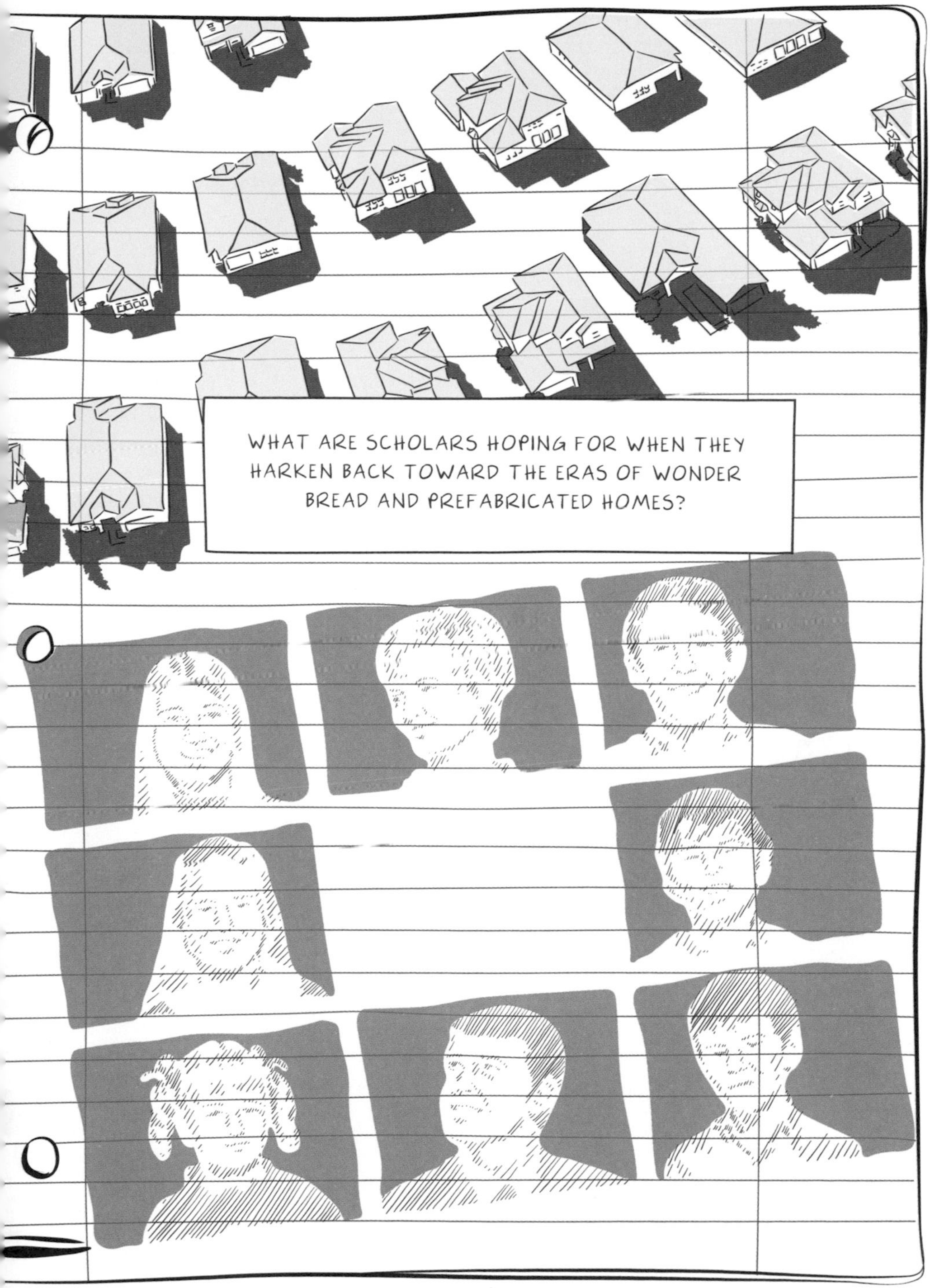
WHAT ARE SCHOLARS HOPING FOR WHEN THEY HARKEN BACK TOWARD THE ERAS OF WONDER BREAD AND PREFABRICATED HOMES?

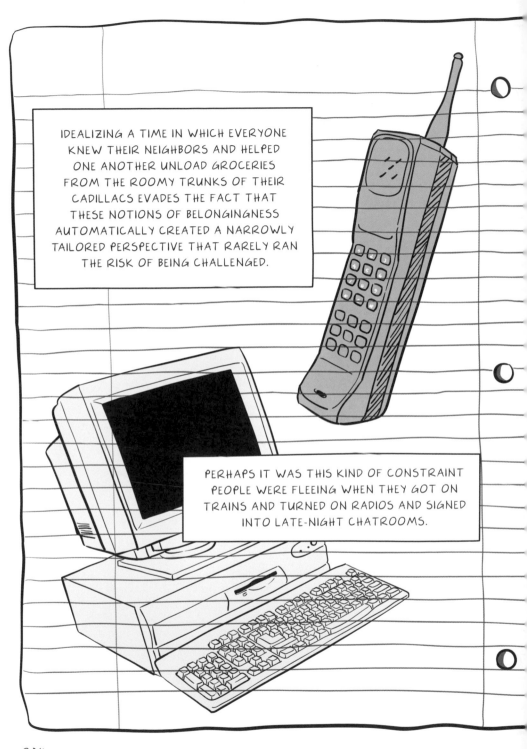

IDEALIZING A TIME IN WHICH EVERYONE
KNEW THEIR NEIGHBORS AND HELPED
ONE ANOTHER UNLOAD GROCERIES
FROM THE ROOMY TRUNKS OF THEIR
CADILLACS EVADES THE FACT THAT
THESE NOTIONS OF BELONGINGNESS
AUTOMATICALLY CREATED A NARROWLY
TAILORED PERSPECTIVE THAT RARELY RAN
THE RISK OF BEING CHALLENGED.

PERHAPS IT WAS THIS KIND OF CONSTRAINT
PEOPLE WERE FLEEING WHEN THEY GOT ON
TRAINS AND TURNED ON RADIOS AND SIGNED
INTO LATE-NIGHT CHATROOMS.

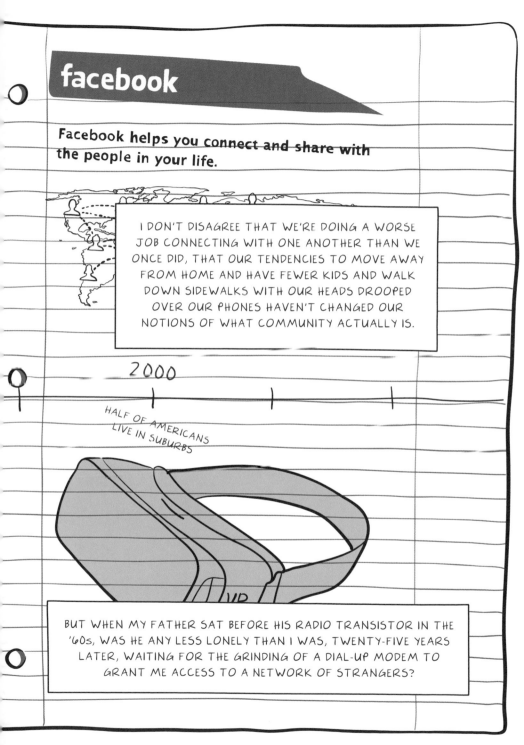

facebook

Facebook helps you connect and share with the people in your life.

I DON'T DISAGREE THAT WE'RE DOING A WORSE JOB CONNECTING WITH ONE ANOTHER THAN WE ONCE DID, THAT OUR TENDENCIES TO MOVE AWAY FROM HOME AND HAVE FEWER KIDS AND WALK DOWN SIDEWALKS WITH OUR HEADS DROOPED OVER OUR PHONES HAVEN'T CHANGED OUR NOTIONS OF WHAT COMMUNITY ACTUALLY IS.

2000

HALF OF AMERICANS LIVE IN SUBURBS

VR

BUT WHEN MY FATHER SAT BEFORE HIS RADIO TRANSISTOR IN THE '60s, WAS HE ANY LESS LONELY THAN I WAS, TWENTY-FIVE YEARS LATER, WAITING FOR THE GRINDING OF A DIAL-UP MODEM TO GRANT ME ACCESS TO A NETWORK OF STRANGERS?

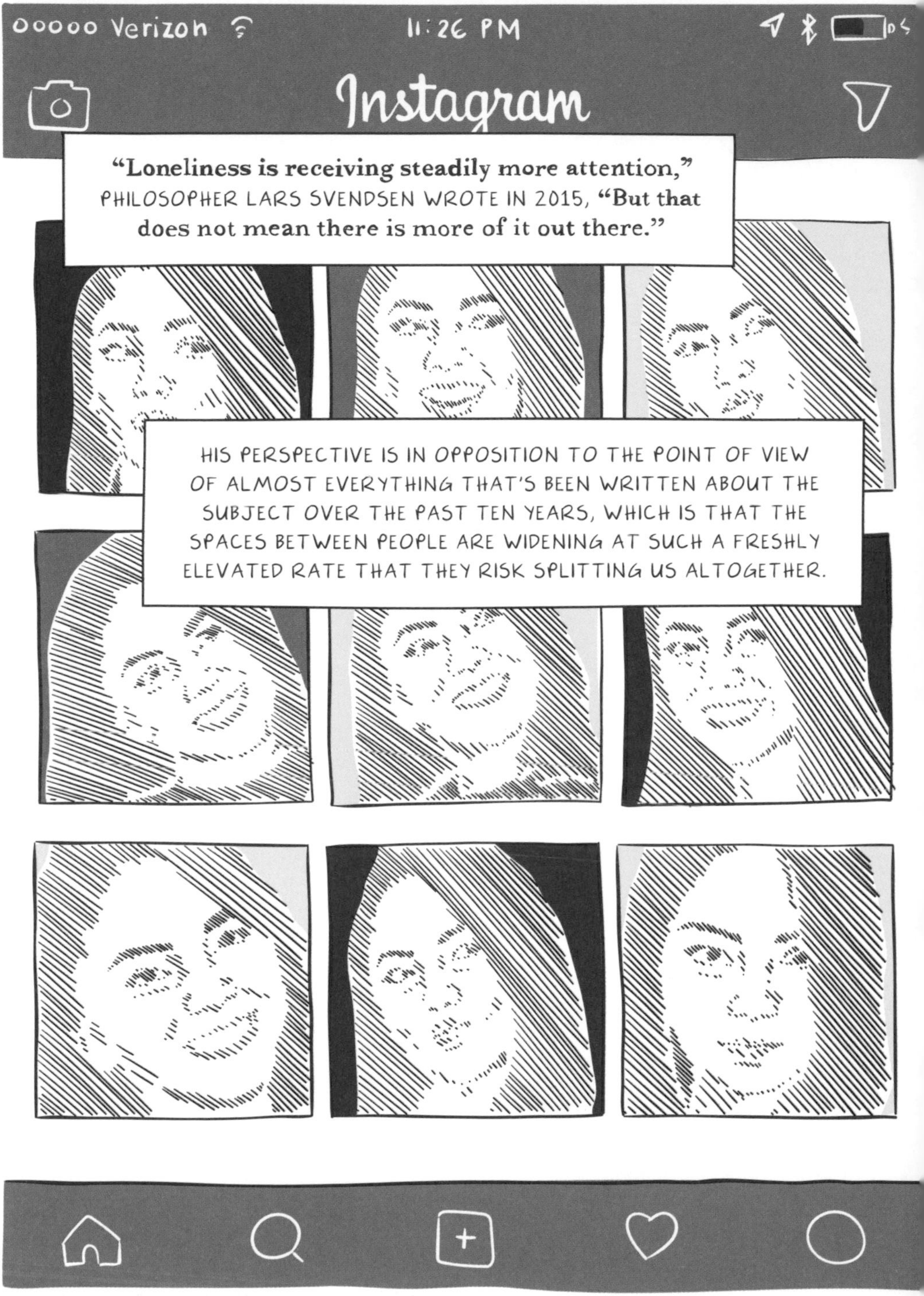
ooooo Verizon
11:26 PM
Instagram
"Loneliness is receiving steadily more attention," PHILOSOPHER LARS SVENDSEN WROTE IN 2015, "But that does not mean there is more of it out there."
HIS PERSPECTIVE IS IN OPPOSITION TO THE POINT OF VIEW OF ALMOST EVERYTHING THAT'S BEEN WRITTEN ABOUT THE SUBJECT OVER THE PAST TEN YEARS, WHICH IS THAT THE SPACES BETWEEN PEOPLE ARE WIDENING AT SUCH A FRESHLY ELEVATED RATE THAT THEY RISK SPLITTING US ALTOGETHER.

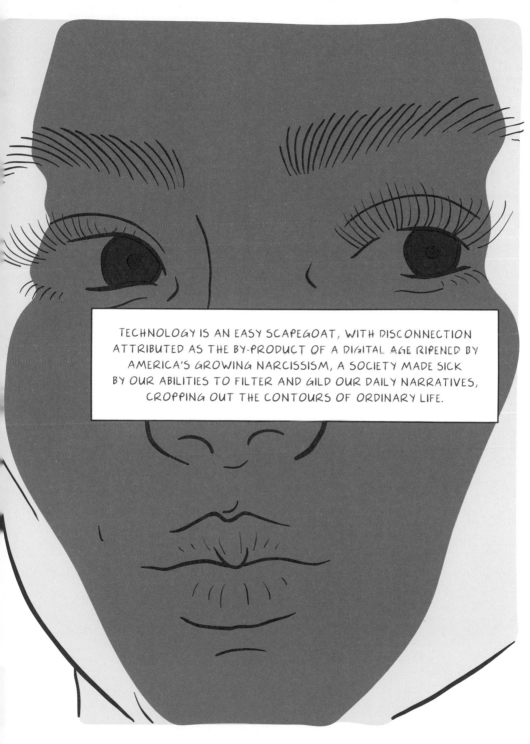

TECHNOLOGY IS AN EASY SCAPEGOAT, WITH DISCONNECTION ATTRIBUTED AS THE BY-PRODUCT OF A DIGITAL AGE RIPENED BY AMERICA'S GROWING NARCISSISM, A SOCIETY MADE SICK BY OUR ABILITIES TO FILTER AND GILD OUR DAILY NARRATIVES, CROPPING OUT THE CONTOURS OF ORDINARY LIFE.

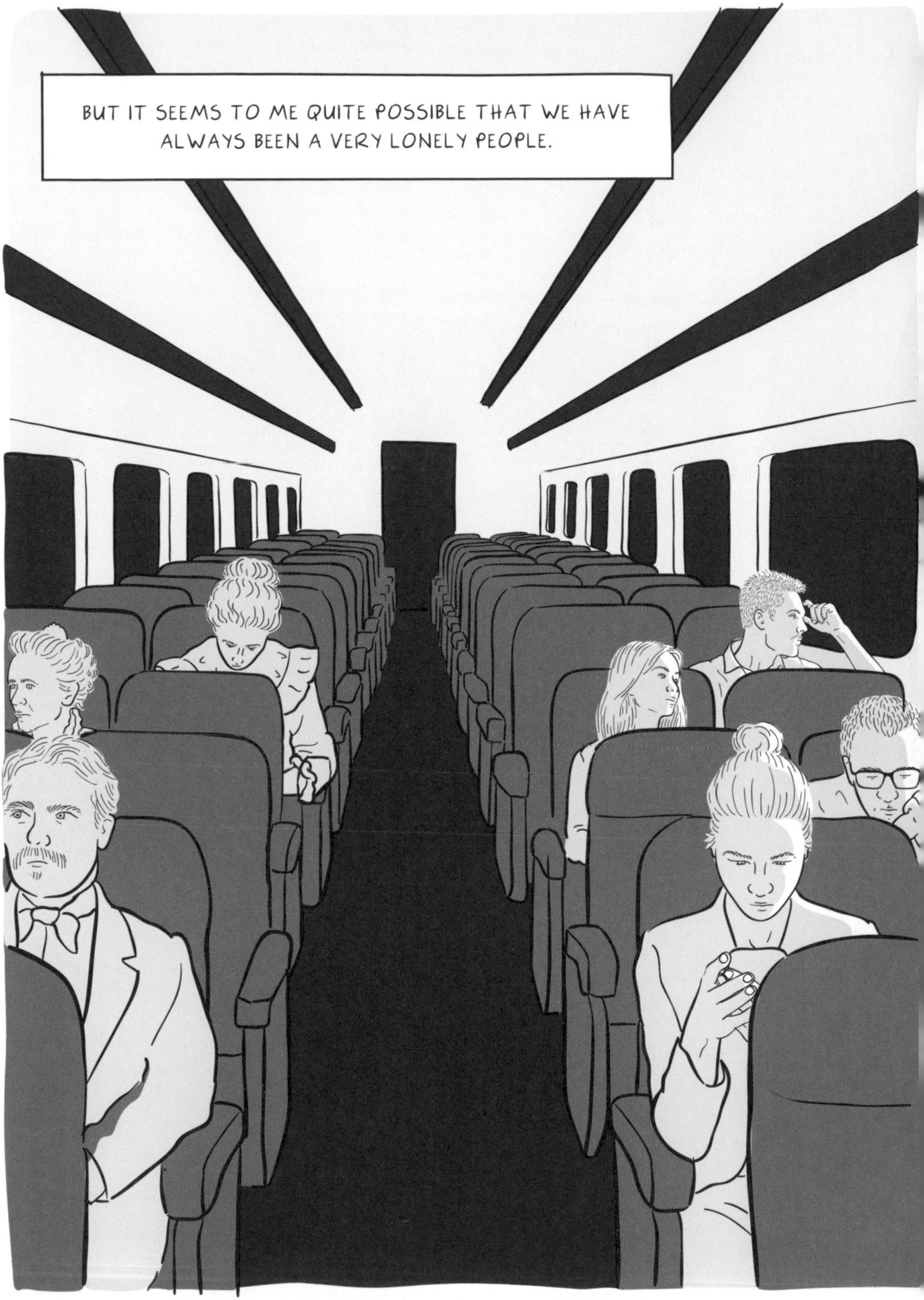
BUT IT SEEMS TO ME QUITE POSSIBLE THAT WE HAVE ALWAYS BEEN A VERY LONELY PEOPLE.

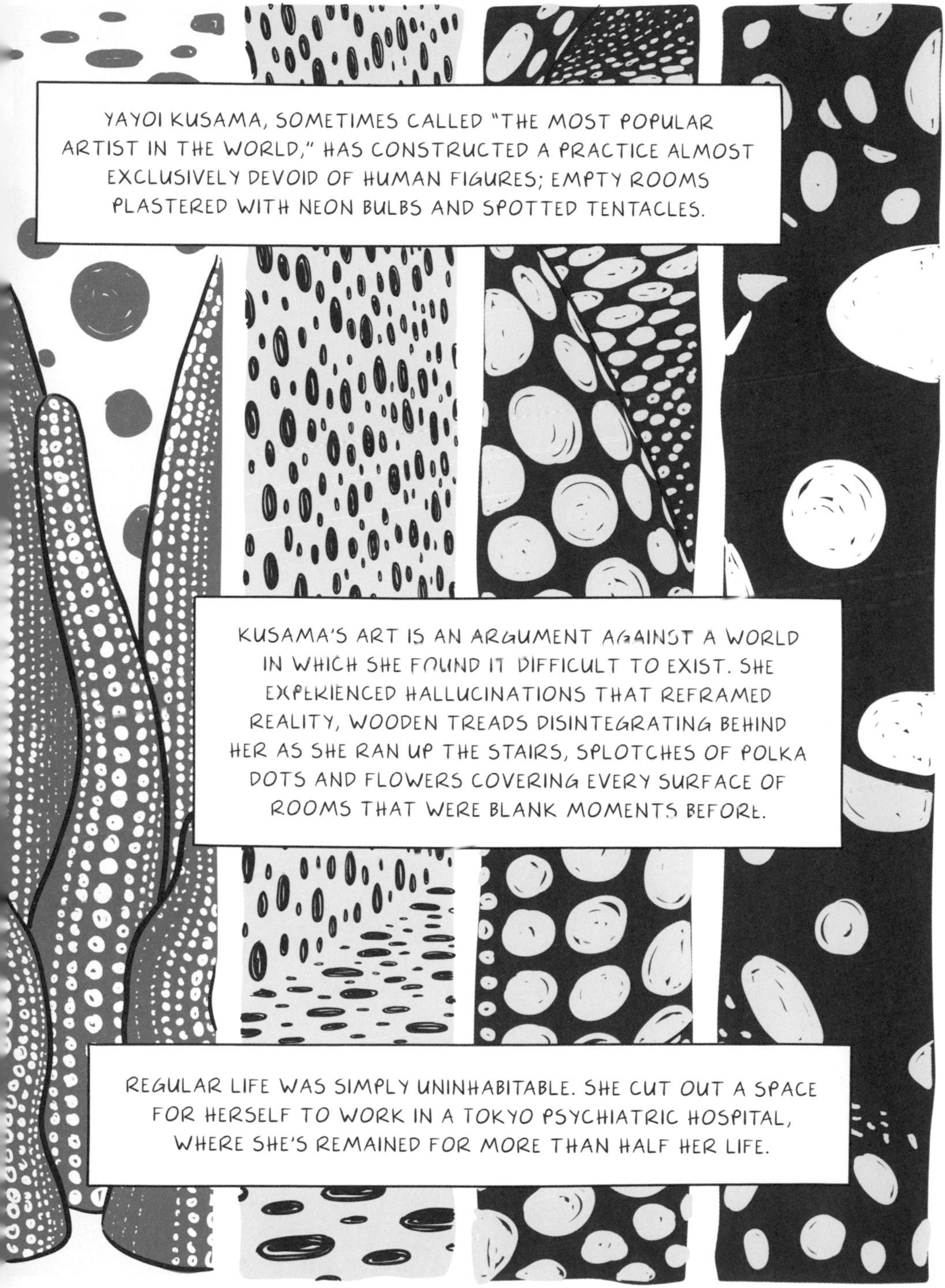
YAYOI KUSAMA, SOMETIMES CALLED "THE MOST POPULAR ARTIST IN THE WORLD," HAS CONSTRUCTED A PRACTICE ALMOST EXCLUSIVELY DEVOID OF HUMAN FIGURES; EMPTY ROOMS PLASTERED WITH NEON BULBS AND SPOTTED TENTACLES.
KUSAMA'S ART IS AN ARGUMENT AGAINST A WORLD IN WHICH SHE FOUND IT DIFFICULT TO EXIST. SHE EXPERIENCED HALLUCINATIONS THAT REFRAMED REALITY, WOODEN TREADS DISINTEGRATING BEHIND HER AS SHE RAN UP THE STAIRS, SPLOTCHES OF POLKA DOTS AND FLOWERS COVERING EVERY SURFACE OF ROOMS THAT WERE BLANK MOMENTS BEFORE.
REGULAR LIFE WAS SIMPLY UNINHABITABLE. SHE CUT OUT A SPACE FOR HERSELF TO WORK IN A TOKYO PSYCHIATRIC HOSPITAL, WHERE SHE'S REMAINED FOR MORE THAN HALF HER LIFE.

SHE DEBUTED THE FIRST ITERATION OF HER INSTALLATION NARCISSUS GARDEN AT THE 1966 VENICE BIENNALE, TO WHICH SHE WAS NOT INVITED. SO SHE STOOD OUTSIDE THE PAVILION DOORS AND SOLD REFLECTIVE ORBS—REPRESENTATIVE OF EACH CUSTOMER'S NARCISSISM, SHE EXPLAINED—TO PASSERSBY.

$45

Simple Modern Yayoi Kusama Wave Point Simulation Pumpkin Plush Pillow

Yayoi Kusama Dots Mousepad-Yellow

2012 Louis Vuitton Red Vernis Leather Dots Infinity Yayoi Kusama

$2,750.00 from Mo deSens

Yayoi
Monog

$9.95 fr

$43.00 from MoMA Store

TODAY HER TRAVELING INSTALLATION OF 1,500 MIRRORED BALLS IS ARRANGED IN SPACES WORLDWIDE, FROM NEW YORK'S HURRICANE-STRIPPED ROCKAWAYS TO A POND IN BRAZIL TO THE FESTOONED CORRIDORS OF THE BELLAGIO HOTEL IN LAS VEGAS.

$20.00 from Ets
DIYPrintings

YOUR
NARCISIUM
FOR SALE
one peice $2

NARCISÌZZATI

al pezzo L. 1200

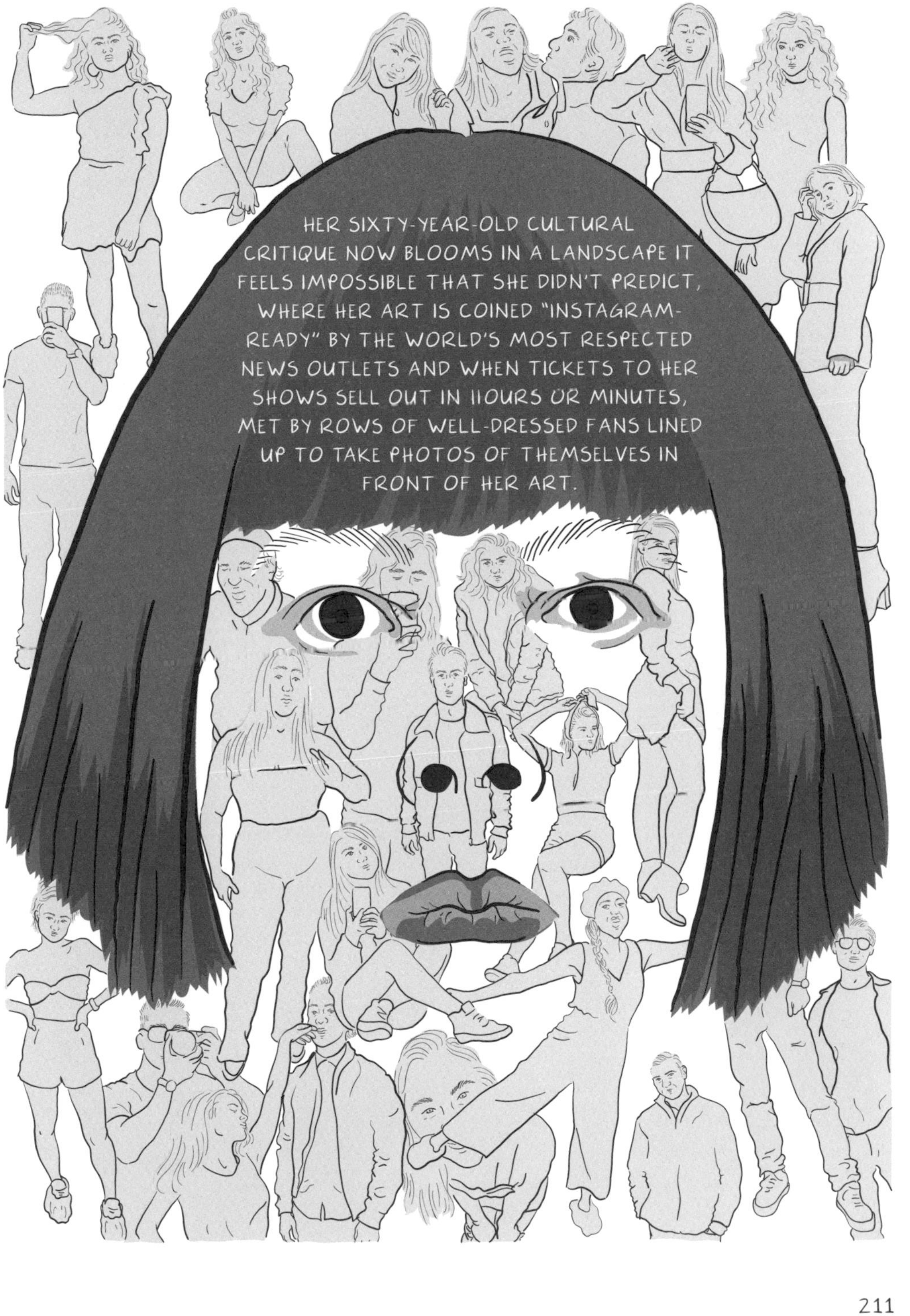
HER SIXTY-YEAR-OLD CULTURAL CRITIQUE NOW BLOOMS IN A LANDSCAPE IT FEELS IMPOSSIBLE THAT SHE DIDN'T PREDICT, WHERE HER ART IS COINED "INSTAGRAM-READY" BY THE WORLD'S MOST RESPECTED NEWS OUTLETS AND WHEN TICKETS TO HER SHOWS SELL OUT IN HOURS OR MINUTES, MET BY ROWS OF WELL-DRESSED FANS LINED UP TO TAKE PHOTOS OF THEMSELVES IN FRONT OF HER ART.

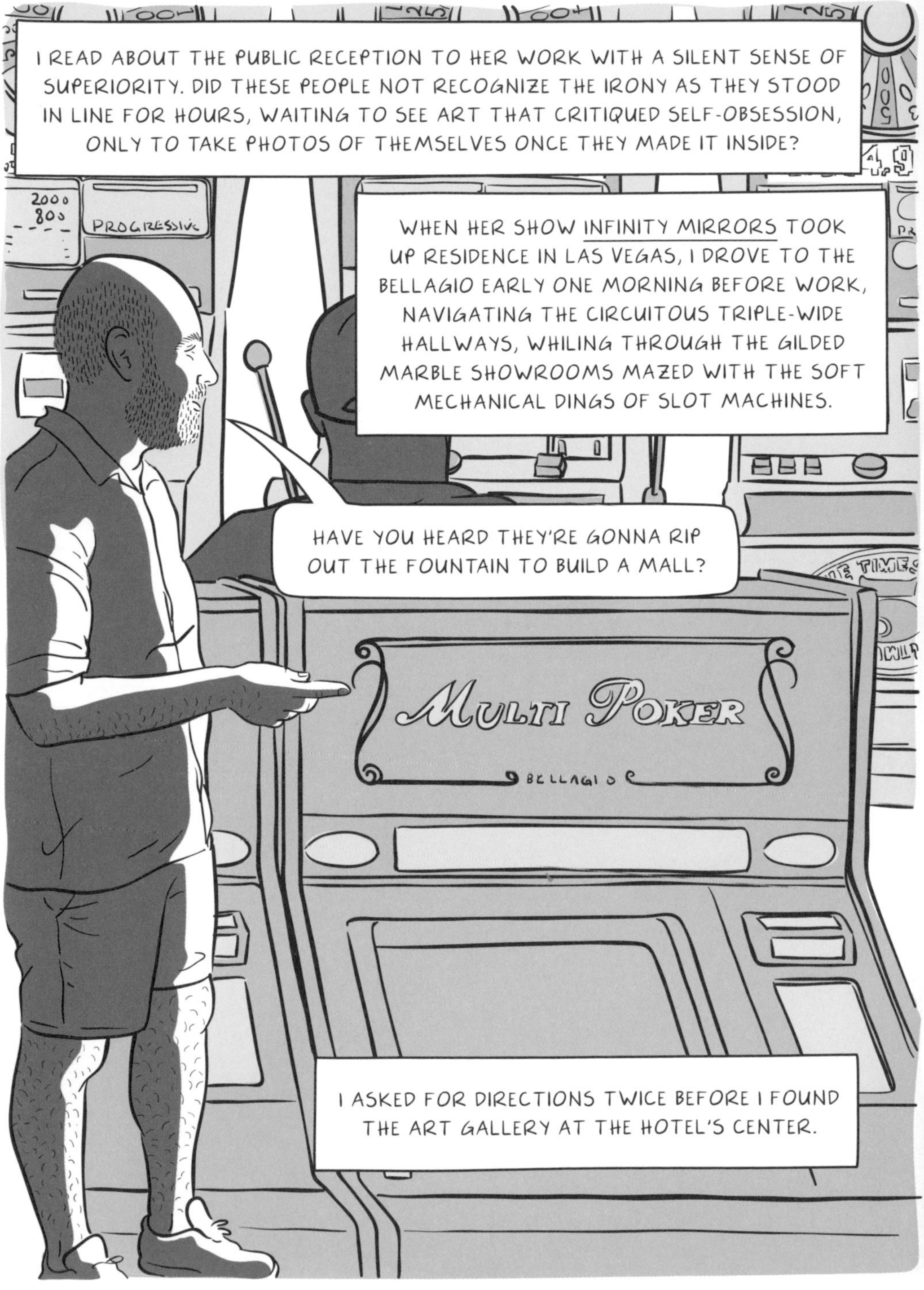
I READ ABOUT THE PUBLIC RECEPTION TO HER WORK WITH A SILENT SENSE OF SUPERIORITY. DID THESE PEOPLE NOT RECOGNIZE THE IRONY AS THEY STOOD IN LINE FOR HOURS, WAITING TO SEE ART THAT CRITIQUED SELF-OBSESSION, ONLY TO TAKE PHOTOS OF THEMSELVES ONCE THEY MADE IT INSIDE?
WHEN HER SHOW INFINITY MIRRORS TOOK UP RESIDENCE IN LAS VEGAS, I DROVE TO THE BELLAGIO EARLY ONE MORNING BEFORE WORK, NAVIGATING THE CIRCUITOUS TRIPLE-WIDE HALLWAYS, WHILING THROUGH THE GILDED MARBLE SHOWROOMS MAZED WITH THE SOFT MECHANICAL DINGS OF SLOT MACHINES.
HAVE YOU HEARD THEY'RE GONNA RIP OUT THE FOUNTAIN TO BUILD A MALL?
PROGRESSIVE
MULTI POKER
BELLAGIO
I ASKED FOR DIRECTIONS TWICE BEFORE I FOUND THE ART GALLERY AT THE HOTEL'S CENTER.

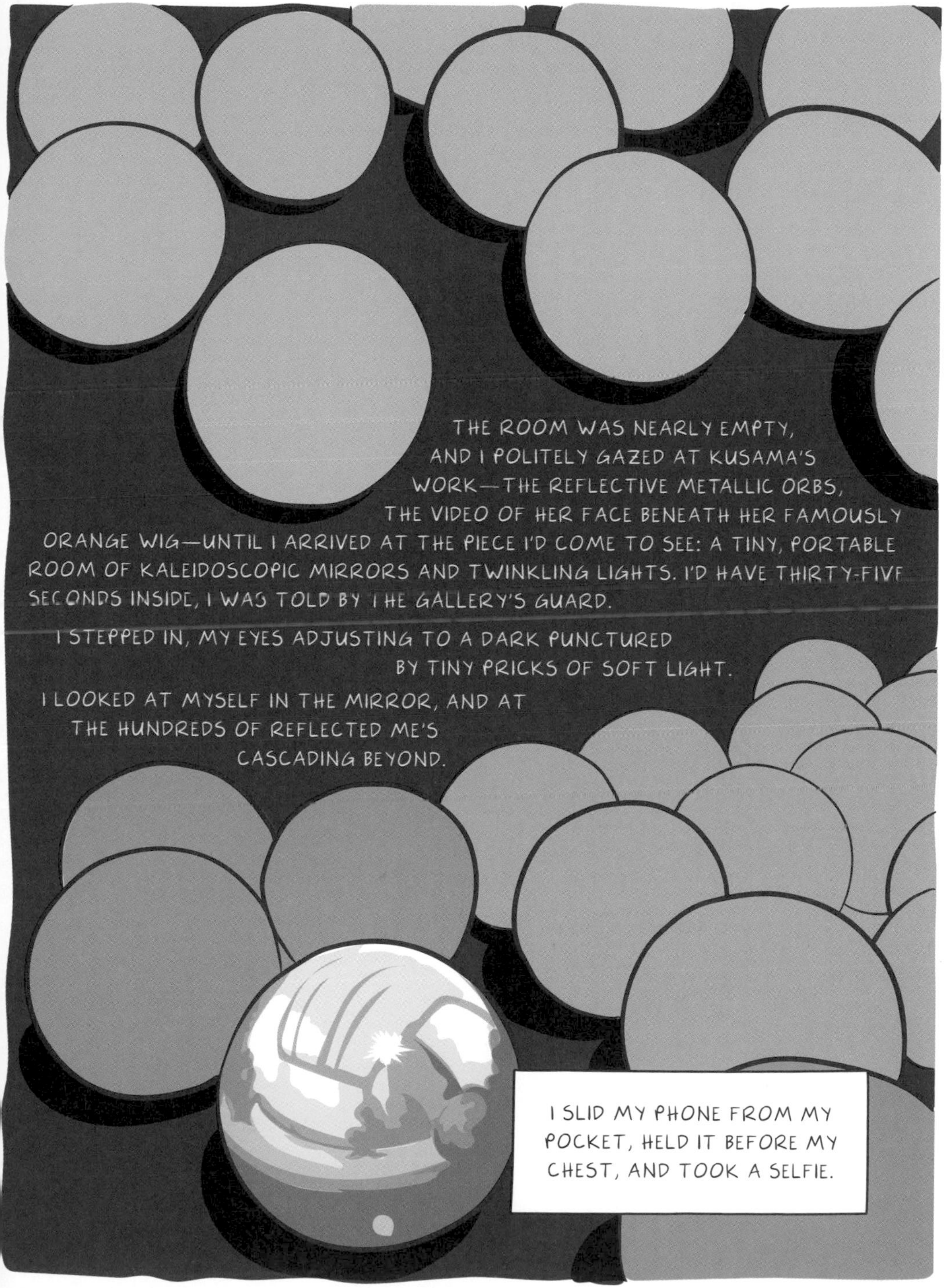
THE ROOM WAS NEARLY EMPTY, AND I POLITELY GAZED AT KUSAMA'S WORK—THE REFLECTIVE METALLIC ORBS, THE VIDEO OF HER FACE BENEATH HER FAMOUSLY ORANGE WIG—UNTIL I ARRIVED AT THE PIECE I'D COME TO SEE: A TINY, PORTABLE ROOM OF KALEIDOSCOPIC MIRRORS AND TWINKLING LIGHTS. I'D HAVE THIRTY-FIVE SECONDS INSIDE, I WAS TOLD BY THE GALLERY'S GUARD.
I STEPPED IN, MY EYES ADJUSTING TO A DARK PUNCTURED BY TINY PRICKS OF SOFT LIGHT.
I LOOKED AT MYSELF IN THE MIRROR, AND AT THE HUNDREDS OF REFLECTED ME'S CASCADING BEYOND.
I SLID MY PHONE FROM MY POCKET, HELD IT BEFORE MY CHEST, AND TOOK A SELFIE.

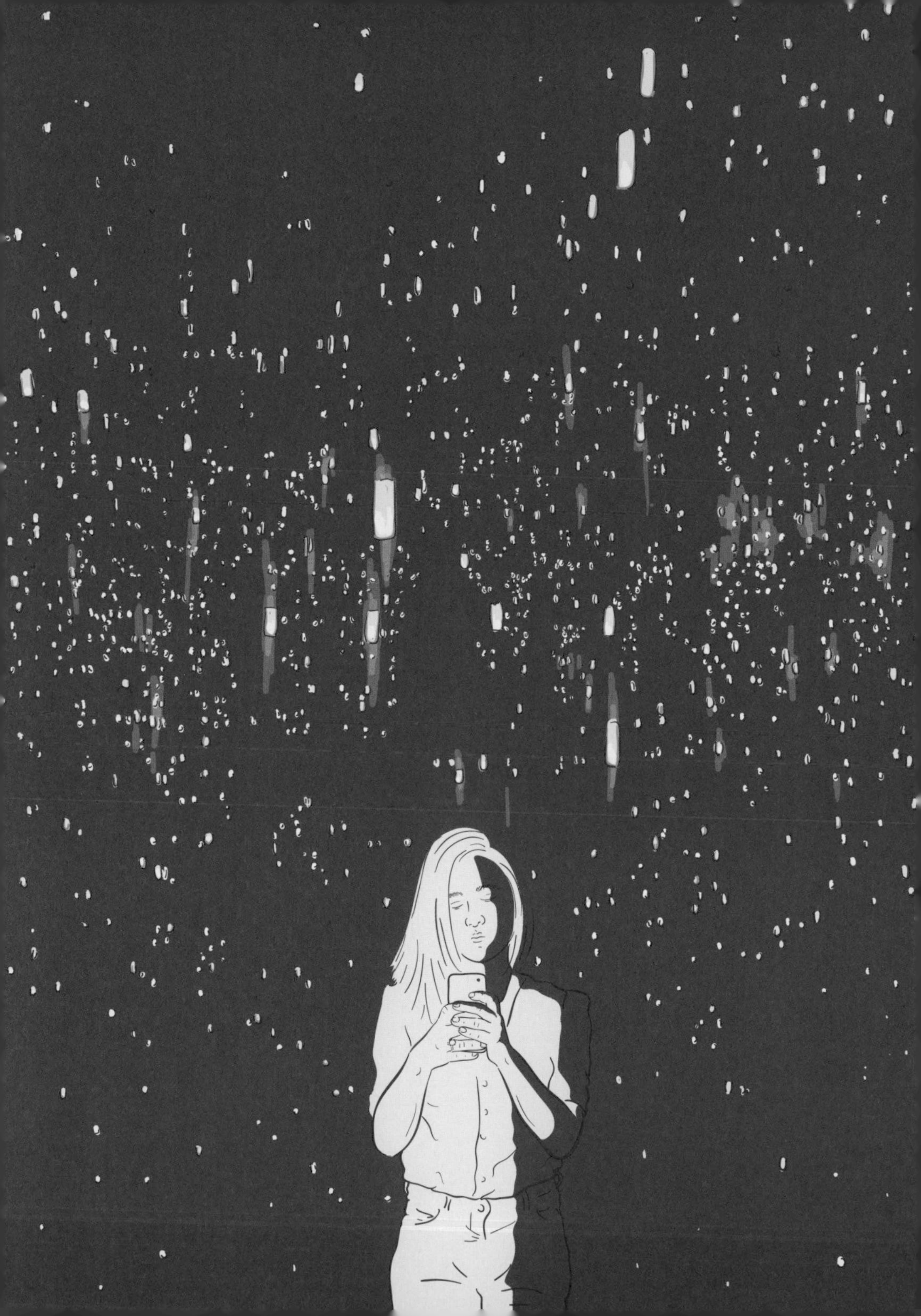

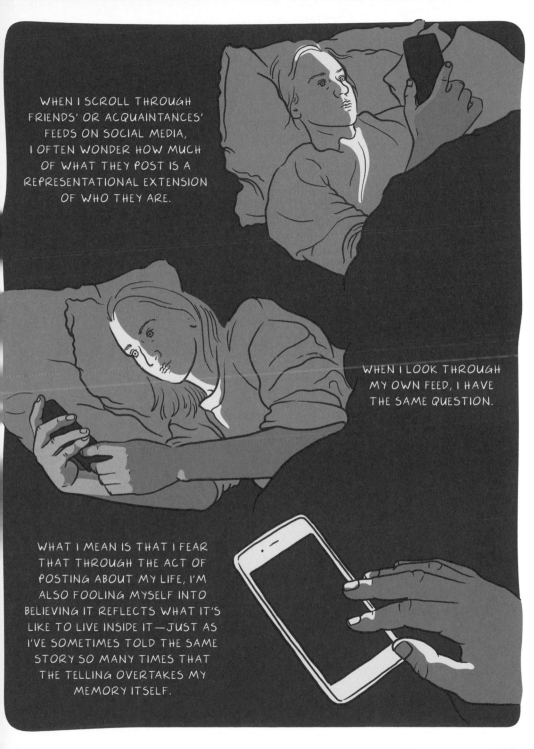

WHEN I SCROLL THROUGH FRIENDS' OR ACQUAINTANCES' FEEDS ON SOCIAL MEDIA, I OFTEN WONDER HOW MUCH OF WHAT THEY POST IS A REPRESENTATIONAL EXTENSION OF WHO THEY ARE.

WHEN I LOOK THROUGH MY OWN FEED, I HAVE THE SAME QUESTION.

WHAT I MEAN IS THAT I FEAR THAT THROUGH THE ACT OF POSTING ABOUT MY LIFE, I'M ALSO FOOLING MYSELF INTO BELIEVING IT REFLECTS WHAT IT'S LIKE TO LIVE INSIDE IT—JUST AS I'VE SOMETIMES TOLD THE SAME STORY SO MANY TIMES THAT THE TELLING OVERTAKES MY MEMORY ITSELF.

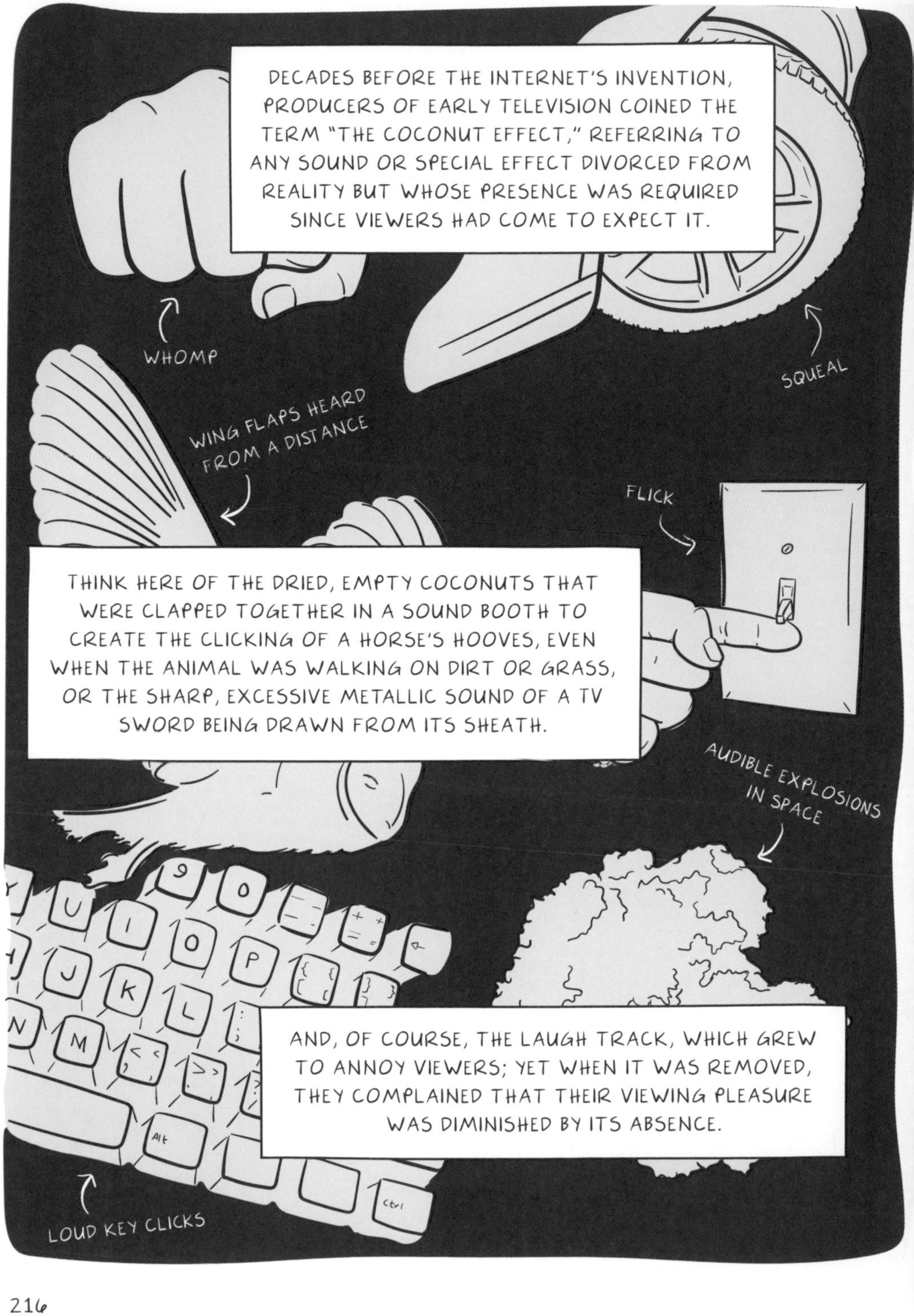
DECADES BEFORE THE INTERNET'S INVENTION, PRODUCERS OF EARLY TELEVISION COINED THE TERM "THE COCONUT EFFECT," REFERRING TO ANY SOUND OR SPECIAL EFFECT DIVORCED FROM REALITY BUT WHOSE PRESENCE WAS REQUIRED SINCE VIEWERS HAD COME TO EXPECT IT.
WHOMP
SQUEAL
WING FLAPS HEARD FROM A DISTANCE
FLICK
THINK HERE OF THE DRIED, EMPTY COCONUTS THAT WERE CLAPPED TOGETHER IN A SOUND BOOTH TO CREATE THE CLICKING OF A HORSE'S HOOVES, EVEN WHEN THE ANIMAL WAS WALKING ON DIRT OR GRASS, OR THE SHARP, EXCESSIVE METALLIC SOUND OF A TV SWORD BEING DRAWN FROM ITS SHEATH.
AUDIBLE EXPLOSIONS IN SPACE
AND, OF COURSE, THE LAUGH TRACK, WHICH GREW TO ANNOY VIEWERS; YET WHEN IT WAS REMOVED, THEY COMPLAINED THAT THEIR VIEWING PLEASURE WAS DIMINISHED BY ITS ABSENCE.
LOUD KEY CLICKS

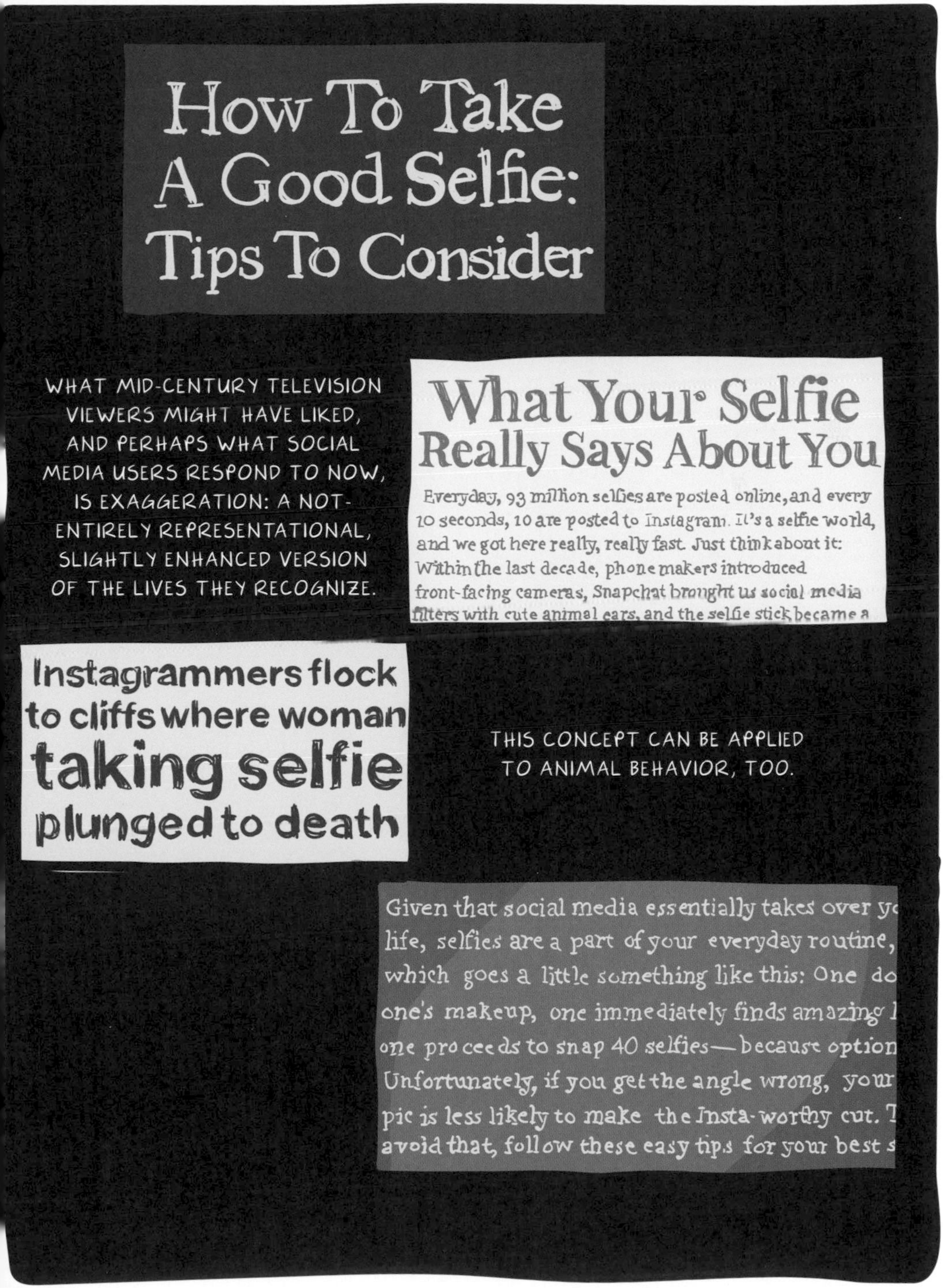
How To Take A Good Selfie: Tips To Consider
WHAT MID-CENTURY TELEVISION VIEWERS MIGHT HAVE LIKED, AND PERHAPS WHAT SOCIAL MEDIA USERS RESPOND TO NOW, IS EXAGGERATION: A NOT-ENTIRELY REPRESENTATIONAL, SLIGHTLY ENHANCED VERSION OF THE LIVES THEY RECOGNIZE.
What Your Selfie Really Says About You
Everyday, 93 million selfies are posted online, and every 10 seconds, 10 are posted to Instagram. It's a selfie world, and we got here really, really fast. Just think about it: Within the last decade, phone makers introduced front-facing cameras, Snapchat brought us social media filters with cute animal ears, and the selfie stick became a
Instagrammers flock to cliffs where woman taking selfie plunged to death
THIS CONCEPT CAN BE APPLIED TO ANIMAL BEHAVIOR, TOO.
Given that social media essentially takes over y
life, selfies are a part of your everyday routine,
which goes a little something like this: One do
one's makeup, one immediately finds amazing
one proceeds to snap 40 selfies—because option
Unfortunately, if you get the angle wrong, your
pic is less likely to make the Insta-worthy cut. T
avoid that, follow these easy tips for your best s

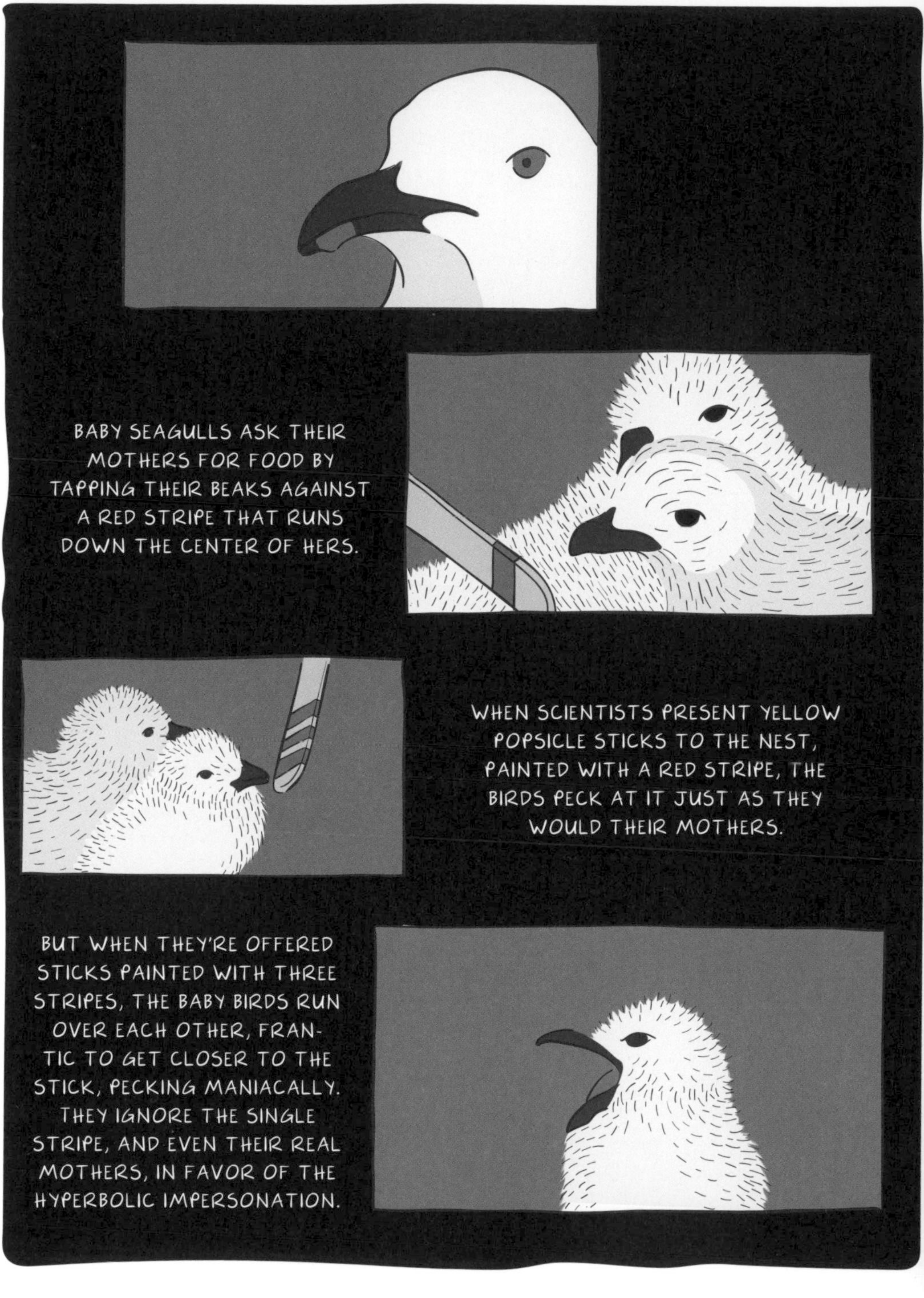
BABY SEAGULLS ASK THEIR MOTHERS FOR FOOD BY TAPPING THEIR BEAKS AGAINST A RED STRIPE THAT RUNS DOWN THE CENTER OF HERS.
WHEN SCIENTISTS PRESENT YELLOW POPSICLE STICKS TO THE NEST, PAINTED WITH A RED STRIPE, THE BIRDS PECK AT IT JUST AS THEY WOULD THEIR MOTHERS.
BUT WHEN THEY'RE OFFERED STICKS PAINTED WITH THREE STRIPES, THE BABY BIRDS RUN OVER EACH OTHER, FRAN-TIC TO GET CLOSER TO THE STICK, PECKING MANIACALLY. THEY IGNORE THE SINGLE STRIPE, AND EVEN THEIR REAL MOTHERS, IN FAVOR OF THE HYPERBOLIC IMPERSONATION.

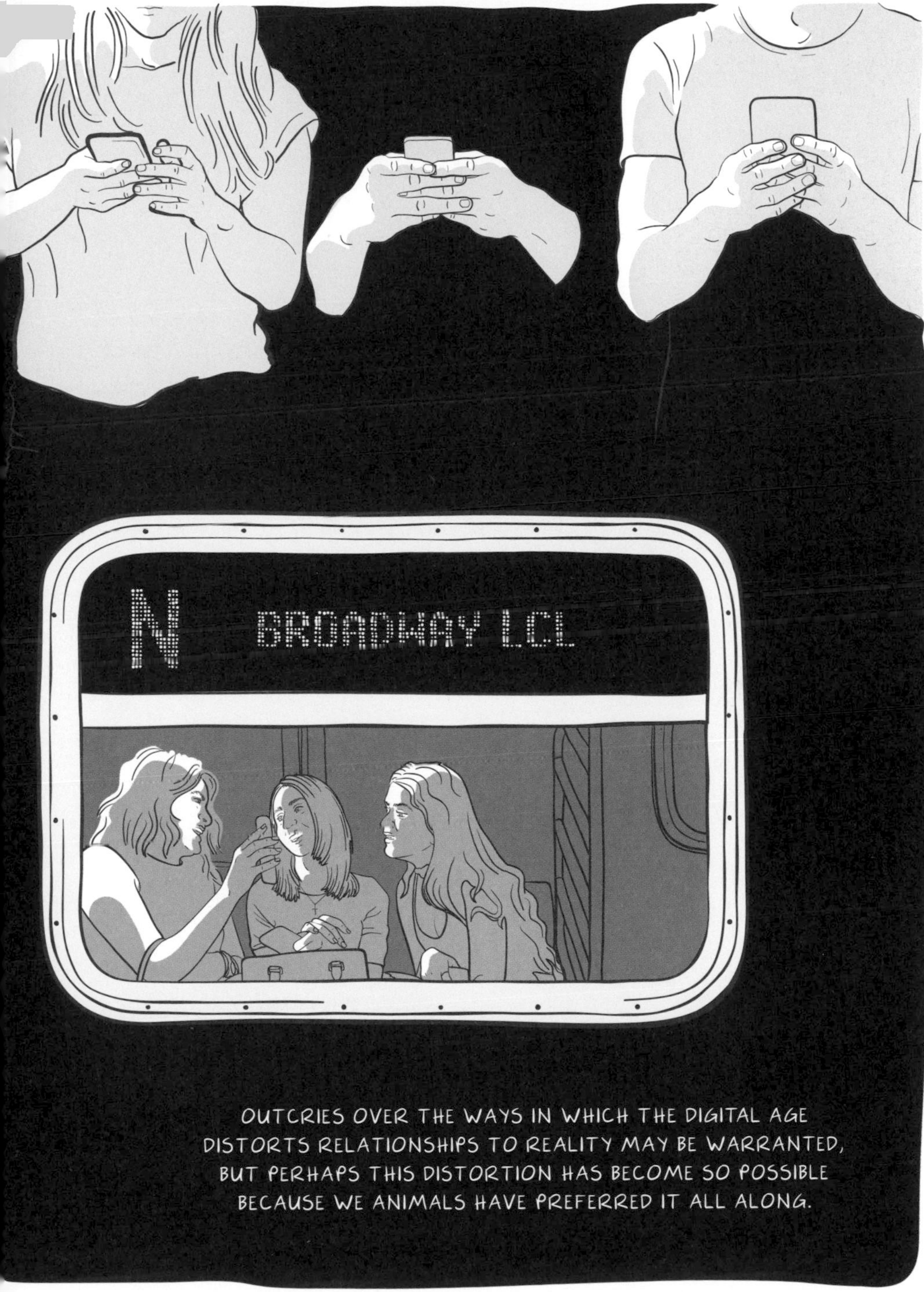
N
BROADWAY LCL
OUTCRIES OVER THE WAYS IN WHICH THE DIGITAL AGE DISTORTS RELATIONSHIPS TO REALITY MAY BE WARRANTED, BUT PERHAPS THIS DISTORTION HAS BECOME SO POSSIBLE BECAUSE WE ANIMALS HAVE PREFERRED IT ALL ALONG.

IF WE NO LONGER FEEL TETHERED TO THE COMMUNITIES OUR SPECIES WAS MOLDED INTO NEEDING, THE ACT OF POSTING A SELFIE OR A CAREFULLY EDITED PORTRAIT OF OUR BANAL DOMESTIC LIVES COULD JUST BE A MUTED FORM OF PERSONAL RESCUE.

IS DISPLAY A FORM OF DILUTION, OR IS THE BROADCAST PART OF WHAT MAKES IT REAL?

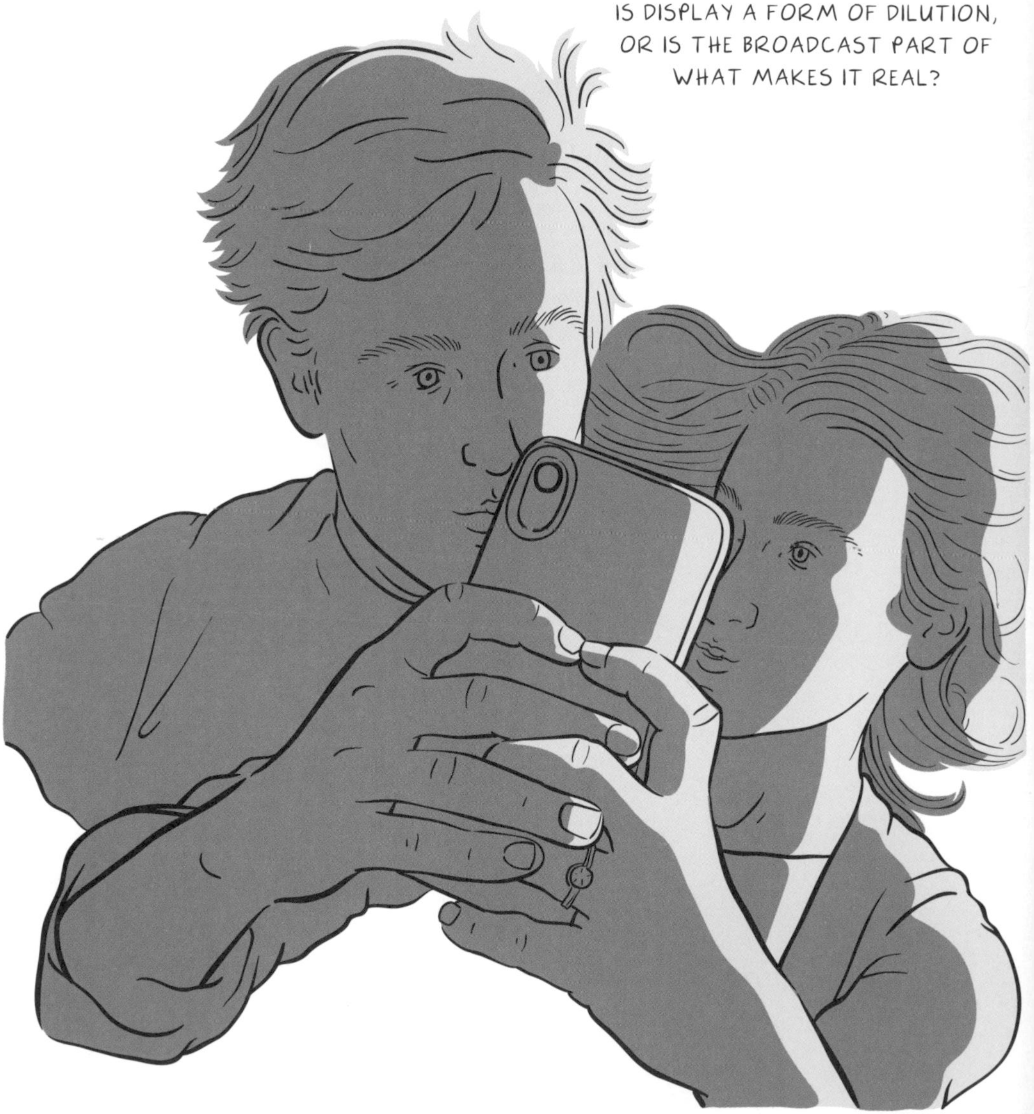

II

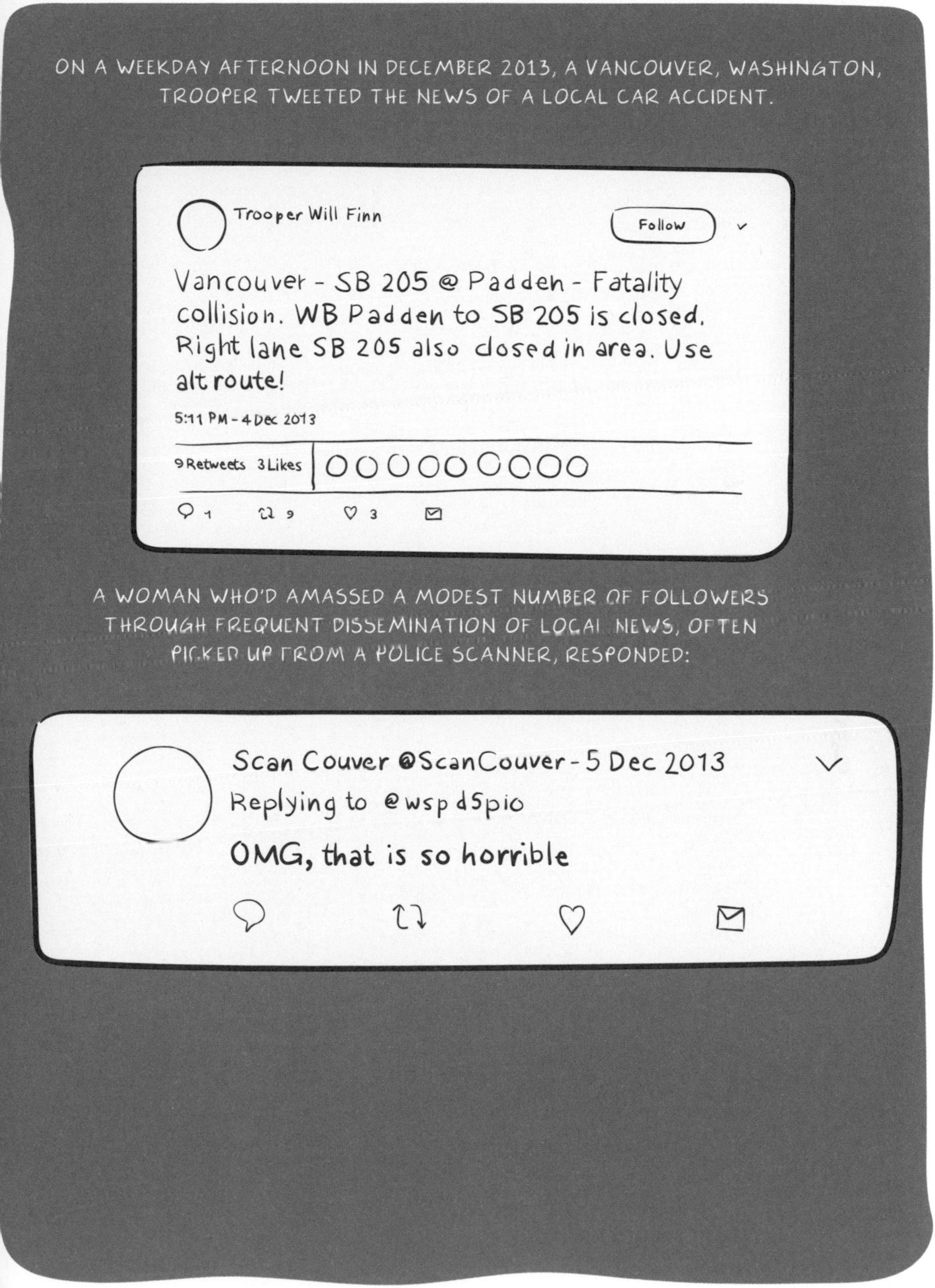
ON A WEEKDAY AFTERNOON IN DECEMBER 2013, A VANCOUVER, WASHINGTON, TROOPER TWEETED THE NEWS OF A LOCAL CAR ACCIDENT.
Trooper Will Finn
Follow
Vancouver - SB 205 @ Padden - Fatality collision. WB Padden to SB 205 is closed. Right lane SB 205 also closed in area. Use alt route!
5:11 PM - 4 Dec 2013
9 Retweets 3 Likes
1
9
3
A WOMAN WHO'D AMASSED A MODEST NUMBER OF FOLLOWERS THROUGH FREQUENT DISSEMINATION OF LOCAL NEWS, OFTEN PICKED UP FROM A POLICE SCANNER, RESPONDED:
Scan Couver @ScanCouver - 5 Dec 2013
Replying to @wspd5pio
OMG, that is so horrible

SHE SHARED THE DETAILS WITH HER FOLLOWERS AS SHE LEARNED THEM:

They said they are so close to SWWWMC, they can take the patient there, instead of Lifeflight. #clark911

A FEW MINUTES LATER, SHE TWEETED:

I'm trying not to panic, but my husband left work early and he drives 205 to get home. He's not answering his phone.

AND THEN:

he's late

AND:

I just called his work and he was feeling faint when he left work.

#Panic

THEN:

and now my kids are home from school...

THE PICTURE OF HER HUSBAND'S CAR, THE METAL OF ITS FRONT END PEELED LIKE BITS OF JAGGED TINFOIL, ITS BLACKENED MECHANICAL PARTS SPLAYED ACROSS THE ASPHALT, LOOKS LIKE A PROTOTYPE FOR EVERY ROAD-SAFETY PHOTO OR VIDEO PRESENTED IN DRIVER'S ED, ALMOST CARTOONISH IN ITS VULGARITY.

THIRTY-FOUR MINUTES AFTER SHE TWEETED THAT HER CHILDREN HAD RETURNED FROM SCHOOL, SHE POSTED:

it's him. he died.

IF SHE RECEIVED VERIFICATION OF HER HUSBAND'S ACCIDENT IN THE HALF-HOUR BETWEEN HER KIDS' ARRIVAL HOME AND HER TWEET ABOUT HIS DEATH, WE CAN PLAUSIBLY ASSUME THAT SHE SHARED THE NEWS WITH HER FOLLOWERS BEFORE SHE TOLD HER CHILDREN, OR THAT SHE PIVOTED BACK TO SOCIAL MEDIA SHORTLY AFTER TELLING THEM THEIR FATHER WAS DEAD.

I am so, so, so, sorry for your loss. I saw this story on the news
and I wanted you to know I am praying 4 U & UR kids

NEWS OUTLETS WORLDWIDE PICKED UP SCANCOUVER'S STORY, AND THE
INTERNET ARRIVED WITH ITS STANDARD SUPPORT WAVE.

Love and Prayers. May he RIP!

praying for you. From Arkansas, US.

I am so sorry. You are in my thoughts.

oh my goodness. Praying

Can't imagine. so sry

this is horrible. RIP

absolutely awful. driving is so dangerous,
thinking of you and your family

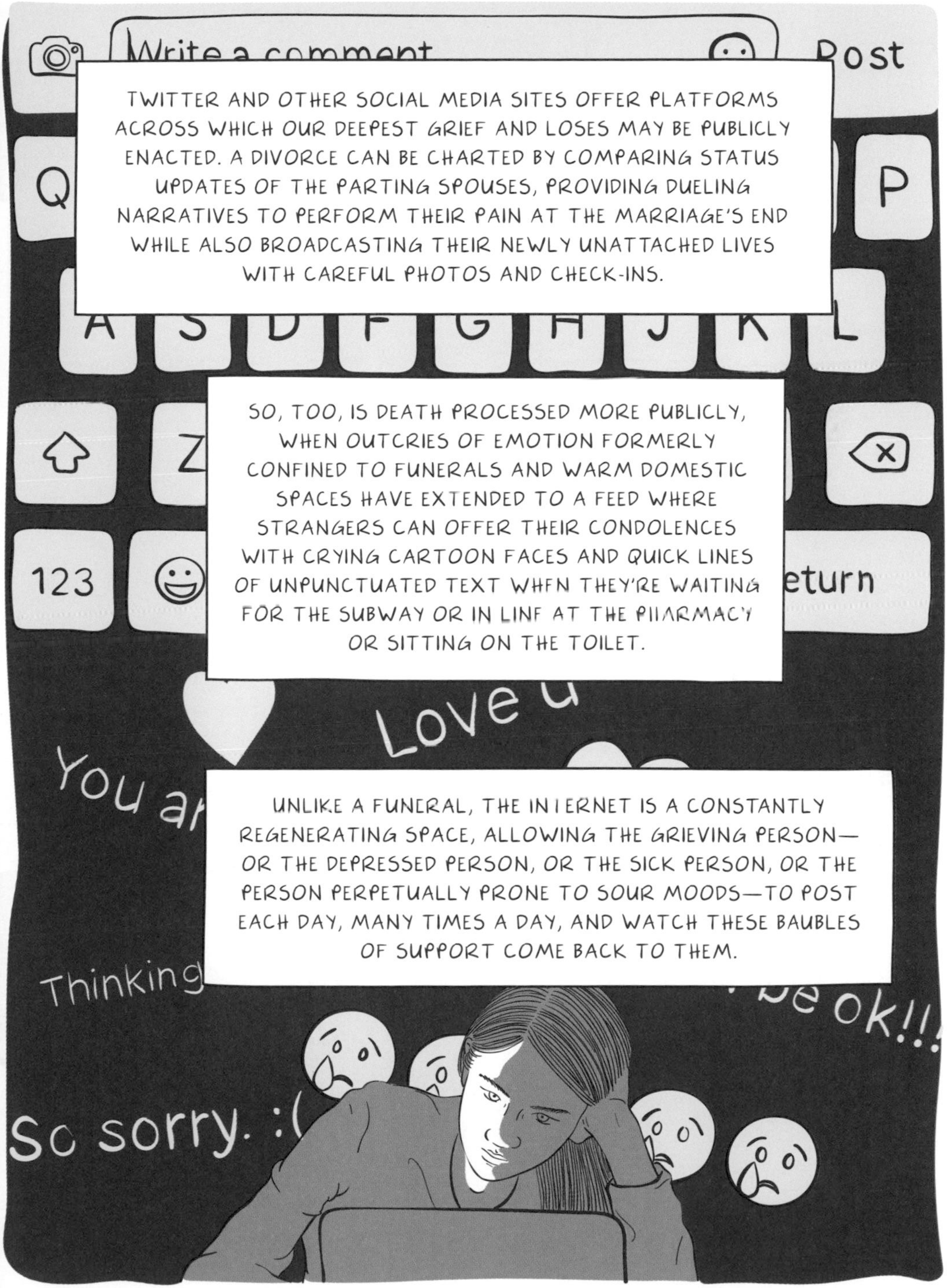
Write a comment
Post
TWITTER AND OTHER SOCIAL MEDIA SITES OFFER PLATFORMS ACROSS WHICH OUR DEEPEST GRIEF AND LOSES MAY BE PUBLICLY ENACTED. A DIVORCE CAN BE CHARTED BY COMPARING STATUS UPDATES OF THE PARTING SPOUSES, PROVIDING DUELING NARRATIVES TO PERFORM THEIR PAIN AT THE MARRIAGE'S END WHILE ALSO BROADCASTING THEIR NEWLY UNATTACHED LIVES WITH CAREFUL PHOTOS AND CHECK-INS.
SO, TOO, IS DEATH PROCESSED MORE PUBLICLY, WHEN OUTCRIES OF EMOTION FORMERLY CONFINED TO FUNERALS AND WARM DOMESTIC SPACES HAVE EXTENDED TO A FEED WHERE STRANGERS CAN OFFER THEIR CONDOLENCES WITH CRYING CARTOON FACES AND QUICK LINES OF UNPUNCTUATED TEXT WHEN THEY'RE WAITING FOR THE SUBWAY OR IN LINE AT THE PHARMACY OR SITTING ON THE TOILET.
123
Love u
UNLIKE A FUNERAL, THE INTERNET IS A CONSTANTLY REGENERATING SPACE, ALLOWING THE GRIEVING PERSON—OR THE DEPRESSED PERSON, OR THE SICK PERSON, OR THE PERSON PERPETUALLY PRONE TO SOUR MOODS—TO POST EACH DAY, MANY TIMES A DAY, AND WATCH THESE BAUBLES OF SUPPORT COME BACK TO THEM.
Thinking
So sorry. :(

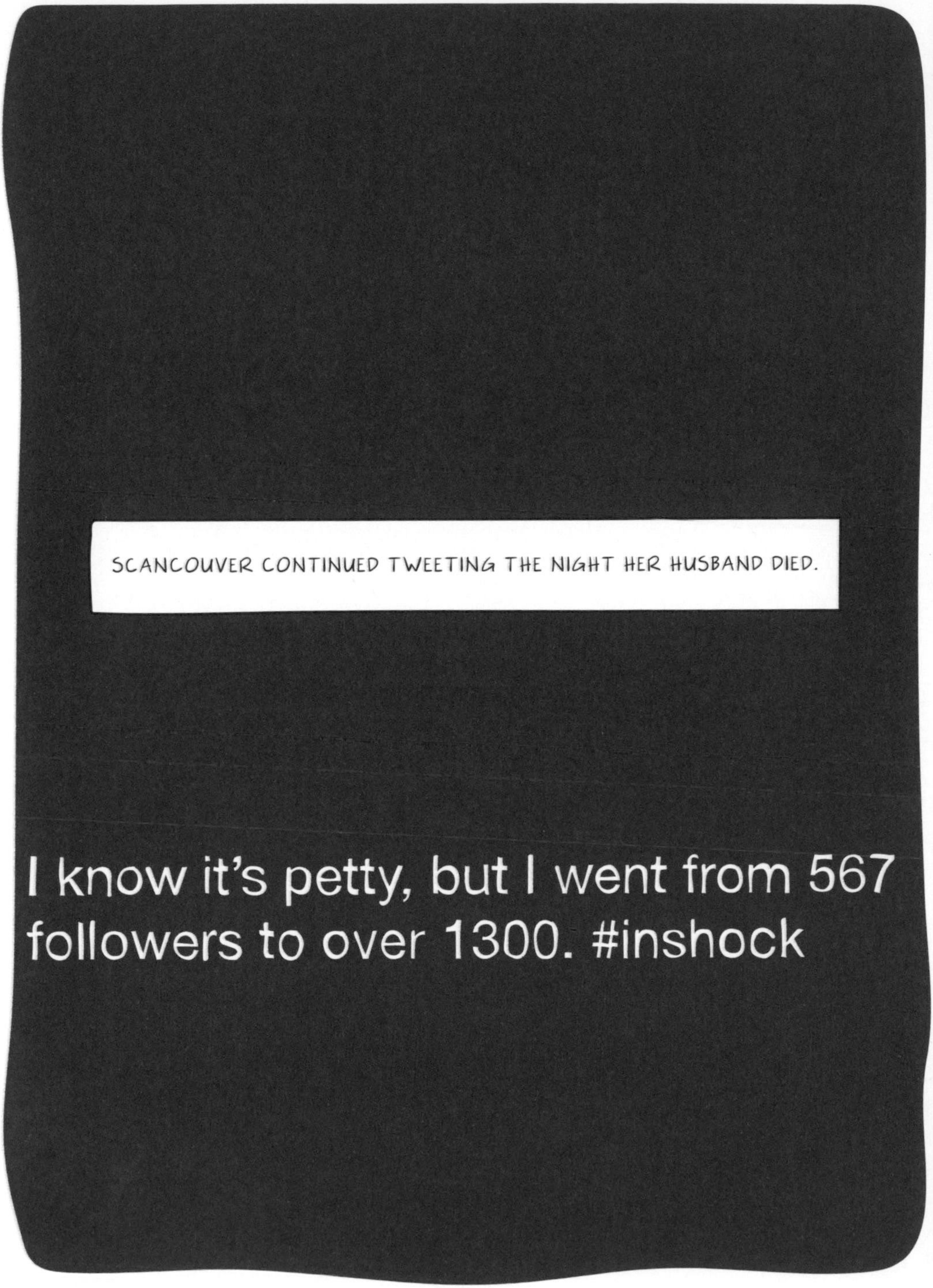
SCANCOUVER CONTINUED TWEETING THE NIGHT HER HUSBAND DIED.
I know it's petty, but I went from 567 followers to over 1300. #inshock

What? You wouldn't be more concerned with your Twitter follower numbers than your dead husband and fatherless children?

Just another reason I don't get Twitter. #GetALife

this woman just wants attention and donations. Oh, and more twitter followers.

I don't know if its heartbreaking. I mean she didn't sound hurt, did she? Live tweeting her husbands death..... Crazy

live posting an accident @ScanCouver finds out it's her own husband dead. Keeps posting abt how fast she's been getting followers. Disturbing

Very hard way to learn how inappropriate it is to tweet details of other people's misfortune...

A women live tweeted her husbands death? What the fuck. Surely the last thing you'd wanna be doing is tweeting.

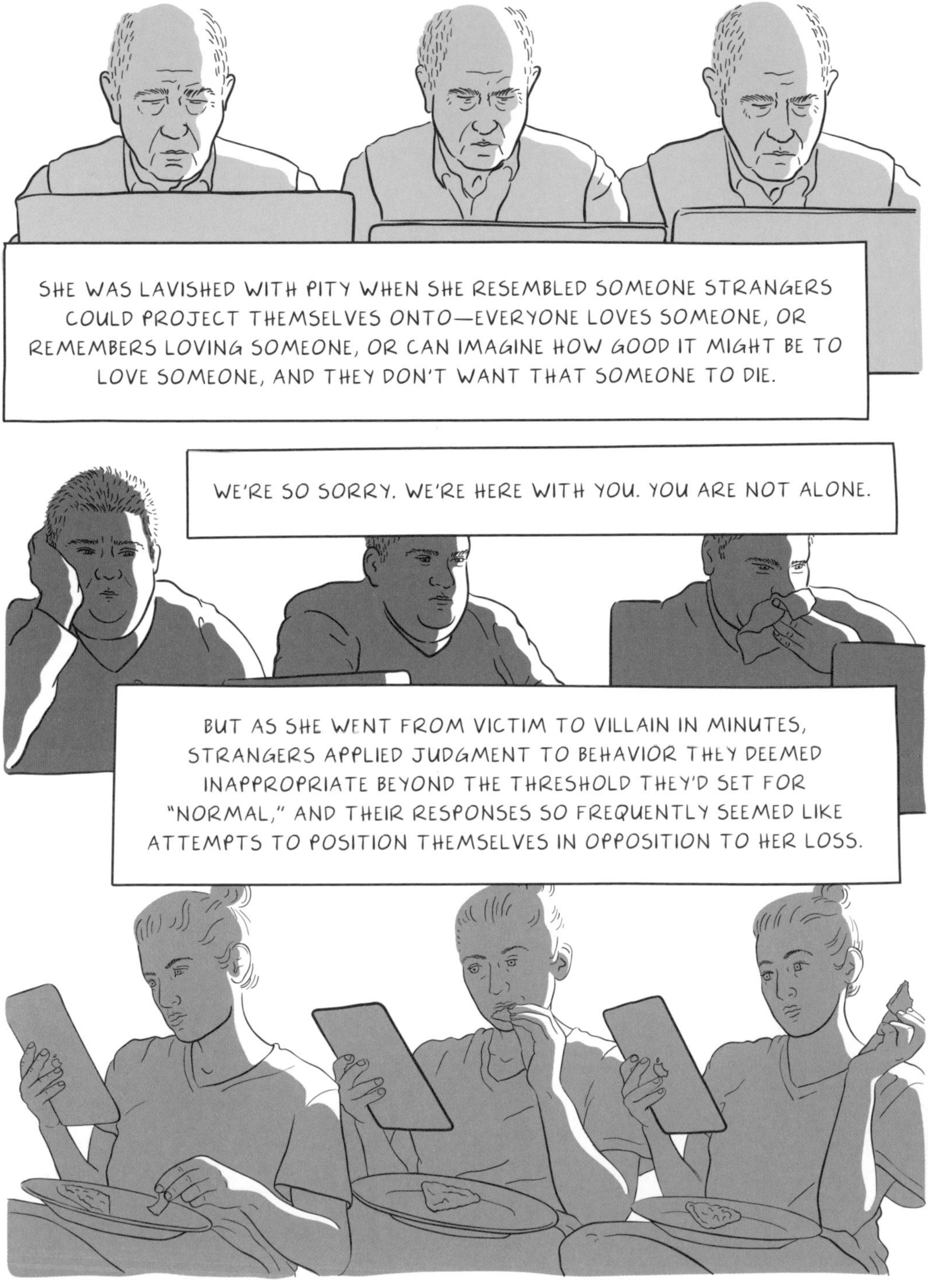
SHE WAS LAVISHED WITH PITY WHEN SHE RESEMBLED SOMEONE STRANGERS COULD PROJECT THEMSELVES ONTO—EVERYONE LOVES SOMEONE, OR REMEMBERS LOVING SOMEONE, OR CAN IMAGINE HOW GOOD IT MIGHT BE TO LOVE SOMEONE, AND THEY DON'T WANT THAT SOMEONE TO DIE.
WE'RE SO SORRY. WE'RE HERE WITH YOU. YOU ARE NOT ALONE.
BUT AS SHE WENT FROM VICTIM TO VILLAIN IN MINUTES, STRANGERS APPLIED JUDGMENT TO BEHAVIOR THEY DEEMED INAPPROPRIATE BEYOND THE THRESHOLD THEY'D SET FOR "NORMAL," AND THEIR RESPONSES SO FREQUENTLY SEEMED LIKE ATTEMPTS TO POSITION THEMSELVES IN OPPOSITION TO HER LOSS.

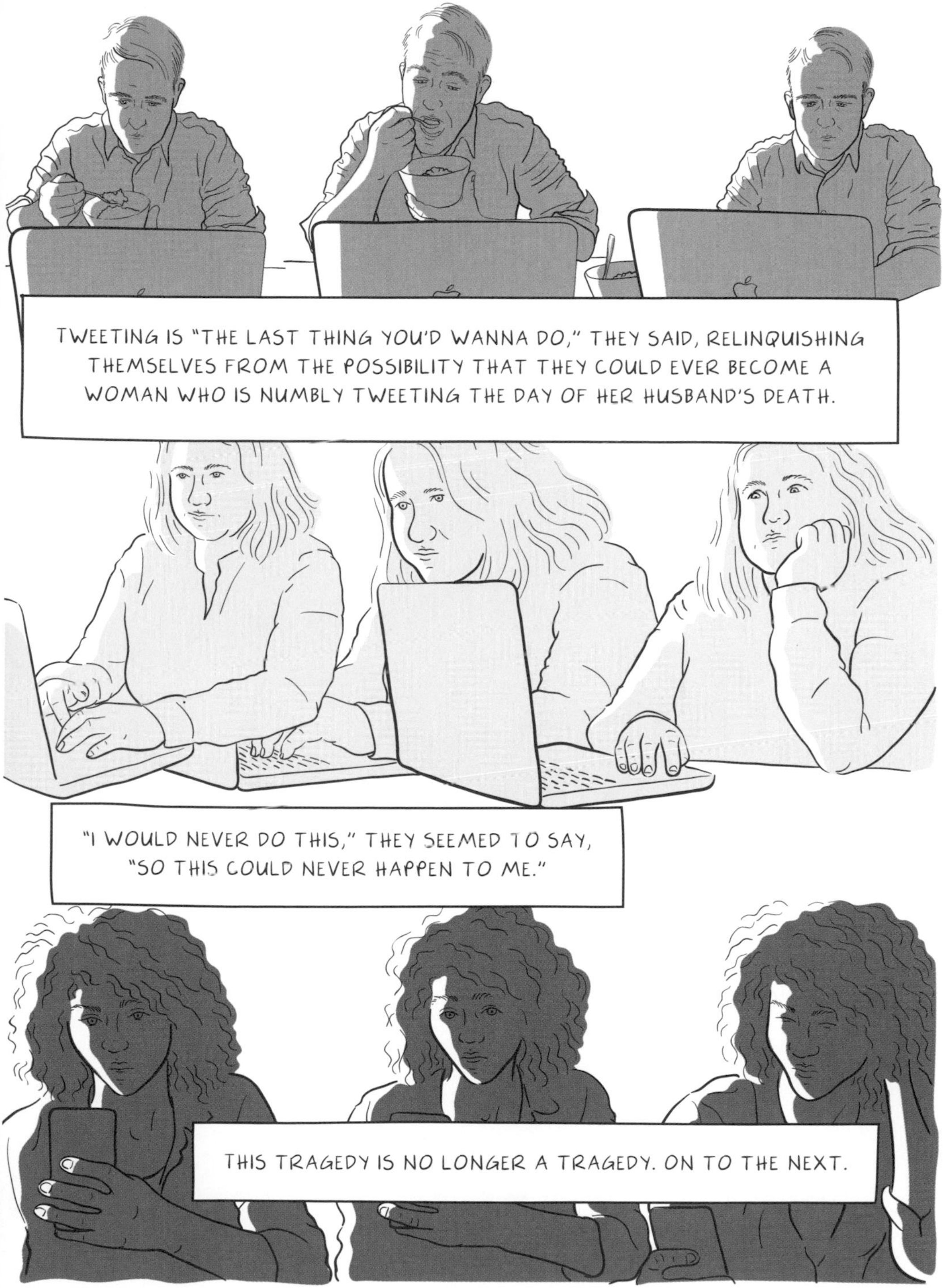

TWEETING IS "THE LAST THING YOU'D WANNA DO," THEY SAID, RELINQUISHING THEMSELVES FROM THE POSSIBILITY THAT THEY COULD EVER BECOME A WOMAN WHO IS NUMBLY TWEETING THE DAY OF HER HUSBAND'S DEATH.
"I WOULD NEVER DO THIS," THEY SEEMED TO SAY, "SO THIS COULD NEVER HAPPEN TO ME."
THIS TRAGEDY IS NO LONGER A TRAGEDY. ON TO THE NEXT.

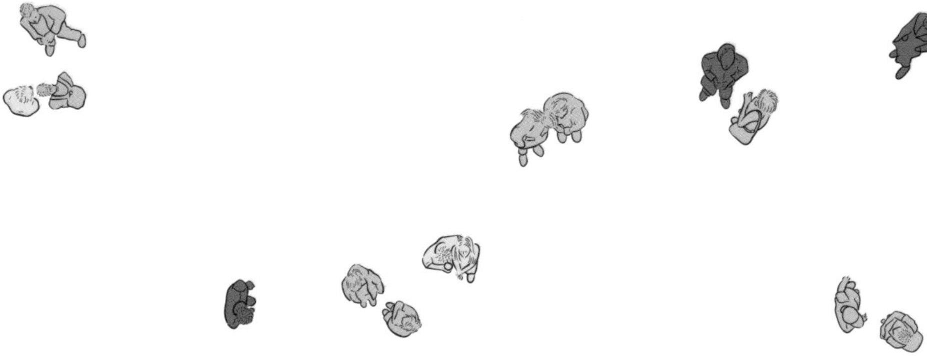

FROM EXPLOITATIVE CELEBRITY NEWS TO NOSY NEIGHBORS TO THE GOSSIP THAT SOMETIMES FUELS OUR FRIENDSHIPS, PEOPLE HAVE FELT THEY HAD A RIGHT TO OTHERS' STORIES LONG BEFORE THE INTERNET OFFERED A PLACE TO DO SO IN SUCH A SPRAWLING, PUBLIC FASHION.

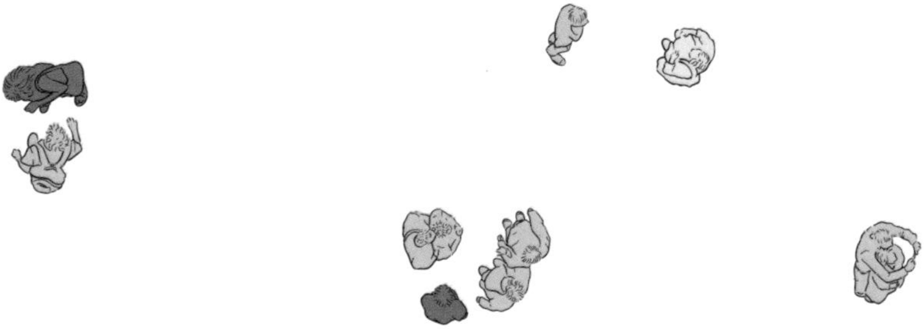

THIS IS FOUNDATIONAL TO STORYTELLING ITSELF.

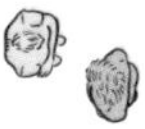

STORIES ARE HOW WE DRAW OURSELVES CLOSER TO ONE ANOTHER, AND HOW WE REMEMBER, AND SOMETIMES HOW WE RESHAPE.

EVERYONE WANTED TO TALK TO SCANCOUVER. REPORTERS APPEARED AT HER DOOR. *GOOD MORNING AMERICA* CALLED. SHE SAID NO TO THEM ALL, BUT SHE GAVE ONE INTERVIEW, WITH A SMALL IDAHO NEWS CHANNEL, TWO YEARS AFTER HER HUSBAND'S DEATH.

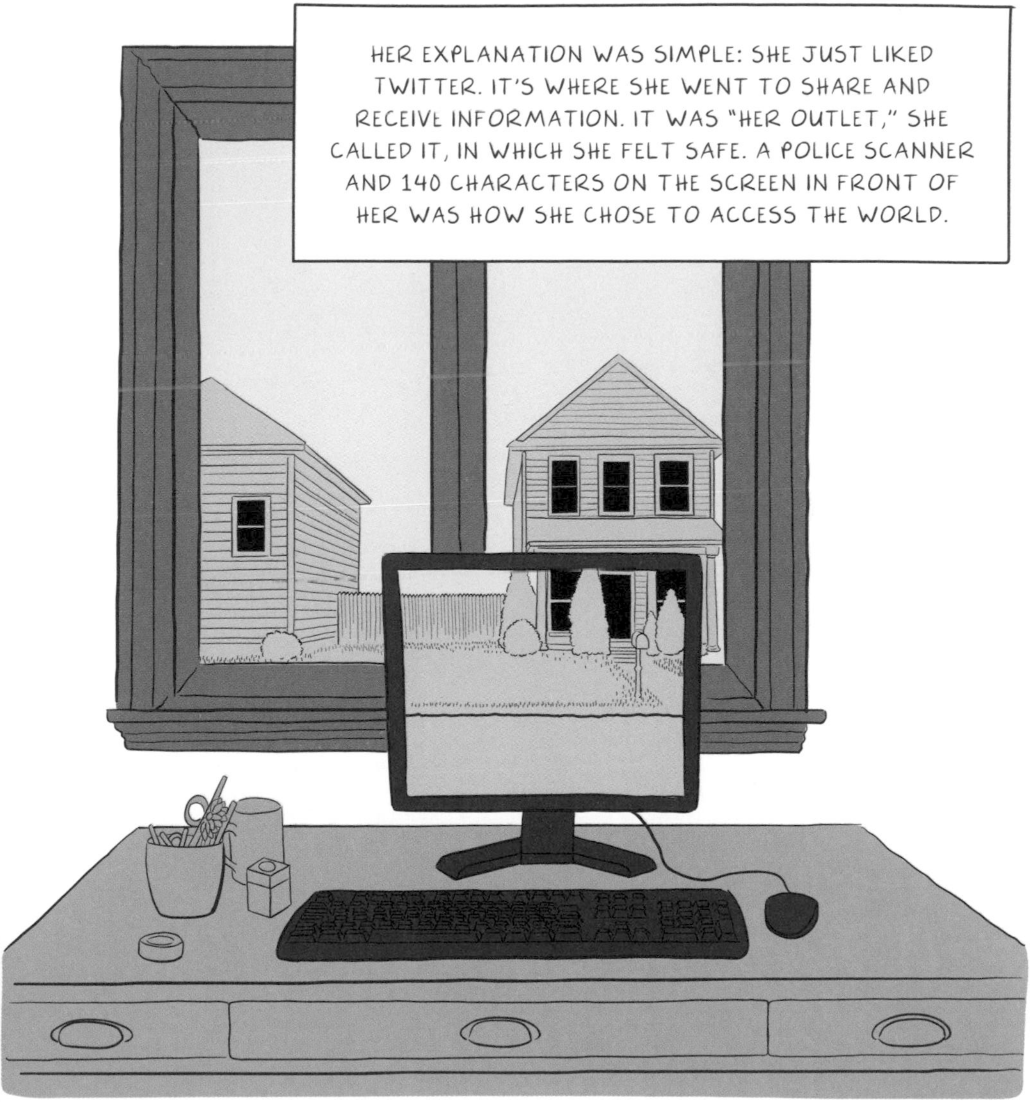
HER EXPLANATION WAS SIMPLE: SHE JUST LIKED TWITTER. IT'S WHERE SHE WENT TO SHARE AND RECEIVE INFORMATION. IT WAS "HER OUTLET," SHE CALLED IT, IN WHICH SHE FELT SAFE. A POLICE SCANNER AND 140 CHARACTERS ON THE SCREEN IN FRONT OF HER WAS HOW SHE CHOSE TO ACCESS THE WORLD.

TOUCH

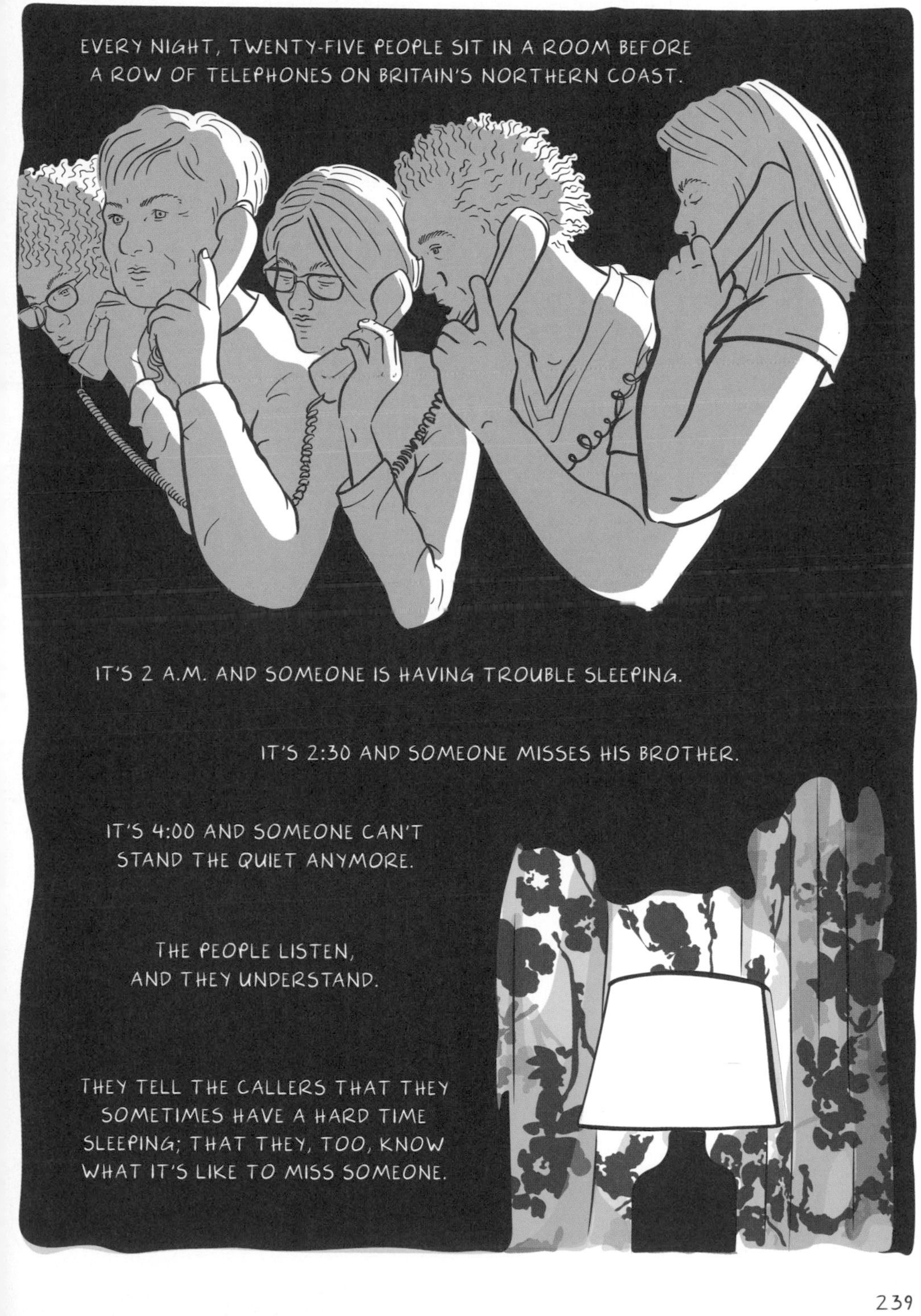
EVERY NIGHT, TWENTY-FIVE PEOPLE SIT IN A ROOM BEFORE A ROW OF TELEPHONES ON BRITAIN'S NORTHERN COAST.
IT'S 2 A.M. AND SOMEONE IS HAVING TROUBLE SLEEPING.
IT'S 2:30 AND SOMEONE MISSES HIS BROTHER.
IT'S 4:00 AND SOMEONE CAN'T STAND THE QUIET ANYMORE.
THE PEOPLE LISTEN, AND THEY UNDERSTAND.
THEY TELL THE CALLERS THAT THEY SOMETIMES HAVE A HARD TIME SLEEPING; THAT THEY, TOO, KNOW WHAT IT'S LIKE TO MISS SOMEONE.

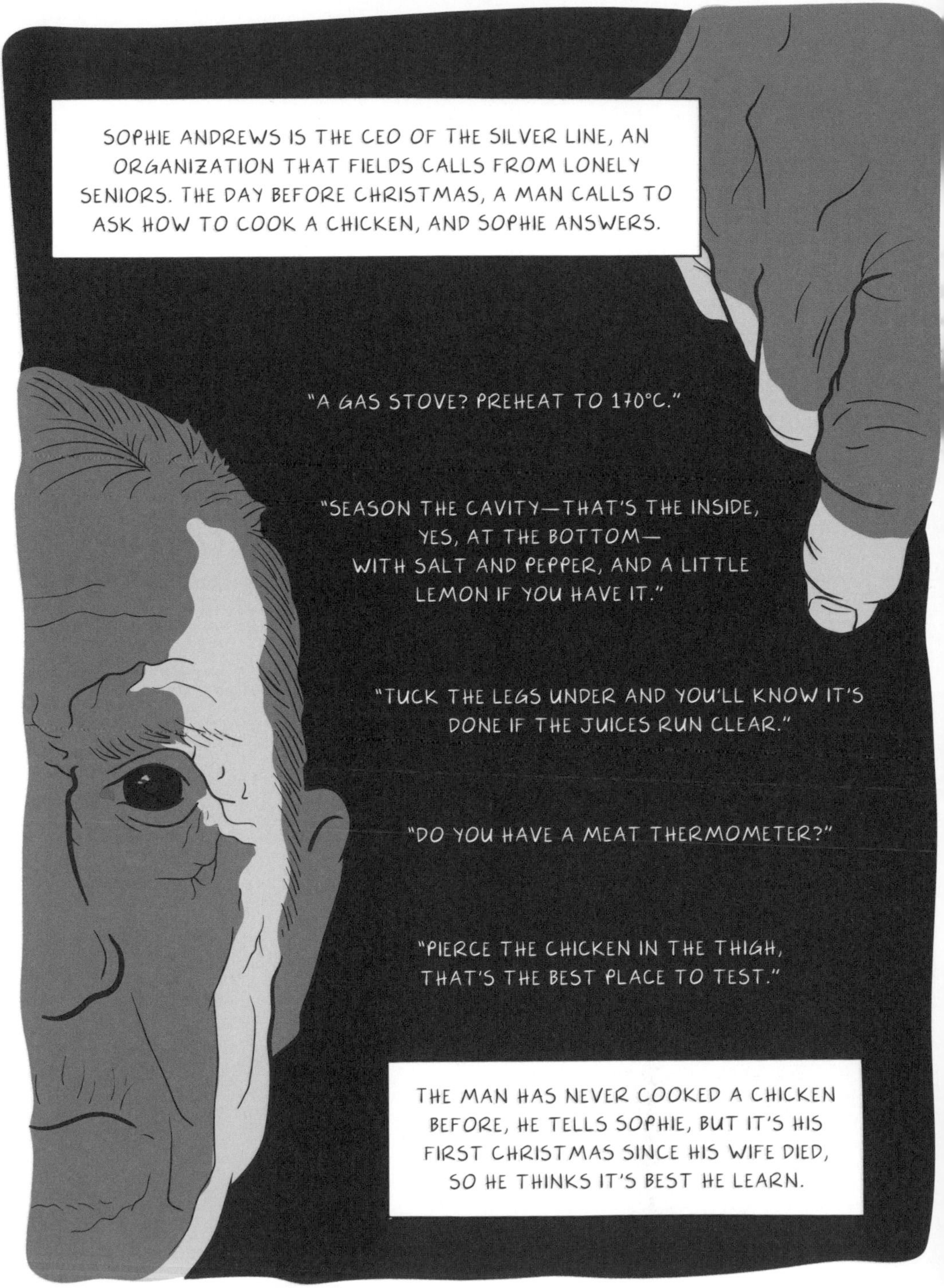
SOPHIE ANDREWS IS THE CEO OF THE SILVER LINE, AN ORGANIZATION THAT FIELDS CALLS FROM LONELY SENIORS. THE DAY BEFORE CHRISTMAS, A MAN CALLS TO ASK HOW TO COOK A CHICKEN, AND SOPHIE ANSWERS.
"A GAS STOVE? PREHEAT TO 170°C."
"SEASON THE CAVITY—THAT'S THE INSIDE, YES, AT THE BOTTOM— WITH SALT AND PEPPER, AND A LITTLE LEMON IF YOU HAVE IT."
"TUCK THE LEGS UNDER AND YOU'LL KNOW IT'S DONE IF THE JUICES RUN CLEAR."
"DO YOU HAVE A MEAT THERMOMETER?"
"PIERCE THE CHICKEN IN THE THIGH, THAT'S THE BEST PLACE TO TEST."
THE MAN HAS NEVER COOKED A CHICKEN BEFORE, HE TELLS SOPHIE, BUT IT'S HIS FIRST CHRISTMAS SINCE HIS WIFE DIED, SO HE THINKS IT'S BEST HE LEARN.

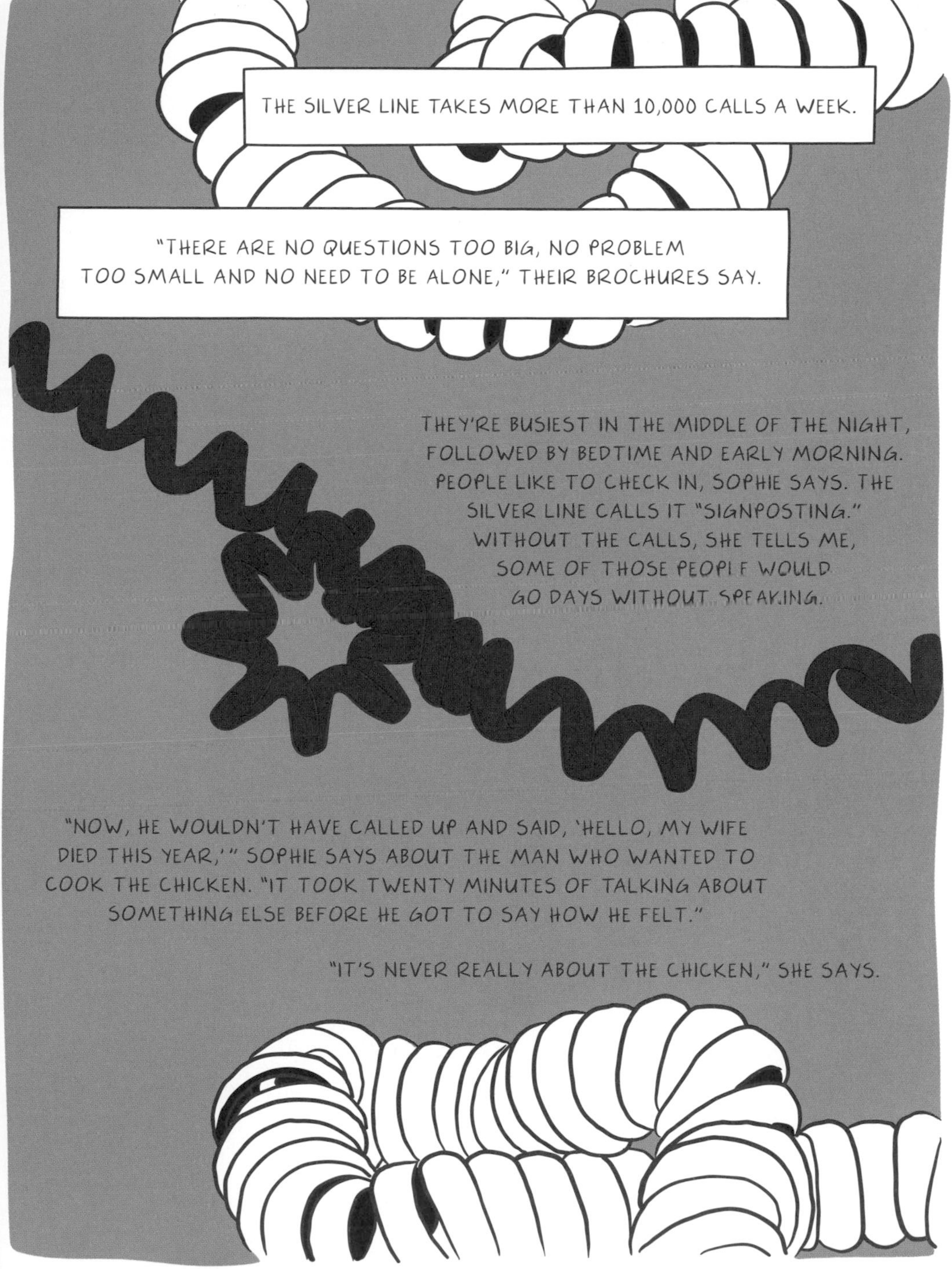
THE SILVER LINE TAKES MORE THAN 10,000 CALLS A WEEK.
"THERE ARE NO QUESTIONS TOO BIG, NO PROBLEM TOO SMALL AND NO NEED TO BE ALONE," THEIR BROCHURES SAY.
THEY'RE BUSIEST IN THE MIDDLE OF THE NIGHT, FOLLOWED BY BEDTIME AND EARLY MORNING. PEOPLE LIKE TO CHECK IN, SOPHIE SAYS. THE SILVER LINE CALLS IT "SIGNPOSTING." WITHOUT THE CALLS, SHE TELLS ME, SOME OF THOSE PEOPLE WOULD GO DAYS WITHOUT SPEAKING.
"NOW, HE WOULDN'T HAVE CALLED UP AND SAID, 'HELLO, MY WIFE DIED THIS YEAR,'" SOPHIE SAYS ABOUT THE MAN WHO WANTED TO COOK THE CHICKEN. "IT TOOK TWENTY MINUTES OF TALKING ABOUT SOMETHING ELSE BEFORE HE GOT TO SAY HOW HE FELT."
"IT'S NEVER REALLY ABOUT THE CHICKEN," SHE SAYS.

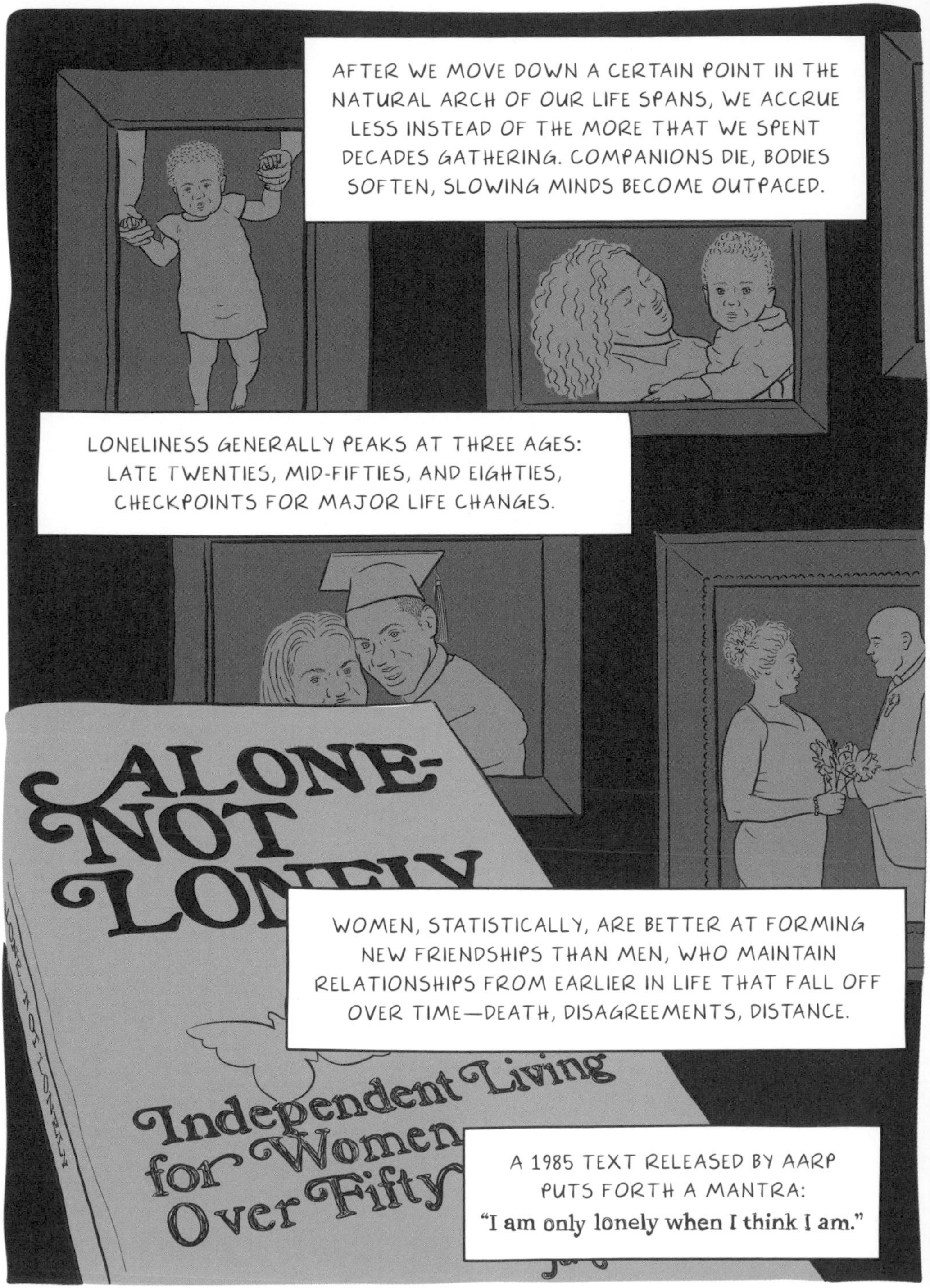
AFTER WE MOVE DOWN A CERTAIN POINT IN THE NATURAL ARCH OF OUR LIFE SPANS, WE ACCRUE LESS INSTEAD OF THE MORE THAT WE SPENT DECADES GATHERING. COMPANIONS DIE, BODIES SOFTEN, SLOWING MINDS BECOME OUTPACED.
LONELINESS GENERALLY PEAKS AT THREE AGES: LATE TWENTIES, MID-FIFTIES, AND EIGHTIES, CHECKPOINTS FOR MAJOR LIFE CHANGES.
ALONE-NOT LONELY
WOMEN, STATISTICALLY, ARE BETTER AT FORMING NEW FRIENDSHIPS THAN MEN, WHO MAINTAIN RELATIONSHIPS FROM EARLIER IN LIFE THAT FALL OFF OVER TIME—DEATH, DISAGREEMENTS, DISTANCE.
Independent Living for Women Over Fifty
A 1985 TEXT RELEASED BY AARP PUTS FORTH A MANTRA:
"I am only lonely when I think I am."

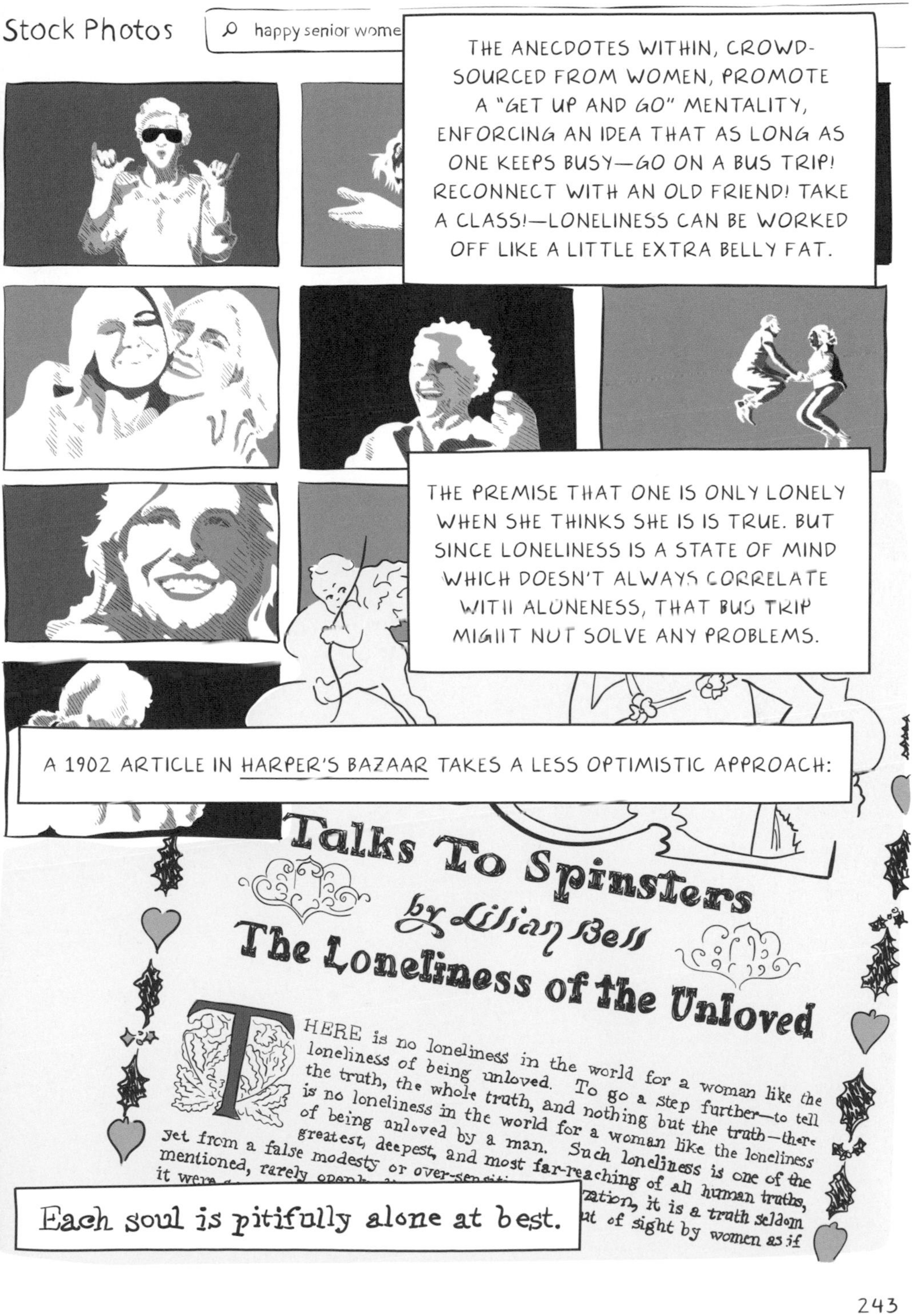
Stock Photos
happy senior wome
THE ANECDOTES WITHIN, CROWD-SOURCED FROM WOMEN, PROMOTE A "GET UP AND GO" MENTALITY, ENFORCING AN IDEA THAT AS LONG AS ONE KEEPS BUSY—GO ON A BUS TRIP! RECONNECT WITH AN OLD FRIEND! TAKE A CLASS!—LONELINESS CAN BE WORKED OFF LIKE A LITTLE EXTRA BELLY FAT.
THE PREMISE THAT ONE IS ONLY LONELY WHEN SHE THINKS SHE IS IS TRUE. BUT SINCE LONELINESS IS A STATE OF MIND WHICH DOESN'T ALWAYS CORRELATE WITH ALONENESS, THAT BUS TRIP MIGHT NOT SOLVE ANY PROBLEMS.
A 1902 ARTICLE IN HARPER'S BAZAAR TAKES A LESS OPTIMISTIC APPROACH:
Talks To Spinsters
by Lilian Bell
The Loneliness of the Unloved
THERE is no loneliness in the world for a woman like the loneliness of being unloved. To go a step further—to tell the truth, the whole truth, and nothing but the truth—there is no loneliness in the world for a woman like the loneliness of being unloved by a man. Such loneliness is one of the greatest, deepest, and most far-reaching of all human truths, yet from a false modesty or over-sensiti
zation, it is a truth seldom mentioned, rarely openl
ut of sight by women as if it were
Each soul is pitifully alone at best.

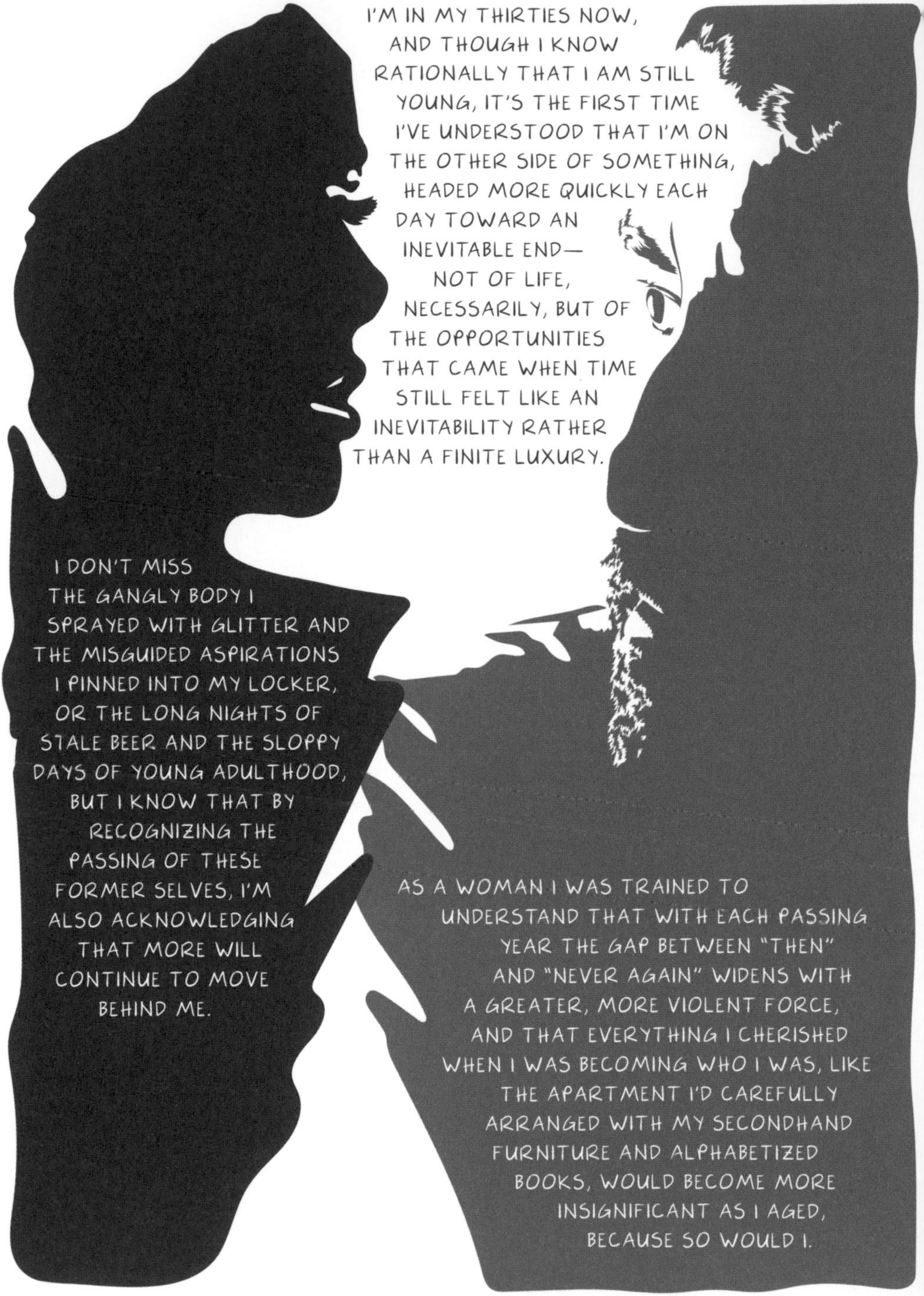
I'M IN MY THIRTIES NOW, AND THOUGH I KNOW RATIONALLY THAT I AM STILL YOUNG, IT'S THE FIRST TIME I'VE UNDERSTOOD THAT I'M ON THE OTHER SIDE OF SOMETHING, HEADED MORE QUICKLY EACH DAY TOWARD AN INEVITABLE END— NOT OF LIFE, NECESSARILY, BUT OF THE OPPORTUNITIES THAT CAME WHEN TIME STILL FELT LIKE AN INEVITABILITY RATHER THAN A FINITE LUXURY.
I DON'T MISS THE GANGLY BODY I SPRAYED WITH GLITTER AND THE MISGUIDED ASPIRATIONS I PINNED INTO MY LOCKER, OR THE LONG NIGHTS OF STALE BEER AND THE SLOPPY DAYS OF YOUNG ADULTHOOD, BUT I KNOW THAT BY RECOGNIZING THE PASSING OF THESE FORMER SELVES, I'M ALSO ACKNOWLEDGING THAT MORE WILL CONTINUE TO MOVE BEHIND ME.
AS A WOMAN I WAS TRAINED TO UNDERSTAND THAT WITH EACH PASSING YEAR THE GAP BETWEEN "THEN" AND "NEVER AGAIN" WIDENS WITH A GREATER, MORE VIOLENT FORCE, AND THAT EVERYTHING I CHERISHED WHEN I WAS BECOMING WHO I WAS, LIKE THE APARTMENT I'D CAREFULLY ARRANGED WITH MY SECONDHAND FURNITURE AND ALPHABETIZED BOOKS, WOULD BECOME MORE INSIGNIFICANT AS I AGED, BECAUSE SO WOULD I.

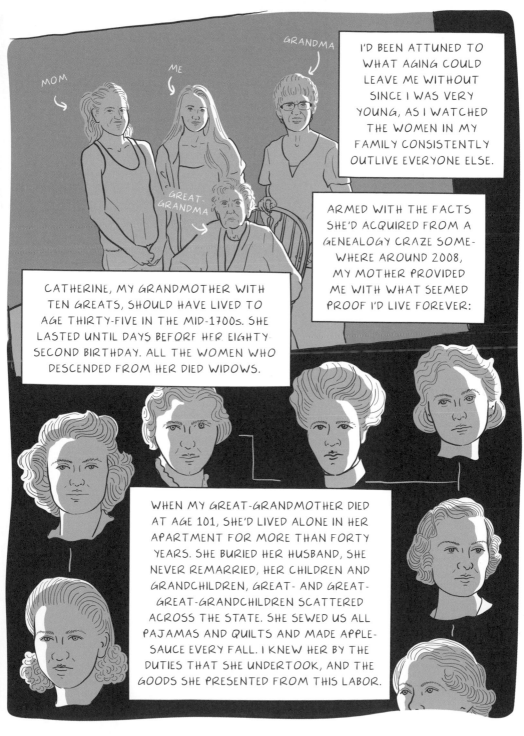

MOM

ME

GRANDMA

GREAT-GRANDMA

I'D BEEN ATTUNED TO WHAT AGING COULD LEAVE ME WITHOUT SINCE I WAS VERY YOUNG, AS I WATCHED THE WOMEN IN MY FAMILY CONSISTENTLY OUTLIVE EVERYONE ELSE.

ARMED WITH THE FACTS SHE'D ACQUIRED FROM A GENEALOGY CRAZE SOME-WHERE AROUND 2008, MY MOTHER PROVIDED ME WITH WHAT SEEMED PROOF I'D LIVE FOREVER:

CATHERINE, MY GRANDMOTHER WITH TEN GREATS, SHOULD HAVE LIVED TO AGE THIRTY-FIVE IN THE MID-1700s. SHE LASTED UNTIL DAYS BEFORE HER EIGHTY-SECOND BIRTHDAY. ALL THE WOMEN WHO DESCENDED FROM HER DIED WIDOWS.

WHEN MY GREAT-GRANDMOTHER DIED AT AGE 101, SHE'D LIVED ALONE IN HER APARTMENT FOR MORE THAN FORTY YEARS. SHE BURIED HER HUSBAND, SHE NEVER REMARRIED, HER CHILDREN AND GRANDCHILDREN, GREAT- AND GREAT-GREAT-GRANDCHILDREN SCATTERED ACROSS THE STATE. SHE SEWED US ALL PAJAMAS AND QUILTS AND MADE APPLE-SAUCE EVERY FALL. I KNEW HER BY THE DUTIES THAT SHE UNDERTOOK, AND THE GOODS SHE PRESENTED FROM THIS LABOR.

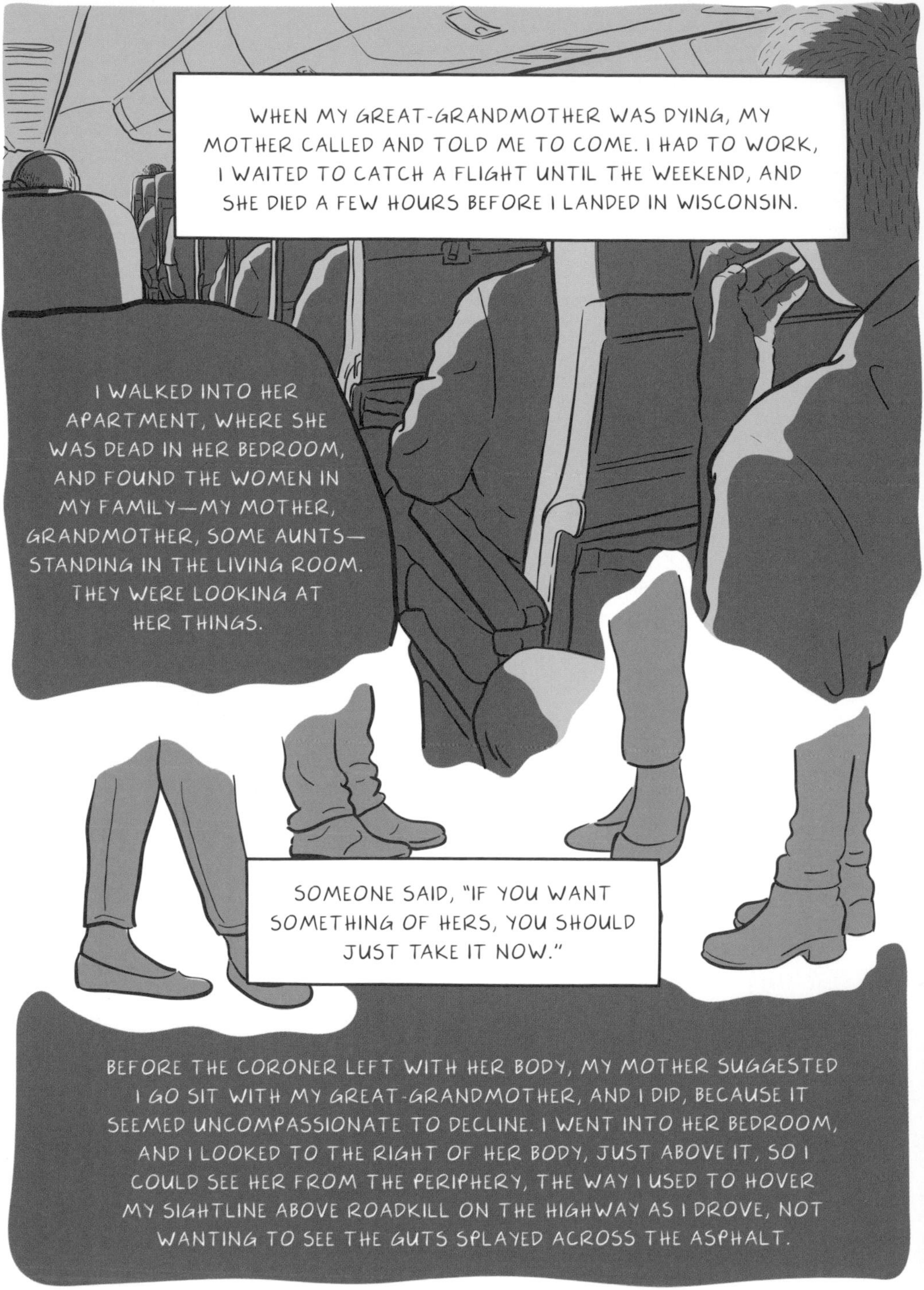
WHEN MY GREAT-GRANDMOTHER WAS DYING, MY MOTHER CALLED AND TOLD ME TO COME. I HAD TO WORK, I WAITED TO CATCH A FLIGHT UNTIL THE WEEKEND, AND SHE DIED A FEW HOURS BEFORE I LANDED IN WISCONSIN.
I WALKED INTO HER APARTMENT, WHERE SHE WAS DEAD IN HER BEDROOM, AND FOUND THE WOMEN IN MY FAMILY—MY MOTHER, GRANDMOTHER, SOME AUNTS—STANDING IN THE LIVING ROOM. THEY WERE LOOKING AT HER THINGS.
SOMEONE SAID, "IF YOU WANT SOMETHING OF HERS, YOU SHOULD JUST TAKE IT NOW."
BEFORE THE CORONER LEFT WITH HER BODY, MY MOTHER SUGGESTED I GO SIT WITH MY GREAT-GRANDMOTHER, AND I DID, BECAUSE IT SEEMED UNCOMPASSIONATE TO DECLINE. I WENT INTO HER BEDROOM, AND I LOOKED TO THE RIGHT OF HER BODY, JUST ABOVE IT, SO I COULD SEE HER FROM THE PERIPHERY, THE WAY I USED TO HOVER MY SIGHTLINE ABOVE ROADKILL ON THE HIGHWAY AS I DROVE, NOT WANTING TO SEE THE GUTS SPLAYED ACROSS THE ASPHALT.

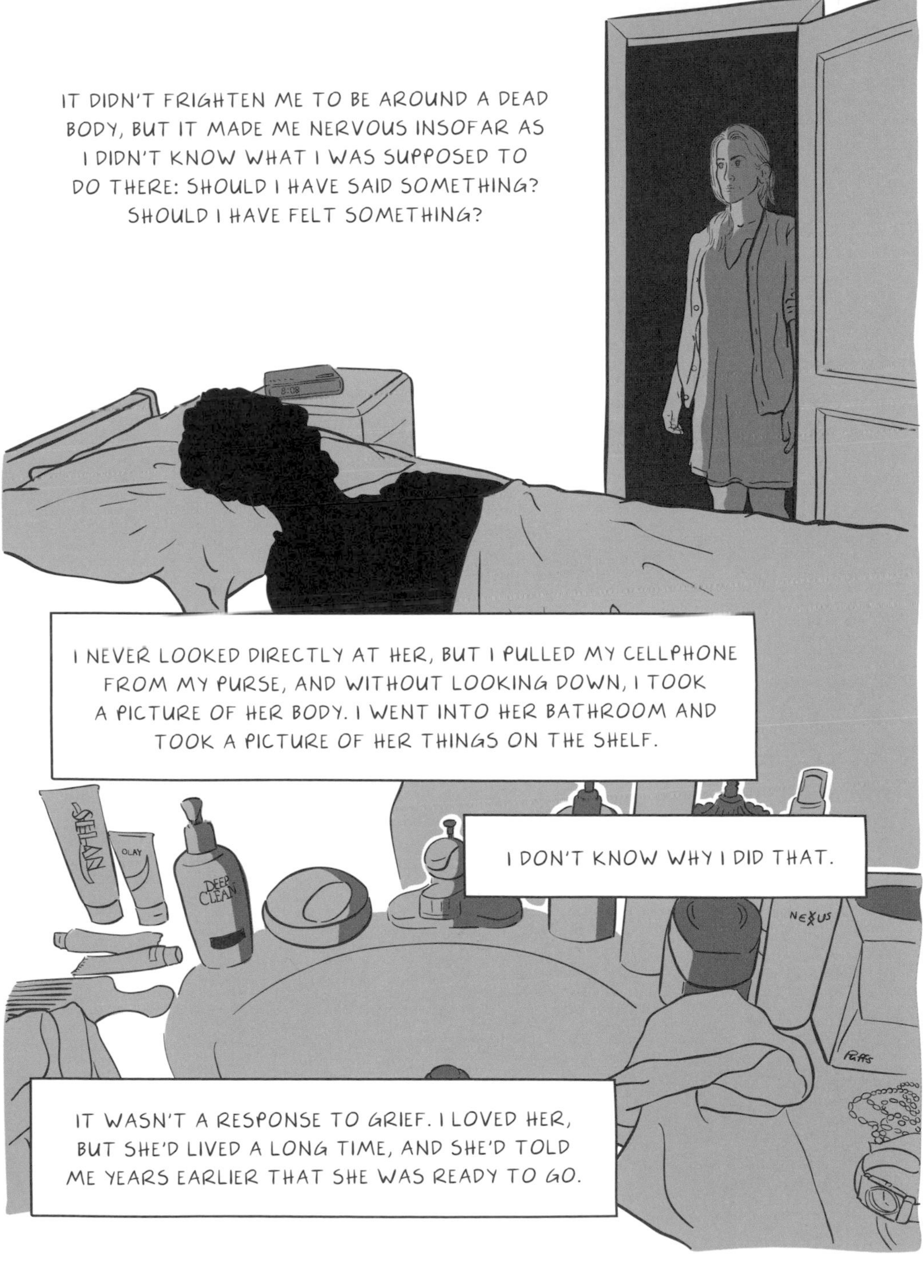
IT DIDN'T FRIGHTEN ME TO BE AROUND A DEAD BODY, BUT IT MADE ME NERVOUS INSOFAR AS I DIDN'T KNOW WHAT I WAS SUPPOSED TO DO THERE: SHOULD I HAVE SAID SOMETHING? SHOULD I HAVE FELT SOMETHING?
8:08
I NEVER LOOKED DIRECTLY AT HER, BUT I PULLED MY CELLPHONE FROM MY PURSE, AND WITHOUT LOOKING DOWN, I TOOK A PICTURE OF HER BODY. I WENT INTO HER BATHROOM AND TOOK A PICTURE OF HER THINGS ON THE SHELF.
SELAN
OLAY
DEEP CLEAN
I DON'T KNOW WHY I DID THAT.
NEXUS
Puffs
IT WASN'T A RESPONSE TO GRIEF. I LOVED HER, BUT SHE'D LIVED A LONG TIME, AND SHE'D TOLD ME YEARS EARLIER THAT SHE WAS READY TO GO.

IT WAS MORE THAT I DIDN'T WANT TO SEE AN END
I COULD ONLY ASSUME WOULD SOMEDAY MIRROR
MINE, BUT THAT LATER, I MIGHT WANT THE OPTION
TO REVIEW WHAT THAT WOULD LOOK LIKE.

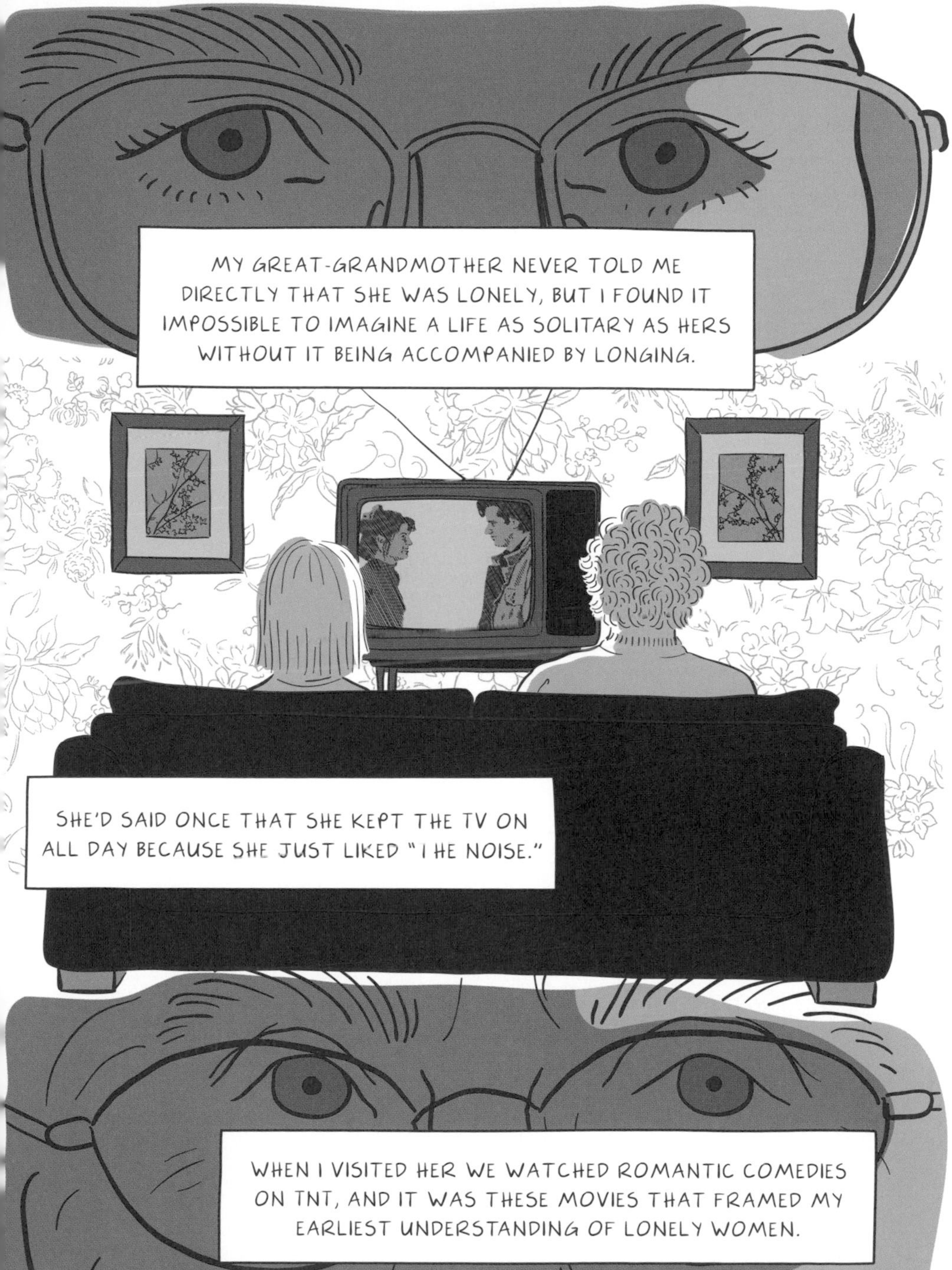
MY GREAT-GRANDMOTHER NEVER TOLD ME DIRECTLY THAT SHE WAS LONELY, BUT I FOUND IT IMPOSSIBLE TO IMAGINE A LIFE AS SOLITARY AS HERS WITHOUT IT BEING ACCOMPANIED BY LONGING.
SHE'D SAID ONCE THAT SHE KEPT THE TV ON ALL DAY BECAUSE SHE JUST LIKED "THE NOISE."
WHEN I VISITED HER WE WATCHED ROMANTIC COMEDIES ON TNT, AND IT WAS THESE MOVIES THAT FRAMED MY EARLIEST UNDERSTANDING OF LONELY WOMEN.

THE STARS WERE BEAUTIFUL AND UNDERTOUCHED, WAITING TO BE SCOOPED OUT OF THEIR SAD, ISOLATED LIVES INTO READY-MADE AND SHINY ONES, WHILE THE SUPPORTING CHARACTERS WERE ROOTED IN A PATHETIC UNMATTERING—THE NOS NEIGHBOR IN HER BATHROBE COMPLAINING ABOUT THE NOISE; THE EMBITTERED, AGING COWORKER TRAPPED FOREVER AT THE ASSISTANT DESK, WITHOUT A SINGLE PHOTC PINNED TO THE CORKBOARD BEHIND HER COMPUTER.

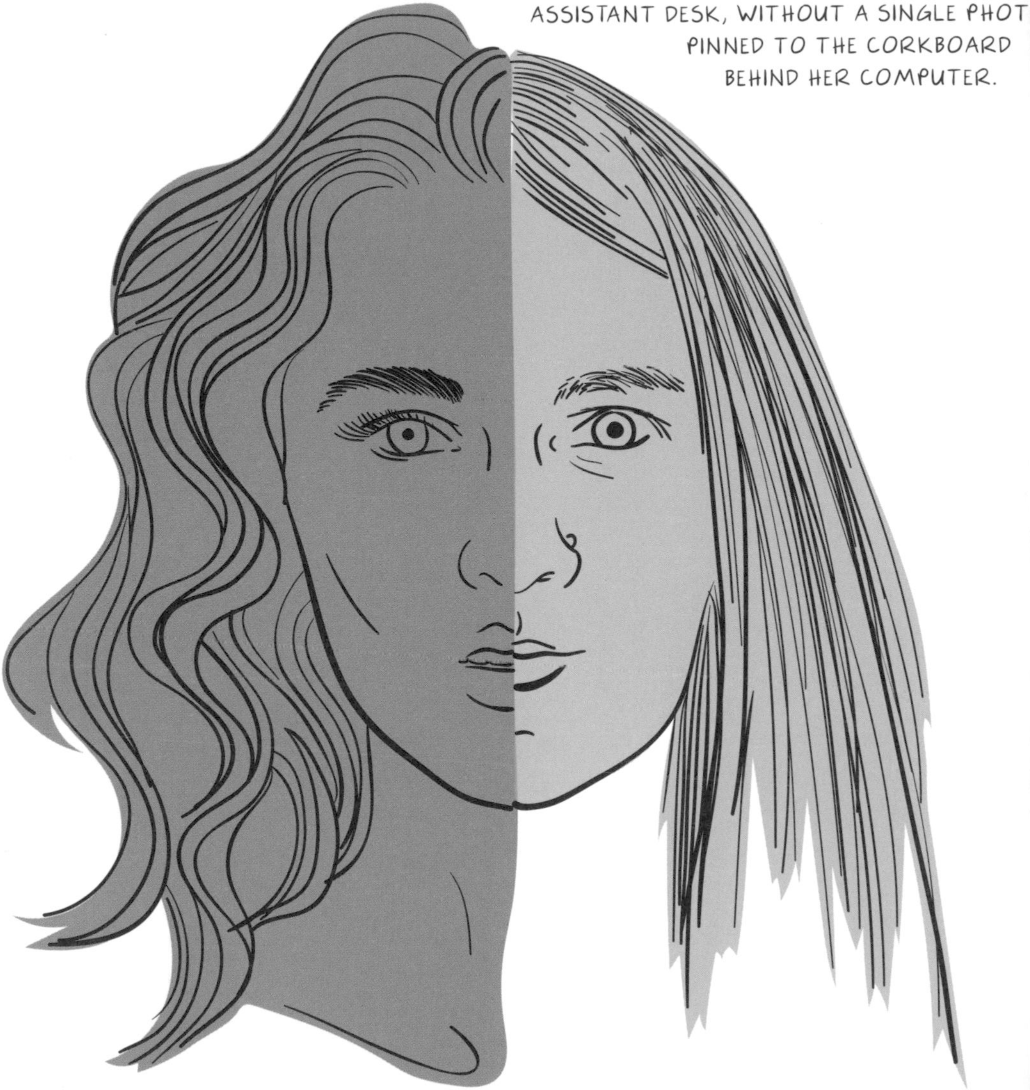

THE NEIGHBOR AND THE SECRETARY CANNOT TRUDGE OUT OF THEIR CRUSTY, UNFILLED LIVES, BUT THE STAR DOES, AND IT'S THE DRIVING FORCE BEHIND HER NARRATIVE.

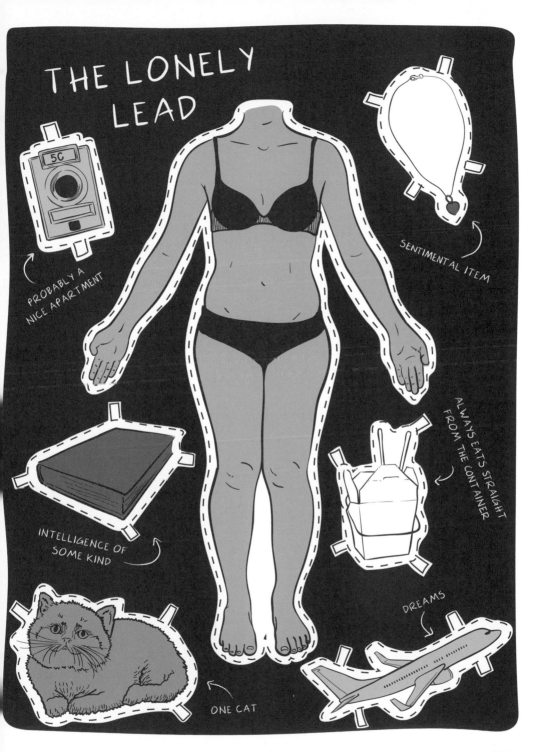

THE LONELY LEAD

5C

PROBABLY A NICE APARTMENT

SENTIMENTAL ITEM

INTELLIGENCE OF SOME KIND

ALWAYS EATS STRAIGHT FROM THE CONTAINER

DREAMS

ONE CAT

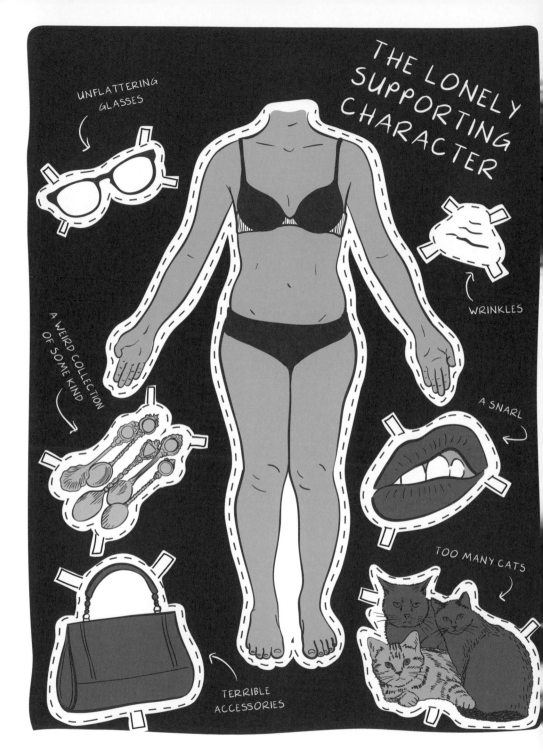

THE LONELY SUPPORTING CHARACTER

UNFLATTERING GLASSES

WRINKLES

A WEIRD COLLECTION OF SOME KIND

A SNARL

TOO MANY CATS

TERRIBLE ACCESSORIES

252

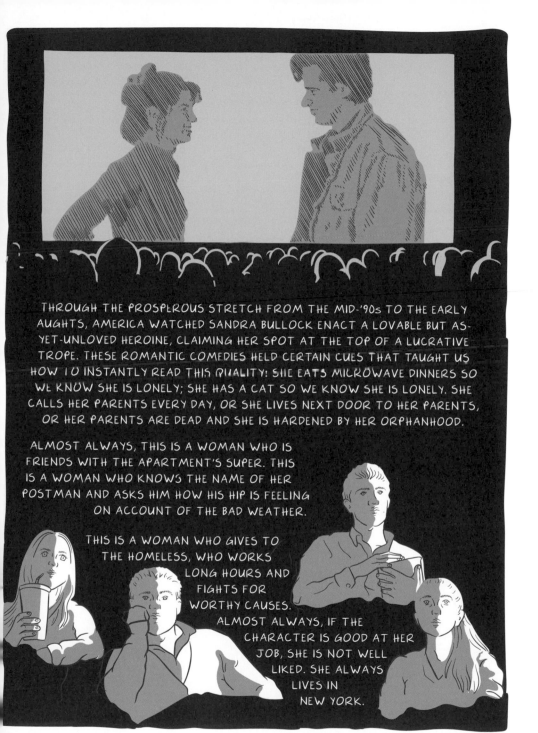

THROUGH THE PROSPEROUS STRETCH FROM THE MID-'90s TO THE EARLY AUGHTS, AMERICA WATCHED SANDRA BULLOCK ENACT A LOVABLE BUT AS-YET-UNLOVED HEROINE, CLAIMING HER SPOT AT THE TOP OF A LUCRATIVE TROPE. THESE ROMANTIC COMEDIES HELD CERTAIN CUES THAT TAUGHT US HOW TO INSTANTLY READ THIS QUALITY: SHE EATS MICROWAVE DINNERS SO WE KNOW SHE IS LONELY; SHE HAS A CAT SO WE KNOW SHE IS LONELY. SHE CALLS HER PARENTS EVERY DAY, OR SHE LIVES NEXT DOOR TO HER PARENTS, OR HER PARENTS ARE DEAD AND SHE IS HARDENED BY HER ORPHANHOOD.

ALMOST ALWAYS, THIS IS A WOMAN WHO IS FRIENDS WITH THE APARTMENT'S SUPER. THIS IS A WOMAN WHO KNOWS THE NAME OF HER POSTMAN AND ASKS HIM HOW HIS HIP IS FEELING ON ACCOUNT OF THE BAD WEATHER.

THIS IS A WOMAN WHO GIVES TO THE HOMELESS, WHO WORKS LONG HOURS AND FIGHTS FOR WORTHY CAUSES. ALMOST ALWAYS, IF THE CHARACTER IS GOOD AT HER JOB, SHE IS NOT WELL LIKED. SHE ALWAYS LIVES IN NEW YORK.

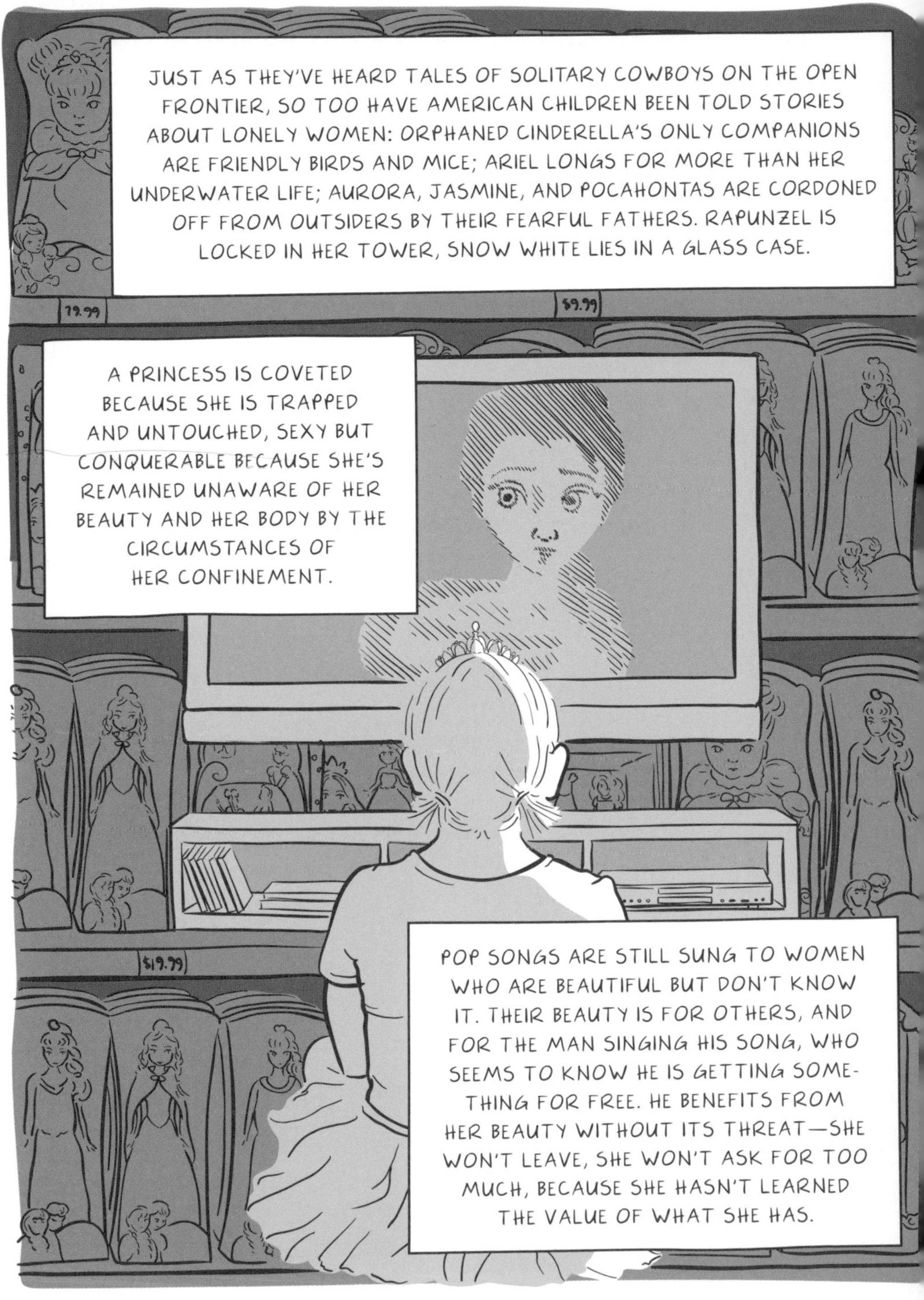
JUST AS THEY'VE HEARD TALES OF SOLITARY COWBOYS ON THE OPEN FRONTIER, SO TOO HAVE AMERICAN CHILDREN BEEN TOLD STORIES ABOUT LONELY WOMEN: ORPHANED CINDERELLA'S ONLY COMPANIONS ARE FRIENDLY BIRDS AND MICE; ARIEL LONGS FOR MORE THAN HER UNDERWATER LIFE; AURORA, JASMINE, AND POCAHONTAS ARE CORDONED OFF FROM OUTSIDERS BY THEIR FEARFUL FATHERS. RAPUNZEL IS LOCKED IN HER TOWER, SNOW WHITE LIES IN A GLASS CASE.
$9.99
A PRINCESS IS COVETED BECAUSE SHE IS TRAPPED AND UNTOUCHED, SEXY BUT CONQUERABLE BECAUSE SHE'S REMAINED UNAWARE OF HER BEAUTY AND HER BODY BY THE CIRCUMSTANCES OF HER CONFINEMENT.
$19.99
POP SONGS ARE STILL SUNG TO WOMEN WHO ARE BEAUTIFUL BUT DON'T KNOW IT. THEIR BEAUTY IS FOR OTHERS, AND FOR THE MAN SINGING HIS SONG, WHO SEEMS TO KNOW HE IS GETTING SOMETHING FOR FREE. HE BENEFITS FROM HER BEAUTY WITHOUT ITS THREAT—SHE WON'T LEAVE, SHE WON'T ASK FOR TOO MUCH, BECAUSE SHE HASN'T LEARNED THE VALUE OF WHAT SHE HAS.

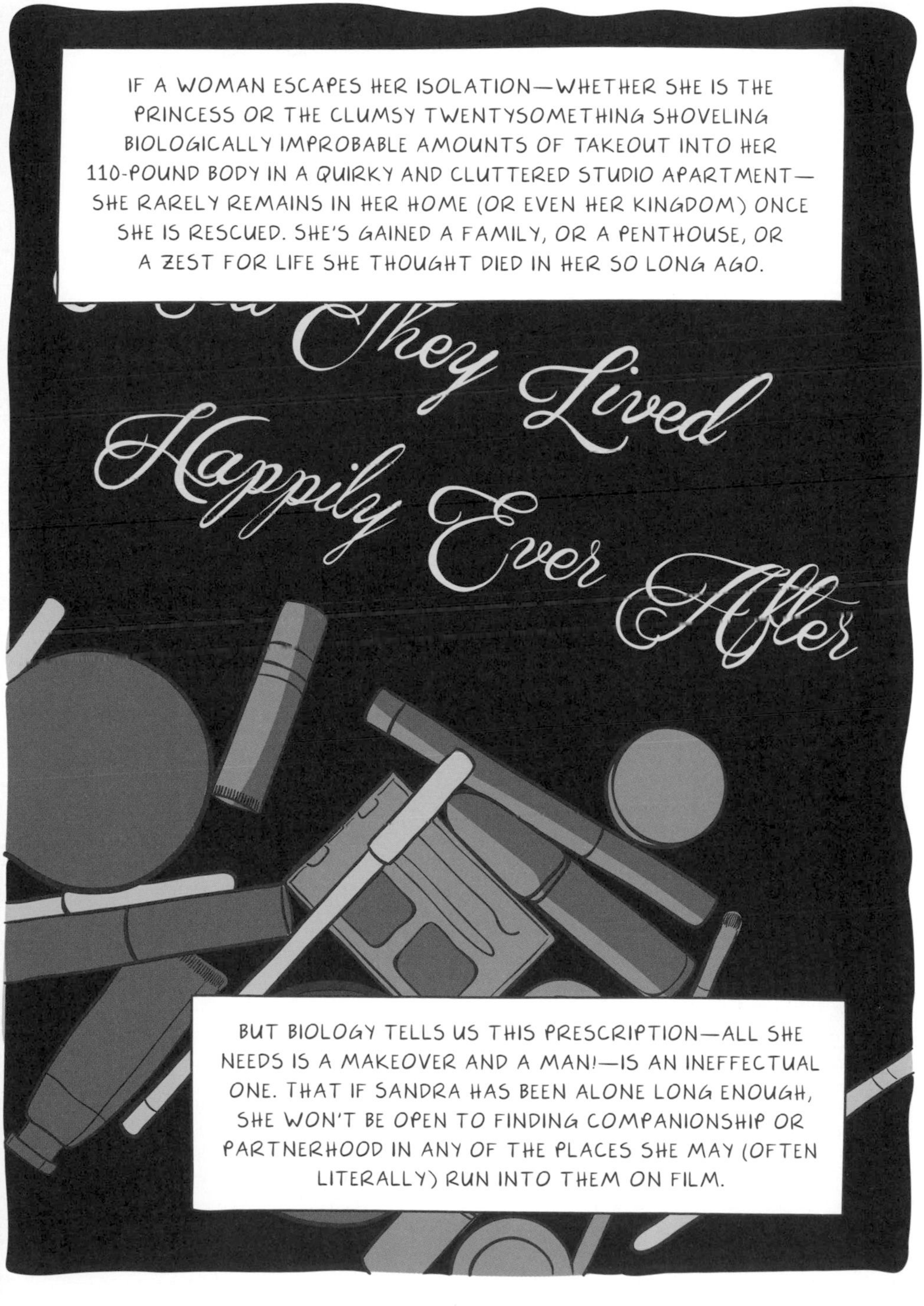
IF A WOMAN ESCAPES HER ISOLATION—WHETHER SHE IS THE PRINCESS OR THE CLUMSY TWENTYSOMETHING SHOVELING BIOLOGICALLY IMPROBABLE AMOUNTS OF TAKEOUT INTO HER 110-POUND BODY IN A QUIRKY AND CLUTTERED STUDIO APARTMENT—SHE RARELY REMAINS IN HER HOME (OR EVEN HER KINGDOM) ONCE SHE IS RESCUED. SHE'S GAINED A FAMILY, OR A PENTHOUSE, OR A ZEST FOR LIFE SHE THOUGHT DIED IN HER SO LONG AGO.
They Lived Happily Ever After
BUT BIOLOGY TELLS US THIS PRESCRIPTION—ALL SHE NEEDS IS A MAKEOVER AND A MAN!—IS AN INEFFECTUAL ONE. THAT IF SANDRA HAS BEEN ALONE LONG ENOUGH, SHE WON'T BE OPEN TO FINDING COMPANIONSHIP OR PARTNERHOOD IN ANY OF THE PLACES SHE MAY (OFTEN LITERALLY) RUN INTO THEM ON FILM.

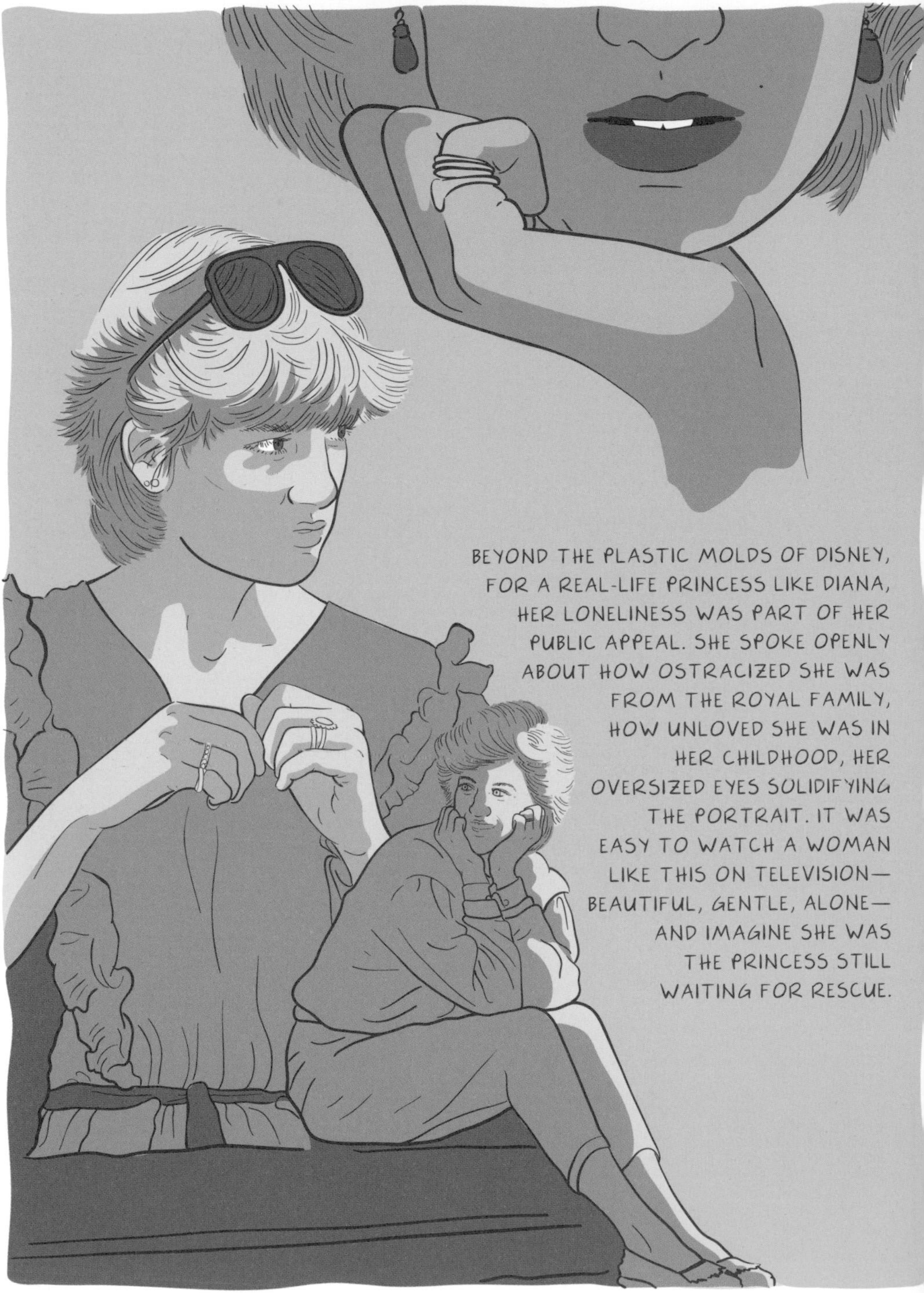
BEYOND THE PLASTIC MOLDS OF DISNEY, FOR A REAL-LIFE PRINCESS LIKE DIANA, HER LONELINESS WAS PART OF HER PUBLIC APPEAL. SHE SPOKE OPENLY ABOUT HOW OSTRACIZED SHE WAS FROM THE ROYAL FAMILY, HOW UNLOVED SHE WAS IN HER CHILDHOOD, HER OVERSIZED EYES SOLIDIFYING THE PORTRAIT. IT WAS EASY TO WATCH A WOMAN LIKE THIS ON TELEVISION— BEAUTIFUL, GENTLE, ALONE— AND IMAGINE SHE WAS THE PRINCESS STILL WAITING FOR RESCUE.

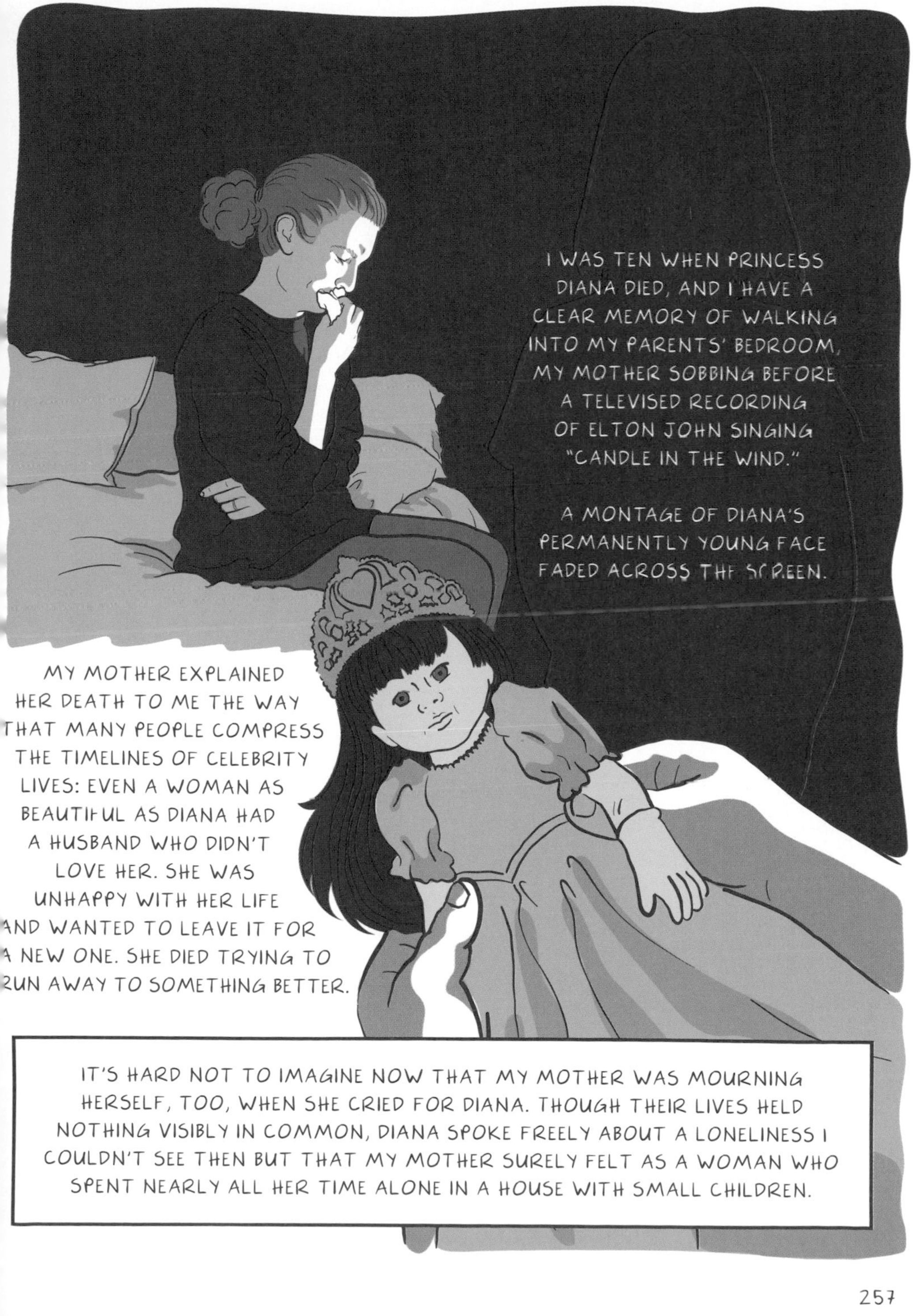
I WAS TEN WHEN PRINCESS DIANA DIED, AND I HAVE A CLEAR MEMORY OF WALKING INTO MY PARENTS' BEDROOM, MY MOTHER SOBBING BEFORE A TELEVISED RECORDING OF ELTON JOHN SINGING "CANDLE IN THE WIND."
A MONTAGE OF DIANA'S PERMANENTLY YOUNG FACE FADED ACROSS THE SCREEN.
MY MOTHER EXPLAINED HER DEATH TO ME THE WAY THAT MANY PEOPLE COMPRESS THE TIMELINES OF CELEBRITY LIVES: EVEN A WOMAN AS BEAUTIFUL AS DIANA HAD A HUSBAND WHO DIDN'T LOVE HER. SHE WAS UNHAPPY WITH HER LIFE AND WANTED TO LEAVE IT FOR A NEW ONE. SHE DIED TRYING TO RUN AWAY TO SOMETHING BETTER.
IT'S HARD NOT TO IMAGINE NOW THAT MY MOTHER WAS MOURNING HERSELF, TOO, WHEN SHE CRIED FOR DIANA. THOUGH THEIR LIVES HELD NOTHING VISIBLY IN COMMON, DIANA SPOKE FREELY ABOUT A LONELINESS I COULDN'T SEE THEN BUT THAT MY MOTHER SURELY FELT AS A WOMAN WHO SPENT NEARLY ALL HER TIME ALONE IN A HOUSE WITH SMALL CHILDREN.

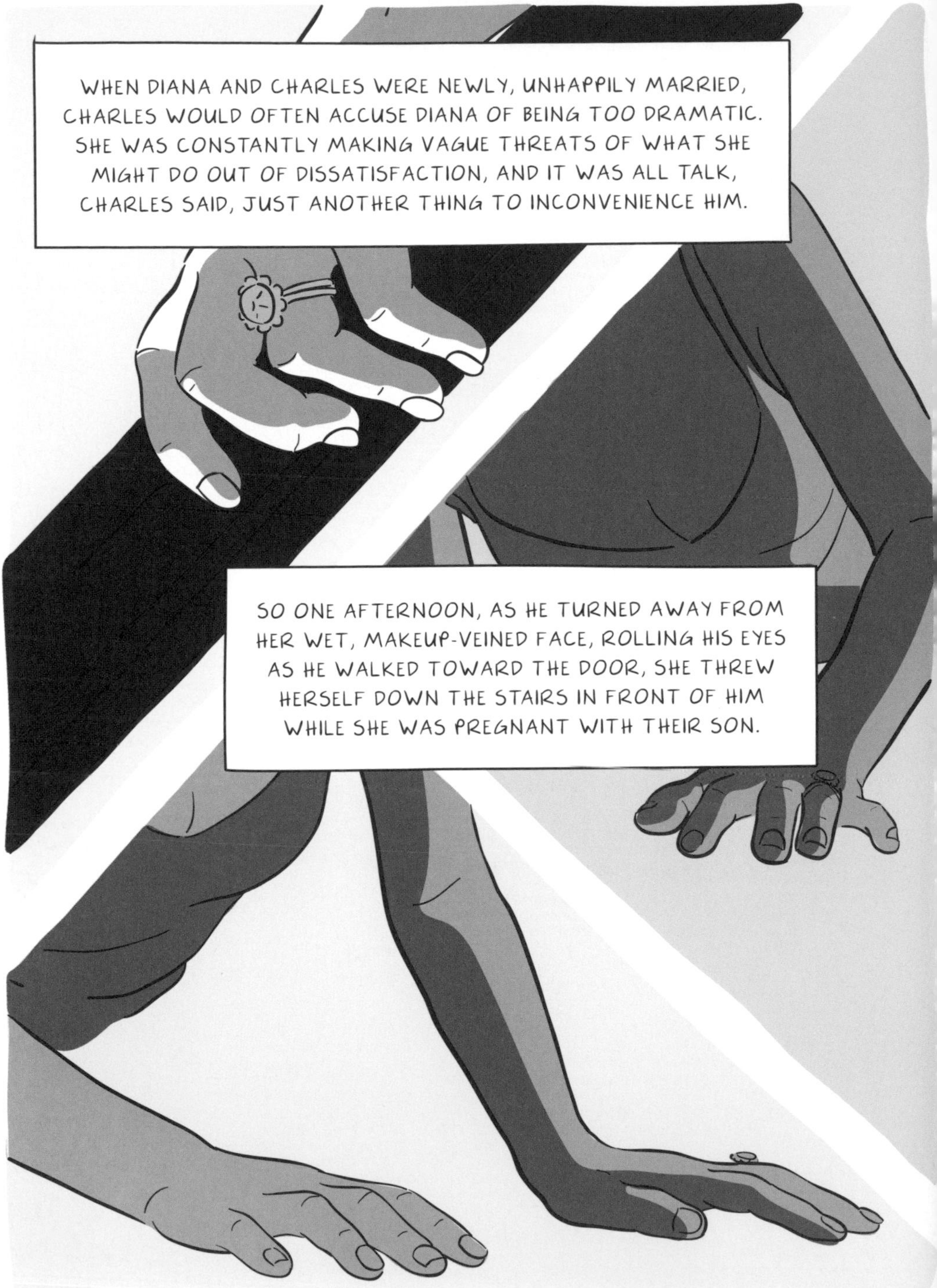
WHEN DIANA AND CHARLES WERE NEWLY, UNHAPPILY MARRIED, CHARLES WOULD OFTEN ACCUSE DIANA OF BEING TOO DRAMATIC. SHE WAS CONSTANTLY MAKING VAGUE THREATS OF WHAT SHE MIGHT DO OUT OF DISSATISFACTION, AND IT WAS ALL TALK, CHARLES SAID, JUST ANOTHER THING TO INCONVENIENCE HIM.
SO ONE AFTERNOON, AS HE TURNED AWAY FROM HER WET, MAKEUP-VEINED FACE, ROLLING HIS EYES AS HE WALKED TOWARD THE DOOR, SHE THREW HERSELF DOWN THE STAIRS IN FRONT OF HIM WHILE SHE WAS PREGNANT WITH THEIR SON.

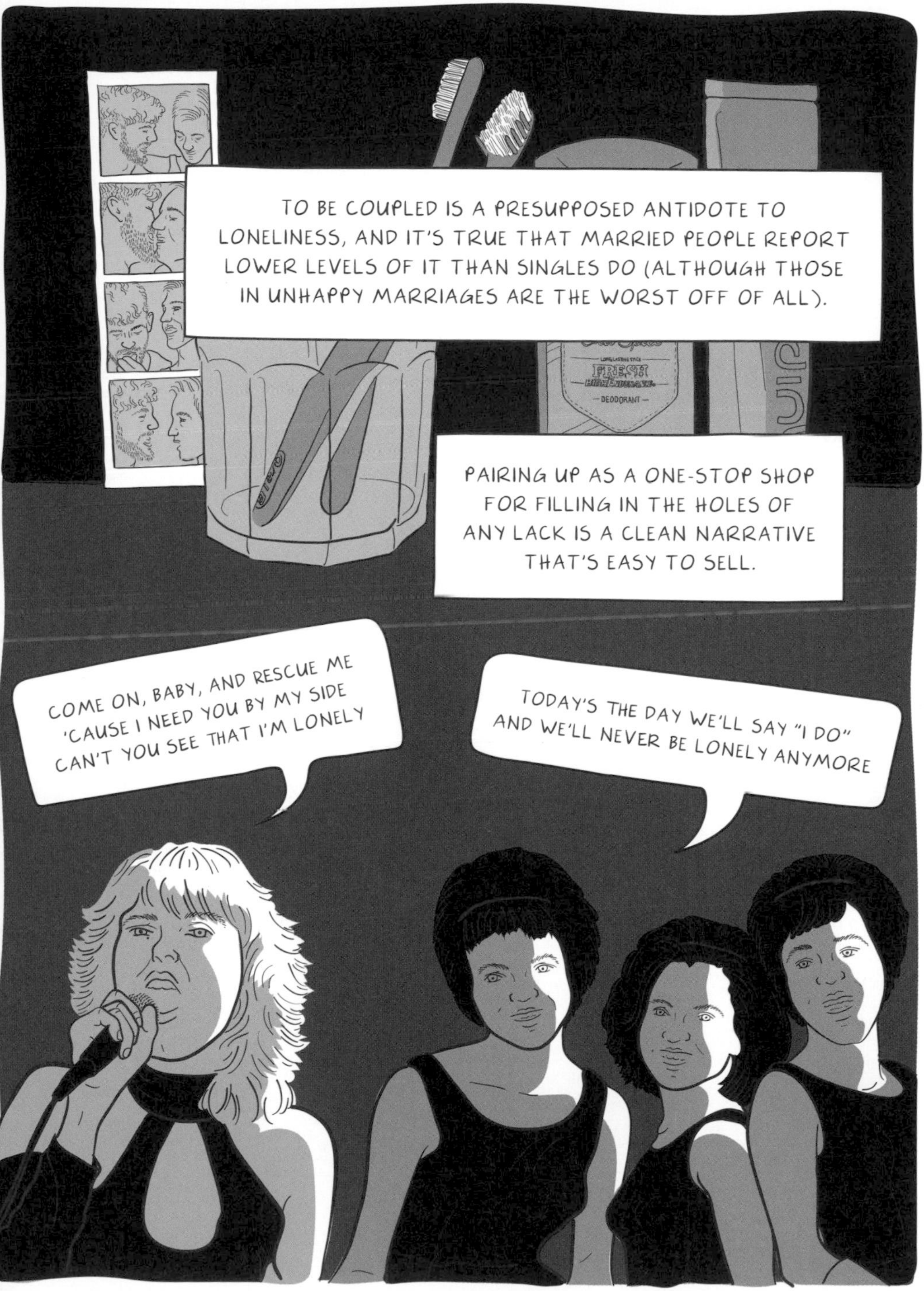
TO BE COUPLED IS A PRESUPPOSED ANTIDOTE TO LONELINESS, AND IT'S TRUE THAT MARRIED PEOPLE REPORT LOWER LEVELS OF IT THAN SINGLES DO (ALTHOUGH THOSE IN UNHAPPY MARRIAGES ARE THE WORST OFF OF ALL).
PAIRING UP AS A ONE-STOP SHOP FOR FILLING IN THE HOLES OF ANY LACK IS A CLEAN NARRATIVE THAT'S EASY TO SELL.
COME ON, BABY, AND RESCUE ME 'CAUSE I NEED YOU BY MY SIDE CAN'T YOU SEE THAT I'M LONELY
TODAY'S THE DAY WE'LL SAY "I DO" AND WE'LL NEVER BE LONELY ANYMORE

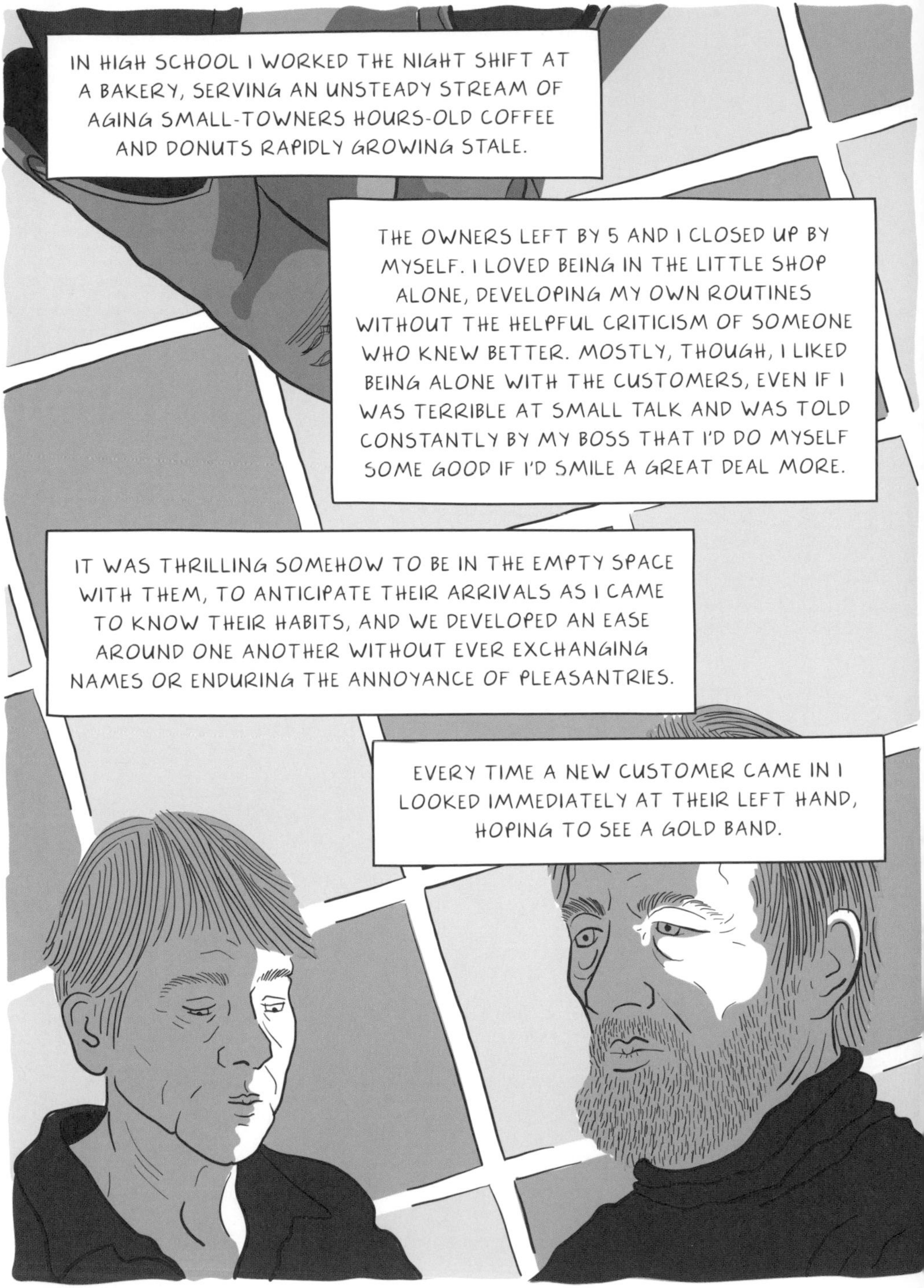
IN HIGH SCHOOL I WORKED THE NIGHT SHIFT AT A BAKERY, SERVING AN UNSTEADY STREAM OF AGING SMALL-TOWNERS HOURS-OLD COFFEE AND DONUTS RAPIDLY GROWING STALE.
THE OWNERS LEFT BY 5 AND I CLOSED UP BY MYSELF. I LOVED BEING IN THE LITTLE SHOP ALONE, DEVELOPING MY OWN ROUTINES WITHOUT THE HELPFUL CRITICISM OF SOMEONE WHO KNEW BETTER. MOSTLY, THOUGH, I LIKED BEING ALONE WITH THE CUSTOMERS, EVEN IF I WAS TERRIBLE AT SMALL TALK AND WAS TOLD CONSTANTLY BY MY BOSS THAT I'D DO MYSELF SOME GOOD IF I'D SMILE A GREAT DEAL MORE.
IT WAS THRILLING SOMEHOW TO BE IN THE EMPTY SPACE WITH THEM, TO ANTICIPATE THEIR ARRIVALS AS I CAME TO KNOW THEIR HABITS, AND WE DEVELOPED AN EASE AROUND ONE ANOTHER WITHOUT EVER EXCHANGING NAMES OR ENDURING THE ANNOYANCE OF PLEASANTRIES.
EVERY TIME A NEW CUSTOMER CAME IN I LOOKED IMMEDIATELY AT THEIR LEFT HAND, HOPING TO SEE A GOLD BAND.

GOOD, I'D THINK:
YOU'RE NOT ALONE.

IT WAS IMMATURE REASONING,
THIS IDEA THAT IF SOMEONE HAS PICKED
YOU AND YOU THEM YOU BELONG TO SOMETHING THAT'S PROTECTED FROM THE HUGE
EXPANSE OF SOLITUDE THAT SEEMED INESCAPABLE AS A TEENAGER
WATCHING THEM BUY DONUTS, COUNTING OUT THEIR CHANGE,
THEN MOPPING THE TILE, LOCKING THE DOOR, AND DRIVING
THE FOURTEEN MINUTES DOWN AN UNLIT COUNTRY ROAD
TO MY FAMILY'S HOUSE, BYPASSING MY PARENTS FOR
THE CONTAINED QUIET OF MY BEDROOM AND THE
ABSTRACT LONGINGS I FILLED IT WITH.

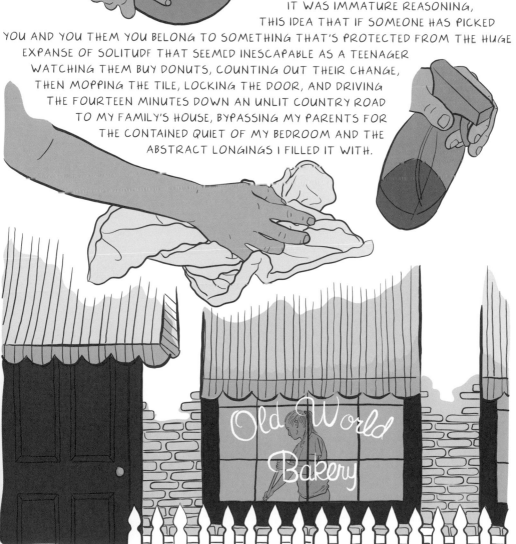

Old World
Bakery

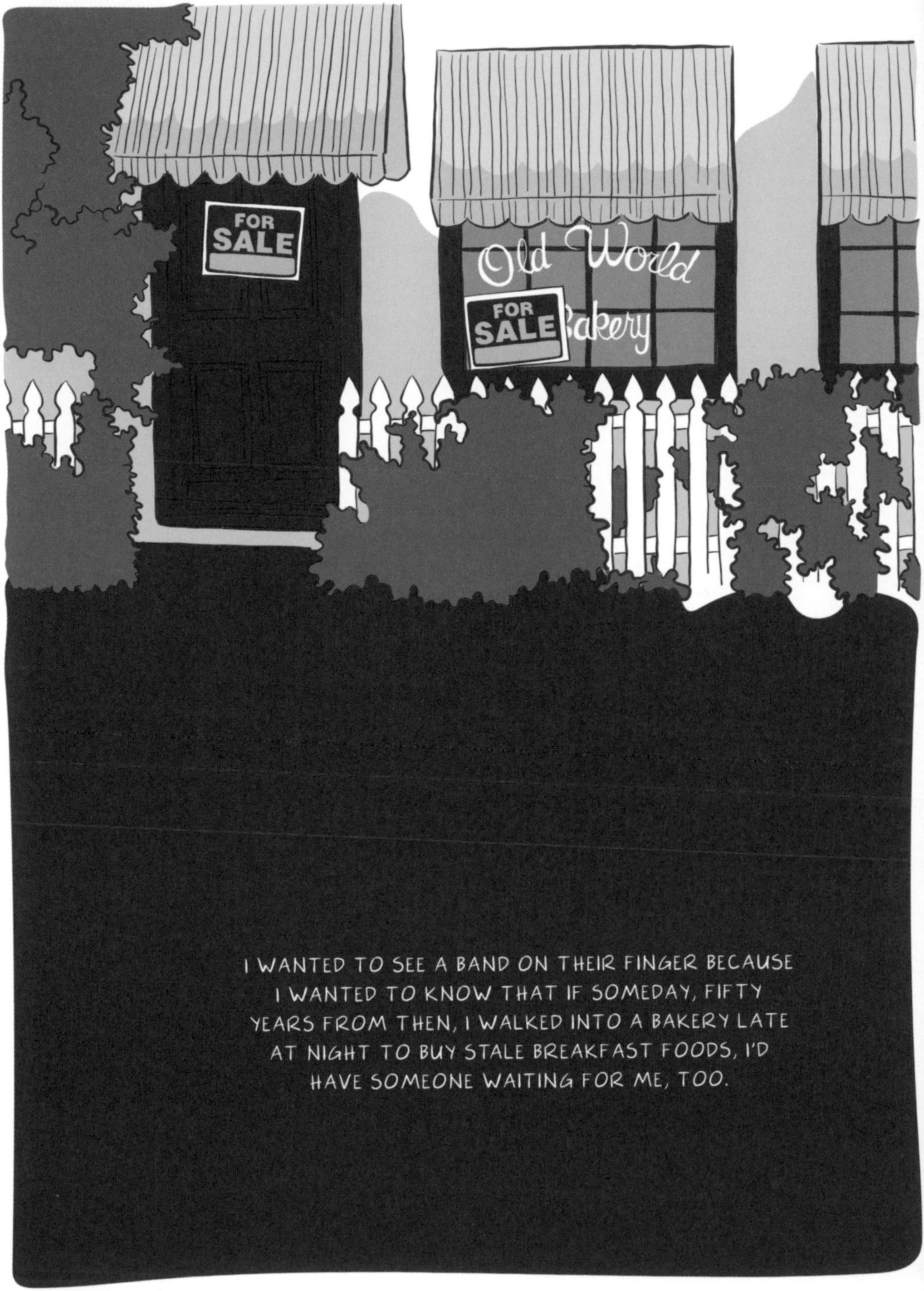
FOR SALE
Old World Bakery
FOR SALE
I WANTED TO SEE A BAND ON THEIR FINGER BECAUSE I WANTED TO KNOW THAT IF SOMEDAY, FIFTY YEARS FROM THEN, I WALKED INTO A BAKERY LATE AT NIGHT TO BUY STALE BREAKFAST FOODS, I'D HAVE SOMEONE WAITING FOR ME, TOO.

II

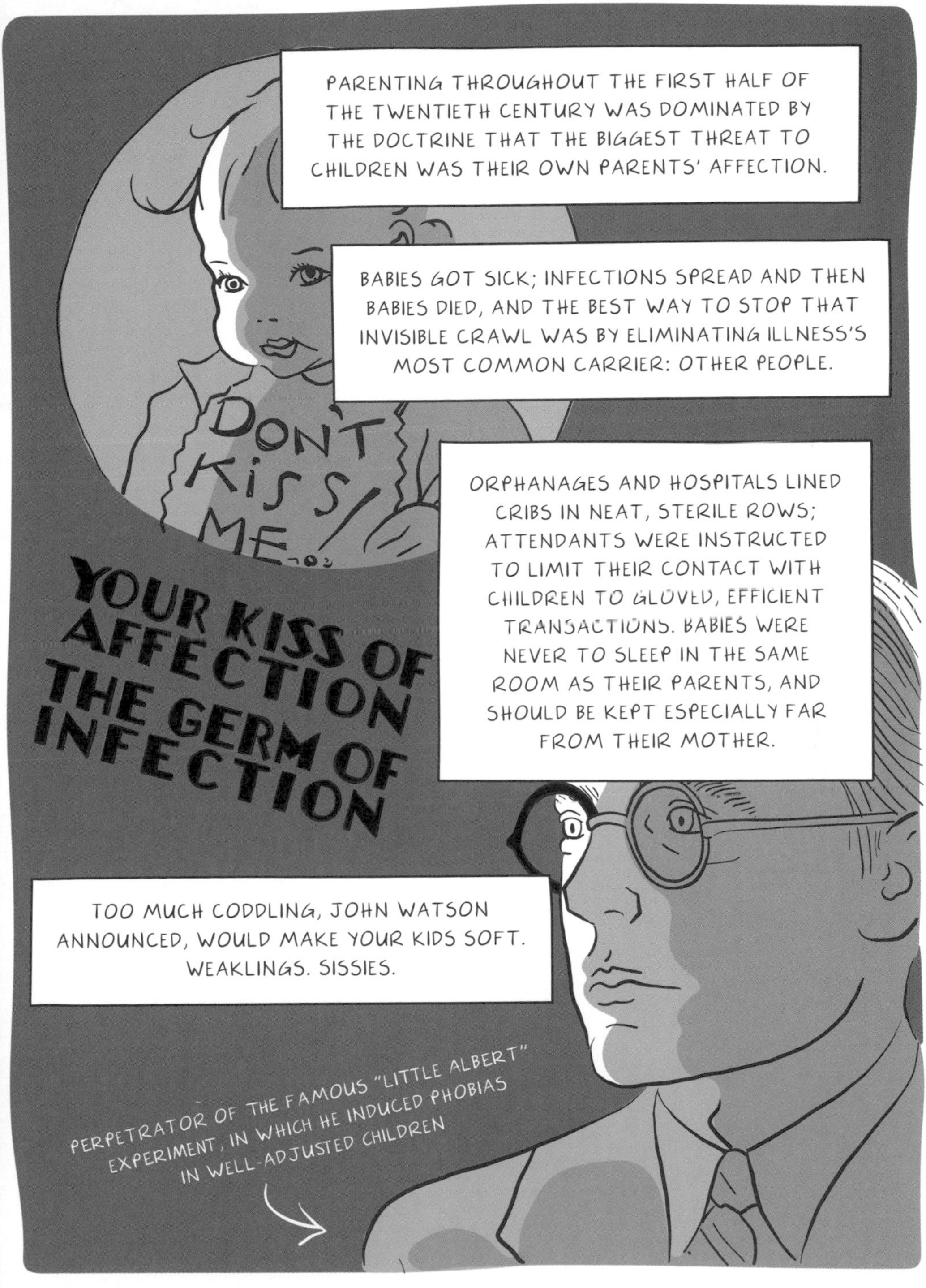
PARENTING THROUGHOUT THE FIRST HALF OF THE TWENTIETH CENTURY WAS DOMINATED BY THE DOCTRINE THAT THE BIGGEST THREAT TO CHILDREN WAS THEIR OWN PARENTS' AFFECTION.
BABIES GOT SICK; INFECTIONS SPREAD AND THEN BABIES DIED, AND THE BEST WAY TO STOP THAT INVISIBLE CRAWL WAS BY ELIMINATING ILLNESS'S MOST COMMON CARRIER: OTHER PEOPLE.
DON'T KISS ME!
YOUR KISS OF AFFECTION THE GERM OF INFECTION
ORPHANAGES AND HOSPITALS LINED CRIBS IN NEAT, STERILE ROWS; ATTENDANTS WERE INSTRUCTED TO LIMIT THEIR CONTACT WITH CHILDREN TO GLOVED, EFFICIENT TRANSACTIONS. BABIES WERE NEVER TO SLEEP IN THE SAME ROOM AS THEIR PARENTS, AND SHOULD BE KEPT ESPECIALLY FAR FROM THEIR MOTHER.
TOO MUCH CODDLING, JOHN WATSON ANNOUNCED, WOULD MAKE YOUR KIDS SOFT. WEAKLINGS. SISSIES.
PERPETRATOR OF THE FAMOUS "LITTLE ALBERT" EXPERIMENT, IN WHICH HE INDUCED PHOBIAS IN WELL-ADJUSTED CHILDREN

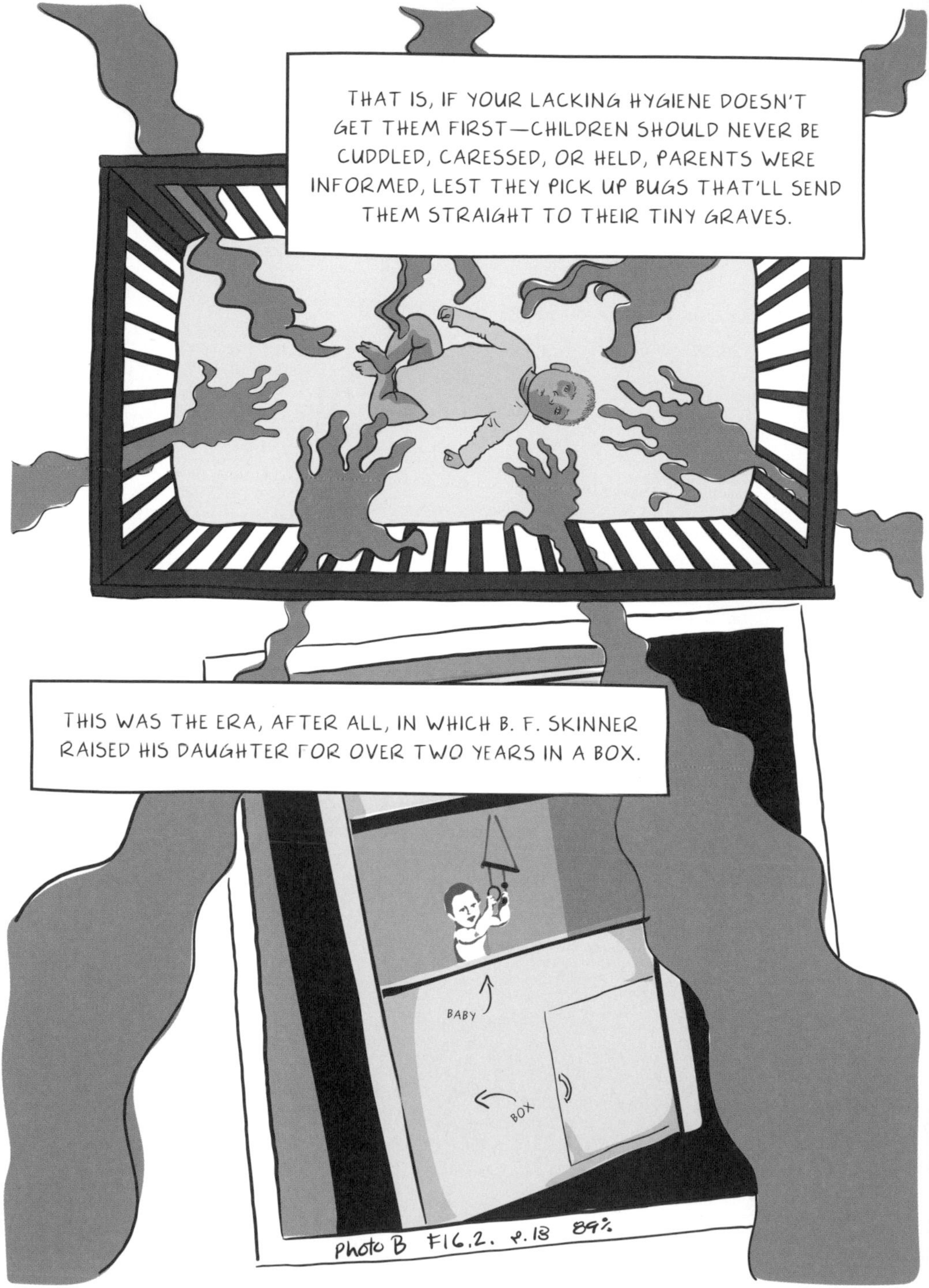
THAT IS, IF YOUR LACKING HYGIENE DOESN'T GET THEM FIRST—CHILDREN SHOULD NEVER BE CUDDLED, CARESSED, OR HELD, PARENTS WERE INFORMED, LEST THEY PICK UP BUGS THAT'LL SEND THEM STRAIGHT TO THEIR TINY GRAVES.
THIS WAS THE ERA, AFTER ALL, IN WHICH B. F. SKINNER RAISED HIS DAUGHTER FOR OVER TWO YEARS IN A BOX.
BABY
BOX
Photo B FIG.2. p.18 89%

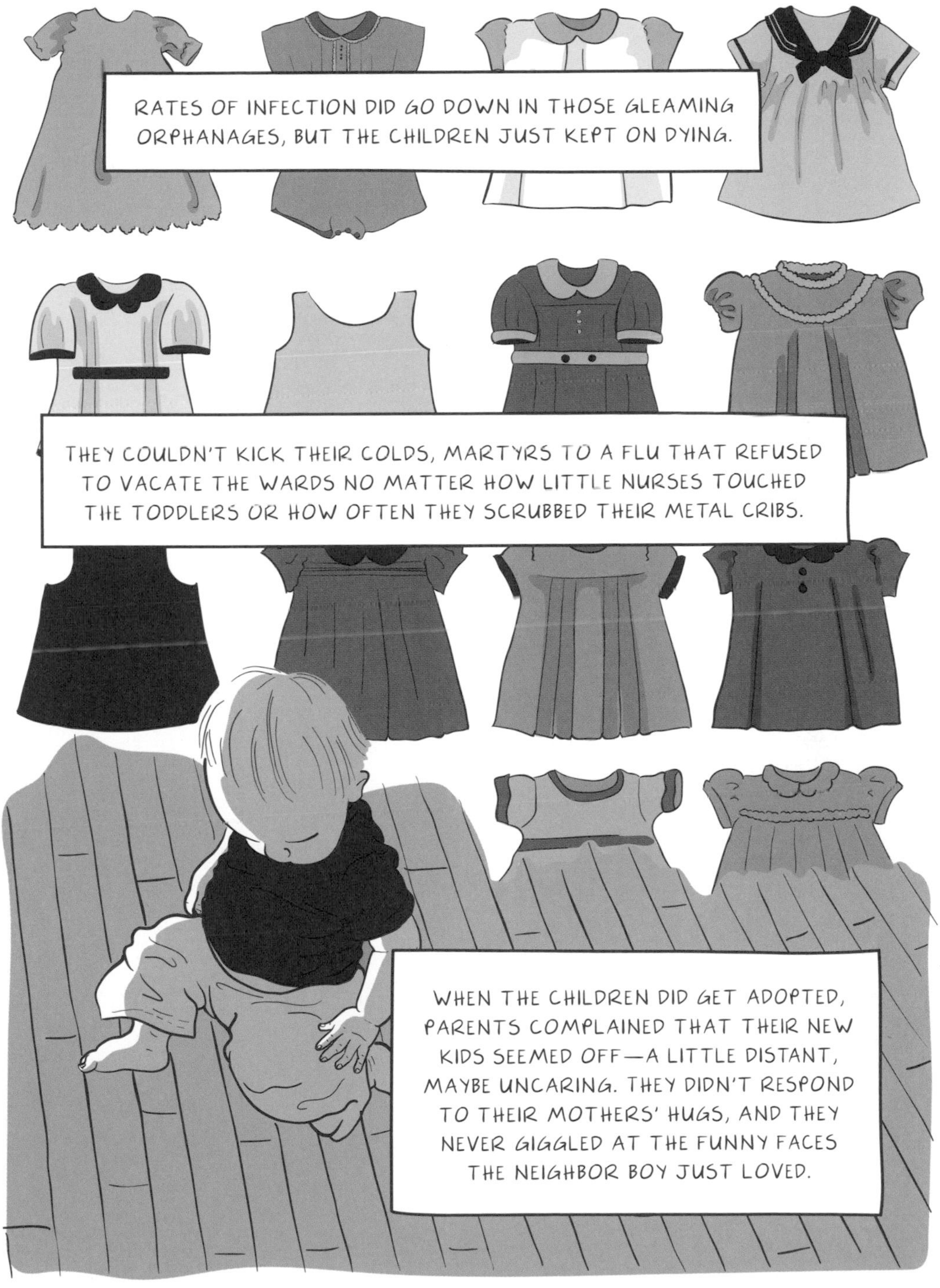
RATES OF INFECTION DID GO DOWN IN THOSE GLEAMING ORPHANAGES, BUT THE CHILDREN JUST KEPT ON DYING.
THEY COULDN'T KICK THEIR COLDS, MARTYRS TO A FLU THAT REFUSED TO VACATE THE WARDS NO MATTER HOW LITTLE NURSES TOUCHED THE TODDLERS OR HOW OFTEN THEY SCRUBBED THEIR METAL CRIBS.
WHEN THE CHILDREN DID GET ADOPTED, PARENTS COMPLAINED THAT THEIR NEW KIDS SEEMED OFF—A LITTLE DISTANT, MAYBE UNCARING. THEY DIDN'T RESPOND TO THEIR MOTHERS' HUGS, AND THEY NEVER GIGGLED AT THE FUNNY FACES THE NEIGHBOR BOY JUST LOVED.

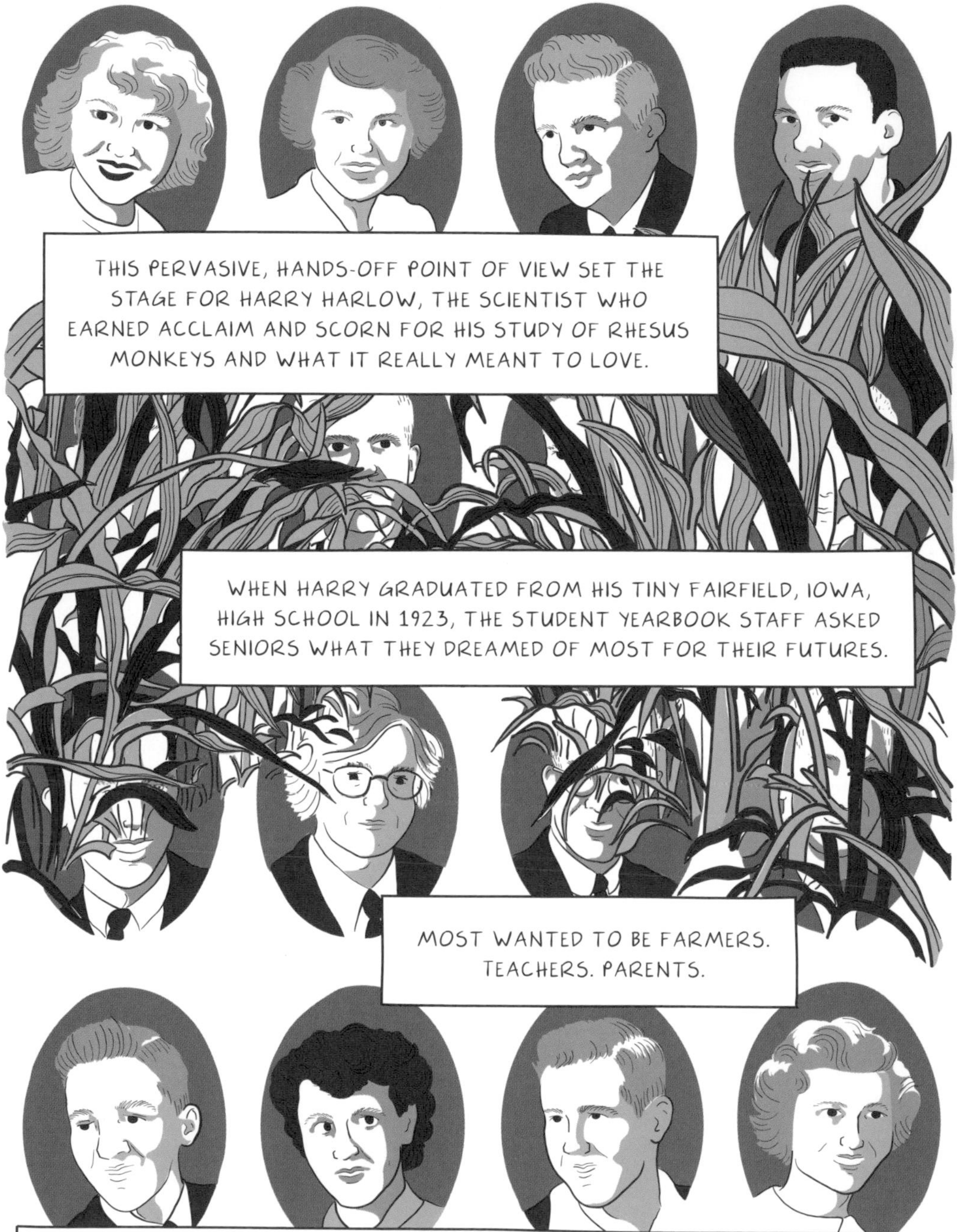
THIS PERVASIVE, HANDS-OFF POINT OF VIEW SET THE STAGE FOR HARRY HARLOW, THE SCIENTIST WHO EARNED ACCLAIM AND SCORN FOR HIS STUDY OF RHESUS MONKEYS AND WHAT IT REALLY MEANT TO LOVE.
WHEN HARRY GRADUATED FROM HIS TINY FAIRFIELD, IOWA, HIGH SCHOOL IN 1923, THE STUDENT YEARBOOK STAFF ASKED SENIORS WHAT THEY DREAMED OF MOST FOR THEIR FUTURES.
MOST WANTED TO BE FARMERS. TEACHERS. PARENTS.
HARRY HARLOW'S WISH, EMBOLDENED NEXT TO HIS PICTURE: "BE FAMOUS."

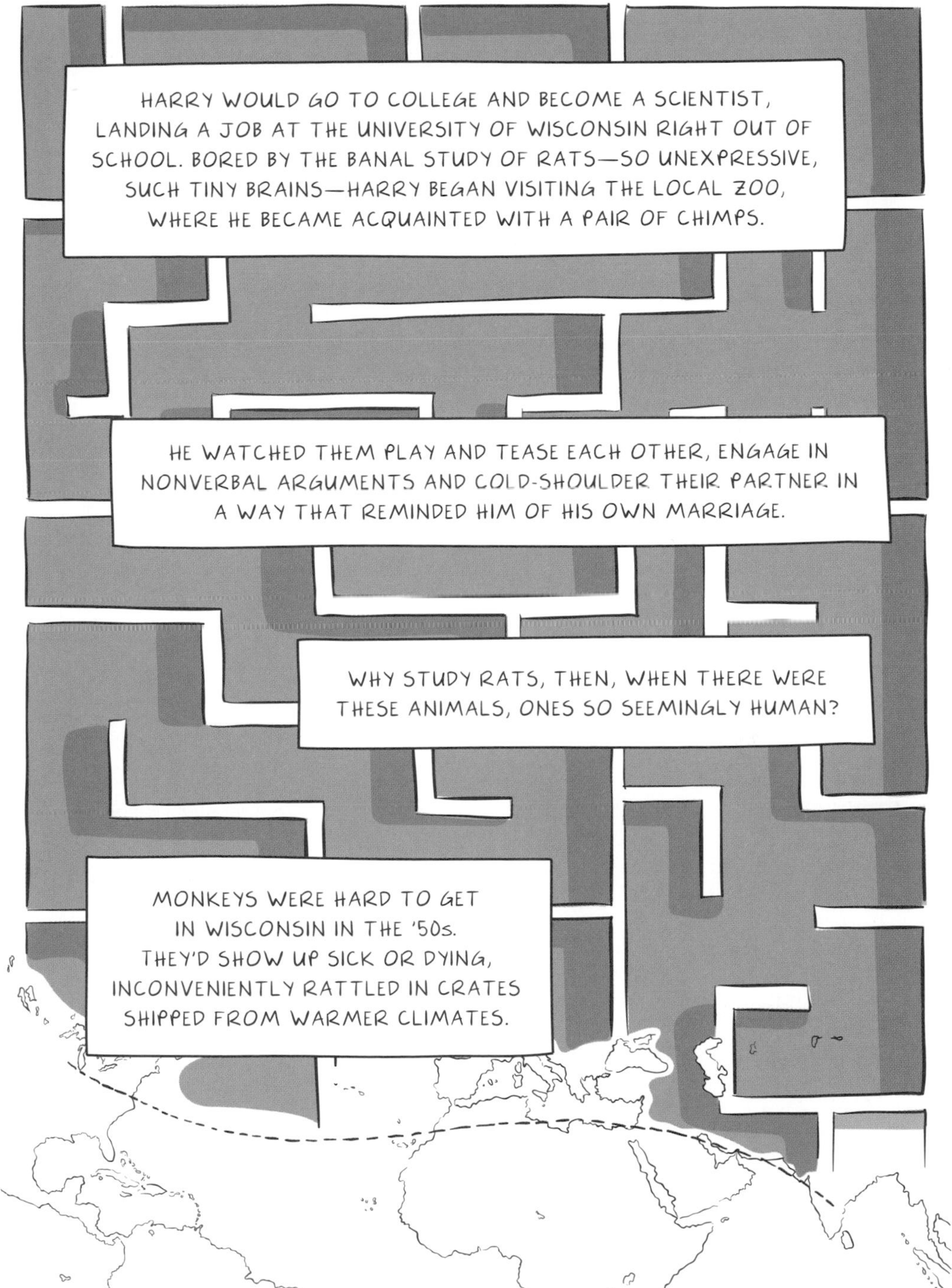
HARRY WOULD GO TO COLLEGE AND BECOME A SCIENTIST, LANDING A JOB AT THE UNIVERSITY OF WISCONSIN RIGHT OUT OF SCHOOL. BORED BY THE BANAL STUDY OF RATS—SO UNEXPRESSIVE, SUCH TINY BRAINS—HARRY BEGAN VISITING THE LOCAL ZOO, WHERE HE BECAME ACQUAINTED WITH A PAIR OF CHIMPS.
HE WATCHED THEM PLAY AND TEASE EACH OTHER, ENGAGE IN NONVERBAL ARGUMENTS AND COLD-SHOULDER THEIR PARTNER IN A WAY THAT REMINDED HIM OF HIS OWN MARRIAGE.
WHY STUDY RATS, THEN, WHEN THERE WERE THESE ANIMALS, ONES SO SEEMINGLY HUMAN?
MONKEYS WERE HARD TO GET IN WISCONSIN IN THE '50s. THEY'D SHOW UP SICK OR DYING, INCONVENIENTLY RATTLED IN CRATES SHIPPED FROM WARMER CLIMATES.

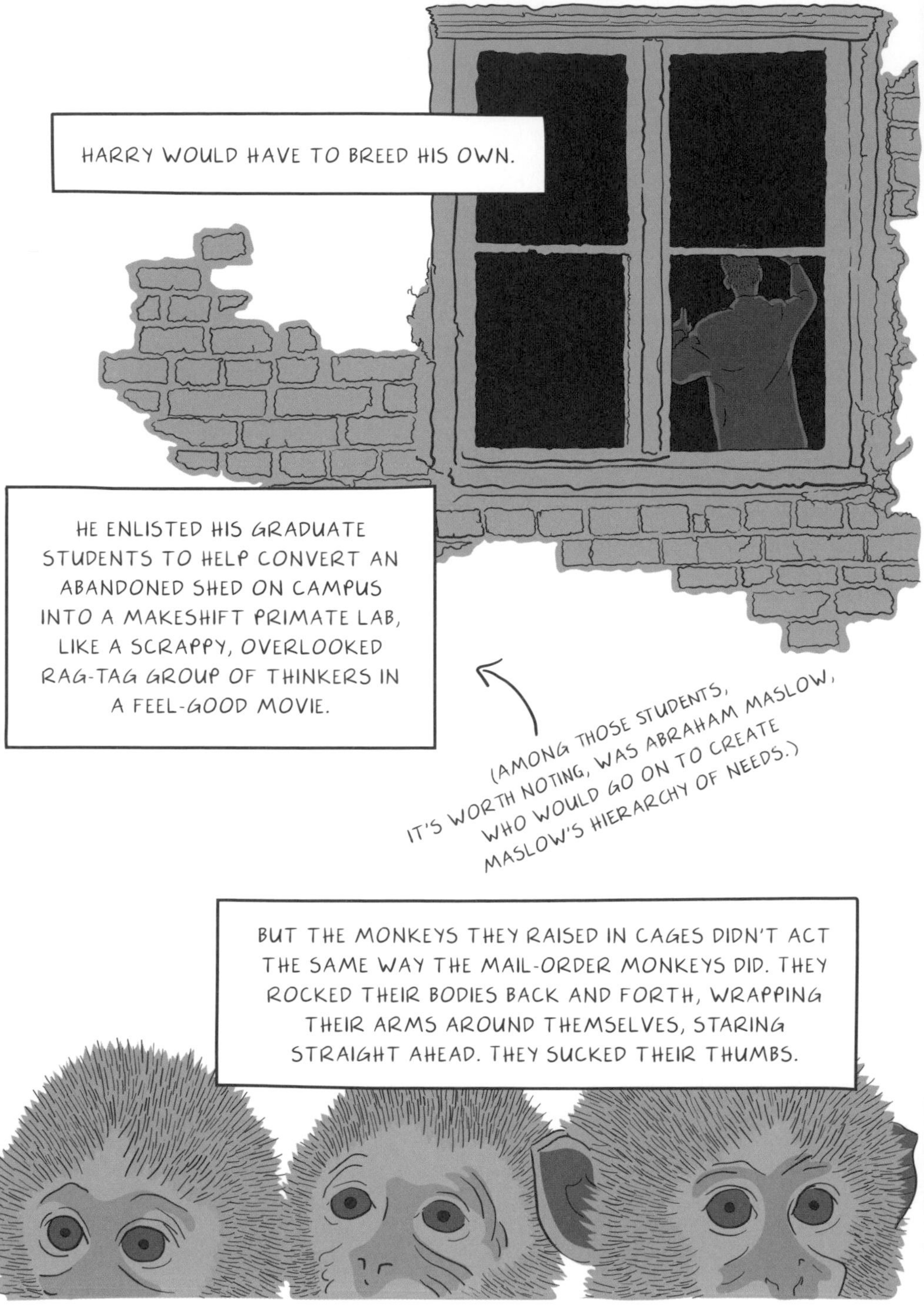
HARRY WOULD HAVE TO BREED HIS OWN.
HE ENLISTED HIS GRADUATE STUDENTS TO HELP CONVERT AN ABANDONED SHED ON CAMPUS INTO A MAKESHIFT PRIMATE LAB, LIKE A SCRAPPY, OVERLOOKED RAG-TAG GROUP OF THINKERS IN A FEEL-GOOD MOVIE.
(AMONG THOSE STUDENTS, IT'S WORTH NOTING, WAS ABRAHAM MASLOW, WHO WOULD GO ON TO CREATE MASLOW'S HIERARCHY OF NEEDS.)
BUT THE MONKEYS THEY RAISED IN CAGES DIDN'T ACT THE SAME WAY THE MAIL-ORDER MONKEYS DID. THEY ROCKED THEIR BODIES BACK AND FORTH, WRAPPING THEIR ARMS AROUND THEMSELVES, STARING STRAIGHT AHEAD. THEY SUCKED THEIR THUMBS.

SO, IF MONKEYS THAT WERE RAISED ALONE, RARELY INTERACTED WITH OR TOUCHED, EXHIBITED SO MANY BEHAVIORAL PROBLEMS, HARLOW WONDERED, WHAT WAS HAPPENING TO THE HUMAN BABIES UPON WHOM DOCTORS WERE PRESCRIBING DISTANCE?

HARLOW AND HIS TEAM BEGAN HIS MOST FAMOUS STUDY, SEPARATING BABY MONKEYS FROM THEIR MOTHERS SHORTLY AFTER BIRTH.

THE BABIES WERE PLACED IN CAGES WITH TWO INANIMATE DOLL-LIKE FIGURES, ONE MADE OF WIRE, ONE OF CLOTH.

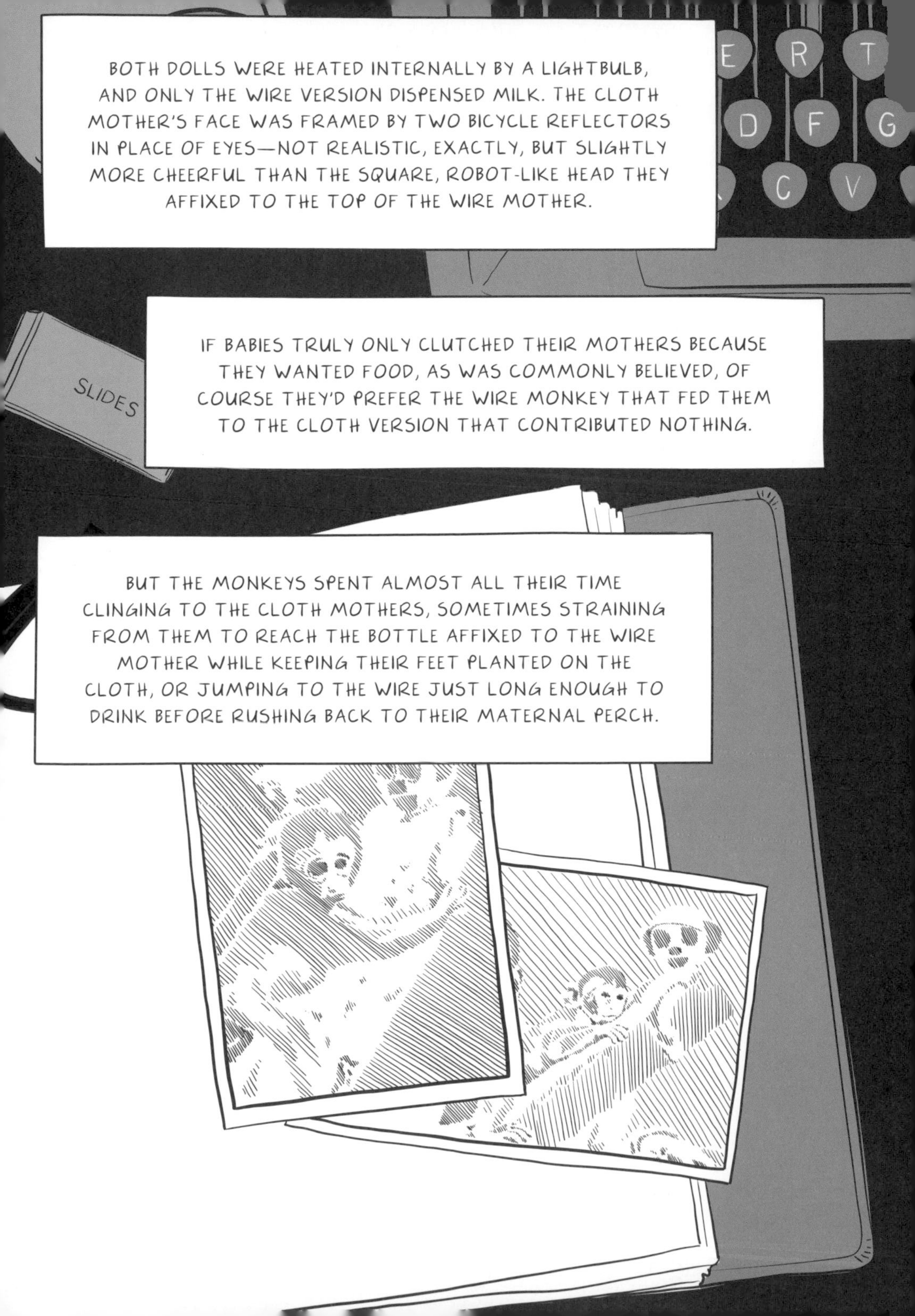
E R T
D F G
C V
BOTH DOLLS WERE HEATED INTERNALLY BY A LIGHTBULB, AND ONLY THE WIRE VERSION DISPENSED MILK. THE CLOTH MOTHER'S FACE WAS FRAMED BY TWO BICYCLE REFLECTORS IN PLACE OF EYES—NOT REALISTIC, EXACTLY, BUT SLIGHTLY MORE CHEERFUL THAN THE SQUARE, ROBOT-LIKE HEAD THEY AFFIXED TO THE TOP OF THE WIRE MOTHER.
SLIDES
IF BABIES TRULY ONLY CLUTCHED THEIR MOTHERS BECAUSE THEY WANTED FOOD, AS WAS COMMONLY BELIEVED, OF COURSE THEY'D PREFER THE WIRE MONKEY THAT FED THEM TO THE CLOTH VERSION THAT CONTRIBUTED NOTHING.
BUT THE MONKEYS SPENT ALMOST ALL THEIR TIME CLINGING TO THE CLOTH MOTHERS, SOMETIMES STRAINING FROM THEM TO REACH THE BOTTLE AFFIXED TO THE WIRE MOTHER WHILE KEEPING THEIR FEET PLANTED ON THE CLOTH, OR JUMPING TO THE WIRE JUST LONG ENOUGH TO DRINK BEFORE RUSHING BACK TO THEIR MATERNAL PERCH.

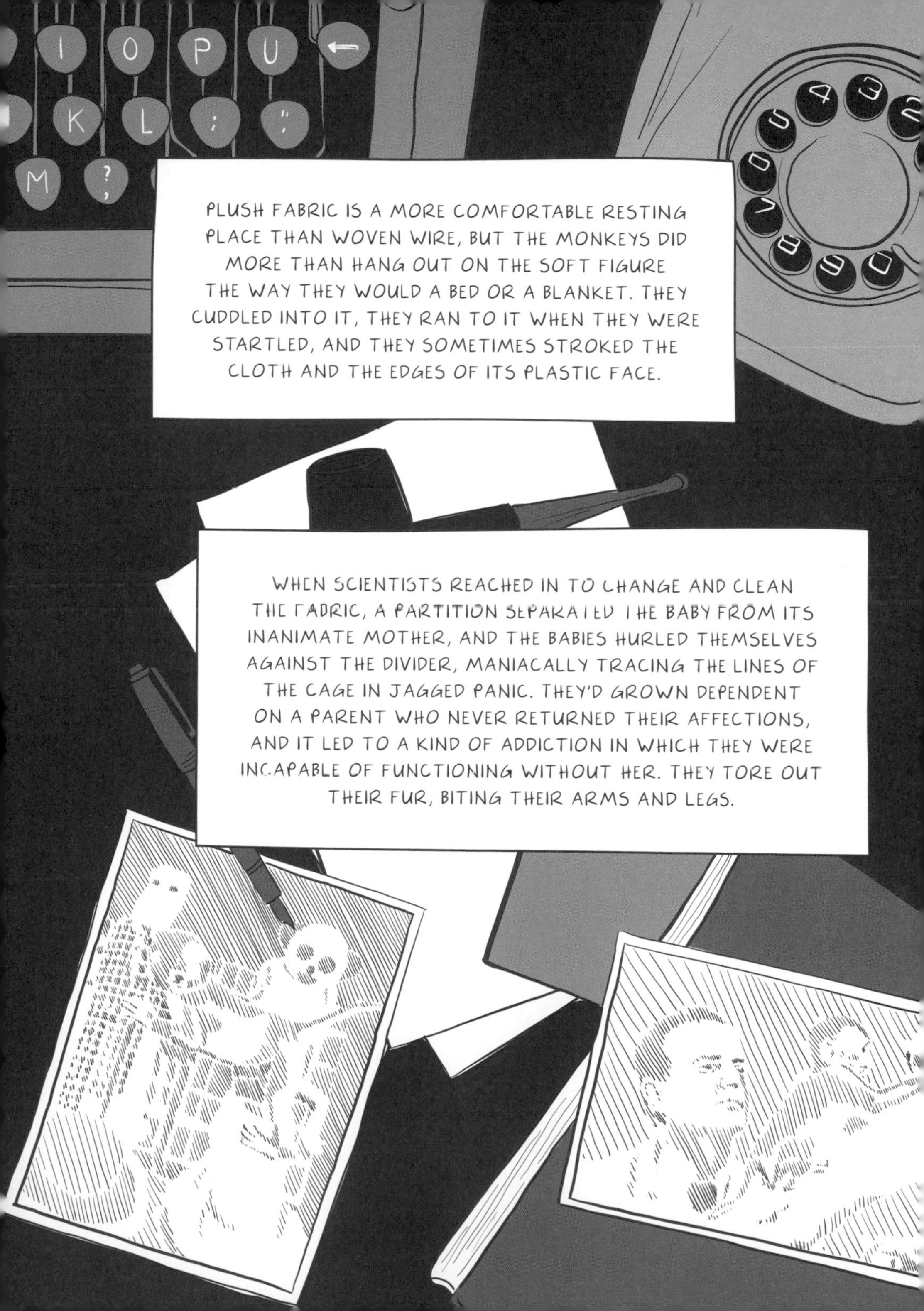
PLUSH FABRIC IS A MORE COMFORTABLE RESTING PLACE THAN WOVEN WIRE, BUT THE MONKEYS DID MORE THAN HANG OUT ON THE SOFT FIGURE THE WAY THEY WOULD A BED OR A BLANKET. THEY CUDDLED INTO IT, THEY RAN TO IT WHEN THEY WERE STARTLED, AND THEY SOMETIMES STROKED THE CLOTH AND THE EDGES OF ITS PLASTIC FACE.
WHEN SCIENTISTS REACHED IN TO CHANGE AND CLEAN THE FABRIC, A PARTITION SEPARATED THE BABY FROM ITS INANIMATE MOTHER, AND THE BABIES HURLED THEMSELVES AGAINST THE DIVIDER, MANIACALLY TRACING THE LINES OF THE CAGE IN JAGGED PANIC. THEY'D GROWN DEPENDENT ON A PARENT WHO NEVER RETURNED THEIR AFFECTIONS, AND IT LED TO A KIND OF ADDICTION IN WHICH THEY WERE INCAPABLE OF FUNCTIONING WITHOUT HER. THEY TORE OUT THEIR FUR, BITING THEIR ARMS AND LEGS.

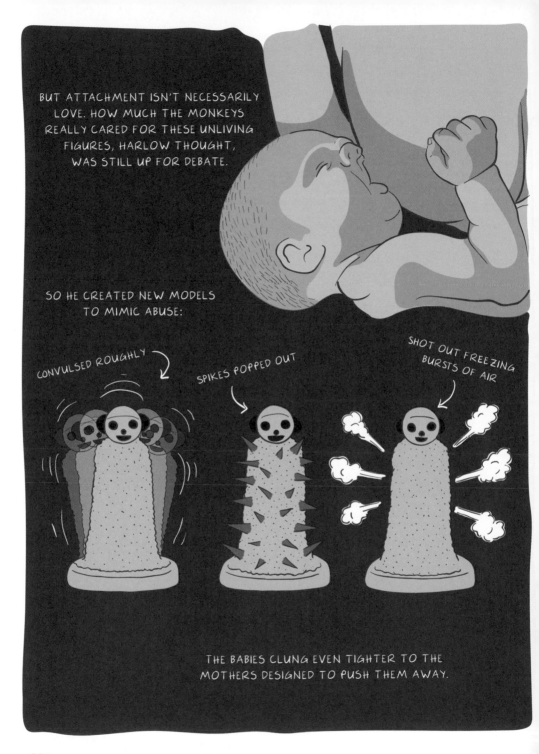

BUT ATTACHMENT ISN'T NECESSARILY LOVE. HOW MUCH THE MONKEYS REALLY CARED FOR THESE UNLIVING FIGURES, HARLOW THOUGHT, WAS STILL UP FOR DEBATE.

SO HE CREATED NEW MODELS TO MIMIC ABUSE:

CONVULSED ROUGHLY

SPIKES POPPED OUT

SHOT OUT FREEZING BURSTS OF AIR

THE BABIES CLUNG EVEN TIGHTER TO THE MOTHERS DESIGNED TO PUSH THEM AWAY.

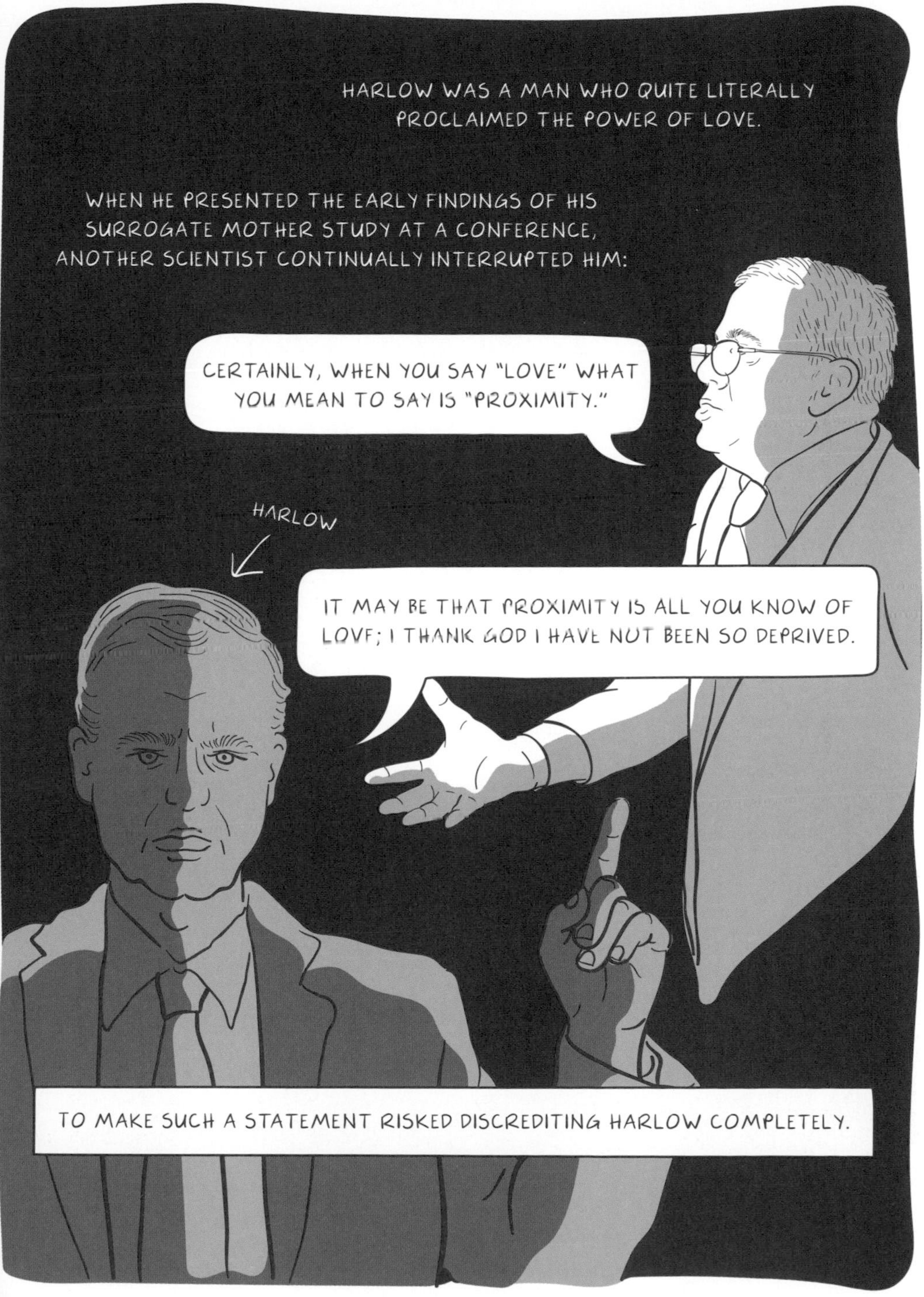
HARLOW WAS A MAN WHO QUITE LITERALLY PROCLAIMED THE POWER OF LOVE.
WHEN HE PRESENTED THE EARLY FINDINGS OF HIS SURROGATE MOTHER STUDY AT A CONFERENCE, ANOTHER SCIENTIST CONTINUALLY INTERRUPTED HIM:
CERTAINLY, WHEN YOU SAY "LOVE" WHAT YOU MEAN TO SAY IS "PROXIMITY."
HARLOW
IT MAY BE THAT PROXIMITY IS ALL YOU KNOW OF LOVE; I THANK GOD I HAVE NOT BEEN SO DEPRIVED.
TO MAKE SUCH A STATEMENT RISKED DISCREDITING HARLOW COMPLETELY.

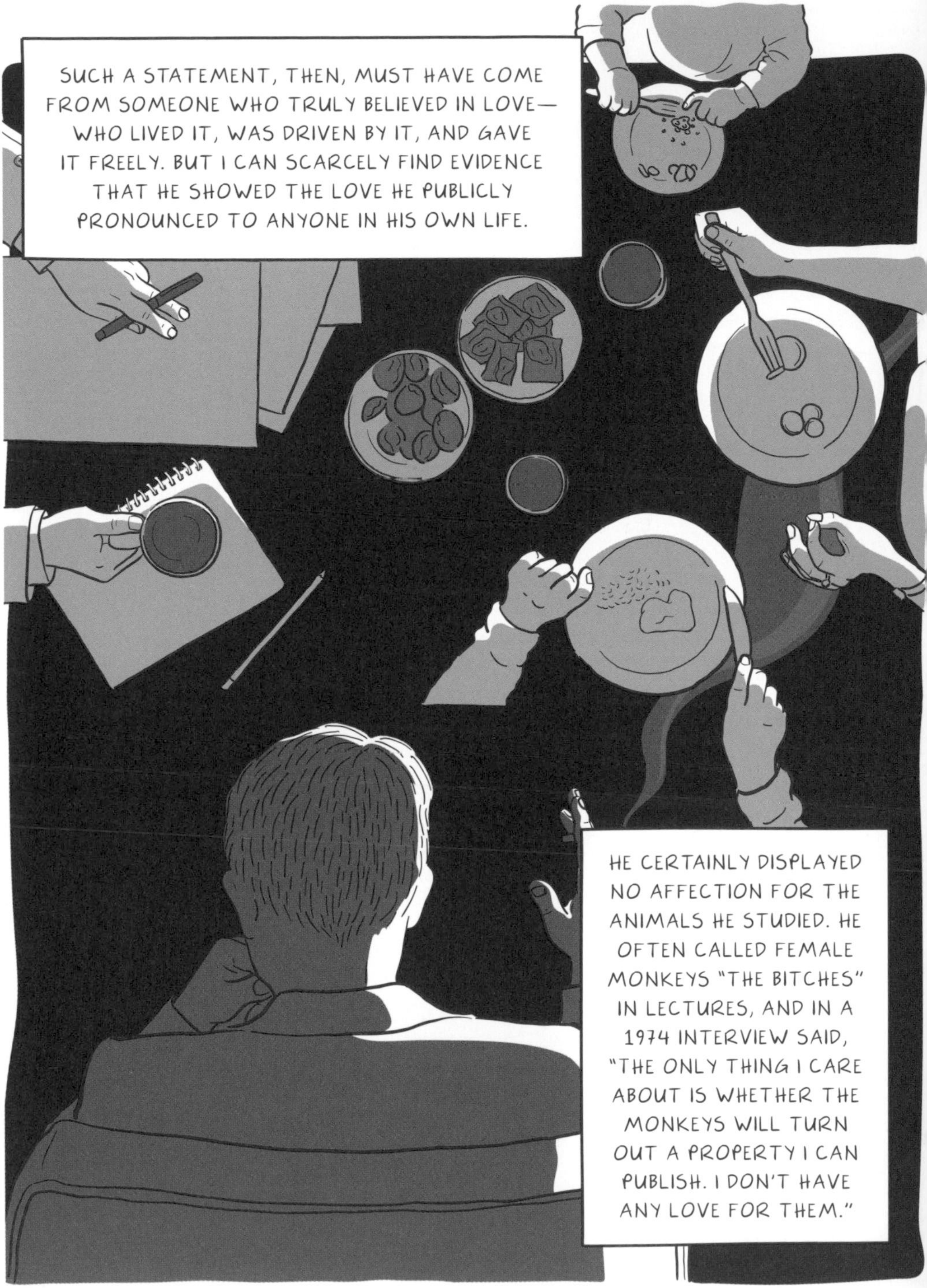
SUCH A STATEMENT, THEN, MUST HAVE COME FROM SOMEONE WHO TRULY BELIEVED IN LOVE—WHO LIVED IT, WAS DRIVEN BY IT, AND GAVE IT FREELY. BUT I CAN SCARCELY FIND EVIDENCE THAT HE SHOWED THE LOVE HE PUBLICLY PRONOUNCED TO ANYONE IN HIS OWN LIFE.
HE CERTAINLY DISPLAYED NO AFFECTION FOR THE ANIMALS HE STUDIED. HE OFTEN CALLED FEMALE MONKEYS "THE BITCHES" IN LECTURES, AND IN A 1974 INTERVIEW SAID, "THE ONLY THING I CARE ABOUT IS WHETHER THE MONKEYS WILL TURN OUT A PROPERTY I CAN PUBLISH. I DON'T HAVE ANY LOVE FOR THEM."

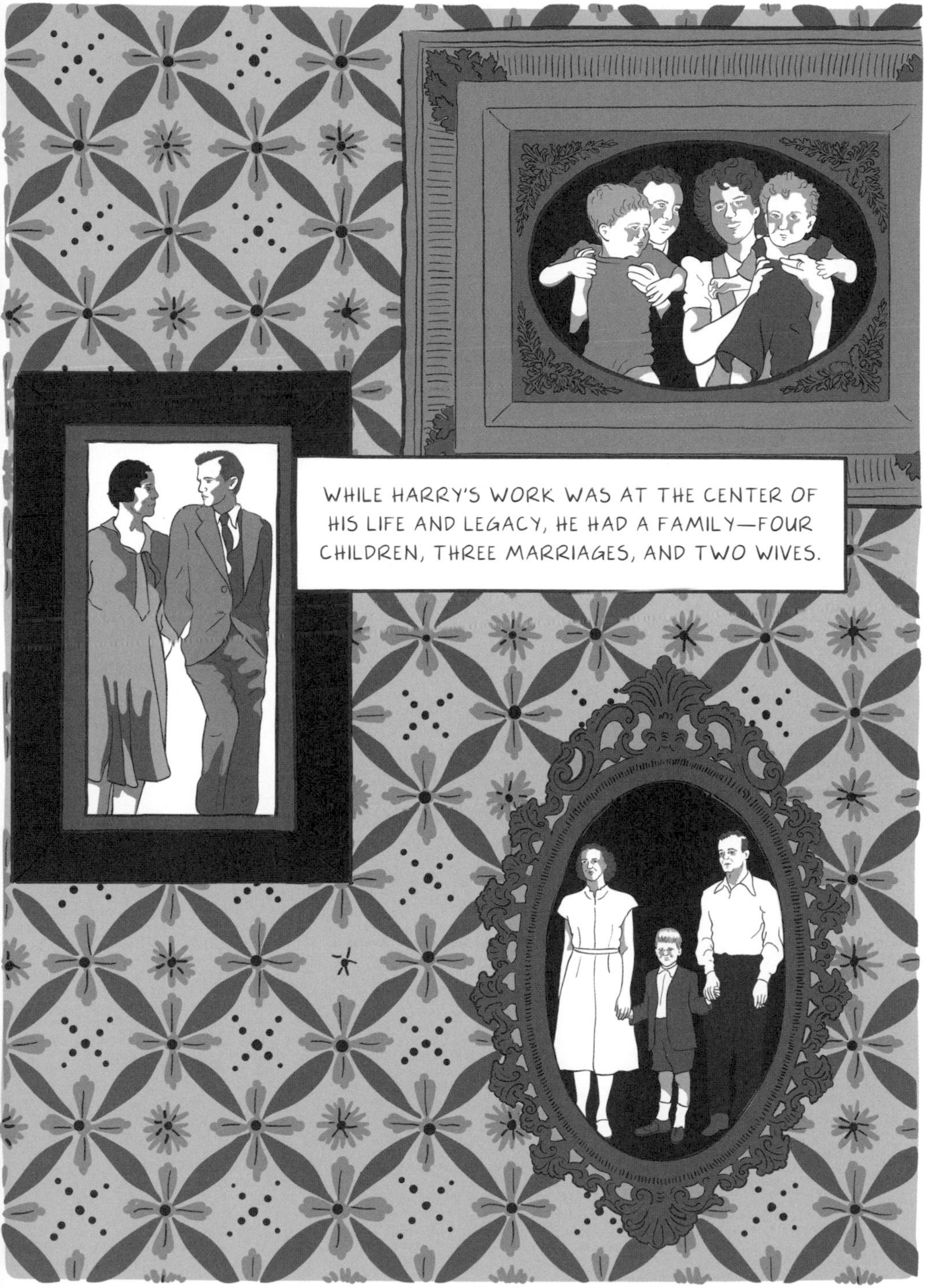
WHILE HARRY'S WORK WAS AT THE CENTER OF HIS LIFE AND LEGACY, HE HAD A FAMILY—FOUR CHILDREN, THREE MARRIAGES, AND TWO WIVES.

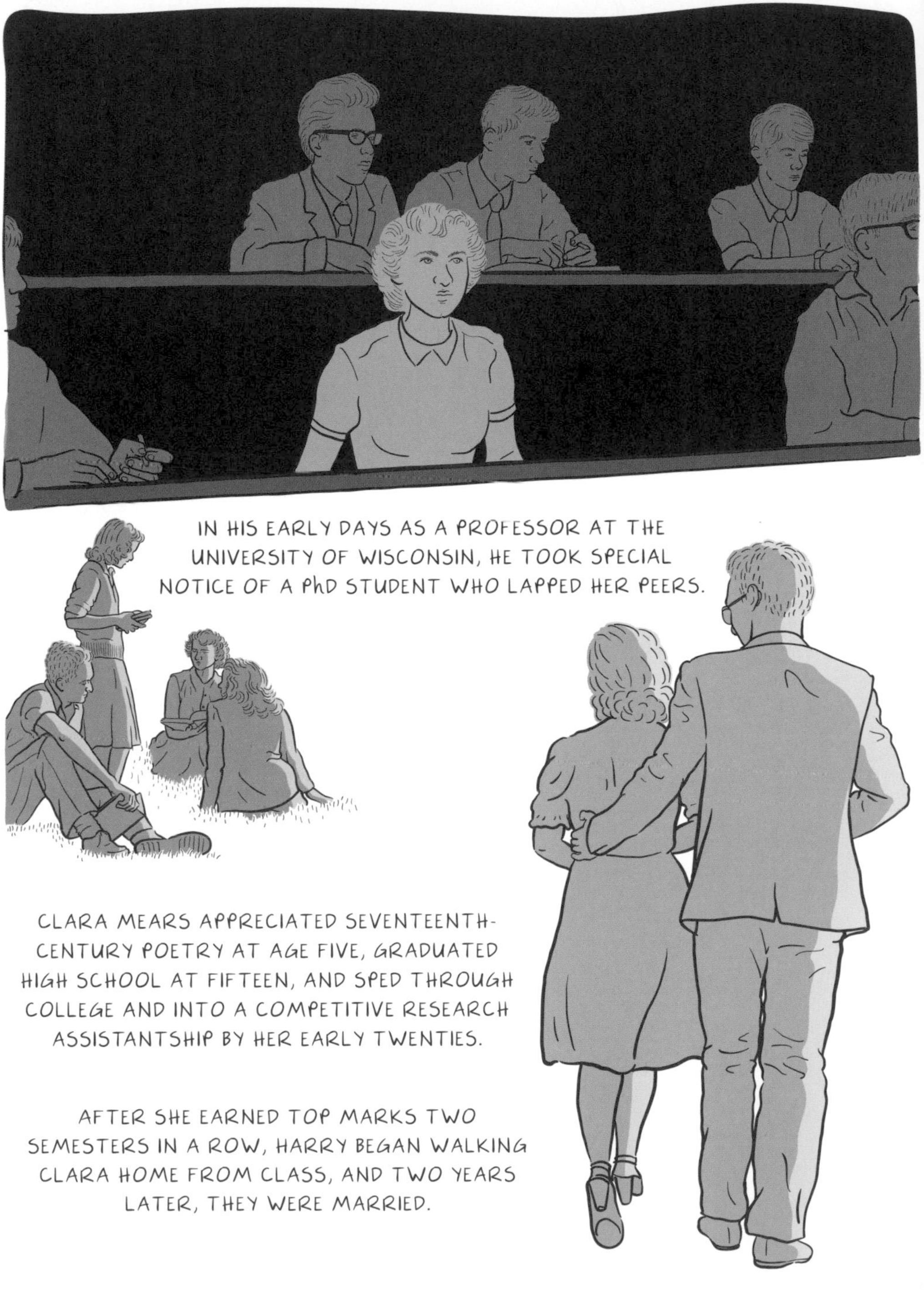
IN HIS EARLY DAYS AS A PROFESSOR AT THE UNIVERSITY OF WISCONSIN, HE TOOK SPECIAL NOTICE OF A PhD STUDENT WHO LAPPED HER PEERS.
CLARA MEARS APPRECIATED SEVENTEENTH-CENTURY POETRY AT AGE FIVE, GRADUATED HIGH SCHOOL AT FIFTEEN, AND SPED THROUGH COLLEGE AND INTO A COMPETITIVE RESEARCH ASSISTANTSHIP BY HER EARLY TWENTIES.
AFTER SHE EARNED TOP MARKS TWO SEMESTERS IN A ROW, HARRY BEGAN WALKING CLARA HOME FROM CLASS, AND TWO YEARS LATER, THEY WERE MARRIED.

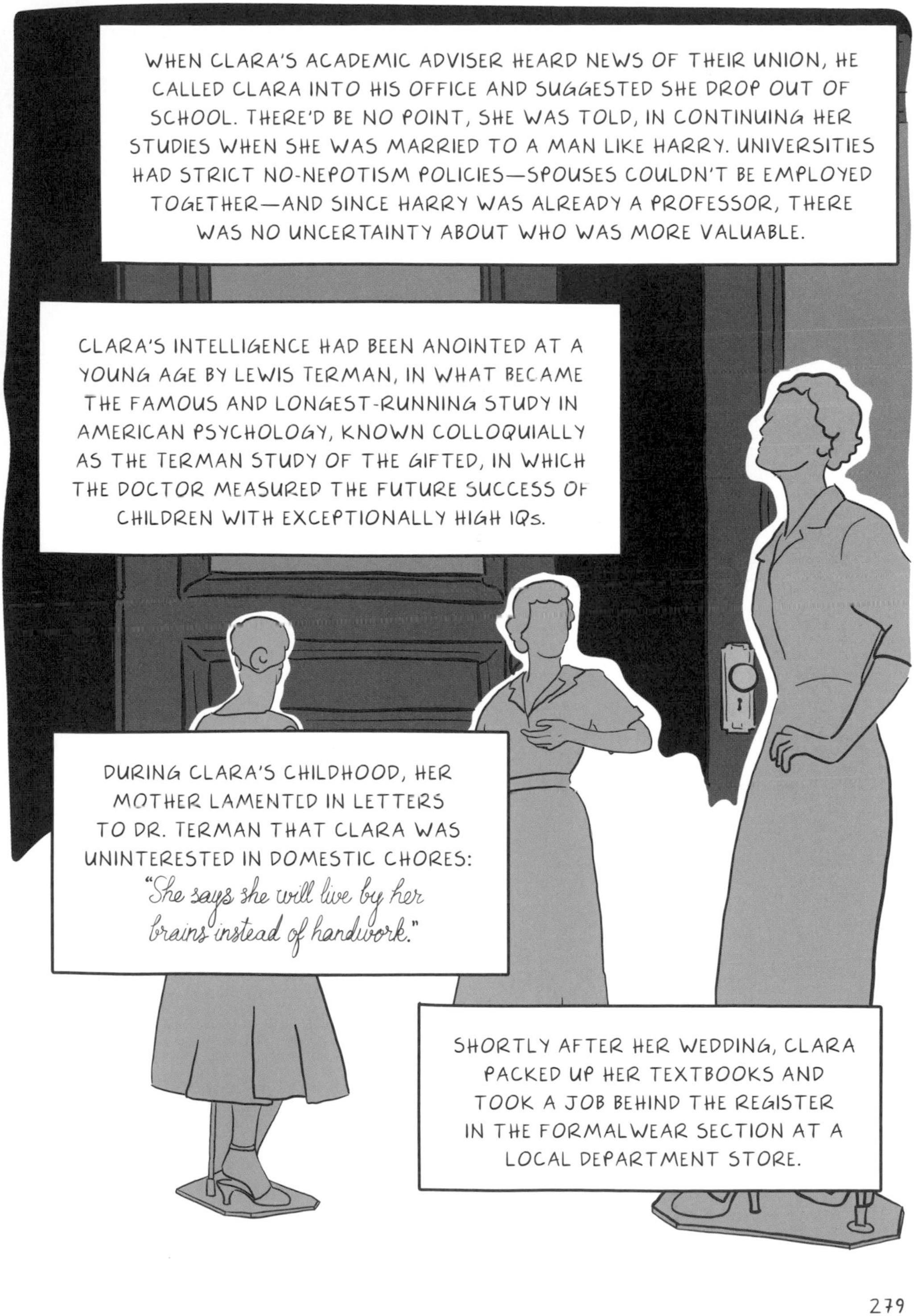
WHEN CLARA'S ACADEMIC ADVISER HEARD NEWS OF THEIR UNION, HE CALLED CLARA INTO HIS OFFICE AND SUGGESTED SHE DROP OUT OF SCHOOL. THERE'D BE NO POINT, SHE WAS TOLD, IN CONTINUING HER STUDIES WHEN SHE WAS MARRIED TO A MAN LIKE HARRY. UNIVERSITIES HAD STRICT NO-NEPOTISM POLICIES—SPOUSES COULDN'T BE EMPLOYED TOGETHER—AND SINCE HARRY WAS ALREADY A PROFESSOR, THERE WAS NO UNCERTAINTY ABOUT WHO WAS MORE VALUABLE.
CLARA'S INTELLIGENCE HAD BEEN ANOINTED AT A YOUNG AGE BY LEWIS TERMAN, IN WHAT BECAME THE FAMOUS AND LONGEST-RUNNING STUDY IN AMERICAN PSYCHOLOGY, KNOWN COLLOQUIALLY AS THE TERMAN STUDY OF THE GIFTED, IN WHICH THE DOCTOR MEASURED THE FUTURE SUCCESS OF CHILDREN WITH EXCEPTIONALLY HIGH IQs.
DURING CLARA'S CHILDHOOD, HER MOTHER LAMENTED IN LETTERS TO DR. TERMAN THAT CLARA WAS UNINTERESTED IN DOMESTIC CHORES: *"She says she will live by her brains instead of handwork."*
SHORTLY AFTER HER WEDDING, CLARA PACKED UP HER TEXTBOOKS AND TOOK A JOB BEHIND THE REGISTER IN THE FORMALWEAR SECTION AT A LOCAL DEPARTMENT STORE.

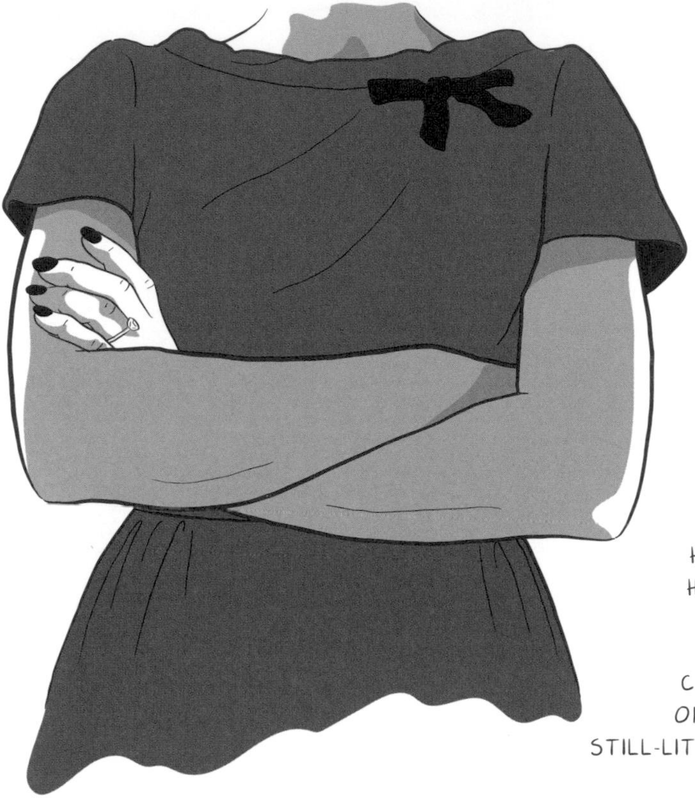

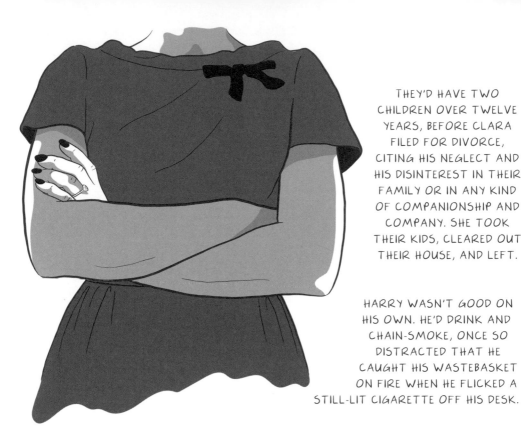

THEY'D HAVE TWO CHILDREN OVER TWELVE YEARS, BEFORE CLARA FILED FOR DIVORCE, CITING HIS NEGLECT AND HIS DISINTEREST IN THEIR FAMILY OR IN ANY KIND OF COMPANIONSHIP AND COMPANY. SHE TOOK THEIR KIDS, CLEARED OUT THEIR HOUSE, AND LEFT.

HARRY WASN'T GOOD ON HIS OWN. HE'D DRINK AND CHAIN-SMOKE, ONCE SO DISTRACTED THAT HE CAUGHT HIS WASTEBASKET ON FIRE WHEN HE FLICKED A STILL-LIT CIGARETTE OFF HIS DESK.

HIS MOODS WERE WORSE THAN USUAL, HIS UNPRESSED SUITS OFTEN MATTED WITH YESTERDAY'S LUNCH.

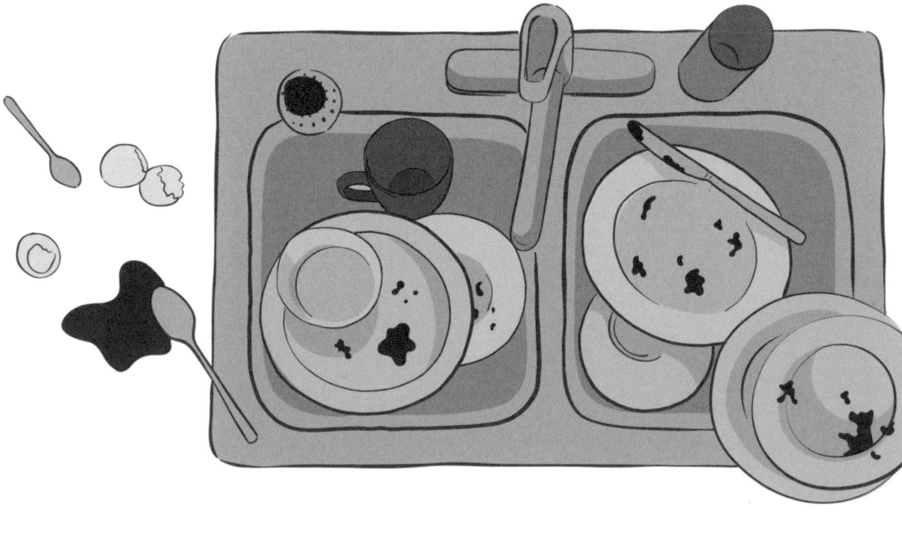

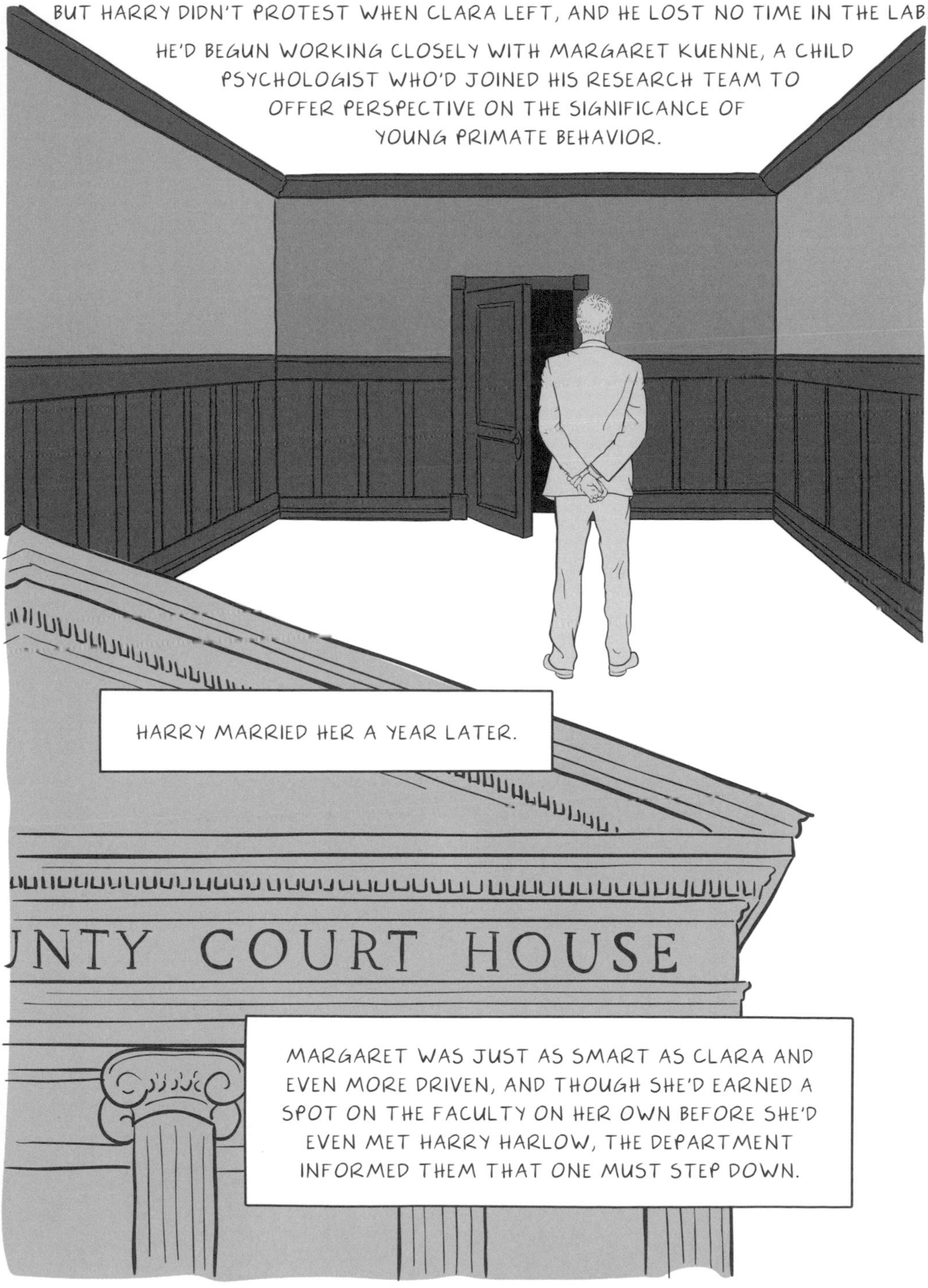
BUT HARRY DIDN'T PROTEST WHEN CLARA LEFT, AND HE LOST NO TIME IN THE LAB.
HE'D BEGUN WORKING CLOSELY WITH MARGARET KUENNE, A CHILD PSYCHOLOGIST WHO'D JOINED HIS RESEARCH TEAM TO OFFER PERSPECTIVE ON THE SIGNIFICANCE OF YOUNG PRIMATE BEHAVIOR.
HARRY MARRIED HER A YEAR LATER.
UNTY COURT HOUSE
MARGARET WAS JUST AS SMART AS CLARA AND EVEN MORE DRIVEN, AND THOUGH SHE'D EARNED A SPOT ON THE FACULTY ON HER OWN BEFORE SHE'D EVEN MET HARRY HARLOW, THE DEPARTMENT INFORMED THEM THAT ONE MUST STEP DOWN.

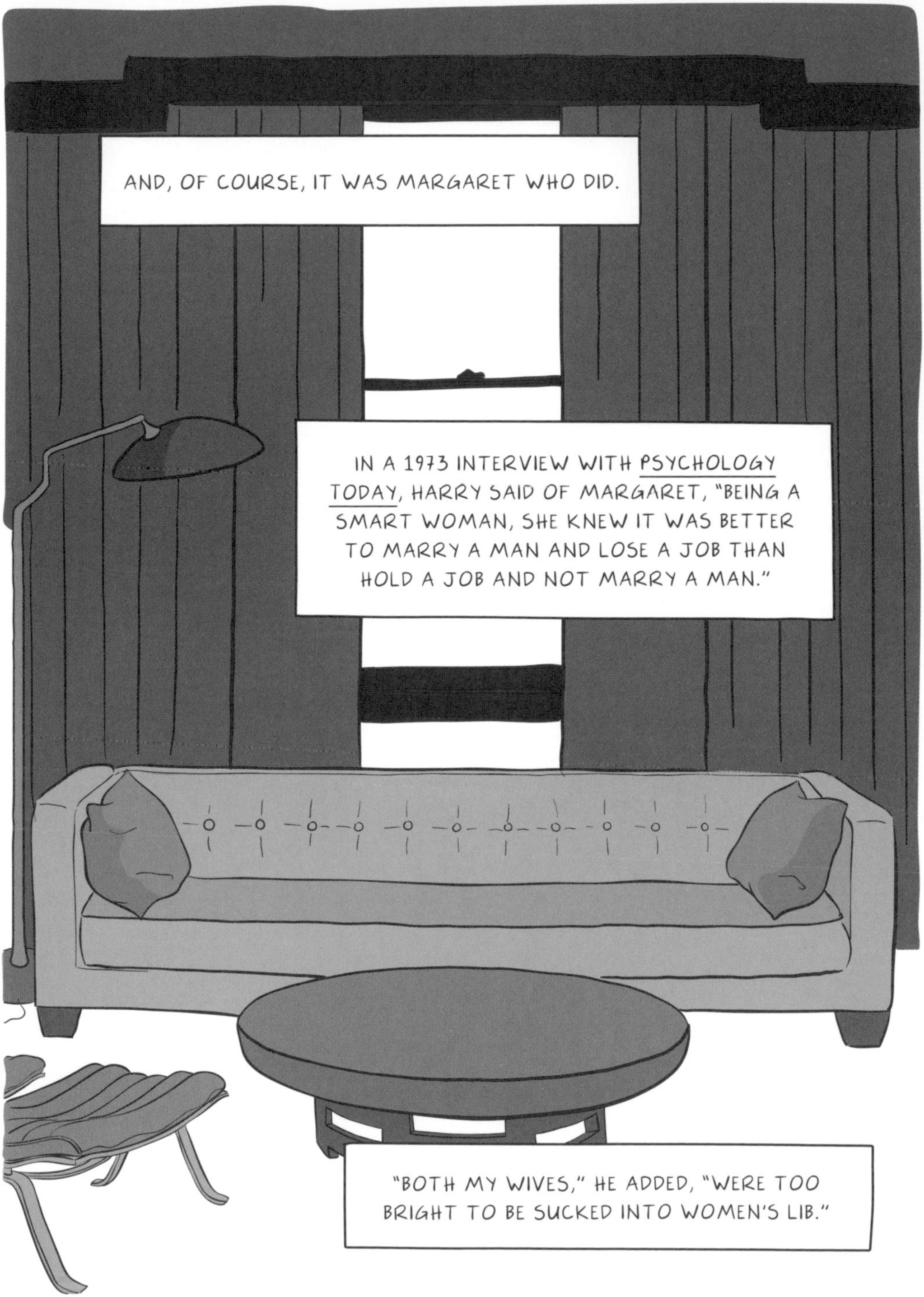
AND, OF COURSE, IT WAS MARGARET WHO DID.
IN A 1973 INTERVIEW WITH PSYCHOLOGY TODAY, HARRY SAID OF MARGARET, "BEING A SMART WOMAN, SHE KNEW IT WAS BETTER TO MARRY A MAN AND LOSE A JOB THAN HOLD A JOB AND NOT MARRY A MAN."
"BOTH MY WIVES," HE ADDED, "WERE TOO BRIGHT TO BE SUCKED INTO WOMEN'S LIB."

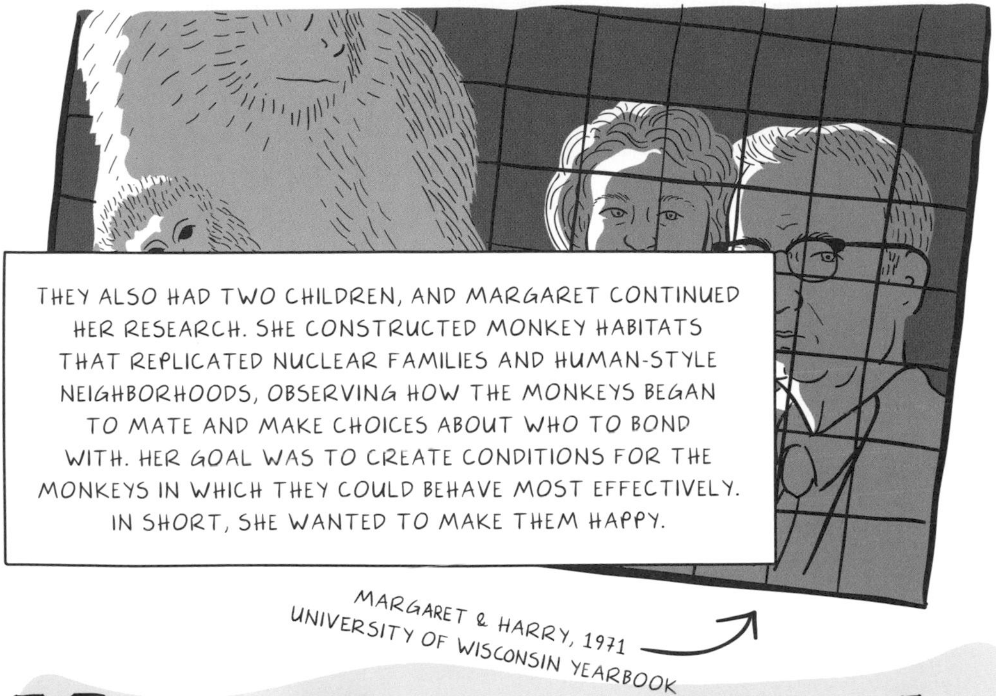
THEY ALSO HAD TWO CHILDREN, AND MARGARET CONTINUED HER RESEARCH. SHE CONSTRUCTED MONKEY HABITATS THAT REPLICATED NUCLEAR FAMILIES AND HUMAN-STYLE NEIGHBORHOODS, OBSERVING HOW THE MONKEYS BEGAN TO MATE AND MAKE CHOICES ABOUT WHO TO BOND WITH. HER GOAL WAS TO CREATE CONDITIONS FOR THE MONKEYS IN WHICH THEY COULD BEHAVE MOST EFFECTIVELY. IN SHORT, SHE WANTED TO MAKE THEM HAPPY.
MARGARET & HARRY, 1971
UNIVERSITY OF WISCONSIN YEARBOOK

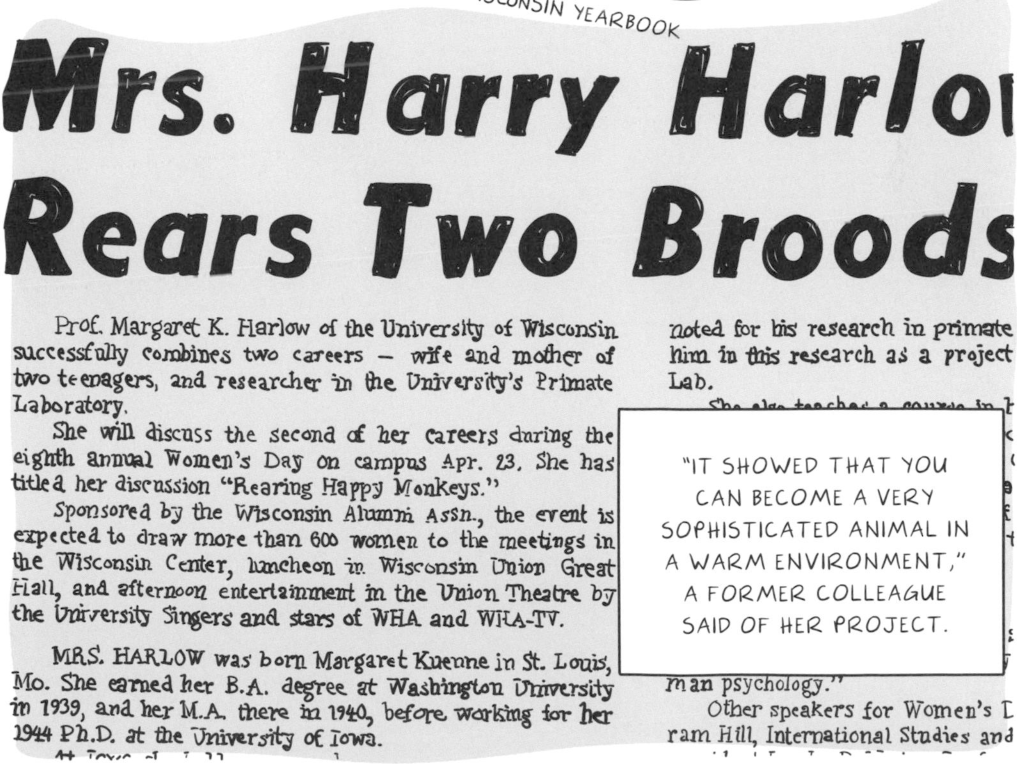

Mrs. Harry Harlo

Rears Two Broods

Prof. Margaret K. Harlow of the University of Wisconsin successfully combines two careers — wife and mother of two teenagers, and researcher in the University's Primate Laboratory.

She will discuss the second of her careers during the eighth annual Women's Day on campus Apr. 23. She has titled her discussion "Rearing Happy Monkeys."

Sponsored by the Wisconsin Alumni Assn., the event is expected to draw more than 600 women to the meetings in the Wisconsin Center, luncheon in Wisconsin Union Great Hall, and afternoon entertainment in the Union Theatre by the University Singers and stars of WHA and WHA-TV.

MRS. HARLOW was born Margaret Kuenne in St. Louis, Mo. She earned her B.A. degree at Washington University in 1939, and her M.A. there in 1940, before working for her 1944 Ph.D. at the University of Iowa.

noted for his research in primate
him in this research as a project
Lab.

man psychology."

Other speakers for Women's D
ram Hill, International Studies and

"IT SHOWED THAT YOU CAN BECOME A VERY SOPHISTICATED ANIMAL IN A WARM ENVIRONMENT," A FORMER COLLEAGUE SAID OF HER PROJECT.

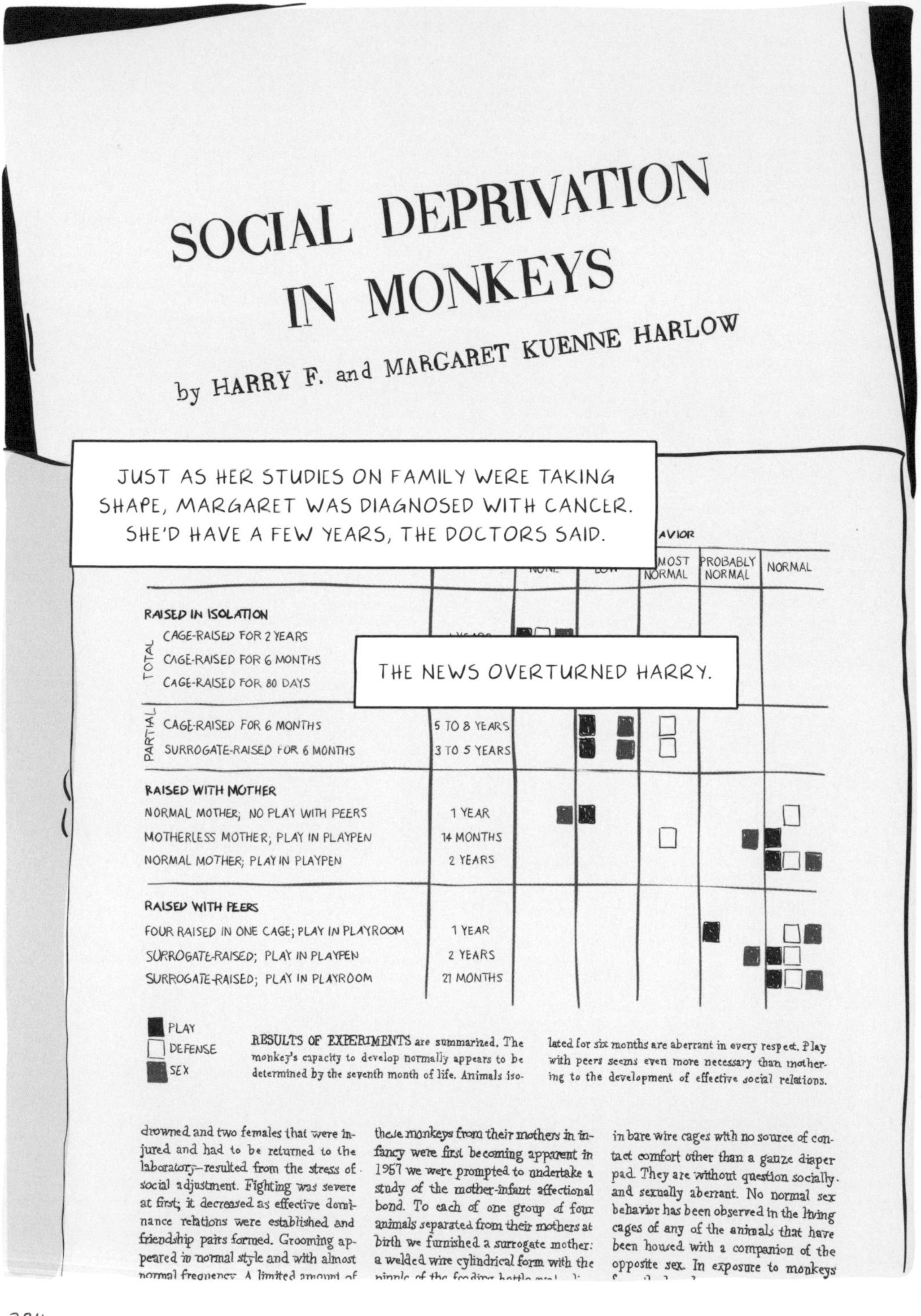

SOCIAL DEPRIVATION IN MONKEYS

by HARRY F. and MARGARET KUENNE HARLOW

JUST AS HER STUDIES ON FAMILY WERE TAKING SHAPE, MARGARET WAS DIAGNOSED WITH CANCER. SHE'D HAVE A FEW YEARS, THE DOCTORS SAID.

THE NEWS OVERTURNED HARRY.

		NONE	LOW	MOST NORMAL	PROBABLY NORMAL	NORMAL
RAISED IN ISOLATION (TOTAL)						
CAGE-RAISED FOR 2 YEARS	LYS 180					
CAGE-RAISED FOR 6 MONTHS						
CAGE-RAISED FOR 80 DAYS						
(PARTIAL) CAGE-RAISED FOR 6 MONTHS	5 TO 8 YEARS	■ ■	□			
SURROGATE-RAISED FOR 6 MONTHS	3 TO 5 YEARS	■ ■	□			
RAISED WITH MOTHER						
NORMAL MOTHER; NO PLAY WITH PEERS	1 YEAR	■ ■				□
MOTHERLESS MOTHER; PLAY IN PLAYPEN	14 MONTHS			□	■ ■	■ □
NORMAL MOTHER; PLAY IN PLAYPEN	2 YEARS					■ □ □
RAISED WITH PEERS						
FOUR RAISED IN ONE CAGE; PLAY IN PLAYROOM	1 YEAR				■	□ □
SURROGATE-RAISED; PLAY IN PLAYPEN	2 YEARS				■	□ ■
SURROGATE-RAISED; PLAY IN PLAYROOM	21 MONTHS					□ ■

■ PLAY
□ DEFENSE
■ SEX

RESULTS OF EXPERIMENTS are summarized. The monkey's capacity to develop normally appears to be determined by the seventh month of life. Animals isolated for six months are aberrant in every respect. Play with peers seems even more necessary than mothering to the development of effective social relations.

drowned and two females that were injured and had to be returned to the laboratory—resulted from the stress of social adjustment. Fighting was severe at first; it decreased as effective dominance relations were established and friendship pairs formed. Grooming appeared in normal style and with almost normal frequency. A limited amount of these monkeys from their mothers in infancy were first becoming apparent in 1957 we were prompted to undertake a study of the mother-infant affectional bond. To each of one group of four animals separated from their mothers at birth we furnished a surrogate mother: a welded wire cylindrical form with the nipple of the feeding bottle emerging in bare wire cages with no source of contact comfort other than a gauze diaper pad. They are without question socially and sexually aberrant. No normal sex behavior has been observed in the living cages of any of the animals that have been housed with a companion of the opposite sex. In exposure to monkeys

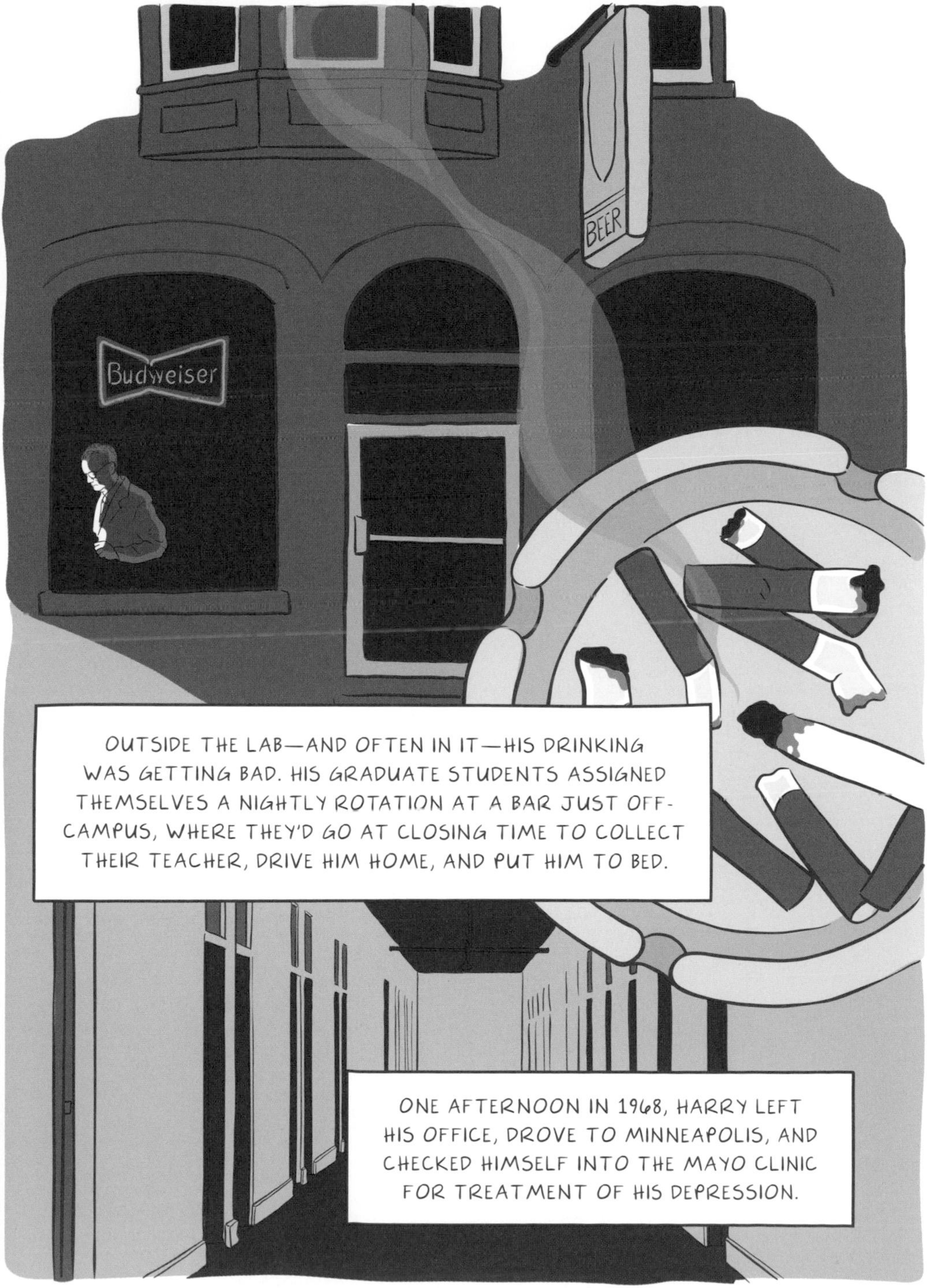
BEER
Budweiser
OUTSIDE THE LAB—AND OFTEN IN IT—HIS DRINKING WAS GETTING BAD. HIS GRADUATE STUDENTS ASSIGNED THEMSELVES A NIGHTLY ROTATION AT A BAR JUST OFF-CAMPUS, WHERE THEY'D GO AT CLOSING TIME TO COLLECT THEIR TEACHER, DRIVE HIM HOME, AND PUT HIM TO BED.
ONE AFTERNOON IN 1968, HARRY LEFT HIS OFFICE, DROVE TO MINNEAPOLIS, AND CHECKED HIMSELF INTO THE MAYO CLINIC FOR TREATMENT OF HIS DEPRESSION.

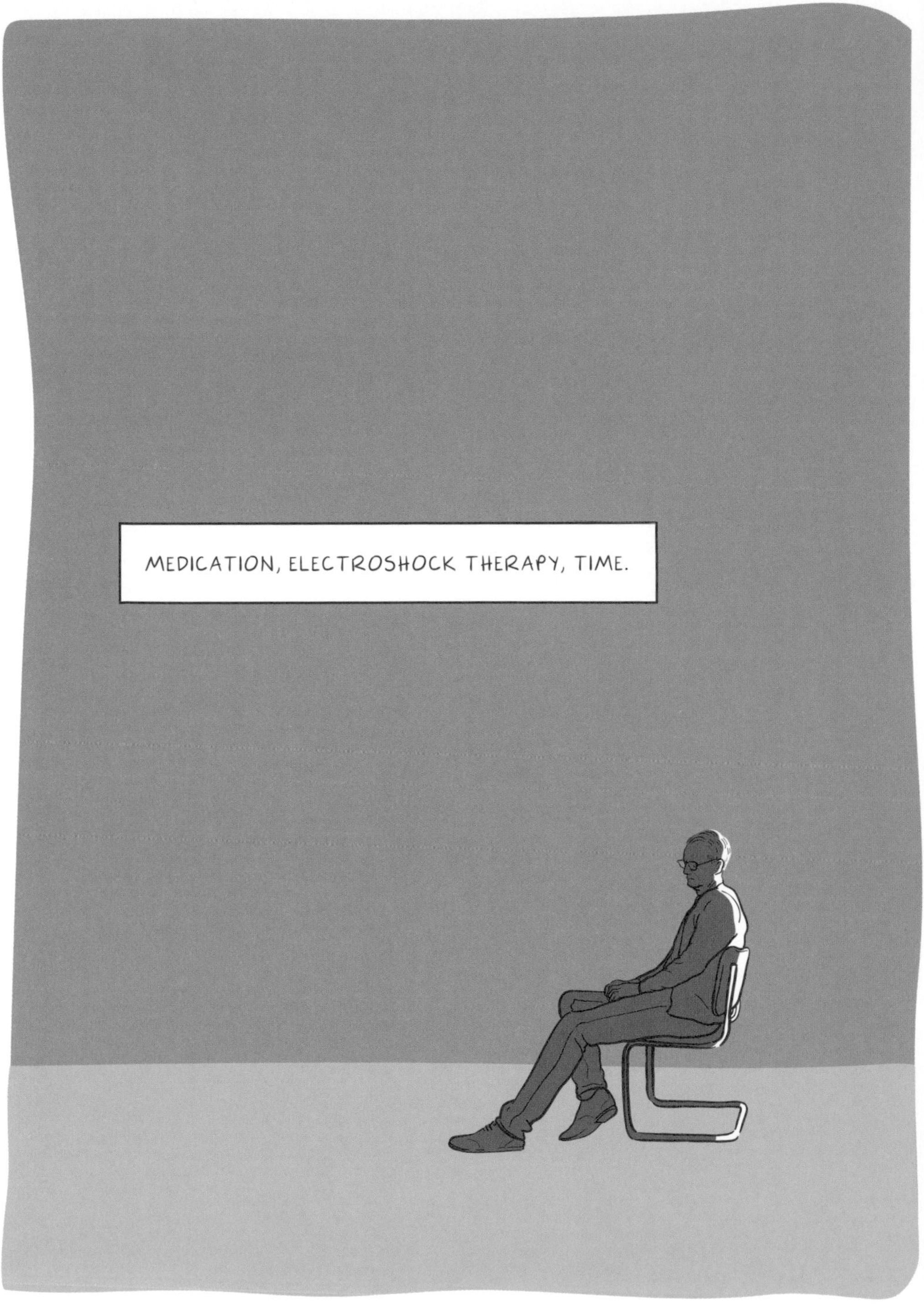
MEDICATION, ELECTROSHOCK THERAPY, TIME.

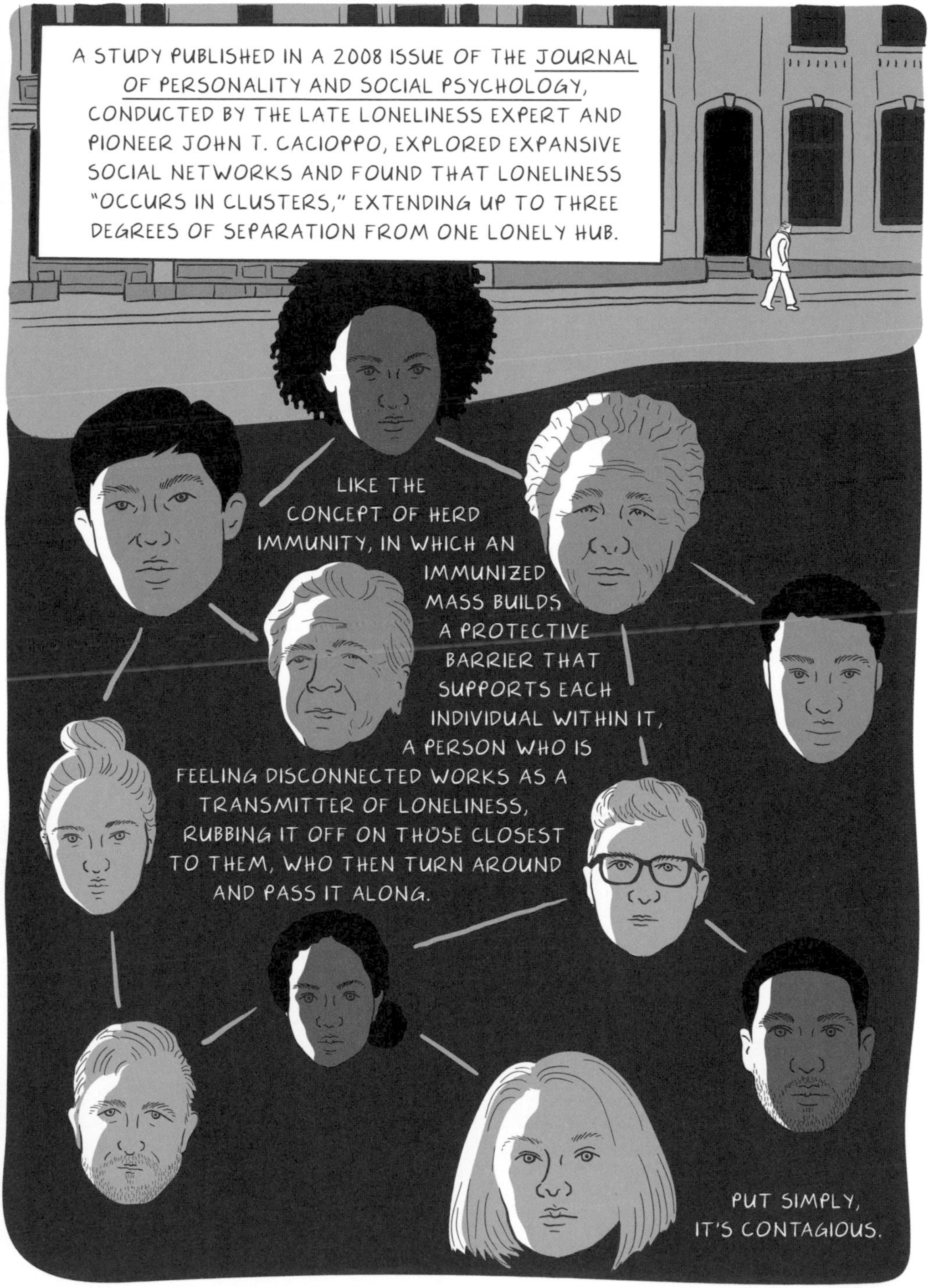
A STUDY PUBLISHED IN A 2008 ISSUE OF THE JOURNAL OF PERSONALITY AND SOCIAL PSYCHOLOGY, CONDUCTED BY THE LATE LONELINESS EXPERT AND PIONEER JOHN T. CACIOPPO, EXPLORED EXPANSIVE SOCIAL NETWORKS AND FOUND THAT LONELINESS "OCCURS IN CLUSTERS," EXTENDING UP TO THREE DEGREES OF SEPARATION FROM ONE LONELY HUB.
LIKE THE CONCEPT OF HERD IMMUNITY, IN WHICH AN IMMUNIZED MASS BUILDS A PROTECTIVE BARRIER THAT SUPPORTS EACH INDIVIDUAL WITHIN IT, A PERSON WHO IS FEELING DISCONNECTED WORKS AS A TRANSMITTER OF LONELINESS, RUBBING IT OFF ON THOSE CLOSEST TO THEM, WHO THEN TURN AROUND AND PASS IT ALONG.
PUT SIMPLY, IT'S CONTAGIOUS.

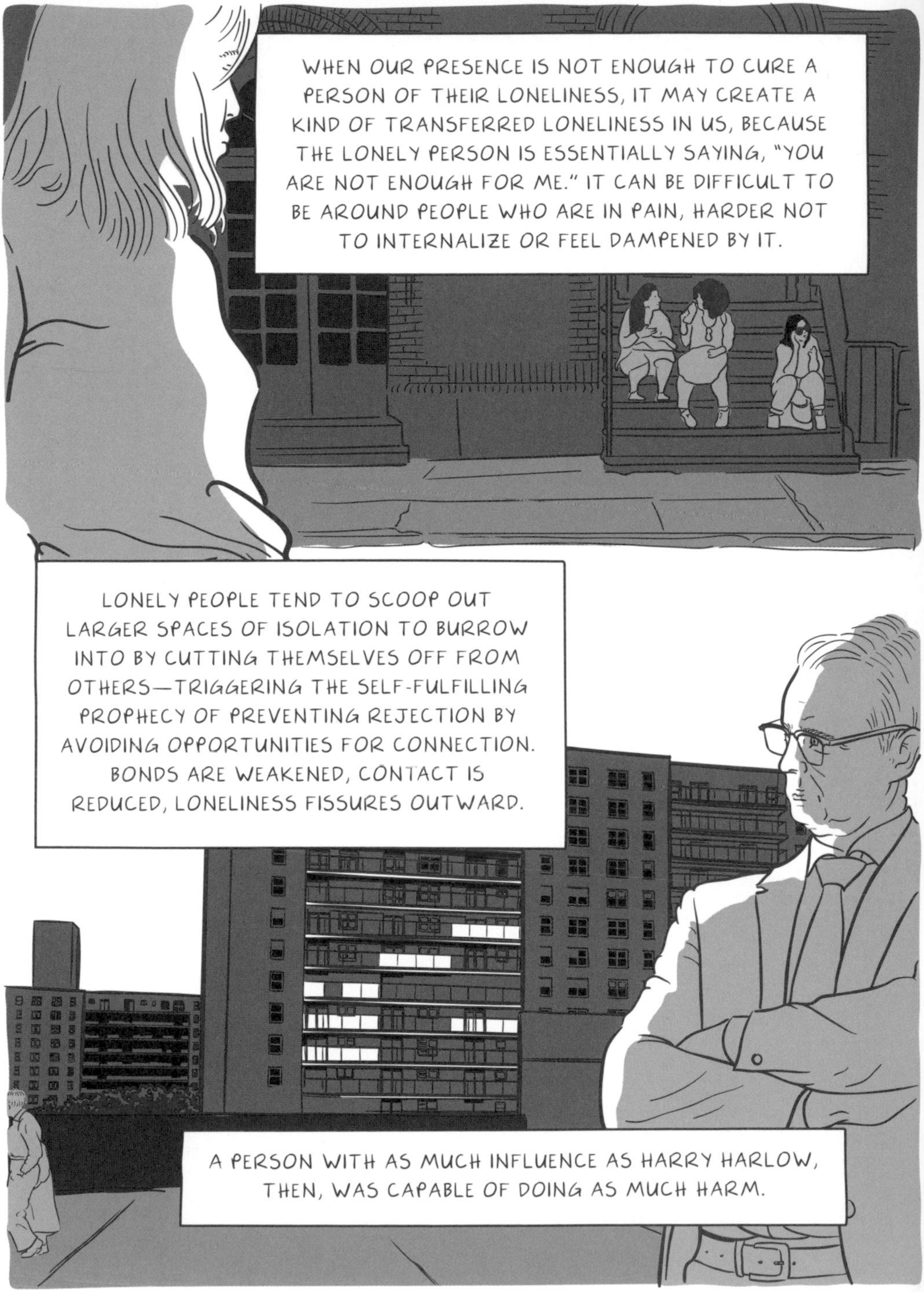
WHEN OUR PRESENCE IS NOT ENOUGH TO CURE A PERSON OF THEIR LONELINESS, IT MAY CREATE A KIND OF TRANSFERRED LONELINESS IN US, BECAUSE THE LONELY PERSON IS ESSENTIALLY SAYING, "YOU ARE NOT ENOUGH FOR ME." IT CAN BE DIFFICULT TO BE AROUND PEOPLE WHO ARE IN PAIN, HARDER NOT TO INTERNALIZE OR FEEL DAMPENED BY IT.
LONELY PEOPLE TEND TO SCOOP OUT LARGER SPACES OF ISOLATION TO BURROW INTO BY CUTTING THEMSELVES OFF FROM OTHERS—TRIGGERING THE SELF-FULFILLING PROPHECY OF PREVENTING REJECTION BY AVOIDING OPPORTUNITIES FOR CONNECTION. BONDS ARE WEAKENED, CONTACT IS REDUCED, LONELINESS FISSURES OUTWARD.
A PERSON WITH AS MUCH INFLUENCE AS HARRY HARLOW, THEN, WAS CAPABLE OF DOING AS MUCH HARM.

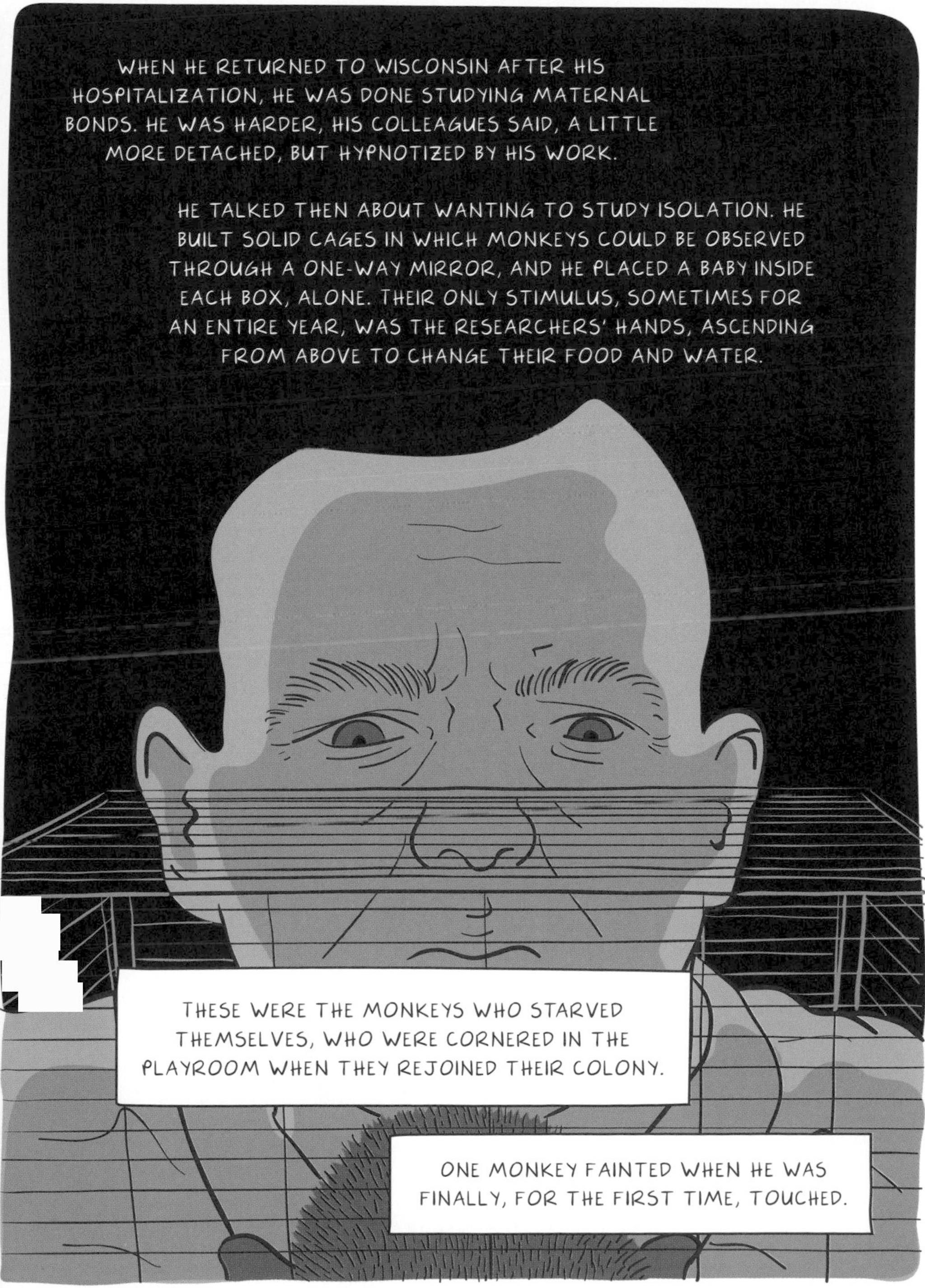
WHEN HE RETURNED TO WISCONSIN AFTER HIS HOSPITALIZATION, HE WAS DONE STUDYING MATERNAL BONDS. HE WAS HARDER, HIS COLLEAGUES SAID, A LITTLE MORE DETACHED, BUT HYPNOTIZED BY HIS WORK.
HE TALKED THEN ABOUT WANTING TO STUDY ISOLATION. HE BUILT SOLID CAGES IN WHICH MONKEYS COULD BE OBSERVED THROUGH A ONE-WAY MIRROR, AND HE PLACED A BABY INSIDE EACH BOX, ALONE. THEIR ONLY STIMULUS, SOMETIMES FOR AN ENTIRE YEAR, WAS THE RESEARCHERS' HANDS, ASCENDING FROM ABOVE TO CHANGE THEIR FOOD AND WATER.
THESE WERE THE MONKEYS WHO STARVED THEMSELVES, WHO WERE CORNERED IN THE PLAYROOM WHEN THEY REJOINED THEIR COLONY.
ONE MONKEY FAINTED WHEN HE WAS FINALLY, FOR THE FIRST TIME, TOUCHED.

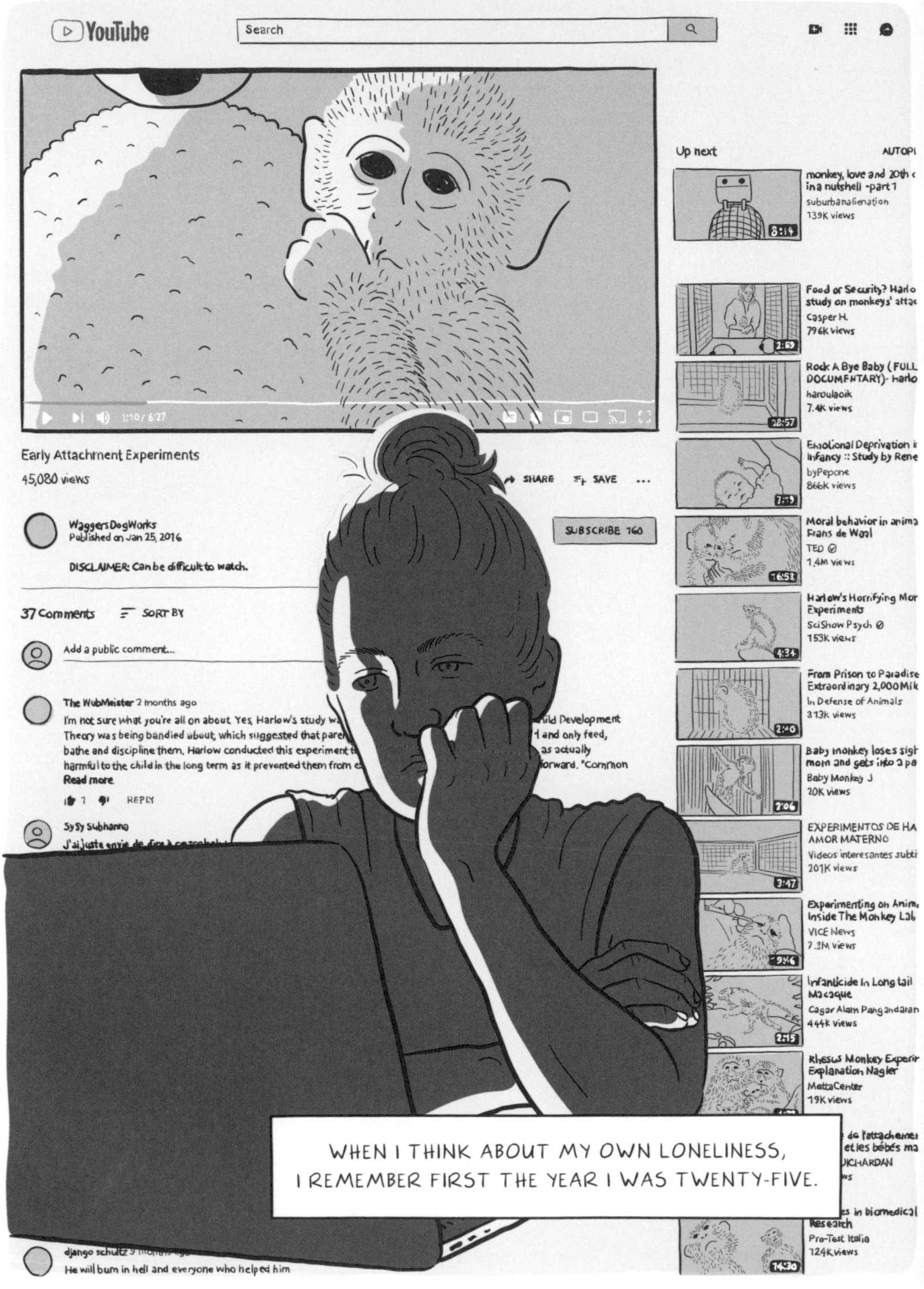
YouTube
Search
Up next
Early Attachment Experiments
45,080 views
SHARE
SAVE
WaggersDogWorks
Published on Jan 25, 2016
SUBSCRIBE 760
DISCLAIMER: Can be difficult to watch.
37 Comments
SORT BY
Add a public comment...
The WubMeister 2 months ago
Read more
REPLY
SySy Subhanna
django schultz
He will burn in hell and everyone who helped him
monkey, love and 20th
in a nutshell - part 1
suburbanalienation
139K views
Casper H.
79.6K views
Rock A Bye Baby (FULL
harouiaoik
7.4K views
byPepone
866K views
Moral behavior in
Frans de Waal
TED
1.4M views
Harlow's Horrifying
Experiments
SciShow Psych
153K views
In Defense of Animals
313K views
Baby Monkey J
20K views
AMOR MATERNO
201K views
Inside The Monkey Lab
VICE News
7.3M views
Infanticide in Long tail
Macaque
444K views
Explanation Nagler
MettaCenter
19K views
Research
Pro-Test Italia
124K views
WHEN I THINK ABOUT MY OWN LONELINESS,
I REMEMBER FIRST THE YEAR I WAS TWENTY-FIVE.

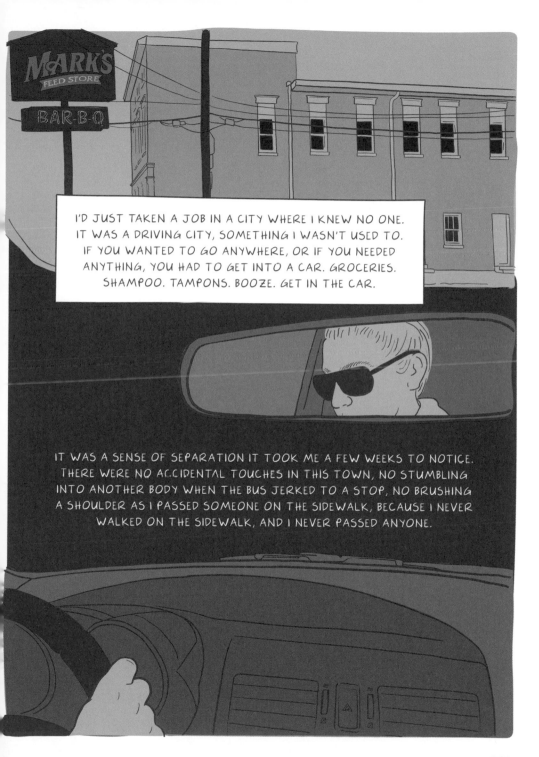

I'D JUST TAKEN A JOB IN A CITY WHERE I KNEW NO ONE. IT WAS A DRIVING CITY, SOMETHING I WASN'T USED TO. IF YOU WANTED TO GO ANYWHERE, OR IF YOU NEEDED ANYTHING, YOU HAD TO GET INTO A CAR. GROCERIES. SHAMPOO. TAMPONS. BOOZE. GET IN THE CAR.

IT WAS A SENSE OF SEPARATION IT TOOK ME A FEW WEEKS TO NOTICE. THERE WERE NO ACCIDENTAL TOUCHES IN THIS TOWN, NO STUMBLING INTO ANOTHER BODY WHEN THE BUS JERKED TO A STOP, NO BRUSHING A SHOULDER AS I PASSED SOMEONE ON THE SIDEWALK, BECAUSE I NEVER WALKED ON THE SIDEWALK, AND I NEVER PASSED ANYONE.

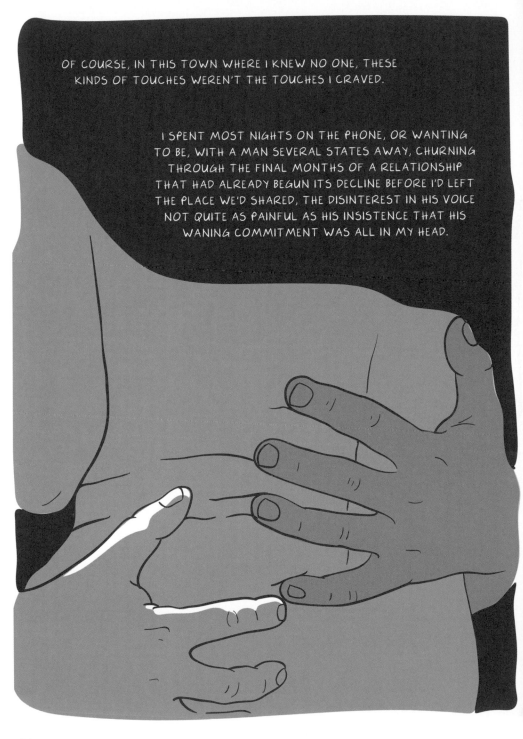

OF COURSE, IN THIS TOWN WHERE I KNEW NO ONE, THESE
KINDS OF TOUCHES WEREN'T THE TOUCHES I CRAVED.

I SPENT MOST NIGHTS ON THE PHONE, OR WANTING
TO BE, WITH A MAN SEVERAL STATES AWAY, CHURNING
THROUGH THE FINAL MONTHS OF A RELATIONSHIP
THAT HAD ALREADY BEGUN ITS DECLINE BEFORE I'D LEFT
THE PLACE WE'D SHARED, THE DISINTEREST IN HIS VOICE
NOT QUITE AS PAINFUL AS HIS INSISTENCE THAT HIS
WANING COMMITMENT WAS ALL IN MY HEAD.

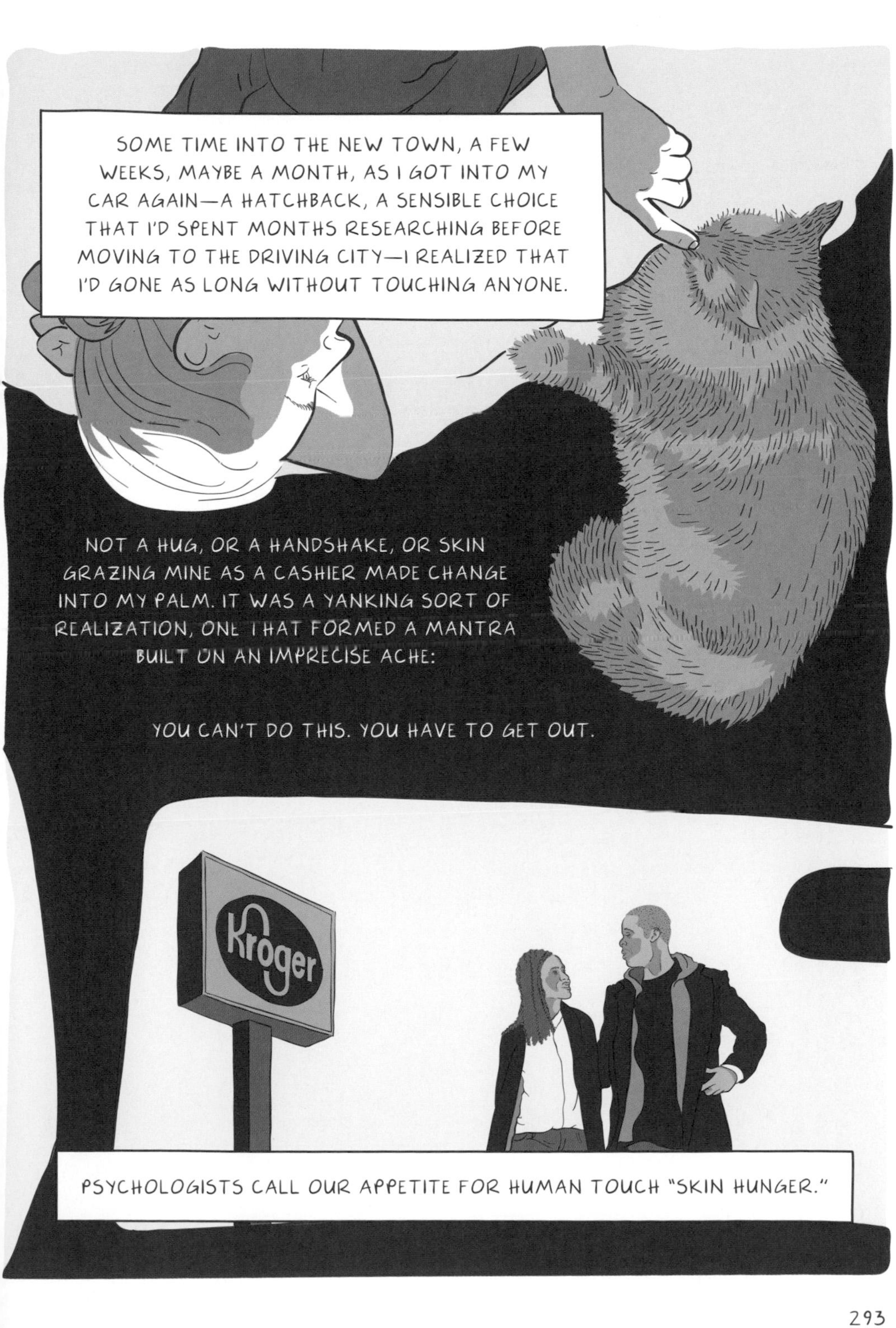
SOME TIME INTO THE NEW TOWN, A FEW WEEKS, MAYBE A MONTH, AS I GOT INTO MY CAR AGAIN—A HATCHBACK, A SENSIBLE CHOICE THAT I'D SPENT MONTHS RESEARCHING BEFORE MOVING TO THE DRIVING CITY—I REALIZED THAT I'D GONE AS LONG WITHOUT TOUCHING ANYONE.
NOT A HUG, OR A HANDSHAKE, OR SKIN GRAZING MINE AS A CASHIER MADE CHANGE INTO MY PALM. IT WAS A YANKING SORT OF REALIZATION, ONE THAT FORMED A MANTRA BUILT ON AN IMPRECISE ACHE:
YOU CAN'T DO THIS. YOU HAVE TO GET OUT.
Kroger
PSYCHOLOGISTS CALL OUR APPETITE FOR HUMAN TOUCH "SKIN HUNGER."

Spooning
strangers
trending?

IT'S AN ODD AND BEAUTIFUL NAME THAT CONNOTES NOT A WANT BUT A NEED. WHEN WE ARE HUNGRY WE MUST EAT. SO, TOO, IS THE BODY'S DESIRE FOR TOUCH DESIGNED TO BRING US TOWARD ANOTHER PERSON, BECAUSE SO MUCH—OUR IMMUNE SYSTEM, OUR HORMONE RELEASE, OUR MENTAL HEALTH—RELIES IN PART ON HUMAN CONTACT TO CONTINUE FUNCTIONING AS IT SHOULD.

No hugging:
are we living
through a

THE LONGING FOR CONTACT IS SO PERVASIVE THAT IT'S CREATED AN INDUSTRY OF PAID PLATONIC TOUCH, STAFFED BY AN ARMY OF SURROGATES TO ENACT THE PHYSICAL INTIMACY THAT'S TRADITIONALLY BEEN A BUILT-IN BY-PRODUCT OF REGULAR LIFE.

Up:

Professional cuddle

are changing the way

pe

DOZENS OF COMPANIES HAVE RESPONDED TO THE CALL, SOME BUILT LIKE OFFSHOOTS OF TOUCH-THERAPY CENTERS, STAFFED BY PROFESSIONAL CUDDLISTS, OTHERS FORMING SOCIAL NETWORKS FOR THOSE WHO WANT TO MEET UP AND SPOON GRATIS.

AT IS PROFESSIONAL CUD

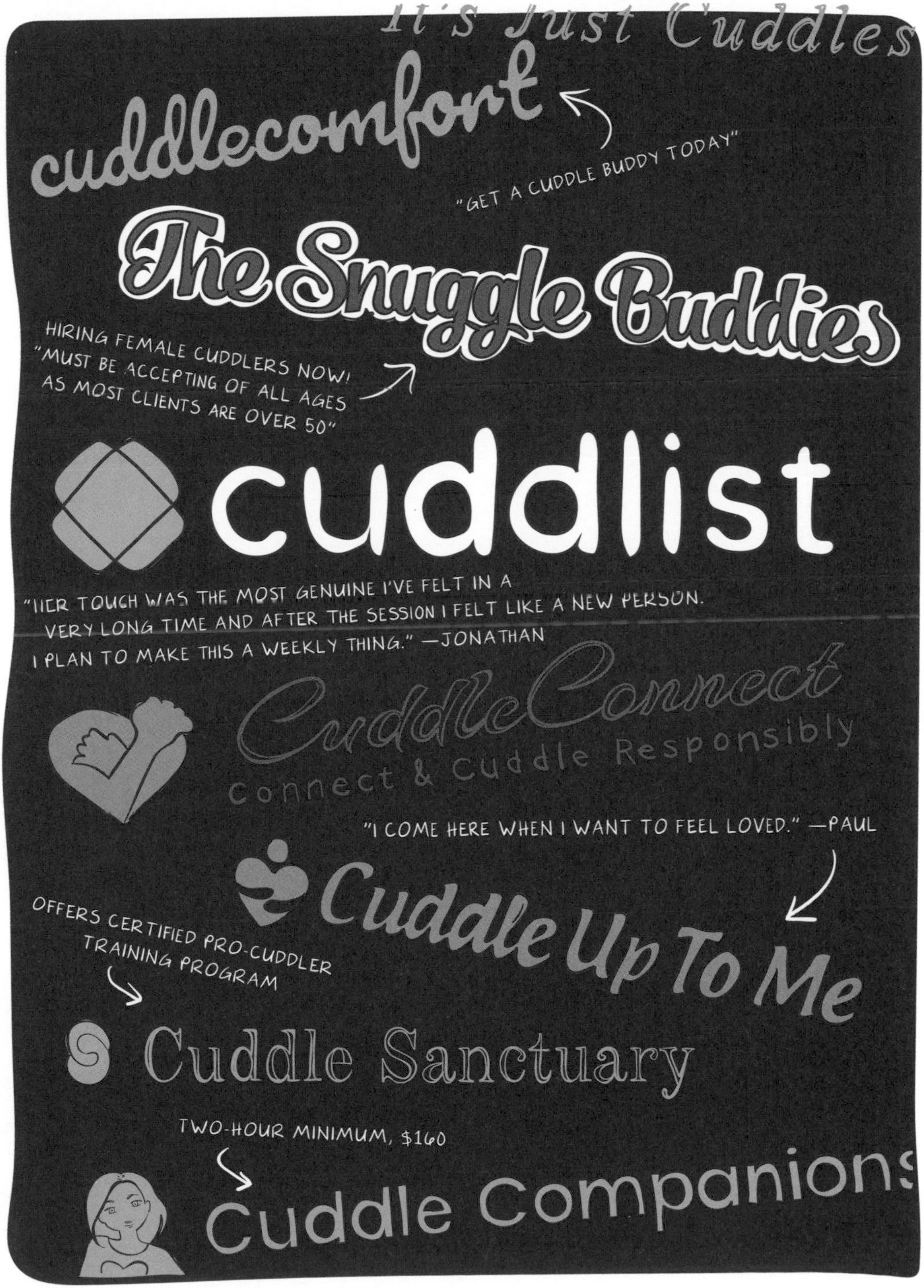
It's Just Cuddles
cuddlecomfort
"GET A CUDDLE BUDDY TODAY"
The Snuggle Buddies
HIRING FEMALE CUDDLERS NOW!
"MUST BE ACCEPTING OF ALL AGES
AS MOST CLIENTS ARE OVER 50"
cuddlist
"HER TOUCH WAS THE MOST GENUINE I'VE FELT IN A
VERY LONG TIME AND AFTER THE SESSION I FELT LIKE A NEW PERSON.
I PLAN TO MAKE THIS A WEEKLY THING." —JONATHAN
CuddleConnect
Connect & Cuddle Responsibly
"I COME HERE WHEN I WANT TO FEEL LOVED." —PAUL
Cuddle Up To Me
OFFERS CERTIFIED PRO-CUDDLER
TRAINING PROGRAM
Cuddle Sanctuary
TWO-HOUR MINIMUM, $160
Cuddle Companions

THE EMERGENCE OF SOMETHING LIKE THE "CUDDLE INDUSTRY" CAN SUGGEST THAT WE'RE REALLY MORE REMOVED FROM ONE ANOTHER THAN WE ONCE WERE; WE CAN WAX ON ABOUT TECHNOLOGY AND DETACHMENT AND "WE'VE ALL JUST GOTTEN SO DARN BUSY." BUT IT ALSO MIGHT IMPLY THAT WE NOW SIMPLY LIVE IN A CULTURE THAT'S SOOTHED BY ACCESSIBLE SELF-HELP AND COMMODIFIABLE EXPERIENCES AND THE BUZZWORDS UTILIZED TO SELL THESE THINGS.

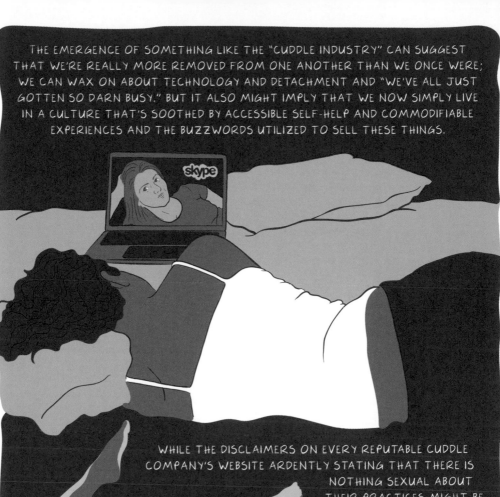

WHILE THE DISCLAIMERS ON EVERY REPUTABLE CUDDLE COMPANY'S WEBSITE ARDENTLY STATING THAT THERE IS NOTHING SEXUAL ABOUT THEIR PRACTICES MIGHT BE TRUE, PERHAPS A CUDDLE BUDDY JUST COMMERCIALIZES THE SAME THINGS WE'VE ALWAYS BEEN PREDISPOSED TO LACK OR CRAVE.

SEX WORK, AFTER ALL, IS ABOUT A LOT MORE THAN SEXUAL GRATIFICATION. ANYONE WHO PAYS FOR SEX CERTAINLY KNOWS HOW TO PRO-CURE THEIR OWN ORGASM FOR FREE.

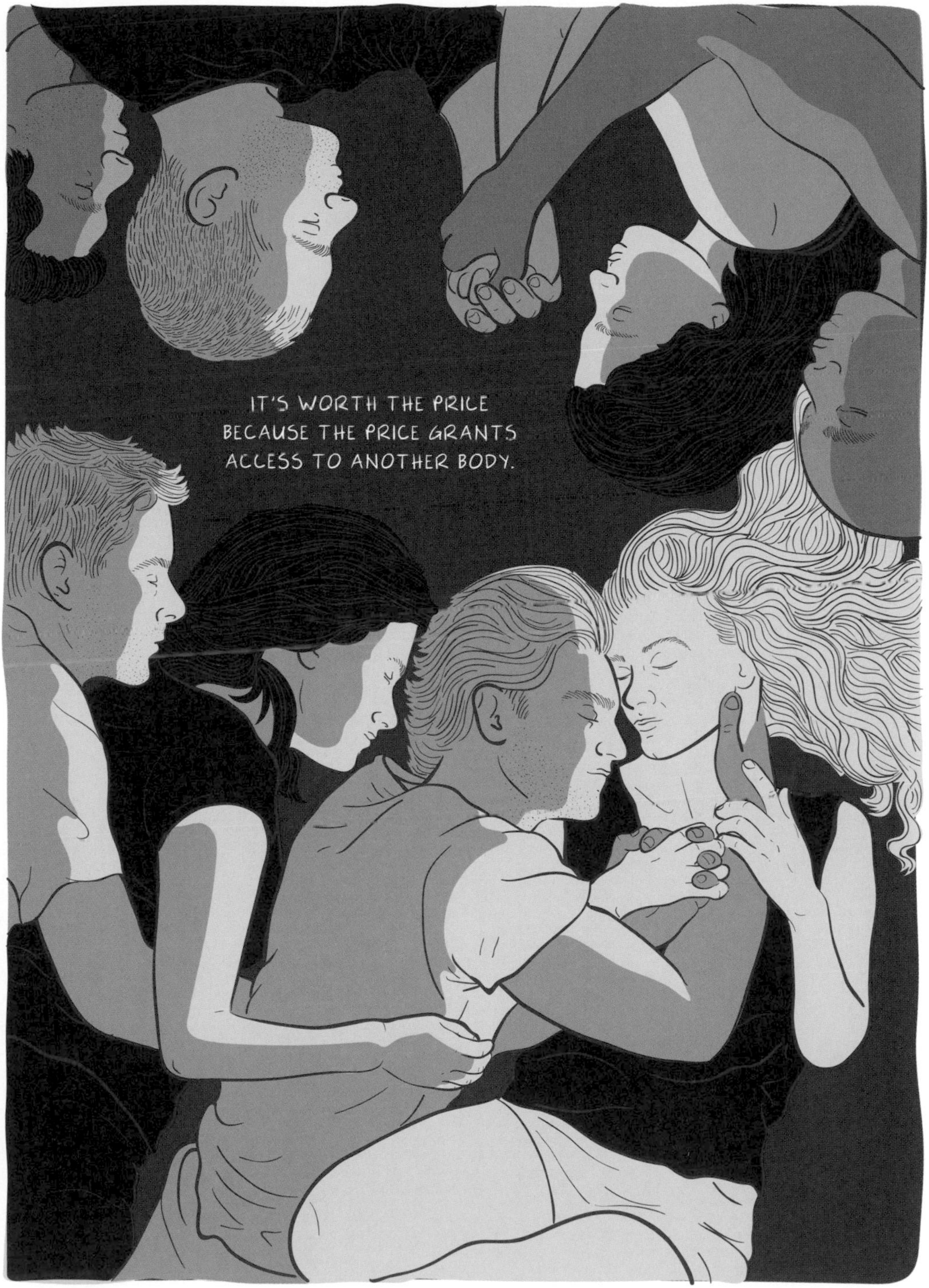
IT'S WORTH THE PRICE BECAUSE THE PRICE GRANTS ACCESS TO ANOTHER BODY.

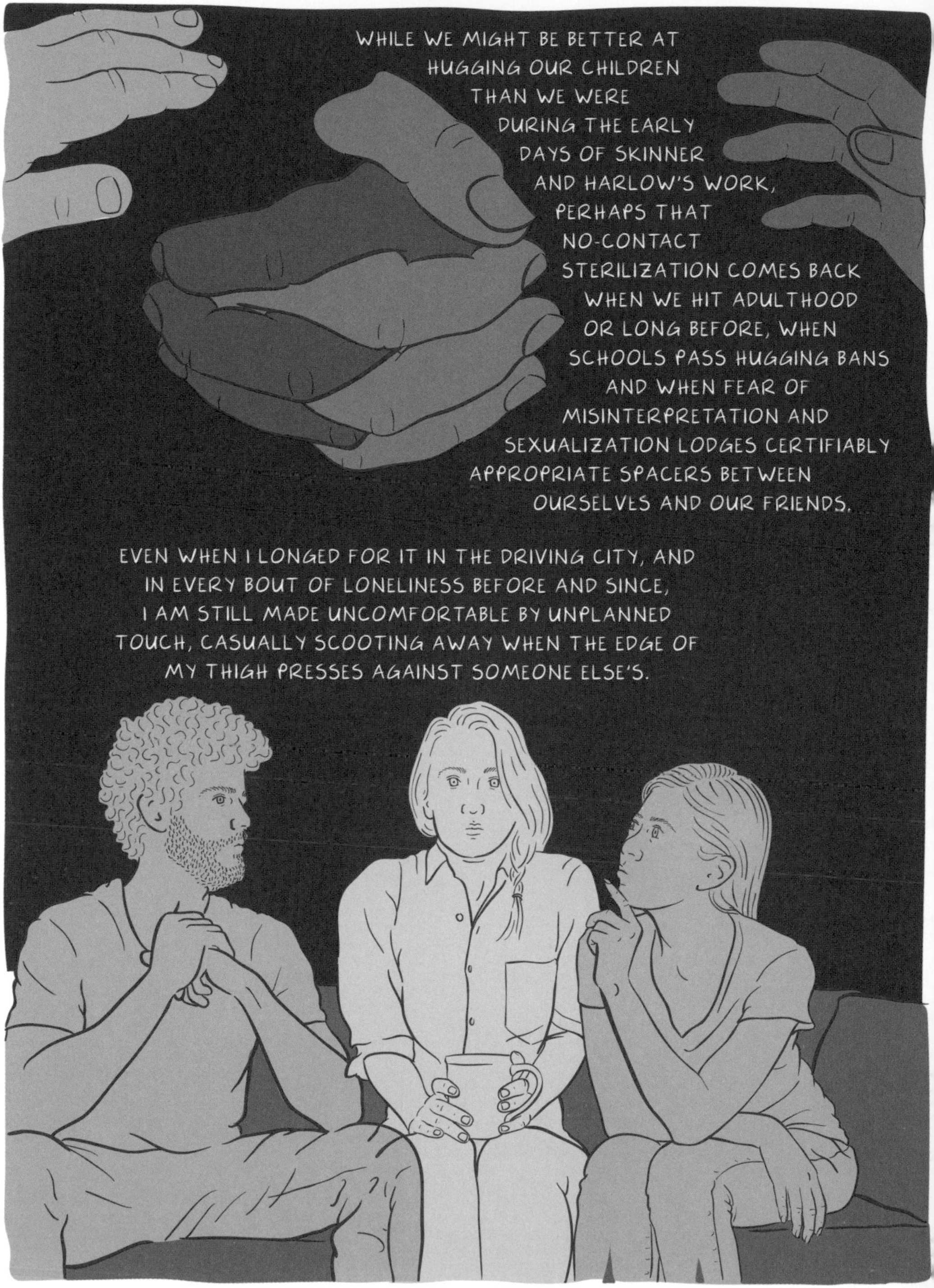
WHILE WE MIGHT BE BETTER AT HUGGING OUR CHILDREN THAN WE WERE DURING THE EARLY DAYS OF SKINNER AND HARLOW'S WORK, PERHAPS THAT NO-CONTACT STERILIZATION COMES BACK WHEN WE HIT ADULTHOOD OR LONG BEFORE, WHEN SCHOOLS PASS HUGGING BANS AND WHEN FEAR OF MISINTERPRETATION AND SEXUALIZATION LODGES CERTIFIABLY APPROPRIATE SPACERS BETWEEN OURSELVES AND OUR FRIENDS.
EVEN WHEN I LONGED FOR IT IN THE DRIVING CITY, AND IN EVERY BOUT OF LONELINESS BEFORE AND SINCE, I AM STILL MADE UNCOMFORTABLE BY UNPLANNED TOUCH, CASUALLY SCOOTING AWAY WHEN THE EDGE OF MY THIGH PRESSES AGAINST SOMEONE ELSE'S.

ONCE, I SAT ACROSS FROM MY FRIEND AND HER SISTER, MY FRIEND CASUALLY PLAYING WITH HER SISTER'S HAIR AS SHE SPOKE, BRUSHING IT OFF HER SHOULDERS, RUNNING THE STRANDS THROUGH HER FINGERS.

I FELT LIKE I SHOULD TURN AWAY.

I WOULD NEVER REGARD A FRIEND OR SIBLING THIS WAY, EVEN THOUGH I MIGHT OCCASIONALLY HAVE AN URGE TO—TO REACH OUT MY HAND TOWARD HERS, TO REST MY HEAD AGAINST THE BOWL OF HER NECK AS WE TALK. BUT IF I DO, I REGRET IT ALMOST IMMEDIATELY, WANTING TO PULL BACK.

I DON'T KNOW WHY I FEEL THIS WAY OTHER THAN THAT I WAS RAISED TO KEEP MY HANDS TO MYSELF, SWATTED BY THE NUNS AT CATHOLIC SCHOOL.

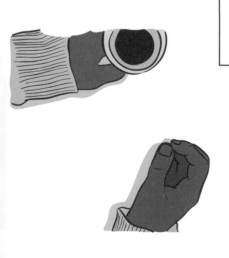

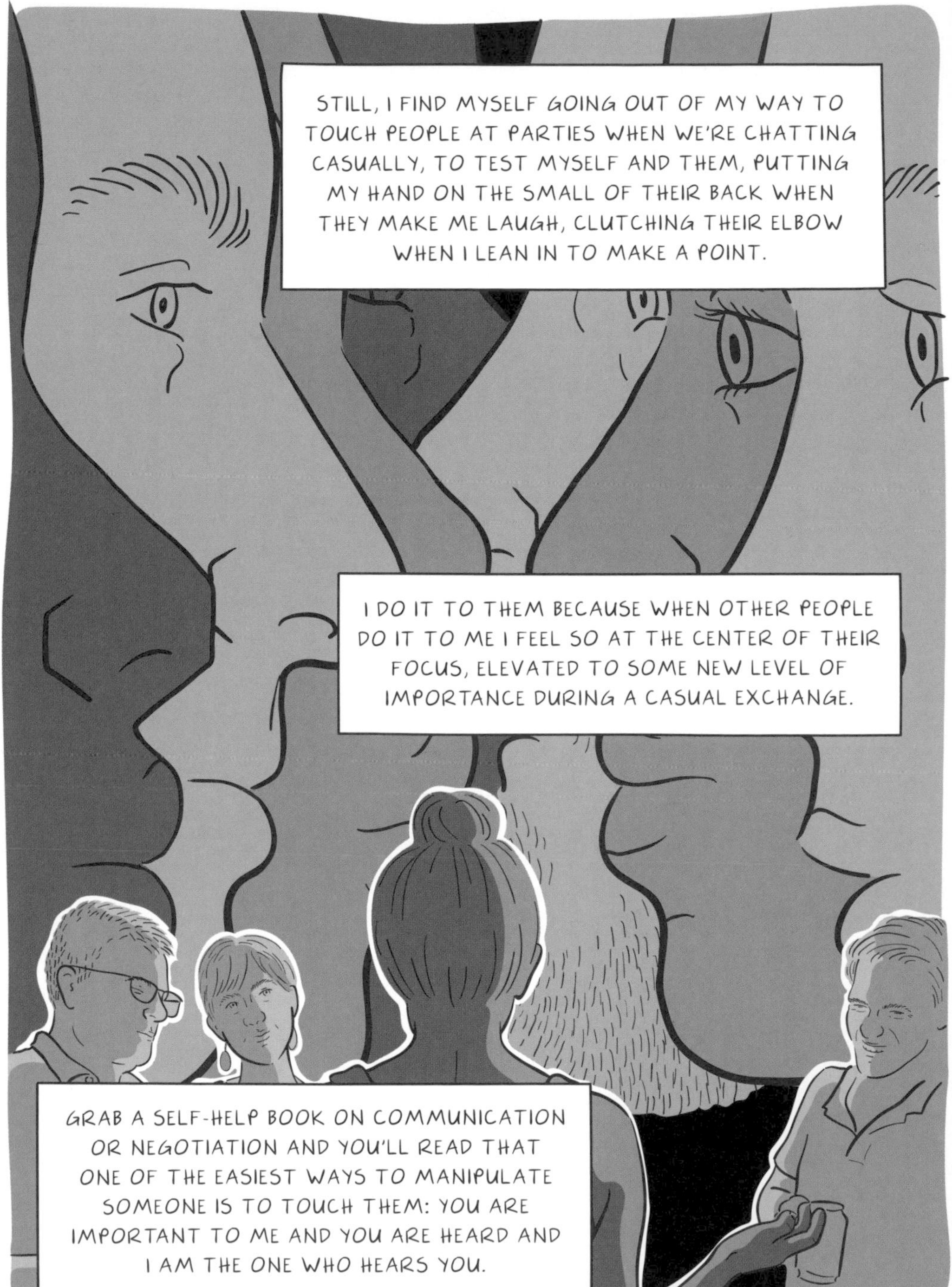
STILL, I FIND MYSELF GOING OUT OF MY WAY TO TOUCH PEOPLE AT PARTIES WHEN WE'RE CHATTING CASUALLY, TO TEST MYSELF AND THEM, PUTTING MY HAND ON THE SMALL OF THEIR BACK WHEN THEY MAKE ME LAUGH, CLUTCHING THEIR ELBOW WHEN I LEAN IN TO MAKE A POINT.
I DO IT TO THEM BECAUSE WHEN OTHER PEOPLE DO IT TO ME I FEEL SO AT THE CENTER OF THEIR FOCUS, ELEVATED TO SOME NEW LEVEL OF IMPORTANCE DURING A CASUAL EXCHANGE.
GRAB A SELF-HELP BOOK ON COMMUNICATION OR NEGOTIATION AND YOU'LL READ THAT ONE OF THE EASIEST WAYS TO MANIPULATE SOMEONE IS TO TOUCH THEM: YOU ARE IMPORTANT TO ME AND YOU ARE HEARD AND I AM THE ONE WHO HEARS YOU.

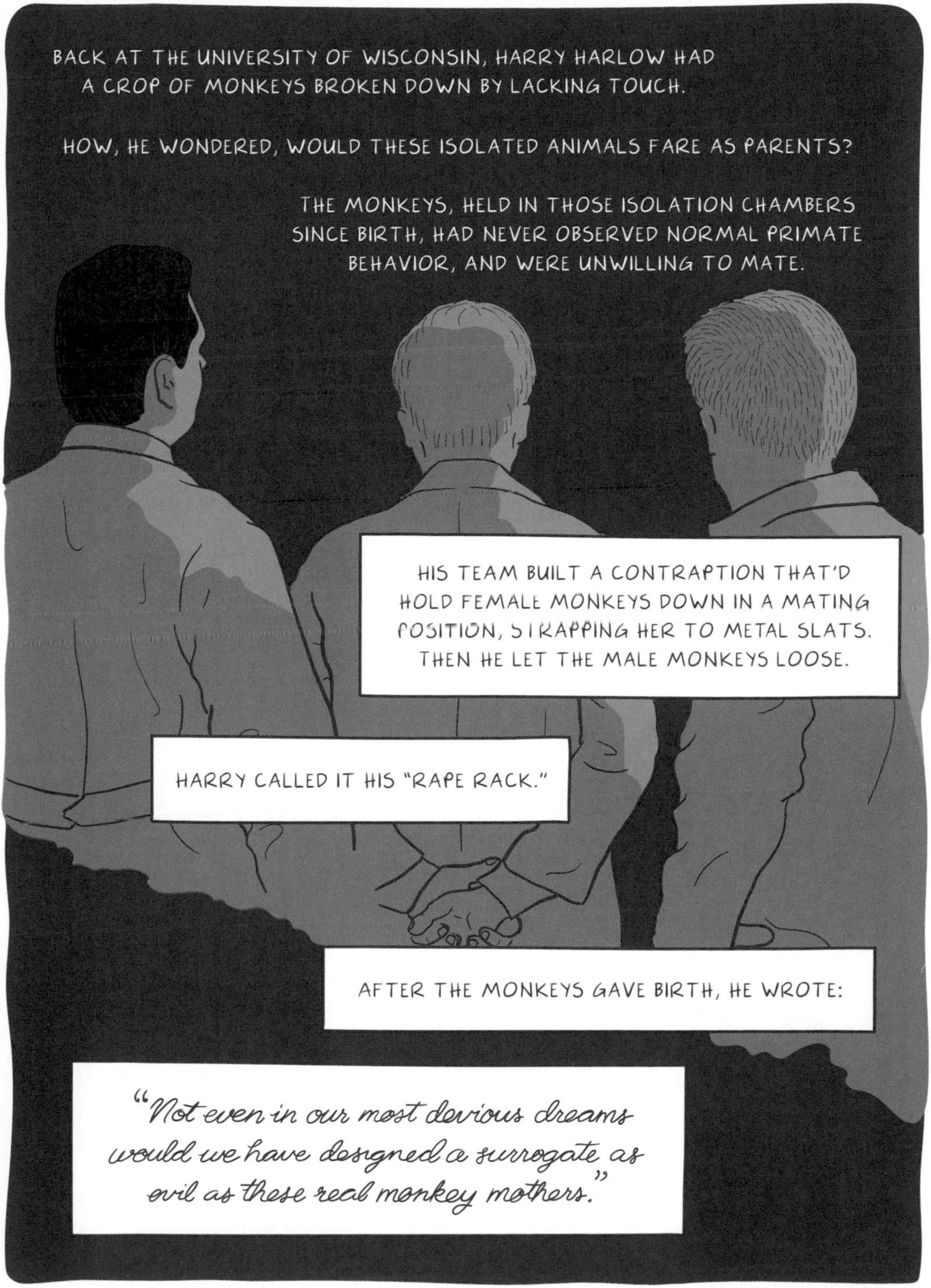
BACK AT THE UNIVERSITY OF WISCONSIN, HARRY HARLOW HAD A CROP OF MONKEYS BROKEN DOWN BY LACKING TOUCH.
HOW, HE WONDERED, WOULD THESE ISOLATED ANIMALS FARE AS PARENTS?
THE MONKEYS, HELD IN THOSE ISOLATION CHAMBERS SINCE BIRTH, HAD NEVER OBSERVED NORMAL PRIMATE BEHAVIOR, AND WERE UNWILLING TO MATE.
HIS TEAM BUILT A CONTRAPTION THAT'D HOLD FEMALE MONKEYS DOWN IN A MATING POSITION, STRAPPING HER TO METAL SLATS. THEN HE LET THE MALE MONKEYS LOOSE.
HARRY CALLED IT HIS "RAPE RACK."
AFTER THE MONKEYS GAVE BIRTH, HE WROTE:
"Not even in our most devious dreams would we have designed a surrogate as evil as these real monkey mothers."

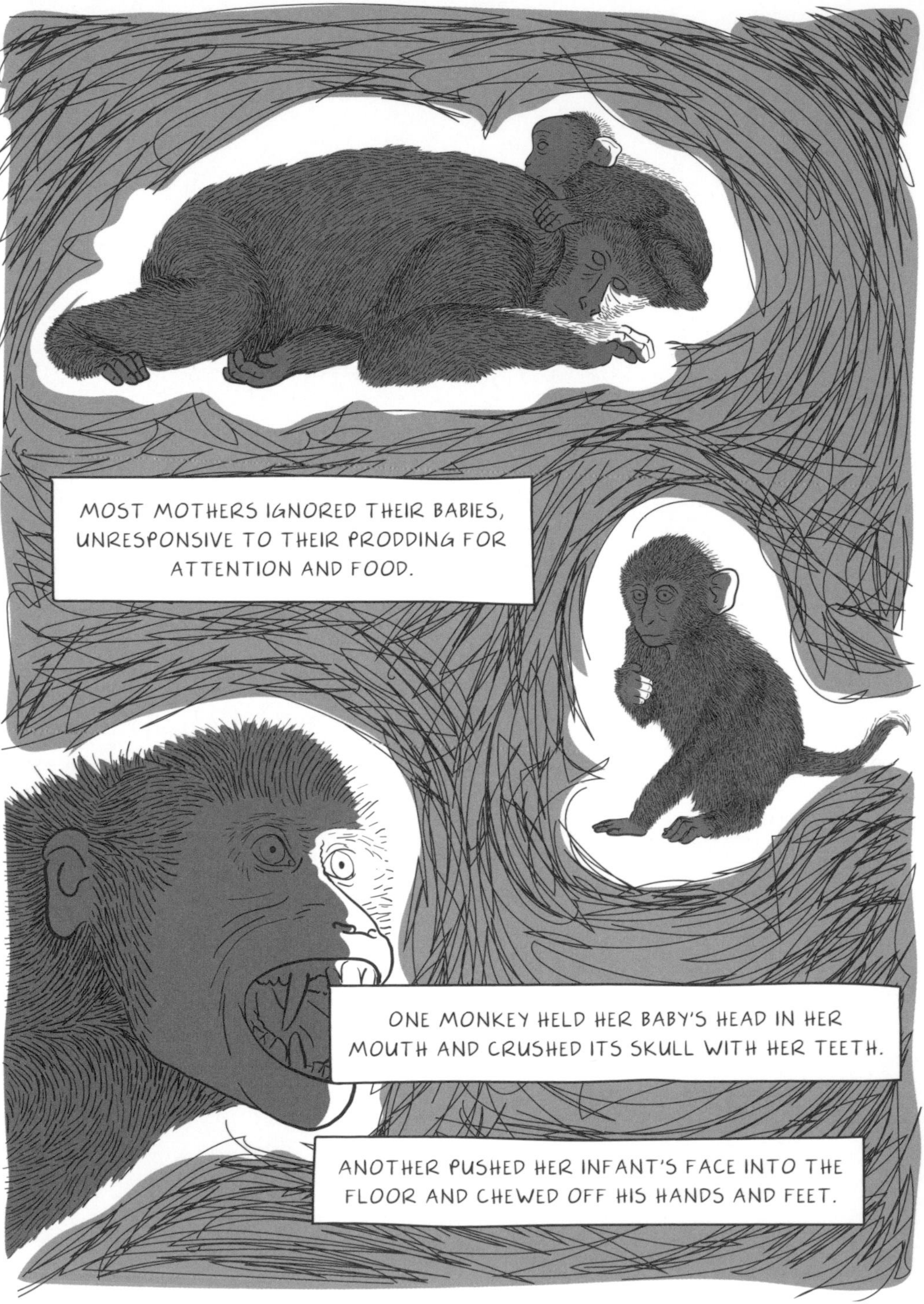

MOST MOTHERS IGNORED THEIR BABIES, UNRESPONSIVE TO THEIR PRODDING FOR ATTENTION AND FOOD.
ONE MONKEY HELD HER BABY'S HEAD IN HER MOUTH AND CRUSHED ITS SKULL WITH HER TEETH.
ANOTHER PUSHED HER INFANT'S FACE INTO THE FLOOR AND CHEWED OFF HIS HANDS AND FEET.

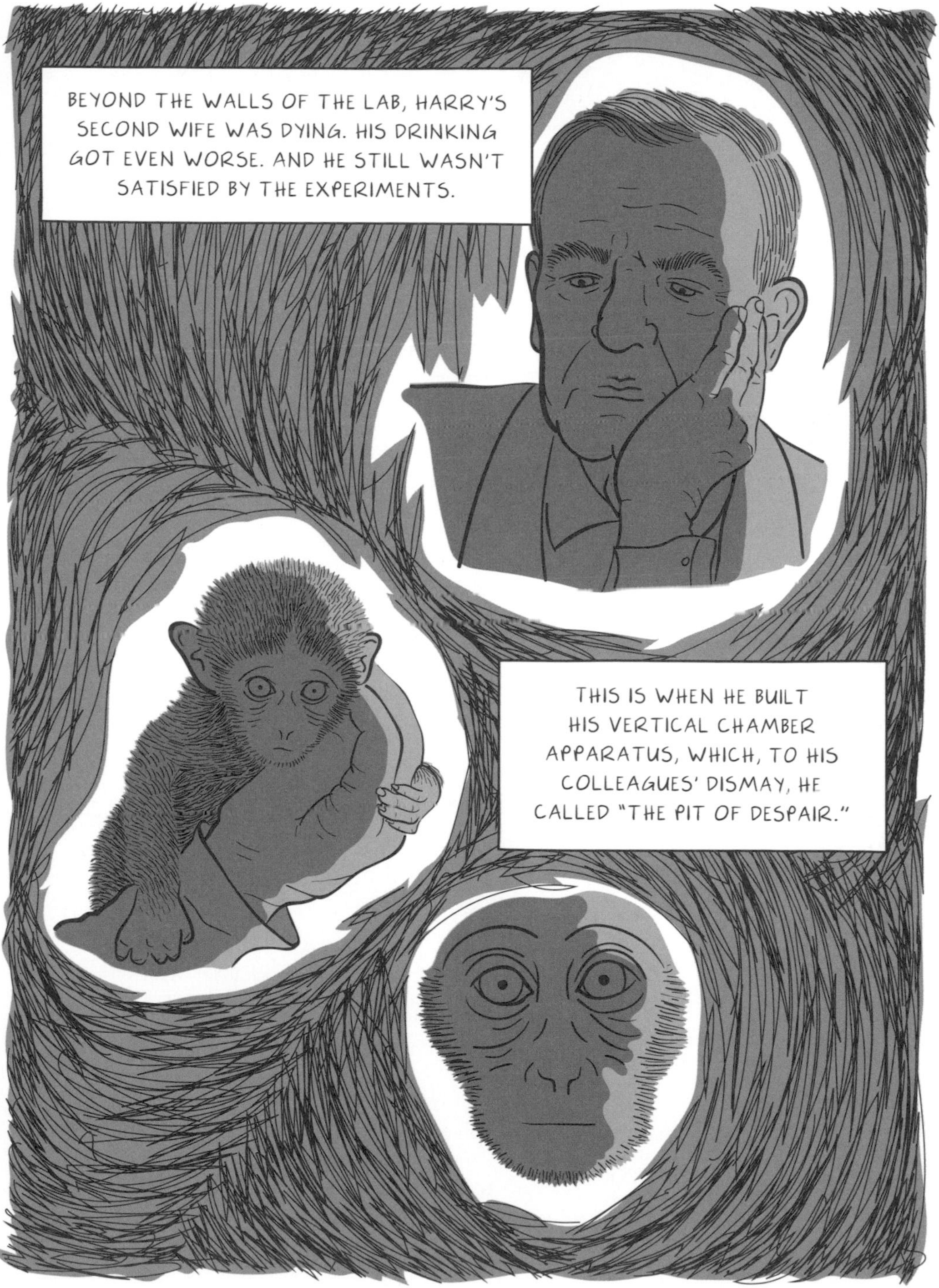
BEYOND THE WALLS OF THE LAB, HARRY'S SECOND WIFE WAS DYING. HIS DRINKING GOT EVEN WORSE. AND HE STILL WASN'T SATISFIED BY THE EXPERIMENTS.
THIS IS WHEN HE BUILT HIS VERTICAL CHAMBER APPARATUS, WHICH, TO HIS COLLEAGUES' DISMAY, HE CALLED "THE PIT OF DESPAIR."

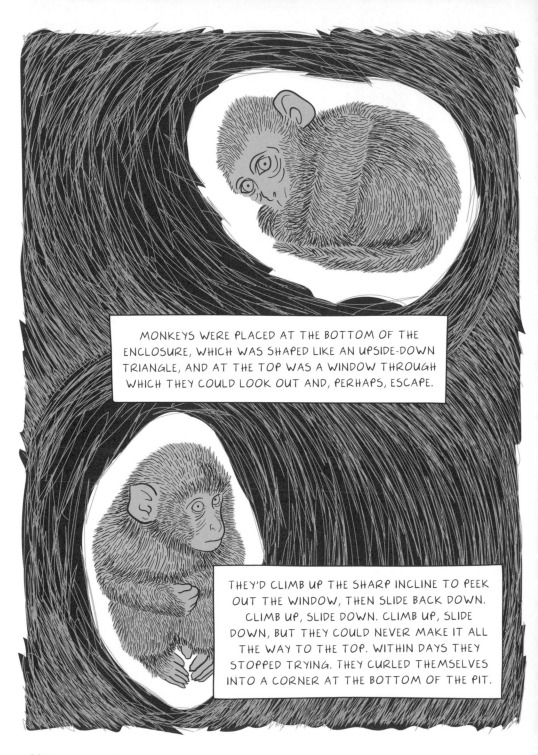

MONKEYS WERE PLACED AT THE BOTTOM OF THE ENCLOSURE, WHICH WAS SHAPED LIKE AN UPSIDE-DOWN TRIANGLE, AND AT THE TOP WAS A WINDOW THROUGH WHICH THEY COULD LOOK OUT AND, PERHAPS, ESCAPE.

THEY'D CLIMB UP THE SHARP INCLINE TO PEEK OUT THE WINDOW, THEN SLIDE BACK DOWN. CLIMB UP, SLIDE DOWN. CLIMB UP, SLIDE DOWN, BUT THEY COULD NEVER MAKE IT ALL THE WAY TO THE TOP. WITHIN DAYS THEY STOPPED TRYING. THEY CURLED THEMSELVES INTO A CORNER AT THE BOTTOM OF THE PIT.

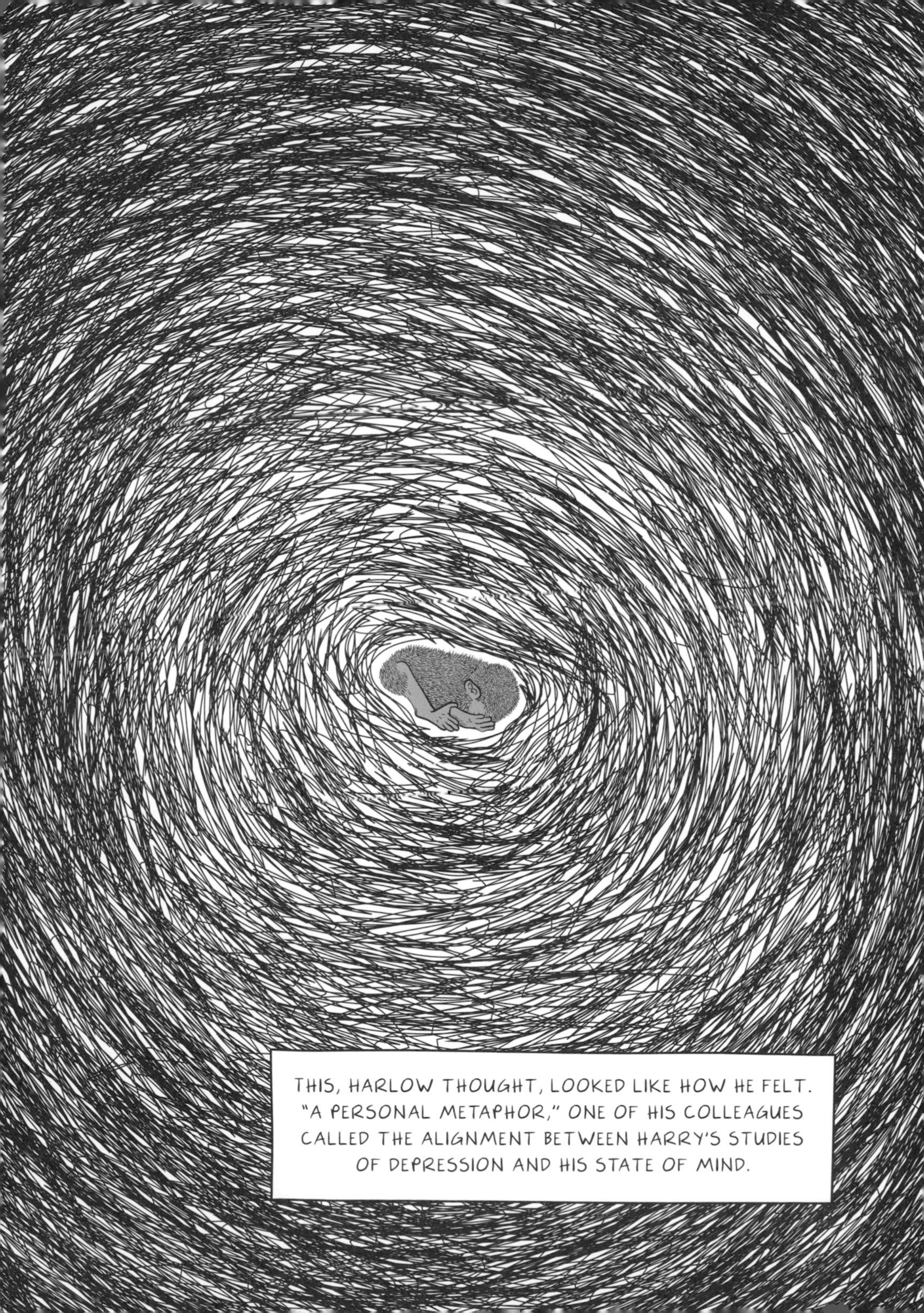
THIS, HARLOW THOUGHT, LOOKED LIKE HOW HE FELT. "A PERSONAL METAPHOR," ONE OF HIS COLLEAGUES CALLED THE ALIGNMENT BETWEEN HARRY'S STUDIES OF DEPRESSION AND HIS STATE OF MIND.

A PERFECTLY HAPPY MONKEY WOULD GO INTO
THE PIT AND, IN LESS THAN A WEEK, COME OUT
INCAPABLE OF INTERACTING WITH ANY OTHER
ANIMAL. HE CALLED A CHAPTER ON THE STUDY,
MANY YEARS LATER, "THE HELL OF LONELINESS."

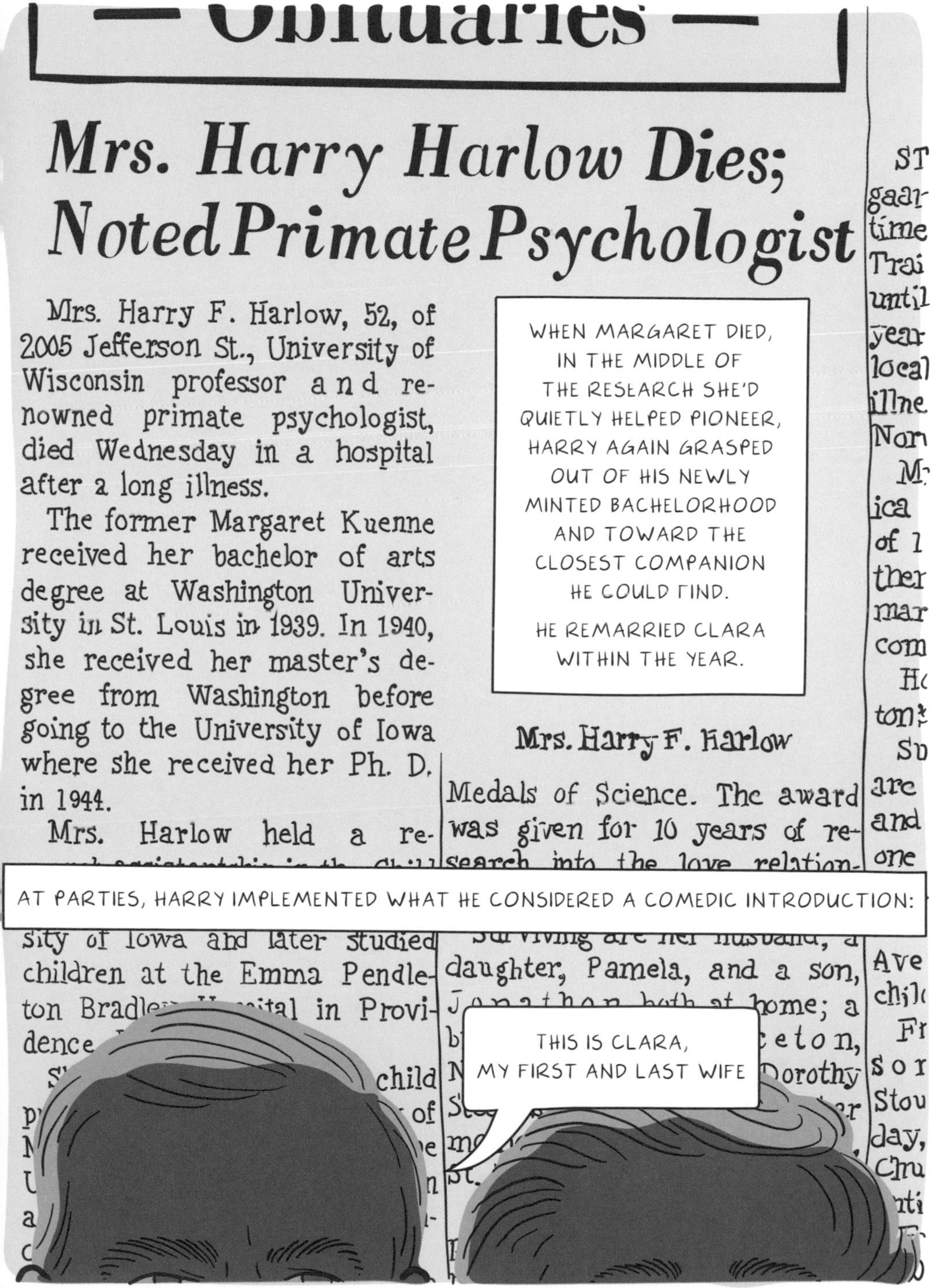

— Obituaries —

Mrs. Harry Harlow Dies; Noted Primate Psychologist

Mrs. Harry F. Harlow, 52, of 2005 Jefferson St., University of Wisconsin professor and renowned primate psychologist, died Wednesday in a hospital after a long illness.

The former Margaret Kuenne received her bachelor of arts degree at Washington University in St. Louis in 1939. In 1940, she received her master's degree from Washington before going to the University of Iowa where she received her Ph. D. in 1944.

Mrs. Harlow held a re-

WHEN MARGARET DIED, IN THE MIDDLE OF THE RESEARCH SHE'D QUIETLY HELPED PIONEER, HARRY AGAIN GRASPED OUT OF HIS NEWLY MINTED BACHELORHOOD AND TOWARD THE CLOSEST COMPANION HE COULD FIND.

HE REMARRIED CLARA WITHIN THE YEAR.

Mrs. Harry F. Harlow

Medals of Science. The award was given for 10 years of research into the love relation-

sity of Iowa and later studied children at the Emma Pendleton Bradley Hospital in Providence

child of

Surviving are her husband, a daughter, Pamela, and a son, Jonathan both at home; a bceton,
N
St
m

AT PARTIES, HARRY IMPLEMENTED WHAT HE CONSIDERED A COMEDIC INTRODUCTION:

THIS IS CLARA, MY FIRST AND LAST WIFE

Dorothy

ST
gaar
time
Trai
until
year
local
illne
Non
M
ica
of 1
ther
mar
com
H
ton
Su
are
and
one

Ave
chil
Fr
sor
Stou
day,
Chu
nti
F

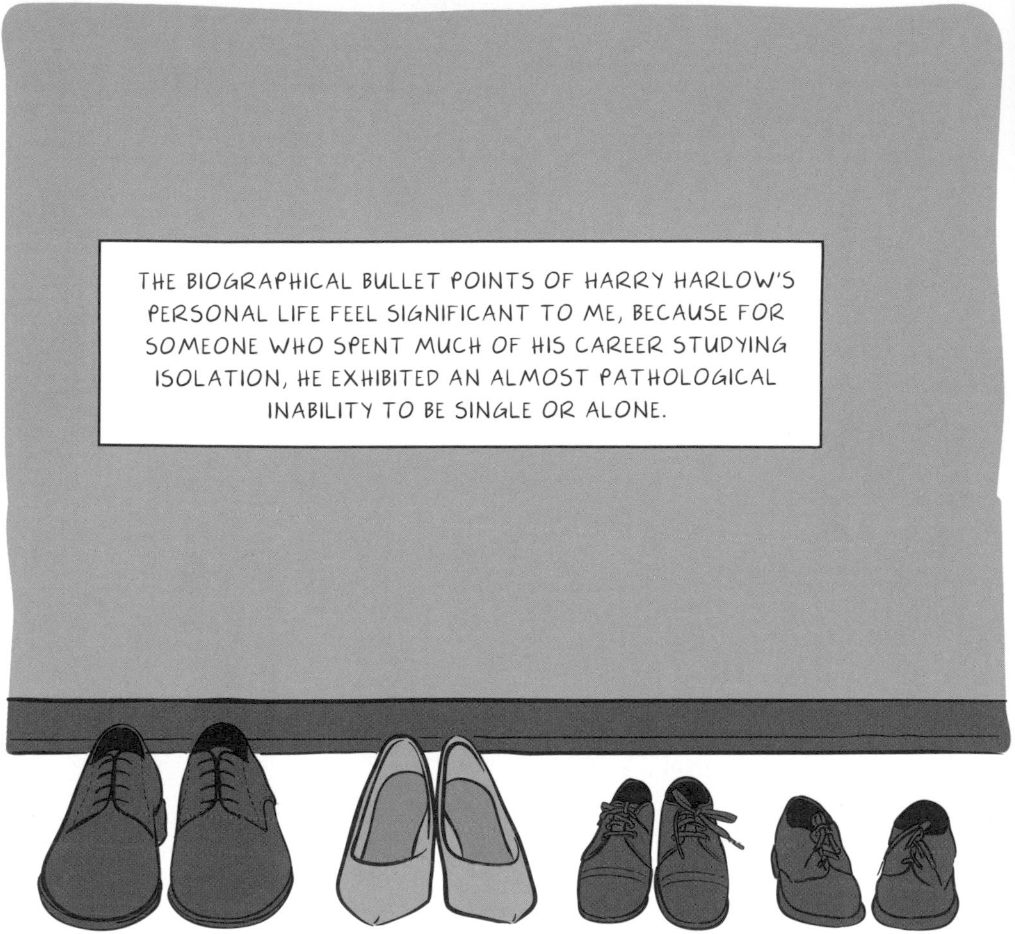
THE BIOGRAPHICAL BULLET POINTS OF HARRY HARLOW'S PERSONAL LIFE FEEL SIGNIFICANT TO ME, BECAUSE FOR SOMEONE WHO SPENT MUCH OF HIS CAREER STUDYING ISOLATION, HE EXHIBITED AN ALMOST PATHOLOGICAL INABILITY TO BE SINGLE OR ALONE.

IF A LINE WERE DRAWN AND I WAS ASKED TO MARK AN X FOR LONELINESS AND AN X FOR LOVE, I MIGHT IMPULSIVELY DRAW THEM AT OPPOSITE POLES. BUT THE DRIVE OF EACH IS SIMILAR. THEY'RE BOTH DESIGNED TO KEEP US TOGETHER.

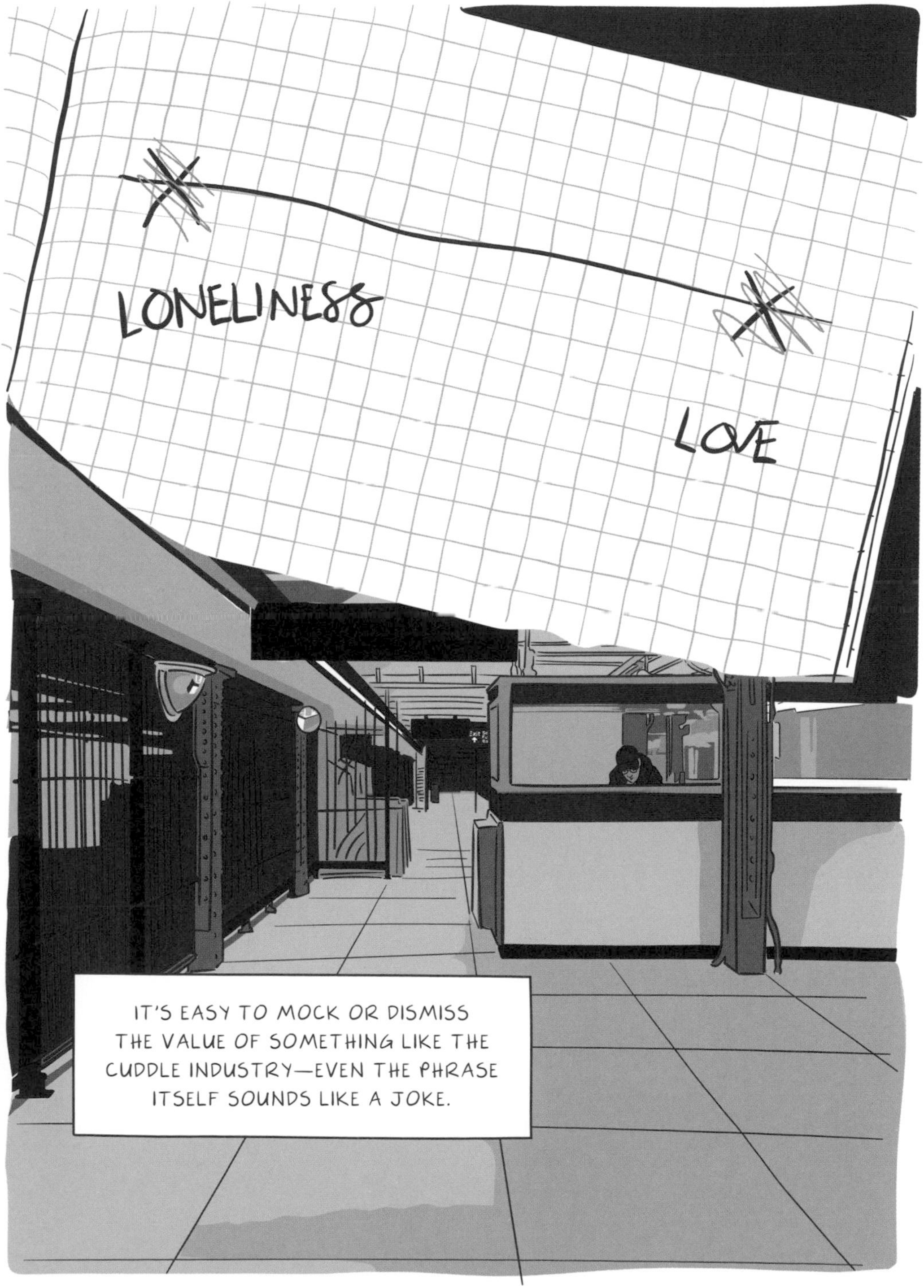
LONELINESS
LOVE
IT'S EASY TO MOCK OR DISMISS THE VALUE OF SOMETHING LIKE THE CUDDLE INDUSTRY—EVEN THE PHRASE ITSELF SOUNDS LIKE A JOKE.

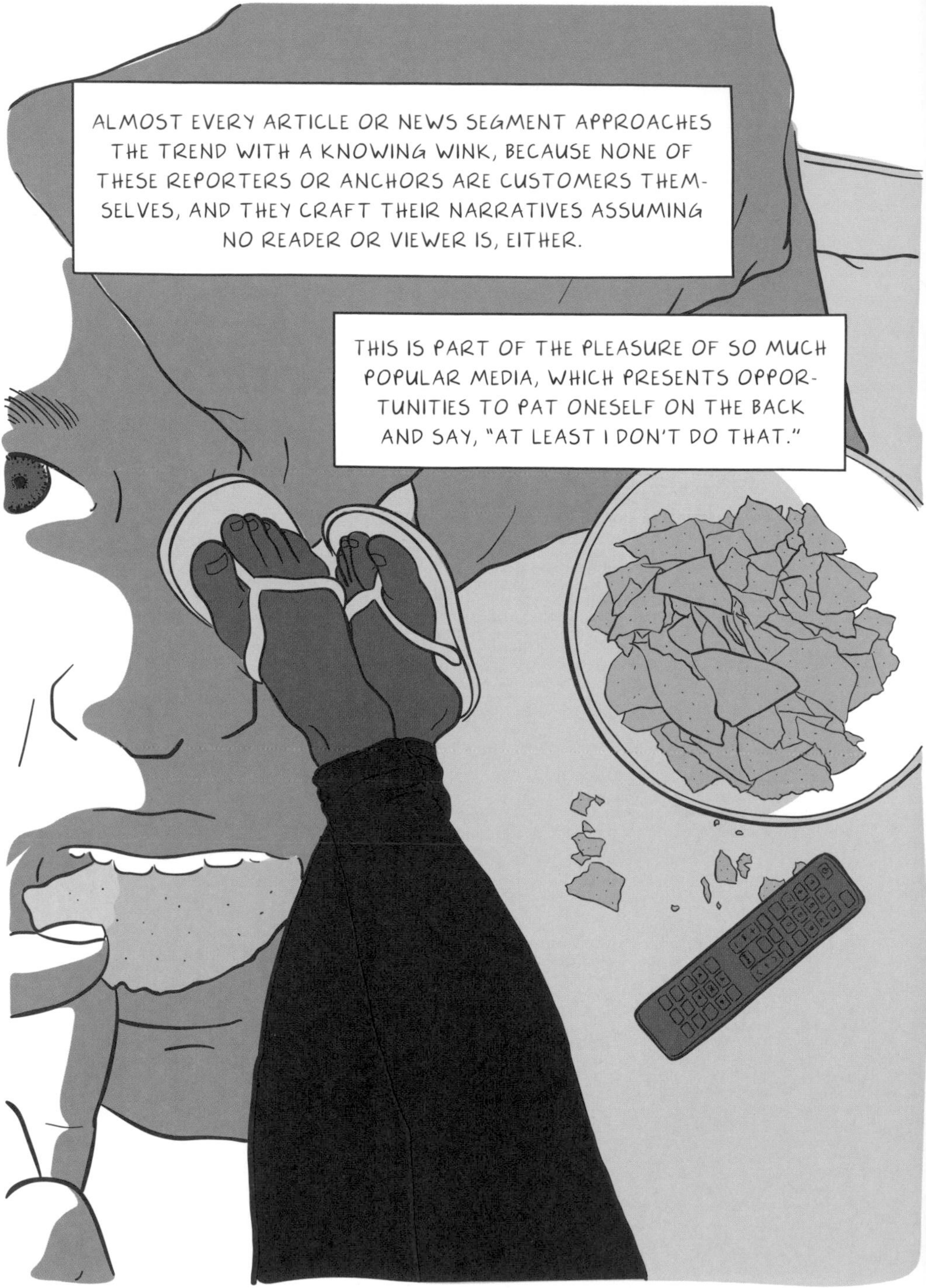
ALMOST EVERY ARTICLE OR NEWS SEGMENT APPROACHES THE TREND WITH A KNOWING WINK, BECAUSE NONE OF THESE REPORTERS OR ANCHORS ARE CUSTOMERS THEMSELVES, AND THEY CRAFT THEIR NARRATIVES ASSUMING NO READER OR VIEWER IS, EITHER.
THIS IS PART OF THE PLEASURE OF SO MUCH POPULAR MEDIA, WHICH PRESENTS OPPORTUNITIES TO PAT ONESELF ON THE BACK AND SAY, "AT LEAST I DON'T DO THAT."

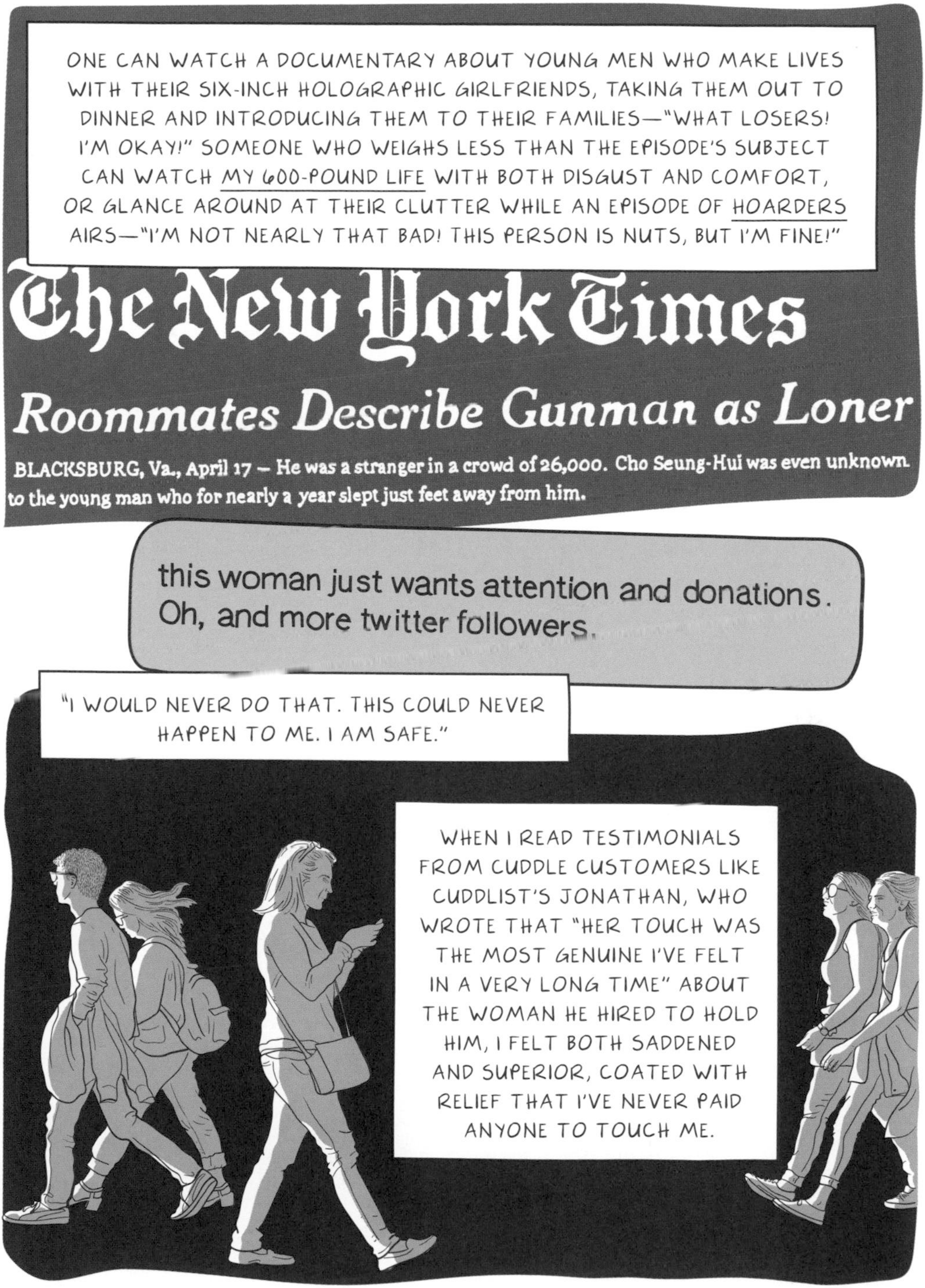

ONE CAN WATCH A DOCUMENTARY ABOUT YOUNG MEN WHO MAKE LIVES WITH THEIR SIX-INCH HOLOGRAPHIC GIRLFRIENDS, TAKING THEM OUT TO DINNER AND INTRODUCING THEM TO THEIR FAMILIES—"WHAT LOSERS! I'M OKAY!" SOMEONE WHO WEIGHS LESS THAN THE EPISODE'S SUBJECT CAN WATCH MY 600-POUND LIFE WITH BOTH DISGUST AND COMFORT, OR GLANCE AROUND AT THEIR CLUTTER WHILE AN EPISODE OF HOARDERS AIRS—"I'M NOT NEARLY THAT BAD! THIS PERSON IS NUTS, BUT I'M FINE!"
The New York Times
Roommates Describe Gunman as Loner
BLACKSBURG, Va., April 17 – He was a stranger in a crowd of 26,000. Cho Seung-Hui was even unknown to the young man who for nearly a year slept just feet away from him.
this woman just wants attention and donations. Oh, and more twitter followers.
"I WOULD NEVER DO THAT. THIS COULD NEVER HAPPEN TO ME. I AM SAFE."
WHEN I READ TESTIMONIALS FROM CUDDLE CUSTOMERS LIKE CUDDLIST'S JONATHAN, WHO WROTE THAT "HER TOUCH WAS THE MOST GENUINE I'VE FELT IN A VERY LONG TIME" ABOUT THE WOMAN HE HIRED TO HOLD HIM, I FELT BOTH SADDENED AND SUPERIOR, COATED WITH RELIEF THAT I'VE NEVER PAID ANYONE TO TOUCH ME.

Someone help me. I need a cuddle buddy. I'm lonely in Philadelphia.

epohon

I'm so lonely and need to cuddle, that's why I came to this site. Hopefully I can cuddle someday. I'm just too lonely I can't concentrate on anything. 😥

BashfulLoner

I get cologne packets from magazines and run them on before a cuddle. I actually do this at Barnes and Nobles so i don't even buy the magazines

ation

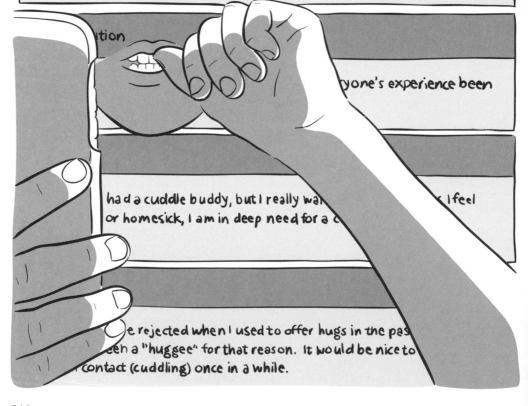

yone's experience been

had a cuddle buddy, but I really wa   I feel
or homesick, I am in deep need for a c

e rejected when I used to offer hugs in the pas
eh a "huggee" for that reason. It would be nice to
contact (cuddling) once in a while.

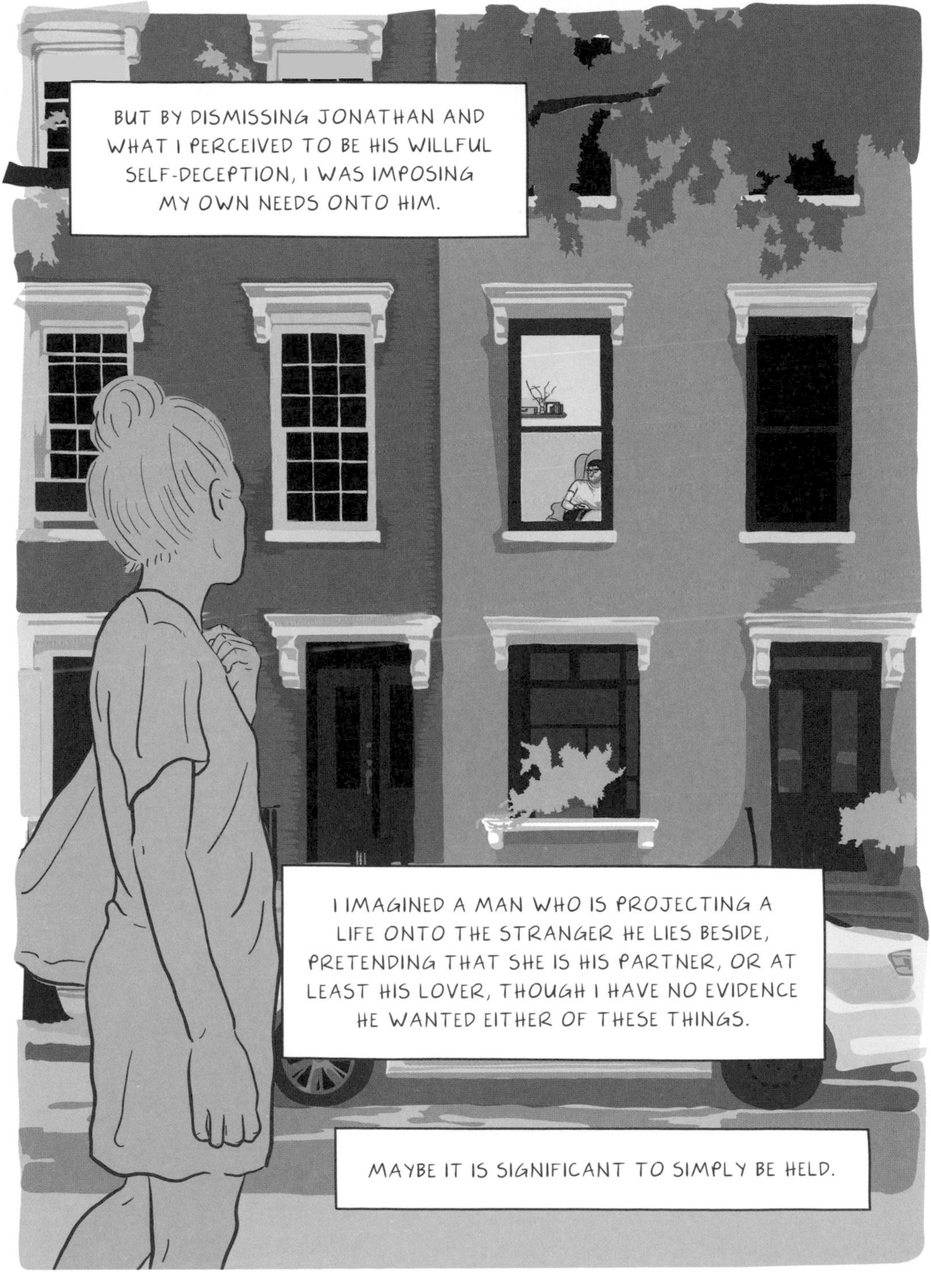
BUT BY DISMISSING JONATHAN AND WHAT I PERCEIVED TO BE HIS WILLFUL SELF-DECEPTION, I WAS IMPOSING MY OWN NEEDS ONTO HIM.
I IMAGINED A MAN WHO IS PROJECTING A LIFE ONTO THE STRANGER HE LIES BESIDE, PRETENDING THAT SHE IS HIS PARTNER, OR AT LEAST HIS LOVER, THOUGH I HAVE NO EVIDENCE HE WANTED EITHER OF THESE THINGS.
MAYBE IT IS SIGNIFICANT TO SIMPLY BE HELD.

WHEN ONE FRIEND EXPLAINED TO ME WHY HE OCCASIONALLY PATRONIZED SEX WORKERS, HE SAID HE WASN'T THERE BECAUSE HE WANTED A RELATIONSHIP.

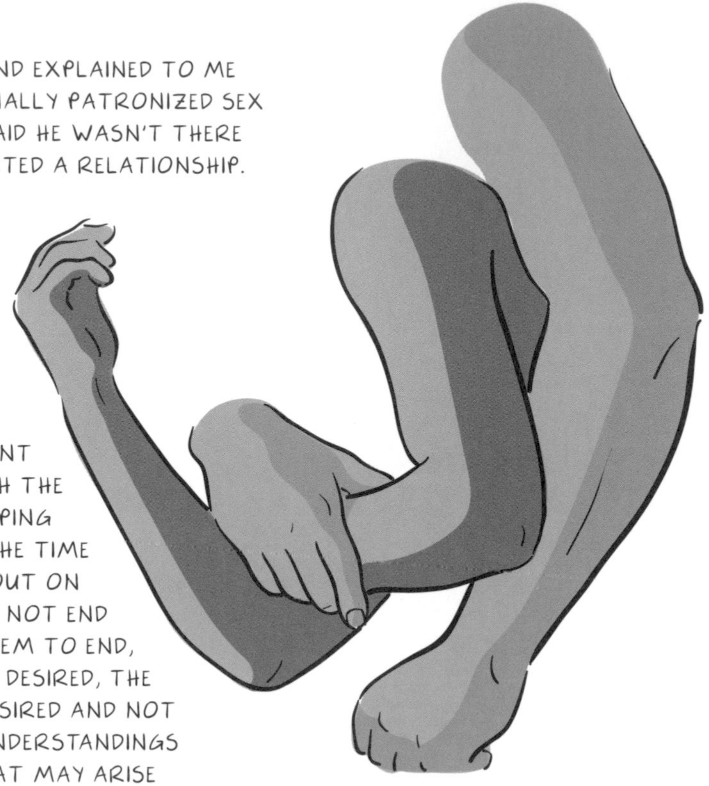

HE DIDN'T WANT TO GO THROUGH THE HASSLE OF SWIPING AND MATCHING, THE TIME IT TOOK TO GO OUT ON DATES THAT MIGHT NOT END WHERE HE WANTED THEM TO END, THE RISK OF NOT BEING DESIRED, THE DISCOMFORT OF BEING DESIRED AND NOT DESIRING BACK, THE MISUNDERSTANDINGS OR COMPLICATIONS THAT MAY ARISE ONCE THEY'VE SLEPT TOGETHER.

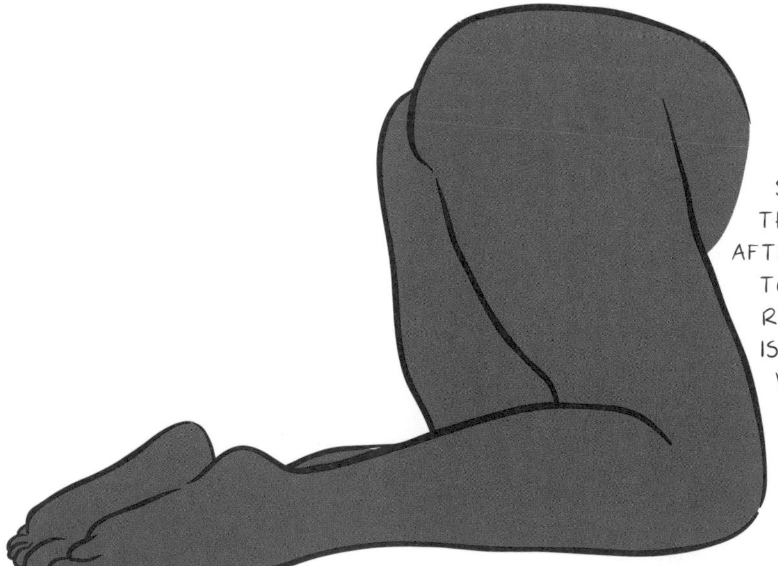

HE DIDN'T WANT TO PUT IN THE TIME IT TOOK TO ARRIVE AT SEX, OR THE TIME THAT WAS REQUIRED AFTER; HE JUST WANTED TO HAVE SEX. SO, HE REASONED, IF THERE IS A CLEAR PATH TO WHAT HE WANTS, WHY WOULDN'T HE TAKE IT?

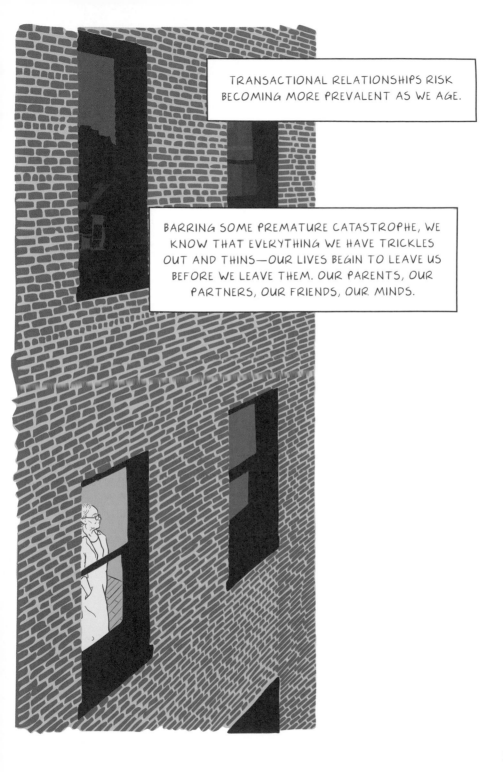

TRANSACTIONAL RELATIONSHIPS RISK
BECOMING MORE PREVALENT AS WE AGE.

BARRING SOME PREMATURE CATASTROPHE, WE
KNOW THAT EVERYTHING WE HAVE TRICKLES
OUT AND THINS—OUR LIVES BEGIN TO LEAVE US
BEFORE WE LEAVE THEM. OUR PARENTS, OUR
PARTNERS, OUR FRIENDS, OUR MINDS.

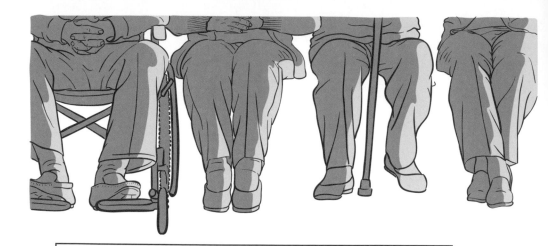

SOME NURSING HOMES HAVE RESPONDED TO THE DESPONDENCY OF LONELY ELDERLY RESIDENTS BY PROVIDING THEM WITH ROBOTIC COMPANIONS, LIKE PARO, AN ANIMATRONIC THERAPY SEAL EQUIPPED WITH VOICE RECOGNITION AND SENSORS THAT TRIGGER RESPONSES TO TOUCH AND LIGHT.

STAFF WHO WORK WITH THE ROBOTS SAY PATIENTS WHO HAVE PARO ARE HAPPIER. THEY'RE MORE ALERT, AND THEY EVEN LIVE LONGER.

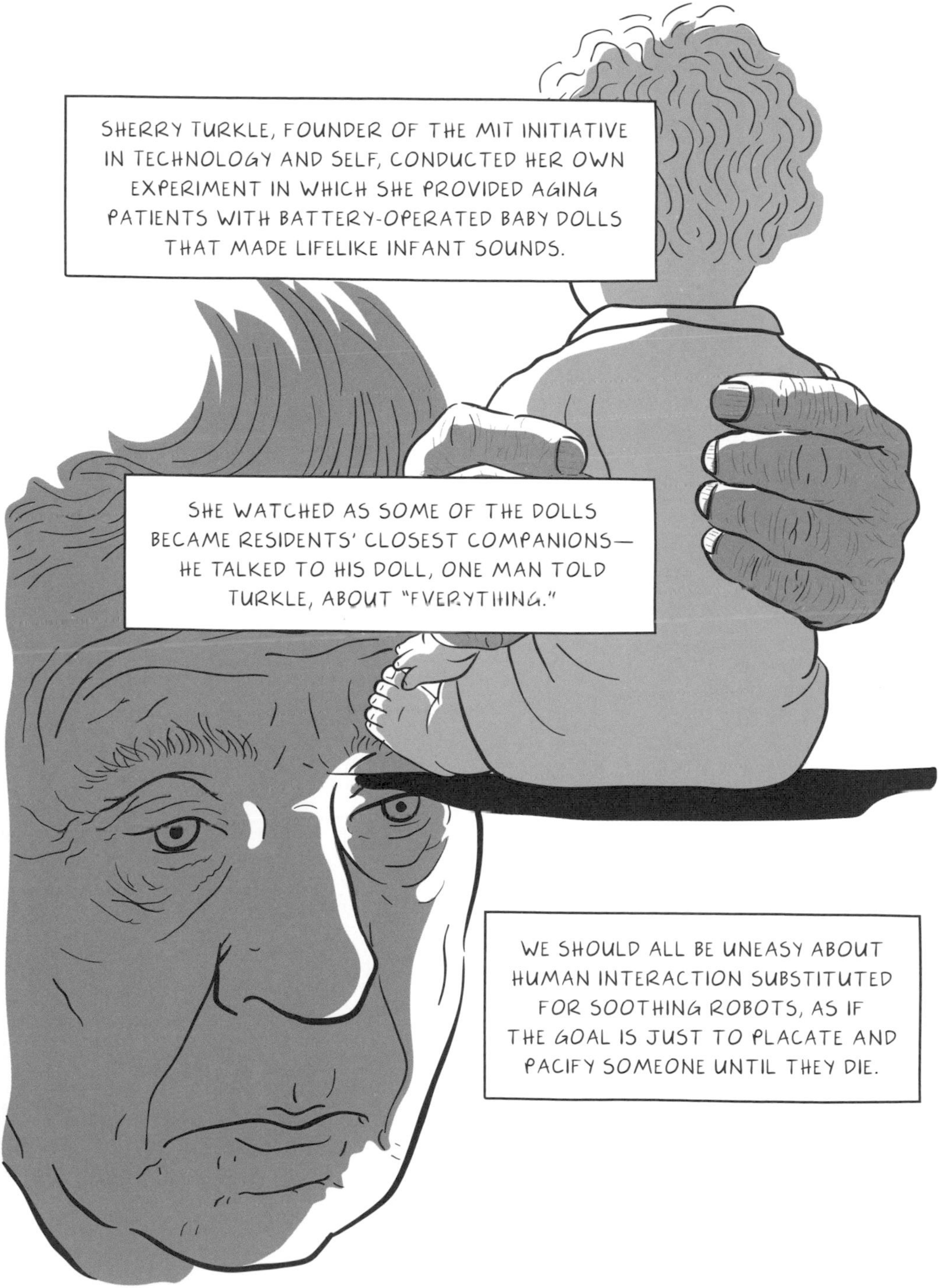
SHERRY TURKLE, FOUNDER OF THE MIT INITIATIVE IN TECHNOLOGY AND SELF, CONDUCTED HER OWN EXPERIMENT IN WHICH SHE PROVIDED AGING PATIENTS WITH BATTERY-OPERATED BABY DOLLS THAT MADE LIFELIKE INFANT SOUNDS.
SHE WATCHED AS SOME OF THE DOLLS BECAME RESIDENTS' CLOSEST COMPANIONS—HE TALKED TO HIS DOLL, ONE MAN TOLD TURKLE, ABOUT "EVERYTHING."
WE SHOULD ALL BE UNEASY ABOUT HUMAN INTERACTION SUBSTITUTED FOR SOOTHING ROBOTS, AS IF THE GOAL IS JUST TO PLACATE AND PACIFY SOMEONE UNTIL THEY DIE.

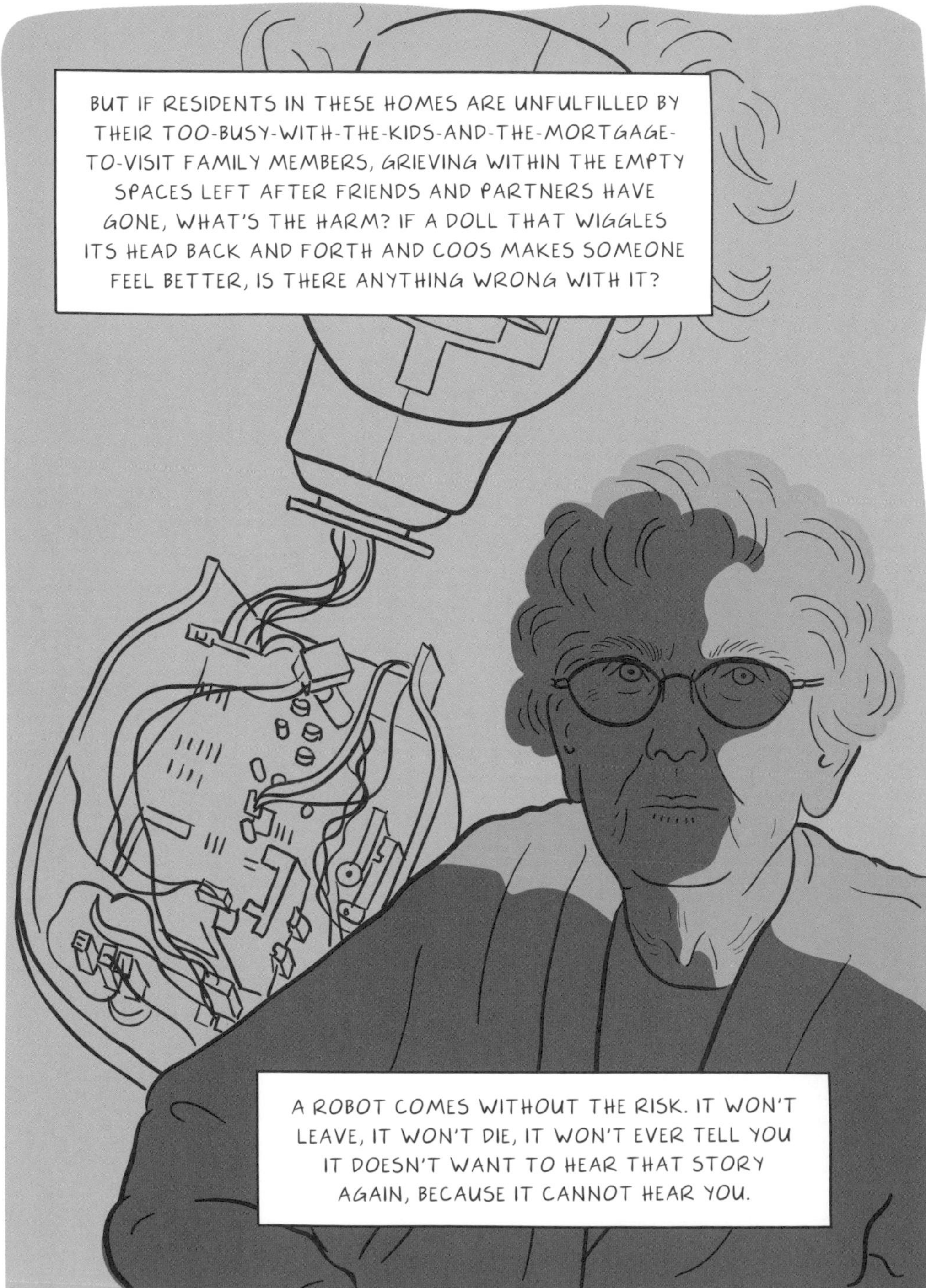
BUT IF RESIDENTS IN THESE HOMES ARE UNFULFILLED BY THEIR TOO-BUSY-WITH-THE-KIDS-AND-THE-MORTGAGE-TO-VISIT FAMILY MEMBERS, GRIEVING WITHIN THE EMPTY SPACES LEFT AFTER FRIENDS AND PARTNERS HAVE GONE, WHAT'S THE HARM? IF A DOLL THAT WIGGLES ITS HEAD BACK AND FORTH AND COOS MAKES SOMEONE FEEL BETTER, IS THERE ANYTHING WRONG WITH IT?
A ROBOT COMES WITHOUT THE RISK. IT WON'T LEAVE, IT WON'T DIE, IT WON'T EVER TELL YOU IT DOESN'T WANT TO HEAR THAT STORY AGAIN, BECAUSE IT CANNOT HEAR YOU.

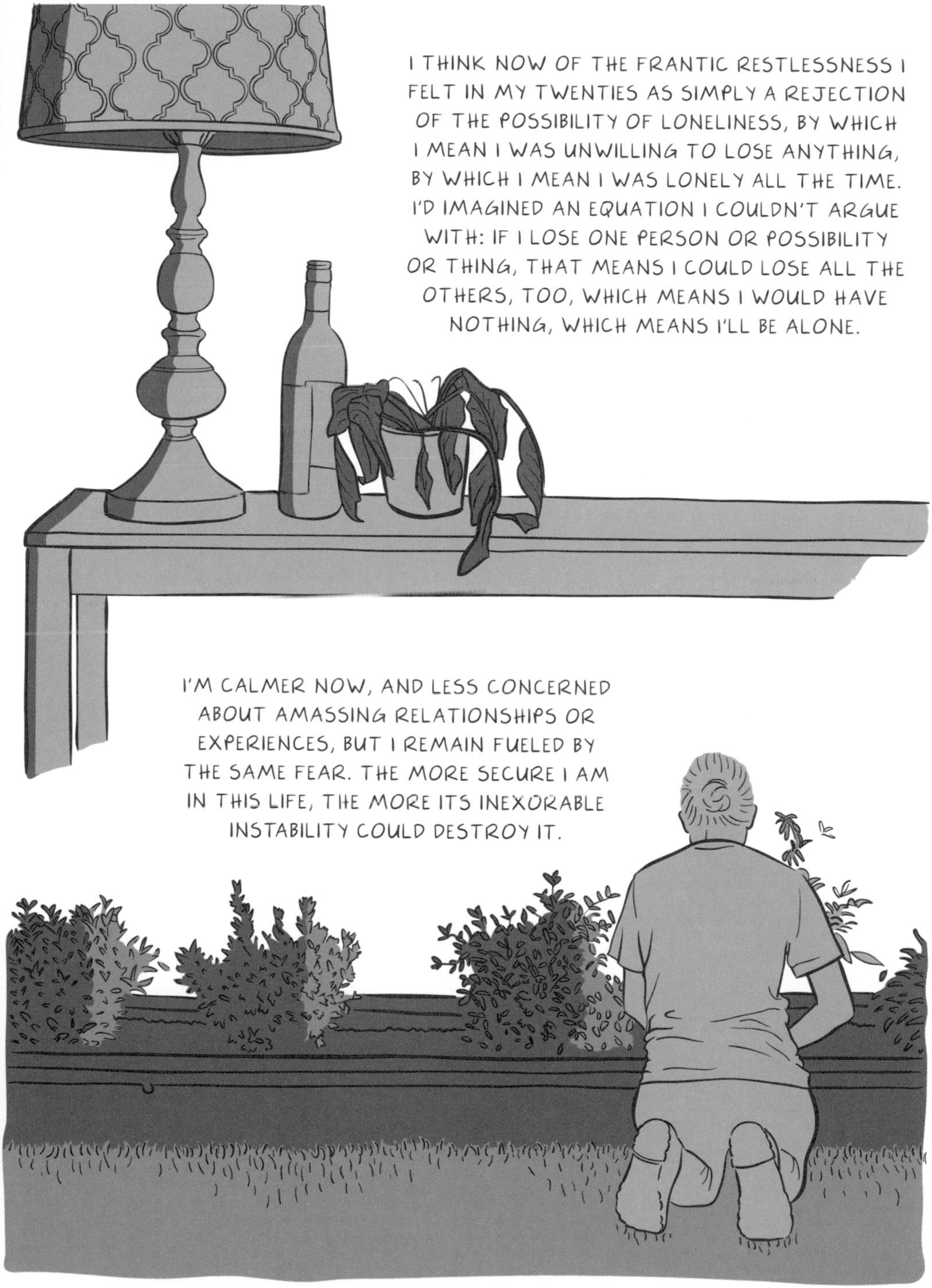
I THINK NOW OF THE FRANTIC RESTLESSNESS I FELT IN MY TWENTIES AS SIMPLY A REJECTION OF THE POSSIBILITY OF LONELINESS, BY WHICH I MEAN I WAS UNWILLING TO LOSE ANYTHING, BY WHICH I MEAN I WAS LONELY ALL THE TIME. I'D IMAGINED AN EQUATION I COULDN'T ARGUE WITH: IF I LOSE ONE PERSON OR POSSIBILITY OR THING, THAT MEANS I COULD LOSE ALL THE OTHERS, TOO, WHICH MEANS I WOULD HAVE NOTHING, WHICH MEANS I'LL BE ALONE.
I'M CALMER NOW, AND LESS CONCERNED ABOUT AMASSING RELATIONSHIPS OR EXPERIENCES, BUT I REMAIN FUELED BY THE SAME FEAR. THE MORE SECURE I AM IN THIS LIFE, THE MORE ITS INEXORABLE INSTABILITY COULD DESTROY IT.

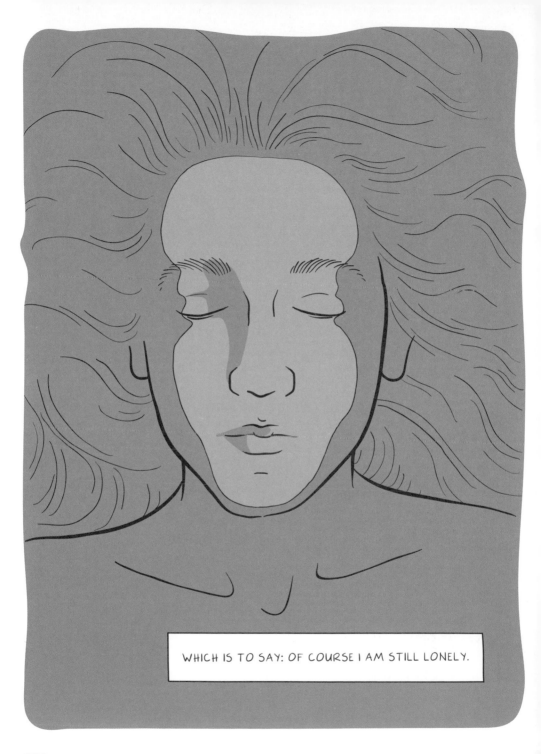

WHICH IS TO SAY: OF COURSE I AM STILL LONELY.

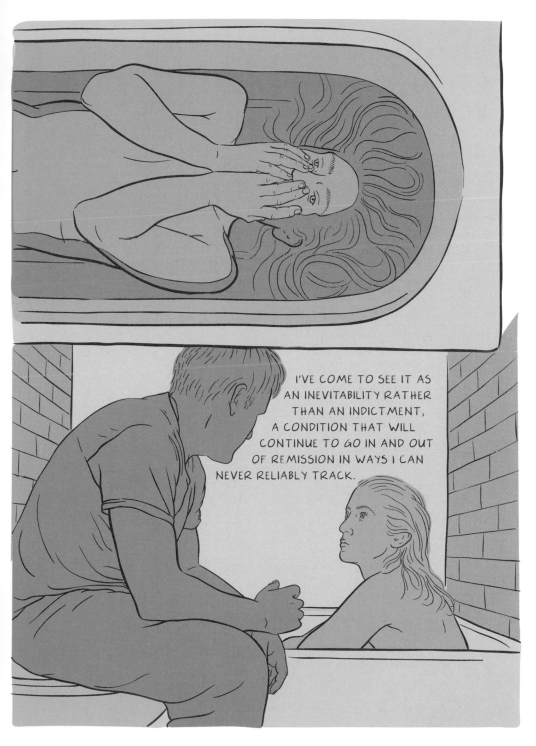

I'VE COME TO SEE IT AS AN INEVITABILITY RATHER THAN AN INDICTMENT, A CONDITION THAT WILL CONTINUE TO GO IN AND OUT OF REMISSION IN WAYS I CAN NEVER RELIABLY TRACK.

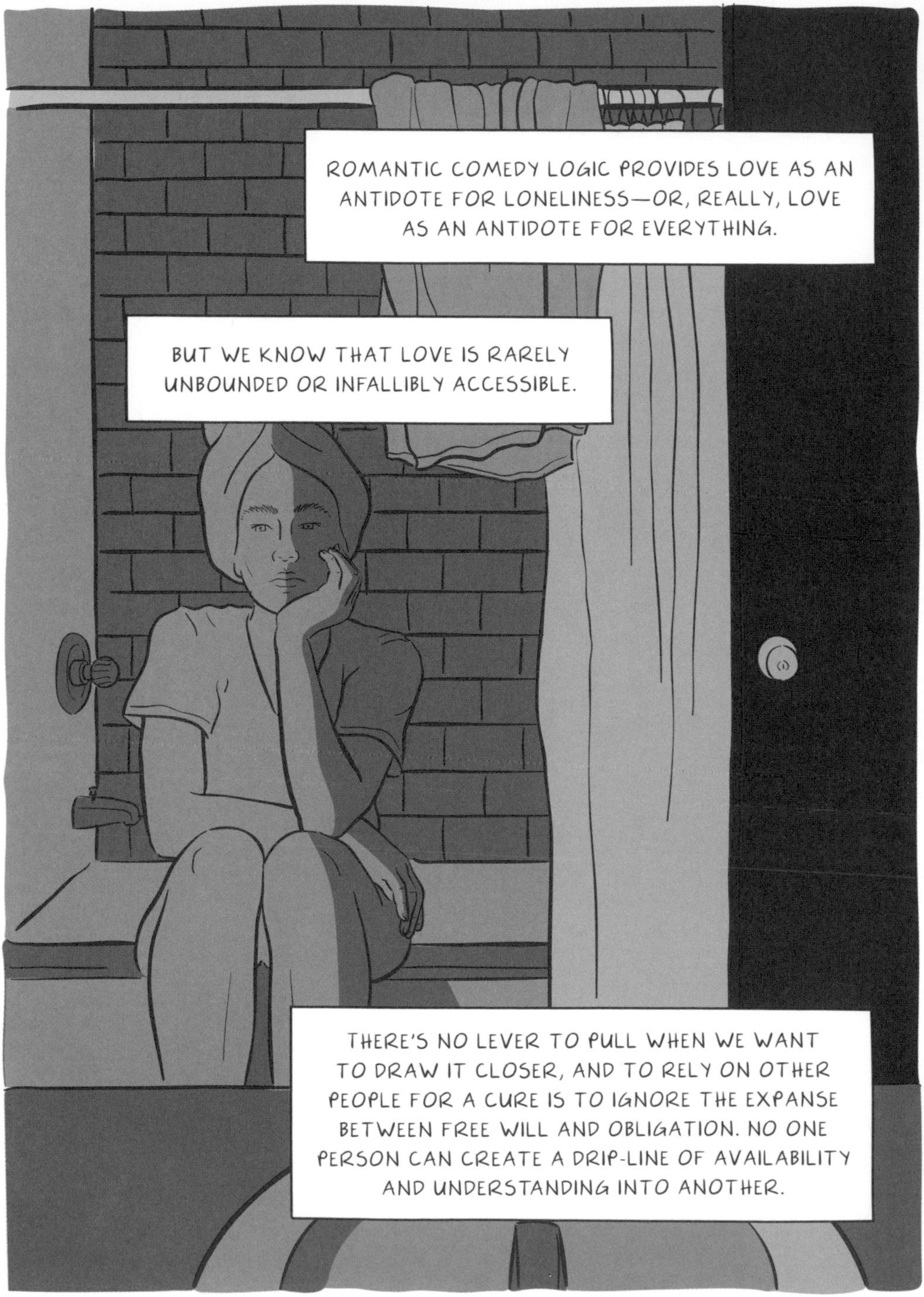
ROMANTIC COMEDY LOGIC PROVIDES LOVE AS AN ANTIDOTE FOR LONELINESS—OR, REALLY, LOVE AS AN ANTIDOTE FOR EVERYTHING.
BUT WE KNOW THAT LOVE IS RARELY UNBOUNDED OR INFALLIBLY ACCESSIBLE.
THERE'S NO LEVER TO PULL WHEN WE WANT TO DRAW IT CLOSER, AND TO RELY ON OTHER PEOPLE FOR A CURE IS TO IGNORE THE EXPANSE BETWEEN FREE WILL AND OBLIGATION. NO ONE PERSON CAN CREATE A DRIP-LINE OF AVAILABILITY AND UNDERSTANDING INTO ANOTHER.

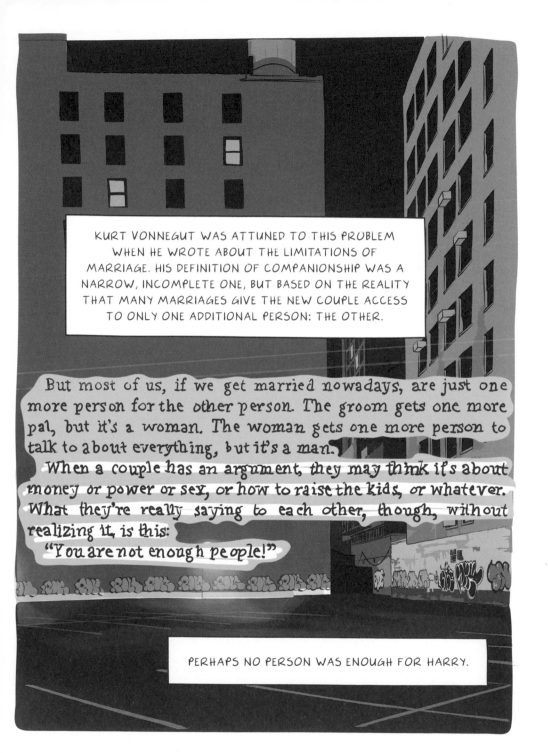

KURT VONNEGUT WAS ATTUNED TO THIS PROBLEM WHEN HE WROTE ABOUT THE LIMITATIONS OF MARRIAGE. HIS DEFINITION OF COMPANIONSHIP WAS A NARROW, INCOMPLETE ONE, BUT BASED ON THE REALITY THAT MANY MARRIAGES GIVE THE NEW COUPLE ACCESS TO ONLY ONE ADDITIONAL PERSON: THE OTHER.

But most of us, if we get married nowadays, are just one more person for the other person. The groom gets one more pal, but it's a woman. The woman gets one more person to talk to about everything, but it's a man.

When a couple has an argument, they may think it's about money or power or sex, or how to raise the kids, or whatever. What they're really saying to each other, though, without realizing it, is this:

"You are not enough people!"

PERHAPS NO PERSON WAS ENOUGH FOR HARRY.

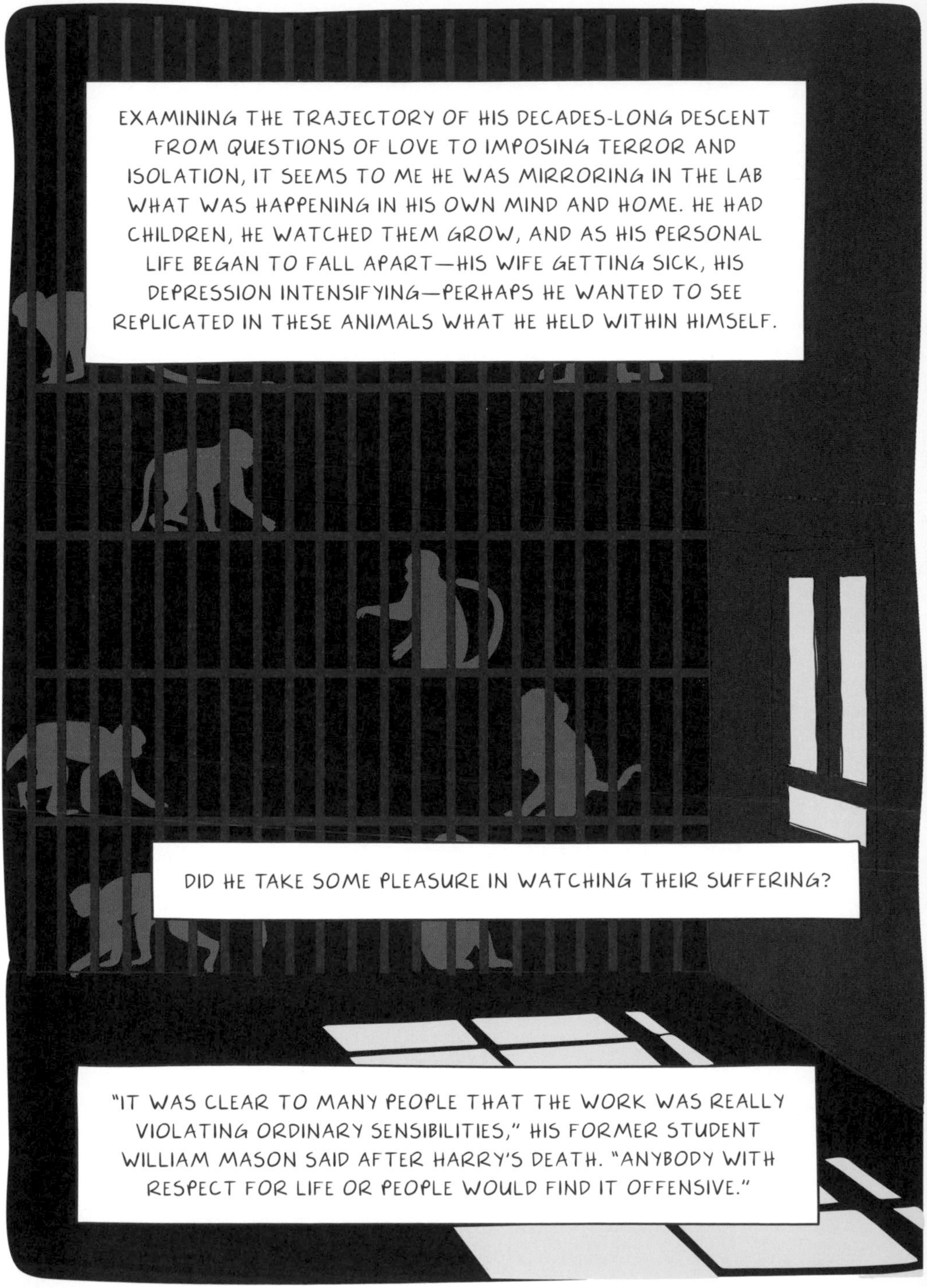
EXAMINING THE TRAJECTORY OF HIS DECADES-LONG DESCENT FROM QUESTIONS OF LOVE TO IMPOSING TERROR AND ISOLATION, IT SEEMS TO ME HE WAS MIRRORING IN THE LAB WHAT WAS HAPPENING IN HIS OWN MIND AND HOME. HE HAD CHILDREN, HE WATCHED THEM GROW, AND AS HIS PERSONAL LIFE BEGAN TO FALL APART—HIS WIFE GETTING SICK, HIS DEPRESSION INTENSIFYING—PERHAPS HE WANTED TO SEE REPLICATED IN THESE ANIMALS WHAT HE HELD WITHIN HIMSELF.
DID HE TAKE SOME PLEASURE IN WATCHING THEIR SUFFERING?
"IT WAS CLEAR TO MANY PEOPLE THAT THE WORK WAS REALLY VIOLATING ORDINARY SENSIBILITIES," HIS FORMER STUDENT WILLIAM MASON SAID AFTER HARRY'S DEATH. "ANYBODY WITH RESPECT FOR LIFE OR PEOPLE WOULD FIND IT OFFENSIVE."

YET THAT WORK CHANGED THE WAY CHILDREN WERE RAISED
AND CARED FOR, GRANTING LICENSE TO PARENTS AND
CARETAKERS TO ENACT THEIR AFFECTION WHERE BEFORE THEY
WERE SEPARATED BY FEARS OF WIMPY OFFSPRING AND DISEASE.

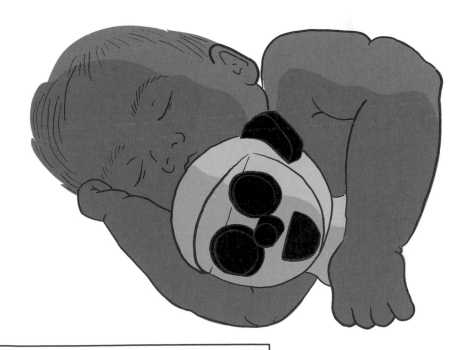

THE WAYS IN WHICH MOST OF US ARE
TAUGHT FROM INFANCY HOW TO REACH
OUT AND FEEL SOMEONE REACHING BACK
ARE DUE IN LARGE PART TO THOSE MONKEYS
CLINGING TO WIRE WRAPPED IN CLOTH,
STROKING THE SIDES OF A PLASTIC FACE.

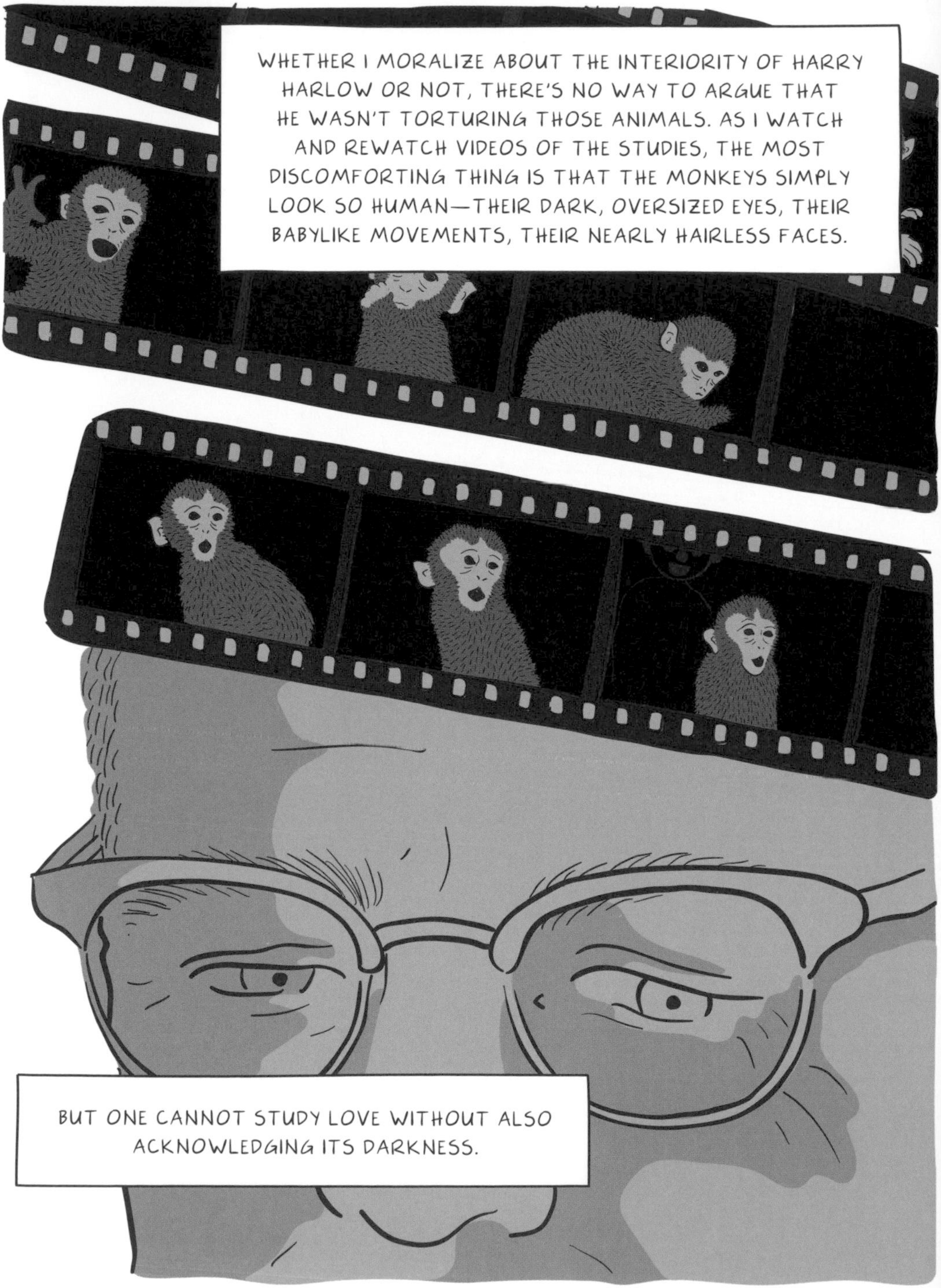
WHETHER I MORALIZE ABOUT THE INTERIORITY OF HARRY HARLOW OR NOT, THERE'S NO WAY TO ARGUE THAT HE WASN'T TORTURING THOSE ANIMALS. AS I WATCH AND REWATCH VIDEOS OF THE STUDIES, THE MOST DISCOMFORTING THING IS THAT THE MONKEYS SIMPLY LOOK SO HUMAN—THEIR DARK, OVERSIZED EYES, THEIR BABYLIKE MOVEMENTS, THEIR NEARLY HAIRLESS FACES.
BUT ONE CANNOT STUDY LOVE WITHOUT ALSO ACKNOWLEDGING ITS DARKNESS.

WHAT IF, INSTEAD OF EGO OR SADISM OR HIS TEENAGE HOPE FOR
FAME, I IMAGINE THAT HIS WORK WAS BORN OUT OF LOVE?

HE PROVED THAT LOVE IS NOT A DISTRACTION
OR A PEDESTRIAN LABEL SLAPPED ONTO ACTION,
BUT THAT LOVE IS THE ACTION ITSELF.

IN EVERY MONSTROUS ACT, THERE WAS ALSO A PERSON SO
DESPERATE TO UNDERSTAND THE CIRCUMSTANCES OF THIS
SADNESS THAT HE SPENT DECADES CREATING IT, OVER AND
OVER, UNTIL HE WAS HIMSELF REFLECTED BACK.

LISTEN

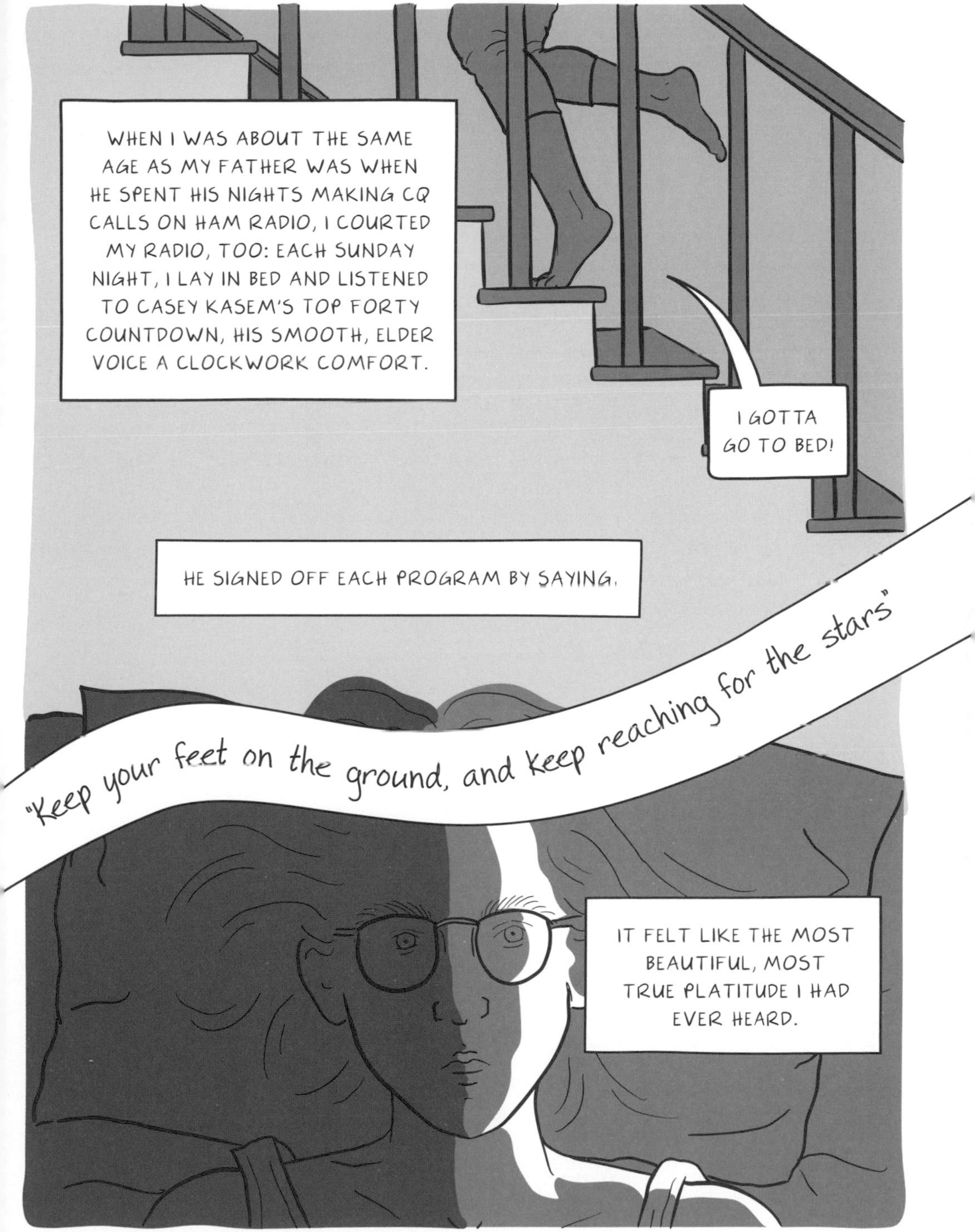
WHEN I WAS ABOUT THE SAME AGE AS MY FATHER WAS WHEN HE SPENT HIS NIGHTS MAKING CQ CALLS ON HAM RADIO, I COURTED MY RADIO, TOO: EACH SUNDAY NIGHT, I LAY IN BED AND LISTENED TO CASEY KASEM'S TOP FORTY COUNTDOWN, HIS SMOOTH, ELDER VOICE A CLOCKWORK COMFORT.
I GOTTA GO TO BED!
HE SIGNED OFF EACH PROGRAM BY SAYING,
"Keep your feet on the ground, and keep reaching for the stars"
IT FELT LIKE THE MOST BEAUTIFUL, MOST TRUE PLATITUDE I HAD EVER HEARD.

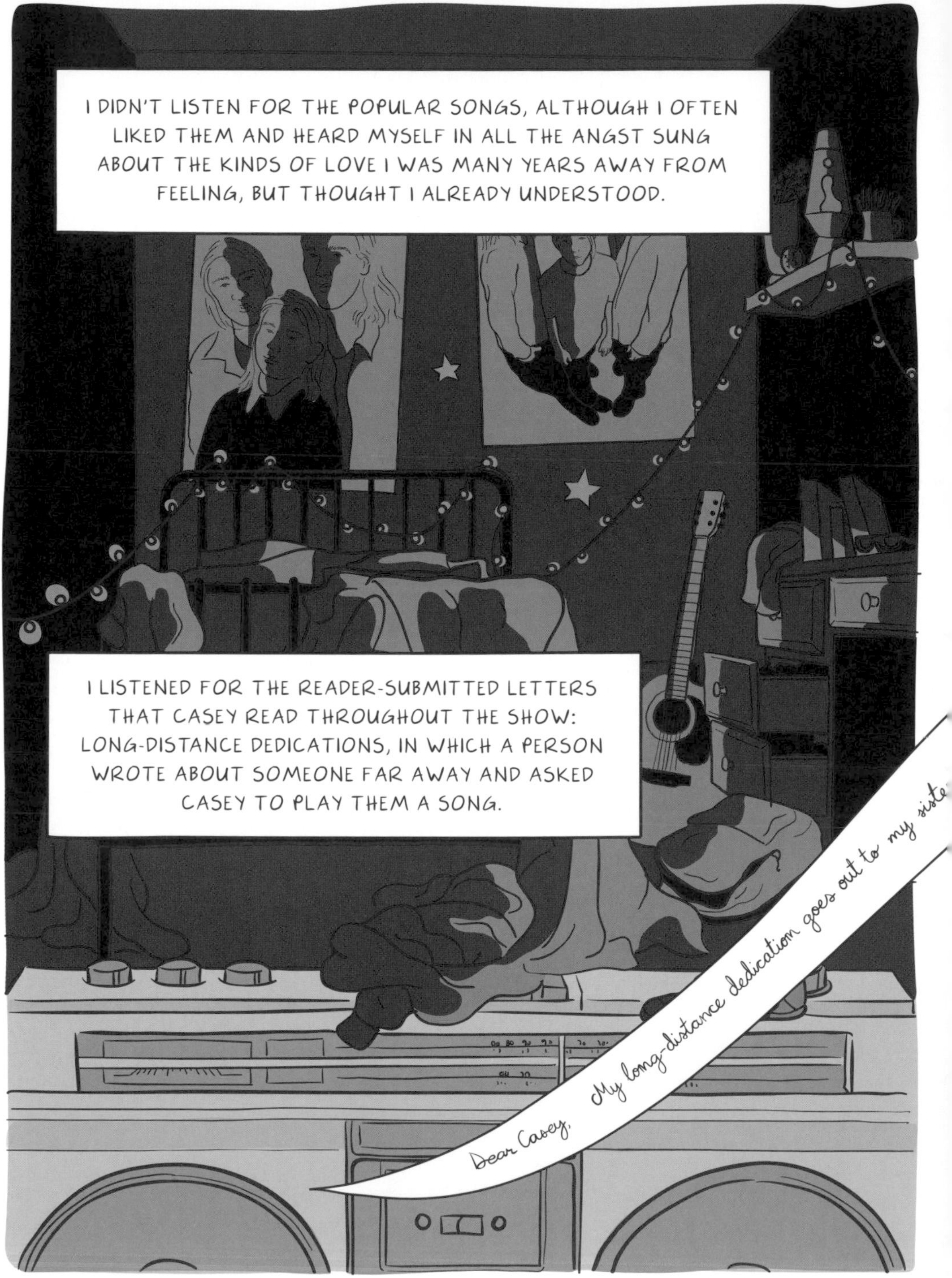
I DIDN'T LISTEN FOR THE POPULAR SONGS, ALTHOUGH I OFTEN LIKED THEM AND HEARD MYSELF IN ALL THE ANGST SUNG ABOUT THE KINDS OF LOVE I WAS MANY YEARS AWAY FROM FEELING, BUT THOUGHT I ALREADY UNDERSTOOD.
I LISTENED FOR THE READER-SUBMITTED LETTERS THAT CASEY READ THROUGHOUT THE SHOW: LONG-DISTANCE DEDICATIONS, IN WHICH A PERSON WROTE ABOUT SOMEONE FAR AWAY AND ASKED CASEY TO PLAY THEM A SONG.
Dear Casey, My long-distance dedication goes out to my siste

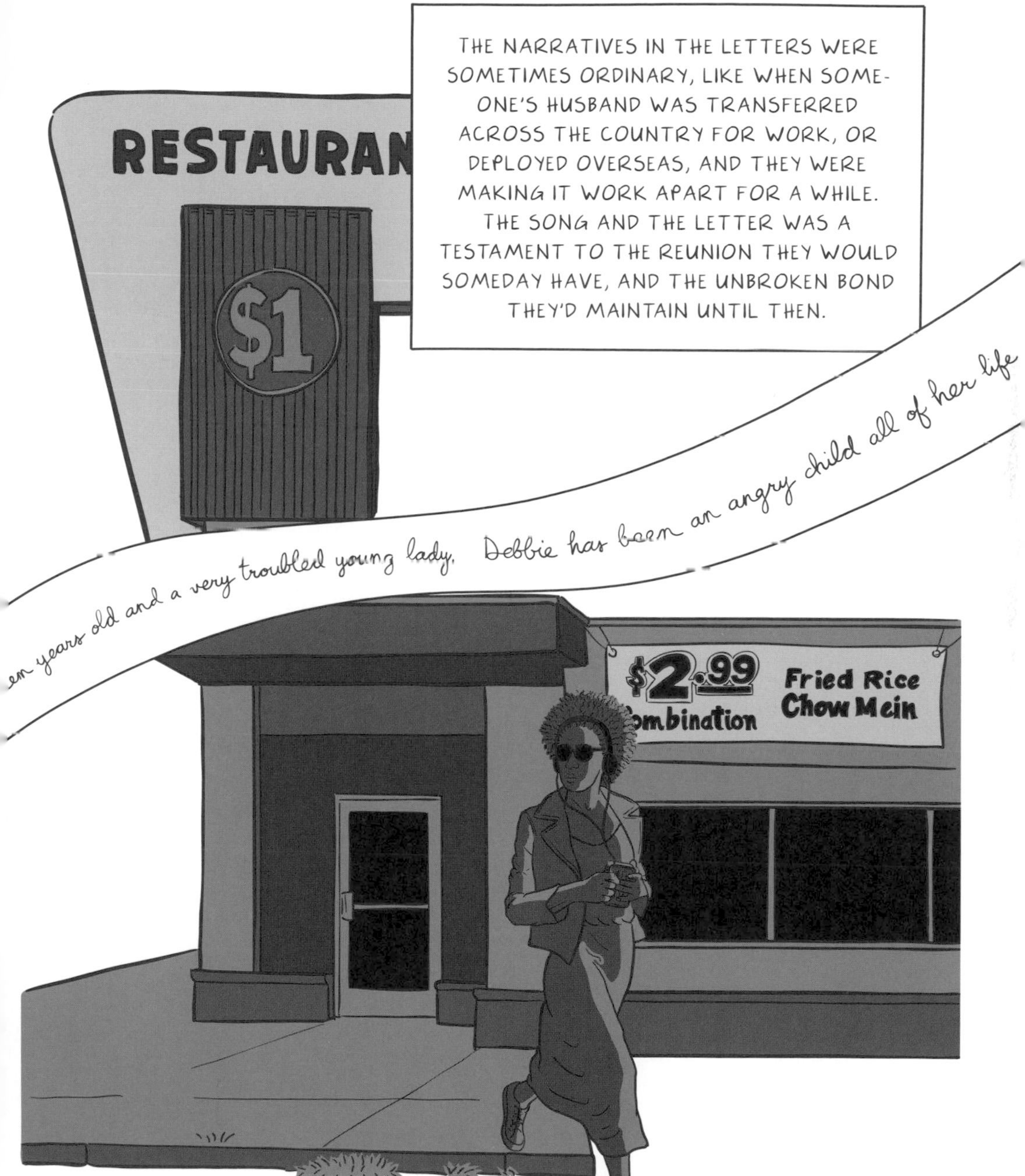
THE NARRATIVES IN THE LETTERS WERE SOMETIMES ORDINARY, LIKE WHEN SOME-ONE'S HUSBAND WAS TRANSFERRED ACROSS THE COUNTRY FOR WORK, OR DEPLOYED OVERSEAS, AND THEY WERE MAKING IT WORK APART FOR A WHILE. THE SONG AND THE LETTER WAS A TESTAMENT TO THE REUNION THEY WOULD SOMEDAY HAVE, AND THE UNBROKEN BOND THEY'D MAINTAIN UNTIL THEN.
RESTAURAN
$1
en years old and a very troubled young lady. Debbie has been an angry child all of her life
$2.99
ombination
Fried Rice
Chow Mein

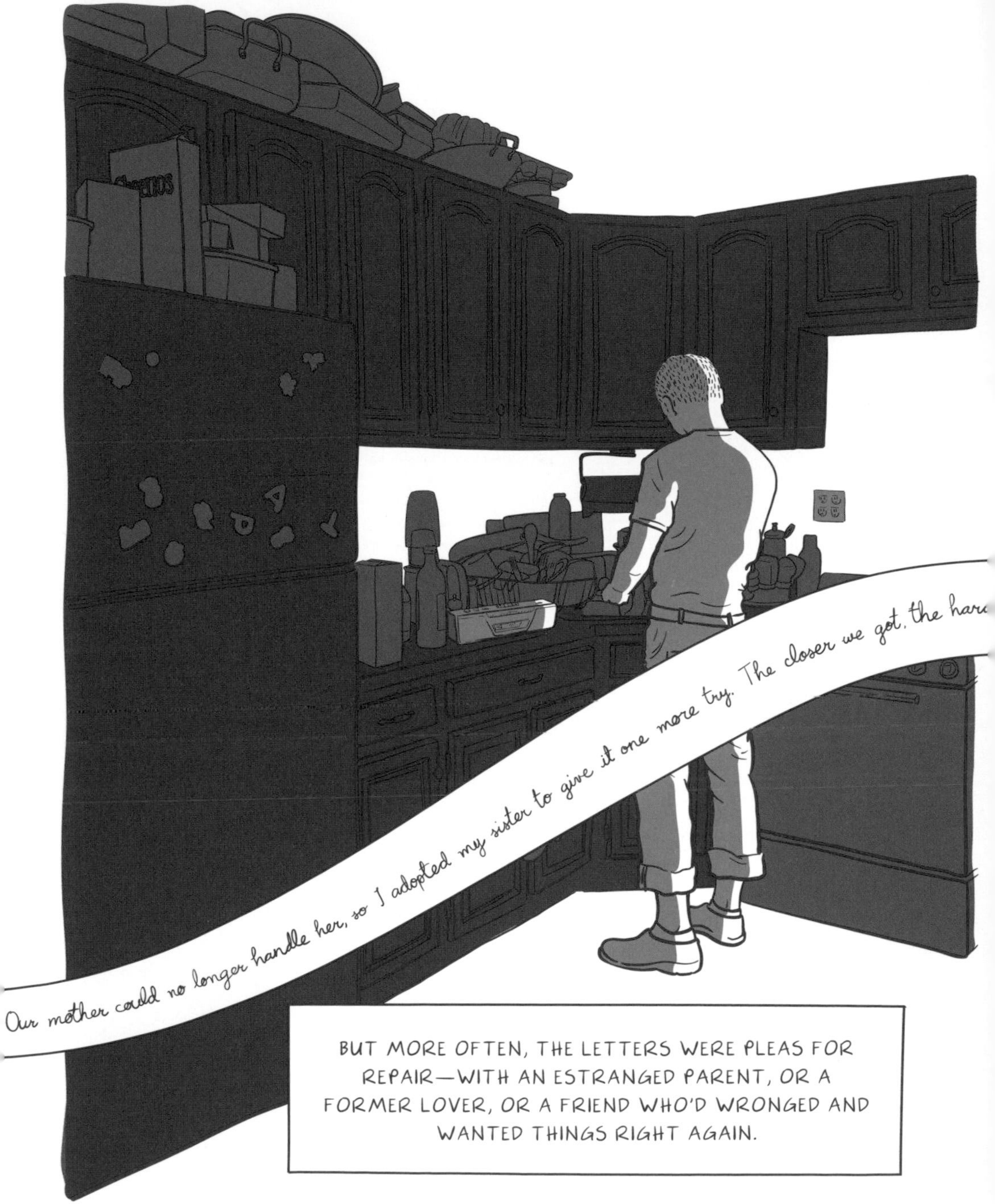
Our mother could no longer handle her, so I adopted my sister to give it one more try. The closer we got, the har
BUT MORE OFTEN, THE LETTERS WERE PLEAS FOR REPAIR—WITH AN ESTRANGED PARENT, OR A FORMER LOVER, OR A FRIEND WHO'D WRONGED AND WANTED THINGS RIGHT AGAIN.

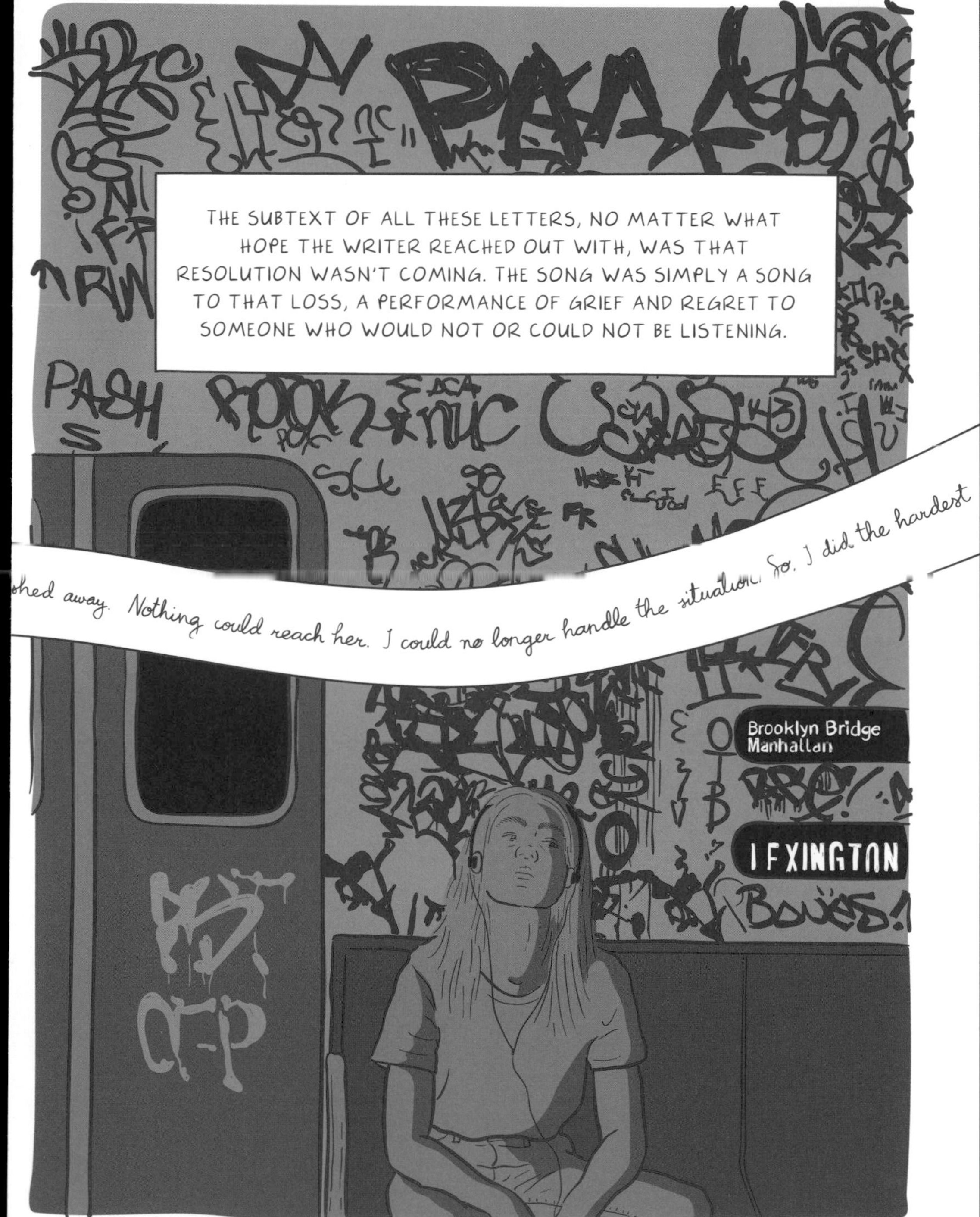
THE SUBTEXT OF ALL THESE LETTERS, NO MATTER WHAT HOPE THE WRITER REACHED OUT WITH, WAS THAT RESOLUTION WASN'T COMING. THE SONG WAS SIMPLY A SONG TO THAT LOSS, A PERFORMANCE OF GRIEF AND REGRET TO SOMEONE WHO WOULD NOT OR COULD NOT BE LISTENING.
away. Nothing could reach her. I could no longer handle the situation. So, I did the hardest
Brooklyn Bridge
Manhattan

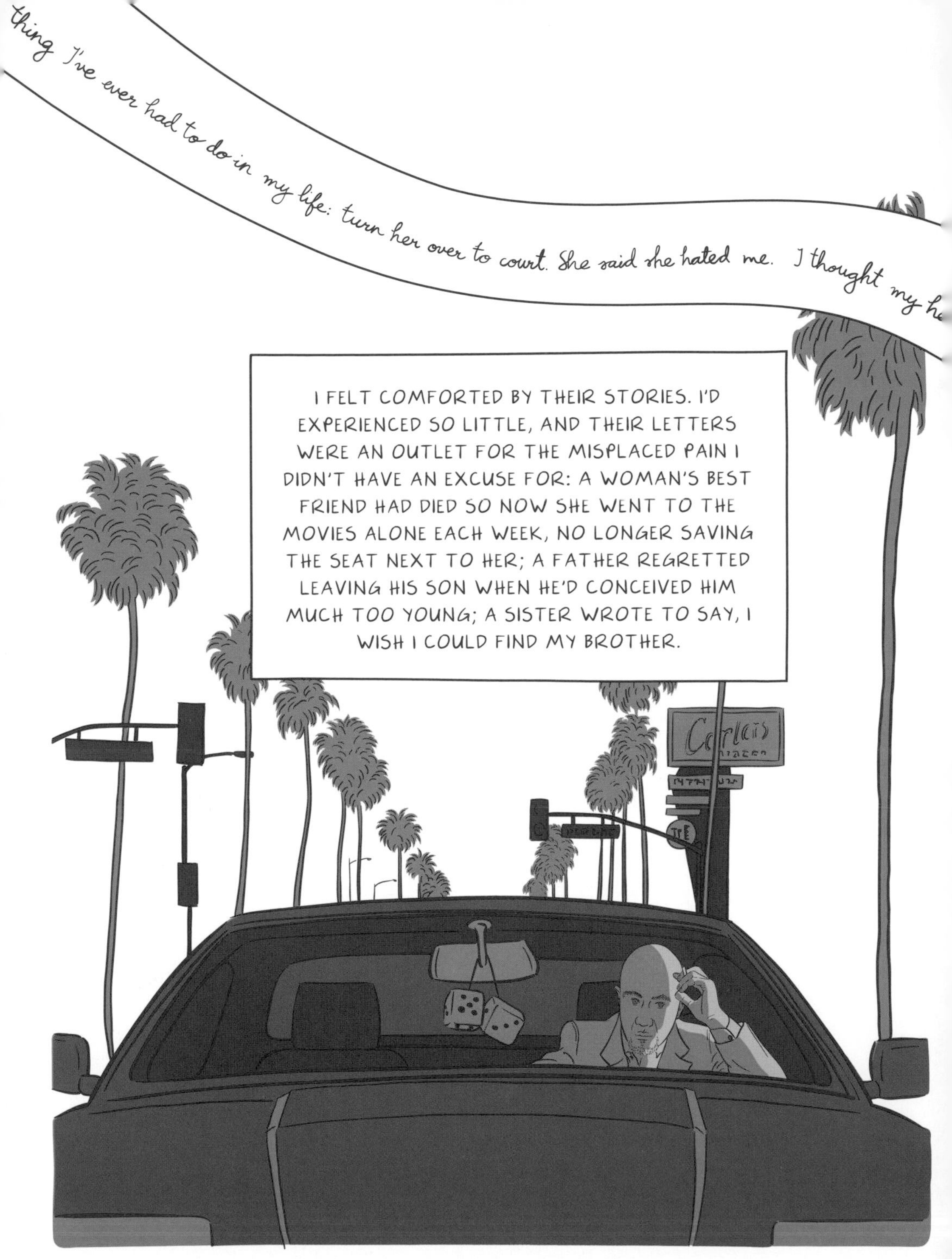
thing I've ever had to do in my life: turn her over to court. She said she hated me. I thought my h
I FELT COMFORTED BY THEIR STORIES. I'D EXPERIENCED SO LITTLE, AND THEIR LETTERS WERE AN OUTLET FOR THE MISPLACED PAIN I DIDN'T HAVE AN EXCUSE FOR: A WOMAN'S BEST FRIEND HAD DIED SO NOW SHE WENT TO THE MOVIES ALONE EACH WEEK, NO LONGER SAVING THE SEAT NEXT TO HER; A FATHER REGRETTED LEAVING HIS SON WHEN HE'D CONCEIVED HIM MUCH TOO YOUNG; A SISTER WROTE TO SAY, I WISH I COULD FIND MY BROTHER.

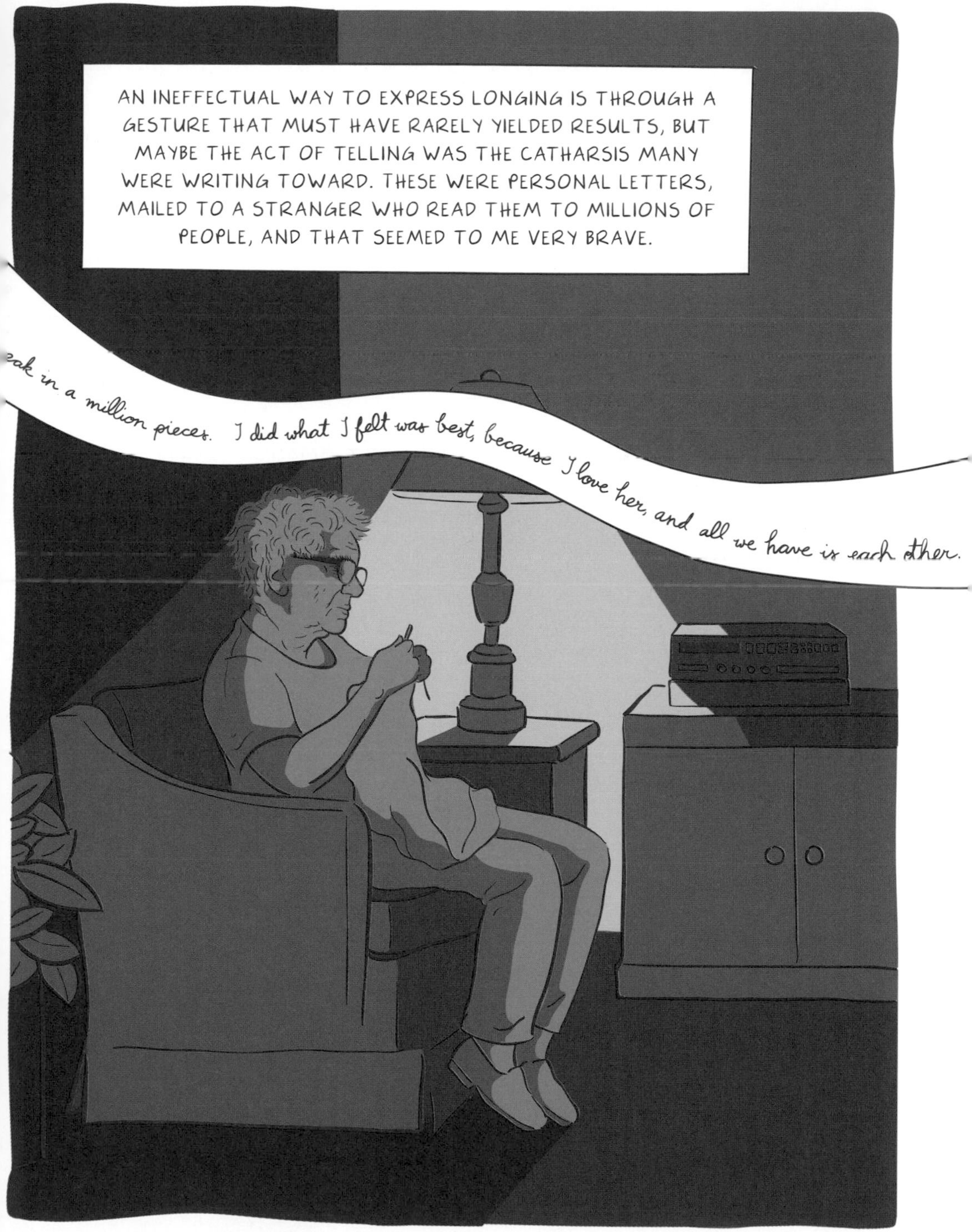
AN INEFFECTUAL WAY TO EXPRESS LONGING IS THROUGH A GESTURE THAT MUST HAVE RARELY YIELDED RESULTS, BUT MAYBE THE ACT OF TELLING WAS THE CATHARSIS MANY WERE WRITING TOWARD. THESE WERE PERSONAL LETTERS, MAILED TO A STRANGER WHO READ THEM TO MILLIONS OF PEOPLE, AND THAT SEEMED TO ME VERY BRAVE.
eak in a million pieces. I did what I felt was best, because I love her, and all we have is each other.

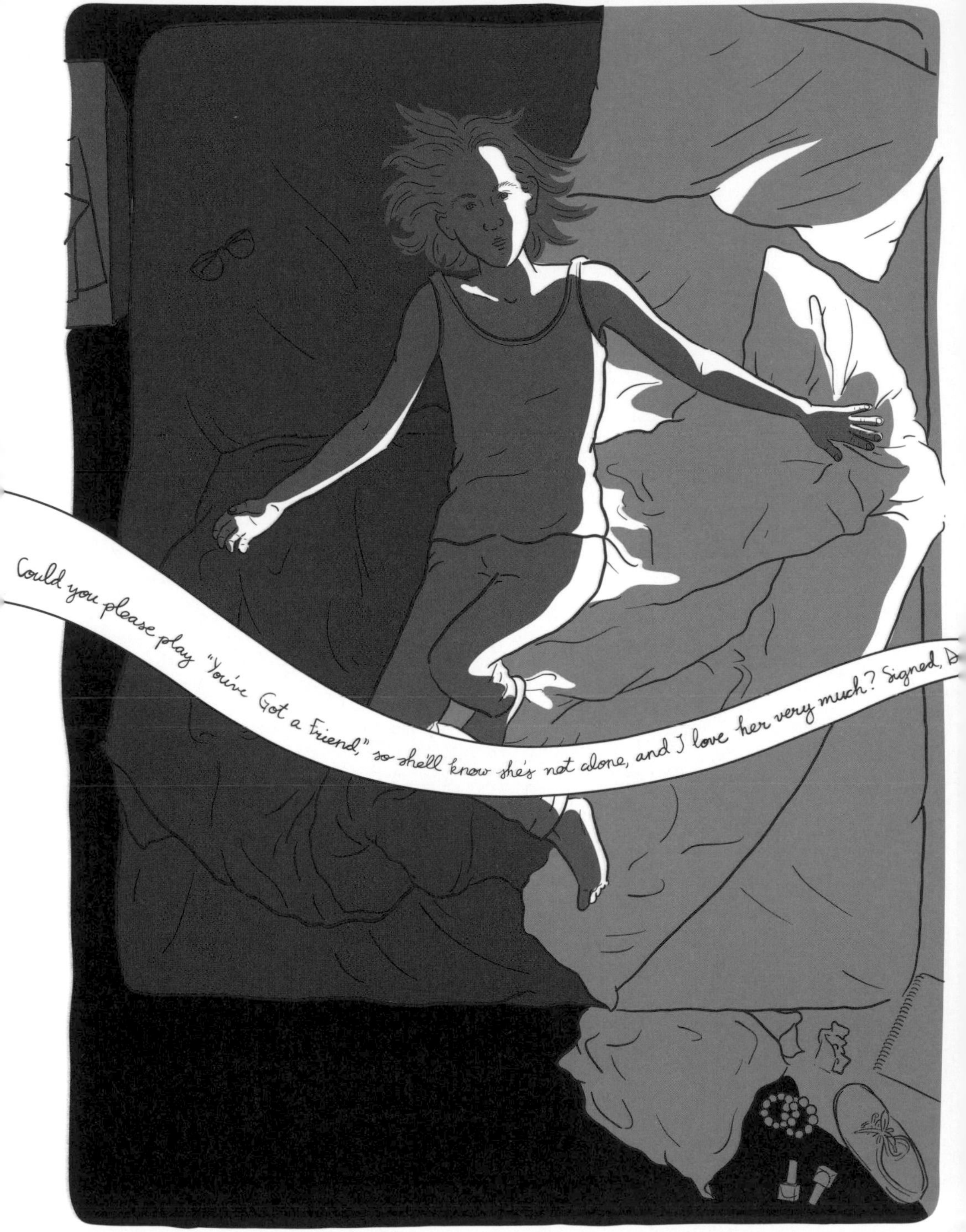
Could you please play "You've Got a Friend," so she'll know she's not alone, and I love her very much? Signed, D

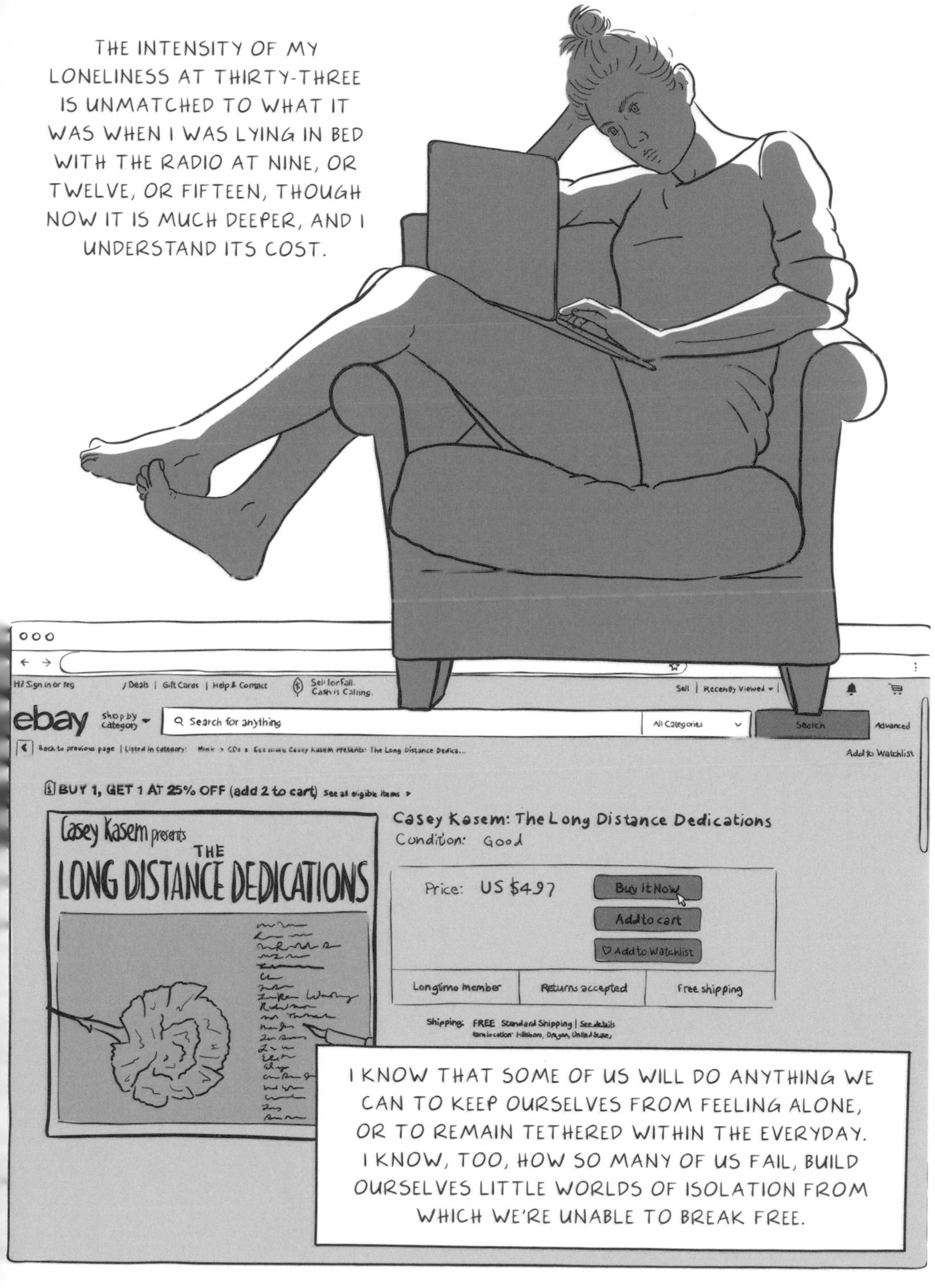
THE INTENSITY OF MY LONELINESS AT THIRTY-THREE IS UNMATCHED TO WHAT IT WAS WHEN I WAS LYING IN BED WITH THE RADIO AT NINE, OR TWELVE, OR FIFTEEN, THOUGH NOW IT IS MUCH DEEPER, AND I UNDERSTAND ITS COST.
ebay
Search for anything
All Categories
Search
Advanced
Add to Watchlist
BUY 1, GET 1 AT 25% OFF (add 2 to cart)
Casey Kasem presents THE LONG DISTANCE DEDICATIONS
Casey Kasem: The Long Distance Dedications
Condition: Good
Price: US $4.97
Buy It Now
Add to cart
Add to Watchlist
Longtime member
Returns accepted
Free shipping
I KNOW THAT SOME OF US WILL DO ANYTHING WE CAN TO KEEP OURSELVES FROM FEELING ALONE, OR TO REMAIN TETHERED WITHIN THE EVERYDAY. I KNOW, TOO, HOW SO MANY OF US FAIL, BUILD OURSELVES LITTLE WORLDS OF ISOLATION FROM WHICH WE'RE UNABLE TO BREAK FREE.

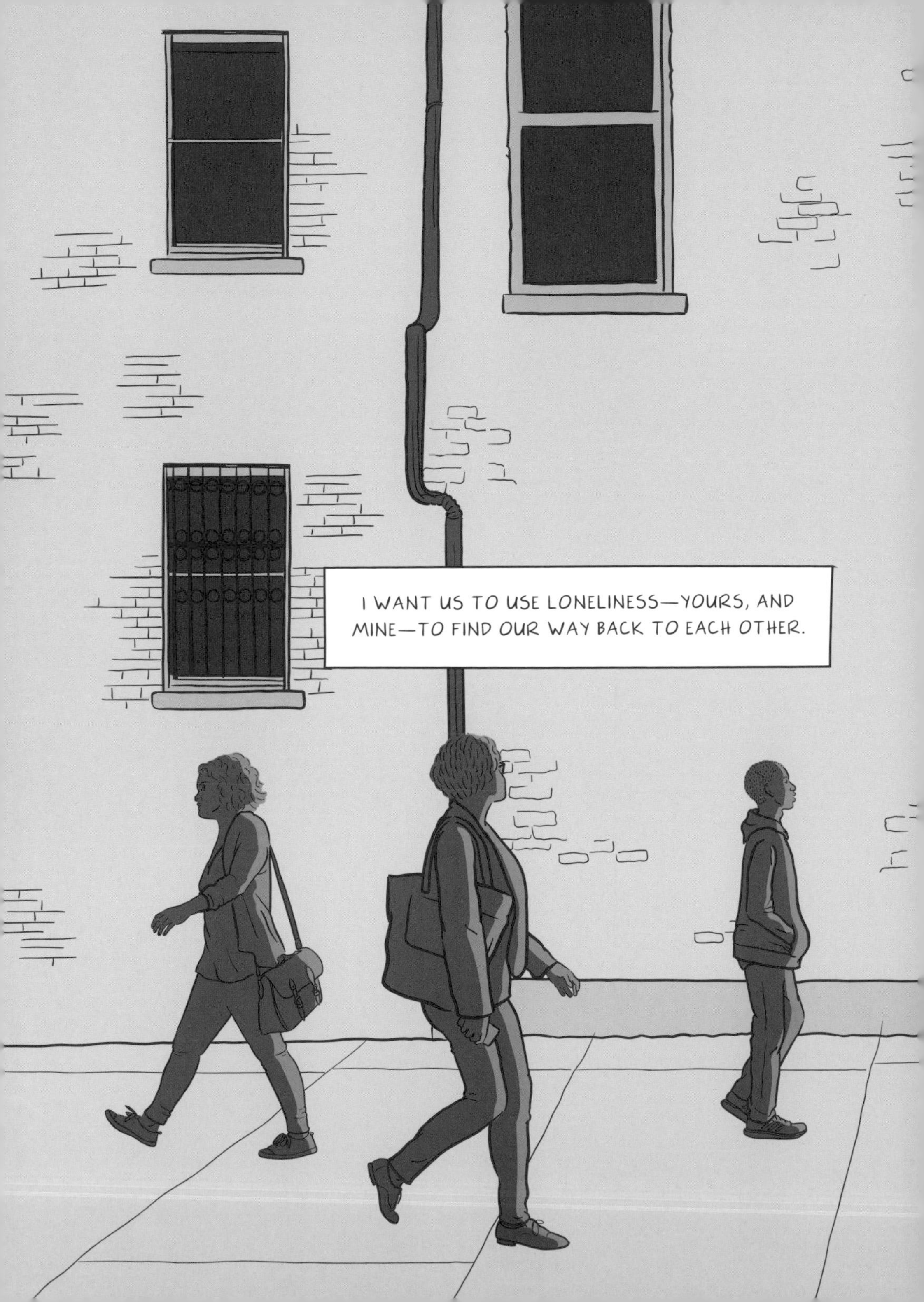
I WANT US TO USE LONELINESS—YOURS, AND MINE—TO FIND OUR WAY BACK TO EACH OTHER.

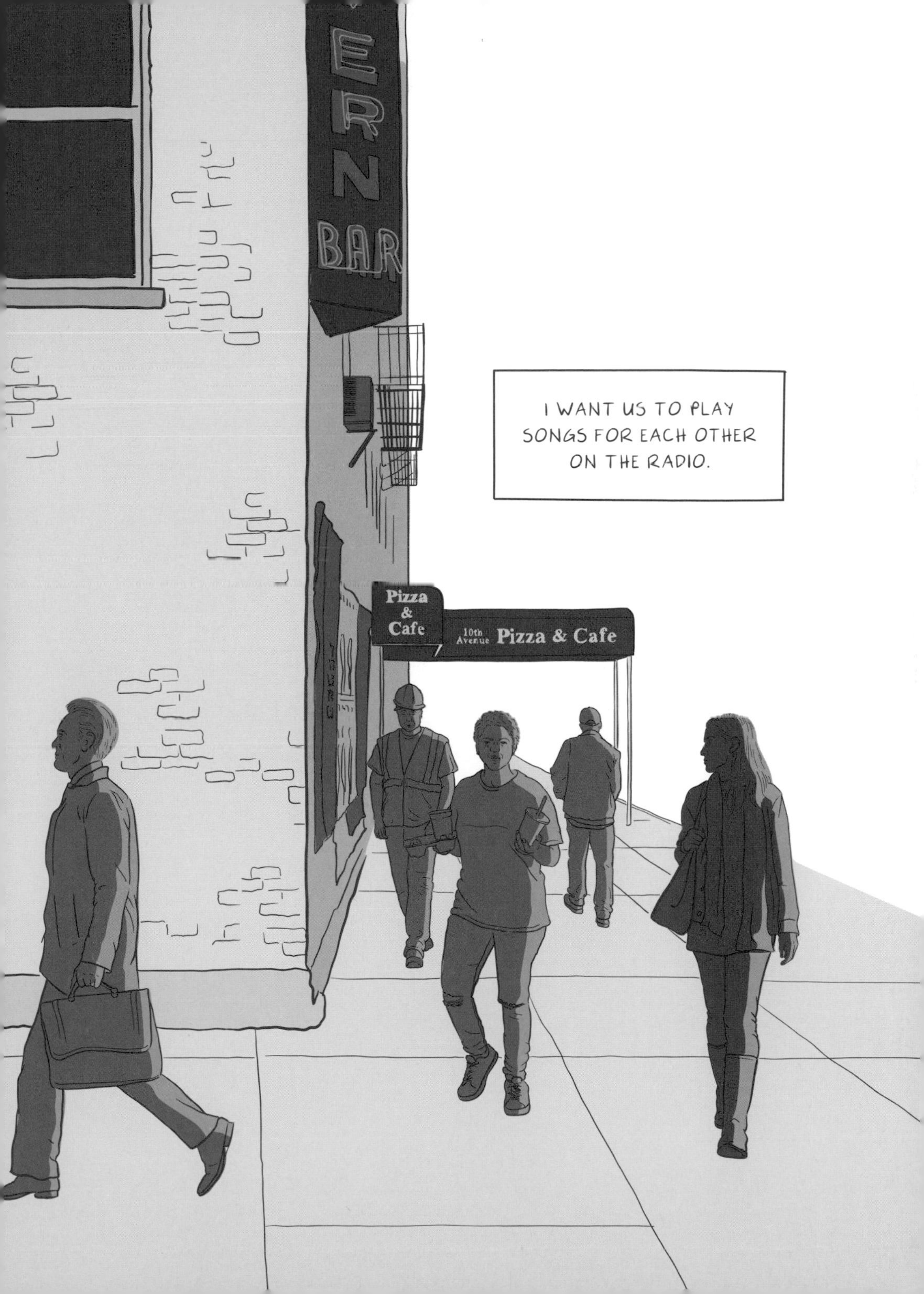
ERN
BAR
I WANT US TO PLAY SONGS FOR EACH OTHER ON THE RADIO.
Pizza & Cafe
10th Avenue Pizza & Cafe

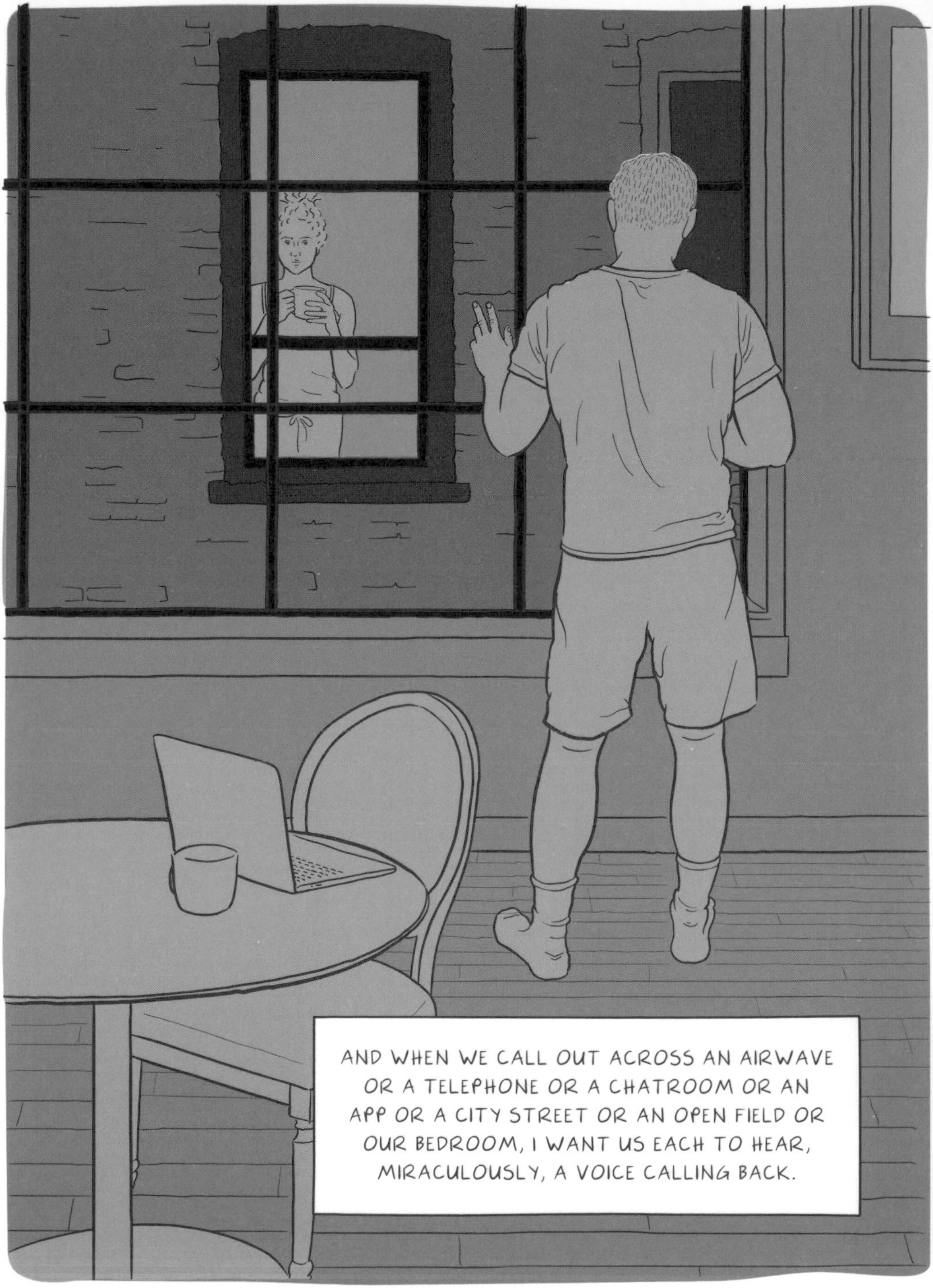
AND WHEN WE CALL OUT ACROSS AN AIRWAVE OR A TELEPHONE OR A CHATROOM OR AN APP OR A CITY STREET OR AN OPEN FIELD OR OUR BEDROOM, I WANT US EACH TO HEAR, MIRACULOUSLY, A VOICE CALLING BACK.

THANKS:

FIRST AND ALWAYS, THANK YOU TO MY AGENT, JIN AUH, ALEXANDRA
CHRISTIE, AND EVERYONE AT THE WYLIE AGENCY.

TIM O'CONNELL, EDITOR AND FRIEND, GENTLY SAW THIS BOOK THROUGH
MANY FORMS. THANK YOU TO EVERYONE AT PANTHEON, ESPECIALLY LISA
LUCAS, ANDY HUGHES, ROSE CORNIN-JACKMAN, ALTIE KARPER, ANNA
KAUFMAN, ROBERT SHAPIRO, MORGAN FENTON, JULIANNE CLANCY, AND
THE BEST PRODUCTION TEAM IN THE BOOKS. AND TO MICHAEL TAECKENS,
AS EVER.

MY PRIMARY READERS ON THIS PROJECT WERE: TONY TULATHIMUTTEE,
MAXWELL NEELY-COHEN, LUCAS MANN, AND ARIEL LEWITON, WHO HELPS
ME BUILD THE BONES OF MORE THAN JUST MY BOOKS. THANKS TO ALL OF
YOU FOR MAKING ME SMARTER. CHRIS RUSSELL SPOTTED EVERY ERRANT
LINE WITH EXTREME KINDNESS AND CARE. AMY KURZWEIL OFFERED A
COZY SPACE FOR WHINING. PAYTON BLESSING SPENT A SEMESTER AS MY
RESEARCH ASSISTANT.

ZAINA ARAFAT, GARNETT CADOGAN, EMILY HA, KERRY HOWLEY, MIRA
JACOB, JONATHAN LEE, DYLAN NICE, MICAH McCRARY, DINA NAYERI,
RACHEL YODER, ELENA PASSARELLO, NANCY WYLAND, MAXWELL NEELY-
COHEN, DANIEL POPPICK, MELISSA XIMENA, AND TONI NEALIE GENEROUSLY
SHARED THEIR LONELIEST MOMENTS AND ALLOWED ME TO INCLUDE
THEM HERE.

I AM STUPENDOUSLY THANKFUL TO THE WHITING FOUNDATION FOR SEEING
SOMETHING IN THIS PROJECT WHEN IT WAS A GERM OF ITSELF. THANK
YOU TO THE JUDGES OF THE CREATIVE NONFICTION GRANT, AND TO
COURTNEY HODELL, ADINA APPLEBAUM, DANIEL REID, ELENA PASSARELLO,
AND JESS ROW.

THE CORPORATION OF YADDO OFFERED THE TRANSFORMATIVE SPACE IN
WHICH THIS PROJECT FOUND ITSELF. THANK YOU TO ALL MY GLOWSTICK
COMPATRIOTS, ESPECIALLY DEAN HASPIEL, VU TRAN, AND WILL BOAST.

THIS BOOK STARTED AS A FOUR-PART SERIES AT THE NEW YORKER'S "PAGE-TURNER," AND I'M GRATEFUL TO DAVID HAUGLAND FOR ALLOWING ME THE ROOM TO THINK CRITICALLY ABOUT LONELINESS FOR THE FIRST TIME. THANKS ALSO TO JANE KIM AT THE ATLANTIC, JAMES DATZ AT THE NEW YORK TIMES, ELLA RILEY-ADAMS AT VOGUE, AND KEVIN NGUYEN DURING HIS TIME AT GQ.

THANK YOU TO MY COLLEAGUES AT THE BELIEVER AND THE BEVERLY ROGERS, CAROL C. HARTER BLACK MOUNTAIN INSTITUTE.

I'M CONTINUOUSLY GRATEFUL TO BOOKSELLING HEROES LIKE NATHAN DUNBAR, MIWA MESSER, SARAH BAGBY, CHRIS ANDERSEN, SARAH HOLLENBECK, JOHN FRANCISCONI, STEPHEN SPARKS, CLAIRE TOBIN, AND SO MANY OTHERS.

THANK YOU, JEFFERY GLEAVES, FOR MAKING ME A LITTLE MORE UNLONELY EVERY DAY.

NOTES:

I RELIED HEAVILY ON THE EXTRAORDINARY RESEARCH AND REPORTING OF
SCIENTISTS, PHILOSOPHERS, AND WRITERS TO COMPLETE THIS PROJECT.
TWO BOOKS WERE ESPECIALLY INDISPENSABLE. LONELINESS: HUMAN NATURE
AND THE NEED FOR SOCIAL CONNECTION BY THE LATE JOHN T. CACIOPPO
AND WILLIAM PATRICK OFFERED A COMPREHENSIVE OVERVIEW FROM WHICH
I BEGAN TO THINK ABOUT THE SCIENCE OF LONELINESS. THE CONTRIBUTIONS
DR. CACIOPPO MADE TO LONELINESS STUDIES ARE UNPARALLELED, AND, AS
DR. STEVEN COLE SAID TO ME, "WE'RE ALL A LITTLE LONELIER" WITHOUT HIM.

DEBORAH BLUM'S WRITING AND RESEARCH ABOUT HARRY HARLOW, PAR-
TICULARLY LOVE AT GOON PARK: HARRY HARLOW AND THE SCIENCE OF
AFFECTION, WAS CRUCIAL TO MY UNDERSTANDING OF HARLOW'S WORK.
INSIGHT INTO THE INNER WORKINGS OF HARLOW'S MIND AND THE ESSEN-
TIAL DETAILS OF HIS LIFE OUTSIDE THE LAB WOULD NOT BE AVAILABLE TODAY
WITHOUT HER WORK.

DOZENS OF TEXTS WERE INSTRUMENTAL IN HELPING REFINE MY THINK-
ING, ESPECIALLY ALONE TOGETHER BY SHERRY TURKLE, SOCIAL: WHY
OUR BRAINS ARE WIRED TO CONNECT BY MATTHEW D. LIEBERMAN,
THE LONELY AMERICAN BY JACQUELINE OLDS AND RICHARD S. SCHWARTZ,
BOWLING ALONE: THE COLLAPSE AND REVIVAL OF AMERICAN COMMUNITY
BY ROBERT D. PUTNAM, LONELINESS AS A WAY OF LIFE BY THOMAS DUMM,
THE VANISHING NEIGHBOR BY MARC J. DUNKELMAN, LONELINESS IN
PHILOSOPHY, PSYCHOLOGY, AND LITERATURE BY BEN LAZARE MIJUSKOVIC,
A PHILOSOPHY OF LONELINESS BY LARS SVENDSEN, THE LONELY CITY: ADVEN-
TURES IN THE ART OF BEING ALONE BY OLIVIA LAING, AND THE SELFISHNESS
OF OTHERS: AN ESSAY ON THE FEAR OF NARCISSISM BY KRISTIN DOMBEK.

THE LINE DRAWINGS ON PAGES 45 AND 49 ARE BASED ON STILLS FROM
I LOVE LUCY, HOGAN'S HEROES, AND FRIENDS.

THE HEADLINES ON PAGE 63 ARE PULLED FROM, IN ORDER: THE TELEGRAPH
(SARAH KNAPTON), TIME (JUSTIN WORLAND), NPR (ANGUS CHEN), THE
NEW YORK TIMES (CEYLAN YEGINSU), AND THE BBC.

THE ART DRAWN ON THE BRICK WALL ON PAGE 67 IS BASED ON NICK WALKER'S THE LOVE VANDAL (2014). I'M GRATEFUL TO NICK FOR HIS PERMISSION TO USE IT HERE.

THE JACQUELINE OLDS AND RICHARD S. SCHWARTZ QUOTE ON PAGE 79 APPEARS IN THE LONELY AMERICAN: DRIFTING APART IN THE TWENTY-FIRST CENTURY.

THE LINE DRAWING ON PAGE 81 IS BASED ON NORMAN ROCKWELL'S 1948 PAINTING THE GOSSIPS.

THE DRAWINGS ON PAGES 86 AND 87 ARE BASED OFF THE FOLLOWING WORKS OF ART, IN ORDER: ROMEO AND FRIAR LAWRENCE BY H. C. SELOUS, THE EMPEROR NAPOLEON IN HIS STUDY AT THE TUILERIES BY JACQUES-LOUIS DAVID, THE ARRIVAL OF CHARON BY GUSTAVE DORÉ, ADAM AND EVE EXPELLED FROM PARADISE, AN ILLUSTRATION FROM PARADISE LOST BY JOHN MILTON: A SERIES OF TWELVE ILLUSTRATIONS, AND A FIFTEENTH-CENTURY ART IMPRESSION OF LUCIFER FROM DANTE'S INFERNO.

THE GREEN TEXT ON PAGE 97 COMES FROM JOHN T. CACIOPPO'S CV.

THE DRAWING ON PAGE 120 IS A MASHUP OF AN AD FOR THE RONALD REAGAN CAMPAIGN AND A VINTAGE MARLBORO AD.

THE LETTERING ON PAGE 122 IS BASED ON THE POSTER FOR THE 1962 MOVIE THE MAN WHO SHOT LIBERTY VALANCE.

THE DRAWING ON PAGE 127 IS BASED ON THE COVER OF THEODORE ROO-SEVELT: THE MAN OF ACTION, PUBLISHED BY THE JOHN HANCOCK MUTUAL LIFE INSURANCE COMPANY, IN 1926.

THE HEADLINES ON PAGE 128 ARE DRAWN FROM THE NEW YORK TIMES ARTICLE "BOUND TO NO PARTY, TRUMP UPENDS 150 YEARS OF TWO-PARTY RULE" BY PETER BAKER, AND POLITICO MAGAZINE'S "THE LONELIEST PRESI-DENT" BY MICHAEL KRUSE.

THE DRAWINGS ON PAGE 148 ARE BASED ON RACIST SIGNAGE SOURCED FROM THE INTERNET, MY HOMETOWN, AND PHOTOS OF TRUMP RALLIES. I CONSISTENTLY FOUND THAT THE MORE RACIST THE SENTIMENT, THE POORER THE DESIGN.

THE DRAWINGS AND QUOTES ON PAGE 155 WERE SOURCED FROM '90s NEWS SEGMENTS ON THE BBC, ABC NEWS, AND FOX 11.

THE HEADLINES ON PAGES 158 AND 159 WERE DRAWN FROM THE FOLLOW-ING ARTICLES, IN ORDER: "NEIGHBORS OF SHOOTER GARY MARTIN DESCRIBE HIM AS A 'LONER,'" IN CBS LOCAL CHICAGO, FEBRUARY 15, 2019; "ROOM-MATES DESCRIBE GUNMAN AS LONER," BY MARC SANTORA, THE NEW YORK TIMES, APRIL 17, 2007; "JAMES HOLMES, AURORA SHOOTING SUSPECT, WAS GRAD SCHOOL DROPOUT AND LONER, SAY NEIGHBORS," BY NANCY DIL-LON AND LARRY MCSHANE IN THE NEW YORK DAILY NEWS, JULY 21, 2017; "THE SOLE SUSPECT OF THE QUEBEC MOSQUE SHOOTING DESCRIBE AS A 'LONER' AND ANTI-FEMINIST 'TROLL,'" BY JEREMY BERKE, BUSINESS INSIDER, JANUARY 30, 2017; "DALLAS SHOOTER MICAH JOHNSON ARMY VETERAN AND 'LONER'" BY WILLIAM ARKIN, TRACY CONNER, AND JIM MIKLASZEWSKI AT NBC NEWS, JULY 8, 2016; "GILROY FESTIVAL KILLER DESCRIBED AS 'KIND OF A LONER,' MOTIVE FOR SHOOTING REMAINS A MYSTERY," ASSOCI-ATED PRESS, JULY 31, 2019; "EL PASO SHOOTER WAS ANTI-SOCIAL LONER, FORMER CLASSMATE SAYS," BY TANYA EISERER, WFAA, AUGUST 4, 2019; "'LONER' DALLAS GUNMAN HAD BOMB MATERIALS AND KEPT JOURNAL OF COMBAT TACTICS" BY MOLLY HENNESSY-FISKE, DEL QUENTIN WILBER, AND MATT PEARCE, LOS ANGELES TIMES, JULY 8, 2016; "'LONER' STUDENT SHOOTS AND KILLS 10 AT TEXAS SCHOOL" BY LIZ HAMPTON AND ERWIN SEBA, REUTERS, MAY 18, 2018; "MUNICH SHOOTING: KILLER WAS BULLIED TEEN LONER OBSESSED WITH MASS MURDER" BY JANEK SCHMIDT, KATE CONNOLLY, AND EMMA GRAHAM-HARRISON FOR THE GUARDIAN, JULY 24, 2016; "ELLIOTT RODGER, A QUIET, TROUBLED LONER, PLOTTED RAMPAGE FOR MONTHS" BY JOSEPH SERNA, KATE MATHER, AND AMANDA COVARRU-BIAS FOR LOS ANGELES TIMES, FEBRUARY 19, 2015; "PLANNED PARENTHOOD SHOOTER DESCRIBED AS A 'LONER'" BY KATIE BO WILLIAMS FOR THE HILL, NOVEMBER 28, 2015; "WHY MANY MASS SHOOTERS ARE 'LONERS'" BY OLGA

KHAZAN AT THE ATLANTIC, AUGUST 5, 2019; "PHOENIX SERIAL STREET SHOOTER SUSPECT SEEMED TO LIVE IN ISOLATION" BY ASTRID GALVAN AND JACQUES BILLEAUD FOR ASSOCIATED PRESS, MAY 10, 2017; AND "EXCLUSIVE: CONGRESS SHOOTER WAS 5'6" RUDE LONER WHO CREEPED OUT FEMALE BAR STAFF AT BBQ RESTAURANT WHERE HE SPENT HAPPY HOURS—AFTER MOVING TO D.C. TO PROTEST AGAINST THE PRESIDENT HE HATED" BY ALANA GOODMAN, LOUISE BOYLE, AND JENNIFER SMITH AT THE DAILY MAIL, JUNE 15, 2017.

THE DRAWINGS OF '90s PRETEEN OBJECTS ON PAGE 180 INCLUDE THE COVER OF FRANCINE PASCAL'S SWEET VALLEY HIGH PLAYING WITH FIRE, AND TEEN SPIRIT DEODORANT BY COLGATE-PALMOLIVE. THE BUTTONS ON THE INTERNET WINDOW ARE DRAWN FROM AN EARLY VERSION OF AOL INSTANT MESSENGER.

THE LINE DRAWINGS ON PAGES 190 AND 191 ARE BASED ON PHOTOGRAPHS FROM PHILIP-LORCA diCORCIA'S HEADS.

THE DRAWINGS ON PAGES 209, 211, 213, AND 214 ARE BASED ON INSTALLATIONS BY YAYOI KUSAMA.

THE DRAWN TEXT ON PAGE 217 IS PULLED FROM, IN ORDER, "HOW TO TAKE A GOOD SELFIE: TIPS TO CONSIDER," BY STEPHANIE SALTZMAN AND GENNA ROSENSTEIN AT ALLURE, "WHAT YOUR SELFIE REALLY SAYS ABOUT YOU" AT REFINERY29, "INSTAGRAMMERS FLOCK TO CLIFFS WHERE WOMAN TAKING SELFIE PLUNGED TO HER DEATH," BY VANITA SALISBURY AT THE NEW YORK POST, AND "5 FLAWLESS TIPS TO TAKING YOUR BEST SELFIE," KRYSTYNA CHÁVEZ AND CARLY CARDELLINO AT COSMOPOLITAN.

THE INFORMATION AND DRAWINGS ON PAGE 218 WERE BASED ON THE BBC'S HOW ART MADE THE WORLD, WITH NIGEL SPIVEY. THANK YOU TO JOHN D'AGATA FOR POINTING ME IN THE RIGHT DIRECTION.

THE TWEETS IN DRAWINGS IN SECTION II WERE COLLECTED FROM A DEEP DIVE CONDUCTED BY MY RESEARCH ASSISTANT PAYTON BLESSING, FROM VARIOUS ACCOUNTS THAT POSTED IN DECEMBER 2013.

THE BOOK COVER DRAWN ON PAGE 242 IS OF ALONE NOT LONELY: INDEPEN-
DENT LIVING FOR WOMEN OVER FIFTY, PUBLISHED BY AARP IN 1985.

THE DRAWING OF THE ARTICLE ON PAGE 243 COMES FROM A 1902 ISSUE OF
HARPER'S BAZAAR. THE DRAWINGS OF THE STOCK PHOTOS ON THE TOP OF
THE PAGE ARE SOURCED FROM ADOBE STOCK.

THE LINE DRAWINGS ON PAGES 249 AND 253 ARE BASED ON A STILL FROM
WHILE YOU WERE SLEEPING.

THE DRAWING ON PAGE 254 IS BASED ON A STILL FROM DISNEY'S FROZEN.

THE SNAPSHOT DRAWING ON PAGE 266 IS BASED ON AN ARCHIVAL PHOTO-
GRAPH OF B. F. SKINNER'S DAUGHTER DEBORAH IN HIS "BABY TENDER."

THE LINE DRAWINGS ON PAGES 272 AND 273 ARE BASED ON ARCHIVAL PHO-
TOGRAPHS OF HARRY HARLOW'S STUDIES, SOURCED FROM "THE NATURE
OF LOVE" IN AMERICAN PSYCHOLOGIST (1958) AND THE UNIVERSITY OF
WISCONSIN ARCHIVES.

THE DRAWINGS ON PAGE 277 ARE BASED ON ARCHIVAL PHOTOGRAPHS
FOUND IN LOVE AT GOON PARK: HARRY HARLOW AND THE SCIENCE OF
AFFECTION BY DEBORAH BLOOM. THE QUOTE FROM CLARA MEARS'S
MOTHER'S LETTER TO LEWIS TERMAN ON PAGE 279 WAS ALSO SOURCED
FROM BLOOM'S BOOK.

THE TOP DRAWING ON PAGE 283 IS BASED ON A PHOTOGRAPH IN THE UNI-
VERSITY OF WISCONSIN 1971 YEARBOOK AT THE UNIVERSITY OF WISCONSIN
ARCHIVES. THE NEWSPAPER ARTICLE DRAWN BENEATH IT APPEARED IN THE
WISCONSIN STATE JOURNAL ON MARCH 11, 1968.

THE DRAWING ON PAGE 284 IS BASED ON MATERIAL FOUND IN THE PAM-
PHLET "SOCIAL DEPRIVATION IN MONKEYS" BY HARRY AND MARGARET
HARLOW, PUBLISHED BY W. H. FREEMAN AND COMPANY AND REPRINTED BY
SCIENTIFIC AMERICAN IN 1962.

PAGE 290 WAS DRAWN FROM A YOUTUBE VIDEO POSTED IN 2016 BY YOUTUBE USER WAGGERSDOGWORKS.

THE HEADLINES ON PAGE 294 WERE DRAWN FROM ARTICLES, FROM TOP TO BOTTOM, BY GINNA ROE FOR KUTV (2019), PAULA COCOZZA FOR THE GUARDIAN (2018), TRIBUNE MEDIA WIRE (2019), AND CERTIFIEDCUDDLERS .COM.

THE LOGOS AND QUOTES ON PAGE 295 WERE DRAWN FROM ITSJUSTCUDDLES .COM (NOW DEFUNCT), CUDDLECOMFORT.COM, SNUGGLEBUDDIES.COM, CUDDLIST.COM, CUDDLECONNECT.COM, CUDDLEUPTOME.COM, CUDDLE SANCTUARY.COM, AND CUDDLECOMPANIONS.ORG.

THE QUOTE FROM HARRY HARLOW'S LETTERS ON PAGE 301 APPEARS IN LOVE AT GOON PARK: HARRY HARLOW AND THE SCIENCE OF AFFECTION BY DEBORAH BLOOM. ON PAGE 305, THE QUOTE ABOUT HARLOW'S STATE OF MIND COMES FROM CHARLES SNOWDEN, AS QUOTED IN THE ABOVE.

MARGARET KUENNE HARLOW'S OBITUARY, DRAWN ON PAGE 307, APPEARED IN THE MADISON CAPITAL TIMES ON AUGUST 12, 1971.

THE NEW YORK TIMES HEADLINE DRAWN ON THE TOP OF PAGE 311 ACCOM-PANIED AN ARTICLE BY MARC SANTORA, PUBLISHED ON APRIL 17, 2007. THE TWITTER POST BENEATH IT WAS WRITTEN BY A TWITTER USER NAMED VERONICA CORNINGSTONE.

THE BACKGROUND TEXT ON PAGE 312 WAS DRAWN FROM POSTS ON THE CUDDLE COMFORT MESSAGE BOARD AT CUDDLECOMFORT.COM.

THE KURT VONNEGUT QUOTE ON PAGE 323 APPEARS IN HIS BOOK A MAN WITHOUT A COUNTRY.